MODERN
HOME
WINEMAKING

Techniques in Home Winemaking
The Comprehensive Guide to Making Château-Style Wines

❖

Kit Winemaking
The Illustrated Beginner's Guide to Making Wine from Concentrate

❖

Wine Myths, Facts & Snobberies
81 Questions & Answers on the Science and Enjoyment of Wine

MODERN
HOME
WINEMAKING

*A Guide to Making Consistently
Great Wines*

DANIEL PAMBIANCHI

Véhicule Press

Published with the generous assistance of the Canada Book Fund of the Department of Canadian Heritage.

Canadä

Cover design: David Drummond
Typeset by David Leblanc of studio oneonone
Technical editing by Arthur Harder and Robert Peak
Illustrations by Don Martin

Library and Archives Canada Cataloguing in Publication

Title: Modern home winemaking : a guide to making consistently great
  wines / Daniel Pambianchi.
Names: Pambianchi, Daniel, author.
Identifiers: Canadiana 20210132019 | ISBN 9781550655636 (softcover)
Subjects: LCSH: Wine and wine making—Amateurs' manuals. | LCGFT:
  Handbooks and manuals.
Classification: LCC TP548.2 .P344 2021 | DDC 641.87/2—dc23

Published by Véhicule Press, Montréal, Québec, Canada

Distribution in Canada by LitDistCo
www.litdistco.ca

Distribution in the U.S.by Independent Publishers Group
ipgbook.com

Printed in Canada

Disclaimer

....

Additives, processing aids, reagents and other products and chemicals referenced in this book have applications in winemaking and lab analysis. With care and caution, these can be safely used in home winemaking although some may be unsafe or may pose a health hazard if not used in the recommended concentrations or if used by unskilled winemakers.

Commercial winemaking regulations may prohibit or limit the use of such chemicals or products, and vary from one country or winemaking region to another. Some commercial wineries also shun the use of additives or similar products because they simply deem these as unnatural and unconventional, going against traditional winemaking methods. For home winemaking use, chemicals approved for enological applications should be used with great care, and recommended concentrations should be strictly followed. Generic substitutes for enological chemicals should not be used.

Neither the author, editors, or the publisher assumes any responsibility for the use or misuse of information contained in this book.

References to winemaking supplies from various manufacturers or vendors are included to illustrate typical use of these supplies from companies whose products are the most prevalent in the home winemaking market. The use of these references and all trademarks and copyrighted material from cited manufacturers, suppliers, wholesalers, retailers, distributors or other constitute neither sponsorship nor affiliation of these companies with the author, editors and publisher, or with this book. Companies have not paid any promotional fees to have their names and/or products listed here.

Contents

....

Acknowledgments

....

A technical, instructional book always involves many, many people who have dedicated precious time and relentless energy to make it all possible.

First and foremost, I would like to thank Simon Dardick and Nancy Marrelli, publishers of Véhicule Press, who once again have provided immense support in making this book project a reality. And I am particularly grateful to two of the most knowledgeable and all-around super individuals and friends, our two Technical Editors, Arthur Harder and Robert (Bob) Peak, who have spent countless hours reviewing and editing the manuscript, suggesting improvements and providing feedback.

I would like to thank Don Martin for his usual wonderful work on illustrations, working from my "sketches" that he somehow understands and interprets without asking questions, typesetter David Leblanc for bringing it all together, and the following individuals for reviewing specific sections: Gordon Specht, Sigrid Gertsen-Schibbye, Eric (Rick) Theiner, David Noone, Richard Sportsman, Dominick Profaci, Zac Brown, Garett Savage, and Tim Vandergrift. A big "thank you" to the many manufacturers, and specifically, Lallemand, Laffort, Lesaffre, White Labs, Wyeast, Renaissance, AB Biotek, and Chr Hansen, and their technical representatives, including Anne-Claire Bauquis, Karen Fortmann, Tamara Logsdon, Hugo Picard, Art Mills and Peter Tudisco, who have responded to my many queries and provided product information, and to the many amateurs and small-winery operators who follow me on social media and contribute enormously to our wonderful home winemaking hobby. Thank you each and every one of you, from the bottom of my heart.

And last but not least, I would like to thank my family — Dalia Ishak, Eric and Justin Pambianchi — who have each contributed in their own ways to my winemaking, from helping with blending bench trials and tasting many "experimental wines," to bottling and, well, simply enjoying my wines at dinner or till late at night just shooting the breeze.

About the Technical Editors

ARTHUR HARDER

Arthur Harder was raised in Vineland Station in the Niagara Viticultural region in Ontario, Canada. Inspired by wine, its culture and the fledgling 'new' Niagara wine industry of the mid 1970's, Harder chose a professional road with degrees in chemistry at Ryerson University in Toronto, Canada in 1981, and in Enology and Viticulture at the famed Geisenheim University in Geisenheim, Germany in 1987. Since 2002 Harder is principal partner in Harder Enology Consulting Services working freelance directing winemaking in a number start-up wineries, while committed to staying at the forefront of technology and dedicated to continuous improvement. Now focusing on his roots and residing in Beamsville, Ontario, he continues to craft fine wines, which express the quality grapes grown in the Niagara region.

ROBERT (BOB) PEAK

Retired from co-owning a home brewing and winemaking supply store, Bob Peak writes and consults about fermentation, including as Technical Editor and Techniques columnist for WineMaker magazine. Before his 14 years helping hobbyists, Bob managed a commercial wine laboratory and fermentation products supplier. That position followed years of managing environmental testing laboratories in California. When the last of those assignments brought him to Sonoma County, Bob realized it was time to plant grapes and make wine, a project he started just before the turn of the century. These experiences are built on Bob's Bachelor of Science degree in chemistry from Harvey Mudd College in Claremont, California, plus extension classes at University of California, Davis.

"In enology, fact is merely what enough people believe, and truth lies only in how fervently they believe it."

– Volker Schneider, Schneider-Oenologie

Preface

....

MODERN HOME WINEMAKING is for winemakers — amateur wine-making enthusiasts and small commercial winery operators — who aspire to raise the bar and make great wines, consistently, even when faced with a challenging harvest. Mother Nature doesn't always deliver perfectly balanced grapes, but the skilled and methodical winemaker will still be able to craft great balanced wine. Skill requires knowledge and experience, and *MODERN HOME WINEMAKING* is based on modern wine science theory and extensive practical experience that will give you the confidence to expertly craft wines vintage after vintage with all the challenges each brings.

As a seasoned winemaker, you can jump right into any section to further your knowledge and try out new techniques for making wine from grapes, fresh juice, processed 100% juice and concentrate. If you are a beginner highly motivated to make superlative wines, you can take a stepwise approach and tackle sections progressively, perhaps skipping more advanced subsections and coming back to these as you grow your knowledge. You will come to develop your own techniques or adapt others you have read about in other literature but now you will have the knowledge to make informed decisions. You will find additional information in the preamble section in the more advanced chapters.

Much of the content is based on my experience, lots of it based on researching and experimenting different techniques, new equipment, and the many new and specialized products that come to market at a very rapid pace. Much of my experience stems from analyzing wine in great details in my lab, and comparing results to theory — there can be great variations owing to the complex beverage that is wine. You will also find many examples not found in other textbooks to illustrate how specific procedures and calculations are performed. Yes, it will get very technical, but as you grow into your hobby and start appreciating the technical aspect of winemaking, you will be better positioned to make better decisions when, for example, faced with harvest challenges or when something has gone wrong.

First review all the terms defined in the **Winemaking Lexicon** so that you understand all the lingo presented in the introductory chapters. The detailed concepts are then presented in their respective chapters. Chapters are laid out to provide all the theory and practical advice first, then followed by chapters on white, rosé and red winemaking.

Chapter 1 first describes the transformation of grapes into wine, that is, what happens in grape juice as it is transformed by fermentation into wine. Knowledge of some of the more important chemical and microbiological transformations is fundamental in winemaking — decisions are based on science, not guesswork, not myths, not even tradition. This chapter also presents an overview and flowchart of each of the process for making white, rosé and red wine — these styles are the focus of this book.

Chapter 2 gives descriptions of some of the more common vinifera, Native American and hybrid grape varieties used for making great wines. There you will find key characteristics of each variety and the type of wine it can produce, along with helpful tips and advice on dealing with specific peculiarities, such as poor color or high acidity, along with yeast recommendations.

Chapter 3 lists all the essential winemaking and laboratory equipment you will need to make great wine — efficiently. You will be able to choose the right equipment to start small and then what upgrades you need to grow your winemaking.

Chapter 4 describes how to clean and sanitize equipment, and the many kinds of products on the market and their applications with recommendations for cleaning and sanitizing glass, plastic (PET and HDPE), and stainless steel.

Chapter 5 outlines the process for conducting bench trials used, for example, to determine precise sugar or acid additions. Bench trials help you avoid having to treat juice or wine that you have over-adjusted with a blind addition.

Chapter 6 gets into the theory of sugar and alcohol analysis, how to measure the amount of fermentable sugars, how to estimate the amount of alcohol that will be produced, how to make corrections if your juice or grapes do not have enough sugar, or maybe too much sugar, and how and why to measure the amount of leftover or residual sugar in wine.

Chapter 7 discusses one of the most important topic in winemaking and wine chemistry — acidity and pH, with a special focus on the chemistry of potassium bitartrate. Along with alcohol, the amount of residual sugar, and tannins in red wines, acidity plays an important role in wine balance — a marker, however objective, of quality in wine.

Chapter 8 discusses another very important topic — sulfur dioxide (SO_2). SO_2 protects wine from chemical and microbiological faults or outright spoilage, and also enhances aromas. The chapter discusses the intricate but necessary theory of sulfites and SO_2, how to measure SO_2 levels, how to manage SO_2 levels throughout the life of a wine from grapes to bottle, including how to make adjustments like an expert with the objective of maximizing SO_2 efficacy while reducing the total amount used. The chapter also offers alternative additives and strategies for reducing the use of sulfites.

Chapter 9 introduces tannins: what they do, what they are, and where they come from. Understanding how tannins work in creating structure, stabilizing color and improving wine aging potential, is fundamental to red winemaking.

Chapter 10 gives an overview of the main enological enzymes used to, for example, improve pressing (of grapes) and increase juice yields, avoid clarification and filtration problems, or hasten color and tannin extraction when making red wine.

Chapter 11 describes alcoholic fermentation (AF), the yeast growth cycle, nutritional needs and choosing an appropriate yeast for the grape variety at hand and winemaking objectives. It describes how to carry out a trouble-free and efficient fermentation. You will find handy charts listed by manufacturer of the many yeast products available. Since no winemaker has never had to deal with a problem fermentation, this chapter outlines a surefire protocol for restarting a sluggish or stuck fermentation. And if you are into making sweet wines, you will find a protocol to stop an active fermentation to preserve some of the natural sugars.

Chapter 12 describes malolactic fermentation (MLF), nutritional needs, choosing an appropriate bacterium for a desired style of wine, how to conduct a trouble-free MLF, and how to test for completion of MLF. It briefly discusses current theories on the timing of the MLF, i.e., should it be done concurrently with the AF or sequentially following the AF. Here too you will find a protocol to deal with a sluggish or stuck MLF.

Chapter 13 describes the most common processing aids used for fining and clarifying wine — and the difference between fining and clarifying — and how to choose the most appropriate for any application. It also describes related processing, including: juice settling in white and rosé winemaking, racking wine, and degassing for those who make wine from kits or who want to bottle quickly.

Chapter 14 discusses the four main topics of wine stabilization: microbial, pectin, protein and tartrate. Microbial stabilization is specifically concerned with how to manage wine that contains residual sugar from alcoholic fermentation or added by the winemaker, and residual malic acid from an incomplete or partial malolactic fermentation. The chapter describes how to test for instability and how to carry out specific stabilization procedures.

Chapter 15 discusses the benefits of aging wine and how to age wine, either in glass, stainless steel or HDPE tanks, or barrels, with or without the use of oak adjuncts, e.g., oak chips, staves, spirals, etc., and on the lees — the dead yeast cells left over from alcoholic fermentation. For more information on barrel-buying considerations and how to store, maintain and prepare oak barrels, please consult reference [1].

Chapter 16 discusses how to fine-tune wine to: improve balance between, for example, acidity and sweetness by either increasing or decreasing acidity or sweetening; enhance body and structure; reduce bitter and astringent tannins; and augment oak aroma and flavor complexity. It also describes the benefits of blending different wines and how to use the Pearson Square to calculate the required proportions of wines to be blended.

Chapter 17 discusses why and when clarifying and sterile filtration are needed, the various setups and necessary equipment to filter efficiently, and how to expertly filter wine.

PREFACE

Chapter 18 discusses packaging and bottling equipment. Packaging includes bottles, corks, capsules and labels. Bottling equipment includes washing and sanitizing equipment, filler and corker. It also describes the different ways of bottling and the necessary setups for small and large batches.

Then we bring everything together we have learned to this point and, in **Chapters 19, 20** and **21**, look at step-by-step, crush-to-bottle protocols for making white wine in a fruity style as well as a fuller-bodied, oaked style, rosé wine in a fresh and fruit-forward style, and red wine in a full-bodied style. These are protocols — not recipes — that walk you through the detailed process for making wine expertly.

Chapter 22 discusses twelve of the most common wine flaws and faults: premature oxidation, volatile acidity, surface film, hydrogen sulfide, tartrates, haze/cloudiness, refermentation in bottle, poor color in reds, vegetal character in Cabernet varietals, unpleasant smell of geraniums, cork taint, and *Brettanomyces*. It describes the most probable causes, how to assess problems, how to evaluate and implement remedial actions, and how to prevent flaws and faults in the first place.

Chapter 23 discusses what judges look for in wines submitted into competitions and how to get wines ready for competitions, i.e., how to self-assess one's wines and find and fix faults.

Appendix A lists conversion factors between Metric, U.S. and Imperial systems for relevant measurements.

Appendix B provides handy tables for converting between Specific Gravity, Brix, potential alcohol and sugar concentration, a table to correct hydrometer readings taken at different temperatures than the instrument's calibration temperature, and tables to help you estimate the amount of residual sugars in wine.

Appendix C has a handy winemaking log chart that can be used to record all winemaking and vinification activities. Keeping records of a wine's progress and treatments is key to successful winemaking.

If you want to explore making styles other than dry wines, such as sparkling wine or sweet styles of wines, please consult reference [1]; or if you are just starting out and want to learn the winemaking process using a concentrate in a kit, please consult reference [2]. If you want to learn about making mead, and fruit and country wines, please consult references [3] and [4], respectively.

There are many enological products — additives and processing aids — and test equipment mentioned in this book and which I have used in my own winemaking and wine analysis. These can help you too, but you will come to choose and adapt those that work best for you and according to your objectives.

CONVENTIONS USED IN THIS BOOK

Commonly used words in other languages appear in italics on the first occurrence; for example *bâtonnage*.

Words or phrases are abbreviated on the first occurrence in each chapter, for example, malolactic fermentation (MLF), then the abbreviation is used in the remainder of the chapter.

Grape variety names and (wine) varietal names are capitalized; for example, Sauvignon Blanc, and Muscat Blanc à Petits Grains.

ICONS USED IN THIS BOOK

 A short explanation or additional information that you may find useful.

 A warning which, if not observed, can result in unexpected or undesirable outcomes or become a health hazard.

 Specific advice or instructions for performing a procedure to avoid potential problems.

 A useful practical tip that can improve efficiency or simplify a certain procedure.

Montreal, Quebec, Canada
Daniel Pambianchi

July 2021

REFERENCES

1. Pambianchi, D. 2008. *Techniques in Home Winemaking: A Practical Guide to Making Château-Style Wines.* Newly-Revised and Expanded. Véhicule Press, Montréal (Québec).

2. Pambianchi, D. 2009. *Kit Winemaking: The Illustrated Beginner's Guide to Making Wine from Concentrate.* Véhicule Press, Montréal (Québec).

3. Piatz, S. 2014. *The Complete Guide to Making Mead: The Ingredients, Equipment, Processes, and Recipes for Crafting Honey Wine.* Voyageur Press, Beverly, MA.

4. Keller, J.B., Jr., 2021. *Home Winemaking: The Simple Way to Make Delicious Wine.* Adventure Publications, Cambridge, MN.

About Units of Measures

....

Winemaking in most parts of the world is greatly influenced by European methods and processes. Therefore, the use of the Metric system (also known as the International System of Units or *Système International d'Unités* (SI) in French) for units of measures has proliferated to most winemaking countries. In the U.S., the Metric system is also widely used in laboratory analysis, but the U.S. system is most often used for winemaking equipment manufactured there. For example, French oak barrels sold in the U.S. are described in liters and American barrels are described in gallons.

Readers are advised to exercise caution with the use of units of measures when obtaining winemaking "recipes" from books and other sources to ensure proper dosage. Many U.S. and Imperial units use the same terms but their quantities are quite different — a U.S. gallon is smaller than an Imperial gallon.

This book expresses all measurements using the Metric system with U.S. conversions in parentheses as required as per common usage in the U.S.; for example, temperature is expressed in degrees Celsius followed by degrees Fahrenheit in parentheses, and similarly, volume in liters followed by gallons in parentheses. Please consult Appendix A for a list of conversion factors for Metric, U.S. and Imperial systems, including abbreviations for units used in this book.

To avoid confusion for those not familiar with the Metric system, volume measurements are expressed in liters and gallons, and not in hectoliters (hL) — equivalent to 100 liters (L) — the industry standard. But laboratory measurements are expressed in milliliters (mL) or liters (L).

And where precise temperature and volume measurements are important, exact conversions are given, otherwise, for simplicity and to be consistent with common usage, rounded numbers are used. For example, we
refer to a standard 23-liter carboy as a 6-gallon carboy, the two being somewhat equivalent although a 6-gallon carboy is about 22.7 liters. Similarly,
temperature may be specified in instructions as, for example, 15 °C (60 °F)
although 15 °C converts to 59 °F.

Concentration measurements are expressed as per de facto industry
standards, i.e., in grams per liter (g/L) and milligrams per liter (mg/L),
with the former followed by grams per gallon (g/gal) in parenthesis. But
parts per million (ppm) and percentage (%) are also in common use. Conversions are simple: 1 ppm by volume or weight is equivalent to 1 mg/L
or 1 mg/kg, respectively, using the Metric system, and 1% is equivalent to
10 g/L when the percentage refers to a ratio of mass to volume. For
example, 30 mg/L free sulfur dioxide (SO_2) is the same as 30 ppm free SO_2,
and 6.5 g/L total acidity (TA) is the same as 0.65% TA.

Pay careful attention to percentages listed in this book and on product
labels. Percentages may represent either a ratio of *weight to volume* (w/v),
volume to volume (v/v), or *weight to weight* (w/w). For example, a TA of
0.65% is understood to mean 0.65% w/v, an alcohol level of 13.5% commonly means 13.5% v/v, and a sugar concentration of 24.0% *in juice* means
24.0% w/w (which is equivalent to 24.0 degrees Brix).

The use of baking measuring tools, i.e., cup, teaspoon (tsp) and table-
spoon (tbsp), is not recommended except where only rough volumes of
additives are to be measured for expediency, for example, if instructed to
dissolve 3 tbsp of sulfite in a gallon of water. These tools are otherwise not
sufficiently accurate to add precise amounts of sulfite or other additives to
wine; a good laboratory scale is recommended for such purposes.

Winemaking Lexicon

The winemaking vocabulary is quite expansive, and many terms are used interchangeably, often incorrectly, or are used differently by winemakers. Here you will find short definitions to help you understand the winemaking processes described in Section 1.3 and the vocabulary to describe working with grape varieties in Chapter 2. The terms are defined in greater details in subsequent relevant chapters.

Wine is usually defined broadly as a fermented beverage from any raw material that contains primarily sugar, such as grapes, fruits, vegetables and flowers, but also starch. In this book, "wine" will refer to those made from grapes or grape derivatives (e.g., must, juice, concentrate).

Words in italics within definitions refer to terms defined elsewhere in this lexicon.

Acetaldehyde: A volatile substance formed in small amounts by *yeast* metabolism during *alcoholic fermentation (AF)*. It is also formed by chemical *oxidation* of *ethanol* and where it can impart a strong bruised-apple smell, a clear marker of advanced oxidative spoilage. Also known as ethanal.

Acetic acid: The most important acid in *volatile acidity (VA)*. It is produced in tiny amounts by *yeast* during *alcoholic fermentation (AF)* and which adds aroma complexity to wine; however, when detected as a distinct vinegar smell, it is considered a *fault*.

Acidification: The process of adding one or more acids to increase the *acidity* of *must* or wine.

Acidity: The general term used to describe the tart, sour taste of the combined effects of acids in wine. It is quantifiable by measuring *total acidity (TA)*.

Additive: A substance, such as a *fining* agent or *sulfur dioxide (SO₂)*, added to and which remains in *must* or wine. Compare *processing aid*.

Adjunct: Any piece of wood, primarily oak, such as, staves, cubes, chips and spirals, used as an alternative to oak barrels for imparting oak *aromas*, flavors and *tannins*. See *oak alternatives*.

Aging: The sojourn of wine in vessels from the end of the *alcoholic fermentation (AF)* to bottling, in the case of bulk aging, or in bottles until consumed, in the case of bottle aging. Also known as maturation.

Aging potential: A qualitative or quantitative description of how long a wine can be expected to age before its quality starts declining.

Airlock: A device used on *carboys* and other winemaking vessels to allow *carbon dioxide (CO₂)* gas to escape during fermentation and aging while keeping air (oxygen), dust and other elements out.

Alcoholic fermentation (AF): The conversion of fermentable sugars — glucose and fructose — into alcohol (*ethanol*) and *carbon dioxide (CO₂)* gas by *yeast*.

Amelioration: A term used to refer to the practice of adding water to *must* for the purpose of lowering the initial sugar level or acidity, i.e., *Specific Gravity (SG)* or *total acidity (TA)*, respectively.

Anthocyanins: The color pigment molecules, belonging to the broad class of *polyphenols*, found in red grape skins and the pulp of certain varieties — called *teinturiers* — that give red wines their color.

Aromas: A term used here to describe all positive odors that can be perceived in wine, i.e., aromas from grapes, from *yeast* metabolism, and from aging in inert vessels as well as barrels, referred to as primary, secondary and tertiary aromas, respectively. Enologists may use the term to refer to the odors of a young wine and differentiate these from the term *bouquet* to refer to the amalgamation of odors only acquired through aging, i.e., tertiary aromas.

Astringency: A tactile sensation of dryness and roughness on the palate caused by wine *tannins* binding with saliva proteins when we taste and drink red wine. Compare *bitterness*.

Autolysis: The breakdown of dead *yeast* cells, or *lees*, as *alcoholic fermentation (AF)* nears completion.

B

Backsweeten: See *sweeten*.

Bacteria: Microorganisms mainly involved in spoilage, such as acetic acid bacteria responsible for producing *acetic acid* when, for example, wine is excessively exposed to oxygen. There are also beneficial bacteria, such as lactic acid bacteria involved in *malolactic fermentation (MLF)*.

Balance: A descriptor for wine where *acidity*, sweetness and sugar, alcohol, and *tannins* coexist in harmony without any one element dominating.

Bâtonnage: A French term commonly used to refer to the technique of stirring *lees*, the dead *yeast* cells leftover from the *alcoholic fermentation (AF)*, to increase *aroma* and flavor complexity, enhance *mouthfeel*, and increase *aging* potential.

Bench trials: Tests performed on a small scale with juice or wine samples to assess the qualitative or quantitative impacts of adding varying amounts of *additives* or *processing aids*, for example, to correct some deficiency. The amount determined that best achieves the desired results is then scaled up to treat an entire batch.

Bitterness: A term used to describe the bitter taste (as opposed to tactile sensation) of *tannins*. Compare *astringency*.

Blend: A wine consisting of two or more different wines, either from different grape varieties, from grapes of the same *variety* but sourced from different vintages or vineyards. If the blend consists of wines all made from a single grape *variety*, it is called a *varietal*. Note that commercial wineries may label a blend as a *varietal* if it meets the rules of that winemaking region, for example, a *varietal* may comprise no less than 85% of wine from that one grape variety. Compare *varietal*.

Body: A term that describes the "weight," "fullness" or "richness" of wine. Body depends mainly on alcohol content, *tannins, acidity, polysaccharides*, color and amount of *residual sugar (RS)*. A richly colored red wine with high alcohol and tannins is said to be full-bodied. A fruity, *dry* white wine is said to be light-bodied. Compare *structure*.

Bottle shock: A condition of "wine stress" that results from excessive handling or vibrations from, for example, a long journey in a car. It is often used interchangeably with *bottle sickness*, though the two terms have different meanings.

Bottle sickness: A temporary condition where a wine has seemingly become devoid of its wonderful pre-bottling *aromas* and flavors. It is believed to be the result of rapid *oxidation* during the bottling process that causes a small amount of *acetaldehyde* to form. It is often used interchangeably with *bottle shock*, though the two terms have different meanings.

Bottle variation: A condition where two or more bottles from the same production run smell or taste somewhat differently, usually due to different amounts of oxygen uptake during bottling or from closure variability. See *OTR*.

Bouquet: A term used to describe the amalgamation of odors only acquired through aging and which develop gradually over the course of time. Also referred to as "tertiary aromas." Compare *aromas*.

Brewing: The production of beer by steeping, for example, malt, barley, or other sources of starch in water and then fermenting the liquid. This term is often used interchangeably, albeit incorrectly, with winemaking.

Brix: A measure of *total dissolved solids (TDS)*. It gives an approximation of the amount of sugars in juice and wine, measured as a percentage of total weight.

Bung: A rubber or silicone stopper, either solid or with a hole to accommodate an *airlock*.

C

Cap: The mass of red grape solids that forms and floats to the top of a vessel as wine ferments. A cap signifies that *alcoholic fermentation (AF)* is in progress with *carbon dioxide (CO₂)* gas pushing red grape solids to the surface.

Carbon dioxide (CO_2): A gas produced primarily during *alcoholic fermentation (AF)* but also during *malolactic fermentation (MLF)*. See *degassing*.

Carbonic maceration: A red winemaking technique where whole grape clusters are placed in a sealed tank without *crushing* or *destemming* and layered with CO_2 gas to trigger fermentation within berries to produce a light-bodied, fruity style of wine.

Carboy: A glass or plastic-type vessel of standard size, mainly 19 L (5 gal) and 23 L (6 gal). See *demijohn*.

Chaptalization: The practice of adding sugar to *must* or fermenting wine for the purpose of increasing *potential alcohol (PA)*, i.e., the expected maximum amount of alcohol that can be produced.

Clarification: The process of clearing wine via natural *sedimentation*, the use of *additives*, for example, a *fining* agent, or *filtration*.

Cleaning: The process of removing dirt, debris and organic matter from equipment in preparation for *sanitizing*.

Cold crashing: A term used in home winemaking to refer to the process of chilling wine at cold temperatures to avoid *tartrates* from forming later in the bottle or to stop an active fermentation. See *cold stabilization*.

Cold settling: The technique of letting white or rosé juice settle at cold temperatures to allow *sedimentation* of grape fragments and other particulates that would otherwise interfere with *yeast* metabolism during *alcoholic fermentation (AF)*.

Cold soak: A red winemaking technique used primarily before *alcoholic fermentation (AF)* where crushed red grapes are kept at cold temperatures to favor color extraction while inhibiting a spontaneous fermentation. It is also used following fermentation as a technique to soften *tannins* to make a wine more approachable in its youth. Also known as cold soak maceration and pre-ferment cold soak.

Cold stabilization: A *tartrate stabilization* process involving subjecting wine to cold temperatures — close to freezing — to avoid *tartrates* from forming later in the bottle. Also referred to as *cold crashing* in home winemaking.

Colloidal matter (colloids): Refers to microscopically dispersed insoluble or soluble particles, such as *proteins*, *pectin*, *anthocyanins* and *tannins*, in *must* or wine.

Concentrate: Juice that has been processed to partially remove water and then stabilized and packaged into a kit. To make wine, water is added to the concentrate and then fermented.

Copigmentation: A phenomenon whereby *anthocyanins* link in a very specific fashion to colorless compounds or other anthocyanins and which increase color intensity and stability when cofermenting a white variety with a red variety, for example, Viognier and Syrah.

Counterfining: The practice of adding a second *fining* agent or other *processing aid* to either improve the efficacy of the first fining agent or, for example, to help it settle once it has flocculated so it can be completely removed by *racking*. See *flocculation*.

Crushing: The process of gently splitting berries open to facilitate release of juice during *pressing* in white winemaking or to expose juice to grape solids during *maceration* in red winemaking.

Cultivar: Short for "cultivated varieties" — the more technical term for "grape variety."

Deacidification: The process of reducing one or more acids to lower the *acidity* of *must* or wine.

Degassing: The process of removing *carbon dioxide* (CO_2) gas from wine prior to *clarification* and bottling, or from wine samples to be analyzed, for example, for *total acidity (TA)*.

Demijohn: A glass vessel with a large body and small neck, most commonly 54 L (14 gal) in volume, traditionally enclosed in wickerwork but now predominantly plastic basket. Known as "damigiana" in Italian. See *carboy*.

Destemming: The process of removing and separating stems from grape berries before or after *crushing*, depending on equipment.

Dry: A wine is said to be "dry" when it has no perceptible sweetness, and therefore, a wine with some *residual sugar (RS)* but high *acidity* may taste dry. However, from a *stabilization* perspective, a wine is considered dry when all fermentable sugars have been consumed by *yeast* during *alcoholic fermentation (AF)* and the amount of *residual sugar (RS)* is less than 2 g/L.

E

Enology: The science and study of wine and winemaking. Spelled "œnology" in Commonwealth countries.

Enzymes: *Proteins* that enable or catalyze reactions without themselves undergoing any change. These reactions could otherwise not happen or could take much longer to occur. For example, naturally occurring or exogenous pectolytic *enzymes*, or pectinases, break down *pectin* transferred from skins into juice and improve *clarification* and *filtration*, and proteases break down naturally occurring *proteins* in grapes.

Esters: A class of compounds responsible for many of the fruity *aromas* and flavors in wine. These compounds are produced either by *yeast* during *alcoholic fermentation (AF)* or by esterification, a chemical reaction between alcohols and acids.

Ethanol: The major alcohol produced by *yeast* during *alcoholic fermentation (AF)*.

F

Fault: A defect, such as oxidized wine or wine afflicted by *volatile acidity (VA)*, resulting from winemaking and which adversely affects the taste or enjoyment of wine. Compare *flaw*.

Fermentation: Refers to *alcoholic fermentation (AF)* when used without a qualifier.

Fermentor: A vessel, such as a *carboy*, vat, tank or barrel, used for fermentation. Also spelled as "fermenter" although this refers in fermentation science to any agent or substance, such as a bacterium, mold or *yeast* that causes microbiological reactions.

Filtration: The process of clarifying wine by mechanical means through filter media, such as filter pads or cartridges, or of removing *yeast* and bacterial cells through special filter media for the purpose of ensuring *microbial stability*.

Fining: Another term for *clarification*, but it also refers to the process of treating, for example, excessive *proteins*, harsh *tannins*, or poor color via the use of *additives* or *fining* agents. Compare *clarification*.

Flaw: An abnormality or a distraction, but not quite a serious defect, which does not adversely affect the taste or enjoyment of wine. Compare *fault*.

Flocculation: A process by which *colloidal matter* aggregates into a floc, either spontaneously or due to the addition of a clarifying or *fining* agent, and which comes out of suspension to then precipitate. See *sedimentation*.

Free-run: Free-run juice or wine obtained by simple drainage of liquid, i.e., without *pressing* grape solids. Compare *press-run*.

Glutathione: A naturally occurring sulfur-containing substance in grapes having very high antioxidant power. Also known as GSH.

Headspace: The space above the surface of the wine in a wine bottle, *carboy*, barrel or other vessel, and which contains air and causes *oxidation* if not otherwise removed by vacuum or displaced with an inert gas. Also referred to as *ullage*.

Heat stabilization: Also known as *protein stabilization*, the process of adding a suitable *fining* agent, such as bentonite, to remove *proteins* in *must* or wine.

Hydrogen sulfide (H_2S): A *volatile sulfur compound (VSC)* with an unpleasant smell of rotten eggs, sewage or struck flint, often the result of lack of fermentation *nutrients* or leaving wine too long on the gross *lees*.

Hybrid: A grape *variety* the result of interspecific crossing, i.e., crossing or hybridization of two species from the same genus.

Hydrometer: An instrument used to measure the amount of *total dissolved solids (TDS)* to get an approximation of the amount of sugar in *must* or wine. It can include one or more scales, including *Specific Gravity (SG)*, *Brix* and *Potential Alcohol (PA)*.

Inoculation: The point at which *yeast* is added to *must* to initiate *alcoholic fermentation (AF)*, or lactic acid *bacteria* added to *must* or wine to initiate *malolactic fermentation (MLF)*.

Inoculum: The *yeast* or bacterium preparation for inoculating juice or *must* to start *alcoholic fermentation (AF)* or *malolactic fermentation (MLF)*.

Lactic acid: An important acid in wine. It results from the conversion of *malic acid* by lactic acid *bacteria* during *malolactic fermentation (MLF)*.

Lees: Sediments that form at the bottom of vessels, mainly during *alcoholic fermentation (AF)* and which are referred to as "gross lees," but also form during aging and which are referred to as "fine lees." Lees contain dead *yeast* cells, grape solid fragments, *tartrates*, *polysaccharides*, *bacteria* and other precipitable matter.

Lees stirring: A technique of stirring *lees*, the dead *yeast* cells leftover from the *alcoholic fermentation (AF)*, to increase *aroma* and flavor complexity, enhance *mouthfeel* and increase *aging potential*. See *bâtonnage*.

M

Maceration: The red winemaking technique of macerating, or "steeping," grape skins in juice pre-fermentation for the purpose of extracting *aromas* and flavors, color and *tannins*, or macerating grape solids in wine post fermentation for the purpose of softening or extracting further *tannins*. It is also used for making *orange wine*.

Malic acid: The second most significant acid, after *tartaric acid*, found in grapes. In reds, it is most often converted into *lactic acid* by lactic acid *bacteria* during *malolactic fermentation (MLF)*.

Malolactic fermentation (MLF): The enzymatic process of converting the sharper-tasting *malic acid* into the softer *lactic acid* by lactic acid *bacteria* for the purpose of reducing *acidity* as well as to add *aromas* and flavors.

Mannoproteins: Large *polysaccharides* found abundantly in *yeast* cell walls and, consequently, in wines aged on the *lees* with stirring, and which contribute *body* to wine. See *bâtonnage*.

Mercaptans: A class of foul-smelling *volatile sulfur compounds (VSCs)*, such as hydrogen sulfide (H_2S), resulting primarily from the post-fermentation interaction between gross *lees* and sulfur compounds.

Methoxypyrazines: A class of compounds found in Cabernet-related varieties that impart a vegetal, green bell pepper character to wine, especially when made from underripe fruit. Often just referred to as pyrazines.

Microbial spoilage: Any kind of spoilage of microbial nature, i.e., caused by microorganisms, for example, *yeast* or *bacteria*.

Microbial stability: The state of wine when it is protected against microorganisms — *yeast* and *bacteria* — that could otherwise cause spoilage. Microbial stability is achieved by adding a preservative, such as *sulfur dioxide (SO_2)*, or by *sterile filtration*.

Micro-oxidation: A physicochemical phenomenon involving the passive and gradual transfer of infinitesimally small amounts of atmospheric oxygen into certain types of vessels, such as barrels and HDPE (high-density polyethylene) tanks. It facilitates polymerization of *tannins* and *anthocyanins*, which causes a "softening" of *tannins* for a smoother *mouthfeel*, and also stabilizes color.

Minerality: An ill-defined term used by some wine tasters to describe a "rocky" or "steely" taste accompanied by *aromas* of gun flint, as if these *aromas* and flavors come from the rocks and soils, although there is no science-based evidence supporting any link to actual minerals found in wines. Winemaker and consultant Clark Smith describes minerality as being neither an aroma nor a flavor, but rather, a sensation occurring at the back of the palate, akin to an "electrical current running through the throat" [1].

Mouthfeel: A term used in conjunction with "body" to describe the tactile sensation felt on the palate and in the mouth due to *tannins*, alcohol, *polysaccharides* and *residual sugar (RS)*. Compare *body*.

Must: The juice used in making white wine, or the juice and all its dissolved solids as well as crushed grapes in making red wine; it is what winemakers refer to as what will be fermented. The term is often used interchangeably with "juice" in white winemaking. Once fermentation has started and alcohol is being produced, it is then referred to as *wine*.

Nutrients: Naturally occurring nitrogen-containing substances used by *yeast* and *bacteria* to successfully carry out their metabolic functions during *alcoholic fermentation (AF)* and *malolactic fermentation (MLF)*. *Musts* are often deficient in nutrients and must therefore be supplemented with *additives*.

Oak alternatives: Pieces of oak wood available in many different forms used to impart oak aromas and flavors to wine as a less expensive alternative to barrels. Also referred to as oak *adjuncts*.

Orange wine: A bolder, more intense style of white wine characterized by a deeper color, orange to amber, made by macerating and fermenting grape skins and solids with the juice. Also known as skin-contact white wine.

OTR: Short for oxygen transfer rate, i.e., the rate at which oxygen moves through a material, such as wood in a barrel or plastic in a HDPE tank, or through and around a closure, such as cork stoppers.

Oxidation: A spoilage condition arising from excessive oxygen in wine. It can cause wine to turn to an orange and then brown color, it can mute *aromas*, or cause the conversion of compounds into undesirable substances, for example, *ethanol* into *acetaldehyde*.

Pearson Square: A simple tool or method to calculate the proportions of two juices or wines needed to create a blend with a desired concentration of, for example, *total acidity (TA)* or alcohol.

Pectin: A class of substances, or *polysaccharides*, found in the cell walls of grape skins, which can cause problems with *clarification* and *filtration* if not broken down by naturally occurring or exogenous *enzymes* known as pectinases.

pH: A measure of the strength of acids (or alkalis) in *must* or wine. Compare *total acidity (TA)*.

Phenolic browning: A phenomenon that causes phenols in *must* to turn brown due to oxidative *enzymes*, known as polyphenol oxidases (PPOs), or in wine to also turn to an orange and then brown color due to chemical *oxidation* of *polyphenols*.

Phenolic ripeness: Refers to the amount of *tannins* and *anthocyanins* in red grape *varieties*.

Piquette: A light-bodied, low-alcohol wine made by adding water to pressed grape *pomace*, and then fermenting on the skins, or re-pressing the pomace and then fermenting. Also known as second-run wine.

Polyphenols: A very broad class of compounds that includes *tannins* and *anthocyanins*. The word is often used interchangeably with "phenolics" for brevity.

Polysaccharides: Long chains of many monosaccharides, such as simple sugar molecules. *Yeast* polysaccharides, or *mannoproteins*, contribute to *body* by giving a sense of "fullness" on the palate. But polysaccharides can also be a source of chemical and physical instabilities due to their high molecular weights.

Pomace: The mass of grape solids either from pressing grapes in white winemaking or pressing crushed grapes that have macerated in wine in red winemaking. Also referred to as "cake."

Potassium: Naturally occurring minerals (K^+ ions) found in grapes and which are translocated to wine. Potassium ions react with *tartaric acid* to form *potassium bitartrate*, which causes *tartrate* crystals to form when wine is subjected to cold temperatures.

Potassium bitartrate: The chemical name for *tartrates*, the salt crystals that form and precipitate from *potassium* and *tartaric acid* when wine is subjected to cold temperatures.

Potassium metabisulfite: The potassium and most common salt of metabisulfite used in winemaking; it is used for *sanitizing* equipment and also as a preservative against *oxidation* and *microbial spoilage*. It is often referred to simply as *sulfite* or "KMS," the "K" being the element symbol for *potassium*.

Potential alcohol (PA): The expected maximum amount of alcohol (*ethanol*) that can potentially be produced if *yeast* converts all fermentable sugars during *alcoholic fermentation (AF)*. It can be estimated by a direct reading on the *hydrometer* or by converting a *Specific Gravity (SG)* or *Brix* reading.

Precursors: Another word for "varietal compounds"; it refers to those grape and wine compounds that would characterize the wine as typical of that variety. See *varietal*.

Pressing: The process of pressing grape solids to extract juice in white winemaking or wine following *maceration* and *alcoholic fermentation (AF)* in red winemaking.

Press-run: Press-run juice or wine obtained by *pressing* grape solids. Compare *free-run*.

Primary fermentation: A confusing term mainly used by amateur winemakers, especially kit winemakers, that refers to the *alcoholic fermentation (AF)* phase when wine is fermenting in a pail. Once transferred to a *carboy* (see *racking*), the continuation of the *alcoholic fermentation (AF)* is referred to as *secondary fermentation*.

Processing aid: A substance used, for example, to clarify wine or precipitate harsh *tannins*, but which itself becomes removed following *racking*. Also referred to as "adjuvant." Compare *additives*.

Protective colloids: Naturally occurring substances or *additives* that protect other substances in wine so that the latter do not react with other wine components or do not precipitate; for example, carboxymethyl cellulose (CMC) is a protective colloid that inhibits the formation of *tartrates*.

Proteins: Very large molecules consisting of long chains of amino acids. Proteins can be a source of cloudiness, or protein haze, in white wines, especially when subjected to warmer temperatures, and must therefore be removed by *fining*. Proteins have a great affinity for *tannins*.

Protein stabilization: Also known as *heat stabilization*, the process of adding a suitable *fining* agent, such as bentonite, to remove proteins in *must* or wine.

Pumpover: The red winemaking technique of pumping juice or wine over the grape solids during maceration and fermentation to favor extraction of *polyphenols*, homogenize temperature, and protect against *microbial spoilage*. Compare *punchdown*.

Punchdown: The red winemaking technique of "punching down" the grape solids by mechanical means into the *must* or wine during maceration and fermentation to favor extraction of *polyphenols*, homogenize temperature, and protect against *microbial spoilage*. Compare *pumpover*.

Quinones: The brown-colored form of certain *polyphenols* and which are responsible for *phenolic browning*.

Racking: The process of transferring *must* or wine from one vessel to another by gravity or using a pump for the purpose of separating the juice or wine from its sediment.

Reduction: In chemistry, reduction is the opposite of *oxidation*, and when a substance is oxidized, the substance causing *oxidation* undergoes reduction. In winemaking, the term is used to refer to a condition in which wine smells of *volatile sulfur compounds (VSCs)*, notably *hydrogen sulfide (H₂S)*, due to, for example, a lack of *nutrients* during *alcoholic fermentation (AF)* or a lack of oxygen in bottled wine. Reduction occurs frequently in bottled wine under screw cap because this type of closure, unlike natural cork, provides a much tighter barrier to oxygen ingress.

Residual sugar (RS): The amount of natural sugars remaining in a wine after completion of the *alcoholic fermentation (AF)*, or the amount of natural and added sugar measured in a wine at bottling, and which impact *body* and *mouthfeel*. Also referred to as "reducing sugars" although the meanings are slightly different.

Rice hulls: Hulls or husks of rice used as *pressing* aids to facilitate the flow of juice or wine through the grape mass in the press; it is particularly useful when dealing with slipskin grape varieties.

Rosé: French for "pink"; refers to any of pink-colored wines.

Saignée: A French term that translates to "bleeding" and which refers to the technique of running off some juice from crushed red grapes to make *rosé* wine. The primary objective is usually to concentrate flavors and color in the rest of the juice in making red wine.

Sanitizing: The process of removing and inhibiting microorganisms from winemaking equipment and vessels down to a level deemed to pose no risk of spoilage. *Cleaning* is a necessary step before sanitizing.

Secondary fermentation: A confusing term mainly used by amateur winemakers, especially kit winemakers, that refers to the *alcoholic fermentation (AF)* phase following *primary fermentation* conducted in a *carboy*. To add to the confusion, it is also used to refer to *malolactic fermentation (MLF)*.

Sedimentation: The natural, physical process whereby suspended, insoluble matter in juice or wine precipitate to the bottom of a vessel. Compare *flocculation*.

SO₂: See *sulfur dioxide (SO₂)*.

Specific Gravity (SG): A measure of the amount of *total dissolved solids (TDS)* relative to the density of pure water, at some specified temperature, usually 20 °C (68 °F) in winemaking, to obtain an estimate of the amount of sugar in a *must*.

Stabilization: Refers to any of the various processes used to protect wine against, for example, *oxidation*, *microbial spoilage* and the formation of *tartrates*.

Sterile filtration: The process of removing *yeast* and bacterial cells through special filter media for the purpose of ensuring *microbial stability*.

Structure: A term often used in conjunction, often interchangeably, with *body* to describe the taste and sensation of wine. Both "structure" and "body" may refer more specifically to the relationship between *tannins* and *acidity* without considering alcohol and *polysaccharides*. Compare *body*.

Sulfite: The short name for any of the sulfite salts (e.g., *potassium metabisulfite*, sodium metabisulfite, ammonium bisulfite) used as preservatives in wine. "Sulfite" is often though incorrectly used interchangeably with *sulfur dioxide (SO₂)*.

Sulfur dioxide (SO₂): A gas, which, when dissolved in wine, acts as a preservative and protects against *microbial spoilage* and *oxidation*. SO₂ is added to wine most commonly using a *sulfite* salt, usually *potassium metabisulfite*.

Sur-lie aging: A winemaking technique of aging wine "sur lies" or on the *lees*, i.e., the dead *yeast* cells left over from the *alcoholic fermentation (AF)*, which releases *mannoproteins* that give wine more *body* and increased *mouthfeel*, and longer *aging potential*.

Sweeten: The practice of adding sugar, juice concentrate or a wine conditioner to a finished wine to create a sweeter style or to offset high acidity. Commonly referred to as "backsweeten" in home winemaking.

T

Tannins: A broad subclass of *polyphenols* found in grape skins, seeds, stems and oak wood, and which are in part responsible for *body* and *structure* in wine, particularly reds. *Tannins* are characteristically bitter and astringent, progressively less so as they polymerize into larger tannin complexes. They are also very effective in protecting wine against *oxidation*.

Tartaric acid: The most important acid in grapes and wine though not necessarily the most abundant; *malic acid* levels can be higher, especially in grapes sourced from cold-climate regions or in Native American and hybrid grape varieties. Tartaric acid also reacts with naturally occurring *potassium* to form *potassium bitartrate*, which crystallizes and precipitates as *tartrates* when wine is subjected to cold temperatures.

Tartrates: The common word for *potassium bitartrate* salt crystals. Also known as "wine diamonds" and cream of tartar.

Tartrate stabilization: A process involving adding *protective colloids* or subjecting wine to cold temperatures to avoid tartrates from forming later in the bottle. Compare *cold stabilization*.

Teinturier: A French word used to refer to any red grape *variety* that has red skin but also red juice and pulp, i.e., it can make red wine without *maceration*. Teinturier varieties are often used as blending wines to improve color in deficient reds or for making *rosé*.

Thiols: A broad but narrower class of highly *volatile sulfur compounds (VSCs)*, including *mercaptans*, which can contribute positive or negative *aromas* and smells. Thiols are responsible for the distinctive character of and (positive) *aromas* in Sauvignon Blanc wines, and notably those from New Zealand.

Titration: An analytical method used to determine the concentration of a specific substance, or analyte, in *must* or wine. A reagent, or titrant, of known concentration is added until a predetermined endpoint is reached; the amount of titrant used is then used to calculate the concentration of the analyte. For example, sodium hydroxide (NaOH) is a titrant used to determine the concentration of acids, or *total acidity (TA)*.

Topping: The practice of adding wine to a *carboy*, barrel or other vessel to minimize *headspace* and reduce the risks of *oxidation* or *microbial spoilage*.

Total acidity (TA): A measurement of the concentration of acids in *must* and wine; it is determined by *titration*. Compare *pH*.

Total dissolved solids (TDS): For all practical purposes, refers to an approximation of the amount of fermentable sugars in winemaking.

Ullage: Also referred to as *headspace*, the space above the surface of the wine in a wine bottle, *carboy*, barrel or other vessel, and which contains air if not otherwise removed by vacuum or displaced with inert gas. Also refers to the process of evaporation that creates the headspace itself.

Varietal: Refers to wine made from a single *variety*; for example, a wine made from 100% Chardonnay grapes is a varietal. The term "varietal compounds," or *precursors*, then refers to those grape and wine compounds that would characterize the wine as typical of that variety; for example, *thiols* are well-known varietal compounds that give Sauvignon Blanc its characteristic grapefruit and passion fruit *aromas*. Compare *variety*. Compare *blend*.

Variety: Refers to "grape variety"; for example, Cabernet Sauvignon is a grape variety. The word "cultivar" is the more correct botanical term, but "variety" is used more commonly among vineyardists and winemakers. Compare *varietal*. See *hybrid*.

Veraison: Refers to the onset of grape ripening. In red varieties, veraison occurs when grapes progress from green to red.

Vessel: Any type of container of food-grade material suitable for fermenting and storing wine. These include glass *carboys* and *demijohns*, PET (polyethylene terephthalate) *carboys*, plastic tubs or vats, stainless steel and HDPE (high-density polyethylene) tanks, and oak barrels.

Vinification: The winemaking process of converting grape juice, or *must*, into wine.

Vintage: The year grapes have been grown. For example, in the northern hemisphere 2019 would mean that grapes were grown in the spring, summer and fall of 2019, and harvested late summer or in the fall, or possibly in the winter and into 2020 in the case of grapes used for making ice wine.

Volatile acidity (VA): Consists primarily of *acetic acid*, an acid produced in tiny amounts by *yeast* during *alcoholic fermentation (AF)* and which adds aroma complexity to wine; however, when detected as a distinct vinegar smell, it is considered a *fault*. In the presence of oxygen, it can be produced by *Acetobacter bacteria*, as in the making of vinegar, or in poorly topped up vessels. It can also be the result of lactic acid *bacteria* metabolizing citric acid during *malolactic fermentation (MLF)*, hence why citric acid is never used to increase acidity in wines that are to go through MLF.

Volatile sulfur compounds (VSCs): A very broad class of highly volatile compounds having sulfur as the core component and which can contribute positive or negative *aromas* and smells. VSCs are also responsible for *reduction* in wine. VSCs include, for example, *sulfur dioxide (SO$_2$)*, sulfides and *mercaptans*, such as *hydrogen sulfide (H$_2$S)*, and *thiols*.

Wine: In this book, "wine" refers to fermented beverages made from grapes or grape derivatives (e.g., *must*, juice or *concentrate*).

Yeast: In winemaking, "yeast" refers primarily to *Saccharomyces cerevisiae* yeast, the microorganism responsible for metabolizing sugar into *ethanol* and the plethora of other by-products that give wines their many *aromas* and flavors.

Yield: The expected or actual volume of juice, raw wine or finished wine that a certain amount of grapes will provide.

REFERENCE

1. Smith, C. 2013. *Postmodern Winemaking: Rethinking the Modern Science of an Ancient Craft.* University of California Press, Berkeley, CA.

1 Making Consistently Great Wine

Making consistently *great* wine goes well beyond following some recipe or set of instructions. Sure, you can make excellent wine relatively easily using a kit or processed fresh juice — that is, juice that your supplier may have adjusted the sugar level, acidity or pH to allow you to make a balanced wine. But as you venture into making wine from grapes or unprocessed fresh juice, you will need to become proficient in all aspects of not only winemaking but also wine science.

To make consistently great wine, you first have to insist on sourcing the best quality raw material you can find and that your budget allows, or on growing fruit adapted to your soil and climate if you have a backyard vineyard. That will be a challenge in itself as you will often have grapes or juice that may not have perfect balance in sugar, acidity, pH and polyphenols to make well-balanced wine. Perhaps you received a load of grapes with a very high sugar level, which you know will be a problem fermenting completely, or perhaps with a high pH, which will require acidification, maybe, maybe not, depending on acidity. Therefore, you will need a solid knowledge of juice and wine chemistry and how to measure the various parameters to be able to understand how to achieve balance — it's not always straightforward — and how and when to intervene when faced with unexpected problems along the way. You will need to be able to assess problems, determine the root cause, and implement corrective actions. Record-keeping will be absolutely essential. You will also need to be familiar with the plethora of commercial winemaking products to help you get more out of your wine. And of course you will need to be familiar with grape varieties so you can make an informed choice for a desired style and decide on processing techniques. We will explore the most common grape varieties in Chapter 2.

If you haven't already done so, first review the terms defined in the *Winemaking Lexicon* section of this book. To help you better manage the winemaking process to make astute decisions, for example, if and how to increase acidity to lower pH, this chapter presents a high-level view of juice and wine chemistry and the transformations that occur from grapes to juice to wine. It provides an overview of the processes for making white, rosé and red wine using grapes, fresh juice, processed 100% juice, and concentrate with detailed protocols presented in later chapters. It also discusses the need and importance of good record-keeping.

1.1 THE TRANSFORMATION OF GRAPES INTO MUST AND WINE

It all starts in the vineyard on vines. After budbreak in the spring, flowers start to grow, pollination and fertilization take place, and then berries form, grow and ripen during the hot, sunny days of summer as fall and harvest approach. The stage at which these ripening changes occur is called veraison. Sugar accumulates, malic acid is slowly metabolized and the high acidity starts declining while tartaric acid remains fairly constant (it doesn't get metabolized), color changes from green to shades of yellow (depending on grape variety) for whites and to hues of deep purple for reds, aromas and precursors develop, and phenolic ripeness increases. Some white varieties, such as Gewürztraminer and Pinot Gris/Grigio, have colored skins that can tinge these white wines with faint pinkish hues.

After veraison, sucrose and other sugars are manufactured by photosynthesis as grapevine leaves convert solar energy and carbon dioxide into sugar in conjunction with soil chemistry to deliver water, minerals and other essential nutrients to allow grape berries to ripen. Most of the sucrose is hydrolyzed into glucose and fructose by invertase enzymes so that there is little sucrose left in fully ripened grapes. In *V. vinifera* varieties, i.e., those of European descent, glucose content starts off considerably higher than that of fructose but then drops as berries start switching from sugar to organic acids as substrates, and levels off to about the same concentration during the maturation phase as berries only use organic acids. Therefore, there are approximately equal amounts of glucose and fructose in berries at harvest. If grapes are left to overripen, fructose continues to accumulate and the glucose-to-fructose ratio drops below 1 (one). The relevance of this ratio from a winemaking perspective is that *Saccharomyces cerevisiae* wine yeast is predominantly glucophilic, therefore it converts glucose at faster rate than fructose, which means that a wine fermented to dryness will have less residual glucose than fructose, and any glucose and fructose remaining in the wine at the end of fermentation contribute to residual sugar. Residual fructose will make wine taste sweeter than glucose as it has about 1.5 times the perception of sweetness. During veraison, pectin also forms in grape skins and soften berries from their hard, green physiology during the development stage.

The critical decision of when to harvest is based on achieving the "right" balance of sugar, acids, phenolic ripeness and flavors to make a desired style of wine. Balance can be corrected in the winery through such procedures as chaptalization to increase sugar content and potential alcohol level, acid adjustments to raise or lower acidity and adjust pH, blending or adding processing aids that can modify taste, flavors and tactile sensations. "Mouthfeel" and "texture" are common terms used interchangeably to describe tactile sensations in the mouth, i.e., viscosity, astringency/dryness, and hotness (burning sensation due to high ethanol concentration).

Figure 1.1 illustrates the composition and distribution of the major types of compounds in ripe grape berries at harvest.

Grape berries consist of a grape skin, flesh or pulp, and seeds. Stems, and especially green stems (as opposed to woody, brown stems) contain undesirable harsh tannins, and therefore, grape bunches are usually destemmed in any winemaking that involves macerating grape solids with their juice, such as in red winemaking, although there is notable success in fermenting Pinot Noir, for example, with a small percentage of whole bunches. There is no crushing or destemming either when making wine by carbonic maceration.

Most white and red grape varieties comprise "white" pulp, and therefore it is possible to make white wine from red varieties. Red wine is made from red varieties by macerating grape skins in juice to extract color. A few varieties, known as teinturiers, such as Alicante Bouschet and Chambourcin, have red pulp and can only make red wine or rosé without the need for maceration.

The pulp, including the area surrounding the seeds, called the endocarp, comprises the majority of fermentable sugars, organic acids and proteins, as well as aroma compounds, some polyphenols, and potassium, copper and iron in the form of ions.

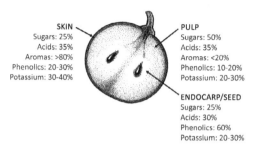

SKIN
Sugars: 25%
Acids: 35%
Aromas: >80%
Phenolics: 20-30%
Potassium: 30-40%

PULP
Sugars: 50%
Acids: 35%
Aromas: <20%
Phenolics: 10-20%
Potassium: 20-30%

ENDOCARP/SEED
Sugars: 25%
Acids: 30%
Phenolics: 60%
Potassium: 20-30%

Figure 1.1: Cross-section of a grape berry showing distribution of key substances in the skin, and pulp, including the area surrounding the seeds; percentages are relative to the whole berry (adapted from [1], [2], [3] and [4]).

Tartaric and malic acid are the two most significant organic acids and, along with those other acids produced during fermentation, give wines their freshness and microbial stability (along with alcohol).

Proteins are very large molecules made up of long chains of amino acids and which can cause haze to develop even in a perfectly clear wine if the wine was not stabilized against proteins, and particularly if it is subjected to rising temperatures. Proteins are generally not an issue in reds because they bind to and precipitate with tannins. They may be an issue in red hybrids and Native American varieties that have unusually high amounts of proteins and particularly if they have low tannins. But in whites where tannin levels are very low, proteins must be removed using a suitable fining agent, such as bentonite, to avoid potential haze problems.

Although the amount of aroma compounds in the pulp is relatively small in non-aromatic varieties, the pulp can contain significant amounts of odorants, called terpenes or terpenoids, in aromatic varieties. These aromas originating in grapes are referred to as primary aromas. TDN, short for the very complex chemical name 1,1,6-trimethyl-1,2-dihydronaphthalene, the compound responsible for the pejorative-sounding petrol aroma found Riesling, is an example of a terpenoid.

Many of the aroma compounds in non-aromatic varieties are not perceptible in berries or juice, that is, they are not volatile yet, and therefore you cannot smell them. During fermentation, yeast will break apart these aroma compounds (and create new ones) and free them from their non-volatile parts (mainly sugars) to make the aromas volatile. Wines also develop aroma complexity during aging as aroma compounds are cleaved and freed by, for example, hydrolysis. Aromas can be smelled in aromatic varieties, such as Muscat, Riesling and Gewürztraminer, because the aroma compounds are already free and not tied to any non-volatile parts.

The pulp contains very little in terms of tannins but small amounts of phenolic acids (which belong to the family of polyphenols) that are responsible for the browning effect when juice is excessively exposed to air. The pulp in teinturiers contains large amounts of anthocyanins.

Potassium ions (K^+) are translocated from the soil into grapes, and are therefore found in significant amounts in juice (must). Potassium is of great significance in winemaking as it raises pH and also impacts tartrate stability. Potassium interacts with tartaric acid to form and precipitate potassium bitartrate crystals, or tartrates, during fermentation and if wine is subjected to cold temperatures, a phenomenon of greater concern in whites given their higher tartaric acid content.

Copper and iron ions are found in minute quantities but can have profound effects. These ions are in fact oxidation catalysts, and can cause wine to age prematurely if present in excessive amounts. That's why must and wine, owing to their relatively high acidity that can extract these substances from materials, should never come into contact with copper or iron-containing alloys, such as brass or steel, unless it is stainless steel.

There are two other important naturally occurring substances found in grape juice: glutathione and polyphenol oxidases.

Glutathione (abbreviated GSH, where G stands for the *gluta* part, and SH refers to the thiol, or sulfur–hydrogen, function) is a sulfur-containing tripeptide (a chain of three amino acids) in grapes and is released relatively abundantly into the must when grapes are crushed or pressed, and which, having very high antioxidant power, protects must and wine from oxidation, at least until it becomes all exhausted.

Polyphenol oxidases, or PPOs, are oxidation enzymes that jump into action as soon as berries are crushed or pressed and the juice becomes exposed to air. PPOs are responsible for oxidation and browning of juice; they can be inhibited with sulfur dioxide (SO_2).

Grape skin contains polyphenols, aroma compounds, pectin, potassium, and some small amounts of sugars and organic acids too.

Polyphenols in white varieties consist mostly of small amounts of tannins, but in red varieties, the skins are rich in polyphenols, specifically anthocyanins and tannins, responsible for color and structure in red wines. These are extracted to various extent during maceration and fermentation in the red winemaking process depending on the grape variety and techniques used to create a specific style. But winemakers also add tannins, or more specifically so-called "fermentation tannins," not necessarily to add body or improve structure, but primarily to stabilize color. Anthocyanins are very unstable on their own, and red wines need a good balance of tannins so that they don't shed their color. Wines aged in barrels also acquire tannins, though different kinds of tannins that contribute further to wine's stability and aging potential.

In aromatic varieties, such as those from the Muscat family, there is also a large concentration of terpenoids, powerful odorants responsible for the many floral aromas in wine, and thiols in such varieties as Sauvignon Blanc and Chenin Blanc, which give these wines their characteristic boxtree, passion fruit and grapefruit aromas. This is why these varieties may benefit from a short maceration — to extract much-desirable aroma compounds from skins. But aroma extraction from skins can also be an issue in red winemaking where it's all about macerating grape solids and juice, as methoxypyrazines, those compounds responsible for herbaceous, green pepper aromas in underripe Cabernet, are transferred from grape skins into the juice.

Pectin is found in the cell walls of grape skins and is transferred into the juice or must during pressing or maceration. Pectin is of concern mainly with non-vinifera varieties and particularly whenever grape solids are macerated in juice, where it can cause clarification and filtration problems if not broken down with pectinases. Grapes have naturally occurring pectinases to deal with pectin but not sufficiently in some non-viniferas, and therefore, juice and must from non-viniferas often have to be treated with additional pectinases.

As reds involve maceration, they will have higher levels of potassium, especially press fractions, which will cause a higher pH. Maceration will also cause small increases in sugars and acids as those are transferred from skins to juice.

Seeds contain mainly harsh tannins as well as phenolic acids, those same polyphenols responsible for the browning effects when wine oxidizes.

During alcoholic fermentation (AF), yeast converts sugars — glucose and fructose — into ethanol, glycerol (glycerin), and great amounts of carbon dioxide (CO_2) gas; the latter dissipates to imperceptible amounts by the time the wine is bottled. Most dry wines contain 11–15% ethanol by volume. Ethanol contributes to body and microbial stability. Glycerol has a slightly sweet taste but does not affect viscosity, as is often believed. By the end of fermentation, the amount of fermentable sugars is very low, below 2 g/L, in dry wine. And as potassium reacts with tartaric acid to form potassium bitartrate, the latter becomes more insoluble as the amount of ethanol produced increases, and then forms and precipitates tartrates. More tartrates will form and precipitate when wine is subjected to colder temperatures.

Yeast performs many other functions. It metabolizes sugars and other substances in grape juice into many, many other by-products, such as succinic acid, which contributes to total acidity, esters, responsible for fruity aromas and flavors, and other compounds that contribute to organoleptic qualities. Esters and other aroma compounds from yeast metabolism are responsible for what are known as secondary aromas, and are part of what some refer to as bouquet. Some yeast strains can specifically metabolize malic acid and reduce total acidity. Yeast also breaks up and frees some of the aroma compounds from their binding components making them volatile. And it also possesses a metabolic engine that produces SO_2, usually more than 10 mg/L (ppm), and therefore there is always some SO_2 present in wine.

The sharper-tasting malic acid is converted by lactic acid bacteria into the softer lactic acid in wines that are put through malolactic fermentation (MLF), which results in a decrease in total acidity and increase in pH. Lactic acid bacteria used in MLF will also produce many other by-products, the most significant is diacetyl, which imparts buttery notes. The amount of diacetyl can be modulated using various winemaking techniques.

As wine ages, either in inert vessels or wood barrels, they develop and acquire other aromas, referred to as tertiary aromas, which are part of a wine's bouquet. Some of these pleasant aromas result from acids forming odoriferous esters during aging via a chemical reaction with alcohol called esterification.

1.2 BALANCE IN WINE

We're going to talk a lot about balance in grapes and especially wine. The topic of balance will come up repeatedly in any wine discussion — it's one of the most important factors for assessing and describing quality. We all look for balance in grapes, juice and the final wine. A wine that is out of balance will not deliver the same pleasure.

Renowned French enologist Émile Peynaud (1912–2004) offers the following guiding principles in his scholarly book *The Taste of Wine* in achieving balance [5]:

"A wine tolerates acidity better when its alcoholic degree is higher; acid, bitter and astringent tastes reinforce each other; the hardest wines are those which are at the same time acid and also rich in tannins; a considerable amount of tannin is more acceptable if acidity is low and alcohol is high.

The less tannic a red wine is, the more acidity it can support (necessary for its freshness); the richer a red wine is in tannins (necessary for its development and for its longevity) the lower should be its acidity; a high tannin content allied to a pronounced acidity produces the hardest and most astringent wines."

Following are additional guiding principles in achieving balance:

- Sweetness and acidity counteract each other — that is, the higher the acidity, the lower the perception of sweetness, and vice versa. This is particularly useful in balancing and mellowing out high-acid whites by leaving a little residual sugar or adding a small amount of table sugar or grape concentrate.

- Acidity and bitterness reinforce each other — that is, the higher the acidity, the higher the bitterness and astringent sensation from tannins in reds. Therefore aim for low acidity in highly tannic wines, and low tannins in high-acid wines. But you need to consider alcohol too, as outlined in the next point.

- High acidity or high bitterness (from high tannin content) is best matched with higher alcohol. Avoid low acidity and low tannins in high-alcohol wines, or high acidity and high tannins in low-alcohol wines.

1.3 OVERVIEW OF WINEMAKING

Depending on your level of expertise, equipment, and budget and effort you are willing to invest in making wine, you have several options as to the choice of raw material: grapes from your own backyard vineyard, grapes sourced from a local grape grower or shipped to you through a third party, fresh juice, frozen must, or kits with concentrated or 100% juice. In this book, we will look at how to make dry white, rosé and red wine from any type of raw material. If you want to explore making styles other than dry wines, such as sparkling wine or sweet styles of wines, please consult reference [6].

1.3.1 GRAPES, FRESH JUICE, FROZEN MUST, KITS

GRAPES

If you have your own backyard vineyard, you have total control over the quality of grapes. You decide when to harvest based on an assessment of sugar level and ripeness, flavor development, and acidity and pH. You are looking for as perfect a balance as possible among all the components. The less imbalance, particularly between sugar and acidity, the less intervention will be required in the winemaking. But even in the best of vintages, adjustments are often necessary, for example, to increase the sugar level, reduce acidity, or lower the pH, to get a balanced must. When ready, you harvest and transport grapes to your home winery for immediate processing.

If you live in a grape-growing area, you can purchase grapes directly from a local vineyard, and then haul the load to your home winery for processing. Unless you have an exclusive relationship with a grower, you have no control or say over the quality of the grapes, therefore, you have to be prepared to deal with the possibility of having to make adjustments.

If you live far away from any grape-growing area, you will likely need to order through a grape purveyor who deals directly with growers and arranges refrigerated transportation to a local facility for pickup. Here too you have no control over the quality and balance of the grapes. Work with a reputable purveyor that deals with known vineyards and who brings in high-quality fruit.

FRESH JUICE

Working with grapes involves extra, messy work and dedicated crushing and pressing equipment that you will only use in the fall winemaking season and perhaps the spring season if you also make wine from southern hemisphere grapes (if you live in the northern hemisphere). Therefore you may opt to purchase juice so that you do not have to crush and press grapes, or even macerate, in the case of reds, as this can be done for you too. The processing is done by the grower or a designated processor, or your purveyor, and then shipped and stored refrigerated or frozen until you are ready to pick up. Therefore here too you have no control over the quality and balance of the juice. Those who want to offer a consistent product to their customers may adjust sugar, acidity and pH levels so you don't have to worry about making adjustments. This is an excellent option if you are not into analyzing and testing the various parameters, but the disadvantage is that you have no further control over color and tannin extraction with red juice.

FROZEN MUST

If you don't want to have to crush grapes but still want control over color and tannin extraction in reds, frozen must is an excellent option for making premium wine. Growers or their designated processors, or your purveyor, can crush grapes into pails, and store and ship them frozen; you still need to press grapes at the end of fermentation. A significant advantage of frozen must is that the freezing process breaks down the cell walls of grapes, and this helps release more color into the juice. Aside from possibly a light sulfite addition, processors do not adjust the chemistry of the must — that will be your responsibility to verify and make adjustments as necessary.

KITS

If you want to invest minimally in winemaking equipment and not have to crush or press grapes, or analyze and adjust must, and you want to make good, balanced wine reliably every single time, then winemaking kits may be your best option.

Kits provide the raw material and all the necessary additives — yeast, clarifying agent, preservatives, etc. — and step-by-step instructions to make wine in as little as four weeks. If you like a certain type or style of wine, you can buy the same kit again and make exactly the same wine.

But with kits too there are different options — and price ranges — in the raw material. Most kits will make 23 L (6 gal) of wine, or about 30 standard bottles. The raw material in kits can be concentrate or a blend of concentrate and juice packaged, for example, in 10- or 16-L formats, or 100% juice packaged in 23-L format. All are processed into shelf-stable products for sales and distribution.

Concentrate is juice with a portion of the water removed and then pasteurized to eradicate wild yeasts and other unwanted spoilage microorganisms; preservatives are added to make the concentrate stable and to extend its shelf life. Some concentrates may also be a blend of concentrate and juice. To make wine, you add sufficient water to the concentrate to get a starting volume of, for example, 23 L (6 gal). The greater the concentration, i.e., the smaller the volume of concentrate, the more water you will have to add. Generally, the greater the concentration, the lower the quality and price.

100% juice is also processed into a shelf-stable product, but no water was removed and, therefore, no water is added to make the wine. Kits with 100% juice will be the most expensive option, but they can produce outstanding wines.

Premium, full-bodied, red-wine kits may also include a separate pack of pasteurized, crushed and destemmed grapes, such as Allgrape Pack, which you re-introduce into the juice to extract more color and tannins.

A question that is often asked is if it is okay to do a malolactic fermentation (MLF) in kit wines. It is not recommended even you have experience conducting an MLF because the manufacturer has balanced the juice to obtain a perfectly balanced wine in a specific style that has been designed and tested as such and to deliver consistent results.

1.3.2 WHITE WINEMAKING

Figure 1.2 illustrates a generalized view of the white winemaking process using grapes or fresh juice. Here, the focus is on creating and preserving aromas and flavors.

Grapes are first crushed and destemmed, then pressed, or possibly just pressed without crushing, i.e., whole clusters, to extract the juice. A short maceration of grape skins in juice before pressing can add aromas and flavors. The juice is chilled to inhibit a spontaneous fermentation while heavy solids and particulates settle at the bottom of the vessel. It is then racked to obtain clearer juice, now called must, which is then warmed up slightly to start the alcoholic fermentation (AF), either spontaneously relying on indigenous yeast or by adding cultured yeast. The AF is done in closed containers, such as glass or stainless steel containers, to minimize oxidation effects as aromas and flavors are very delicate in whites. Except for very few grape varieties, most whites are not put through malolactic fermentation (MLF) so as to preserve the fruity style and all the acidity that gives whites their freshness.

For fuller-bodied styles of white wine, the AF is either conducted in oak barrels or the wine is aged in oak barrels post fermentation. Full-bodied whites are usually allowed to go through MLF to reduce acidity for better balance with tannins, but also to add more aroma and flavor complexity. The wine can also be aged on the lees for extra body, aromas and flavors.

Once the AF (or AF and MLF) is complete, the wine is clarified, stabilized with sulfite to protect it from spoilage microorganisms, stabilized against proteins that can cause haze as well as against tartrates. The wine is racked to separate out the sediment, with optional filtering to get a crystal-clear wine, and then bottled.

For making orange wine, the crushed grapes are macerated with the juice and fermented for several days or weeks depending on the grape variety and desired style, much like in red winemaking. When the desired extraction is achieved or when fermentation is complete, the mass of grape solids is pressed but lightly to avoid extracting excessive tannins, and is then clarified and stabilized as any white wine.

Chapter 19 describes detailed protocols for making white wine.

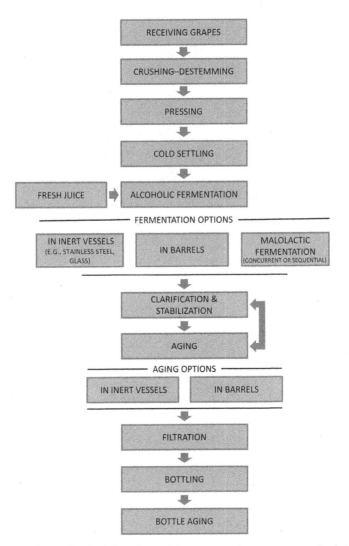

Figure 1.2: Generalized white winemaking process from grapes or fresh juice

1.3.3 ROSÉ WINEMAKING

Figure 1.3 illustrates a generalized view of the rosé winemaking process from grapes. The process is very similar to white winemaking except for a short maceration to extract color. Therefore, in addition to creating and preserving aromas and flavors, the focus here is on extracting just the right amount of color, and protecting that color from the effects of oxidation.

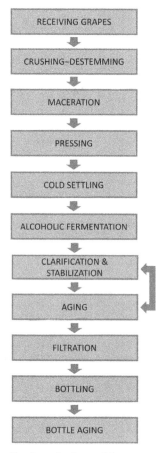

Figure 1.3: Generalized rosé winemaking process from grapes

Grapes are first crushed and destemmed into a vat and the grape solids allowed to macerate with the juice for a short period, in the order of a couple to several hours or more depending on the grape variety and desired color. When the desired color is achieved, the mass of crushed grapes is pressed and the juice is transferred to fermentation vessels. High-anthocyanin varieties, such as Syrah, are whole-cluster pressed, i.e., without crushing, since too much color would be extracted otherwise.

The juice is chilled to inhibit a spontaneous fermentation while heavy solids and particulates settle at the bottom of the vessel. It is then racked to obtain clearer juice, now called must, which is then warmed up slightly to start the alcoholic fermentation (AF), either spontaneously relying on indigenous yeast or by adding cultured yeast. The AF is done in closed containers, such as glass or stainless steel containers, to minimize oxidation effects as aromas and flavors are very delicate in rosés. Generally, rosés are not put through malolactic fermentation (MLF) so as to preserve the fruity style and all the acidity that gives rosés their freshness.

Once the AF is complete, the wine is clarified, stabilized with sulfite to protect it from spoilage microorganisms, stabilized against proteins that can cause haze as well as against tartrates. The wine is racked to separate out the sediment, with optional filtering to get a crystal-clear wine, and then bottled.

Chapter 20 describes a detailed protocol for making rosé wine.

1.3.4 RED WINEMAKING

Figure 1.4 illustrates a generalized view of the red winemaking process from grapes or frozen must. As reds are about color and tannins, in addition to creating and preserving aromas and flavors as in all wines, there is a strong focus here on extracting color and tannins.

Grapes are first crushed and destemmed into an open vat or similar vessel to allow the grape solids to macerate with the juice for the duration of the alcoholic fermentation (AF), or a shorter period if a lighter-colored style is desired. Enzymes and tannins are added right at crush to help extract and stabilize color. The mass of grape solids and juice are referred to as must at this point.

The must is then allowed to start the AF, either spontaneously relying on indigenous yeast or by adding cultured yeast. The AF is done in an open vessel, i.e., plastic vat, oak wood vat or barrel, or stainless steel tank. Anthocyanins and tannins are extracted during maceration and fermentation with greater extraction at higher temperatures; color is extracted mostly early on in the first couple of days while tannins are progressively extracted throughout as alcohol increases.

Once to three times daily, the cap is re-submerged into the fermenting must, now wine, by punchdowns or pumpovers to help extract color and tannins, to homogenize temperature to ensure good fermentation dynamics, and to keep spoilage microorganisms in check. The AF generally lasts 5–7 days, but it can be made to last longer depending on the desired style.

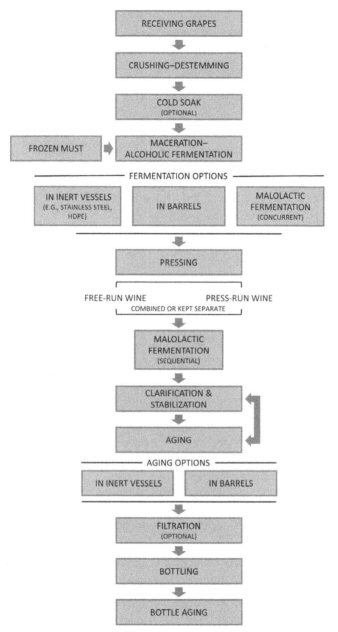

Figure 1.4: Red winemaking process from grapes or frozen must

Once the AF is complete, or earlier when desired, free-run wine is transferred to closed vessels, i.e., carboys, tanks or barrels. Grape solids are
pressed and press-run wine is transferred to closed vessels too. Free- and

press-run wines are generally kept separate given their different chemistries; they can be blended now or later if the wines are similar.

Almost all reds are put through malolactic fermentation (MLF) to reduce acidity, to increase aroma and flavor complexities, and to improve microbial stability. The MLF can be initiated soon after the start of the AF so that both fermentations occur concurrently, or sequentially after completion of the AF so that there is no interference between the two fermentations. The MLF too can be allowed to occur spontaneously relying on indigenous lactic acid bacteria, but it is often conducted using cultured bacteria for more reliable and predictable results.

Following completion of both the AF and MLF, the wine is stabilized with sulfite to keep spoilage microorganisms in check.

Wine can undergo aging in glass carboys, or stainless steel or HDPE tanks, with or without oak adjuncts, or in oak barrels for a fuller-bodied style of wine. The wine is racked to separate out the sediment, with optional filtering for extra clarity, and then bottled.

Chapter 21 describes a detailed protocol for making red wine.

1.4 RECORD-KEEPING

To make great wines consistently, you have to manage your process diligently. That means keeping meticulous and detailed records of all activities, additives and processing aids used, measurements taken, as well as progress tasting notes. Not only will you have a documented history of your process, which you can consult in future vintages to reliably replicate a specific style, but you will have all the detailed data to be able to perform a root-cause analysis if you run into a problem.

Among other key data, I record the brand name of all additives, the type of filter system and filter media (down to the lot number) as well as the bottling system, as I use different systems for processing small versus large batches, and the exact characteristics of corks. I also track grape yield data to help me better plan future vintages; specifically, I track both gross and final volumes of juice or wine per unit weight for each variety.

There are various online apps you can use to track your winemaking activities. I like not only the simplicity and flexibility of a spreadsheet-based log chart (see Appendix C) but also that all the data is visible in chronological order in a single view; this makes it easier to perform a root-cause analysis when trying to identify and resolve a problem. Other log sheets or apps may break it down into blocks, one for each winemaking step — crushing/pressing, fermentation, etc. It boils down to personal preference, and perhaps you'll come to develop your own log sheet tailored to your specific needs.

The log sheet in Appendix C can be downloaded from ModernHome-Winemaking.com. Create one log sheet per batch — it will be easier to manage and less confusing than having all batches of a single wine on the same log sheet. If you are proficient at editing MS Excel spreadsheets, you can customize the log sheet to, for example, perform some simple calculations and post to a "dashboard" line, create a fermentation progress chart, and automatically highlight potential problems with color codes based on defined parameters, as in Figure 1.5.

2020	Cabernet Sauvignon	Dry										

BATCH ID:	54DJ-A

DASHBOARD: 1.112   15.1   5.3   3.70   25   Not Started

DATE	CHECKPOINT / OPERATION	Additive or Processing aid	Quantity added	VOLUME (L)	TEMP. (°C)	Temp. Adjusted SG	PA or Actual %ABV	TA (g/L)	pH	FSO2 (mg/L)	MLF Check	COMMENTS
2-Oct-20	MICROBIAL STABILIZATION	KMS	4.3 g	100.0	15.0							
	MUST ANALYSIS			100.0	15.0	1.112	15.1	4.3	3.80	25	Not Started	Do sequential MLF
	ACIDIFICATION	Tartaric acid	1.0 mg/L									
	CONTROL							5.3	3.70			Watch pH

Figure 1.5: Winemaking log chart (selected columns shown)

You also need to be disciplined in managing your winemaking. Create a 4-month calendar view (Figure 1.6) of any processing or analysis for all wines; it's a rigid process, but rigidity forces you to perform tasks — when they're due. You can use your electronic calendar with reminders or have a paper copy posted up on the wall where it is visible — that way it's always on your mind and makes it easier to plan upcoming activities. Why a 4-month view? As we'll see throughout this book, you'll be taking SO_2 measurements every 3 months, therefore, you need to have that activity recorded again in 3 months from the current month.

And establish a routine for regular activities. For example, if you are working with barrels, you need to top up every two weeks or once a month; pick a date or dates, for example, the 15th and 30th of the month to top up barrels. It's easier to remember that way, and even easier if you jot it down on your calendar.

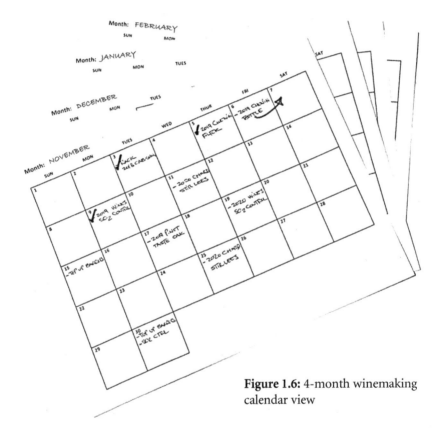

Figure 1.6: 4-month winemaking calendar view

REFERENCES

1. Coombe, B.G. 1987. *Distribution of Solutes within the Developing Grape Berry in Relation to Its Morphology.* Am. J. Enol. Vitic. 38:120-127.

2. Conde, C., P. Silva, N. Fontes, A.C.P. Dias, R.M. Tavares, M.J. Sousa, A. Agasse, S. Delrot and H. Gerós. 2007. *Biochemical changes throughout grape berry development and fruit and wine quality.* Food. 1:1-22.

3. Jackson, R.S. 2008. *Wine Science: Principles and Applications.* Third. Academic Press, Burlington (MA).

4. Fontes, N., H. Gerós and S. Delrot. 2011. *Grape Berry Vacuole: A Complex and Heterogeneous Membrane System Specialized in the Accumulation of Solutes.* Am. J. Enol. Vitic. 62:270-278.

5. Peynaud, É. 1987. *The Taste of Wine: The Art and Science of Wine Appreciation.* Michael Schuster (tr.), Macdonald & Co, London (GB).

6. Pambianchi, D. 2008. *Techniques in Home Winemaking: A Practical Guide to Making Château-Style Wines.* Newly-Revised and Expanded. Véhicule Press, Montréal (Québec).

2 A Guide to Popular Grape Varieties

There are many, many grape varieties from which to choose to make white, rosé and red wine, and which can be made in varied styles, from dry to sweet to sparkling. This chapter provides a list of the most common grape varieties and some of the styles of wines they can produce along with some winemaking tips and considerations — you will not necessarily be processing Pinot Noir in the same fashion as Norton.

Grape varieties used for making wine are commonly classified as vinifera, native varieties, and hybrids. They all belong to the genus *Vitis*, Latin for vine. The genus name is usually abbreviated as *V.*, and therefore, *Vitis vinifera* is written as *V. vinifera*. Related varieties that share botanical characteristics are grouped by species, such as *vinifera* and *aestivalis*. Pinot Noir is an example of a variety belonging to *V. vinifera*, and Norton is an example of a variety belonging to *V. aestivalis*.

Grape varieties can be from a specific species, for example, *V. vinifera* or *V. labrusca*, or from crossing two varieties from the same or different species, for example, Cabernet Sauvignon is an intraspecific cross between Cabernet Franc and Sauvignon Blanc, while Baco Noir is an interspecific cross between *V. vinifera* and *V. riparia*. Interspecific crossings are commonly referred to as hybrids.

Species are not that relevant here other to know which varieties are *V. vinifera* since they are by far the most common given their global reach, success and recognition, which are *V. labrusca* given their very characteristic "gamey" and "foxy" aromas, and which have a *V. riparia* lineage that tends to have herbaceous aromas and flavors.

Varieties can also have several clones, such as Pinot Noir, the result of vegetative propagation, and Pinot Gris/Grigio a mutant of Pinot Noir, and which may have different soil or climate adaption, for example. Different clones of the same variety will produce similar wines but perhaps with some differences, for example, in the aroma and flavor profile. There may not always be differences in the wines.

This chapter presents and describes some of the more popular or readily available *V. vinifera*, Native American and hybrid grape varieties for making wine. For additional reading or to learn more about pedigree, origins and viticultural characteristics of grape varieties, please consult references [1], [2] and [3].

ABOUT GRAPE VARIETY DESCRIPTIONS, PROFILES AND YEAST RECOMMENDATIONS

Grape variety descriptions presented here include common types and styles of wines possible. The name of regions are provided in some cases only to inform of origins or where they are best known, which often dictate the style, such as Pinot Noir in Burgundy (France), Nebbiolo in Barolo (Piemonte, Italy), or Marquette in Minnesota (USA). Many varieties are now grown the world over in different climates and soils, and produced into varying styles of wines, and therefore, your results, including aromas and flavors, may vary depending on your source of fruit or juice, choice of yeast, and winemaking techniques. Grape characteristics can vary depending on many factors, for example, vintage and where the grapes are grown. A Cabernet Sauvignon grown in California's Central Valley will have a very different profile than that grown in Washington State (USA) or Chile.

Grapes from colder climates will tend to have lower sugar levels and higher acidity due to higher amounts of malic acid. These may require adding sugar, or chaptalization, to bring the expected amount of alcohol to be produced within standard wine range, or may require deacidification (the lowering of acidity by removing acids). On the flip side, grapes grown in hot climates will tend to have higher sugar levels and lower acidity, which may require the addition of water to produce a wine without excessive alcohol and the addition of acids for better balance.

For additional information on viticultural aspects of growing grapes, you can consult the many references available in print or online. When researching varieties further, be sure that you identify these clearly as they all have many synonyms, many of which are also synonyms for different varieties altogether.

Each grape variety has a pictogram depicting its profile along with a list of recommended yeasts following its description. The profile is to help you quickly identify *typical* characteristics so you can better plan and adapt your winemaking where, for example, you may require to chaptalize a low-sugar harvest or deacidify a high-acid variety.

For white varieties, the profile includes typical SG/Brix and acidity levels, and the most common type of wine in terms of body. Figure 2.1 illustrates the profile for Chardonnay where SG/Brix level would yield a typical alcohol level and with lower acidity, and which would produce a medium-bodied wine.

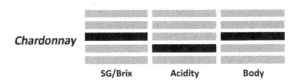

Figure 2.1: Grape profile example – Chardonnay

For red varieties, the profile includes typical depth of color, SG/Brix, acidity and tannin levels, and the most common type of wine in terms of body. Figure 2.2 illustrates the profile for Cabernet Sauvignon, which is characterized by high color, higher SG/Brix than the average but lower acidity and high tannins, which would produce a full-bodied wine.

Figure 2.2: Grape profile example – Cabernet Sauvignon

As a winemaker, you should measure all relevant parameters within your means and abilities to be able to make corrections towards making great wine, even if from unbalanced fruit. You will have to call upon different techniques, for example, to either increase or lower the amount of alcohol to be produced, or to adjust acidity up or down. Many varieties, especially from cool or cold growing regions and non-vinifera varieties, will have low sugar levels and high acidity.

To avoid repetition in descriptions, it is understood that white wines are almost always put through a chilling process — known as cold stabilization and cold crashing in home winemaking — to avoid having tartrates form in bottles. Tartrate stabilization and the process for stabilizing wines are discussed in Section 14.4. But cold stabilization can also be used specifically for deacidification, i.e., reducing acidity in high-acid wines — both whites and reds.

There is a plethora of yeast strains from the many manufacturers of dry and liquid yeast cultures. Many are only available in large formats, usually 500 g (just over 1 lb), for making wine on a commercial basis. Fewer are available in small formats, e.g., 5 g, 35 mL or 125 mL, geared to amateur winemakers. Yeast strains best suited for each varietal are presented, regardless of format; those available in carboy-sized formats are identified in **bold**. You can search out vendors who repackage yeast cultures into smaller formats, e.g., 8 g, 50 g, 80 g or 100 g, or purchase a larger format and split it with a group of winemakers. Yeast recommendations for each yeast are primarily from manufacturers' product sheets complemented by winemakers' recommendations.

Section 11.7 presents a listing per manufacturer of the most commonly available yeasts and some of their specifications. Be sure to consult manufacturers' product sheets or web pages for complete information on each yeast strain regarding rate of fermentation, flocculation, volatile acidity (VA) production, sulfur dioxide (SO_2) production, malolactic fermentation (MLF) compatibility, and hydrogen sulfide (H_2S) production.

2.1 *VITIS VINIFERA* VARIETIES

The most well-known and most popular wines of the world are made from *V. vinifera* grapes, and are referred to as "vinifera grapes" or simply "viniferas," or as "European varieties" being native to Europe. Viniferas include, for example, Chardonnay, Riesling and Sauvignon Blanc as white varieties, and Cabernet Franc, Pinot Noir and Syrah as red varieties.

The following sections introduce 10 white and 21 red *V. vinifera* varieties to choose from to make exquisite wines.

2.1.1 WHITE VINIFERA VARIETIES

With white viniferas, you will need to make specific winemaking decisions when working with varieties having dominant characteristics. For example, you would approach aromatic whites differently from thiolic varieties, choosing a suitable yeast strain and fermenting at cooler or warmer temperatures that enhance the dominant traits characteristic of each variety.

The most common aromatic whites include Gewürztraminer, Muscat, Riesling and Viognier, but also include Albariño, Chenin Blanc, Pinot Gris and Sauvignon Blanc. Aromatic whites are characterized by high levels of terpenes, compounds that impart very distinctive floral aromas.

Thiolic varieties include Sauvignon Blanc and Grenache as the most common but also Chenin Blanc and Riesling, and are characterized by high levels of thiols, sulfur-based compounds that impart, for example, boxtree, passion fruit and grapefruit aromas.

SG/Brix   Acidity   Body

ALBARIÑO (ALVARINHO)

Albariño is a popular Spanish grape variety that produces light but very aromatic whites redolent of citrus fruit, peaches and nectarines. It is also found in Portugal where it is known as Alvarinho and made into the popular spritzy-style Vinho Verde, which translates to "green wine" for its refreshing acidity.

Albariño usually has high acidity that may require deacidification or sweetening for balance. It can age in oak barrels for added complexity and extra body if acidity is lowered.

As it is a thick-skinned variety, it does pose a challenge at the press. It is recommended to first crush and then use rice hulls in the press. A light pressing is best to minimize extraction of bitter tannins from seeds.

Recommended Yeasts

LALLEMAND	LAFFORT	ENARTIS	RED STAR	WHITE LABS	WYEAST	RENAISSANCE
71B-1122, Cross Evolution, DV10, **QA23**, R2, VIN 13	DELTA, VL1, X16	Q Citrus, Q9	**Côte des Blancs**, **Premier Blanc**	**WLP730**	**4028**, **4783**	Allegro

Auxerrois

| SG/Brix | Acidity | Body |

What we know today in North America as Auxerrois is specifically named Auxerrois Blanc de Laquenexy, a thin-skinned variety known to make delicious wines in northeast France as well as in other cool-climate grape-growing areas in the US and Canada. It should not be confused with other varieties that are also commonly referred to simply as Auxerrois, including Malbec (a red variety) as it is called in Southern France, or Auxerrois Gris, which is really Pinot Gris. And according to Jancis Robinson, even Chardonnay was once known as Auxerrois Blanc. Auxerrois is in fact a sibling of Chardonnay [1].

Auxerrois tends to have low acidity, especially in warmer vintages, and therefore the must (juice) may need a small acidification for a wine style other than dry. It produces very good, albeit alcoholic wines with honey aromas. It is otherwise often blended with one or more of its Pinot relatives, such as Pinot Gris, or Pinot Noir (when made as a white wine), or Chardonnay or Seyval Blanc for better acidity balance.

Recommended Yeasts

LALLEMAND	LAFFORT	ENARTIS	RED STAR	WHITE LABS	WYEAST	RENAISSANCE
71B-1122, Alchemy I	CX9, VL1, X16	ES181, Vintage White, VQ10	**Côte des Blancs**, **Premier Blanc**	**WLP715**, **WLP730**	**4021**, **4783**	Bella

SG/Brix   Acidity   Body

CHARDONNAY

Chardonnay is one of the world's most popular white grape varieties. It is believed to be a cross between a little-known variety called Gouais Blanc and Pinot Noir, and is therefore often referred to misleadingly as Pinot Chardonnay.

Chardonnay does exceptionally well in cool-climate growing regions. It can be made into various types or styles from a fresh, fruity, dry wine with no oak influence to a richer, creamy, barrel-fermented or barrel-aged style with good aging potential, to sparkling wine. It can also be used to make orange wine.

The simpler unoaked style of Chardonnay is all about expressing freshness (i.e., acidity) and aromas of citrus and tropical fruit, dried fruit and green apples. It is made in a dry style, rarely off-dry, using a long and cool fermentation and optional MLF depending on acidity and desired complexity so as to preserve as much freshness and fruitiness as possible.

Barrel-fermented or barrel-aged Chardonnays are fuller bodied with toasted oak and vanilla aromas and flavors owing to the interactions with oak wood, and with lower acidity to balance the higher tannin content. The lower acidity is achieved by putting the wine through MLF with a diacetyl-producing lactic acid bacterium strain, which imparts the tell-tale sign of buttery aromas. Aging on the lees adds creaminess and body and also increases aging potential.

Some well-known and interesting blends are possible with Auxerrois, Chenin Blanc, Sauvignon Blanc, Seyval Blanc and Viognier.

In sparkling wine, Chardonnay can be made as a varietal or as a blend, a style that would be referred to as a *blanc de blancs*, meaning a white wine from one or more white varieties, or, for example, as a blend with Pinot Meunier and Pinot Noir, two red varieties, in making Champagne.

Recommended Yeasts

LALLEMAND	LAFFORT	ENARTIS	RED STAR	WHITE LABS	WYEAST	RENAISSANCE
Alchemy I, **BM4X4**, BM45, BRG, Cross Evolution, CY3079, DV10, ICV-D21, ICV-D254, **ICV-D47**, **QA23**, VIN 13	CX9, VL1, VL2, X16	ES123, Q9, Vintage White, VQ10	**Côte des Blancs**, **Premier Blanc**, **Premier Classique**, **Premier Cuvée**	WLP707, WLP718, WLP730, WLP740, WLP760, WLP770	4021, 4028, 4242	Allegro, Bella, Vivace

CHENIN BLANC

SG/Brix   Acidity   Body

Chenin Blanc, or simply Chenin, does not enjoy anywhere the popularity of Chardonnay but, given its high acidity, it can be made into as many if not more styles from fresh, aromatic, dry or off-dry wines, to sparkling, to rich, mouth-filling, sweet wines that can age years, decades and much longer. It is however very popular in South Africa where it is also known as Steen. Chenin Blanc has a range of aromas including honey, quince, pears and apples, and perhaps a touch of floral scents that develop with aging.

Chaptalization may be required as sugar levels are typically low. Ferment at cooler temperatures for a fruitier style. A short maceration on the skins, a touch of oak, or a short aging on the lees can add extra aroma complexity and body. Given its high acidity, MLF with a neutral bacterium strain is a good option when wanting to soften that lively acidity.

Chenin Blanc wines shine best on their own, particularly with some aging, but can be blended with Chardonnay or Sauvignon Blanc, or any other white wine in need of an acidity boost. It also blends very well with Niagara (a hybrid) when a flavorful style with extra zippy acidity is desired.

Recommended Yeasts

LALLEMAND	LAFFORT	ENARTIS	RED STAR	WHITE LABS	WYEAST	RENAISSANCE
Alchemy I, CY3079, ICV-GRE, **K1V-1116**, **QA23**, R2, VIN 13	DELTA, VL1, VL3, X16	Aroma White, ES181, Q Citrus, Q9, Vintage White	**Côte des Blancs**, **Premier Cuvée**	**WLP735**	**4028**, **4242**	Allegro, TR-313

❖

GEWÜRZTRAMINER

SG/Brix   Acidity   Body

In spite of its hard-to-pronounce name, Gewürztraminer, or simply Gewürz, which means "spice," is one of the most easily identifiable white wines owing to the grape's intense aromas and flavors of spices, honey, lychees, roses and grapefruit, and possibly musky notes. The floral/rose aromas are due compounds known as monoterpenols, which are found abundantly in Muscat Blanc à Petits Grains. It grows best in cool-climate regions. Being a pink-skinned "white" variety, wines tend to have a deeper color.

Gewürztraminer can be made into various styles ranging from dry to sweet, including late-harvest and ice wines, and light to fuller bodied, and which have good aging potential. It is a perfect blending partner with Riesling because of their many organoleptic and geographical similarities.

Because of the grape's relatively low acidity, wines are never subjected to MLF; the aroma and flavor profiles could otherwise be compromised. Low acidity also implies higher pH, and therefore, grapes and wines must be processed with extra care to minimize risks of oxidation and microbial spoilage.

Recommended Yeasts

LALLEMAND	LAFFORT	ENARTIS	RED STAR	WHITE LABS	WYEAST	RENAISSANCE
Cross Evolution, DV10, **QA23**, R2	DELTA, VL1, VL3	Aroma White, ES181, Q Citrus, Q9, VQ Assmanshausen, VQ10	**Côte des Blancs**	**WLP720**, **WLP727**	**4021**, **4242**, **4783**	Bella, TR-313

MUSCAT BLANC À PETITS GRAINS (MOSCATO BIANCO)

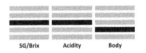

SG/Brix   Acidity   Body

"Muscat" refers to a large family of clone varieties sharing common compounds known as monoterpenols that give grapes their intense characteristic floral, grapey aromas, but which can range in color from white or yellow, to pink and dark blue. Yellow-colored Muscat Blanc à Petits Grains (which translates to "white Muscat with small berries") is the most popular variety and most common in home winemaking. It is also known in various grape-growing regions of the world as Muscat Blanc, Moscato Bianco, and Muscat Canelli. There are also red Muscat varieties. Muscat varieties have no relationship to Muscadine (*V. rotundifolia*) varieties.

Muscat Blanc à Petits Grains can be made in many different early-drinking styles from dry and off-dry to medium-sweet and sweet, as well as fortified wines and in a lightly spritzy style such as Asti Spumante of Asti (Piemonte, Italy) fame. In addition to its unmistakable floral aromas, Muscat Blanc à Petits Grains wines also reveal citrus fruit and peach aromas.

Recommended Yeasts

LALLEMAND	LAFFORT	ENARTIS	RED STAR	WHITE LABS	WYEAST	RENAISSANCE
Cross Evolution, **QA23**, R2, VIN 13	VL1	ES123, Q9, Q Citrus	**Côte des Blancs**, **Premier Blanc**	**WLP720**	**4021**, **4242**	Bella

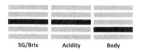

PINOT GRIS (PINOT GRIGIO)

Pinot Gris, known as Tokay in Alsace (France), can range in style from gently perfumed and dry to rich and sweet but is best appreciated as light dry or off-dry with low to moderate acidity. Fuller-bodied styles can also age well for several years. Aromas include tropical fruit, cantaloupes, peaches and mangos. It is known as Pinot Grigio in Northeastern Italy where wines can be very different in style, usually lighter with crisper acidity with citrusy aromas and flavors, or a copper-hued *ramato* (it means "coppery" in Italian), a style that is not quite a rosé nor an orange wine.

As the French name implies, berries can have a grayish-blue to brownish-pink skin as it is a mutation of Pinot Noir, a red-skinned grape, and so, wines produced with short maceration can show a slightly copper or pink hue. Whites produced without maceration will show an attractive pale-yellow color. When tannin extraction is to be limited, whole-bunch pressing (no maceration) is recommended. Fermentation is carried out at cooler temperatures to maximize production of fruity esters.

Pinot Gris is a fun variety to experiment with different maceration periods and possibly some oaking for different styles and colors. It is a good blending partner with Auxerrois.

Recommended Yeasts

LALLEMAND	LAFFORT	ENARTIS	RED STAR	WHITE LABS	WYEAST	RENAISSANCE
71B-1122, Alchemy I, CY3079, DV10, **QA23**, R2, SVG	DELTA	Aroma White, Q Citrus, Q9, VQ10	**Côte des Blancs**, **Premier Cuvée**	**WLP735**	**4021**, **4242**	Allegro, Vivace

RIESLING

Riesling wines have the unfortunate reputation of being always sweet due to the mass production of low-quality but quaffable sweet German wines that once appealed greatly to neo wine drinkers. Riesling can however produce highly aromatic wines in a wide range of styles from bone-dry to sweet, including late-harvest wine and ice wine (*Eiswein* in German) as well as sparkling wine. The best Rieslings of the world have impeccable balance between green-apple acidity and residual sugar, and can age for many years and even decades. As Riesling ages, color progresses from straw to deep yellow.

Being a cool-climate variety, the high acidity may be overwhelming in a poor vintage or if not managed well in the vineyard or balanced with sweetness. But undesirable sensory consequences of MLF do not make this a viable option to reduce acidity. Riesling wines also do not benefit from any oak influence.

A characteristic of some aged Riesling wines is their unmistakable smell of petrol that intensifies with aging. The petrol smell is the result of a naturally occurring compound simply referred to as TDN, short for the very complex chemical name 1,1,6-trimethyl-1,2-dihydronaphthalene. Depending on the grape-growing area, Riesling can also exhibit aromas of lime, honey, minerality, as well as floral notes, the latter due to the same monoterpenols found in Muscat Blanc à Petits Grains. A very short maceration with the skins and fermentation at lower temperatures can increase aromatic intensity.

Riesling wines are best enjoyed as varietals but they can be blended in varying proportions with Gewürztraminer. And given its petrol character, it is a natural blending partner with Niagara (a hybrid).

Recommended Yeasts

LALLEMAND	LAFFORT	ENARTIS	RED STAR	WHITE LABS	WYEAST	RENAISSANCE
71B-1122, Alchemy I, ICV-GRE, **QA23**, R2, SVG	DELTA, VL1, VL3, X5	Aroma White, ES123, ES181, Q Citrus, Q9, VQ Assmanshausen, VQ10	**Côte des Blancs**	**WLP720**, **WLP727**, **WLP749**	4783	Bella, TR-313, Vivace

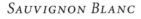

Sauvignon Blanc

SG/Brix   Acidity   Body

Sauvignon Blanc, or simply Sauvignon, is another popular variety the world over as it can produce very enjoyable aromatic wines with refreshing and vibrant but balanced acidity in dry and off-dry styles that are easy to drink. It is also used for making orange wine as well as sparkling and dessert (sweet) wines.

Sauvignon is laden with flavor compounds belonging to two classes known as thiols and methoxypyrazines that give Sauvignon wines their varietal character.

Thiols give Sauvignon wines their characteristic aromas of boxtree, passion fruit and grapefruit, and what is described as the pejoratively sounding but highly desirable "cat pee" as is most obvious in New Zealand Sauvignons. As we will see in Chapter 19 on making white wine, the amount of thiols produced can be augmented, when desired, by choosing an appropriate thiol-expressing strain and fermenting at warmer temperatures. As thiols are very sensitive to oxygen, every precaution should be taken to avoid excessive exposure to air to prevent varietal character loss. For this same reason, Sauvignon wines should be drunk young as they do not generally age well except for sweet styles. Another consequence of oxygen reactivity is a phenomenon known as pinking, a reaction that gives some varieties a slightly grayish-pink to pink color; it usually does not affect organoleptic qualities. Sauvignon is at risk of pinking if grapes are sourced from a hot, dry vintage when the skins have much higher levels of phenolics, which can be mitigated with a PVPP treatment (see Section 13.4.4). For a fruitier style with little or no thiols, ferment at cooler temperatures to preserve as much esters as possible.

Methoxypyrazines impart unmistakable, vegetative aromas of green peppers, grass and asparagus that are detectable at very low levels. These aromas will persist and seemingly more present as wine ages. They can in part be masked with oak. Aging in oak and/or on the lees can also add body and more flavor complexity in lower-acid Sauvignons.

Sauvignon is an excellent blending varietal with Chardonnay, Chenin Blanc and Niagara.

Recommended Yeasts

LALLEMAND	LAFFORT	ENARTIS	RED STAR	WHITE LABS	WYEAST	RENAISSANCE
Alchemy I,	DELTA,	Aroma White,	**Côte des**	**WLP740,**	**4021,**	TR-313,
QA23,	VL1,	ES181,	**Blancs**	**WLP750,**	**4028,**	Vivace
R2,	VL3,	Q Citrus, Q9,		**WLP770**	**4267**	
SVG,	X5	VQ10,				
VIN 13		Vintage				

VIOGNIER

SG/Brix   Acidity   Body

Viognier is a lesser known but stellar variety that can make excellent, intensely aromatic wines. It has low acidity but it can benefit from a partial MLF to increase organoleptic complexity if acidity is not too low. Since grapes tend to be high-sugar and therefore higher in alcohol than typical whites, acidity needs to be managed carefully to preserve good balance. Aggressive acidification may be required, particularly in the case of high pH, to bring acidity to "normal" levels.

Viognier can also be used for making sweet wine using the grapes' natural sugars. It also makes excellent sparkling wine.

Viognier is however very sensitive to oxygen and therefore requires careful treatment and processing to avoid varietal character loss. As with Sauvignon Blanc, Viognier too is a variety at risk of pinking if grapes are sourced from a hot, dry vintage; pinking can be mitigated with a PVPP treatment (see Section 13.4.4).

Aromas are reminiscent of Muscat varieties and include apricots, peaches, tropical fruit, violets, roses, honey and spices with some minerality. A short aging on the lees adds extra complexity and fullness on the palate; this can be done in inert vessels, possibly with oak adjuncts, or in oak barrels.

Other than adding finesse and aromas, one of the most interesting traits of Viognier from a winemaking perspective is that, owing to its high flavonol content, it is used up to 10% to coferment with Syrah, a red variety, to increase color intensity and stability via a phenomenon known as co-pigmentation (see Chapter 21). Flavonols are naturally occurring polyphenols partly responsible for the yellowish color in grape skins. Viognier can also be blended with Chardonnay post fermentation or prior to bottling for a style that showcases the best of both varieties.

Recommended Yeasts

LALLEMAND	LAFFORT	ENARTIS	RED STAR	WHITE LABS	WYEAST	RENAISSANCE
Cross Evolution, ICV-D254, **ICV-D47**, ICV-GRE, **QA23**, R2, SVG, VIN 13	DELTA, VL2	Aroma White, ES181, Q Citrus, Q9	**Premier Blanc**	**WLP715**, **WLP735**	**4028**, 4267	Allegro

❖

2.1.2 RED VINIFERA VARIETIES

In the following descriptions, Bordeaux varietals refer to Cabernet Sauvignon, Cabernet Franc, Merlot, Malbec, Petit Verdot, and to a lesser extent, Carménère. These are often blended in various combinations in classic red Bordeaux blends, which are known as Meritage — an American designation for Bordeaux-style wines. Super Tuscan wines were similarly created as Tuscany's answer to premium Bordeaux reds that were previously not permitted under Italian winemaking laws.

Many red wines have an affinity for oak wood and are therefore aged in barrels to not only increase organoleptic qualities and aging potential, but also polymerize and soften tannins via the minuscule amounts of oxygen entering barrels; it also stabilizes color. This oxygen exchange phenomenon is known as micro-oxygenation or micro-oxidation. We'll explore tannins and their properties further in Chapter 9.

Cabernet Franc and related varieties, i.e., Cabernet Sauvignon, Carménère and Merlot, as well as Malbec, share a common trait: they can exhibit green, bell pepper aromas and to varying degrees due to methoxypyrazines, the same compounds we had encountered in Sauvignon Blanc, a child of Cabernet Franc. Methoxypyrazines and their characteristic vegetal-like aromas are much more pronounced in a weak (cold, wet) vintage or underripe fruit from a precipitous harvest. Methoxypyrazines can be limited in the vineyard through proper canopy management, such as selective leaf removal in the grape zone, or mitigated in the cellar by adding untoasted oak at crush or during fermentation. Untoasted oak masks the vegetal character in wines by intensifying the fruity expression and exhibiting more "ripe" fruit notes without the aromas of toasted oak. Toasted oak can be used to mask methoxypyrazines but where toasted notes are desired.

Some red varieties, for example, Cabernet Sauvignon, Grenache, Merlot and Pinot Noir, also contain thiols, those same compounds found in some white varieties, which makes them suitable for rosé wine when boxtree, passion fruit and grapefruit-like aromas are desired.

2

AGLIANICO

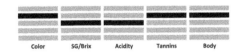

| Color | SG/Brix | Acidity | Tannins | Body |

Aglianico is a famous dark-skinned Southern Italian variety that can produce outstanding, richly colored, full-bodied tannic wines with moderate acidity and good aging potential. The aromas are redolent of chocolate, plums and black cherries. Aromas, flavors and overall quality greatly improve with short aging in oak barrels.

Owing to its relatively high acidity, wines are put through MLF. They can be blended with Cabernet Franc, Cabernet Sauvignon or Merlot. Aglianico can also be used for making delightful, brightly colored rosé wines.

Recommended Yeasts

LALLEMAND	LAFFORT	ENARTIS	RED STAR	WHITE LABS	WYEAST	RENAISSANCE
BM4X4, CLOS, ICV-D80, SYRAH	F15, FX10	ES454	**Premier Rouge**	**WLP740**, **WLP750**	4028, 4267, 4946	Bravo, Maestoso

❖

ALICANTE BOUSCHET

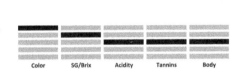

| Color | SG/Brix | Acidity | Tannins | Body |

Alicante Bouschet is a thick-skinned French teinturier that makes deeply colored, good quality wines either as a varietal or as a blending component to enhance color in light reds; it is also used to make fortified wine, such as port-style wine.

It is commonly but confusingly referred to as Alicante, which was the old name for Garnacha (Grenache) in Spain. It was a very popular variety with new Italian immigrants to America because of its availability and accessibility during Prohibition, and because of its higher yields in both free- and press-run fractions.

Being a teinturier, it can still be made into a lighter-bodied, fruitier style by foregoing any maceration. Alcohol levels can however be high when grapes come from a hot climate or vintage, but its deep color allows for amelioration, when required, to scale back alcohol with only minimal loss of color.

Aging allows more complex aromas and flavors to develop and add character to wine.

Recommended Yeasts

LALLEMAND	LAFFORT	ENARTIS	RED STAR	WHITE LABS	WYEAST	RENAISSANCE
CLOS, ICV-D80, SYRAH	F15	Red Fruit	**Premier Rouge**	**WLP740, WLP750**	**4028, 4267, 4946**	Maestoso

❖

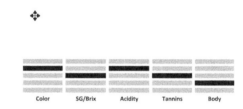

BARBERA

Barbera is an Italian variety predominantly from the Piemonte region and northern Italy. It makes easy-drinking, quaffable, light- to medium-bodied wines with high acidity, which makes this variety well-suited for growing in hotter climates where grapes can shed some of their acidity. MLF is de rigueur with Barbera to further lower acidity. The variety has relatively lower tannins, which complements its high acidity.

Barbera varietals are deep-ruby colored and express an array of berry aromas, such as cherries, blackberries, raspberries and blueberries depending on ripeness, and aromas of licorice and black pepper. Aging in oak barrels can further increase aromatic complexity and enhance structure. It is however known to be susceptible to reduction, responsible for producing what are known as reductive smells, such as the smell of rotten eggs due to hydrogen sulfide (H_2S). To minimize the effects of reduction, wines are supplied some oxygen during racking operations.

Being grown in the same region, Barbera is often blended with Nebbiolo to add color to the latter, but this does not solve the former's high acidity; for this purpose, a variety such as Cabernet Sauvignon or Cabernet Franc may provide more balance. It is however blended with low-acid wines to increase acidity. It can also make a very flavorful, fruity rosé by fermenting at cooler temperatures and foregoing MLF.

2

Recommended Yeasts

LALLEMAND	LAFFORT	ENARTIS	RED STAR	WHITE LABS	WYEAST	RENAISSANCE
BRL97, CLOS	F83	ES454, MB15, Q5, VQ Assmanshausen, VQ51	**Premier Rouge**	**WLP760**	**4028, 4244, 4267**	Bravo

CABERNET FRANC

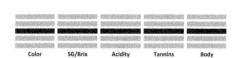

Color SG/Brix Acidity Tannins Body

Cabernet Franc, a parent of Cabernet Sauvignon, Merlot and Carménère, is one of the five Bordeaux varietals. It grows best in cooler climates where it produces lighter-colored, light- to medium-bodied reds that do well as varietals but are better known for blending to tame aggressive Cabernet Sauvignon or Merlot wines, and to add aromas of raspberries, tobacco and cassis. Though less so commonly now, Cabernet Franc is also blended with Petit Verdot and Malbec as was done in many Bordeaux reds. It can create interesting blends with Carménère, Aglianico, Barbera, Baco Noir, Gamay and Grenache, and for an interesting twist, with Chambourcin.

Cabernet Franc is highly prone to methoxypyrazines and their characteristic bell pepper, vegetal aromas in a weak vintage or underripe fruit.

Recommended Yeasts

LALLEMAND	LAFFORT	ENARTIS	RED STAR	WHITE LABS	WYEAST	RENAISSANCE
BDX, CSM, ICV-254, ICV-GRE, RP15	F15	D20, ES488, VQ51	**Premier Blanc, Premier Classique, Premier Rouge**	**WLP750, WLP760**	**4021, 4028, 4267**	Bravo

CABERNET SAUVIGNON

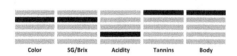

Color SG/Brix Acidity Tannins Body

Cabernet Sauvignon wine has long been the undisputed king of reds, except to Pinot Noir enophiles. Cabernet Sauvignon is now recognized as a cross between Cabernet Franc and Sauvignon Blanc, which explains why it shares many of the odoriferous compounds found in its parents. It is one of the five Bordeaux varietals.

Given its widespread appeal and consumer recognition, Cabernet Sauvignon is grown the world over and which therefore gives rise to many different styles of wines. However, the best-quality Cabernet Sauvignons, or "Cabs" as they are referred to, are appreciated for their intense aromas of black cherries, blackcurrant, tobacco and cedar, their full-bodied style, and very long aging potential, particularly those aged in oak barrels. It performs exceptionally well as a varietal but the richer styles often need to be tamed with one or more of the Bordeaux varietals, as is done in Bordeaux reds and Meritages. It also blends perfectly with Sangiovese and Syrah as is done in Super Tuscans, with Grenache or Tempranillo as done in Spain, and with Aglianico, Barbera, Nebbiolo, Baco Noir and Chambourcin. Typically, each varietal is fermented, processed and aged separately in barrels, and then the best components of each are selected and blended just before bottling.

Full-bodied Cabs may go through an extended maceration either before or after fermentation, possibly both, for greater extraction of tannins, and fermented relatively hot (up to 30 °C/86 °F) for maximum color extraction. Fermentation can be carried out in oak barrels, or in vats to promote color stability and to reduce the taste of "wood" and almond and toasted aromas compared to aging wine in barrels. More commonly, wines are simply aged in oak barrels to increase organoleptic qualities and aging potential, and to soften tannins.

High sugar and low acidity in Cabernet Sauvignon grapes grown in hot climates or from a hot vintage may pose a challenge in achieving good balance — amelioration, acidification or both may be required. Those from a poor vintage or precocious harvest will have the characteristic green bell pepper, vegetal character due to methoxypyrazines as with other related varieties.

Lighter styles are fermented cooler in stainless steel tanks to preserve more of the fruity character. Oak chips or other types of oak products can be used to add just a hint of oak and vanillin aromas if desired.

2

Cabernet Sauvignon wines are usually put through MLF to reduce acidity further, if required, to allow for better integration with natural as well as oak-derived tannins; MLF also greatly enhances organoleptic qualities.

Recommended Yeasts

LALLEMAND	LAFFORT	ENARTIS	RED STAR	WHITE LABS	WYEAST	RENAISSANCE	AB BIOTEK
BDX, BM45, **BM4X4**, CSM, ICV-D21, ICV-D254, ICV-D80, ICV-GRE, **RC 212**, RP15	F15, FX10	D20, ES454, ES488, VQ51	**Premier Blanc, Premier Classique, Premier Cuvée, Premier Rouge**	**WLP707, WLP750, WLP760**	4028, 4267, 4946	Andante, Bravo	Maurivin B

CARMÉNÈRE

Color	SG/Brix	Acidity	Tannins	Body

Carménère can make delicious deep-colored, medium- to full-bodied wines as varietals, but which can be excellent blending partners with one of the other Bordeaux varietals where it contributes aromas of cherries, plums, dark chocolate and leather, and aromas of raspberries and bell peppers that it shares with its Cabernet Franc parent. It also blends well with Sangiovese. Fuller-bodied, oak-aged Carménères can age very well too. Jancis Robinson describes Carménère wine as having "the potential to make very fine wines, combining some of the charm of Merlot with the structure of Cabernet Sauvignon" [1].

One challenge with Carménère is that it tends to produce higher amounts of methoxypyrazines, hence more pronounced bell pepper, herbaceous aromas, even in a good vintage, which will need to be mitigated right from crush as pyrazines can be very difficult to remove in wine.

Recommended Yeasts

LALLEMAND	LAFFORT	ENARTIS	RED STAR	WHITE LABS	WYEAST	RENAISSANCE
BDX, CSM, ICV-D80	F15, F83, FX10	ES488, VQ51	**Premier Rouge**	**WLP740, WLP750, WLP750**	4028, 4267	Andante, Bravo, Brio

GAMAY

| Color | SG/Brix | Acidity | Tannins | Body |

Gamay (Gamay Noir) is a purple-colored variety with bright acidity and low tannins that produce light-bodied fruity wines best enjoyed young. If you have had Beaujolais Nouveau, you have had Gamay as young as it gets. Beaujolais Nouveau is a popular French wine from Beaujolais, a region immediately south of Burgundy, and which is fermented and produced in just a few weeks and released for sale on the third Thursday of November. Gamay is also popular, though to a lesser extent, further northwest in the Loire Valley. It grows very well in the Niagara Peninsula (Ontario, Canada) where it produces exquisite wines that express sour cherry and black cherry aromas and flavors and minerality found in fuller-bodied styles as well as in Oregon's Willamette Valley.

Commercial wineries produce Gamay wine by carbonic maceration, a technique not only used for showcasing fruity aromas but also to tame acidity. But great, age-worthy Gamays are possible by implementing a maceration–fermentation program focused on maximum color and tannin extraction and full MLF.

Gamay is an excellent blending wine with Cabernet Franc and Malbec.

Recommended Yeasts

LALLEMAND	LAFFORT	ENARTIS	RED STAR	WHITE LABS	WYEAST	RENAISSANCE	AB BIOTEK
71B-1122, BRG, **RC 212**	F15, RB2	Red Fruit , Q5, VQ51	**Premier Rouge**	**WLP707** **WLP770**	**4028,** **4242**	Brio	Maurivin B

GRENACHE

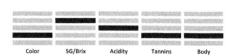

| Color | SG/Brix | Acidity | Tannins | Body |

Grenache, also known as Garnacha from its Spanish origins, can make excellent flavorful wine as a red varietal or as a blend, for example, Côtes du Rhône (French) or South Australian-style GSM blends, i.e., Grenache, Syrah (Shiraz) and Mourvèdre (Monastrell), particularly if grapes are

2

lightly-colored, or as a Spanish-inspired Priorat-style blend with Cabernet Franc, Cabernet Sauvignon, Merlot and Syrah. It also blends well with Petite Sirah and Tempranillo.

Given Grenache's lighter-colored skin, it is a popular grape for making dry or sweeter, berry-flavored rosés that can express many of the same thiol-derived aromas as Sauvignon Blanc. And because of the grape's and thiols' general sensitivity to oxygen, rosés from Grenache need to be protected from air during processing to minimize varietal character loss and to limit the amount of orange color (due to phenolic browning) and to preserve more of the red color. Fermentation is carried out at cooler temperatures to maximize fruity expression, or warmer to increase thiol production. MLF is generally not desirable so as not to affect the delicate fruity aromas.

For making red Grenache as a varietal, warmer fermentation temperatures are recommended with frequent punchdowns to favor color extraction given the low amounts of anthocyanins found in skins, along with an MLF for added aroma and flavor complexity. A short sojourn in oak barrels can also help stabilize color.

Grenache does produce high levels of sugar, and therefore high alcohol, when grown in hot climates, and as such, winemakers often opt to ameliorate the must or stop fermentation slightly prematurely for lower alcohol and some residual sugar to make a more approachable off-dry or medium-dry rosé style. It does however have relatively lower acidity due to low malic acid, which may not yield any significant acidity drop during MLF.

Recommended Yeasts

LALLEMAND	LAFFORT	ENARTIS	RED STAR	WHITE LABS	WYEAST	RENAISSANCE	AB BIOTEK
71B-1122, BM45, **BM4X4**, CLOS, ICV-GRE, **RC 212**, RP15	F83, RX60	D20, ES488, MB15, VQ51	**Premier Rouge**	**WLP760**	**4028**	Brio	Maurivin B

MALBEC

Malbec is one of the five Bordeaux varietals. It is a thick-skinned variety packing lots of anthocyanins and tannins that can produce high-quality, richly colored, full-bodied varietal wines. Following the drop in Malbec production due to the sap-sucking root louse *Phylloxera* that devastated many vineyards in Europe beginning in the late 19th century, the variety is now enjoying renewed success with excellent fruit from Argentina and Chile. It is a perfect blending partner with the other Bordeaux varietals as well as Carménère, where it adds body, structure and color, and contributes aromas of plums, blackberries, chocolate and tobacco. Try it with Gamay too.

Low acidity in Malbec from hot climates may pose a challenge, perhaps requiring acidification to make sure the wine is not too flabby, particularly after MLF. And underripe Malbec too is known to exhibit bell pepper aromas due to methoxypyrazines.

Recommended Yeasts

LALLEMAND	LAFFORT	ENARTIS	RED STAR	WHITE LABS	WYEAST	RENAISSANCE
BRL97, CLOS, ICV-D254, RP15	FX10	ES454, VQ51	**Premier Rouge**	**WLP750**	**4028**, **4244**, **4267**	Bravo

MERLOT

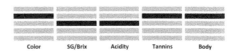

Merlot is one of the five Bordeaux varietals. It is a deep-colored variety but has less tannins than Cabernet Sauvignon and therefore produces smoother, softer and more approachable varietal wines when young. The softer tannins make Merlot a perfect blending partner for taming richly tannic, aggressive Cabernet Sauvignon and other varietals, such as is commonly done with Cabernet Franc, Malbec, Petit Verdot, Sangiovese and Carménère, as well as with Aglianico, Baco Noir, Chambourcin and Grenache.

Merlot wines are characterized by a wide range of aromas including plums, blackberries, raspberries, strawberries, cassis, chocolate, dried herbs, leather, cedar and tobacco. Barrel aging gives Merlot greater complexity and body. As with all varieties in the Cabernet family, underripe fruit will exhibit green bell pepper aromas that may detract from the fruity aromas.

Merlot can also make delicious fruity rosés, or White Merlot, in a dry style with more of a red color than Grenache as it is not as sensitive to oxygen; it only requires a very short maceration with no MLF. The pressed grape solids (pomace) can then be used with other varieties being fermented to add more color, aromas and flavors.

Recommended Yeasts

LALLEMAND	LAFFORT	ENARTIS	RED STAR	WHITE LABS	WYEAST	RENAISSANCE
BDX, BRL97, CSM, ICV-D21, ICV-D80, ICV-GRE, RP15, SYRAH	F15, F83, FX10, RB2	D20, ES454, ES488, VQ51	**Premier Rouge**	**WLP740, WLP750**	4028, 4267, 4767	Bravo, Maestoso

MOURVÈDRE (MONASTRELL)   Color   SG/Brix   Acidity   Tannins   Body

Mourvèdre, or Monastrell in Spain, is a thick-skinned variety that can produce richly colored, bold and full-bodied varietals high in tannins and alcohol, especially when grown in hot climates. They require some aging to tame and soften tannins as they can be very aggressive in their youth. Mourvèdre is often blended with Grenache and Syrah in so-called GSM blends to add body, structure, color, earthy aromas, tobacco notes, and meaty flavors.

Mourvèdre does pose some winemaking challenges as wines are prone to both oxidation and reduction, the latter being responsible for producing reductive smells, such as the unpleasant smell of rotten eggs due to hydrogen sulfide (H_2S). And therefore these wines have to be monitored carefully throughout processing.

Mourvèdre can also make rosés — as a varietal or in a blend — in a dry style with more of a red color than Grenache but requires the same precautions as the latter owing to its sensitivity to oxygen. It only requires a very short maceration with no MLF. The pomace can then be used with other varieties being fermented to add more color, tannins, aromas and flavors.

Recommended Yeasts

LALLEMAND	LAFFORT	ENARTIS	RED STAR	WHITE LABS	WYEAST	RENAISSANCE
SYRAH	F83	ES454, Q5, VQ51	**Premier Rouge**	**WLP750, WLP760**	**4028, 4267, 4767**	Bravo, Maestoso

❖

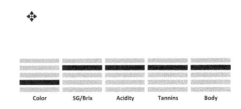

Color   SG/Brix   Acidity   Tannins   Body

NEBBIOLO

Nebbiolo is better known as Barolo and to a lesser extent as Barbaresco, two of the most important producing towns in Piemonte (Italy), although these are not varietal synonyms. Though lightly colored, it can produce outstanding, tannin-packed, full-bodied wines that need aging to be appreciated. Barolos are known to age well for years and decades. Due to the nature of Nebbiolo anthocyanins and susceptibility to oxidation, wines take on a characteristic orange color followed by a brown color with aging if color is not stabilized more aggressively than with other reds. We'll explore color stabilization in Chapter 9.

Barolo and Barbaresco wines exhibit characteristic aromas of tar and leather, which intensify with aging and which make Nebbiolos easy to identify, as well as aromas of cherries, roses, truffles and tobacco.

Given the lighter color of grape skins, juice and solids may undergo an extended pre-ferment cold soak and possibly a cooler fermentation to extend the maceration period to extract as much color as possible. And given their higher acidity, Nebbiolo wines are always put through MLF and possibly through cold stabilization to reduce acidity further when required.

Although Nebbiolo can be aged in new oak, a long sojourn in older barrels is preferable to allow micro-oxygenation to soften tannins without adding more. New oak is recommended when more tannins are desired, always being careful not to over-extract.

For a deeper-colored, younger, more approachable style that does not need years of aging, Nebbiolo can be blended with, for example, Barbera, Cabernet Sauvignon or Syrah.

Recommended Yeasts

LALLEMAND	LAFFORT	ENARTIS	RED STAR	WHITE LABS	WYEAST	RENAISSANCE
BRL97	RX60	ES454, MB15, VQ Assmanshausen, VQ51	Premier Rouge	WLP760	4244	Andante, Bravo

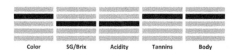

| | Color | SG/Brix | Acidity | Tannins | Body |

PETIT VERDOT

Petit Verdot is one of the five Bordeaux varietals, but it can make exquisite deeply colored, well-balanced, full-bodied, age-worthy wines on its own. The wines express aromas of cedar, violets, black cherries, pepper and spices. It grows very well in Virginia (USA).

Given its high tannins, Petit Verdot is often used as a blending wine to enhance structure and body in weaker varietals.

Recommended Yeasts

LALLEMAND	LAFFORT	ENARTIS	RED STAR	WHITE LABS	WYEAST	RENAISSANCE
BDX, BRL97, CLOS, CSM, ICV-D254, RP15, SYRAH	FX10	D20, VQ51	Premier Rouge, Premier Cuvée	WLP740, WLP750, WLP760	4028, 4244, 4267	Bravo, Brio

Petite Sirah (Durif)

Petite Sirah, a descendant of Syrah and also known as Durif, produces deeply colored, richly flavorful, full-bodied wines with high alcohol and moderate acidity but which pack plenty of tannins that give these wines long aging potential. Pressing before the wine reaches dryness is advisable to avoid extracting excessive tannins.

Petite Sirah wines express aromas of plums, blueberries and black pepper. They blend well with Alicante Bouschet, Barbera, Cabernet Sauvignon, Grenache, Syrah and Zinfandel, and any wine in need of a color boost. It also makes vibrant and delicious rosé requiring only a very short maceration.

Recommended Yeasts

LALLEMAND	LAFFORT	ENARTIS	RED STAR	WHITE LABS	WYEAST	RENAISSANCE
BM4X4, CLOS, ICV-D80, RP15, SYRAH	F15, FX10	D20, Q5	**Premier Rouge**	**WLP740**, **WLP750**	**4028**, **4267**, **4946**	Bravo, Maestoso

❖

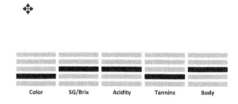

Pinot Noir

Pinot Noir is the famous red grape of Burgundy, hence why generic Pinot Noir wines are referred to as Red Burgundy, and is now grown the world over in cool climates. Its popularity or stature is often compared to that of Cabernet Sauvignon though the comparison is not necessarily valid. Whereas Cabernet Sauvignon is about muscles backed by solid tannins, Pinot Noir is about finesse and elegance. And whereas Cabernet Sauvignon grows relatively well in various climates and poses few winemaking challenges, Pinot Noir is hard to cultivate and work with in the cellar, hence why it is known as the "heartbreak grape." And this makes it a challenge to source for home winemakers. And to complicate matters, there are many clones of Pinot Noir, which make it difficult to replicate consistently a de-

2

sired style when fruit is sourced from different purveyors, even grapes grown in the same vineyard but on different clones.

As a thin-skinned, cool-climate variety, Pinot Noir tends to have much less color and relatively lower tannins and therefore tends to make lightly colored, light- to medium-bodied wines. And expect lower juice yields than most other red varieties. Techniques such as cold-soak maceration, using a small portion of whole clusters (i.e., uncrushed, non-destemmed), and higher maceration/fermentation temperatures in conjunction with aggressive punchdowns can help achieve greater color and tannin extraction. Barrel-fermented or barrel-aged wines from top-quality fruit can make exceptionally well-balanced, medium-bodied Pinot Noirs with soft tannins and long aging potential.

Young Pinot Noirs express primarily cherry and raspberry aromas as well as gamey odors, and take on more subtle and complex earthy, truffle aromas while aging. Those from warmer climates will reveal more berry fruit aromas and a deeper color. It does not perform well in warmer and especially hot climates; wines tend to become too "jammy."

Pinot Noir can also make very fruity, dry and refreshing early-drinking rosés although the color will lean more towards copper. It is also used along with Chardonnay and Pinot Meunier in making Champagne and other traditional-method sparkling wines, or on its own in *blanc de noirs*, which means "white sparkling wine from red grapes," where grapes are pressed without destemming and maceration to extract white juice. It is otherwise rarely blended although a deep-colored varietal, often Syrah, may be blended in to add color.

Recommended Yeasts

LALLEMAND	LAFFORT	ENARTIS	RED STAR	WHITE LABS	WYEAST	RENAISSANCE	AB BIOTEK
BRG, BRL97, RC 212	F15, RB2	ES454, ES488, MB15, VQ Assmanshausen, WS	Premier Rouge	WLP707, WLP740, WLP749, WLP770	4028, 4946	Brio	Maurivin B

| Color | SG/Brix | Acidity | Tannins | Body |

PINOTAGE

Pinotage is synonymous with South African red wine, and as the name implies, Pinot Noir is one of its parent, but the similarities end there. Pinotage wines can be deep-colored and full-bodied with high alcohol, and contributing plenty of tannins to match the relatively low acidity. They have solid structure and backbone, especially when aged in oak barrels, which gives them long aging potential. The wines express aromas of cherries and blackberries, and smoky, earthy and meaty flavors. Wines can be fairly neutral if grapes are over-cropped. Acidity needs to be managed carefully, requiring perhaps acidification with tartaric acid as MLF can drop total acidity to very low levels.

Pinotage wines may develop two inherent flaws if not mitigated in the cellar. They tend to develop a compound called isoamyl acetate that may impart banana and pear aromas but more likely a pungent paint-like odor. This can be mitigated by fermenting at warmer temperatures. And they are also prone to acetic acid, or volatile acidity (VA) (see Section 7.2), which can give wine a slight vinegar smell, and therefore, a low-VA-producing, alcohol-tolerant yeast strain is recommended for fermentation, making sure to protect the wine from the elements.

Pinotage also makes delicious rosé wines though they may need a slight acidification when a more refreshing or perhaps off-dry style is desired.

Recommended Yeasts

LALLEMAND	LAFFORT	ENARTIS	RED STAR	WHITE LABS	WYEAST	RENAISSANCE	AB BIOTEK
BM4X4, ICV-D80	F15, FX10, RX60	MB15, Q5, Q7	**Premier Rouge**	**WLP740**, **WLP750**	**4021**, **4946**	Maestoso	Maurivin B

SANGIOVESE

Color	SG/Brix	Acidity	Tannins	Body

Sangiovese is a thin-skinned variety used widely in quaffable reds in central Italy but known primarily in making Chianti, a blend including other indigenous varieties and possibly a little Cabernet Sauvignon, and which is named after the Chianti region in central Tuscany. It is also famous as Sangiovese or Brunello varietals. Brunello was originally believed to be a different variety but it is simply one of many clones of the same variety. It is also a major component of Super Tuscans, premium blends that can include, for example, Cabernet Sauvignon, Merlot and Syrah.

On its own, it can produce medium-bodied varietals with moderate to high tannins and fairly high acidity, and which have great affinity for oak as well as chestnut barrels. Varietal or Sangiovese blends can have long aging potential, and in fact, Sangiovese wines can take time to "open up" before they can be appreciated.

Wines are put through MLF to tame the high acidity. In warmer climates or hot vintages, color and acidity are better balanced, in which case you may opt to forego the MLF to keep the acidity.

Aromas can vary depending on the source of fruit; they range from roasted tomatoes in young Sangioveses, to cherries, strawberries and violets, earthy and coffee notes, and vanilla and tar when aged in barrels.

Given their relatively lighter color when over-cropped and being thin-skinned, grapes benefit from an extended pre-ferment cold soak to extract more color. Alternatively, a portion of the juice can be run off and made into a rosé wine in the *saignée* method; this increases the skin-to-juice ratio and improves color in making red wine. Blending with a deeper-colored wine is always an option to improve color.

Recommended Yeasts

LALLEMAND	LAFFORT	ENARTIS	RED STAR	WHITE LABS	WYEAST	RENAISSANCE
BM45,	F83	D20,	**Premier**	**WLP760**	**4028**,	Andante
BM4X4,		MB15,	**Rouge**		**4244**,	
ICV-D254		VQ Assmanshausen,			**4267**,	
		VQ51			**4767**	

| Color | SG/Brix | Acidity | Tannins | Body |

SYRAH (SHIRAZ)

Syrah is a warm-climate, dark-skinned grape variety of great popularity in the Rhône Valley (France) where it is used primarily in GSM blends in the southern Rhône, and as a varietal known as Hermitage in the northern Rhône. It makes for great GSM blends in South Australia and Paso Robles (CA) too. It is also cofermented with Viognier, a white variety, where its high flavonol content help increase color intensity and stability via a phenomenon known as copigmentation. Syrah is also used for making dry rosé and sparkling wine.

Syrah has gained renewed popularity as a varietal and in Cabernet Sauvignon blends in Australia where it is known as Shiraz, and is also used as a blending component in some Super Tuscans.

As a varietal, Syrah can make excellent flavorful, medium- to full-bodied, age-worthy wines with moderate to high levels of alcohol and tannins and balanced acidity, and with a wide range of aromas, including blackberries, peppercorn, chocolate, espresso coffee, leather and tobacco, and earthy notes, depending on the clone, the climate and soil where grapes are grown, and the extent of aging in the cellar. It also has an affinity for oak; it enhances aroma and flavor complexity, increases color intensity and stability, and increases aging potential. Full-bodied Syrahs can require long aging before they are approachable; go for a lighter style with less tannin extraction for an earlier-drinking wine.

As Syrah grows well in warmer climates, the must may require acidification to compensate for low acidity and high pH, and to mitigate the changes due to MLF.

Recommended Yeasts

LALLEMAND	LAFFORT	ENARTIS	RED STAR	WHITE LABS	WYEAST	RENAISSANCE	AB BIOTEK
BDX, CLOS,	F83,	D20,	**Premier**	**WLP740**	**4028,**	Andante,	Maurivin B
ICV-D21,	RX60	ES454,	**Rouge**		**4267,**	Bravo,	
ICV-D254,		Q5,			**4946**	Brio	
ICV-D80,		Q7,					
ICV-GRE,		VQ Assmanshausen,					
RP15,		VQ51					
SYRAH							

TEMPRANILLO

	Color	SG/Brix	Acidity	Tannins	Body

Tempranillo is Spain's most famous red variety where, for example, in Rioja and Ribera del Duero, it can make richly colored, medium- to full-bodied wines with superb balance among alcohol, acidity and tannins, and with great affinity for long aging in oak barrels. As a varietal, it expresses light aromas of dried figs, plums, raspberries, cherries and herbs, and of cedar and tobacco from aging. The choice of a suitable yeast, maximum extraction during fermentation, and the use of oak are key to increase aromatic intensity. Alternatively, it can be blended with Cabernet Sauvignon, Grenache, Merlot or Syrah, as is often done to add more aromas and flavors. It is also grown in the Central Valley of California where it is known as Valdepeñas and is very popular with home winemakers. Tempranillo from warm climates may require acidification with tartaric acid or blending with a high-acid varietal if total acidity is too low. Tempranillo is also used for making rosé.

Tempranillo grapes can have high amounts of malic acid and potassium as well, which can cause pH to spike up as a proton (H^+) is lost in the process in exchange for every potassium ion (K^+) (see Section 7.2 for a discussion on the effects of pH on wine quality). Malic acid is easily addressed by putting wines through MLF. Potassium and pH may be reduced via a small tartaric acid addition at crush and cold stabilization during aging.

Recommended Yeasts

LALLEMAND	LAFFORT	ENARTIS	RED STAR	WHITE LABS	WYEAST	RENAISSANCE
CLOS, RP15	RX60	Q5	**Premier Cuvée**	**WLP750, WLP760**	**4028,** 4244, 4267, 4767	Maestoso

Color	SG/Brix	Acidity	Tannins	Body

TOURIGA NACIONAL

Touriga Nacional has long been one of the several varieties used in making Port wine, but it has become popular as Portugal's signature varietal wine as well. Grapes are packed with high sugar, high tannins but moderate acidity, which all translates into high-alcohol, full-bodied wines expressing intense black fruit aromas of raspberry and blackcurrant.

Grape clusters have relatively small berries and therefore contain smaller amounts of pulp, and therefore, expect lower juice yields than most other red varieties. But the greater skin-to-pulp ratio makes for deeper-colored wines. To avoid over-extraction of tannins, monitoring maceration and fermentation closely by tasting the wine often, and pressing early.

Recommended Yeasts

LALLEMAND	LAFFORT	ENARTIS	RED STAR	WHITE LABS	WYEAST	RENAISSANCE
BDX, CLOS, ICV-D21, ICV-D254, ICV-D80, ICV-GRE, RP15, SYRAH	F15, F83, FX10, RX60	Q5	Premier Rouge	WLP740	4028, 4767, 4946	Maestoso

❖

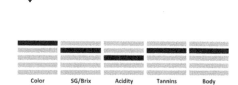

Color	SG/Brix	Acidity	Tannins	Body

ZINFANDEL (PRIMITIVO)

Zinfandel, also known as Primitivo in Puglia (Italy), is a very popular variety in California and with home winemakers as it is fun to work with because it can be made into various styles of wines from semi-sweet rosés (think White Zinfandel), to fruity, light-bodied reds to alcohol-charged, fuller-bodied styles, to sweet dessert-style or fortified port-style wines. But Zinfandel seems to perform best as a varietal as it has a bit of everything, and therefore it is seldom blended. High sugar levels in "Zins" are not uncommon, and often require amelioration to reduce alcohol levels. As a bonus, it also has higher juice yields compared to other red varieties.

2

Wine aromas too can vary greatly depending on the climate where grapes are grown. The range of aromas includes raspberries, strawberries, blueberries, anise, cinnamon and pepper. Full-bodied varietals can age very well, particularly those aged in oak barrels.

Recommended Yeasts

LALLEMAND	LAFFORT	ENARTIS	RED STAR	WHITE LABS	WYEAST	RENAISSANCE	AB BIOTEK
BDX, BM45, **BM4X4**, BRL97, CLOS, ICV-D21, ICV-D254, ICV-D80, RP15	F15	D20, ES454, MB15, Q7, VQ Assmanshausen, VQ51, WS	**Premier Rouge**	**WLP749**, **WLP760**	**4028**, 4767, 4946	Andante	Maurivin B

2.2 NATIVE AMERICAN VARIETIES AND HYBRIDS

Native varieties are those that are indigenous to a specific grape-growing region, and include *Vitis* varieties from, for example, *labrusca, rotundifolia, riparia, rupestris* and *aestivalis* species. Scuppernong (*V. rotundifolia*) and Concord (*V. labrusca*) are examples of Native American varieties.

Hybrids are varieties resulting from crossing two or more varieties from different *Vitis* species. Hybrids are created to take advantage of the best characteristics of the crossed varieties and, ideally, eliminating their weaknesses, for example, to improve their winter hardiness or their resistance to specific diseases. American hybrids are varieties resulting from the crossing of varieties from Native American species. French–American hybrids are varieties resulting from the crossing of varieties from *V. vinifera* and from American species, e.g., *V. labrusca*. Baco Noir is an example of a French–American hybrid resulting from the cross of *V. vinifera* and *V. riparia* varieties. Modern winemaking hybrids have come a long way and are capable of making some first-rate wines and can be grown in some climates where vinifera don't thrive or simply cannot be grown.

Many *V. labrusca* varieties — not to be confused with Lambrusco, an Italian red variety — are slipskin, meaning that they have a tough skin that separates readily from the pulpy flesh, and therefore require the use of rice hulls and light pressing to avoid problems in the press and to allow for better juice drainage through the grape mass. They typically contain higher levels of pectin, which must be broken down with pectolytic enzymes (pectinases) so that they don't cause any downstream problems. *V. labrusca* varieties also have characteristic "grapey" and "foxy" aromas — the latter is best described as a musty, earthy, musky odor and flavor that becomes unappealing at high concentrations. It is due to a substance known as methyl anthranilate, which is not found in *V. vinifera* varieties or other varieties with non-*V. labrusca* parentage. Varieties with *V. riparia* lineage tend to have herbaceous aromas and flavors, which can be mitigated using untoasted oak at crush or during fermentation.

From a winemaking perspective, non-vinifera varieties may need to be approached differently from viniferas owing to their significantly different sugar, acidity, and aroma and flavor profiles.

Since the vast majority of non-vinifera varieties are grown in cool or cold climates, sugar levels tend to be lower than in viniferas due to the shorter growing season, and acidity levels are relatively high (and low pH) due to high malic acid levels. And therefore, such varieties often require chaptalization and/or deacidification to bring acidity down to more palatable levels. Malic acid levels can be relatively high, which may require the use of complementary processing techniques, such as, deacidifying, fermenting using a yeast strain that metabolizes malic acid, putting the wine through malolactic fermentation (MLF), and cold stabilizing the wine. As MLF can impart various aromas and flavors that may not bode well with some varieties, it is only encouraged where acidity needs to be dropped *and* where such aromas and flavors complement the wine's organoleptic profile. Be sure to use lactic acid bacteria that can perform at low pH levels. And you'll need to pay particular attention to red hybrids and Native American varieties that may have unusually high proteins levels, more so if they have low tannins, which may cause protein stability issues (see Section 14.3).

The following sections introduce 7 white and 11 red hybrid and Native American varieties to choose from to make equally exquisite wines. We will refer to these varieties collectively as "non-vinifera varieties."

2.2.1 WHITE NON-VINIFERA VARIETIES

Cayuga White

Cayuga White is an American hybrid crossed from Seyval Blanc with origins in the Finger Lakes region in upstate New York and grown predominantly in northeastern United States. It produces wine with a good structure and balanced acidity in a dry, fruity style often compared to Riesling and Viognier. In cooler climates or in a poor vintage, deacidification may be required to achieve the proper acid balance, or alternatively, it can be sweetened or blended with other wines. Its high acidity makes Cayuga White ideal for making sparkling wine where freshness is key. Also give it a try as an orange wine.

Recommended Yeasts

LALLEMAND	LAFFORT	ENARTIS	RED STAR	WHITE LABS	WYEAST	RENAISSANCE
QA23	DELTA, VL2	Aroma White, ES181, Q Citrus	**Premier Cuvée**	**WLP735**	4021, 4242	Allegro

La Crescent

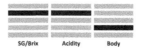

La Crescent is a cold-climate variety that can produce very aromatic wines reminiscent of Riesling but without the characteristic *V. labrusca* foxy aromas and herbaceous aromas of *V. riparia*. It expresses very pleasant aromas of citrus fruit, peach, apricot, pineapple and Muscat. It can be made into a dry style but fares better in a sweeter style given its high acidity that can often exceed 10 g/L. In spite of its high acidity, the result of a shorter growing season, La Crescent can produce fairly high sugar levels. Fermentation is best carried out at cooler temperatures to preserve as much of the fruity esters as possible. It is a great blending wine to add aromatics to more neutral white varietals.

Recommended Yeasts

LALLEMAND	LAFFORT	ENARTIS	RED STAR	WHITE LABS	WYEAST	RENAISSANCE
71B-1122, Alchemy I, Lalvin C, **QA23**, R2, SVG, VIN 13	Delta, VL1	Q9, Q Citrus	**Côte des Blancs**, **Premier Blanc**	**WLP715**, **WLP735**	**4021**, **4242**	TR-313

SG/Brix   Acidity   Body

NIAGARA

Niagara is a thin-skinned, slipskin hybrid variety, a cross of Concord and Cassady, from Niagara County, New York. Grapes tend to have low sugar and high acidity, which may require chaptalization or deacidification, or both, to produce a balanced wine.

Niagara makes very flavorful dry or sweeter-style wines but which can have strong characteristic gamey and foxy aromas, much like its one red-variety parent, Concord. It can also express petrol-like aromas akin to Riesling. To minimize these traits, grapes should be whole-cluster pressed, which can be a challenge in itself for a slipskin variety, or crushed and moved to the press very quickly to avoid any maceration of juice and solids.

Niagara is a great blending partner with Seyval Blanc if acidity can be adequately balanced, though it can make some interesting blends with viniferas, such as Chenin Blanc, Gewürztraminer, Riesling and Sauvignon Blanc.

Recommended Yeasts

LALLEMAND	LAFFORT	ENARTIS	RED STAR	WHITE LABS	WYEAST	RENAISSANCE
71B-1122	DELTA	Q9	**Côte des Blancs**	**WLP720**	**4242**	Allegro

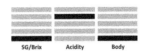

SCUPPERNONG

Scuppernong, often referred to as White Muscadine (see *Muscadines* in Section 2.2.2), is a greenish-bronze colored, thick-skinned white variety that produces dark-gold wines. This slipskin variety can prove to be a challenge when pressing; rice hulls as pressing aid are highly recommended to ease the pressing operation and improve juice flow through the mass of grapes. The extra pressure needed to press grapes can cause higher amounts of tannins to be extracted than desired, which can make for overly bitter wines compounded by naturally high acidity. Significant sweetening is often require for balance. And given the variety's low sugar production, chaptalization is almost always required to obtain alcohol levels in typical wine range. It can also be used to make orange wine.

Recommended Yeasts

LALLEMAND	LAFFORT	ENARTIS	RED STAR	WHITE LABS	WYEAST	RENAISSANCE
Lalvin C, VIN 13	DELTA	Top Essence	**Premier Blanc**	**WLP720**	4028, 4783	Allegro

SEYVAL BLANC

Seyval Blanc, or simply Seyval, is a cool-climate, pale-skinned French–American hybrid grown predominantly in northeastern Unites States and Canada. It can make crisp, early-drinking wines to fuller-bodied styles.

Wines have low to moderate alcohol, which may require chaptalization in lesser vintages, and are made typically in a dry style with moderate to high acidity that may benefit from MLF and for stylistic reasons too. They express citrusy and green apple aromas and flavors with hints of minerality, but which can be fermented or aged in oak barrels for added complexity.

Grapes should ideally be whole-cluster pressed to minimize harsh skin tannins, which can otherwise be excessively bitter in high-acid wines; alternatively, wine can be treated post-fermentation with a suitable fining agent to reduce bitter tannins.

Seyval Blanc is a perfect blending partner with low-acid varieties such as Chardonnay and Auxerrois, or with Niagara when acid can be balanced. It is a great variety for making sparkling wine because of its high acidity and lower alcohol. It can also be used to make orange wine.

Recommended Yeasts

LALLEMAND	LAFFORT	ENARTIS	RED STAR	WHITE LABS	WYEAST	RENAISSANCE
71B-1122, Alchemy I, **QA23**, SVG	DELTA, VL2	Q9, Top Essence, Vintage White	**Côte des Blancs**, **Premier Cuvée**	**WLP735**	**4021**, **4028**, **4783**	Allegro

TRAMINETTE

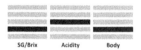

SG/Brix   Acidity   Body

Traminette is a cross of a French–American hybrid and, as the name suggests, Gewürztraminer, from Illinois but now popularly grown in Indiana and other regions in the United States. Traminette varietals exhibit some of the fragrant monoterpenols-derived odoriferous characteristics of Gewürztraminer, including apricots and honey. Cooler fermentation temperatures are recommended to preserve the delicate aromas. And as with Gewürztraminer, MLF is never recommended, but a short maceration with skins can enhance spicy Gewürz-like aromas and flavors.

Recommended Yeasts

LALLEMAND	LAFFORT	ENARTIS	RED STAR	WHITE LABS	WYEAST	RENAISSANCE
Alchemy I, **QA23**, R2, VIN 13	Delta, VL1	Q9, Q Citrus, VQ Assmanshausen, VQ10	**Côte des Blancs**, **Premier Cuvée**	**WLP735**	**4021**, **4242**, **4783**	TR-313

VIDAL BLANC

SG/Brix   Acidity   Body

Vidal Blanc, or simply Vidal, is a thick-skinned French–American hybrid variety with Ugni Blanc (Trebbiano) and Seyval Blanc lineages. It is a versatile variety used for crafting many different styles of fruit-forward wines. Because of its moderate to high acidity, it is well suited for making sparkling wine when sugar levels are low. It can be used to make sweeter styles of wines as well as sweet dessert wines, including ice wine. It does well in cool climates, particularly in Canada's Niagara region and the US Midwest and Northeast, where it can easily produce high amounts of sugars and, therefore, Vidal varietals can be high in alcohol compared to what would be more typical in white wines. MLF is a viable option for Vidal Blanc when needing to reduce high acidity.

Vidal wines express aromas of grapefruit, apples, peaches and pineapples. Some untoasted or lightly toasted oak can augment aroma and flavor complexity.

Recommended Yeasts

LALLEMAND	LAFFORT	ENARTIS	RED STAR	WHITE LABS	WYEAST	RENAISSANCE
71B-1122, Alchemy I, **K1V-1116,** **QA23,** R2	DELTA, VL1, VL2	Q9, Q Citrus, Vintage White, VQ10	**Côte des** **Blancs,** **Premier** **Cuvée**	**WLP715,** **WLP735**	**4783**	Bella

2.2.2 RED NON-VINIFERA VARIETIES

Generally, interspecific red Native American and hybrid grapes produce wines with lower tannin concentrations than *V. vinifera* varieties, often greater than a four-fold difference, likely due to significantly stronger binding by flesh cell wall proteins. Therefore you will need to pay special attention to tannins when working with Native American and hybrid grapes, particularly with regard to color stabilization in highly pigmented varieties. Specifically, you will likely need to use proteases to reduce protein binding and increase tannin levels, or alternatively, you can add more tannins. Chapter 9 describes tannins and protein binding in more details.

If you want to reduce certain aromas and flavors, for example, if you are not partial to the foxy character of *V. labrusca* varieties or if dealing with underripe grapes, you'll want to go easy on extraction techniques, reduce maceration/fermentation time by pressing earlier than at dryness, and complete fermentation without grape solids in other vessels. You can also make use of the same technique as with methoxypyrazine-prone vinifera varieties: adding untoasted oak at crush or during fermentation to mask the foxy character by intensifying the fruity expression and exhibiting "ripe" fruit notes without the aromas of toasted oak.

If you have timely access to viniferas, consider blending in some small amount into your non-vinifera crush to deal with some of the technical challenges of high acidity or low tannins, for example, or even to add complementary aromas and flavors. Try the same by cofermenting hybrids and Native American varieties. You can also experiment with adding a small amount of concentrate from a wine kit if you cannot source vinifera grapes or juice, or if the timing is not good.

Baco Noir

| Color | SG/Brix | Acidity | Tannins | Body |

Baco Noir is a French–American hybrid (*V. vinifera* var. Folle Blanche × *V. riparia*) where it grows well in the cooler regions in northern United States and Canada. It produces richly colored wines with relatively low tannins but moderate to high acidity, and strawberry aromas and light caramel notes with possibly an herbaceous taste.

Baco can also have high potassium (K^+) that can result in very high pH by the end of fermentation; a tartaric acid addition is therefore recommended at crush. Naturally high acidity is likely due to malic acid, and therefore wines will benefit from a malic-degrading yeast for the AF and from a MLF.

Baco has an affinity for oak where it will acquire more tannins, and therefore it can age well for several years when made into a full-bodied style. Chambourcin is a good blending partner; also try with a Cabernet variety.

Recommended Yeasts

LALLEMAND	LAFFORT	ENARTIS	RED STAR	WHITE LABS	WYEAST	RENAISSANCE	AB BIOTEK
71B-1122,	F15,	ES488,	Premier Rouge,	WLP740,	4267,	Andante,	Maurivin B
RC 212	RB2	Q5	Premier Cuvée	WLP770	4946	Maestoso	

2

CATAWBA

| Color | SG/Brix | Acidity | Tannins | Body |

Catawba is a deep-pink, thick-skinned North American variety likely the result of crossing of *V. vinifera* and Native American *V. labrusca* varieties, which means that wines have a characteristic "foxy" aroma.

Being very lightly colored, Catawba is used for making white and light rosé (Pink Catawba) wines in a range of styles from dry to semi-sweet or sweet, as well as sparkling wine. Chaptalization is often required to bring alcohol to white-wine levels.

Catawba can also make light- to medium-bodied reds with moderate acidity; however, it usually does not have sufficient anthocyanins to make a fully colored red wine. A cool fermentation with no MLF is recommended to preserve as much of the red berry and sweet fruit esters as possible.

Deacidification, blending with other wines or sweetening may be required in poor vintages to tame high acidity.

As with other *V. labrusca* slipskin varieties, rice hulls are recommended at the press.

Recommended Yeasts

LALLEMAND	LAFFORT	ENARTIS	RED STAR	WHITE LABS	WYEAST	RENAISSANCE
71B-1122, K1V-1116	F15	ES401	Côte des Blancs	WLP740, WLP770	4028	Andante, Bella

⚜

CHAMBOURCIN

| Color | SG/Brix | Acidity | Tannins | Body |

Chambourcin is a deep-colored French–American teinturier variety that can make richly colored and strongly flavored wines in dry or off-dry styles, or used to add color in weaker wines. Given its low tannin content, an extended post-fermentation maceration, a tannin addition, blending with another varietal, or barrel aging may be required to improve body and structure. Chambourcin expresses fruity and spicy aromas. It is an excellent blending partner with Baco Noir and Maréchal Foch as well as viniferas, such as Cabernet Sauvignon or Franc and Merlot.

Recommended Yeasts

LALLEMAND	LAFFORT	ENARTIS	RED STAR	WHITE LABS	WYEAST	RENAISSANCE
71B-1122, BM45, **BM4X4**, CLOS, CSM, ICV-D254, ICV-D80, **RC 212**	F15, F83, RX60	Q5, VQ51	**Premier Rouge**	**WLP740**	**4946**	Bravo

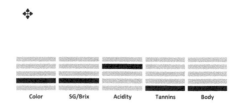

| | Color | SG/Brix | Acidity | Tannins | Body |

CONCORD

Concord is a Native American, slipskin variety of *V. labrusca* with a deep-blue to purple color that produces wines with a highly distinct "foxy" aroma. It is most commonly used to make medium-sweet to sweet wines although it is possible to make a dry style when grapes have reached good balance of sugars and acids at full ripeness. With balance often lacking, Concord requires chaptalization to increase alcohol and balance high acidity, and perhaps coupled with a deacidification. Concord is the most popular variety for bottled purple grape juice and grape jelly; those products provide good examples of foxy aromas.

The foxy character of Concord can be reduced by doing a short, cold-soak maceration until the desired color is achieved, being sure to use pectinases to break down the great amounts of pectin, and then pressing the grapes *before* fermentation. Add rice hulls to the grape solids when loading the press.

MLF and oak influence are not recommended so as not to detract from the fruity character of the wine.

Recommended Yeasts

LALLEMAND	LAFFORT	ENARTIS	RED STAR	WHITE LABS	WYEAST	RENAISSANCE	AB BIOTEK
71B-1122	F15	Red Fruit	**Côte des Blancs**	**WLP770**	**4028, 4267**	Andante	Maurivin B

FRONTENAC

| Color | SG/Brix | Acidity | Tannins | Body |

Frontenac (Noir) is a deeply colored French–American hybrid developed at the University of Minnesota. It can achieve high sugar levels that make this variety ideal for making port-style wines or when residual sugar is desired. It does however have high acidity, which, for making a balanced table wine, may require deacidification in conjunction with MLF, and perhaps some sweetening if fermented completely dry. It can also be made into a fuller-bodied, off-dry style of rosé.

Given its relatively low tannin content, wines may require a small tannin addition being mindful that tannins and acidity reinforce each other. As a red varietal, Frontenac expresses bold cherry and plum aromas with possibly slightly herbaceous notes.

Recommended Yeasts

LALLEMAND	LAFFORT	ENARTIS	RED STAR	WHITE LABS	WYEAST	RENAISSANCE	AB BIOTEK
BM4X4, CSM, Lalvin C, RC 212, RP15	F15	ES401, ES488	Premier Rouge, Premier Cuvée	WLP750, WLP760	4028, 4267, 4946	Andante	Maurivin B

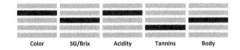

LÉON MILLOT

| Color | SG/Brix | Acidity | Tannins | Body |

Léon Millot, a sibling of Maréchal Foch, is a blue-skinned French–American hybrid variety ((*V. riparia* × *V. rupestris*) × *V. vinifera*) from Alsace (France). Berries can be very small, and therefore, expect yields to be low. It can however produce very concentrated wines often compared to Syrah and, naturally, to Maréchal Foch. It expresses earthy aromas, perhaps with some barnyard and chocolate aromas.

Léon Millot can be made into many styles from a rosé using a very short maceration, to a light- or medium-colored red to a richer, fuller-bodied red with MLF to reduce the naturally high malic acid levels. If acid levels are high, in any style, a malic-degrading yeast is recommended for the AF.

Medium- and full-bodied Léon Millot wines have an affinity for oak and can age well for several years but, given the variety's tannin deficiency, tannin additions may be necessary at the crusher and/or post fermentation to stabilize color and prevent a drop in color intensity. As Léon Millot can also have high pH, it can make color stability a further challenge. Quite counterintuitively given that it also has high acidity, it will require a tartaric acid addition to drop the pH. We'll explore the chemistry and application of this technique in Section 7.5.3.

Recommended Yeasts

LALLEMAND	LAFFORT	ENARTIS	RED STAR	WHITE LABS	WYEAST	RENAISSANCE	AB BIOTEK
71B-1122, RP15	F15	ES488, Q5, Red Fruit	**Premier Rouge**, **Premier Cuvée**	**WLP750**, **WLP760**	4028, 4267, **4946**	Andante, Bella, Maestoso	Maurivin B

| Color | SG/Brix | Acidity | Tannins | Body |

MARÉCHAL FOCH

Maréchal Foch, or simply Foch, a sibling of Léon Millot, is a French–American hybrid variety from Alsace. It is used to make a range of wines from light reds to fuller-bodied styles including port-style. It has an affinity for oak that also improves aging potential. The wines are often said to be of "Burgundian" character although "Beaujolais" would be more appropriate given their similarities to Gamay wines.

Maréchal Foch grapes are naturally high in acidity, often exceeding 10 g/L, and may require a combination of deacidification at the juice stage, the use of a malic-degrading yeast for the AF, and putting the wine through MLF.

Aromas can vary significantly depending on the age of the vines and climate where grapes are grown, and may include black fruit, coffee, chocolate, vanilla bean, and possibly gamey notes.

Recommended Yeasts

LALLEMAND	LAFFORT	ENARTIS	RED STAR	WHITE LABS	WYEAST	RENAISSANCE	AB BIOTEK
71B-1122, BM45, BRL97, **RC 212**, RP15	F15, RB2	ES488, Q5	**Premier Rouge**, **Premier Cuvée**	**WLP750**, **WLP760**	4946	Andante, Bravo, Maestoso	Maurivin B

2

MARQUETTE

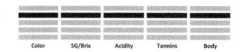

| Color | SG/Brix | Acidity | Tannins | Body |

Marquette is a relatively new French–American hybrid teinturier variety related to Pinot Noir and Frontenac developed at the University of Minnesota. It can ripen to high sugar levels and still moderate to high acidity with pronounced tannins. It can produce excellent wines, either fruity reds and rosés, or full-bodied reds with cherry and blackcurrant aromas and notes of spices, leather and tobacco. A malic-degrading yeast coupled with MLF is recommended to lower high acidity. Given the potentially very low pH, below the typical 3.2 threshold of lactic acid bacteria used in MLF, an appropriate low-pH culture is recommended.

Recommended Yeasts

LALLEMAND	LAFFORT	ENARTIS	RED STAR	WHITE LABS	WYEAST	RENAISSANCE	AB BIOTEK
71B-1122, **BM4X4,** CLOS, CSM, ICV-D254, **RC 212,** RP15	F15, RB2, RX60	ES488, Q5	**Premier** **Cuvée**	**WLP750,** **WLP760**	**4028,** **4267,** **4946**	Andante	Maurivin B

MUSCADINES

The term "Muscadines" refers to a number of red and white grape varieties belonging to the species *V. rotundifolia* (also known as Muscadinia) native to the southeastern and south-central United States, and which, as the name suggests, produce wines with characteristic musky, grapey flavors. Muscadines don't form bunches as other varieties, but rather, as clusters of sparse berries.

The name "Muscadine" is often used to refer to specific North American red grape varieties, for example, Noble. Red varieties used for making wine have large, very thick-skinned, dark-purple berries, almost black in color, and are very rich in polyphenols. They often have low sugar and therefore require chaptalization to bring the alcohol to red-wine levels.

NOIRET

Noiret is a hybrid with *V. labrusca* and *V. vinifera* lineages, developed at Cornell University in upstate New York. It makes richly colored reds packed with tannins and exhibiting aromas of pepper, raspberry and blackberry but without the foxy characteristics of other *V. labrusca* varieties. Acidity is not as high as in other hybrids, which makes for well-balanced wines after MLF.

Recommended Yeasts

LALLEMAND	LAFFORT	ENARTIS	RED STAR	WHITE LABS	WYEAST	RENAISSANCE
71B-1122, BRL97, CLOS	F15	Q5, Red Fruit	**Premier Rouge**, **Premier Cuvée**	**WLP750**, **WLP760**	**4028**, **4267**	Brio

❖

NORTON (CYNTHIANA)

Norton, also known as Cynthiana, is a dark-skinned American hybrid (*V. aestivalis*) with possibly some lineage to *V. labrusca* too. It is widely and successfully grown in Missouri as well as in Virginia. It is capable of producing flavorful, deep-colored, high-quality red wines, often deemed of vinifera quality. The wines express coffee and spicy aromas but with almost none of the foxy *V. labrusca* aromas.

Acidity can be very high, as high as 15 g/L with up to 6 g/L of malic acid [2], and therefore, must may require deacidification and wines put through MLF. Given the high levels of tartaric acid coupled with possibly great amounts of potassium, up to 6 g/L [2], cold stabilization will be required to avoid post-bottling tartrates.

And given the higher anthocyanin levels in this variety compared to other hybrids, special attention is required at crush and post fermentation in adding tannins — either as grape tannins or oak powder — to stabilize color.

2

Recommended Yeasts

LALLEMAND	LAFFORT	ENARTIS	RED STAR	WHITE LABS	WYEAST	RENAISSANCE	AB BIOTEK
71B-1122, BRL97, CLOS, ICV-D254, Lalvin C, RP15	F15, RB2	ES401, ES488	**Premier Cuvée**	**WLP750, WLP760**	**4028,** 4267, **4946**	Andante	Maurivin B

St. Croix

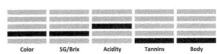

Color   SG/Brix   Acidity   Tannins   Body

St. Croix is a thin-skinned American hybrid from a cross of various *Vitis* genera grapes, and which performs well in cold-climate growing areas such as the US Midwest and Québec (Canada) although it poses a challenge in the vineyard in achieving higher sugar levels as well as in the cellar in extracting color. Chaptalization is most often required.

Wines tend to be light- to medium-bodied with moderate acidity and low alcohol, and may need to be supplemented with tannins to improve structure. It has good fruit aromas and can exhibit heavy flavors of tobacco, tar or smoke if overripe or overly macerated [1], but without the foxy or herbaceous character from its *V. labrusca* and *V. riparia* lineages.

Recommended Yeasts

LALLEMAND	LAFFORT	ENARTIS	RED STAR	WHITE LABS	WYEAST	RENAISSANCE
71B-1122, CLOS, CSM	F15	ES454, ES488	**Premier Rouge,** **Premier Cuvée**	**WLP740,** **WLP750**	**4028,** 4267	Bravo

REFERENCES

1. Robinson, J., Harding, J., Vouillamoz, J. 2012. *Wine Grapes: A Complete Guide to 1,368 Vine Varieties, Including Their Origins and Flavours.* Ecco, UK.

2. Iowa State University. 2016. *A Review of Cold Climate Grape Cultivars.* https://store.extension.iastate.edu/Product/A-Review-of-Cold-Climate-Grape-Cultivars-pdf. Last accessed December 23, 2020.

3. Hawkins, A. J. 2007. *The Super Gigantic Y2K Winegrape Glossary.* http://www.wineloverspage.com/wlp_archive/wineguest/wgg.html. Last accessed December 23, 2020.

3

3 Essential Winemaking Equipment

If you are just starting out in winemaking, you only need basic equipment to make a standard 23-L (6-gal) batch. Home winemaking supply shops sell a basic starter kit (Figure 3.1) that includes:

- a pail or bucket (referred to as a primary fermentor in kit wine-making) for fermenting juice
- a 23-L (6-gal) glass or PET carboy (referred to as a secondary fer-mentor in kit winemaking) for completing fermentation and for storing wine; PET (polyethylene terephthalate) is a type of durable plastic
- a hydrometer and test cylinder
- a fermentation lock (airlock) and stopper (bung)
- a racking cane and siphon hose for transferring wine from one fermentor to another
- a long-handle spoon for stirring

Figure 3.1: Basic winemaking starter kit

A starter kit may also include some extra equipment such as:

- a wine thief for drawing wine samples from fermentors
- a thermometer for monitoring fermentation temperature
- a bottle brush for washing used bottles
- a simple bottle filler
- a hand corker for inserting corks into bottles

You can invest in other equipment for greater efficiency and flexibility as you grow your hobby to larger batches or if you'll be making different types of wines at once, or if you decide to go full out and make wine from grapes.

Filtration and bottling equipment are discussed in Chapters 17 and 18, respectively.

3.1 CRUSHERS AND PRESSES

The first important decision and investment you will make as you take the plunge into winemaking using grapes is the purchase of a crusher and press. If you make red wine from frozen must, you only need a press. The decision on the type of crusher and press is based on your expected annual production, desired efficiency and budget. Be sure to forecast your future needs as your hobby will likely grow very quickly.

There are various models of manual and motorized crushers and crusher–destemmers (Figure 3.2) to suit any budget.

The purpose of the crusher is to split berries open to allow them to be exposed to yeast and release juice in red winemaking, or simply to facilitate pressing and release juice when processing white grapes. Stems are usually removed, or destemmed, as these can impart harsh tannins and unpleasant green aromas, except when you want to press whole clusters, for example, in white winemaking where grapes may go straight to the press without crushing or destemming. If you intend to make more than just a few 16.3-kg (36-lb) cases, consider investing in a motorized crusher–destemmer as destemming by hand is messy and laborious. A crusher–destemmer crushes grapes into a large vat while removing and expelling stems out.

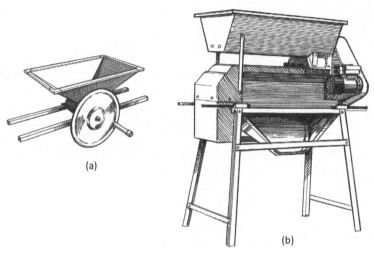

Figure 3.2: a) Manual crusher; b) Motorized crusher–destemmer with stand/chute

You typically crush right into a large vat, but if you are making smaller volumes or your crusher–destemmer is larger than your vat, use a crusher stand/chute (Figure 3.2) to crush into pails, then transfer the crushed grapes to fermenting vessels.

In red winemaking, you need a punchdown tool (Figure 3.3) to submerge several times a day crushed grapes back into the wine as it ferments and carbon dioxide (CO_2) gas pushes grape solids to the surface and form what is called a cap. This helps extract color and tannins, promotes a healthy fermentation, uniforms temperature distribution, and keeps surface spoilage microorganisms in check. You can also do pumpovers where wine is pumped from the bottom valve of a vat, tank or other fermentor and onto the cap to douse and resubmerge it. It is more efficient than punchdowns although it is a fairly aggressive procedure that some will argue it causes excessive oxygen uptake; it also requires a fairly expensive pump that can move grape solids.

Figure 3.3: Punchdown tool

Then you need a press if making wine from grapes, including frozen must. In white winemaking, the press is used to release juice from crushed grapes or from whole bunches. In red winemaking, the press is used to release wine from grape solids that have macerated and fermented in the wine.

If your winemaking is limited to making single-pail, 23-L (6-gal) batches from grapes or frozen must, a small stainless steel press (Figure 3.4) is all you need. You will need a basket or bladder press (Figure 3.4) for larger batches.

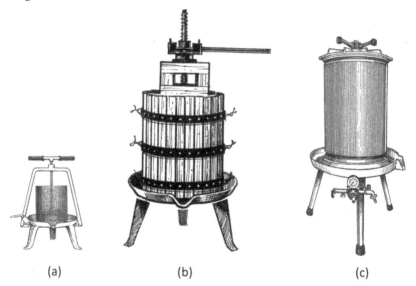

(a)   (b)   (c)

Figure 3.4: a) Small stainless steel press; b) basket press; c) bladder press

Presses can be a significant investment, therefore be sure to pick a size that will keep pace with your growing production, keeping in mind that it will be very difficult to press a small load in a large press and a lot more work to press a large load in a small press. You have to work as fast as possible during pressing cycles to limit the exposure of juice or wine to the elements.

Basket presses range in size from small to very large to handle up to 500 kg (1100 lbs) or more of crushed grapes. Basket size or capacity is typically denoted by a number, such as 45, which simply indicates the diameter of the basket in centimeters. A #45 press can handle about 140 kg (300 lbs) of crushed grapes, or about 90 L (25 gal) in volume.

Bladder presses come in as small as 20 L (5 gal) and as large as 300 L (79 gal) or more; the larger models come on casters making them easy to move around. A 90-L (25-gal) press will meet the needs of most amateurs processing 140 kg (300 lbs) or more of grapes. Bladder presses come with a nylon mesh that is inserted inside the stainless steel screen to keep grape fragments in and to facilitate removing the pressed pomace, and an outer plastic bag or cover to prevent the juice or wine from being squeezed out and making a mess all over.

The decision of a ratchet-type basket press versus a bladder press is a personal one: both are very efficient though you need to exert force — a lot of force — with a basket press whereas you let air or water pressure do the work for you with a bladder press. A bladder press also recovers more juice or wine than a basket press.

The most common bladder presses use water. In hydropresses, as they are known, the bladder is slowly filled with water and exerts pressure on grapes to release juice or wine. You can set the water flow from a tap to a low level so that the bladder pressure increases slowly and remains below the operating maximum, and presses the entire load in one quick but gentle cycle. Hydropresses are equipped with a pressure relief valve that automatically cuts off the flow of water to the bladder when the maximum operating pressure is exceeded — typically around 3 bar or 45 psi. With a basket press, you have to press the load and then wait for pressure to subside before applying pressure again; press cycles tend to be much longer.

 When loading a bladder press (Figure 3.5), distribute the load of grapes evenly over the whole volume of the basket, from bottom to top, to allow for efficient pressing and longer press life. When working with smaller loads than the press capacity, this requires that you partially fill the bladder with water and only then load the press, and maybe releasing some water if more room is needed. If the bladder is inflating with the basket loaded only partway, the bladder will reach maximum pressure against the load towards the bottom of the basket but it will continue to inflate disproportionally towards the top and possibly become damaged.

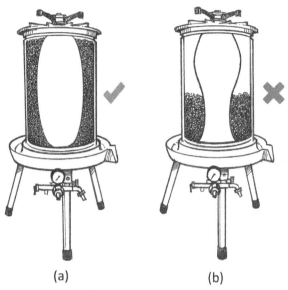

(a)   (b)

Figure 3.5: Loading a bladder press; a) the correct way and b) the wrong way

For hydropresses, once you start the flow of water into the bladder, be sure to open the vent at the top of the bladder at the start of the press cycle to flush out all the air out. As soon as the valve spits out a steady stream of water, close the valve; this way, the bladder fills up with only water and will not get damaged.

If you have to press white and red grapes with a wood-type basket press, always press whites first, then reds. If you press red grapes first, red color absorbed in the wooden slats will leach into the white juice and give it a pinkish or reddish color.

When done for the vintage, thoroughly rinse the wooden-slat basket with high-pressure water, remove the red staining with a mild percarbonate solution (see Section 4.4.1) followed by another rinse with high-pressure water, let dry and store away the basket until next season.

Another piece of equipment that will prove useful in making red wine is the WineEasy (Figure 3.6). The WineEasy is an integrated fermentor and press that makes use of a "piston-like" lid that presses the pomace under the action of vacuum pump, and delivers the pressed wine into a carboy under vacuum. The stainless steel tanks are available in 80, 120 and 220-L

3

Figure 3.6: WineEasy

(20, 30 and 55-gal) sizes, and can also be used as variable-capacity tanks (VCT) for storing and aging wine.

3.2 FERMENTATION AND STORAGE VESSELS

A pail or bucket made of, for example, polypropylene (PP, plastic code 05) or low-density polyethylene (LDPE, plastic code 04), and one glass or PET carboy may be all you need to make a single 23-L (6-gal) batch of wine. A second carboy will come in handy when you have to rack from one carboy to another, avoiding having to rack from the carboy to the pail and back into the carboy. The pail or bucket is used to conduct the initial or primary fermentation and, as such, is commonly referred to as a primary fermentor. The second carboy, referred to as a secondary fermentor, is used to finish fermentation.

As your hobby grows, you will need many different kinds and sizes of fermentors and storage vessels (Figure 3.7). These may include food-grade plastic vats (or tubs) for macerating and fermenting red wine, glass or PET carboys, glass demijohns, stainless steel or HDPE tanks, and oak barrels. PET carboys are made of polyethylene terephthalate (plastic code 01); HDPE tanks and fermentors are made of high-density polyethylene (plastic code 02). If you intend to tartrate stabilize by chilling wine down to cold

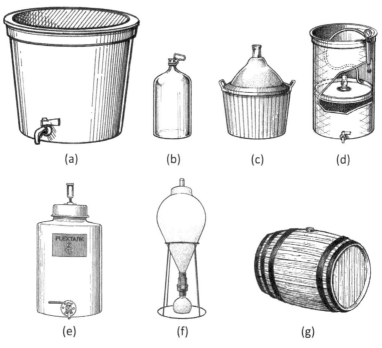

(a)   (b)   (c)   (d)

(e)   (f)   (g)

Figure 3.7: Vessels for fermenting and storing wine: a) food-grade plastic vat/tub; b) glass carboy; c) glass demijohn; d) stainless steel variable-capacity tank (VCT); e) Flextank – an HDPE tank; f) Fast-Ferment (HDPE fermentor); g) oak barrel

temperatures (see Section 14.4), you will need PET carboys or stainless steel tanks — not glass — as these don't pose a breakage danger when exposed to cold temperatures.

 Handle glass carboys with extreme caution. Glass carboys are manufactured from soft glass that can cause severe injuries when they shatter if dropped. Never carry a glass carboy by the neck, and be aware that even lifting a full glass carboy off a counter by placing your hands around its base can cause it to crack wide open. Use milk crates available from your local hardware store to safely move glass carboys around.

As plastic is permeable to oxygen, which will cause wine to slowly oxidize and spoil, only use PET and HDPE vessels for fermenting or storing wine for short term, less than 3 months. You can however use HDPE tanks, such as Flextanks (Figure 3.7), for aging wine, but this has to be done in

3

conjunction with oak wood, wine style permitting; this is discussed in Section 15.4.

 On the ECO line of Flextanks, dab the lid gasket with several drops of olive or mineral oil for a tighter seal against oxygen ingress, but don't over-tighten! You may need to make use of an adjustable belt strap wrench to unscrew a stubborn lid.

For red winemaking, choose a fermenting vat with a diameter-to-height ratio equal to or greater than 1:1 for optimal extraction of color and tannins. Fermentors that are tall and narrow reduce the amount of grape solids in contact with fermenting wine, which reduces extraction.

When buying fermentors and storage vessels, what is important to consider here is that, whatever vessels you use for post-fermentation storage, they must always be topped up so there is minimal headspace to avoid oxidation and microbial spoilage.

Predicting the exact yield of wine from grapes is not an exact science, and what may have yielded a certain volume one vintage may yield more or less the next, making vessel capacity a challenge to manage. And every time you rack — where the wine is separated from its sediment — you end up with less volume and greater headspace to deal with now. It's usually best to make a little more wine, for example, 10% or an extra 4-L (one-gal) jug when making a demijohn (54 L, 14 gal) of wine, so that when the demijohn is racked, the jug should perfectly fill it. And when fermenting in carboys or demijohns, you have to allow extra volume for foaming. There is also the possibility that you may have to ameliorate (add water) to your must, and just like that, unexpectedly, you need a vessel of greater capacity than you had planned.

It can become quite the task managing wine volume and ensuring that all vessels are topped up. Having different-size carboys and demijohns or variable-capacity tanks will help you manage this dilemma. See Section 3.6 for solutions to manage headspace when topping up is not desired or possible.

For fermenting juice only and at relatively warm temperature, and especially with a yeast strain known for producing a lot of foam, choose a fermentor that will be filled three-quarters to allow for foaming during fermentation. If fermenting cool, you can use more of the capacity as there will be much less foaming.

In red winemaking with grapes, you have to estimate the total volume of the must, i.e., grape solids and juice, for the variety at hand and choose a fermentor that will be filled three-quarters — no more — to allow for a cap forming during fermentation. For example, for the fruit I work with, I use an estimate of 85 L per 100 kg of crushed grapes and juice or about 10 gal per 100 lbs, and therefore, if I am processing ten 16.3-kg (36-lb) cases, that's a total volume of roughly 140 L (36 gal), which means I would need a fermentor of at least 187 L (48 gal) filled at three-quarter capacity.

You'll often have to do the reverse calculation, that is, figure out how many kg or lbs of grapes you can process in your fermentor. For example, if you have a 200-L (50-gal) vat, it can accommodate 150 L (38 gal) at three-quarter capacity, which means you can process about 175 kg (380 lbs) of grapes.

And then you need to determine your storage/aging vessels needs based on wine yield once grapes are pressed. For example, I estimate a yield of 15% less than the gross volume calculated above, and then a loss of approximately 15% due to gross lees after the first racking following pressing. And therefore, for the 140 L (36 gal) from above, I would have about 120 L (30 gal) of wine at pressing, which means I will need two 54-L (14-gal) demijohns and figure out at pressing how I will handle the leftover volume of about 12 L (3 gal). But the wine will still drop a lot of lees (10–15% is my estimate) over the next couple of days, so now, I need to plan for just over 100 L (25 gal) of wine, which is just short of two 54-L (14-gal) demijohns. Therefore now I would need to find some combination of the various-sized carboys and other vessels I have to accommodate this volume so that there is no headspace in any vessel.

And now you see the challenges of managing wine volumes and headspace. When working with larger volumes and to avoid these headaches, consider using stainless steel variable-capacity tanks (VCTs). These are equipped with a lid and inflatable bladder that is made to float on the surface of the wine, the bladder is then inflated to seal the tank and protect the wine from the elements. And don't be concerned inflating the bladder past the red line.

As the lid can be positioned at any level, the VCT can be made to hold any volume of wine. In the examples above, I transfer free- and press-run fractions (assuming I keep them together) to a 200-L (50-gal) VCT, let the

3

lees settle, and then rack the wine to another VCT. There will be more losses, albeit much smaller volumes, at subsequent rackings. When buying a VCT, get a spare bladder and pump while you're at it; you don't want a bladder or pump to fail on you late at night with no spare. These can last a lifetime but tend to break down or fail, especially the bladder, if not handled or maintained properly.

Fixed-volume tanks are fine for fermenting, and storage too, but they have to be kept full to avoid spoilage problems — that's not always easy as we have just seen.

To ease racking operations when using large plastic vats, VCTs or HDPE tanks, install appropriately sized stainless steel valves or spigots. A plastic strainer (Figure 3.8) that mounts on the inside of plastic vats/tubs will prove useful for drawing free-run wine when making reds. You can also fit your VCT or HDPE tank with an adjustable rotating racking arm (Figure 3.8) to control the racking operation, for example, if you need to rack wine to just above the lees.

When working with VCTs, you will need to be able to determine with some accuracy how much wine is in the tank so that you can add the right amount of additives for that volume. A simple way is to measure the height of headspace above the wine surface to the top of the tank, subtract that from the total height of the tank, and then calculate the volume using the known relationship for determining the volume of a cylinder. Let's look at an example.

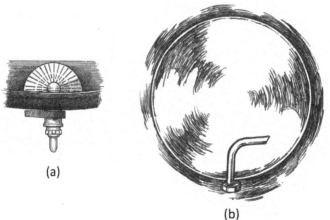

(a)

(b)

Figure 3.8: a) Plastic strainer inside a vat/tub; b) rotating racking arm in a VCT

EXAMPLE 3.1

Measuring wine volume in a VCT

You have a 200-L (50-gal) VCT having a total height of 100 cm (39 in) and a diameter of 50 cm (20 in). These dimensions work out to a total volume of just about 200 L, or 53 gal. Do *not* make any assumptions on the wine volume relative to tank volume as you don't know where the 200-L (50-gal) point is.

With a measuring tape, you measure exactly 35 cm (14 in) from the wine surface to the top of the tank, and therefore, you have 65 cm (25.5 in) of wine in height. Now calculate as follows the actual volume of wine in liters (L) knowing that *r* is the radius of the tank and is equal to half its diameter, i.e., 25 cm and *h* is the height of the wine, i.e., 65 cm, making sure to divide by 1000 to get the volume in liters (L) and dividing by 3.79 to convert into gallons:

$$Volume\ (L) = \pi r^2 h = \frac{3.14 \times 25^2 \times 65}{1000} = 127.6\ L\ (33.7\ gal)$$

Floating lids usually have a single eyelet or hook placed right in the center to which you attach a rope to lift or lower the lid in the tank. This makes it hard to stabilize the lid and have it leveled as you inflate the gasket. To solve this, place three cord clips or hooks secured with double-sided tape at the perimeter of the lid, just inside (Figure 3.9), and then attach a piece of rope to each, collect them into one, and attach to a single rope. Then you can use an eyelet or hook attached to the ceiling just over the tank to help you lift or lower the lid in balanced fashion.

If working with larger volumes, consider installing 1½-inch tri-clamp sanitary fittings (also called tri-clover fittings) on your VCTs or Flextanks. Tri-clamp fittings are made of stainless steel and allow you to quickly install all sorts of attachments, such as ball valve, rotating racking arm (Figure 3.8), and various-sized hose barb adaptors, to increase processing efficiency.

And if you are interested in making oaked wines that benefit from micro-oxidation, you can certainly consider investing in barrels — these

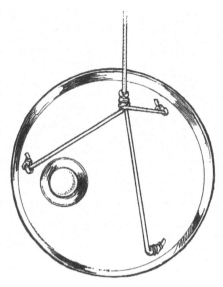

Figure 3.9: Modifying a floating lid for easy insertion and removal

tend to be expensive, particularly premium barrels, and require careful planning, care and maintenance. But they don't have to be complicated. The simplest way to use barrels is to always have wine ready for transferring into barrels when oak-aged wine is ready to be transferred out. You can usually get, on average, three to four vintages rotated in and out from a new barrel before it becomes neutral. A barrel is said to be "neutral" when it no longer imparts any oak substances to wine. Alternatively, you can use pieces of oak wood, referred to as oak adjuncts or oak alternatives — available in different shapes, sizes, American or French oak, and toast levels for any desired oak profile — in any type of vessels or even neutral barrels. Oak barrels and alternatives are discussed in Section 15.4. Consult reference [1] for a complete discussion on barrel care and maintenance.

3.3 STOPPERS AND AIRLOCKS

During fermentation in a closed fermentor, such as in a glass carboy in white winemaking, and for storing and aging wine, you will need rubber stoppers, also called bungs, and fermentation locks, or airlocks. Figures 3.10 and 3.11 show the different types of bungs and airlocks.

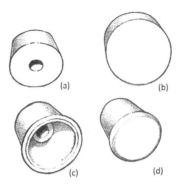

Figure 3.10: Bungs/stoppers: a) standard rubber bung with hole; b) standard solid rubber bung; c) Buon Vino bung with hole; d) silicone breathable bung

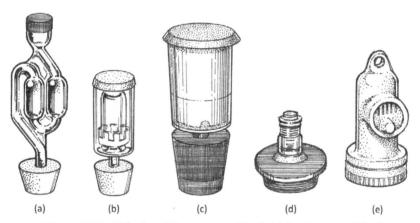

Figure 3.11: Airlocks: a) S-type wet airlock; b) 3-piece wet airlock; c) Speidel rubber airlock; d) Flextank dry airlock; e) marble-type dry airlock for VCTs

You will need a good supply of rubber stoppers — both solid stoppers and with a hole to accommodate the airlock — and of various sizes to fit all your fermentors and storage vessels. A #7 or Buon Vino Medium stopper fits standard glass carboys. Choose bungs made of soft material as hard bungs may not expand back to their original shape when removed from carboys, and therefore, they may not provide a tight seal on subsequent use.

3

The function of the airlock is to let out carbon dioxide (CO_2) gas produced by fermentation while protecting wine from the elements. The most common types are the S-style and 3-piece wet airlocks (Figure 3.11) where water or sulfite solution acts as the barrier between wine and the atmosphere.

S-style airlocks are molded and may have some extra plastic protruding along the seams that may create a gap when inserted into a rubber stopper. This gap will cause air to penetrate the carboy and spoil wine. File or sand down the extra plastic to a smooth finish on first use.

To avoid stoppers from popping up when inserted in glass carboys, dry both the stopper and the mouth of the carboy with a paper towel, then re-insert the stopper down tightly.

Change the sulfite solution (see Section 4.5.1) in airlocks at each 3-month interval when you measure and adjust SO_2 (sulfur dioxide) levels. If you use vodka, it's still good — no need to change.

There are also dry airlocks (see Figure 3.11) that make use of a mechanical device that lifts under the pressure of CO_2 gas and closes in the absence of pressure, such as marble airlocks common on Italian VCTs, dry airlocks on Flextanks, and so-called "breathable bungs" that have several holes and a flap that lifts under the pressure of CO_2 and falls back down to block the holes when there is no gas being produced. Once wine no longer releases any residual CO_2, you can switch from a stopper–airlock to a solid stopper for storing and aging.

Replace the marble airlock on the floating lid of VCTs with a regular stopper and airlock. The marble airlocks are notorious for not providing adequate protection against air ingress.

3.4 RACKING EQUIPMENT AND PUMPS

You will be moving, or what is referred to as racking, a lot of wine from one vessel to another to separate the sediment resulting from, for example, fermentation lees or from a fining treatment. This is accomplished using a racking cane and siphon hose (Figure 3.12) or an auto-siphon.

Starter kits include a ¼- or ⅜-inch racking cane and clear food-grade tubing, which you will want to upgrade to ½ inch for quicker processing, especially once you start using a pump for transferring wine. The racking cane includes an anti-dreg tip to minimize sediment uptake during racking.

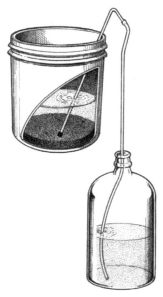

Figure 3.12: Racking cane and siphon hose

Racking by gravity works well for small batches, but when you have to rack larger or multiple batches, a pump will come in very handy. You will also be able to use the pump for filtering if you choose to set up your own filtration system and perhaps even for bottling.

There are two kinds of pumps and in various sizes and power ratings used in home winemaking: positive-pressure pumps and vacuum pumps (Figure 3.13).

In positive-pressure pumps, such as diaphragm and impeller types, wine runs through the pump as it is being transferred from one vessel to another. Some models cannot create sufficient pressure to automatically start the flow of wine and therefore require priming, i.e., you need to add wine into the inlet tube or pump head to start the flow of wine. A good ¼-hp positive-pressure self-priming pump with ½-inch (ID) fittings that can dis-

3

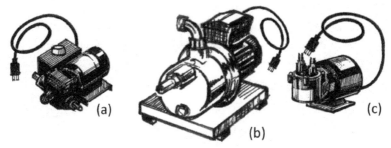

Figure 3.13: a) Positive-pressure diaphragm pump; b) positive-pressure impeller pump; c) vacuum pump

place some 10–15 L (2.5–4 gal) per minute will serve most needs; choose a model with an in-line strainer, or install one (Figure 3.14), to prevent grape solids from entering and possibly damaging the pump head. Variable speed is another feature you will come to appreciate; it gives you better control when filling vessels. And as you start working with pumps and pressurized equipment, you will need a supply of stainless steel hose clamps to secure tubing and hoses; get the Easy-Turn Butterfly kind that can be tightened by hand.

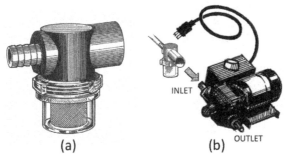

INLET

OUTLET

(a)   (b)

Figure 3.14: a) In-line strainer; b) Fitting an in-line strainer on pump inlet

As you scale up your production, a ½- or 1-hp or more powerful pump with ¾-inch or even 1-inch fittings capable of displacing larger volumes of wine per minute when racking will greatly increase your productivity. Be sure to choose a model with stainless steel fittings — not brass. Brass fittings are not appropriate for handling acidic beverages such as wine; they leach damaging metals into wine.

With vacuum pumps, wine is moved under the action of a vacuum (negative pressure) and therefore never runs through the pump. Transferring wine under vacuum provides protection against the elements and oxygen uptake in the receiving vessel, and also helps degas wine in the process. A good ¼-hp vacuum pump will serve most needs.

We will look at the various types of setups used for filtering and bottling wine in Chapters 17 and 18, respectively, using both types of pumps.

3.5 TEMPERATURE-CONTROL EQUIPMENT

You will often be required to adjust temperature up or down for specific operations. In general, and depending on your winemaking area, it is easier to heat a batch than it is to cool or chill. Usually you can simply increase the temperature of your winemaking area to generate the little heat needed to, for example, restart a stuck fermentation. But you may have to drop temperature by as much as 15 °C (27 °F) or more for cold stabilizing wine for tartrate stabilization (see Section 14.4) — that's more of a challenge. You can time your procedures to take advantage of natural heat or cold, but this is not always practical, particularly when you work with larger volumes where you cannot move a large tank outdoors for cold stabilizing.

For increasing temperature of a batch, a space heater will do the job, but at times you will want to raise the temperature of the batch of wine and not necessarily waste energy heating the rest of the area. Heating belts (Figure 3.15) work well on glass carboys and small tanks. Heating belts can be placed in series to wrap around larger vessels.

For cooling small batches, you can use frozen jugs of water, or place a carboy in the refrigerator or outdoors — and remember to use PET carboys if you intend to chill batches close to or below 0 °C (32 °F) — but for large batches and when you need to drop the temperature significantly, you may want to invest in a home winery-sized glycol cooling system. You may be doing a lot of cooling and chilling, including cold settling juice (see Section 13.1), cold soaking crushed grapes in their juice, fermenting whites and rosés at cooler temperatures, cooling a dangerously hot fermentation, and cold stabilizing.

Figure 3.15: Heating belt

A glycol cooling system (Figure 3.16) includes a glycol chiller and the necessary cooling equipment. The glycol chiller uses one or more pumps and controllers, which may be sold separately, to recirculate chilled propylene glycol at a set temperature to one or more vessels. Determine your chilling needs and consult with a chiller expert to help you choose a suitable unit. You will need to provide such information as how quickly you need to drop temperature and how cold, and the number and size of batches you need to chill concurrently. The chiller expert may recommend, for example, a ¼-hp unit rated for 3,000 BTU/hour with a 30-L (8-gal) glycol-holding reservoir.

The glycol chiller can be hooked up directly to cooling jackets on stainless steel tanks, if you are working with large tanks and batches; otherwise, for small batches, you can use a stainless steel immersion-type device (Figure 3.16), such as a cooling plate or coil for use in open-top vessels, or a cooling rod, such as the BrewBuilt CoolStix (Figure 3.16), for carboys.

Never use copper or other non-stainless steel (e.g., brass) equipment in your winemaking as it will negatively affect the quality of wine and potentially pose a health hazard.

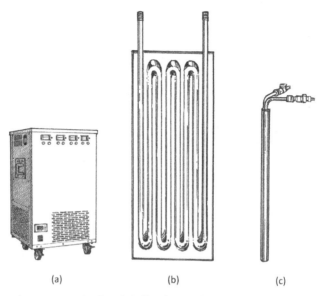

(a)   (b)   (c)

Figure 3.16: a) Glycol chiller; b) cooling immersion plate;
c) BrewBuilt CoolStix cooling rod

3.6 MISCELLANEOUS EQUIPMENT

There are various pieces of equipment you will need to make wine, some of which might be included in a starter kit. As you gain more experience, you will come to learn what works best in your winemaking, and you may decide to upgrade to better equipment.

You will be doing a lot of stirring, for example, to mix in additives and to degas (remove CO_2) wine prior to bottling. For standard 23-L (6-gal) batches, a long-handled plastic spoon (Figure 3.17) will do the job for stirring in additives, but you will need a lot of elbow grease when comes time to degas (see Section 13.3).

A lees stirrer will prove to be indispensable for degassing and for stirring in general. A lees stirrer (Figure 3.17) consists of a rod with two paddles or blades at the bottom that flip up to create a very effective stirring action when the rod is spun using a power drill. Alternatively you can use the Headspace Eliminator or Gas Getter (Figure 3.18) (see Section 13.3).

Figure 3.17: a) Stirring with a long-handled plastic spoon;
b) stirring with a lees stirrer

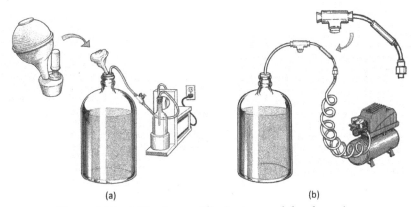

Figure 3.18: a) Headspace Eliminator used for degassing
wine; b) Gas Getter

You will need an ordinary kitchen baster or wine thief (Figure 3.19) to retrieve wine samples for tasting and lab analysis. Choose a glass or stainless steel model that can be easily cleaned and sanitized. If you work with larger vessels, you will need a long wine thief or baster, the idea being that you should be taking samples from as close to the center of the vessel as possible.

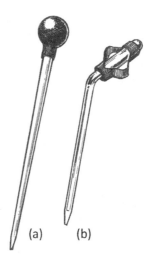

(a)   (b)

Figure 3.19: a) Kitchen baster; b) wine thief

In red winemaking you will need a small container or, better yet, a specially designed plastic scoop (Figure 3.20) for scooping up and transferring crushed and fermented grapes and wine from your fermenting vat to the press. Pressing may release seeds and grape fragments with the wine being collected into a pail, and which must be separated out using a plastic or stainless steel colander or strainer (Figure 3.20) so that you transfer clean wine into storage and aging vessels. Make sure that whichever type of colander or strainer you choose that it can be easily supported on a pail when collecting press-run wine.

A cone-shaped stainless steel strainer (Figure 3.21) will be useful when you need to retrieve wine samples when making red wine with grapes; it makes pulling wine with a thief or baster that much easier.

A set of different-size funnels (Figure 3.22) will be indispensable for transferring wine into carboys, demijohns and barrels.

3

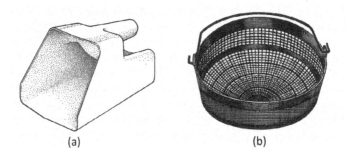

(a) (b)

Figure 3.20: a) Scoop; b) plastic colander

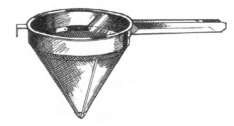

Figure 3.21: Stainless steel strainer for collecting wine sample in must and fermenting wine

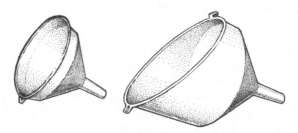

Figure 3.22: Funnels

You will need a set of soft-bristle, non-abrasive brushes or sponges and a carboy cleaner (Figure 3.23) to remove stubborn stains and clean the many different types of vessels and surfaces, e.g., glass, PET, stainless steel and HDPE.

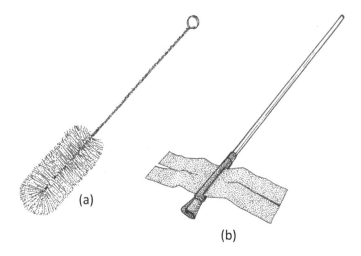

Figure 3.23: a) Soft-bristle, non-abrasive brush; b) carboy cleaner

Although you can get away with measuring chemicals using kitchen teaspoons and tablespoons in some cases, at least where only rough amounts are needed, you will need a good balance (Figure 3.24) that can measure wine additives fairly accurately down to 1 g but preferably down to 0.1 g. Keep in mind that the smaller your batches, the smaller the amounts of additives you will be measuring, making a balance with 1 g accuracy difficult to use. As you'll be doing a lot of wine analysis and measuring small amounts of reagents, a good 0.01-g accuracy scale is the best investment, budget permitting.

Figure 3.24: Balance

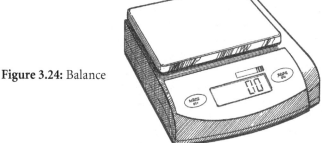

If you expect to move large batches around or to have to place heavy demijohns on shelves, consider buying a dolly or mechanically operated lift (Figure 3.25) or other type of device that can securely and safely lift and move heavy loads around.

Figure 3.25: Mechanically operated lift

And anything that will come into contact with wine needs to be sanitized (see Chapter 4). You will also want to have a second plastic pail or bin for soaking small equipment in cleaning or sanitizing solution and maybe a spray bottle (Figure 3.26) too for sanitizing small tools.

Figure 3.26: Spray bottle

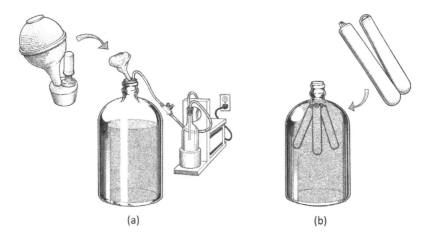

(a)   (b)

Figure 3.27: a) Headspace Eliminator; b) Better Top-Up

Topping up vessels may not always be desirable or possible, for example, if you don't have a similar wine to fill up the headspace. You can flush the headspace with inert gas or pull the air out with a vacuum pump, or use a device to displace wine.

The Headspace Eliminator (Figure 3.27) and the use of inert gas are excellent for short-term headspace inerting; it is recommended to run a vacuum or flush with gas weekly. The Better Top-Ups (Figure 3.27) displace wine volume to reduce headspace, and therefore, these can be left in the wine without worrying about oxidation. One Better Top-Up displaces about 100 mL of wine, and therefore, you would need, for example, five to displace 500 mL of headspace with wine. Many home winemakers also use food-safe glass marbles for displacing wine and reducing headspace. These work well for small headspace in small 4-L (1-gal) batches, but become cumbersome to use with larger headspace because you would need to drop a lot of marbles down a carboy, some 430 standard-sized marbles to displace a mere 500 mL of wine.

 Better Top-Ups will become covered with tartrate crystals if wine is subjected to cold temperatures, or become stained if used with deeply colored red wines. You can remove tartrates and red stains with a mild percarbonate solution (see Section 4.4.1).

And don't forget protective gear as there will be a lot of splashing, almost certainly many mishaps, and as you will be working with chemicals for cleaning and sanitizing winemaking equipment. Basic essentials include protective goggles, or better yet, a face shield, protective gloves, and water-proof overalls and boots. A headlamp with adjustable lighting direction (Figure 3.28) will also prove useful, if not indispensable, when working in dim areas or dark cellar (to keep temperature down) or when you need to clean and inspect the inside of tanks.

Figure 3.28: Headlamp

3.7 LAB EQUIPMENT

Winemaking — at least making consistently great wines — involves a lot of analysis of juice and wine as well as bench trials. Invest in some basic but good analytical equipment; it will greatly simplify your routine of analyzing wine accurately and efficiently.

A hydrometer (and cylinder) is the most important piece of equipment as you will need to determine the amount of sugar in the grape juice that you will be fermenting, and to monitor fermentation progress and completion. Commonly available triple-scale hydrometers (SG, Brix and Potential Alcohol) (Figure 3.29) are inexpensive and do the job fairly well. Some higher-quality hydrometers (Figure 3.29) also include a thermometer and a scale for adjusting hydrometer readings to compensate for temperature. A precision, low-range hydrometer (Figure 3.29) that can measure sugar in the range SG 0.940–1.010 or –5 Brix to +5 Brix will be

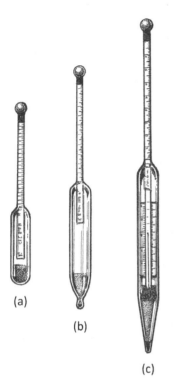

Figure 3.29: a) Triple-scale hydrometer; b) precision, low-range hydrometer; c) hydrometer/thermometer combination

(a)

(b)

(c)

useful to get significantly more accurate readings when nearing the end of fermentation. Hydrometers and their use are described in more details in Section 6.3.

You will also need a thermometer or perhaps even a floating thermometer (Figure 3.30) that will remain in the wine for the duration of fermentation to measure temperature to ensure that fermentation is progressing well and within prescribed maxima and minima, and to make corrections to hydrometer readings. As glass is fragile and there is always the risk of breakage in wine, you can use a digital thermometer with either a short or long probe (Figure 3.30). A long probe allows you measure temperature down low in tall fermentors.

Equip your lab with some essentials, including beakers and Erlenmeyer flasks of various volumes, graduated cylinders (100, 250 and 1000 mL), volumetric flasks (100, 250, 500 and 1000 mL), an eyedropper, burettes (10 and 25 mL) with stopcock, a burette stand with clamp, good 10-mL pipettes and pipette fillers, syringes (1 and 10 mL), a magnetic stir plate and

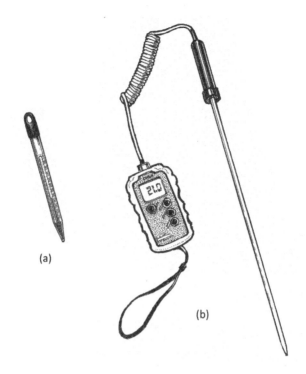

(a)

(b)

Figure 3.30: a) Floating thermometer; b) digital thermometer with probe

stir bars, laboratory wash bottles for rinsing glassware, and wine tasting glasses. Get glass labware for the lab and plasticware for the cellar to minimize breakage, especially if working on a concrete floor.

 Never taste wine in beakers or other lab glassware — only from wine tasting glasses — as lab glassware may have been previously used with harsh chemicals and may have toxic residues.

You will need a pH meter and a strong recommendation for a sulfur dioxide (SO_2) analyzer; these are discussed in Sections 7.3 and 8.3, respectively. The need and use of a paper chromatography kit for testing for malolactic fermentation (MLF) is discussed in Section 12.5.

Here too, don't forget to wear protective equipment — safety googles or face shield, lab coat and nitrile gloves — when working in the lab and handling chemicals.

REFERENCE

1. Pambianchi, D. 2008. *Techniques in Home Winemaking: A Practical Guide to Making Château-Style Wines.* Newly-Revised and Expanded. Véhicule Press, Montréal (Québec).

4 Cleaning and Sanitizing Equipment

Making consistently flawless wines starts with rigorous sanitization of all winemaking equipment. Inadequately cleaned or sanitized equipment — or a dirty winemaking area — can lead to contamination and possibly wine faults or outright spoilage.

Everything — carboys, racking cane, stirring spoon, hoses, pump, etc. — that will come into contact with juice or wine must be thoroughly cleaned and properly sanitized to avoid microbial contamination and possible spoilage. Ambient rogue microorganisms are always present and ready to strike at the most opportune moment. Once wine is infected, it can be very difficult to eradicate the culprit and perhaps impossible to fix if severely flawed. The proverb that "an ounce of prevention is worth a pound of cure" is most appropriate when it comes to implementing a sound cleaning and sanitization protocol in your winemaking.

This chapter describes the difference between cleaning and sanitizing, how to implement an effective cleaning and sanitizing protocol, and how to choose from the many kinds of products available from your winemaking supply shop.

4.1 CLEANING VERSUS SANITIZING

Cleaning and sanitizing are not the same and are not interchangeable; cleaning always precedes sanitizing. And each step is only as good as the previous, that is, if not cleaned properly, then the sanitizing is not effective.

Cleaning is the process of removing organic and inorganic contaminants or residues, such as grape fragments, dried juice, soil and dust from the surface of equipment and from every nook and cranny in preparation for sanitizing. This is accomplished by applying mechanical or physical force, such as water pressure or using a scrubbing device, in conjunction with a cleaning agent suitable for the type of contaminants to be removed and compatible with the material (glass, stainless steel, plastics, silicone and wood) to be treated. Dirt may be cleaned using a simple water rinse whereas sticky residues may require a hot-water treatment and possibly some mechanical force. Some types of residues, like polysaccharides, may require a cleaning agent with good dispersing power, while other residues with lower solubility in water, like mineral salts, may require alkaline (caustic) or acidic cleaning agents.

Cleaning agents by definition do not possess any inherent antimicrobial properties. Some cleaning products are formulated to include a sanitizing agent to allow cleaning and sanitizing to be performed in a single step. These are carefully formulated to ensure that the cleaning action does not inhibit sanitizing efficiency, and vice versa, as the cleaning–sanitizing agent comes into contact with the contaminants. Since contaminants are seldom identifiable in practice, these effects are difficult to predict, and it is therefore best to use dedicated products and perform cleaning and sanitizing steps separately.

Winemakers often use the terms "sanitization" and "sterilization" interchangeably; however, these are not equivalent.

Sterilization is the process of irreversibly eradicating greater than 99.9999% of living microorganisms by using specialized technology and methodologies, such as autoclaving, which involves exposing items to high pressure and saturated steam at 120 °C (250 °F) for 15–20 minutes. Simply pouring boiling water on or into equipment is not the same as autoclaving and doing so will not sterilize; it is unlikely to be as effective as using chemical sanitizing agents and can damage equipment. But this level of decontamination is not necessary in winemaking.

Sanitization is a limited form of sterilization; it is the process of eradicating living microorganisms down to an acceptable level (99.9% is the wine industry norm) using a sanitizing agent suitable for the type of material at hand. The sanitizing agent is left in contact with the equipment for a minimum amount of time without the need for mechanical force, although that may be necessary or recommended at times. Sanitization is the process used in winemaking.

The choice of cleaning and sanitizing agents and the protocol to implement should consider: the nature of contaminants and extent of contamination; compatibility with material at hand; work hazard; and consideration for the environment. Dealing with sticky juice residues will require a different treatment and agents than, for example, stained carboys from red winemaking or mold on a barrel.

All cleaning and sanitizing agents have an SDS (Safety Data Sheet, previously called Material Safety Data Sheet) that lists ingredients and relative concentrations, health hazards, handling instructions, and instructions on how to safely dispose in an environmentally responsible manner. SDSs for specific products can be downloaded from the internet by simply googling the product name, for example, Star San SDS.

4.2 SAFETY FIRST

Cleaning and sanitizing involve handling potentially hazardous and toxic chemicals. Read SDSs to familiarize yourself on the handling, preparation, use and storage of chemicals.

1. Always follow manufacturers' instructions and warnings for handling chemicals and preparing solutions. Work in a well-ventilated area, never exceed recommended concentrations, and never mix chemicals unless provided and instructed by the manufacturer.

2. Store chemicals in approved containers in a cool, well-ventilated area. Store different classes of chemicals, e.g., acids, bases, oxidizers, etc., in separate areas or on separate shelves if extra space is not available. Clearly label solutions, concentrations and preparation dates, and store away from the reach of children. You should never have to smell or taste a chemical to identify it.

3. Always wear proper protection (e.g., eye protection, gloves, and clothing that covers exposed skin) when handling cleaning and

sanitizing chemicals, as well as nonskid, chemical-resistant foot-
wear as the cellar floor can be very slippery with the use of detergents.

4. Clean up spills immediately as many chemicals are corrosive and
   can adversely affect surfaces.

5. Dissolve dry chemicals in cold or lukewarm water — not hot, and
   never add water to chemicals (always the reverse) as it can damage
   the container or cause serious injury from a spontaneous explo-
   sive reaction.

4.3 WATER

Fresh, good-quality potable water that is neither too soft nor too hard is
essential for effective cleaning and sanitizing, particularly in preparing dilute cleaning and sanitizing solutions.

Soft water has a low mineral content whereas hard water causes scaling,
or the formation of limescale, when minerals precipitate, and requires
much more cleaning agent compared to soft water to clean effectively. Limescale, or calcium carbonate, is the result of calcium ions in hard water
reacting with naturally occurring carbonate ions, and greater amounts
form at higher temperatures or with the use of caustic chemicals.

You can easily assess the hardness of your municipal or well water by
pouring a small amount of liquid soap — not detergent — in some water
in a flask or closed container and shaking vigorously, or alternatively, rub-
bing your hands with a bar of soap under running water. The soap should
foam easily; otherwise, the water is hard. You can also use test strips used
for measuring water hardness of pool water. Generally, water hardness
should be less than 50 mg/L and should be "softened" if it measures above
150 mg/L. If your water is hard, consider an alternative source of water or
install a water softener.

And if your municipal-treated water contains high levels of chlorine,
you should consider installing an inline carbon water filter. Chlorine is a
source of spoilage known as TCA, short for 2,4,6-trichloroanisole, a

powerfully odorant molecule responsible for cork taint (see Sections 4.5.2 and 22.11) and may possibly contaminate your whole winemaking area. You can buy treated water, but keep in mind that you will be using vast amounts and you will also have to use a pump for all your cleaning and sanitizing. Alternatively, you can dechlorinate with a sulfite salt, such as potassium metabisulfite (see Section 4.5.1), at a rate of up to 0.5 g per 100 L (25 gal).

More and more commonly, municipalities are adding ammonia along with chlorine to tap water to form chloramine. This compound has the benefit of being more stable in water supply lines, which is helpful for keeping water sanitary, but results in a compound that can be more difficult to remove. Using sulfite salts to remove chloramines works very well, but not all carbon filters are effective. If you are uncertain if your water contains chloramines, run your tap water through a Brita filter (or similar) and test for chlorine. A Brita filter will remove free chlorine, but not 100% of chloramines. Try calling your municipality or local water department and ask if they use chloramines. If they use chlorine only, you have no further need to investigate.

4.4 CLEANING AGENTS

Cleaning products can contain several "active" ingredients, including oxidizing agents (e.g., hydrogen peroxide), acids, alkalis, surfactants that break down dirt and greasy residues, and chelating agents that sequester minerals — the culprits in hard water. Surfactants work by reducing surface tension so that the entire surface will be wet with the cleaning solution and to help the solution to remove soils by penetrating and interposing the solution between the soil and the surface. Carbonates and silicates are the most common alkaline agents, which neutralize acidic soils and help disperse solid soils, and carbonates can provide a secondary function by chelating water hardness via complexation. Polyphosphates have good chelating properties but can be harmful to the environment. Plant-based and synthetic chelating agents are environmentally friendly and as effective, if not more. Do not use any kind of soap as these can leave a residue that can affect the quality of wine.

There are many cleaning agents. Here we describe the most common: sodium carbonate, sodium percarbonate, and sodium and potassium hydroxide. Bleach (sodium hypochlorite) can also be used as a cleaning agent; it is discussed as a sanitizing agent in Section 4.5.2, but must always be rinsed carefully and thoroughly.

Table 4.1 in Section 4.7 presents a material-compatibility chart with recommended concentrations and contact time for common cleaning products.

4.4.1 CARBONATE AND SODIUM PERCARBONATE

Wine soils are generally acidic, therefore an alkaline-based cleaner is generally used. Sodium carbonate (soda ash) and sodium percarbonate are the most common alkaline chemicals found in cleaning products, being very effective in dislodging heavy deposits, such as tartrates, and coloring matter from tank walls, or removing greasy residues. Both are relatively mild (pH 10.0–10.5) at the recommended concentrations but the percarbonate form is more effective. PBW (Powdered Brewery Wash), One Step No-Rinse Cleanser (known as Aseptox in Canada), Barrel OxyFresh (specifically designed for cleaning or reclaiming barrels), B-Brite Cleanser, and OxiClean, a popular household detergent used by home winemakers, are examples of products that contain sodium carbonate and/or sodium percarbonate. Follow the manufacturers' instructions for these products.

Use sodium carbonate at a rate of 10 g per liter of water or about 40 g per gallon.

Sodium percarbonate, also known as sodium carbonate peroxyhydrate and often simply referred to as percarbonate, is commonly found in household laundry detergents and is produced from sodium carbonate through chemical bonding with hydrogen peroxide, a well-known, effective disinfectant and bleaching agent. When dissolved in water, percarbonate releases sodium carbonate and hydrogen peroxide. It is particularly effective in removing red-wine stains from equipment and treating mold on barrels. Use sodium percarbonate at a rate of 1–3 g/L of water or 4–12 g/gallon.

4

These salts do not dissolve easily in water, so first dissolve in a little warm water and then add cool water to dilute to the required concentration. Only make up as much solution as you need as percarbonate is unstable, and store away from heat and light. Hydrogen peroxide in percarbonate tends to break down quickly; the dry powder form is much more stable. If you need to hold a solution and only for several days, you can store percarbonate solution in a properly stoppered glass or chemically resistant container away in a cool and dark area.

Disperse either solution on the equipment to be cleaned and leave in contact with the surface to be cleaned for 10–20 minutes. Then thoroughly rinse with plenty of water followed by a sulfite–citric rinse to neutralize any traces of alkali residue. Complete with one last water rinse. Section 4.5.1 gives instructions for preparing a sulfite–citric solution.

Sodium percarbonate is most effective for dealing with barrel problems, such as slight volatile acidity (VA) contamination inside the barrel or mold on the exterior surface or between stave joints. It is also much more effective than sodium carbonate in removing tartrates. Consult reference [1] for detailed instructions on dealing with barrel problems.

4.4.2 CAUSTIC CHEMICALS

Caustic alkaline chemicals (pH>13), notably sodium hydroxide (also known as caustic soda and NaOH) and potassium hydroxide (also known as caustic potash and KOH), are very effective for breaking down organic residues. Sodium hydroxide is more commonly used than potassium hydroxide because it is cheaper and less is needed although potassium hydroxide has greater solubility in water. Both are available in pellet or granular form and then diluted in water to the appropriate concentration.

 Caustic chemicals even in low concentrations can be extremely hazardous and toxic; they can cause permanent skin burns or blindness. Handle with great care to avoid scalding injuries, particularly when preparing solutions as they give off great amounts of heat.

Avoid caustic chemicals if you are on a septic system as high levels of chemicals risk killing the bacteria needed to break down sewage pathogens both in the tank itself and also in the soil into which the septic tank effluent is discharged.

For most stains, use a 1% solution, i.e., 10 g/L, with a short soak or contact time of 10–20 minutes followed by a light scrubbing; the concentration can be increased up to 3% (30 g/L) for tough stains while being careful as these chemicals are very corrosive and can damage certain materials, especially soft, soda lime glass (but not laboratory-grade, borosilicate glassware), depending on concentration and contact time. In all cases, a thorough rinse with a sulfite–citric solution is always recommended to neutralize any alkaline residue and to prepare the surface to receive wine — an acidic medium.

Since caustic chemicals have high surface tension and have no surfactant activity, these do not provide good penetration of soils. Strong mechanical force from a power washer or scrubbing may be required.

Since these chemicals tend to absorb atmospheric moisture and lose effectiveness, store powders and solutions in sealed, chemical-resistant glass or plastic containers in a cool, low-humidity area.

4.5 SANITIZING AGENTS

Sanitizing products incorporate a range of chemicals that inhibit or kill microorganisms. Although there is a plethora of sanitizing agents used in the food and beverage industry, the most common products used in winemaking for sanitizing include sulfites, oxidizing agents, acids, and iodophors. Ozone has also become a more affordable option and is becoming more common with serious enthusiasts, but it requires special equipment and handling. Very hot water (85 °C/185 °F) or steam can also be used but it too requires special equipment capable of maintaining high temperature and sufficiently long contact time. For sanitizing laboratory equipment, a 1% sulfite–citric solution or 70%-ethanol solution work best.

Table 4.2 in Section 4.8 presents a material-compatibility chart with recommended concentrations and contact time for common sanitizing products.

4.5.1 SULFITES

4

Potassium metabisulfite and sodium metabisulfite, commonly referred to simply as sulfites, are the most widely used sanitizing agents in winemaking.

Sulfites are dissolved in water but must be used with an acid to lower the pH of a 1% sulfite solution from about 4.5 to the 3.0 range to inhibit or kill spoilage microorganisms. You can use citric or tartaric acid though the latter is more expensive, but tartaric acid is recommended if a sulfite solution is to be used for long-term storage of oak barrels. The reason is that if barrels are not properly rinsed and allowed to dry completely when ready to introduce wine, lactic acid bacteria in wine that has undergone malolactic fermentation (MLF) may metabolize excessive residual citric acid into spoilage acetic acid and volatile acidity (VA) (see Sections 7.2 and 22.2). There are otherwise no concerns in using a sulfite–citric solution for sanitizing equipment.

To prepare a 1% sulfite–citric solution, dissolve 10 g of sulfite powder and up to 3 g of citric acid powder — sufficient to get to pH 3.0 — in one liter of cool distilled or fresh water. You can prepare a solution very quickly using 3 tbsp of sulfite powder and ½–1 tbsp of citric acid per 4 L or 1 gallon of water. Store the solution in an airtight glass or chemical-resistant plastic container; it will last up to 6 months.

 Always wear protective clothing, respirator and goggles, and work in a well-ventilated area when handling a sulfite solution as it can cause skin and respiratory irritations.

To sanitize, spray or soak equipment and allow contact for approximately 10 minutes, then, optionally, rinse thoroughly with fresh, clean water. If you decide not to rinse or if you do not have fresh water suitable for rinsing, be sure to let the equipment drain well; the tiny amount of residual sulfite after draining is compatible with wine.

Do not allow sulfite solution to stay in contact for an extended period of time (e.g., overnight) with certain materials; it can cause pitting in stainless steel tanks, cracking in silicone bungs, and hoses to become translucent and lose much of their flexibility and suppleness.

4.5.2 CHLORINE BLEACH

 The use of chlorine bleach is presented here as it is still commonly used by many home winemakers; however, its use is strongly discouraged for reasons presented below. There are equally if not more effective and more environmentally friendly sanitizing agents.

Chlorine bleach solutions have long been used for cleaning and sanitizing equipment owing to their strong oxidizing power and specifically for removing stubborn stains on glass carboys, for disinfecting, and for decolorizing equipment when switching from red to white winemaking. Liquid chlorine bleach is made from sodium hypochlorite, whereas dry chlorine bleach is made from calcium hypochlorite or an organic chlorine releasing compound such as chloroisocyanuric acid. Diversol BXA, also known as Sani-Brew and "the pink stuff" uses dry chlorine bleach. Some products also use chlorinated trisodium phosphate (CTSP).

Chlorine bleach is generally more effective than acid sanitizers and the cheapest of sanitizers but probably the least environmentally friendly. Some are irritants and very strong oxidizers and highly corrosive; they will cause pitting on stainless steel. It is also not recommended on plastic equipment as the material will absorb chlorine, making it difficult to remove and likely cause spoilage, and the bleach may also damage the plastic, causing cracking and embrittlement; they should never be used in or come close to oak barrels.

Aside from its strong oxidizing power that make chlorine incompatible with many kinds of materials, a major drawback is that these can be a source of 2,4,6-trichloroanisole, or TCA, the compound responsible for the moldy, musty smell in so-called "corked" wines. Chlorinated powder dust can easily become airborne, find its way into the winemaking area and contaminate equipment, which could then spread out of control throughout the whole area. Eradicating a TCA infection could prove to be a formidable challenge, if not impossible. If you want to use bleach, prepare and use solutions outdoors well away from any winemaking equipment or area.

For sanitizing, prepare a 0.01% (100 mg/L) bleach solution by dissolving 2 mL (or about ½ tsp) of household chlorine bleach (which is a 5.25% sodium hypochlorite solution) per liter of water, or 7 mL (about ½ tbsp) per gallon, and spray or apply to equipment or fill glass carboys with the solution, and let stand for approximately 5 minutes. If using a powdered chlorine product such as Diversol BXA, follow the manufacturer's instructions, but, generally, use 18 g (or one heaped tbsp) per liter (68 g/gal), stir to dissolve, and use in the same way described above. Never leave glass carboys (or any containers in general) full of bleach solution to sit overnight as this may adversely affect the integrity of the material. Thoroughly rinse at least three times with plenty of water as chlorine is hard to rinse and can leave a strong smell. There should be absolutely no trace of chlorine solution or smell after the water rinse; otherwise, wine will inherit an off-odor or off-flavor.

4.5.3 ACIDS

Products containing acetic acid (i.e., vinegar), phosphoric acid or peroxyacetic acid are effective sanitizers used extensively in the food and beverage industry because they leave equipment in an acidic condition that eliminates water spotting. It is not the acid per se that provides the sanitizing effect, but the acid is necessary to maintain the conditions needed for the biocidal agent to work properly.

Star San, Saniclean and San Step are examples of acid sanitizers that use phosphoric acid to ensure that the biocidal surfactant penetrates the membranes and cell walls of microorganisms. Because of the presence of surfactants, they have been recommended as a one-step cleaner/sanitizer, but best practice is always to carry out cleaning and sanitizing in separate steps.

Saniclean and San Step have the advantage of being non-foaming and are therefore ideal for sanitizing pumps and other equipment that generate a lot of turbulence. OxySan sanitizes through the action of peroxyacetic acid (sometimes simply called peracid), which is created by a reaction between acetic acid and hydrogen peroxide. The reaction method requires the presence of both acetic acid and hydrogen peroxide to stabilize the peracid, therefore a peracetic acid-based sanitizer smells strongly of vinegar and is also a strong oxidizing agent, although not as strong as chlorine bleach. Always follow manufacturers' instructions for these products to ensure both proper performance and safety.

4.5.4 IODOPHORS

Iodophors are sanitizing agents comprising iodine as the active ingredient, surfactants and, possibly, phosphoric acid to enhance the bactericidal activity of iodine by stabilizing the compound in solution. BTF Iodophor Sanitizer and IO-Star are common iodophor products.

Iodine has similar activity as chlorine in killing microorganisms though it is much safer. It has low toxicity and easily attaches to organic matter to provide good sanitizing action. Though not as effective as other sanitizing agents, its major advantage is that it evaporates when used in the recommended proportions, and therefore leaves no residues on compatible equipment and, as some manufacturers suggest, requires no rinsing; however, iodophors tend to produce a lot of foam and can leave an odor, and therefore do in fact require quite a bit of rinsing. They are generally not recommended on plastic equipment as they can leave unattractive orange-brown stains — they also stain hands — but they are ideal for application on glass material. They require a short contact time of only a couple of minutes.

Carefully read and follow the manufacturer's instructions for your product as a minimum amount of iodine, e.g., 12.5 mg/L, is needed when making an iodophor solution. For example, BTF Iodophor Sanitizer recommends 1 tsp per 1½ gal (5.7 L). Only make as much solution as you need for immediate use as it tends to deteriorate fairly quickly; color fades as it deteriorates, but is not the most reliable indicator of activity. The sanitizing effect is provided by iodine that is not bound by surfactant or organic materials, but the bound iodine still produces a color. When in doubt, there are iodine test strips that will reliably indicate the level of free, or active, iodine.

4.6 CLEANING AND SANITIZING PROTOCOL

An effective cleaning and sanitizing protocol consists of the following steps:

1. Pre-rinsing with water

2. Cleaning with a suitable cleaning agent

3. Rinsing with water

4. Sanitizing with a suitable sanitizing agent

5. Final rinsing with water

The sanitizing step will only be effective if the cleaning operation is also effective and thorough; trying to sanitize poorly cleaned equipment can leave residues or contaminants that may negatively impact wine quality.

 Some products are advertised as "no rinse." These products are safe if used without rinsing as any potential residues are deemed to pose no health risks and will not adversely affect the quality of wine. If you have access to fresh, clean, low-alkalinity water, it is always recommended to rinse with plenty of water after any cleaning and sanitizing operation.

This protocol is very rigorous, but it does consume vast quantities of water. To the extent possible, always look for opportunities to save and reuse water; for example, water used to pre-rinse your pump and filtration line can be saved in a pail and then re-used to perform the first rinse following the filtration run. For instructions on preparing and sanitizing filter pads and cartridges, please see Section 17.4.

 Do not dump or flush spent chemicals down the sink or toilet. Always dispose in an environmentally responsible way according to your local laws. Your municipality may have a program for collecting hazardous waste.

 If you work with glass carboys and demijohns very frequently, you can just pour some sulfite–citric solution and stopper the vessel with a solid bung wrapped in plastic (e.g., cling film, food wrap, etc.) to protect it from sulfur dioxide (SO_2) after cleaning

up. On the next use, you can then simply pour out the sulfite–
citric solution, and rinse the carboy or demijohn with plenty of
water, then you're all set to go with the next batch.

Prepare fresh cleaning and sanitizing solutions ahead of time in suitable chemically resistant containers. Make sure you choose products suitable for the kinds of contaminants to be removed and which are compatible with the equipment material to be treated. In my own winemaking, I use sodium percarbonate for cleaning and a sulfite–citric solution for sanitizing.

For lab equipment, assuming it had been cleaned after the last use and set aside to dry, there is no need to sanitize it if wine samples to be analyzed are not returned to their vessels. A simple rinse with distilled water is usually sufficient. If you are working with small volumes and want to be able to take a sample out of a carboy, for example, for measuring and monitoring the sugar level during fermentation, and return the sample to the carboy, then you will need to clean and sanitize all equipment that will come into contact with the wine.

PRE-RINSING

First remove any dirt, loose soil or dried residues on surfaces using warm water and a wet sponge, a soft, non-scratch scouring pad, or a soft-bristle brush. You may need hot water to dissolve and remove stubborn residues. Be careful not to scratch surfaces, particularly on plastic equipment.

Using a water hose or, preferably, a pressure washer, thoroughly spray all surfaces with tap water to dislodge the bulk of the washed dirt and residues. You can use hot tap water not exceeding 50 °C (125 °F), but it is not necessary for effective pre-rinsing; it can damage many types of plastic equipment, cause soft (soda-lime) glass carboys to expand unevenly and crack, and some soils are "set" or made more difficult to remove by high temperatures. Keep rinsed equipment wet until ready to clean. For pumps, hoses, connectors and fittings, you can simply circulate warm (not hot) water through the equipment by running the pump for at least 10 minutes.

CLEANING

Disperse the cleaning solution over the entire surface of the equipment using a sponge. For stubborn stains or for equipment with hard-to-reach spots, you may need to soak the equipment in the cleaning solution. You may need to disassemble and soak equipment such as pump heads or bottle fillers. You can run and recirculate the cleaning solution through hoses.

The contact time depends on the cleaning agent, type of stain, and type of material. For example, red wine stains in glass carboys are easily removed with a mild percarbonate solution. Table 4.1 in Section 4.7 gives some general guidelines for contact time. Do not soak equipment for long periods in cleaning solutions because they can cause the material to deteriorate or break.

You may need to apply mechanical force on stubborn stains; use a soft-bristle hand brush, soft sponge, or a carboy brush specifically designed for cleaning carboys.

 Only use non-abrasive materials that will not scratch the surface of equipment. Scratches will make the equipment more difficult to wash the next time and can become a breeding ground for microorganisms and other contaminations.

RINSING

Rinse all cleaned equipment thoroughly with plenty of water to remove all contaminants and cleaning agent; the idea is to get all surfaces to neutral pH with no residues of the cleaning agent. Remember! Sanitizing agents will not sanitize dirty surfaces effectively. If you detect any odor in the equipment, you may need to repeat the cleaning and rinsing steps, and perhaps, more aggressively or with a different cleaning agent.

SANITIZING

Disperse the sanitizing solution over the entire surface of the equipment using a spray bottle, by soaking small parts in the solution in a pail, or using a pump and dousing the entire surface while recirculating the solution. Leave the sanitizing agent in contact with all surfaces for the recommended duration as per the product's instructions (see Table 4.2 in Section 4.8). Some sanitizing agents can be very aggressive and can damage equipment if left in contact for too long.

FINAL RINSE

Rinse all sanitized equipment thoroughly with plenty of water to rinse away all the sanitizing solution; here too the idea is to get all surfaces to neutral pH with no residues of the sanitizing agent. If there are any concerns that the rinse did not remove all the sanitizing solution, for example, because of hard-to-reach spots, you can neutralize alkaline sanitizing agents with an acidic solution, for example, a sulfite–citric solution. It is always better to leave the equipment in an acidic state than an alkaline state, and therefore, if you used an acidic sanitizing agent, there is no need to do any neutralization — a water rinse is sufficient.

After the final rinse, let the equipment drain. Make sure that there are no residual odors from the use of sanitizing solution.

Manufacturers of some sanitizing agents may state that their products do not require a water rinse as they are deemed "compatible" with wine; however, a final water rinse is always a good idea if you have access to fresh, clean water.

4.7 CLEANING AGENTS MATERIAL COMPATIBILITY AND USE

4

Table 4.1: Cleaning agent material compatibility and use

Product or Brand Name	Dilution rates, contact times, and special instructions	Soft glass carboys	Stainless steel (304)	Food-grade plastics	PET carboys	Silicone equipment	Wood barrels
Sodium carbonate (soda ash)	10 g/L — Allow 10–20 minutes contact — Follow with sulfite–citric rinse	◆	●	●	◆	●	■
Sodium percarbonate	1–3 g/L — Allow 10–20 minutes contact — Follow with sulfite–citric rinse	◆	●	●	◆	●	●
Sodium hydroxide (caustic soda) Potassium hydroxide (caustic potash)	10–30 g/L — Allow 10–20 minutes contact — Follow with sulfite–citric rinse	■	●	●	■	■	✖
PBW (Powdered Brewery Wash) (Five Star Chemicals)	5–10 g/L — If soaking, heat to 60 °C (140 °F) and soak for 4 hours or allow to soak cold overnight	◆	●	●	◆	●	✖
One Step No-Rinse Cleanser (Aseptox) (Logic)	5–10 g/L — For heavy soils, use 30 g/L, heat to 50–70 °C (120–160 °F) and allow 30 minutes contact	◆	●	●	◆	●	✖
Barrel OxyFresh (Logic)	1.5 g/L — Allow 4 hours contact time (follow with a citric acid treatment as per manufacturer's instructions)	◆	●	●	◆	●	●
B-Brite Cleanser (Crosby & Baker)	4 mL/L — Use warm water and soak up to 24 hours as required	◆	●	●	◆	●	■
OxiClean (Church & Dwight)	20–30 g/L — Allow 5–30 minutes contact	◆	●	●	◆	●	✖

Legend:
● Safe to use on material
◆ Use caution; may affect material
■ Generally NOT recommended; may affect material integrity; use caution
✖ Do NOT use; will likely have adverse effects on material

4.8 SANITIZING AGENTS MATERIAL COMPATIBILITY AND USE

Table 4.2: Sanitizing agent material compatibility and use

Product or Brand Name	Dilution rates, contact times, and special instructions	MATERIALS					
		Soft glass carboys	Stainless steel (304)	Food-grade plastics	PET carboys	Silicone equipment	Wood barrels
Potassium metabisulfite / Sodium metabisulfite / Campden tablets	10 g/L sulfite + 1–2 g/L citric acid Allow min. 10 minutes contact	◆	●	●	●	●	●
Star San (Five Star Chemicals)	1.5 g/L[1] Allow min. 3 minutes contact	■	◆	●	●	●	✖
Saniclean (Five Star Chemicals)	2.5 g/L[1] Allow min. 3 minutes contact	■	◆	●	●	●	✖
San Step (Logic)	1.5 g/L[1] Allow min. 3 minutes contact	■	◆	●	●	●	✖
Diversol BXA (Sani-Brew, "the pink stuff") (Diversey)	6 g/L Allow min. 10 minutes contact	■	✖	●	●	●	✖
OxySan ZS (Ecolab)	1 g/L Allow min. 5 minutes contact	◆	◆	◆	■	■	✖
Iodophor BTF Sanitizer (National Chemicals)	1 g/L Allow 2 minutes contact	■	■	◆	●	■	✖

[1] pH must remain below 3 to ensure effective sanitizing

Legend:
● Safe to use on material
◆ Use caution; may affect material
■ Generally NOT recommended; may affect material integrity; use caution
✖ Do NOT use; will likely have adverse effects on material

REFERENCE

1. Pambianchi, D. 2008. *Techniques in Home Winemaking: A Practical Guide to Making Château-Style Wines.* Newly-Revised and Expanded. Véhicule Press, Montréal (Québec).

5 Conducting Bench Trials

You will often have to use additives or processing aids to make adjustments to must or wine or to perform specific treatments for a number reasons, such as:

- To increase or decrease acidity for taste or to adjust pH (Section 7.5)

- To determine how much fining agent (e.g., bentonite) to add to treat proteins (Section 14.3)

- To sweeten to balance gripping acidity (Section 16.1)

- To add or soften tannins to improve mouthfeel (Sections 16.2 and 16.3)

- To determine how much copper sulfate ($CuSO_4$) to add to eliminate a stinky hydrogen sulfide (H_2S) smell left over from fermentation (Section 22.4)

 These adjustments are discussed in section numbers shown in parenthesis. We will look at conducting bench trials for the purpose of blending two of more wines to create a certain style or to correct deficiencies in Section 16.5.

All these scenarios require finding the optimal amount of a substance — e.g., tartaric acid, bentonite, sugar — needed to achieve some desired results. This requires performing tests on a small scale with juice or wine samples with varying amounts of the substance and doing some comparative assessments, and then scaling up the trial results to treat an entire batch — this process is referred to as conducting bench trials.

Bench trials are necessary to avoid blindly treating an entire batch and possibly adding too much of a substance, which could have irreversible adverse effects on the chemistry of the wine, taste, or possibly be hazardous to your health in the case of an excessive copper sulfate treatment.

Let's take a look at how to conduct bench trials like an expert.

5.1 PREPARING FOR BENCH TRIALS

First set out a plan with specific objectives of what you want to accomplish. For example, if you are wanting to increase acidity not only for better balance but also to lower pH, then you will trial adding tartaric acid in increments of, for example, 0.5 g/L, and assess each treated sample for taste, acidity and pH. Similarly, knowing that bentonite is added at a rate of up to 1 g/L to achieve protein stability and that greater amounts can potentially strip aromas and flavors, you will trial adding bentonite in increments of, for example, 0.25 g/L, i.e., 0.25, 0.50, 0.75 and 1.0 g/L, to smaller volumes.

Now figure out how many samples and what volumes you need to run proper trials. You will typically need to compare 3–5 samples against an untreated sample — the "control." If you are working with small batches of wine, for example, 23 L (6 gal), you will likely want to run the trial with 50-mL samples to minimize loss although 100-mL samples are easier to work with as calculations are much simpler, and that they allow at least two people to taste and re-taste treated samples. Keep in mind too that the smaller the volume size you choose, the greater the expected error, which can possibly cause a fairly large discrepancy from your trial results when you come to treat the entire batch.

 Do not return trial samples to your batch of wine as you risk contamination. Instead, run your trial, perform the adjustment to the batch, and either immediately bottle the wine or, if the batch needs topping up, use a similar wine to top up the carboy so that it can be left to age without worry until you are ready to bottle.

To run the actual trial, you will need tasting glasses if the trial involves tasting, and lab glassware — a 100-mL volumetric flask for preparing a dilute solution of the substance to be added and trialed, a 100-mL graduated cylinder, and various beakers if you are analyzing, for example, pH. If the trial involves tasting, invite one or two friends whose palate you trust; you want as much feedback as possible, especially from those who you will be sharing your wines with. Make sure to evaluate samples at the serving temperature, and that means chilling samples if you are working on adjusting acidity or sweetness in a white or rosé wine.

5

5.2 CALCULATIONS

Once you have established the rates of addition and sample size, you will need to determine the concentration of the additive or processing aid to use, and calculate the amount to add to each sample to be treated. This is the most important step, and you will need to brush up on your math skills; be sure to double-check all calculations. For example, if you want to add, say tartaric acid, at a rate of 0.5 g/L to 100-mL samples, this means that you need to add 0.05 g (0.5 g/L × 0.1 L) of tartaric acid to each sample. You would need an expensive laboratory scale to accurately measure such a small quantity, and therefore, it is best to prepare a dilute solution that you can then accurately measure with a relatively inexpensive pipette.

A 10%-solution works best for our tartaric acid example as there is 10 g of acid per 100 mL of solution, which means you need to add 0.5 mL to 100-mL wine samples to add tartaric acid at a rate of 0.5 g/L. Measuring 0.5 mL accurately with a good 1-mL syringe is now much easier. And preparing a 10% solution is very simple: thoroughly dissolve 10 g of tartaric acid crystals in approximately 75 mL of distilled water in a 100-mL volumetric flask or a good 100-mL graduated cylinder, and add water to the 100-mL mark. You will find it easier to first dissolve the acid crystals in a 100-mL beaker using a magnetic stirrer, if so equipped, and then transferring the solution to the 100-mL volumetric flask or graduated cylinder; rinse the beaker with distilled water and pour into the flask or cylinder.

You can make use of the downloadable worksheet at ModernHome-Winemaking.com to help you with these calculations.

5.3 CONDUCTING TRIALS

Next we will look at how to conduct bench trials using a couple of specific examples. Here's a piece of advice for treating the entire batch once you have determined the optimal amount of tartaric acid, sugar, fining agent, or whatever other substance you are trialing:

Only add half of the calculated amount to treat the entire batch, then evaluate the addition by taste or measuring relevant parameters, then add the second half if everything is as expected. This will prevent you from overshooting your adjustments if you have miscalculated any amounts. This will be particularly useful when using estimated volumes in calculations, for example, when having to treat a batch of crushed red grapes.

You can make use of the downloadable worksheet at ModernHome-Winemaking.com to help you with these calculations presented in the following examples.

EXAMPLE 5.1

Determining the amount of sugar to add to sweeten to taste

The objective here is to slightly sweeten a fairly dry wine of unknown residual sugar content by a maximum of 5 g/L for an off-dry style. Since a dry wine has less than 5 g/L of residual sugar, we will prepare six samples in this trial: the control, and then samples with +1 g/L, +2 g/L, +3 g/L, +4 g/L and +5 g/L.

1. Prepare 100 mL of a 10% sugar solution (see Section 16.1 for detailed instructions). Each mL of this 10% solution adds 1 g/L of sugar in 100 mL.

2. Prepare six tasting glasses and label them, say, 0, 1, 2, 3, 4, and 5, for the control and the planned rates of addition. Pour some of the control wine into the glass labeled "0." Pour your tasting mates too if you have someone helping you with your bench trials.

3. Pour exactly 100 mL of wine in a 100-mL graduated cylinder. Using a good 10-mL pipette or a 1-mL syringe, add 1 mL of 10% sugar solution. Place a piece of paraffin film on the cylinder and invert it several times to get a homogeneous sample. Pour some of this wine into the glass labeled "1." Repeat for the other samples by adding 2, 3, 4 and 5 mL of 10% sugar solution.

 Have the wine at your usual serving temperature for that particular wine. That means keeping the wine chilled during the bench trials if you are working with white or rosé wine. Otherwise, the chilled wine once treated may taste less sweet than in your trials.

4. Taste and compare the sweetened wines with the control. See which has the best balance and which best matches your desired taste profile. Seek input from other invited tasters.

5. Scale up your sugar addition and immediately treat the batch based on your bench trial results. Let's say you preferred the sample with +3 g/L and you need to sweeten a 23-L (6-gal) batch, then you will need to add 23 L × 3 g/L or 69 g of sugar.

Note that, in Example 5.1, we were looking for small residual sugar increments of 1 g/L. When doing bench trials in trying to sweeten with larger increments, for example, in balancing a high-acid wine, pick larger increments and a larger range that you think will cover your desired sweetness; for example, try 10, 20 and 30 g/L. Once you have prepared and tasted those samples and you need to zero in on a sugar level, say in the 20–30 g/L range, start with 25 g/L by simply making a 50/50 sample using the 20- and 30-g/L previously prepared samples, and if that's too sweet, make a 50/50 sample using this 25-g/L sample and the 20-g/L sample to get 22.5 g/L — this saves work.

EXAMPLE 5.2

Determining the amount of tartaric acid to lower pH

We have a must with acidity in the desired range but with slightly high pH of 3.80, which we wish to lower to around 3.60 by adding tartaric acid.

We will assume that 1.0 g/L of tartaric acid decreases pH by up to 0.1, therefore we will likely need to add 2.0 g/L, and perhaps a little more in case 2.0 g/L is not enough, to get our pH down to the 3.60 range. And we will use 50-mL samples as that is sufficient for measuring pH — samples are not consumed.

 You may need more than 1.0 g/L of tartaric acid per 0.1 pH drop due to buffering — something we will learn in Chapter 7. For simplicity in this example, we will assume there is no buffering.

1. Prepare 100 mL of a 10% tartaric solution. Each mL of this 10% solution adds 1 g/L of tartaric acid in 100 mL, but since we are working with 50-mL samples, 1 mL of 10% solution adds 2 g/L of tartaric acid. And therefore, we need to add 0.5 mL and 1.0 mL to the 50-mL samples to achieve the desired rates of addition of 1.0 g/L and 2.0 g/L.

2. Pour 50 mL of the control wine into a 100-mL beaker, place the beaker on a magnetic stirrer with stir bar, insert the pH electrode into the sample, and measure and confirm the pH — 3.80 in our case.

3. Using a good 1-mL syringe add 0.5 mL of 10% tartaric acid solution. Wait for the magnetic stirrer to homogenize the sample, then take a pH reading once stable. Let's say you measured 3.72.

4. Add another 0.5 mL of 10% tartaric acid solution. Wait for the magnetic stirrer to homogenize the sample, then take a pH reading. Let's say you measured 3.64. Therefore now you are very close to the desired pH of 3.60. But you know that if you add another 0.5 mL (for a total of 1.5 mL or the equivalent of 3.0 g/L of tartaric acid), it might take the pH down to the 3.50 range. This might actually be a better pH but you feel that adding 3.0 g/L of tartaric acid might be a tad too much acid. You have a good syringe and therefore we'll go with a 0.25-mL addition.

5. Add 0.25 mL of 10% tartaric acid solution. Wait for the magnetic stirrer to homogenize the sample, then take a pH reading. Let's say you measured 3.58. This is very good and very close to the desired pH of 3.60, and you decide this is good. Therefore now you have added 1.25 mL of 10% tartaric acid solution to a 50-mL sample, which represents an addition of 2.5 g/L of tartaric acid. Taste this sample to make sure you have not created a taste imbalance in the must.

6. Now place the sample in the fridge for 7–10 days to give time for the tartaric acid to come to chemical equilibrium, then taste and test again for TA and pH to make sure all is good.

7. Scale up your tartaric acid addition and immediately treat the batch based on your bench trial results. If treating a 23-L (6-gal) batch, then you will need to add 23 L × 2.5 g/L or 57.5 g of tartaric acid.

8. Treat the whole batch, and then take a sample and re-measure the pH to make sure it is around 3.58 as you measured in the trial. You should also re-measure the acidity to confirm that it increased by 2.5 g/L.

6 Wine Analysis and Control: Sugar and Alcohol

You can certainly make wine — good wine — without any knowledge of wine chemistry or analysis. When making wine from a kit or some "recipe" you found on the internet, you can simply follow the instructions and have a very good chance of making good wine. Concentrate in kits or processed juice have sugar, acidity and pH levels adjusted to make a well-balanced wine.

However, if you want to make great wine with impeccable balance from grapes or unprocessed juice, and consistently, you will need some basic knowledge of wine chemistry and analysis; more often than not, you will be faced with unbalanced must chemistry or perhaps subpar grapes that will necessitate making adjustments. This knowledge and analytical skills will also help you replicate a style from year to year, or help you identify and resolve winemaking problems — you can only make as great wine as your ability to fix problems.

Sugar, acidity and pH are the three most basic essential control parameters in winemaking. This chapter discusses analysis and control of sugar and alcohol, and how to make adjustments to increase or decrease sugar or alcohol. Chapter 7 discusses the same for acidity and pH. Sulfur dioxide (SO_2) chemistry too is an essential control parameter; it is a more advanced topic and is discussed in detail in Chapter 8.

6.1 SUGAR AND ALCOHOL

Wine is the transformation of sugars into alcohol, more specifically the transformation by yeast fermentation of glucose and fructose into ethanol, and therefore, the amount of sugar in grapes or juice dictates the *maximum* amount of alcohol possible, or potential alcohol, in the final wine. When all fermentable sugars have been converted into alcohol, the wine is said to be dry — a term used to mean there is no perceptible sweetness. If fermentable sugars are not completely converted, the final alcohol level will be less than the measured potential alcohol, and the wine is said to be off-dry, medium-dry (or semi-sweet) or sweet depending on the amount of unfermented residual sugars.

We'll get technical now.

6.2 SPECIFIC GRAVITY, BRIX AND POTENTIAL ALCOHOL

There are several units for measuring and reporting the amount of sugars in must and wine.

In North America, Specific Gravity and degrees Brix are the standard units for measuring and reporting the amount of *fermentable* sugars with Specific Gravity more common in home winemaking and degrees Brix more so in commercial winemaking. Specific Gravity is abbreviated as sp gr though most commonly as SG, while degrees Brix is abbreviated as °Bx or simply Brix, as is common practice. Here we will use both SG and Brix (in brackets) as many home winemakers also use Brix.

 These measurements actually reflect the amount of total dissolved solids (TDS), which, for all practical purposes, approximates the amount of fermentable sugars in winemaking. It is assumed here that the amount of other dissolved solids is negligible.

Specific Gravity (SG) is a measure of must or wine density relative to the density of water, i.e., SG of water is 1.000, both measured at 20°C (68°F). For example, a must with a SG of 1.092 means that its density due to sugars is 1.092 times the density of water, or its weight due to sugars is 1.092 times the weight of water for the same volume. Note that SG measurements are always specified to a minimum of three decimal digits. These three decimal digits are referred to as points, a term often used when discussing SG changes; for example, if SG drops from 1.092 to 1.080 during fermentation, it is said that SG dropped 12 points.

Degrees Brix (°Bx or B°) is a measure of the amount of sugars, in grams, in 100 g of juice at 20 °C (68 °F). For example, a reading of 22.0 Brix means that the juice contains 22.0 g of sugars in 100.0 g of must at 20 °C (68 °F), or 22.0 percent sugar by weight, or 22% w/w.

Often it will be more convenient to work with sugar concentrations expressed as mass (weight) to volume, i.e., g/L, for example, to determine the amount of sugar to add to must to achieve a desired density. Here we will refer to this sugar concentration as "sugars (g/L)."

6

Other winemaking regions of the world and beer-brewing use different scales: Baumé (B°, Bé°) in France and Australia, Oechsle (°Oe) in Germany, Balling in South Africa, and Plato (°P) in the beer industry. Baumé is approximately equivalent to Potential Alcohol (PA); Oechsle is equivalent to the density minus 1 (one) multiplied by 1000 so that, for example, a density of 1.092 equals 92 °Oe; and Balling is the same as Brix but calibrated at 17.5 °C (63.5 °F).

Since consumers (and tax agencies for commercial operations) are interested in a wine's alcohol level, winemakers also refer to the amount of fermentable sugars as Potential Alcohol (PA), which is expressed as a percentage of ethanol volume to total volume, written as % alc/vol or simply % ABV to mean percent Alcohol By Volume. PA is an estimate of the *expected maximum* amount of ethanol that can be produced if all fermentable sugars are fermented.

When fermentation is complete, the final amount of alcohol produced is the actual, measured % ABV, and any amount of unfermented sugars left in the wine is referred to as residual sugar (RS), expressed in grams per liter (g/L) or simply as a percentage of sugar mass to wine volume.

Let's look at the relationships among SG, Brix, sugars (g/L) and PA.

The relationships are neither simple nor straightforward since these units do not measure the same physical properties of must or wine, and they are often measured using different instruments. The relationships, which are not perfectly linear, also change due to alcohol production as juice is converted into wine during fermentation. The conversions are therefore based on expressions derived from polynomial fits to experimental data, and therefore, you have to expect that there is much approximating when doing conversions. You will find many mathematical formulae in the literature as well as many online calculators that convert very differently among units. Here, we will use Table B.1 in Appendix B instead of using conversion formulae.

Table B.1 tabulates the relationships among Brix, SG, sugars (g/L) and PA at a temperature of 20 °C (68 °F). The amount of fermentable sugars in g/L at a certain SG (Brix) has been approximated to be 10 times the Brix value, and therefore, for example, must with SG 1.105 (25.0 Brix) is assumed to contain approximately 250 g/L of fermentable sugars (Figure 6.1). This assumption and simplification will serve our purpose well and greatly simplify calculations, at least for SG above 1.040 (Brix above 10.0). This approximation scheme has a greater error as SG approaches 1.000, which is 0.0 Brix by definition; however, there is still considerable amounts of sugars to be fermented, possibly up to 20 g/L, at SG 1.000 (0.0 Brix).

Brix	SG	Sugar (g/L)	Sugar (g/gal)	PA (% alc/vol)
25.0	1.105	250	948	14.3

Figure 6.1: Example of conversions among Brix, SG, sugars (g/L) and PA at a temperature of 20 °C (68 °F)

Estimating PA is trickier. SG and Brix measurements are only approximations due to the presence of other substances, such as non-fermentable sugars, acids, salts, proteins, and color pigments in rosé and red musts. These substances and the general chemistry of must cause sugars to be metabolized at different rates in whites, rosés and reds. Fermenting with indigenous yeast results in lower PA, and different yeast strains also metabolize sugars at slightly different rates. Therefore, you can seldom expect PA and final % ABV to match when fermentation is complete, but they should be very close when wine is fermented to dryness.

Let's define "dryness" before looking at the relationship between PA and SG/Brix in Table B.1.

A wine is said to be fermented "dry" when the final SG is 0.995 or lower (Brix is −1.5 or lower). If fermentation stops on its own or is purposely halted when the SG is greater than 0.995 (Brix greater than −1.5), less alcohol would have been produced than the measured PA with the wine having some residual sugar that will affect taste. Other than taste impacts, residual sugar in wine will be a source of instability. If conditions become ideal for yeast, it can restart fermenting that residual sugar, and if it happens in bottles, corks can pop out or, in the worst case, bottles can explode. SG 0.995 (−1.5 Brix) is the generally accepted threshold although, as we will see in Section 6.5, there can still be sufficient sugar to cause problems if the amount of residual sugar is not confirmed by analytical means. We will look at residual sugar and how to measure RS in Section 6.5 below, and discuss how to stabilize wine with residual sugar in Section 14.1.1.

Although it is generally accepted that 16.83 g of fermentable sugars per liter of must produces 1% of alcohol (v/v), empirical data shows that it can vary from 16 g/L to as much as 19 g/L [1,2]. Some enologists have proposed using a factor of 17–17.5 g/L for white wines and 17.5–18 g/L for reds [1]. I have adopted a conversion factor of 17.5 g/L for all types of wines, i.e., whites, rosés and reds, based on my own experimental and winemaking data; this has served me well in my work. Therefore, for example, a must with SG 1.105 (25.0 Brix), which is approximated to contain 250 g/L, will have a calculated PA of about 250 ÷ 17.5 or 14.3%. If you work in Brix, it's very simple: the conversion factor is 0.57, so that 0.57 × 25.0 Brix equals 14.3%.

Table 6.1 lists ranges of SG, Brix, PA and RS to produce various styles of wines. The final % ABV should fall within the ranges of PA. RS may be a combination of natural, unfermented sugars and added sugar. Remember: to express RS as a %, simply divide the value in g/L by 10, so that, for example, 5.0 g/L is equivalent to 0.5%.

Table 6.1: SG, Brix, PA and RS ranges for different styles of wines.

Style of wine	SG	Brix	PA (% alc/vol)	RS (g/L)[1]
Dry, light, fruity white or rosé	1.080–1.090	19–22	11–12.5	<4
Off-dry, light, fruity white or rosé	1.080–1.090	19–22	11–12.5	5–10
Medium-sweet, fruity white or rosé	1.080–1.090	19–22	11–12.5	10–50
Sweet, fruity white or rosé	1.080–1.090	19–22	11–12.5	>50
Fuller-bodied or oak-aged white	1.090–1.100	22–24	12.5–13.5	<4
Light- to medium-bodied red	1.090–1.100	22–24	12.5–13.5	<4
Full-bodied red	1.100–1.110	24–26	13.5–15	<4

[1]Note that "dry" does not equate to microbially stable. Only dry wines with RS less than 2 g/L are considered microbially stable; those with 2–4 g/L RS would still require to be properly stabilized, as outlined in Section 14.1.1.

Data presented in Table 6.1 is different from those in [2] as it uses Table B.1 in Appendix B for the relationships among SG, Brix and PA.

We will look at examples on using these parameters in winemaking and how to use Table 6.1 to understand how this all works, but first, let's look at how SG, Brix and PA are measured.

6.3 MEASURING SG, BRIX AND PA

SG and Brix are measured using a hydrometer (Figure 6.2). PA too can be measured with a hydrometer if wanting to use the hydrometer's conversions.

The hydrometer consists of a hollow glass tube with a wider bottom portion for buoyancy and a narrow stem with graduations for measuring; it comes with a cylinder to introduce the wine and hydrometer to make a measurement.

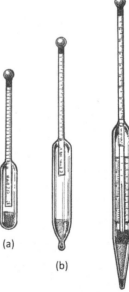

Figure 6.2: a) Triple-scale hydrometer; b) precision, low-range hydrometer; c) hydrometer/thermometer combination

(a)

(b)

(c)

The most common hydrometers used in home winemaking include all three scales, i.e., SG, Brix and PA (Figure 6.2). Higher-end models may incorporate a thermometer for temperature compensation and usually include a single scale, either SG or Brix. Higher-end hydrometers are calibrated at 20 °C (68 °F), which means that if you measure must at a different temperature, the reading needs to be adjusted. Older or more basic hydrometers may be calibrated at different temperatures, for example, 15.5 °C (60 °F), therefore, be sure to confirm the calibration temperature as identified on the scale, and measure and adjust your SG or Brix readings accordingly.

 SG and Brix hydrometer measurements are fairly good approximations of the amount of fermentable sugars in must above SG 1.040 (10.0 Brix). However, as we have seen above, the PA scale is a calculation, and different hydrometer manufacturers use different sugar-to-ethanol conversion factors, which means you may get different PA readings using two different hydrometers; the difference can be as much as ±1% ABV. Decide whether you want to use your hydrometer's PA reading or Table B.1.

If you want more accurate results to better assess completion of fermentation and to better estimate the amount of residual sugar (see Section 6.5), buy a low-range, high-precision hydrometer with a scale of, for example, SG 0.940–1.010 or –5 Brix to +5 Brix (Figure 6.2).

It is always preferable and more accurate to measure samples at the hydrometer calibration temperature rather than using temperature correction. Cool or warm samples, as required, to bring them to hydrometer calibration temperature. When that is not possible, you can adjust readings using Table B.2 in Appendix B. If the sample is colder than the calibration temperature, the SG (Brix) reading must be adjusted *down*; if a sample is warmer than the calibration temperature, the SG (Brix) reading must be adjusted *up*.

Brix in must can also be measured using a digital refractometer (Figure 6.3), which operates by measuring the index of refraction of a liquid. The advantage of the digital refractometer is that it only requires a single drop to make a measurement, and therefore, there is no sample preparation, no sanitizing. Once the juice starts fermenting, the presence of alcohol skews the measurement. There are online tables to help you convert SG/Brix re-fractometer readings taken during fermentation to "real" SG/Brix meas-urements. This is fine to monitor fermentation progress, but a low-range hydrometer is much more accurate for assessing fermentation completion.

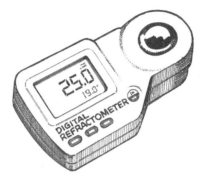

Figure 6.3: Digital Brix refractometer

Measure SG (Brix), PA and temperature of the must, i.e., at the juice stage before fermentation starts, during fermentation to monitor fermen-tation progress, and when fermentation is complete so that you can make a final determination of % ABV and estimate RS.

To take a reading with a hydrometer, sanitize the hydrometer and cyl-inder as per instructions in Section 4.6, insert the hydrometer into the cyl-inder, then pour in a sample of must or wine right to the top of the cylinder, let the hydrometer float and stabilize, and take a reading on any or all scales. The hydrometer must float freely without touching the base or sides of the cylinder; if it does, the cylinder is too small or you have not poured enough sample. Be sure to take a reading at the meniscus level (Figure 6.4). The cleaner the juice, the more accurate your reading will be. If there are a lot of grape fragments and other solids, filter the sample through a fine sieve — sanitized, of course.

To transfer a sample from a pail, carboy or other vessel, use a sanitized gravy baster or wine thief.

When making red wine where grape skins macerate in the juice, make sure the must and grape solids are thoroughly mixed, immerse a sanitized cone-shaped strainer deep enough into the grape solids (Figure 6.5) to separate solids from the juice, then use a sanitized gravy baster or wine thief to draw a sample.

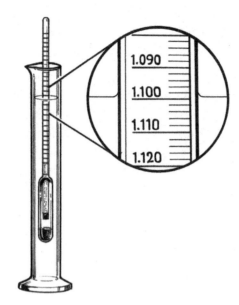

Figure 6.4: How to take a hydrometer reading; SG is 1.100 here

Figure 6.5: Drawing a juice or wine sample in red winemaking

Set aside a 200-mL sample in the refrigerator; you may need to come back to it later on to perform some extra analysis, for example, when doing a root-cause analysis.

If the wine has fermented to complete dryness, your final % ABV should be close (up to ±0.5% ABV is quite acceptable) to your calculated PA based on measured SG/Brix. However, if the wine has stopped fermenting or you deliberately stopped fermentation for a sweeter style of wine, then you have to subtract the PA at the final SG/Brix from the initial PA. Section 11.6 describes how to halt a fermentation for retaining some residual sugar and sweetness.

If you want to measure the actual amount of alcohol in your wine to see how close it is to the measured PA at the juice stage, there are analytical techniques, equipment and kits available, but these tend to involve work, handling dangerous reagents, or expensive equipment. If you want to explore this further as you progress in your winemaking, you can research ethanol analysis by ebulliometry, chemical oxidation (e.g., Vinmetrica's Alcohol By Volume Kit), or distillation.

Let's look at an example to understand how all this works in practical terms.

EXAMPLE 6.1

Estimating PA from SG, Brix

You just received your pail of white juice and it is very cold. You measured a SG of 1.093 (22.5 Brix) at 10 °C (41 °F) using your hydrometer calibrated at 20 °C (68 °F). Using Table B.2 in Appendix B, the SG is corrected by −0.003, so that the adjusted SG is 1.090 (21.9 Brix).

To calculate PA, convert 21.9 Brix to 219 g/L of fermentable sugars, which, using a factor of 17.5 g/L, gives an estimated PA of 219 ÷ 17.5 or 12.5%. If fermented to dryness, i.e., SG below 0.995 (Brix below −1.5), the wine can be expected to have a final % ABV close to 12.5%.

EXAMPLE 6.2

Estimating % ABV from initial and final PA

From Example 6.1, you estimated PA to be approximately 12.5%.

Let's say you halted fermentation at SG 1.020 (5.2 Brix), which represents a PA of approximately 3.0%, then, the final % ABV is calculated as 12.5 − 3.0, or 9.5%.

6

MEASURING SG/BRIX DURING FERMENTATION
AND DEGASSING SAMPLES

During fermentation you will need to monitor how sugar conversion is progressing using your hydrometer to see if fermentation is progressing normally as expected or if it has stopped for whatever reason. We will explore causes of problem fermentations in Section 11.5.

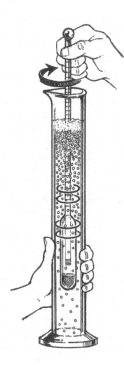

Once fermentation has started and is producing carbon dioxide (CO_2) gas, hydrometer readings are skewed by CO_2. To get a more accurate reading, degas the wine sample, i.e., remove as much CO_2 as possible. This is not that critical during an active fermentation as you are really interested in making sure that everything is progressing well — you don't need an accurate hydrometer measurement at this point. A simpler method that gives good results if you still want to remove at least some of the CO_2 is to stir the sample with the hydrometer in the cylinder and then spin the hydrometer several times (Figure 6.6). You should however completely degas your sample when taking the very final SG/Brix reading when fermentation is over so that you have a more accurate measurement. You will get higher readings in samples that are not degassed.

Figure 6.6: Removing CO_2 from a fermenting wine sample when taking a hydrometer reading

There are several ways to properly degas a wine sample. First, transfer about 250 mL of wine to a 500-mL Erlenmeyer flask. Place a rubber stopper and shake vigorously until there is no more foaming visible in the sample. As you shake, remove the stopper to evacuate the CO_2, and repeat. Alternatively, you can use a vacuum pump with a tube fitted on the stopper to "pull" the CO_2 out, or you can inject nitrogen gas from a small tank through the sample to displace the CO_2 more efficiently.

6.4 ADJUSTING SUGAR AND POTENTIAL ALCOHOL

Often when working with grapes sourced from a third party or from an atypical vintage (too wet, or too hot and dry), the sugar level might be too low or too high for your needs, and therefore, you will need to make adjustments up or down.

6.4.1 CHAPTALIZATION

If you want to make a wine with, for example, 14.0% ABV but your PA is 12.5, you will need to add some form of sugar, a practice known as chaptalization. You can chaptalize with sucrose (table sugar) or a simple sugar, such as glucose or fructose, or using concentrate.

As a rule of thumb, based on the theory presented in Section 6.2, you need to add approximately 17.5 g/L of sugar to raise PA by 1%; alternatively, you can use Table B.1 in Appendix B if you prefer to work with SG or Brix.

If using sugar, glucose is most ideal since most yeast have a preference for glucose over fructose, which reduces the risk of fermentation problems. Fructose is also twice as sweet as glucose, and therefore, unfermented fructose can make the wine taste sweeter than with the same amount of unfermented glucose.

Dissolve sugar in a small volume of juice preferably; water is okay although it will slightly dilute the juice or must. You will need about 1 L of juice (or water) per 500 g of sugar, or about ¼ gal per 1 lb. Thoroughly stir the syrupy solution for 5–10 minutes or until all the sugar is completely dissolved. No heating is necessary; it is never advisable to heat juice (or wine). The sugar will dissolve adequately at room temperature, though it will take longer at cooler temperatures.

Note that your total must volume will increase by about 625 mL per 1000 g (2.2 lbs) of sucrose added to each liter of must if dissolved in juice; you will have to account for water volume too if you choose to dissolve sucrose in water.

If you decide to use water, the small amount will dilute acidity, but it should be minimal. You can first acidify the water using tartaric acid to the same level as the juice or must, then dissolve the sugar in the water.

Once the sugar is completely dissolved, add the syrupy solution to the rest of the juice or must and stir thoroughly, let rest for about an hour, stir thoroughly again, then take a sample and re-measure SG/Brix and PA.

A word of caution! Adding the exact amount of sugar in chaptalization can be tricky, particularly in red winemaking where you need to estimate the volume of juice — you won't know the exact volume until you rack the wine after fermentation, i.e., when you separate the wine from the grape solids. To avoid overcompensating, add half the calculated amount of sugar, take a measurement, and add the second half with any adjustments, if necessary. If you overcompensate on the first and only addition by estimating too low a volume of juice, you will either have to accept the higher PA or ameliorate (see Section 6.4.2).

Use the downloadable worksheet at ModernHomeWinemaking.com to help you determine the required amount of sugar for chaptalization using a two-step approach to avoid overcompensating.

Let's look at an example of chaptalization.

EXAMPLE 6.3

Chaptalization using sucrose (table sugar)

You just crushed some 45 kg (100 lbs) of red grapes, taken a sample, and measured SG 1.091 (22.0 Brix), which gives a PA of 12.6% ABV, but you want a dry wine with 14.0% ABV — an increase of 1.4%. Based on your experience working with this same variety, you estimate a yield of approximately 58 L per 100 kg of grapes, which translates into 26 L for the 45 kg, or about 7 gal for the 100 lbs of grapes.

Using Table B.1 in Appendix B, you determine that at SG 1.091 (22.0 Brix), your must has approximately 220 g/L (834 g/gal) of sugars, and that you need to chaptalize to SG 1.102 (24.5 Brix) to get 14.0% ABV, where you need about 245 g/L (929 g/gal). Therefore, you need to add about 25 g/L (95 g/gal) of table sugar. Using the 17.5 g/L conversion factor to confirm the calculation, you would need 17.5 g/L × 1.4%, or 25 g/L. Then the total amount of sugar to add is:

$$Total\ amount\ of\ sugar\ to\ add\ (g) = 25\ ^{g}/_{L} \times 26\ L$$

$$= 650\ g$$

Since the must volume is an estimate, you need to be careful and only add about half the calculated amount of sugar, say, 325 g or about 11 oz.

Completely dissolve the sugar in a little amount of juice (preferably) or water, about 1.5 L or ½ gal, and then add to the must and stir thoroughly.

Adding half the sugar should result in a PA increase of half the difference between the desired PA (14.0%) and the initial PA (12.6%), or 1.4 ÷ 2 = 0.7. And therefore you should expect a PA of about 13.3.

Wait about one hour, stir thoroughly again, then take another sample, transfer it to your sanitized cylinder, and take a SG/Brix reading. Let's say you now measure 1.095 (23.0 Brix), which is a PA of about 13.1% ABV. This means that half the calculated amount of sugar raised the PA from 12.6 to 13.1, or an increase of 0.5, instead of an expected increase of 0.7, which means that the estimated volume of juice is more than 26 L or 7 gal. So you now need to raise PA another 0.9 from 13.1 to 14.0, and therefore, you need to adjust as follows the second half of the amount you had calculated:

$$Amount\ of\ sugar\ to\ add\ (g) = 325\ g \times \frac{0.9}{0.5}$$

$$= 585\ g$$

Since your first addition was short of the target, your second addition now needs more sugar — specifically, 585 g or 21 oz.

The bonus of this calculation is that you can now better estimate the volume of juice. This will be useful in determining all your subsequent additions, for example, enzymes, tannins, etc.

Calculate the estimated volume as follows knowing that a total of 325 + 585 or 910 g (32 oz) of sugar instead of the original 650 g (23 oz) is needed to increase PA from 12.6 to 14.0:

$$Estimated\ volume\ (L) = 26\ L \times \frac{910}{650}$$

$$= 36\ L\ (9.6\ gal)$$

6

Your expected yield is therefore 36 L (9.6 gal). Use this volume for all subsequent additions. If you want a more accurate number to adjust the volume due to the sugar addition, add 910 g × 625 mL ÷ 1000 g, or 569 mL (0.15 gal); also add the volume of water if you dissolved the sucrose in water instead of juice.

Note that, if you worked with the original volume estimate, you would be adding considerably less additives than your desired amounts since you would be using a volume of 26 L (7 gal) instead of 36 L (9.6 gal), about 38% less!

And to double-check your calculations, you have now added a total of 910 g (32 oz) of sugar in 36 L (9.6 gal) of juice, which works out to 910 ÷ 36, or 25 g/L, as expected. The new SG should be around 1.102 (24.5 Brix) after the second chaptalization; record this value in your log book.

Alternatively, if you prefer to add natural grape flavors in addition to sugar, you can use a commercial sugar-rich grape concentrate specifically developed for chaptalizing must or use a concentrate from a kit. Commercial concentrate is very effective for adding sugar as it can have a SG of up to 1.300 (60 Brix), but it is not readily available to home winemakers. Instead opt for concentrate from a kit, for example, one with 10 L (2.6 gal) or 16 L (4.2 gal) of concentrate; these would have a SG in the range 1.130–1.150 (30–35 Brix) and 1.230–1.260 (50–55 Brix), respectively, assuming the kits are for making 23 L (6 gal) of wine. Note, however, that concentrates still contain significant amounts of water, which can impact quality, and therefore, evaluate these options carefully against your objectives.

Let's take a look at Example 6.3 again but now chaptalizing using a concentrate from a kit with a SG of 1.150 (35 Brix), which you have measured with a high-range hydrometer or with your regular hydrometer by first diluting a sample two-fold.

EXAMPLE 6.4

Chaptalization using concentrate from a kit

Let's first recap the parameters from Example 6.3, still using the estimated volume.

	SG	Brix	PA	Volume (L)	Volume (gal)
Measured	1.091	22.0	12.6	26	7
Desired	1.102	24.5	14.0		

Here we want to add a concentrate with a SG of 1.155 (35 Brix) to must to raise SG from 1.091 to 1.102, or Brix from 22.0 to 24.5. We now need to determine the amount of concentrate needed. This is accomplished using the Pearson Square, which we will learn in Section 16.5.

The amount of concentrate needed works out to about 6 L (1.6 gal).

You'll use the same procedure as in Example 6.3 of adding half the required amount and re-measuring SG (Brix) to determine the second half of the addition.

From Examples 6.3 and 6.4, note that the addition of 910 g of sugar increases volume by about 0.5 L whereas the concentrate increases volume by 6 L, and therefore a lot more concentrate is required to achieve similar results, which also requires extra vessel capacity.

Note that, since increasing alcohol causes potassium bitartrate to become less soluble and to precipitate, chaptalization can cause a drop in acidity in the order of 0.2–0.3 g/L per 1% ABV increase [3]. We will learn about potassium bitartrate and its solubility properties in Section 7.4.1.

And when should you chaptalize? It is always best to chaptalize pre-ferment, the idea is that you have a balanced must heading into fermen-tation. Adding sugar or concentrate during an active fermentation, even in small amounts in successive steps, can unduly stress yeast that could lead to a stuck fermentation, not to mention that it can cause excessive foaming and create a big mess in your winemaking area.

6

6.4.2 AMELIORATION

Now, if your PA is 17.0%, for example, aside from making an overly alco-holic wine, yeast will likely give up at around 16%, maybe less depending on yeast choice, and leave you with enough sugar to make the wine taste overly sweet; the wine will also be unstable from a microbiological stand-point — more on this in Section 14.1.1. There are yeasts that can ferment to 17% or even 18%, but there is always a risk of fermentation stopping, and that much alcohol does not make for a balanced dry wine, though it is great for a port-style wine, for example.

To lower the PA you will need to add acidulated water — a practice known as amelioration — though this may dilute aromas, flavors and, in reds, color, if done heavy-handedly. You may have no other alternatives but to ameliorate.

Amelioration usually involves adding substantial amounts of water. For example, if you measured a PA of 16.5% and you want to make a wine with 14.0 % ABV, you will need to add just over 4 L or about a gallon of water to your 23-L (6-gallon) batch. That's a lot of water! That much water will significantly lower acidity and, therefore, you need to acidulate (add acid to) water to the same acidity as the must or juice. To acidulate, add the same amount of tartaric acid as the acid concentration (see Section 7.2) of the must or juice.

The same caution applies here as with chaptalization in red winemak-ing. Adding the exact amount of acidulated water in amelioration can be tricky as you won't know the exact volume until you rack the wine after fermentation. To avoid overcompensating, add half the calculated amount of water, take a measurement, and add the second half with any adjustments, if necessary. If you overcompensate on the first and only addition by estimating too low a volume of juice, you will either have to accept the lower PA or chaptalize.

Use the downloadable worksheet at ModernHomeWinemaking.com to help you determine the required amount of water for amelioration using a two-step approach to avoid overcompensating.

Let's look at an example of amelioration.

EXAMPLE 6.5

Amelioration

You just crushed some 45 kg (100 lbs) of red grapes, taken a sample, and measured SG 1.123 (28.9 Brix), which gives a PA of 16.5% ABV, but you want a dry wine with 14.0% ABV. Based on your experience working with this same variety, you estimate a yield of approximately 58 L per 100 kg of grapes, which translates into 26 L for the 45 kg, or about 7 gal for the 100 lbs of grapes.

To lower PA by 2.5 from 16.5% to 14.0%, you need to increase the volume proportionally to 26 L × 16.5 ÷ 14.0, or 30.6 L (8.1 gal), and therefore adding 30.6 − 26 = 4.6 L or 1.2 gal of acidulated water. Now you need to acidulate the water with tartaric acid, and for this, you need to measure the acidity (see Section 7.3) of the juice. Let's say you measured 6.5 g/L of acidity. Prepare a little more water, say, 7 L (1.8 gal), in case you have underestimated your juice volume, and to this volume of water, add 6.5 g/L × 7 L, or 46 g (1.6 oz) of winemaking-grade tartaric acid crystals and dissolve thoroughly. This way the water to be added has the same acidity as the juice, therefore you will not be changing the acidity.

Since the juice volume is an estimate, you need to be cautious and only add about half the calculated amount of acidulated water, or 2.3 L (0.6 gal). Add the acidulated water and stir thoroughly. Adding half the water should result in a PA decrease of half the difference between the desired PA (14.0%) and the initial PA (16.5%), or 2.5 ÷ 2=1.25 — let's call it 1.3.

Take another sample, transfer it to your sanitized cylinder, and take SG/Brix and PA readings. Let's say you now measure 1.115 (27.2 Brix) and 15.5, respectively. This means that half the calculated amount of water lowered the PA from 16.5 to 15.5, or a decrease of 1.0, instead of an expected decrease of 1.3, which means that the estimated volume of juice is more than 26 L or 7 gal. Therefore now you need to lower it another 1.5 from 15.5 to 14.0, and therefore, you need to adjust as follows the second half of the amount you had calculated:

$$Amount\ of\ acidulated\ water\ to\ add\ (L) = 2.3\ L \times \frac{1.5}{1.0}$$

$$= 3.5\ L\ (0.9\ gal)$$

Since your first addition was short of the target, your second addition now needs more water — specifically, 3.5 L or 0.9 gal in this case.

As in the chaptalization example, these calculations now allow you to better estimate the volume of must, which will be useful in determining all your subsequent additions of enzymes, tannins, etc.

Calculate the estimated volume as follows knowing that a total of 2.3 + 3.5, or 5.8 L (1.5 gal) of water instead of the original 4.6 L (1.2 gal) is needed to decrease PA from 16.5 to 14.0:

$$Estimated\ volume\ (L) = 26\ L \times \frac{5.8}{4.6}$$

$$= 32.8\ L\ (8.6\ gal)$$

Your expected yield is therefore 32.8 L (8.6 gal) to which you added 5.8 L (1.5 gal) of acidulated water for a new total volume of 38.6 L (10.2 gal). Use this volume for all subsequent additions.

And to double-check your calculations, the adjusted PA is now 16.5 × 32.8 ÷ 38.6 = 14.0%. The new SG should be around 1.102 (24.5 Brix) after the second amelioration; record this value in your log book.

6.5 ESTIMATING AND MEASURING RESIDUAL SUGAR

If wine is not fermented to dryness, i.e., SG < 0.995 (Brix < −1.5), there will be sufficient residual sugars (see sidebar on *WHAT DOES RESIDUAL SUGAR REALLY MEAN?*) to make the wine taste anywhere from off-dry to sweet depending on the final SG/Brix, but more important, the wine will be microbially unstable, meaning that yeast can start a new fermentation feeding on the little amount of sugar remaining. The residual sugar (RS) threshold amount is generally accepted to be 4.0 g/L but no more than 2.0 g/L is recommended here to be safer and to minimize risk; some enologists and commercial analytical services laboratories recommend no more than 1.0 g/L. Wine with a RS greater than 2.0 g/L will need to be treated to avoid the risk of refermentation; stabilization in wine with residual sugar is discussed in Section 14.1.1.

Estimating RS is very complex given the intricacies of wine chemistry, and formulae and methods in the literature can only provide rough estimates, and particularly at low sugar levels. RS can be significantly different even at the same final SG/Brix. It is therefore always best to measure RS by laboratory analysis to get more accurate estimates.

There are relatively inexpensive, easy-to-use kits on the market, such as Vinmetrica's Reducing Sugar Assay Kit and Laboratoires Dujardin-Salleron's Fermentest kit (Figure 6.7), which give very good approximations. Alternatively, you can send samples to a laboratory.

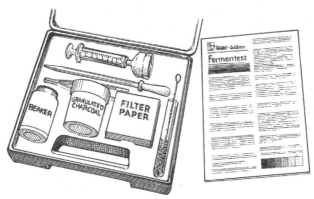

Figure 6.7: Laboratoires Dujardin-Salleron's Fermentest kit

WHAT DOES RESIDUAL SUGAR REALLY MEAN?

The topic of residual sugar uses various terms, such as glucose+fructose, reducing sugars and residual sugar, often confusingly interchanged.

A very important aspect of residual sugar chemistry concerns wine stability where only unfermented but fermentable sugars are relevant; these sugars are glucose and fructose. It is generally accepted that a wine is stable if the sum of residual (unfermented) glucose and fructose, or G+F, is less than 2 g/L. If there is any residual sucrose, a disaccharide of glucose and fructose, it will not be measured unless it is first inverted into its monosaccharides. Isolating and measuring glucose and fructose is well beyond the means of home winemakers.

Methods, equipment and kits for sugar analysis measure what is called reducing sugars, often abbreviated as RS. Reducing sugars include glucose and fructose, and some *unfermentable* sugars (those that cannot be fermented), such as rhamnose, arabinose and ribose. The amount of unfermentable sugars is usually very small, well under 1 g/L, and therefore, RS is only slightly greater than G+F. Unfermentable sugars can contribute sweetness to wine.

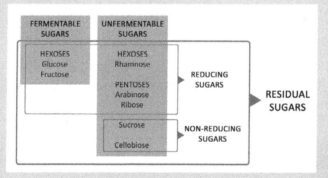

But when discussing how dry a wine is, most use the more common term residual sugar, which we also often abbreviate to RS. Residual sugars include glucose and fructose, reducing sugars, and other unfermentable sugars, such as sucrose and cellobiose. The latter two unfermentable sugars are known as non-reducing sugars and can contribute considerable sweetness, as in the case of sucrose if present in significant amounts, such as just after chaptalization without prior hydrolysis.

For all practical purposes as home winemakers, assuming that sucrose has hydrolyzed, here we will assume that these measurements are all fairly close, and therefore, we will use RS to mean any of the three sugar descriptors discussed above.

If you are still interested in estimating RS based on routinely measured wine parameters, following are two formulae and techniques that you can try.

 Home winemakers often convert SG to RS using a simple formula that provides the same results as Sugars (g/L) in Table B.1 in Appendix B. Sugars (g/L) in Table B.1 are valid for SG greater than 1.040 (Brix greater than 10.0). Sugars (g/L) below SG 1.040 (10.0 Brix) are only to be used to determine final % ABV when fermentation stops above SG 1.000 (0.0 Brix) (see Example 6.2). At SG 1.000 (0.0 Brix), RS is not zero; there are a lot of sugars still to be fermented, but these were already taken into account in the PA calculation.

Method 1, adapted from reference [4], is a predictive calculation based on the final SG (SG_f) reading at the end of fermentation, and a correction factor (cf) to account for dry extract, determined from the initial SG (SG_i) and total acidity (TA), as per the following equation:

$$RS\left(\frac{g}{L}\right) = (SG_f - 1) \times 2000 + 2 \times cf$$

Find cf in Table B.3 in Appendix B using SG_i and TA readings of the must.

Dry extract represents all the dry matter left over after "boiling off" the liquid in wine, and includes, for example, sugars, fixed acids, minerals, glycerin and tannins.

EXAMPLE 6.6

Estimating RS in a white wine using method 1

You fermented a Riesling to dryness to a final SG of 0.995. The must measured SG 1.090, which would give a PA of 12.5%, and a TA of 7.5 g/L.

From Table B.3 in Appendix B, locate 7.5 g/L in the TA column on the left and move across to the SG column under 1.090 to obtain the correction factor (cf) of 6.4. Calculate RS as follows:

$$RS\left(\frac{g}{L}\right) = (0.995 - 1) \times 2000 + 2 \times 6.4$$

$$= 2.8\ g/L$$

EXAMPLE 6.7

Estimating RS in a red wine using method 1

You fermented a Sangiovese to dryness to a final SG of 0.994. The must measured SG 1.100, which would give a PA of 13.7%, and a TA of 5.0 g/L.

From Table B.3 in Appendix B, locate 5.0 g/L in the TA column on the left and move across to the SG column under 1.100 to obtain the correction factor (*cf*) of 9.4. Calculate RS as follows:

$$RS \left(\frac{g}{L}\right) = (0.994 - 1) \times 2000 + 2 \times 9.4$$
$$= 6.8 \ g/L$$

6

In method 2, adapted from references [5,6], RS is determined from tables that are derived from empirical data based on the final SG (SG_f) reading at the end of fermentation and the final % ABV, which will be your PA if you cannot measure the actual % ABV. Then use Tables B.4 and B.5 in Appendix B for determining RS in white/rosé wine and red wine, respectively. These tables have correction factors already built in.

EXAMPLE 6.8

Estimating RS in a white wine using method 2

Using the same wine as in *Example 6.6*, you fermented a Riesling to dryness to a final SG of 0.995. The must measured SG 1.090, which would give a PA of 12.5%.

From Table B.4 in Appendix B, locate 0.995 in the SG column on the left and move across to the % ABV column under 12.5% to obtain a RS of 8.7 g/L.

EXAMPLE 6.9

Estimating RS in a red wine using method 2

Using the same wine as in *Example 6.7*, you fermented a Sangiovese to dryness to a final SG of 0.994. The must measured SG 1.100, which would give a PA of 13.7%.

From Table B.5 in Appendix B, locate 0.994 in the SG column on the left and move across to the % ABV column under 13.5% to obtain a reading of 1.0 g/L. Since our estimated % ABV is 13.7, RS is slightly higher, around 1.6 g/L.

Ostensibly, each method yields very different estimates. Method 1 calculates an estimate more in line with expectations and with some experimental data reported in the literature in the case of a white wine, while method 2 yields an estimate more in line with expectations for a red wine and with my own experimental data.

What's important to notice here is that a wine must be lower than SG 0.995 (−1.5 Brix) to give you sufficient confidence that RS is below 2 g/L and that there are no refermentation concerns. Again, you will obtain much greater confidence by measuring RS — it's well worth investing in a kit and learning the techniques.

As to when to measure RS, at a minimum, take the first measurement immediately after the completion of the AF and MLF, if done, to determine if microbial stability will be an ongoing concern, and at bottling, in case a sorbate treatment or sterile filtration is needed and also as information to have on hand and share when you drink with family and friends.

You can make use of the downloadable worksheet at ModernHome-Winemaking.com to help you with these calculations using either method.

In Section 16.1, we will look at adding sugar to wine for adding sweetness, a practice commonly known as backsweetening in home winemaking.

REFERENCES

1. Blouin, J., Peynaud, É. 2001. *Connaissance et travail du vin*. Dunod, Paris.

2. Pambianchi, D. 2008. *Techniques in Home Winemaking: A Practical Guide to Making Château-Style Wines*. Newly-Revised and Expanded. Véhicule Press, Montréal (Québec).

3. Ribéreau-Gayon, P., D. Dubourdieu, B. Donèche and A. Lonvaud. 2012. *Traité d'œnologie, Tome 1 - Microbiologie du vin. Vinifications*. 6e édition. Dunod, Paris.

4. Dienstleistungzentrum Ländlicher Raum Mosel. *Praxisleitfaden Oenologie 2020*. Rheinland Pfalz. https://www.dlr-mosel.rlp.de/Inter net/global/themen.nsf/Web_DLR_Mosel_Aktuell_All_XP/6F653FC BE0D5CD93C125830B00361153/$FILE/2020-08-13%20Praxisleit faden%20Oenologie%202020%20DLR.pdf, pp. 87 –88.

5. Ims, D. *Extract, Residual Sugar & ABV: Developing a simple way to estimate Residual Sugar and Alcohol in finished wine*. http://www. rochesterwinemakers.org/winemaking-information/winemaking-articles-by-members/determining-abv-and-residual-sugar/.

6. Ims, D. *Quick Reference Guide: Estimating a Wine's ABV and Residual Sugar in 3 Easy Steps*. http://www.rochesterwinemakers.org/wine making-information/winemaking-articles-by-members/guide-est-abv-and-res-sugar/.

6

7 Wine Analysis and Control: Acidity and pH

PREAMBLE

Acidity and pH chemistry is one of the most complex topics in winemaking, second to sulfur dioxide (SO_2) chemistry, which we explore in Chapter 8. The fact that expected results when acidifying or deacidifying rarely match actual results is testament to the complexity of managing acidity and pH.

The acidity and pH adjustment approaches presented in this chapter go well beyond the theory; they reflect practical experience that will give you confidence in managing acidity and pH beyond guesswork. This requires that we delve into some acidity theory and concepts, though this is a review of high school or college chemistry.

HOW TO USE THIS CHAPTER

If you are a beginner and are not ready for acidity/pH chemistry, you can skip Sections 7.1 and 7.4. Without a solid knowledge of acidity/pH theory and concepts, making adjustments to must (juice) or wine can be hit-and-miss that can very likely lead to undesirable results, perhaps irreversible. Make small adjustments to small batches, experiment, to the extent possible, and learn — it will help avoid huge disappointments. As you gain experience and confidence, come back to these sections; you'll become more comfortable tackling acidity and pH concepts.

Acidity and pH are very important chemistry topics in winemaking as they impact taste and balance, microbial stability, tartrate stability, oxidative potential, as well as color intensity and stability in reds.

Wines with little acidity will taste flat, insipid, and perhaps off-dry if there is sufficient residual sugar. As acidity and pH are closely but inversely related, wines with low acidity will likely have high pH, which reduces color intensity and stability in reds, and because microbes thrive at higher pH, wines become at greater risk of microbial spoilage.

Wines with high acidity will taste sour, acerbic, particularly at low alcoholic strength, and can taste very dry even with higher amounts of residual sugar, but, given the inverse relationship with pH, these wines will have much lower risk of microbial spoilage. High acidity can also increase the bitter taste and astringent sensation of tannins in medium- or full-bodied reds and make such wines taste hard and harsh.

Maintaining acidity and pH balance is therefore critical to making sound wines particularly that these parameters change, perhaps significantly, throughout winemaking.

Let's first review some general concepts in acid chemistry towards gaining a better understanding what acidity and pH measurements can tell us about the state of the wine, and what actions to take to make corrections in cases of deficiencies or excesses.

7.1 GENERAL CONCEPTS IN ACID CHEMISTRY

We'll get technical here for just a bit and refresh you on some high school-level chemical principles that may now seem like graduate-level material since those years. But this is important, so try and stick with it.

An acid is a substance — a molecule or an ion — capable of donating a proton, i.e., a hydrogen ion (H^+). This ability to donate protons is referred to as dissociation. Acidity is the concentration of that substance in a solution, such as juice or wine. But acids at the same concentration can have significantly different strengths because each acid dissociates to a lesser or greater extent. For example, hydrochloric acid (HCl) is a very strong acid because it is able to dissociate completely and donate all protons. All acids in juice and wine are weak acids, which means they only donate protons partially. Strengths of acids is measured in pH.

If we define an acid with the general chemical formula HA to represent a substance with a proton (H^+) and the rest of the molecule (an anion) as A^-, we can represent the dissociation using the following chemical equation:

$$HA \leftrightharpoons H^+ + A^-$$

This equation states that an acid in an aqueous solution will dissociate into its protons and anions until an equilibrium is reached. This means that a solution made up of a weak acid comprises all three components: molecules of undissociated or free acid (HA), protons (H^+) and anions (A^-). The right-and-left-pointing arrows ($\leftrightharpoons$) denote partial dissociation and equilibrium.

If HA is a strong acid like HCl, then HCl would dissociate practically completely into protons (H^+) and chloride ions (Cl^-) and the chemical equation is represented as follows with the right-pointing arrow ($\rightarrow$) denoting complete dissociation:

$$HCl \rightarrow H^+ + Cl^-$$

It is that ability of acids to donate protons that determines their strengths, and each acid's ability to donate a proton is characterized by a dissociation constant, or pK_a, and the smaller the pK_a, the stronger the acid. Tartaric, malic and lactic acids, the three most important acids in winemaking, have pK_a values of 2.98, 3.48 and 3.86 [1], respectively, which makes tartaric acid the strongest of the three. For comparison, HCl has a pK_a of –7.0 [2].

Therefore, two acids at the same concentration can have different strengths based on the amounts of protons released. The concentration of protons, denoted $[H^+]$, in a defined volume of solution is measured in moles (M). Since $[H^+]$ numbers tend to be very small, for example, 0.0000001 M in pure water (a very weak acid) or 0.0005 M in a typical wine, these concentrations are best expressed using a base 10 logarithm, and more specifically as the negative of the base 10 logarithm since the logarithm of numbers smaller than 1 are negative. Therefore now we can denote the strength of an acid, or pH, as a function of the concentration of protons as per the following equation:

$$pH = -log_{10}[H^+]$$

Water then has a pH of $-\log_{10}(0.0000001)$ or 7.0 while an acid with $[H^+]=0.0005$ has a pH of $-\log_{10}(0.0005)$ or 3.3. Solutions with a pH below 7 are said to be acidic while those with a pH above 7 are said to be alkaline (or basic). A solution of sodium hydroxide (NaOH) is an example of an alkaline solution. Grape juice and wine are generally in the pH range 3–4. And looking back at tartaric, malic and lactic acids and their respective pK_a values, we see that, *at the same concentration*, a tartaric acid solution would have a lower pH than a solution of malic acid, which in turn would have a lower pH than a solution of lactic acid. This is why tartaric acid is best when wanting to lower pH in must, as we'll see in Section 7.5.

Given the inverse relationship between $[H^+]$ and pH, as the acidity or $[H^+]$ of a solution increases, pH decreases; similarly, as the acidity or $[H^+]$ of a solution decreases, pH increases.

Monoacids are acids that have a single proton they can donate. Many acids, including those found in grape juice and wine, are di-acids or tri-acids that have two or three protons, respectively. Tartaric acid, the major acid in wine, is an example of a di-acid; citric acid found in tiny amounts in grape juice is an example of a tri-acid. Each proton in a multi-acid molecule or ion have successively higher pK_a values. For example, the second pK_a values for tartaric and citric acids are 4.34 and 4.76 [1], respectively, and since these pK_a values are greater than must or wine pH, the acids only dissociate their second protons minimally.

Let's consider a general di-acid HAH, or simply as H_2A. In solution, the di-acid first donates a proton according to its first pK_a, then the second proton according to its second pK_a as the pH of the solution increases. The dissociation equilibrium equation can be written as follows:

$$H_2A \rightleftharpoons H^+ + HA^- \rightleftharpoons 2H^+ + A^{2-}$$

If we denote tartaric acid simply as H_2T where T represents its anion, we can write the above equilibrium equation for tartaric acid and its ions and to include the first and second pK_a values as follows:

$$H_2T \quad \overset{pK_{a1}=2.98}{\rightleftharpoons} \quad H^+ \quad + \quad HT^- \quad \overset{pK_{a2}=4.34}{\rightleftharpoons} \quad 2H^+ \quad + \quad T^{2-}$$

If we wanted to know the concentration of tartaric acid, that would be the sum of the concentrations of molecular tartaric acid (H_2T) and its ionic form, bitartrate ions (HT^-), since it has an undissociated proton that can be donated; pH would measure all dissociated protons, mostly from the dissociation of H_2T and a very small amount from the dissociation of HT^-.

Why is this all important?

Once we look at the chemistry of weak acids in juice and wine, you will get a better appreciation of their relative strengths, why we will favor one acid over another, and how tartaric acid behaves when wine is subjected to cold temperatures. It will also help us understand in Chapter 8 the very important chemistry of sulfur dioxide (SO_2) and its role in winemaking; SO_2 is in fact an acid in solution.

7

Let's look at one last important concept in acid chemistry — buffering — a concept that throws off many winemakers when trying to rationalize inconsistent acid or pH adjustments vis-à-vis expected results.

If you were to add a strong acid to an acid solution, you would see a significant decrease in pH as vast amounts of protons are released. But juice and wine are solutions comprising weak acids, and the way weak acids behave in solutions is more complex. We'll keep it simple here.

Because of the weak-acid composition and chemistry of juice and wine, you may add some amounts of acid and quite possibly see no change in pH. You keep adding more acid, still no change, and then at some point pH finally starts dropping. This is due to a phenomenon in weak-acid chemistry known as buffering, and must and wine are buffer solutions. Because of buffering, you may not always see a drop in pH when acidifying for the specific purpose of dropping pH in, for example, a high-pH must, or you may not see a rise in pH when deacidifying high-acidity must.

7.2 TOTAL ACIDITY AND PH

As we have just learned, acidity refers to the concentration of acids while pH is a measure of the concentration of dissociated protons and therefore a measure of the strength of all acids in a solution.

Grape juice and wine are very complex solutions that contain many acids, both organic and inorganic, in varying concentrations and of varying strengths.

Organic acids comprise fixed acids and volatile acids. Fixed acids are those that we can taste but which have no smell, while volatile acids are those that we can taste and smell. Tartaric and malic acids are the major naturally occurring fixed acids in grapes with much smaller amounts of citric acid. There are also significant amounts of other acids, such as gluconic and glucuronic acids, in grapes affected by *Botrytis cinerea*, a fungus responsible for grey rot (a spoilage infection) and noble rot, so-called because it can turn grapes into superlative sweet, dessert wines. In wine, lactic and succinic acids are other important fixed acids. There are many, many other acids, such as phenolic acids and amino acids, present in very small amounts but which play a significant role in wine chemistry. Acetic acid is the major volatile acid naturally occurring in grapes, found in tiny amounts in sound grapes but in more significant amounts in spoiled grapes or wines that have been excessively exposed to air and affected by acetic acid bacteria.

Inorganic acids include carbonic acid, the acid due to the presence of residual carbon dioxide (CO_2) gas dissolved in wine, sulfurous acid (H_2SO_3) from the addition of sulfite (a preservative, described in Chapter 8) or from yeast metabolism, and sulfuric acid (H_2SO_4) resulting from the oxidation of sulfurous acid.

The sum of all these acids in grape juice or wine is referred to as total titratable acidity. For simplicity, winemakers refer to total titratable acidity as total acidity, or TA, although this term is not quite correct technically because, to a chemist, total acidity also includes neutralized acids in their salt forms. For example, potassium (K^+), an abundantly and naturally occurring mineral will bind to bitartrate ions (HT^-) from dissociated tartaric acid to form potassium bitartrate, the potassium salt of tartaric acid. But it is clear in winemaking that "total acidity" means "total titratable acidity."

Given that these acids have varying strengths and are present in different concentrations, expressing a measurement of acidity would be complicated, and therefore, the measurement of total acidity (TA) is simply expressed as if all acids are tartaric acid since this is the major acid in wine. The component of total acidity which is volatile is known as volatile acidity, or VA, and is expressed as if all acids are acetic acid since this is the major volatile acid in wine. Figure 7.1 summarizes this terminology.

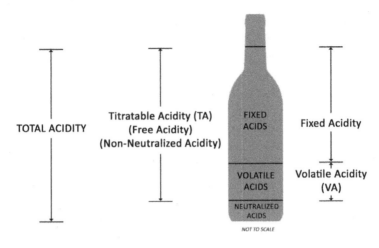

Figure 7.1: Acidity terminology used in winemaking

TA is expressed in g/L or as a weight-to-volume percentage, which means g/100 mL. TA numbers in the literature often specify that TA is expressed as "tartaric acid equivalents" since other countries use different acids as the reference, for example, France uses sulfuric acid. A wine with a TA of 6.5 g/L or 0.65% expressed as tartaric acid equivalents means that if you were to convert all the acids to tartaric acid, the wine would measure 6.5 g of tartaric acid per liter of wine, or 0.65%, i.e., 0.65 g/100mL.

VA is expressed in g/L, but most often in mg/L since values tend to be well below 1 g/L.

The definition of pH does not change since it is a measurement of the amount of dissociated protons — it does not distinguish protons among the many acids. However, juice and wine are complex solutions that also contain significant amounts of potassium translocated from the soil into berries and into wine, and therefore protons (H^+) are "exchanged" for potassium ions (K^+) and raise the pH accordingly. And, for example, the greater the amount of rainfall in a poor vintage, the greater the amount of potassium in grapes and consequently the higher the pH.

Table 7.1 lists recommended ranges for TA and pH in must (juice) and for different styles of wines from vinifera grapes. These ranges will be significantly different when making wine from hybrid or Native American grapes, or from grapes from cool- or cold-climate growing areas or from a very poor vintage where TA of grapes can often exceed 12 g/L, making it a challenge to create those styles of wines. Always go by taste, using these ranges as guidelines only, as other factors, namely, amount of residual sugar, tannins and alcohol, can affect the way acidity is perceived. You'll come to develop your own palate and taste; your numbers may become different from these guidelines, likely in a narrower range, and that's okay.

Table 7.1: Recommended TA and pH ranges for must (juice) and different styles of wines (divide TA by 10 to convert from g/L to %)

Style of wine	MUST	WINE	
	TA range (g/L)	TA range (g/L)	pH range
Dry white or rosé	5–10	5–8	3.1–3.4
Off-dry white or rosé	7–12	6–10	3.1–3.4
Light-bodied red	5–8	5–7	3.3–3.6
Full-bodied red	4–7	4–6	3.3–3.6

Reds generally have lower TA and higher pH than whites. Since reds have tannins, higher acidity could make those tannins taste very harsh; it's also one reason why reds are drunk at warmer temperatures — colder temperatures increase the sensation of acidity, which would in turn make tannins taste harsh. The challenge with reds is that the lower acidity means higher pH, and as pH increases, color becomes weaker and more unstable. Therefore it will be important to keep sight of both TA and pH throughout winemaking. There are also microbial management considerations at higher pH — we'll discuss those in Chapter 8.

7.3 MEASURING ACIDITY AND PH

Total acidity (TA) and pH should be measured at key control points or when a change in either is expected, or when making adjustments, for example, when increasing or decreasing acidity, to confirm those adjustments. Specifically, measurements should be made at a minimum at the following key control points or events:

- At the juice stage, following crushing or pressing

- After any acidification or deacidification treatment

- If you suspect a problem, for example, volatile acidity due bacterial infection

- At SO_2 control to determine how much sulfite to add (see Chapter 8)

- After alcoholic fermentation (see Chapter 11) and malolactic fermentation (see Chapter 12)

- After tartrate stabilization (see Sections 7.4.1 and 14.4)

- After any blending to confirm calculations (see Section 16.5)

- Before bottling as a final check (see Section 18.5)

Set aside a 200-mL sample in the refrigerator; you may need to come back to it later on to perform some extra analysis, for example, when doing a root-cause analysis.

TA is measured very easily and inexpensively by titration using an acid titration kit that includes: a 10-mL syringe, small beaker, a 10-mL pipette, phenolphthalein solution (a color indicator), and sodium hydroxide (NaOH) solution with a concentration of $0.1N$, $0.133N$ or $0.2N$. Either look for a kit with a 10-mL burette with a Teflon stopcock and optional stand, or simply replace the syringe with a more accurate burette to get more accurate results.

Titration involves adding NaOH to a must or wine sample until the acids are neutralized. There is a color change when the titration endpoint is reached: the color turns pink for whites or greenish for reds when using phenolphthalein as the indicator. The volume of NaOH dispensed to neutralize the acids is then used to determine TA.

The color change to pink for white samples is easy to detect although some wonder how deep a pink it should be — it should be a faint and persistent pink. The color change for red samples is more challenging because of the darker color. The sample turns a greyish color while adding NaOH, then a greenish color at the titration endpoint.

To obtain more accurate and more consistent results and avoid having to deal with color changes, forego the use of phenolphthalein and use instead a pH meter and titrate to an endpoint of 8.2. Why 8.2 and not the neutral endpoint of 7.0? Other winemaking regions of the world, for example, France, titrate to a neutral endpoint of 7.0. However, you'll recall that weak acids are somewhat more complicated; these behave differently than when dealing with strong acids, and the neutralization endpoint is actually closer to 8.2. In North America, the standard method is to titrate to an endpoint of 8.2.

To measure TA using a pH meter, transfer *exactly* 10 mL of must or *degassed* wine to a 100-mL beaker, and add *fresh distilled water* to bring the volume to about 50 mL. The amount of distilled water does not need to be precise. Your kit's instructions as to the sample volume and amount of water to add may be different, but the process is identical.

Fill the burette to the zero mark with NaOH solution. Insert the electrode of the pH meter into the sample and wait for the reading to stabilize. During titration, gently stir the sample to get a proper pH reading; either swirl the beaker, stir gently with the electrode, or use a magnetic stirrer.

Slowly open the burette over the beaker to start the flow of NaOH into the sample. You will notice the pH starting to rise slowly. Continue adding NaOH solution until the pH reaches about 6.0 or so, then close the burette and again open slightly to now deliver NaOH *one drop at a time*, waiting for the pH reading to stabilize between each drop. You have to be careful here as the pH will now shoot up very quickly to 8.2. When the pH reading hits 8.2, titration is complete. Read the volume of NaOH solution dispensed from the burette, and follow your kit's instructions to calculate TA. The calculation provided with kits assumes that you are using a NaOH solution with a given concentration, usually $0.1N$, $0.133N$ or $0.2N$. That calculation is based on the following formula that you can use for any NaOH concentration or sample volume:

$$TA\,(g/L) = \frac{75 \times mL\ NaOH \times N\ NaOH}{mL\ of\ sample}$$

Simply divide by 10 the result of the above calculation to express TA as a %; for example, 6.4 g/L can be expressed as 0.64%.

EXAMPLE 7.1

Calculating TA from titration

You used 8.5 mL of $0.1N$ NaOH to titrate a 10-mL sample of wine. Calculate TA, expressed in g/L as tartaric acid equivalents, as follows:

$$TA\,(g/L) = \frac{75 \times 8.5\;mL \times 0.1N}{10.0\;mL}$$

$$= 6.4\,g/L$$

Juice samples should be as clear as possible, or at least free of grape fragments or other heavy particulates, to get more accurate titration results. For wine samples, and more so for samples taken immediately after completion of fermentation, you will need to degas those to remove residual CO_2 that will otherwise skew your titration results by as much as 2 g/L. Carbonic acid from residual CO_2 will naturally dissipate over time from processing wine in your cellar, and therefore, it should not figure in your TA measurements. Follow the instructions outlined in Section 6.3 on how to degas wine samples, but degas a bit more volume than required for titration as the volume will reduce slightly as CO_2 is pulled out.

NaOH solution will lose its strength over time, therefore make sure to use a fresh solution not older than six months. Store the solution in a cool, dark place. If you suspect your NaOH solution is old and weak, or if you are no longer sure if it is $0.1N$ or $0.2N$, you can standardize — meaning, you can find out its strength — by titrating against potassium hydrogen phthalate (KHP), which is more stable and has a longer shelf-life than NaOH. You can substitute the KHP solution with a pH 4.01 buffer as most pH 4.01 reference solutions are $0.05N$ KHP.

To standardize your NaOH solution, titrate a 10-mL sample of $0.05N$, $0.1N$ or $0.2N$ KHP solution like you would a wine sample, then use the following formula to determine the actual concentration of the NaOH solution based on the volume dispensed:

$$Actual\;N\;NaOH = \frac{mL\;KHP \times N\;KHP}{mL\;NaOH}$$

Once you have determined the actual concentration of the NaOH solution, adjust your measured TA value using the following formula:

$$Corrected\ TA\ (g/L) = \frac{Measured\ TA \times Actual\ N\ NaOH}{Theoretical\ N\ NaOH}$$

EXAMPLE 7.2

Standardizing NaOH solution with KHP

You used 11.0 mL of "0.1N" NaOH to titrate a 10-mL sample of 0.1N KHP. Calculate the actual concentration of the NaOH solution as follows:

$$Actual\ N\ NaOH = \frac{10.0\ mL \times 0.1N}{11.0\ mL}$$

$$= 0.091N$$

If you had measured a TA of 6.4 g/L with the weaker "0.1N" NaOH solution, calculate your corrected TA is as follows:

$$Corrected\ TA\ (g/L) = \frac{6.4\ g/L \times 0.091N}{0.1N}$$

$$= 5.8\ g/L$$

Volatile acidity (VA) is measured by a technique called Cash distillation or by enzymatic analysis; these involve equipment, analytical techniques and skills beyond the scope of this book. For additional information on measuring VA, please consult [3].

pH is measured with a pH meter. There are three types of pH meters; pen-style portable meter with integrated electrode, benchtop meter with separate electrode, and portable meter with separate electrode. Benchtop models are pricier as they usually include more features, but you must bring wine samples to your lab to perform measurements. You can take measurements right in your cellar or winemaking area with a pen-style or portable meter; this may be an important consideration if you regularly measure many samples in one session. There are portable pH meters with Bluetooth capability that automatically record measurements for later upload to your electronic log book.

Modern meters are equipped with automatic temperature compensation (ATC) that adjust pH to compensate for temperature differences between a sample and calibration temperature. Some benchtop models may have a separate thermometer probe. pH measurements are usually taken at a standard temperature of 25 °C (77 °F). Measurements will be slightly higher at colder temperatures, but a pH meter with ATC will make the needed correction. If your meter does not have ATC, adjust the temperature of the sample up or down to 25 °C (77 °F).

And since pH measurements are absolutely critical in winemaking, spend a little more money to buy a meter having an accuracy of ±0.01. A meter with an accuracy of ±0.1 means that a measured pH of 3.4, for example, can be anywhere between 3.3 and 3.5, and this being a log scale, there is a big difference. A meter with an accuracy of ±0.01 that reads a pH of 3.40, for example, means that the pH can be anywhere between 3.39 and 3.41 — a much narrower range. Inexpensive pH meters may have a resolution of 0.01 and an accuracy of ±0.1, meaning that, although the meter reads, for example, 3.40, the actual pH is still between 3.3 and 3.5.

To measure pH with a pH meter (with ATC or the sample is brought to standard temperature), dip the electrode in the sample and *stir gently* either with the electrode or with a magnetic stirrer. Wait for the reading to stabilize — it should take no more than 30 seconds. If the reading drifts without ever stabilizing, the electrode is either out of calibration, dirty or no longer good. Electrodes can last easily two years or more when properly maintained.

PROPER USE, CARE AND MAINTENANCE OF PH METERS

Following are some calibration, usage, maintenance and storage tips to get a faster response time from your electrode and meter, more accurate results and prolonged life.

1. Calibrate your electrode and meter as often as you can, or at least once a week, making sure to calibrate at the calibration temperature of your buffer solutions, usually 25 °C (77 °F). If your meter has 2-point calibration, calibrate using a 7.01 buffer and a 3.00 or 4.01 buffer; if it has multipoint calibration, also calibrate with a 10.01 buffer. Calibration points should "bracket" the pH of solutions you'll be measuring. Wine will normally be in the pH range 3–4, but you'll also be doing a lot of TA titrations and measuring to an endpoint of 8.2.

2. Double-check calibration using a potassium bitartrate (KHT, cream of tartar) buffer with a pH of 3.55 at 25 °C (77 °F). To prepare a 3.55 pH KHT buffer, add approximately ¼ tsp KHT to 50 mL of distilled water, mix thoroughly for several minutes, and let undissolved crystals settle, then decant into an appropriate beaker and measure the pH; it should read 3.55±0.04. If the reading is outside this range, then the electrode/meter is out of calibration.

3. Verify the condition of the electrode by measuring its offset and slope percentage.

   To measure the offset and slope percentage, switch the meter to mV (potential) mode, and measure and record readings for 4.01 and 7.01 buffers. The offset is simply the measured mV in the 7.01 buffer and should be between −30 and +30. The slope percentage (%) should be in the range 85–105% and is calculated as follows using measured mV values of the 4.01 and 7.01 buffers, $mV_{4.01}$ and $mV_{7.01}$, respectively:

$$\text{Slope percentage (\%)} = \frac{(mV_{4.01} - mV_{7.01})}{177.48} \times 100\%$$

   For example, if you measured $mV_{4.01}$ and $mV_{7.01}$ to be 187.1 and 17.3, respectively, then the offset is 17.3 and the slope percentage is:

$$\text{Slope percentage (\%)} = \frac{(187.1 - 17.3)}{177.48} \times 100\%$$

$$= 95.7\%$$

   The offset is between −30 and +30 and the slope percentage is within 85–105%, which confirm that the electrode is in good condition.

4. Store the electrode wet in a storage solution; never let an electrode dry. If you expect some delays between taking measurements, dip the electrode in tap water or storage solution. Never store an electrode in distilled water; the electrolyte solution in the electrode will become depleted of ions and the electrode may no longer work properly.

5. Clean the electrode on a regular basis depending on frequency of usage and types of wines analyzed. Richly colored red wines will tend to stain the electrode and skew measurements, and therefore, if you analyze mostly reds, clean the electrode more frequently. You can use a 0.1N (0.1M) HCl (hydrochloric acid) solution with an optional pre-treatment using a 0.1N NaOH solution to loosen adsorbed "films," or use a cleaning solution specifically formulated for this purpose.

6. If your electrode is of the refillable type, make sure that the fill level is just below the fill hole. Use a reference electrolyte solution specifically formulated for your electrode model, for example, "3.5M KCl" for double-junction electrodes or "3.5M KCl + AgCl" for single-junction electrodes. During measurements, remove the fill cap to allow a free flow of ions in the electrolyte solution.

7. Rinse the electrode with distilled water in between readings. Shake off any excess water before immersing the probe in the next sample; do *not* dry with a paper towel or tissue as it can affect the performance of the electrode and possibly shorten its life.

7.4 UNDERSTANDING HOW ACIDS CHANGE DURING WINEMAKING

In making great wines — consistently — you need a good understanding of what happens to the various acids during winemaking to better predict changes and how these will impact your desired style of wine, and also so that you can better formulate any required TA or pH adjustment strategy. TA and pH adjustments is one of the most complicated topics to put into practice.

Here we look first at the chemistry of potassium bitartrate as it is one of the most fundamental principles to understanding acidity, and TA and pH changes in wine, then we will look at how specific acids change and transform, and how new ones are created.

7.4.1 THE CHEMISTRY OF POTASSIUM BITARTRATE

 This section deals with some advanced chemistry principles. You can skip this section if you so choose, but it is essential if you want to be able to better predict acid and pH changes.

Must is supersaturated in (meaning there is an excess of) potassium bitartrate, which we simply abbreviate to KHT (this is not its chemical formula). KHT forms when naturally occurring potassium ions (K^+) react with bitartrate ions (HT^-), the anions of tartaric acid (H_2T).

$$H_2T \overset{pK_{a1}\,=\,2.98}{\rightleftharpoons} H^+ \;+\; HT^- \overset{pK_{a2}\,=\,4.34}{\rightleftharpoons} 2H^+ \;+\; T^{2-}$$

$$K^+ + HT^- \rightarrow KHT \downarrow$$

KHT is rather insoluble but much more so with increasing alcohol and decreasing temperature. And therefore, excess KHT will start to crystallize and precipitate tartrate crystals, or simply tartrates (cream of tartar), which look like tiny shards of glass. You may have witnessed tartrates in a bottle of white wine long forgotten at the back of the fridge. This is why wines — generally most whites and rosés — have to be stabilized against the possibility of tartrates forming. This is referred to as tartrate stabilization and is accomplished by cold stabilization, i.e., chilling the wine down to close to freezing temperature. As potassium bitartrate becomes more insoluble with increasing alcohol, you cannot expect to cold stabilize juice (i.e., pre-fermentation) and hope for a stable wine — the wine will still likely be unstable post fermentation.

Tartrate stabilization can also be accomplished using protective colloids that inhibit tartrate formation. Section 14.4 describes how to evaluate a wine's tartrate stability and the procedure to stabilize using either method.

During processing and wine aging, KHT will continue to form as long as there is sufficient potassium and bitartrate available, dropping tartrates if the wine is subjected to colder temperatures. This crystallization and precipitation causes a drop in tartaric acid and TA and a *change* in pH. Given the drop in TA, tartrate stabilization is often used specifically to reduce TA in high-acid wines. Red wines are less impacted than whites as tannins interfere with KHT formation.

Notice that we said that KHT crystallization and precipitation cause a "change" in pH; it does not necessarily increase as you would expect when TA decreases. Whether pH increases or decreases depends on the pH of the wine. Let's take a closer look as this is an important factor when trying to predict TA and pH changes.

From the equilibrium equation for tartaric acid, we see that the amount of bitartrate ions (HT⁻) is a function of pH; this is also illustrated in Figure 7.2. And here is the most relevant and interesting part: As pH increases, HT⁻ concentration increases and reaches a maximum at pH 3.65, and decreases from thereon. This means that, at pH below 3.65, as HT⁻ and K⁺ form KHT and crystals form and precipitate, TA decreases as tartaric acid drops; however, counterintuitively, pH also decreases as tartaric acid will want to re-establish its equilibrium and release more HT⁻ and protons (H⁺), and more protons means that pH will drop.

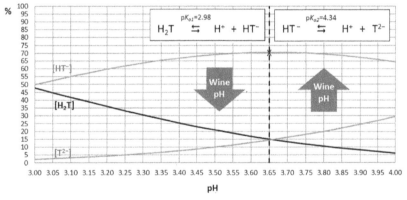

Figure 7.2: Relative concentrations of H_2T, HT^- and T^{2-} in wine pH range

At pH above 3.65, as HT⁻ and K⁺ form KHT and crystals form and precipitate, TA here too decreases as tartaric acid drops, however, HT⁻ will want to re-establish equilibrium by decreasing tartrate ions (T^{2-}) and protons, and less protons means that pH will increase.

Let's recap in practical terms this bit of confusing behavior to understand exactly what to expect during cold stabilization.

- When wine pH is *lower* than 3.65, both TA and pH will decrease during cold stabilization.

- When wine pH is *greater* than 3.65, TA will decrease and pH will increase during cold stabilization.

The drop in TA and change in pH, and the amount of tartrates that form depend mainly on the relative amount of tartaric acid that makes up TA, the amount of potassium ions, and stabilization temperature. This means that a wine with a very high proportion of malic acid may not have sufficient tartaric acid to cause tartrates; and a wine with a high proportion of tartaric acid but with little potassium will likely throw very little tartrates. This poses an added challenge for home winemakers as we cannot easily and inexpensively measure the relative proportions of individual acids and the concentration of potassium, and therefore, cold stabilization really is an art here.

7.4.2 HOW ACIDS CHANGE AND TRANSFORM DURING WINEMAKING

Now that we understand potassium bitartrate chemistry, we know that KHT crystallizes and precipitates first during the alcoholic fermentation (AF) as alcohol production increases. This causes a drop in tartaric acid and TA, but which will be offset by succinic acid, a new acid produced by yeast during AF. Some specific yeast strains can also metabolize significant amounts of malic acid and drop TA further as we will see in Section 7.5.2.

In red winemaking, and to a much lesser extent in white winemaking, wines are put through a second fermentation called malolactic fermentation (see Chapter 12), or MLF, where specific bacteria are added to enable the microbiological conversion of harsher malic acid into softer lactic acid. MLF results in a drop in TA and increase in pH proportional to the amount of malic acid converted.

And lastly, just before bottling, wines, and whites more so because they are bottled sooner than reds, are cold stabilized to further prevent tartrates from forming in bottles.

Now, if you are dealing with must with a TA just slightly over your desired TA, you can expect an overall decrease in TA due to MLF (if done) and cold stabilization, and may therefore not require any adjustments if you predict that TA will fall to within the desired range. But if you are dealing with must with low TA, for example, 4 g/L, TA will drop but only min-imally given the smaller amounts of tartaric and malic acids, and therefore, adding tartaric acid will raise TA (but keep in mind that there will be a slight decrease during cold stabilization). And if you have must with very high TA, say above 10 g/L, you likely have a situation of high malic acid and low tartaric acid, in which case you can expect a large drop in malic acid during MLF (if done) and possibly no change in tartaric acid, in which case you may need to add tartaric acid to compensate for the large drop in malic acid.

7

Tartrate stabilization using protective colloids does not impact TA or pH.

Let's tackle the topics of how to manage acids and pH and how to make necessary adjustments with some examples.

7.5 ADJUSTING ACIDITY AND PH

In a perfect vintage, grapes are harvested at the ideal level of ripeness where taste, SG/Brix/PA, TA and pH are in perfect balance. But all too often Mother Nature gives us a late start to the growing season, perhaps a cool season or excessive rainfall, and one or more parameters that are out of balance.

Acidity can be very low in a very hot vintage as much of the malic acid in grapes has been metabolized, whereas acidity can be very high in a poor vintage because excessive malic acid has not been metabolized to the extent that it should have. And therefore, low-acid juice may require the addition of an acid to boost TA, a practice known as acidification (also as acidula-tion), and high-acid juice may require the reduction or removal of one or more acids, or deacidification, to lower TA. Acidification and deacidifica-tion are also used to decrease or increase pH, respectively.

But as home winemakers we are only equipped to measure TA (and pH), not the concentration of individual acids. This makes choosing and im-plementing acidification and deacidification techniques tricky as we have to guess on the relative concentrations of tartaric and malic acids (Figure 7.3) and predict how those acids and TA and pH will change throughout winemaking and end up with a final TA within a desired range. Different

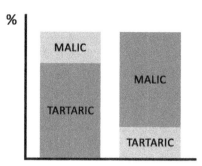

Figure 7.3: Musts or wines with
different relative tartaric and malic
concentrations will require different approaches to adjusting TA or
pH

acidification and deacidification approaches are required depending on
the relative concentrations of tartaric and malic acids.

 *If you are inclined to try enzymatic assaying, you can use Vin-
metrica's SC-50 MLF Analyzer Kit to quantify malic acid (see
Section 12.5).*

And given the complexity of weak-acid chemistry in buffered solutions,
these techniques seldom yield textbook results — the addition of 1 g/L of
tartaric does not always cause a 0.1 drop in pH, or any drop for that matter.
And, as we have seen, a drop in TA due to cold stabilization does not necessarily translate into an increase in pH. It can seem like an overwhelming
challenge managing TA and pH — it is!

The same goes for online calculators that help you figure out your acid
adjustments — these may not take these factors into consideration, and
will therefore often yield results much different from expected theoretical
results.

There will be a lot of guesswork involved in making adjustments, hence
why bench trials are absolutely necessary. Here are tips to improve your
chances of balancing TA, pH and taste when making adjustments.

TIPS FOR ACIDIFYING AND DEACIDIFYING

1. Don't make acidity adjustments with the sole objective of hitting some target numbers. Yes, do use the numbers to guide your adjustments, but be sure to let your palate be the ultimate deciding factor.

2. Always conduct bench trials (see Chapter 5) with different rates of addition to quantify TA and pH changes and to assess taste impacts. For example, if you calculated that you need to add 1.5 g/L of tartaric acid, conduct bench trials adding 1.0, 1.25, 1.5, 1.75 and 2.0 g/L of tartaric acid.

2. As the volume of must to be treated is an estimate in red wine-making, once you have determined the rate of addition from your bench trials, add only half the calculated amount to treat your batch, then re-measure TA and pH and adjust the second addition accordingly, much like we did with sugar adjustments in Section 6.4. You want to avoid, for example, adding too much acid during acidification and then having to deacidify. Over-processing can compromise quality of the wine.

3. Always adjust TA in *must*, i.e., before fermentation, especially when "large" adjustments are necessary, and only make small adjustments in *wine*. We'll come back in just a moment on this very important point of when to make large versus small acidity adjustments.

4. When deacidifying, keep the juice at low temperature to favor carbonate salt formation and precipitation.

5. Do not add tartaric acid or even a small amount of potassium carbonate or bicarbonate to wine after cold stabilization as you may run the risk of tartrates forming again, perhaps in bottles.

Table 7.2 summarizes recommended treatments to address various scenarios of low/high TA and low/high pH discussed in the following sections.

Table 7.2: Summary of options and recommended actions for adjusting low/high TA and/or low/high pH

Condition	Primary objectives	Suspected likely causes	Options / Recommended actions
Low TA (low pH)	Increase TA (minimize decrease in pH)	Low tartaric/malic acid Low potassium	• No adjustments pre-ferment • Re-evaluate post-ferment
Low TA (high pH)	Increase TA (decrease pH)	Low tartaric/malic acid	• Acidify with: 　▸ Tartaric acid 　▸ Tartaric/malic blend if no MLF 　▸ Lactic acid for fine-tuning wine 　▸ Citric acid if no MLF • Blend with high-TA/low-pH juice or wine
High TA (low pH)	Reduce TA (increase pH)	High tartaric acid	• Deacidify with a carbonate salt + cold stabilize • Cold stabilize only (pH decreases if less than 3.65) • Blend with low-TA/high-pH juice or wine • Ameliorate
		High malic acid	• Ferment using malic-degrading yeast • Perform MLF (style permitting) • Blend with low-TA/high-pH juice or wine • Ameliorate
High TA and High pH	Reduce pH Reduce TA (if needed)	High tartaric acid, possibly high potassium	• Acidify with tartaric acid + MLF + cold stabilize • Blend with low-TA/low-pH juice or wine
		High malic acid, possibly high potassium	• Acidify with tartaric acid + ferment with malic-degrading yeast + MLF (style permitting) + cold stabilize • Blend with low-TA/low-pH juice or wine

WHEN IS THE BEST TIME TO MAKE ACIDITY ADJUSTMENTS?

Small acidity adjustments in wine can be beneficial for optimizing balance, however, winemakers will always recommend to make "large" acidity adjustments at the juice (must) stage and only small adjustments in wine, often citing that acids become better integrated over the course of fermentation and aging. But what does this really mean?

First, a large acid addition in juice is preferred as it decreases pH, which, in turn, increases microbial stability. And when a significant deacidification is required, the rise in pH increases the microbial risk, however, the risk is much greater in wine than in juice.

A large deacidification in wine using carbonate salts results in large amounts of CO_2 that can hasten release of volatile aroma substances and potentially strip wine of subtle aromas, especially in delicate whites. Deacidification may also require handling juice or wine for relatively long durations, and therefore, with wine being more fragile, it is best performed pre-AF. And deacidification at the juice stage helps preserve natural potassium and maintain the sensation of volume on the palate, particularly in whites. Conversely, deacidification in a young wine will give a more slender style as more potassium is precipitated during fermentation.

We have seen in Section 7.4 how acids change during winemaking, and one of those important changes is the formation and precipitation of KHT as ethanol production increases during AF. If you make any significant tartaric acid addition post AF, you can then expect further large changes in TA and pH, depending on the availability of potassium, as the more-insoluble KHT will continue precipitating and especially at colder temperatures.

As for better integration during aging, tartaric acid slowly loses some of its tartness due to esterification [4], a very slow reaction where a portion of tartaric acid reacts with ethanol to form ethyl esters (e.g., ethyl ester tartrate), which have a mellowing effect on acidity. A large or late tartaric acid addition can delay or offset esterification.

Since additions of tartaric acid to wine can cause problems as described above, other acids may provide better choices when late adjustments are needed. Malic and lactic acid are fine, as is citric acid if no MLF has occurred or is planned.

7.5.1 ACIDIFICATION

Tartaric acid is invariably the acid of choice to increase TA or reduce pH since it is naturally occurring in grapes and is the strongest of wine acids, and has an immediately perceptible impact on taste. And it is not metabolized under normal winemaking conditions by yeast or bacteria, and therefore it is seldom a cause of spoilage.

Most books will instruct you to add 1.0 g/L to increase TA by 1.0 g/L; however, if you want to retain as much of that tartaric acid you will be adding, you may need to increase additions by up to 2.0 g/L, maybe more, to allow for some potassium bitartrate salt (KHT) to form and drop during AF and cold stabilization. And considerably more tartaric acid than expected may be required for dropping pH in a high-pH must due to buffering.

One way to circumvent tartrates from forming and precipitating is to add malic acid *if the wine will not be put through MLF* (see Chapter 12) as malic acid does not form an insoluble salt like tartaric acid. Malic acid will be converted into lactic acid if the wine goes through MLF — a deacidification technique we explore in see Section 7.5.2.

Lactic acid is recommended for fine-tuning *wine* (as opposed to juice) to avoid possible tartrates when the wine has already been cold stabilized and when malic acid is not desirable if the wine has already undergone MLF. Lactic acid is the softest of the wine acids and is therefore ideal for small tweaks in taste. Lactic acid is not recommended for increasing TA in must as high lactic acid levels (from the addition and that which would be produced during the MLF) can inhibit lactic acid bacteria and MLF.

Citric acid is the acid of choice for acidifying fruit or country wines and white wines because it is the second strongest after tartaric acid and much smaller amounts are needed to increase TA — citric acid is also a lot cheaper. But citric acid or acid blends containing citric acid are not recommended in grape juice or wine that will be put through MLF as malic-converting bacteria will also metabolize citric acid into acetic acid, which will increase VA, and a substance known as diacetyl, which gives wine a buttery taste.

Table 7.3 lists the amount of each acid required to increase TA by 1.0 g/L in tartaric acid equivalents. Due to buffering effects, conduct bench trials to determine impacts on pH. These acids can be dissolved directly in juice (must) or wine, or first in water when dissolution and mixing might be difficult, for example, in red must.

Table 7.3: Amounts of the various acids needed to increase TA by 1.0 g/L in tartaric acid equivalents

Acid to be added	Form	Amount (g/L)
Tartaric	Powder	1.0
Malic	Powder	0.9
Lactic	Liquid[1]	1.2–1.3
Citric	Powder	0.8

[1]Typically available as an 80–88% solution

Let's look at a couple of examples on making acid adjustments. You can make use of the downloadable worksheet at ModernHomeWinemaking. com to help you with these calculations.

EXAMPLE 7.3

Acidification with tartaric acid for the purpose of increasing TA

You just crushed 160 kg (350 lbs) of red grapes, then taken a sample to the lab and measured a TA of 3.5 g/L and a pH of 3.35. You have estimated a yield volume of approximately 100 L (25 gal).

You want to increase TA to 5.0 g/L, no more as you intend to make a richly tannic, full-bodied wine and you don't plan to cold stabilize the wine but you still expect a small drop in TA, maybe in the order of 0.5 g/L, due to KHT precipitation during fermentation. You decide to go with tartaric acid and shoot for a TA of 5.5 g/L, an increase of 2.0 g/L that requires 2.0 g/L of tartaric acid. We'll add it in two steps to avoid over-acidifying.

Calculate the expected *total* amount of tartaric acid needed:

Expected total amount of tartaric acid to add(g)

$$= 2.0 \, g/L \times 100 \, L$$

$$= 200 \, g$$

<u>Add half that amount</u>, i.e., 100 g (3.5 oz), to the must and mix thoroughly, take a new sample and re-measure TA and pH. Theoretically, TA should be 4.5 g/L, which is half the desired increase of 2.0 g/L, but let's say you measured 4.7 g/L — this means that your estimated volume is less than 100 L (25 gal). Adjust the second addition accordingly knowing that the first addition increased TA by 1.2 g/L with 0.8 g/L to go:

$$\textit{Amount of tartaric acid to add } (g) = 100 \, g \times \frac{0.8}{1.2}$$

$$= 66.7 \, g$$

Add the 66.7 g (2.4 oz) of tartaric acid to the must and mix thoroughly, take a new sample and re-measure TA and pH; TA should be 5.5 g/L dead on and the pH still in the desired range if it has dropped.

Your total amount of tartaric acid you added is about 167 g (5.9 oz) instead of the planned 200 g (7.0 oz) owing to the smaller volume than estimated. Just like when adjusting SG (see Section 6.4), you can now estimate the juice yield more accurately using these results:

$$\textit{Estimated volume } (L) = 100 \, L \times \frac{167}{200}$$

$$= 84 \, L \; (22 \, gal)$$

Your expected yield is therefore 84 L (22 gal) and all subsequent additions (e.g. tannins, clarifying agent, etc.) should be based on this volume.

Now let's say that the measured TA after adding half the tartaric addition is lower than the expected 4.5 g/L; let's say you measured 4.3 g/L, which means that half the tartaric acid amount, i.e., 100 g (3.5 oz), increased TA by only 0.8 g/L and that you still need to add 1.2 g/L. Adjust the second addition as follows:

$$\textit{Amount of tartaric acid to add } (g) = 100 \, g \times \frac{1.2}{0.8}$$

$$= 150 \, g$$

Your total here is 250 g (8.8 oz) instead of the planned 200 g (7.0 oz) owing to the larger volume than estimated. You can now estimate the juice yield more accurately using these results:

$$Estimated\ volume\ (L) = 100\ L \times \frac{250}{200}$$

$$= 125\ L\ (33\ gal)$$

Your expected yield is therefore 125 L (33 gal) and all subsequent additions should be based on this volume.

7

EXAMPLE 7.4

Acidification with tartaric acid for the purpose of decreasing pH

You just crushed a load of red grapes, taken a sample to the lab, and measured a TA of 6.0 g/L and a pH of 3.80. TA is good but the pH is a bit high — you wish to reduce it to around 3.60.

Since tartaric acid is the acid that has the biggest impact on pH, the best approach here is to run bench trials with stepwise additions of tartaric acid as a 10% solution and monitoring pH changes to determine how much tartaric acid is needed to drop pH from 3.80 to around 3.60.

Example 5.2 in Section 5.3 describes the procedure for running these bench trials. Since you know about buffering now, don't make any assumptions as we did in Example 5.2; you may need more tartaric acid than expected (i.e., more than 1.0 g/L for each 0.1 pH drop).

If, as in Example 5.2, your TA is 6.0 g/L and you determined that you need 2.5 g/L of tartaric acid, this raises TA to 8.5 g/L — somewhat high for a red wine, particularly a tannic red. But you will likely put the wine through MLF, and that will reduce TA although it will raise pH. The extent of TA and pH changes depend on the amount of malic acid. If TA is still too high after MLF, you have the option of cold stabilizing the wine.

If this were a white wine, a TA of 8.5 g/L might be just okay knowing that it will drop once the wine is chilled at the cold stabilization stage. Predicting pH from cold stabilization is tricky and is best estimated by doing bench trials.

7.5.2 DEACIDIFICATION

Deacidification is used to lower TA or increase pH by reducing or removing one or more acids. It can be achieved by chemical means using carbonate salts, by chilling wine, by microbiological means using malic-degrading yeast or bacteria, or by blending or amelioration.

CHEMICAL DEACIDIFICATION USING CARBONATE SALTS

Chemical deacidification involves adding a carbonate salt, either potassium carbonate (K_2CO_3), potassium bicarbonate ($KHCO_3$), or calcium carbonate ($CaCO_3$). Let's look at the reaction chemistry of these salts in must (or wine) to understand some of their limitations and implementation considerations.

When a carbonate salt is added to must or wine, it dissolves and ionizes into potassium (K^+) or calcium (Ca^{2+}) ions and carbonate (CO_3^{2-}) ions. Carbonate ions react with protons (H^+) to form water and CO_2, then potassium or calcium ions neutralize tartaric acid anions (HT^- or T^{2-}) and form potassium bitartrate (KHT) or calcium tartrate (CaT), respectively.

Given the relatively higher pK_a of malic acid and greater solubility of its salts, carbonate salts used in deacidification only neutralize and drop out tartaric acid, which means that these will have little or no effect in high-TA musts due to malic acid. High-malic musts need different deacidification techniques.

 High-TA musts due to both high tartaric acid and malic acid can be deacidified by a technique known as double-salt precipitation. It uses a special calcium carbonate formulation, found in such products as Acidex and Sihadex, which neutralizes both acids in part by forming calcium tartrate malate — a double salt. This technique is risky and very difficult to implement in home winemaking. You can research this technique further if you are so inclined to give it a try.

As we know now, KHT becomes more insoluble with increasing alcohol and decreasing temperature. This means that excess KHT drops tartrate crystals during fermentation and cold stabilization.

CaT is unstable and can take a very long time to drop crystals, possibly long after wine has been bottled. But unlike KHT, CaT does not impact TA any further, if and when it precipitates, as it does not have a proton. The main concern with calcium carbonate is that calcium residues can impart an earthy or chalky taste if added excessively, therefore you have to be very careful.

As for CO_2, the reaction can cause a lot of foaming and uncontrollable eruptions, especially with potassium bicarbonate. To circumvent this problem, deacidify in a larger container, or place the carbonate salt in the receiving vessel and slowly introduce the must or wine at the bottom using a hose and while stirring continuously. Alternatively, you can either deacidify in a separate vessel a small volume, say 20%, of juice or wine to release as much CO_2 as possible, and then transfer the deacidified volume back into the rest of the batch, or deacidify in small steps the entire batch in its vessel. Excessive foaming in *wine* can cause loss of precious secondary (fermentation) and tertiary (aging) aromas, hence why deacidification using carbonate salts is best done in *juice* where aromas are to a large extent either bound or not yet created as there has been no fermentation.

Table 7.4 lists theoretical amounts for each salt required to decrease TA by 1.0 g/L in tartaric acid equivalents. Always conduct bench trials to determine the required amounts needed and to quantify impacts on pH, making sure that pH does not get too high and become a microbial spoilage concern.

Table 7.4: Theoretical amounts of carbonate salts needed to decrease TA by 1.0 g/L in tartaric acid equivalents

Carbonate salt to be added	Amount (g/L)
Potassium carbonate (K_2CO_3)	0.46
Potassium bicarbonate ($KHCO_3$)	0.67
Calcium carbonate ($CaCO_3$)	0.67

A word of caution when deacidifying with potassium carbonate salts. Chemical reactions are often not complete or there may not be sufficient tartaric acid to react with the amount of carbonate added, therefore, greater amounts than the theoretical amounts are often needed, and therefore, always run bench trials to determine the rate of addition. Be extra careful when needing to deacidify aggressively large amounts of tartaric acid; potassium carbonate salts, and especially potassium carbonate due to its greater potassium content, may leave great amounts of potassium that may impact taste and tartrate stability, in which case, if possible, a complementary deacidification, such as cold stabilization (see below), may be best.

To treat juice (must) or wine, first place the juice or wine in as cold an area as possible or use a glycol chiller, and let cool down. Add the carbonate salt to the juice or wine, or vice versa depending on the method you choose to manage foaming, and stir gently but thoroughly. Gently stir over several hours making sure to place an airlock on the vessel between stirs; the juice or wine is protected in the headspace due to CO_2 from the reaction. Then rack the juice or wine back into its original vessel.

Let's look at some specific examples on determining the amount of carbonate salt needed for deacidification.

You can make use of the downloadable worksheet at ModernHome-Winemaking.com to help you with these calculations.

EXAMPLE 7.5

Deacidification with potassium bicarbonate (KHCO₃)

You just crushed 160 kg (350 lbs) of Gamay grapes, taken a sample to the lab, and measured a TA of 8.0 g/L and a pH of 3.35. You have estimated a yield volume of approximately 100 L (25 gal). With a TA of 8.0 g/L, you are expecting tartaric and malic acids are both present in relatively high amounts and that each will drop TA; from tartaric acid precipitating as KHT during AF, and from malic acid being converted into lactic acid during MLF.

You want to make a light, dry red and wish to decrease TA by 2.0 g/L to 6.0 g/L pre-ferment by adding potassium bicarbonate ($KHCO_3$). You expect the MLF will reduce TA further, perhaps by another 1.0–1.5 g/L.

First run bench trials, with a 1000-mL sample. It will be very difficult to run bench trials on smaller volumes given that tiny amounts of $KHCO_3$ are needed — you would need a higher-accuracy (read, expensive) scale. The amount of $KHCO_3$ to add to a 1000-mL sample is calculated as follows:

$$Amount\ of\ KHCO_3\ to\ add\ (g) = 2.0\,g/L \times 1\,L \times 0.67$$

$$= 1.34\,g$$

Add the $KHCO_3$ to the sample and allow the reaction to occur until there is no more CO_2 produced. Transfer the treated sample to a glass bottle, cap the bottle, and place the sample in the refrigerator. Let stand for 7–10 days. Refer to Section 14.4.1 for more information on this test.

After the wait period, take out the bottle and allow the sample to warm up to room temperature, then measure TA. Theoretically, TA should measure 6.0 g/L. If your measured TA is 6.0 g/L, treat the entire batch with the required amount of $KHCO_3$ calculated as follows:

$$Amount\ of\ KHCO_3\ to\ add\ (g) = 2.0\,g/L \times 100\,L \times 0.67$$

$$= 134\,g$$

If your measured TA is more or less than 6.0 g/L because you suspect that you under- or over-estimated the yield volume, carry out the adjustment calculations as we had done in the examples in Section 7.5.1. Be sure to taste the treated sample to make sure there have been no negative impacts from the deacidification.

 To obtain the full benefit of deacidification, you will need to chill the batch of wine to precipitate the KHT, as per your bench trials. If you do not refrigerate the sample when performing bench trials and you do not intend to cold stabilize the batch, you may need as much as double the amount of $KHCO_3$ used.

If your bench trials resulted in only a relatively small drop in TA, it means that there is very little tartaric acid to react with $KHCO_3$ and that the high TA of the must is due to high malic acid. Therefore now you know that you need to focus on reducing malic acid by one of the other techniques.

DEACIDIFICATION BY CHILLING (COLD STABILIZATION)

As we have seen, cold stabilization is an important aspect of winemaking in, not only preventing tartrates from forming in bottles, but also as a deacidification technique. It does not require the use of a deacidifying agent — just cold temperatures. Although some KHT forms and crystallizes during fermentation, it can only be performed on wine as alcohol is needed to sufficiently reduce solubility of KHT to allow it to drop.

The problem with this technique for deacidification is that predicting the drop in TA (and change in pH) is guesswork. You can however get a good idea of the drop in TA and change in pH by measuring TA and pH after doing a fridge test as described in Section 14.4.1.

DEACIDIFICATION BY MICROBIOLOGICAL MEANS

Microbiological deacidification refers to the use of malic-degrading yeast or bacteria during AF and MLF, respectively.

When must is known to have high malic acid from grapes grown in cool or cold climates or from a poor vintage, as a first step in reducing TA, choose a yeast strain known to be able to metabolize some portion of the malic acid into small amounts of ethanol, or water and CO_2 depending on fermentation conditions — *it is not a conversion of malic acid into lactic acid*. Examples of such strains and the amount of malic acid they can metabolize in brackets, according to manufacturers, include: Lalvin 71B-1122 (20–40%), Laffort Actiflore BO213 (40–80%), and Maurivin B (up to 56%). Consult the yeast charts provided in Section 11.7 for other malic-degrading yeast choices. You will not be able to predict the TA drop since you don't know the malic acid concentration and how much will be metabolized.

High levels of malic acid will produce great amounts of lactic acid, which can inhibit lactic acid bacteria during MLF (see Section 12.4), and therefore, the use of a malic-degrading yeast for the AF is recommended first, and then wine put through MLF.

A further deacidification by partial or complete malic degradation is possible during MLF in those wines that also benefit from the organoleptic changes induced by MLF. Here too you cannot predict the drop in TA since you don't readily know the amount of malic acid in the juice or wine. You can either submit a sample to a lab to measure the amount of malic acid or use Vinmetrica's SC-50 MLF Analyzer Kit (see Section 12.5).

Then you can estimate the change in TA knowing that every 1 g/L of malic acid (expressed as malic acid) converted to lactic acid causes a theoretical TA drop of 0.56 g/L (expressed as tartaric acid equivalents), or about 0.5 g/L in practical terms. For example, if a wine has a TA of 6.0 g/L of which 2.0 g/L is malic acid and which is completely converted by MLF, TA would be expected to drop by about 1.0 g/L for a final TA of approximately 5.0 g/L.

Let's look at an example to illustrate how to plan for acidity changes from microbiological processes.

EXAMPLE 7.6

Microbiological deacidification

You just crushed your Frontenac harvest from a cold and short growing season. You measured a relatively high TA of 10 g/L. You were also able to have a lab measure malic acid; they reported 7 g/L (expressed as malic acid).

Now you need to figure out your game plan knowing that you want a TA in the 6–7 g/L range by the end of both the AF and MLF. Your desired strategy is to reduce TA without chemical deacidification, and instead use a malic-degrading yeast, Lalvin 71B-1122, and put the wine through MLF.

Assuming a 30% degradation by 71B-1122 yeast, the wine will have approximately 5 g/L of malic acid (expressed as malic acid) left following the AF, a drop of about 2 g/L as malic acid, which corresponds to a TA drop of about 2.2 g/L (2 g/L × 1.12 malic-to-tartaric conversion factor) to 7.8 g/L. This is a malic acid degradation, not conversion into lactic acid.

Now let's say that the TA drop is offset by, for example, 1.2 g/L of succinic acid (expressed as tartaric acid) produced by yeast for a net TA drop of about 1.0 g/L. So the TA at this point is about 9.0 g/L; it would otherwise be around 11.2 g/L without the use of 71B-1122 yeast or any malic-degrading yeast.

A full conversion of the remaining 5 g/L of malic acid by MLF will drop TA by about 5 g/L × 0.5 or 2.5 g/L for a final TA of 6.5 g/L, which is right in the desired range.

DEACIDIFICATION BY BLENDING OR AMELIORATION

Acidity can be adjusted up or down by blending or reduced by amelioration.

Blending is an effective technique for reducing — and also increasing — acidity in juice or wine where a high-TA juice or wine in need of acid reduction is blended with a low-TA juice or wine, or vice versa. This technique depends on the availability of blending components; it may not be possible, for example, if you have harvested high-TA grapes and you have no other low-TA grapes coming in or you want to preserve the varietal and not blend in another variety.

Amelioration is not highly recommended as significant amounts of water may be needed to reduce acidity, which would dilute everything else in the juice or wine. For example, you would need about 7.7 L (2 gal) of water to lower TA from 8.0 to 6.0 g/L in 23 L (6 gal) of juice or wine — that's a lot of water; it represents 25% of the total volume!

Amelioration does not impact pH much, if at all, depending on the amount of water. But you will need to account for the change in sugar level, i.e., SG/Brix/PA, when you ameliorate to lower TA.

7.5.3 SPECIAL CASES

So far we have looked at cases where TA was either low or high with pH high or low, respectively, such that either TA or pH was the focus of the adjustment and which would not adversely affect the other parameter. A change to one involved either no change (due to buffering) or a change in the opposite direction for the other.

But now you are faced with a scenario of a must with high TA and high pH; if you deacidify, you might drive pH even higher. And similarly for a must with low TA and low pH; if you acidify, you might drive pH even lower. What to do?

HIGH TA AND HIGH PH

You have a must with high TA and high pH, for example, 10 g/L and 4.0, respectively, and you need to bring *both* down — a not uncommon scenario in reds. If you deacidify by chemical deacidification, it could raise pH even further, increase oxidative potential, reduce color (in reds), and increase the risk of microbial spoilage. Chances are that the high TA is due to high malic acid and the high pH is due to high potassium — but you can't confirm either and definitely not the potassium content as a home winemaker. How do we solve this?

7

Here you need to perform what may seem counterintuitive — an acidification. We'll first add tartaric acid to increase TA, which will lower pH, and we'll do this by running some bench trials to determine the extent of pH changes. The idea is to bring the pH to 3.65 or lower. Why 3.65? Refer back to Section 7.4.1 for the answer.

Run bench trials using a 100-mL sample and adding tartaric acid in increments of 1.0 g/L using a 10% solution and while monitoring pH (refer back to Example 5.2 in Section 5.3) until pH is just below 3.65. Try not to add more than 4–5 g/L of tartaric acid.

Now the must has much more tartaric acid to interact with the high potassium to form and precipitate KHT during fermentation, and cause a drop in *both* TA and pH. If this is a red wine you are making and will be doing an MLF, TA will drop significantly depending on the extent of the MLF and with a corresponding increase in pH, but which should remain within a good range now. There will still be tartaric acid that can be dropped as tartrates during cold stabilization to further reduce TA, if need be, provided there is sufficient potassium.

You see the importance of getting balanced fruit or must — it can get very tricky and complicated making adjustments and predicting the outcome.

Another option is to blend in low-TA/low-pH juice or wine, if available, or with low-TA/low-pH wine post-AF/MLF in the event the AF and MLF did not provide sufficient drops in TA and pH in the problem wine.

You will also find in the literature discussions on phosphoric acid for dealing with cases of high TA and high pH must or juice, however, its use is not recommended as it can negatively affect taste and texture.

LOW TA AND LOW PH

You have a must with low TA and low pH, for example, a Riesling with 5.0 g/L and 3.0, respectively, and you need to increase TA to about 7.0 g/L. Ideally you would want to increase pH too, but this low pH is actually good here and not of concern, as opposed to issues associated with a high pH.

It's best not to make any pre-ferment adjustments and, instead, carry out fermentation and re-assess TA, pH and taste post ferment. Depending on the acid profile in the must, i.e., relative amounts of tartaric and malic acids, there will likely be only a minimal drop in TA, if any, due to potassium bitartrate and a corresponding *drop* in pH. But succinic acid produced by yeast will increase TA by 1-2 g/L, and cause pH to drop further. In the above example, you may well end up with 7.0 g/L TA and pH around 2.9, maybe less. Taste the wine post ferment and determine if any adjustment is warranted.

REFERENCES

1. Schneider, V. and S. Troxell. 2018. *Acidity Management in Musts & Wines: Acidification, deacidification, and crystal stabilization.* Wine Appreciation Guild Press, San Francisco, CA.

2. McMurry, J. 2008. *Organic Chemistry.* 7th. Brooks/Cole (Thomson Learning), Belmont (CA).

3. Pambianchi, D. 2008. *Techniques in Home Winemaking: A Practical Guide to Making Château-Style Wines.* Newly-Revised and Expanded. Véhicule Press, Montréal (Québec).

4. Edwards, T.L., Singleton, V.L. and Boulton, R., 1985. *Formation of ethyl esters of tartaric acid during wine aging: Chemical and sensory effects.* American Journal of Enology and Viticulture, 36(2), pp. 118-124.

8 Wine Analysis and Control: Sulfur Dioxide

PREAMBLE

Sulfur dioxide (SO_2) chemistry is one of the most complex topics in wine-making, and certainly an intimidating one to new hobbyists. It's a tough one to master without understanding the underlying chemistry. And then, there are as many approaches to managing SO_2 as there are winemakers. But with knowledge and experience, you will come to expertly manage SO_2 and adopt your own protocol that works best for you.

In this chapter, I share my years of experience in measuring SO_2 extensively and rigorously — that is, not only free SO_2, but also total SO_2 and dissolved oxygen (DO) — and correlating the parameters. I have amassed and analyzed a wealth of data, which have helped me optimize SO_2 management practices in my winemaking. I am a strong advocate of SO_2 use in winemaking, but I also strive to use the "right" amount — no more, no less — and this work has translated in lower amounts of total SO_2 in my wines.

HOW TO USE THIS CHAPTER

If you are a beginner and are not ready for SO_2 chemistry or if you are not inclined to measure SO_2 levels, still read Section 8.1 to get an appreciation of why SO_2 is needed and how it protects wine, and then jump to Section 8.5 for instructions on how to blindly add sulfite — you should still be adding sulfite to your wines. Then come back to this chapter as you gain more knowledge and experience and become more comfortable tackling SO_2 concepts.

Sulfur dioxide (SO_2) has long been used in winemaking as a sanitizing agent (see Section 4.5.1) but more importantly as a preservative against oxidative and microbial spoilages, and aroma loss. But the chemistry and mode of action of sulfur dioxide is not always well understood and is often a source of frustration amongst winemakers — novice and experienced alike.

Although SO_2 analysis and control is considered an advanced topic in home winemaking, these concepts and techniques will help you better manage SO_2 towards making consistently, technically better wines. All too often wines become prematurely tired — past their peak and lost precious aromas and flavors — due to oxidation from underuse of SO_2; or they lack aroma freshness from blind overuse of SO_2.

Here you will learn about the importance of the use of SO_2 in winemaking, how to add the "right" amount of SO_2, and how to manage SO_2 from crush to bottle.

This chapter presents principles in SO_2 chemistry and the differences among the terms sulfur dioxide, bisulfite and sulfite — the terms are used interchangeably but they have very different meanings and have different mechanisms of action in protecting wine. Specifically, we will learn about:

- The different sources of SO_2
- How SO_2 protects against oxidation and microbial spoilage
- How SO_2 interacts with wine components
- Practical aspects of SO_2 management in the cellar
- Methods and strategies to optimize and minimize the use of SO_2

8.1 WHY THE NEED FOR SO_2?

Sure! Wine can be made "naturally" without adding any SO_2. But the judicious use of SO_2 will not only improve microbial stability, it will also protect against chemical oxidation and vastly improve the wine's ageing potential, maintain freshness, and protect against aroma loss or degradation.

As an illustrative example, let's look at what happens in red wine during chemical oxidation in the absence of SO_2 and how it protects against spoilage in its presence.

Wine contains thousands of substances, either naturally occurring, derived from yeast or bacterial metabolism during alcoholic and malolactic fermentations, or from chemical interactions among those substances during aging. Alcoholic fermentation (AF) and malolactic fermentation (MLF) are discussed in Chapters 11 and 12, respectively.

Substances of relevance in understanding wine oxidation include: oxygen, ethanol, copper and iron ions, and polyphenols in red wine. Polyphenols include: tannins, those substances responsible for astringency and bitterness; anthocyanins, the color pigment molecules that give red wines their color; and a whole array of other compounds such as phenolic acids, responsible for the browning effect in oxidized must. Tannins and anthocyanins are described in Chapter 9.

8

The tiny amounts of copper and iron ions catalyze oxidation of colorless polyphenols into their brown-colored forms, known as quinones. Polyphenols turning into quinones are what cause red wine to turn to an orange and then brown color during aging or from premature oxidation if there is no protection from SO_2. Coupled to this oxidation reaction is the reduction (the opposite of oxidation) of oxygen (O_2) into one of its most powerful radicals, hydrogen peroxide (H_2O_2) — itself a strong oxidizer.

In the absence of any protection from SO_2, quinones continue forming, which can now react with anthocyanins and other substances to form pigmented polymers, adversely affecting the color of red wine. And hydrogen peroxide will oxidize ethanol into acetaldehyde, which, like quinones, can form undesirable pigmented polymers. Acetaldehyde is a highly volatile substance that is easily identified by its bruised-apple smell in wines affected by oxidative spoilage.

Now, if instead the wine is protected with SO_2, there follows a bit of chemical magic in polyphenols. SO_2 transforms brown-colored quinones back into their colorless polyphenols, and any quinones not transformed can become "bound" to SO_2 and shed its brown color. SO_2 also intercepts and reacts with hydrogen peroxide, preventing it from going after ethanol, and binds to acetaldehyde in the event that some ethanol was oxidized.

Once acetaldehyde is bound to SO_2, it is non-volatile and can no longer be smelled.

Therefore we see that SO_2 binds to certain substances and is also consumed in some reactions as in the reconversion of quinones and interception of H_2O_2. This means that SO_2 levels in wine decline over time, and also because some small amounts dissipate into the atmosphere. Therefore, wine must be replenished with more SO_2 to ensure ongoing protection. And, as all winemakers know, carboys, tanks and barrels must always be topped up, i.e., there should be no headspace, which could otherwise favor chemical and microbial spoilage reactions. From an SO_2 management perspective, headspace accumulates gaseous SO_2 as SO_2 equilibrium between the wine and headspace above it is re-established every time the bung is removed, contributing to SO_2 loss. Large headspace would quickly reduce SO_2 to a critically low level.

Oxidation in juice (must) involves similar reactions, although these are more complicated and beyond the scope of this book. However, it is important to note that grape juice contains oxidation enzymes known as polyphenol oxidases, or PPOs. As soon as berries are split and juice is exposed to the elements and PPOs, PPOs go to work and start oxidizing phenolic acids (these belong to the class of polyphenols). SO_2 is added at crush to inhibit PPOs and oxidation.

Let's take another look at acetaldehyde, which we have seen to be an undesirable substance associated with spoilage.

Yeast produces small amounts of acetaldehyde as part of its metabolism during AF, and this little acetaldehyde is desirable in rosés and reds as it bridges anthocyanins and tannins during polymerization and stabilizes color; we'll explore this bit of chemistry in Section 9.1. If we were to add SO_2 immediately upon completion of the AF, SO_2 would quickly bind and sequester acetaldehyde, leaving less SO_2 to protect wine. A hasty SO_2 addition would not be efficient, and therefore, it is best to delay that first SO_2 addition to give acetaldehyde a chance to perform its bridging action. We'll come back to this in Section 8.4 and give specific guidelines on when to add SO_2.

So far we have referred to "SO_2" in describing reactions, and "SO_2" is most often used interchangeably with "sulfite" and other related terms. In the following sections we clarify and set the correct terminology for describing SO_2 chemistry in wine.

8.2 SO_2 CHEMISTRY

Here we look at SO_2 chemistry from the addition of one of its sulfite salt forms, for example, potassium metabisulfite, to how SO_2 is generated and transformed into its various forms that protect wine.

Although SO_2 gas can be injected and dissolved directly into wine, as is often done in large wineries, it is more readily and inexpensively available as a crystalline salt form, for example, as potassium metabisulfite or sodium metabisulfite. Potassium metabisulfite is the preferred form to limit the amount of sodium added to wine; the sodium salt can however be used as a sanitizing agent (see Section 4.5.1).

When potassium metabisulfite ($K_2S_2O_5$), simply abbreviated to KMS, is added to wine, the crystalline structure breaks up as it dissolves, and dissociates into potassium (K^+) and metabisulfite ($S_2O_5^{2-}$) ions, which, in the presence of water in an aqueous medium like wine, forms un-ionized molecular SO_2 (the form that is correctly referred to as SO_2), bisulfite ions (HSO_3^-) and protons (H^+) until an equilibrium is formed. Bisulfite ions (HSO_3^-) can further dissociate into sulfite ions (SO_3^{2-}) and more protons until an equilibrium is formed again. Figure 8.1 shows these dissociations and equilibria between the various forms of SO_2, where we denote molecular SO_2 in an aqueous solution as $SO_2 \cdot H_2O$.

$$SO_2 \cdot H_2O \quad \overset{pK_{a1}=1.81}{\rightleftharpoons} \quad H^+ + HSO_3^- \quad \overset{pK_{a2}=7.20}{\rightleftharpoons} \quad 2\,H^+ + SO_3^{2-}$$

Figure 8.1: Equilibrium between SO_2, HSO_3^- and SO_3^{2-} with pK_a values at 20 °C (68 °F)

Note that SO_2 dissolved in an aqueous solution behaves as an acid as it releases protons. It is indeed an acid, specifically a di-acid, called sulfurous acid, as it can release two protons and therefore, similar to tartaric acid, it has two dissociation constants. The first dissociation occurs at around pH 1.81 and the second at around 7.20. The equilibrium and extent to which these substances are formed depends primarily on pH and to a lesser extent on temperature and to an even lesser extent on alcohol concentration. Increasing temperature causes reduced dissociation, and therefore greater amounts of molecular SO_2 and less HSO_3^-. Sulfite ions (SO_3^{2-}) are not found in wine as HSO_3^- dissociation happens at a much higher pH (7.20) than found in wine.

What does this all mean in practical terms?

It means that a wine with a higher pH has greater SO_2 dissociation and therefore a smaller amount of molecular SO_2 but a greater amount of HSO_3^- than a wine with a lower pH. This has important consequences in terms of how well wine is protected.

Let's look now at how molecular SO_2 and HSO_3^- protect juice and wine.

Molecular SO_2 protects against rogue yeast and bacteria — this is known as microbial protection — and does so by penetrating their cell walls and disrupting cell functions.

Bisulfite ions (HSO_3^-) protect against oxidation — this is known as chemical protection — and do so by chemically reacting with other substances, such as hydrogen peroxide and quinones, which produce sulfates (SO_4^{2-}), or binding to other substances, such as quinones and acetaldehyde. You likely already know that you can add KMS to bind acetaldehyde in flawed wine stricken by advanced oxidation (see Sections 22.1 and 22.2).

The sum of molecular SO_2 and HSO_3^- (and SO_3^{2-} to be correct) concentrations is referred to as free sulfur dioxide, abbreviated to FSO2, and therefore, FSO2 is what protects wine. As molecular SO_2 gets consumed or dissipates out of the wine and into the atmosphere, and as HSO_3^- reacts with or becomes bound over time to those other substances, protection in wine diminishes as FSO2 decreases. Once all HSO_3^- is reacted or bound, it no longer provides protection. The concentration of HSO_3^- that has become bound is referred to as bound sulfur dioxide, or BSO2, and the sum of FSO2 and BSO2 is referred to as total sulfur dioxide, or TSO2. These definitions are depicted in Figure 8.2.

Figure 8.3 graphs the equilibrium equation presented in Figure 8.1 showing the relative concentrations of molecular SO_2, HSO_3^- and SO_3^{2-} as a function of pH. Focusing on wine pH range, i.e., 3.0–4.0, note that there

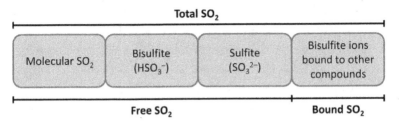

Figure 8.2: The various forms of SO_2 and sulfite ions (no scale is implied)

is about 6% molecular SO_2 and 94% HSO_3^- at pH 3.0 with molecular SO_2 dropping to about 0.6% and HSO_3^- increasing to 99.4% at pH 4.0. This is significant in that microbes thrive at higher pH, meaning, a wine at pH 4.0 is at much higher risk of microbial spoilage than a wine at pH 3.0, yet there is less molecular SO_2 at higher pH. You will recall that molecular SO_2 is needed to protect against microbial spoilage. This means that more FSO2 — and therefore more KMS — is needed at higher pH to get more molecular SO_2.

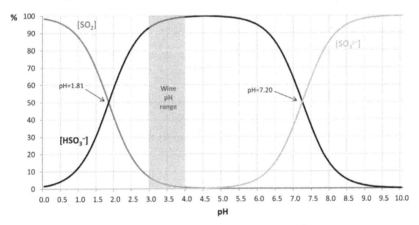

Figure 8.3: Relative concentrations of SO_2, HSO_3^- and SO_3^{2-} as a function of pH

Winemakers most often talk about SO_2 and sulfite concentrations in parts per million (ppm). Here we use the more standard unit of mg/L; it is equivalent to ppm.

Additionally, as temperature increases, the relative amount of free SO_2 increases while that of bound SO_2 decreases. This is because increased temperatures cause partial dissociation of the bound SO_2 form, resulting in increased free SO_2 and hence increased molecular SO_2 concentrations. This means that less KMS is needed at higher temperatures.

How much molecular SO_2 (MSO2) is needed for adequate protection against microbial spoilage?

Red wines are loaded with tannins, which are known to have some inhibitory effects against microbes, and therefore, reds generally require lower MSO2 levels than whites. MSO2 in the range 0.2–0.5 mg/L is recommended for reds depending on tannin levels; for example, a light red is best protected with 0.5 mg/L while a richly tannic red may only need 0.2 mg/L. MSO2 in the range 0.5–0.8 mg/L is recommended for whites and rosés; for example, a young, fruity white is best protected with 0.8 mg/L while an oak-aged white may only need 0.5 mg/L. Although the sensory threshold is generally considered to be around 2 mg/L, it is recommended not to exceed 0.8 mg/L MSO2 as a stricken-match smell can become detectable on the nose by more sensitive tasters.

And how much FSO2 is needed to adequately protect wine against chemical oxidation?

Figure 8.4 illustrates the amount of FSO2 needed as a function of pH. There are three curves: the bottom two curves can be used for reds for a desired MSO2 of 0.2 mg/L or 0.5 mg/L, and the top curve can be used for whites and rosés for a desired MSO2 of 0.8 mg/L along with the middle curve when a MSO2 of 0.5 mg/L is desired. For example, a red wine with pH 3.40 requires about 20 mg/L FSO2 at 0.5 mg/L MSO2 for adequate protection.

For the mathematically inclined, you can calculate FSO2 using the following equation:

$$FSO2 = MSO2 \times \left[1 + 10^{(pH-1.81)}\right]$$

Once you have measured the pH of the wine and you have established your desired MSO2, you can then determine the amount of FSO2 to protect wine adequately.

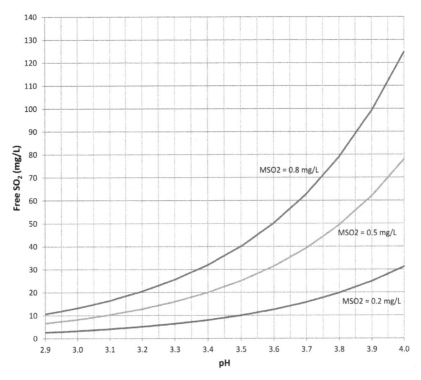

Figure 8.4: Free SO$_2$ as a function of pH at different molecular SO$_2$ levels

What about high-pH wines? Is it okay to add large amounts of KMS?

A high-pH wine may need as much as 100 mg/L FSO2, maybe even more. This much FSO2 will bleach color in red wine — absolutely. If you intend to bottle red wine early and not cellar it for long periods, you can cut back your KMS addition to add, for example, only 50 mg/L FSO2. However, a high FSO2 does not necessarily mean that you will smell "sulfites." What you would smell is molecular (free) SO$_2$ gas, i.e., MSO2, and more so at higher serving temperatures; and if you have added KMS using recommended MSO2 values, you will not smell molecular SO$_2$ at 100 mg/L FSO2. If you do intend to bulk age, you can let FSO2 drop down to, for example, 50 mg/L until you are ready to bottle; SO$_2$–color equilibrium re-establishes itself and some color will come back.

EXAMPLE 8.1

Determining the amount of FSO2 needed based on pH and MSO2

You have a 23-L (6-gal) batch of medium-bodied red wine with a pH of 3.35 which you wish to protect it with 0.5 mg/L MSO2. Therefore:

$$FSO2\ (mg/L) = 0.5 \times \left[1 + 10^{(3.35-1.81)}\right]$$

$$= 17.8\ mg/L$$

Your wine requires about 18 mg/L FSO2 for adequate protection.

Great! We know how much FSO2 is needed, but how much KMS do we need to add?

Looking at the molecular weight of KMS ($K_2S_2O_5$) and how much SO_2 it delivers, we see that 1 mg of KMS delivers approximately 0.57 mg of SO_2, so that the amount of KMS to add per volume is the amount of FSO2 divided by 0.57.

EXAMPLE 8.2

Determining the amount of KMS needed based on FSO2

You determined that your 23-L (6-gal) batch of wine needs 18 mg/L FSO2. Determine the amount of KMS to add, as follows:

$$KMS\ (mg) = \frac{18\ mg/L}{0.57} \times 23\ L$$

$$= 726\ mg\ (0.73\ g)$$

Use the SO2 CALCULATOR (Figure 8.5), downloadable from ModernHomeWinemaking.com, to calculate FSO2 requirements more readily and accurately as calculations will become trickier and more complicated as we get further into SO_2 management and control; the SO2 CALCULATOR will be indispensable.

Before we look at how to measure and adjust FSO2 levels, let's go back and understand a bit better what happens as bisulfite ions (HSO_3^-) bind to other substances and the implications on measuring and managing FSO2 levels.

SO2 CALCULATOR

Version 6.0

© Daniel Pambianchi, 2021

STEP 1. Choose your preferred method of potassium metabisulfite (KMS) addition

10% KMS solution	To prepare a 10% KMS solution: Dissolve 10 g KMS in about 75 mL of cool water, then add water to bring to exactly 100 mL.

STEP 2. Enter your wine information and parameters

Wine identifier	2019	Cabernet Sauvignon		200L-VCT-A
Type of wine	RED			
Estimated/measured % ABV	13.5	% alc/vol	default: 12.0	
pH	3.35			
Cellar temperature	13.0	°C	default: 15°C/59°F	
Current (measured) Free SO_2	23.5	mg/L	default: 0	
Dissolved Oxygen (DO)	700	µg/L	default: 0	
Volume to be treated	100.0	L		

STEP 3. Enter your desired Molecular SO_2 and Binding Factor

Molecular SO_2	0.5	mg/L	default: 0.5 if RED, 0.8 if WHITE/ROSÉ
Binding adjustment factor	50	%	default: 0

STEP 4. Calculated RECOMMENDED Free SO2 at 0.5 Molecular SO2

30.8 mg/L

STEP 5. Enter your DESIRED Free SO_2

Desired Free SO_2	30.8	mg/L	default: RECOMMENDED Free SO2 in Step 4

STEP 6. Calculated amount of KMS to add according to your preferred method

12.7 mL 10% KMS solution

Comments

Figure 8.5: The SO2 CALCULATOR, downloadable from ModernHomeWine-making.com

As we have seen, certain substances have an affinity for binding with HSO_3^- ions, and this can happen relatively quickly (in as little as one day) depending on wine chemistry and cellar temperature. Once completely bound, HSO_3^- ions are no longer available to protect wine. These substances are referred to as binders, and certain binders have a greater affinity to binding than others.

Acetaldehyde is one of the strongest binders, hence why it is dealt with a KMS addition in wines affected by advanced oxidation. Anthocyanins too are very strong binders, followed by tannins. To witness the bisulfite–anthocyanin binding effect, dissolve a little KMS in some water, add just a few mL in a glass of red wine and notice how the color quickly lightens. As red wines are very rich in anthocyanins and tannins, there will be a lot of binding on the first KMS addition, typically by as much as 30–50%, which means that initial KMS additions are not as effective, i.e., a lot of FSO2 becomes BSO2, leaving less FSO2 to protect wine. And therefore, you need to compensate for that binding, and particularly in reds and full-bodied whites, e.g., an oak-aged Chardonnay, to maintain adequate FSO2 levels. For example, if you expect 50% binding, you need to increase the first KMS addition by 100% to hit your desired FSO2 target. For example, if you want to add 20 mg/L FSO2, which would drop to 10 mg/L after binding, you would need to add 40 mg/L, which would drop to 20 mg/L, your desired FSO2 level.

To assess the extent of binding, measure FSO2 some 3 days after a KMS addition, or measure and monitor *both* FSO2 and TSO2. Bound SO_2 (BSO2) is not measured, but rather, it is simply calculated by subtracting FSO2 from TSO2.

To illustrate the value of monitoring TSO2, not just FSO2, consider the scenario in Figure 8.6(a): two wines (A and B) with the same measured FSO2 (30 mg/L), pH (3.56) and MSO2 (0.5 mg/L), but unknown TSO2. Both wines are adequately protected at the same FSO2 level but we have no indication of the efficacy of SO_2 additions; we have no knowledge of the extent of binding. Now consider the scenario in Figure 8.6(b): the same

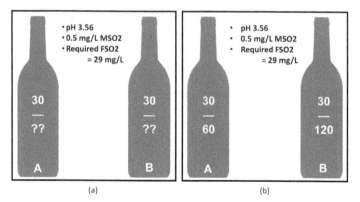

Figure 8.6: Illustrating the value of measuring TSO2, not just FSO2: a) TSO2 is unknown; b) TSO2 is measured and known

wines (A and B) and again with the same measured FSO2, pH and MSO2, but now we measure TSO2 in wines A and B to be 60 mg/L and 120 mg/L, respectively. We can conclude that SO_2 additions in wine B are much less effective as there is a lot of binding. And now you understand why you have been adding a lot of KMS to maintain that FSO2 level of 30 mg/L.

Let's look at some examples to understand this binding phenomenon, how SO_2 measurements are impacted, and how to account for binding in your SO_2 additions. (We will assume here for illustrative purposes that both FSO2 and TSO2 are 0 mg/L initially. As yeast produces some small amount of free SO_2 during fermentation, FSO2 may still measure 0 mg/L as it has become bound, consumed or dissipated, but TSO2 will likely not be 0 mg/L, likely in the 10–20 mg/L range.)

8

EXAMPLE 8.3

Binding in red wine

You just added KMS for the first time to your full-bodied red wine to add 25 mg/L FSO2.

A couple of weeks later, you take samples and measure 10 mg/L and 20 mg/L for FSO2 and TSO2, respectively.

From this, you can deduce that, since TSO2 is 20 mg/L — not 25 mg/L as expected — 10 mg/L FSO2 went to binding and that 5 mg/L FSO2 was consumed or lost through dissipation to the environment. And therefore, considerable FSO2 went to binding leaving only 10 mg/L instead of the 25 mg/L FSO2 you added. This means that you will need to add more KMS to bring FSO2 back up from 10 to 25 mg/L.

EXAMPLE 8.4

Binding (or lack thereof) in white wine

You just added KMS for the first time to your white wine to add 25 mg/L FSO2.

A couple of weeks later, you take samples and measure 20 mg/L for both FSO2 and TSO2.

Here, you can deduce that, since both FSO2 and TSO2 are 20 mg/L, there is no binding and that 5 mg/L FSO2 was consumed or lost through dissipation. This means that the KMS addition was effective with no binding and only minimal FSO2 loss, and that 5 mg/L FSO2 is needed to bring FSO2 back to the desired level of 25 mg/L.

EXAMPLE 8.5

FSO2 loss (no binding)

This example further illustrates the value of measuring TSO2 in addition to FSO2.

You just added KMS for the first time to your red wine to add 25 mg/L FSO2.

A couple of weeks later, you take samples and measure 10 mg/L for both FSO2 and TSO2.

Here too you can deduce that, since both FSO2 and TSO2 are 10 mg/L, there is no binding; however, 15 mg/L FSO2 was consumed or lost through dissipation. This points to a processing problem or some other problem with the wine's chemistry; for example, there may be some oxidation going on, or that perhaps you miscalculated your addition, but you would not know that if you only measured FSO2 as you measured 10 mg/L FSO2 just as in Example 8.3.

Let's take a look at the equipment and techniques used in measuring FSO2 and TSO2 and then we will look at how to make FSO2 adjustments like an expert.

8.3 MEASURING SO$_2$ LEVELS

Winemakers most often only measure free SO$_2$ (FSO2), not total SO$_2$ (TSO2) or perhaps not until bottling as a last check, in spite of the valuable information TSO2 provides in understanding the efficacy of KMS additions. And lactic acid bacteria used for conducting MLF (see Chapter 12) have maximum TSO2 tolerances, beyond which bacteria may be inhibited and unable to proceed with MLF. The additional cost and work for measuring TSO2 is minimal once you make measuring FSO2 a part of your analysis routine.

There are two commonly used methods for measuring FSO2 and TSO2: Aeration–Oxidation (AO) and Ripper. Each method has its advantages and disadvantages. The AO method gives more accurate results but requires more equipment and expertise to implement than the easier Ripper method.

In the AO method, a sample is first acidified with phosphoric acid (to lower pH) to convert bisulfite ions into molecular SO_2, which can then be liberated owing to its volatility as a gas. The liberated SO_2 is removed from the sample by aspiration — hence why it is often referred to as the aspiration method — by passing an air stream through the sample, and then bubbled into and collected in a hydrogen peroxide solution to oxidize it into sulfuric acid. This is then titrated using a standard $0.01N$ sodium hydroxide (NaOH) solution and color indicator. FSO2 is calculated from the amount of NaOH used. To measure TSO2, a second sample is strongly acidified and then heat applied to free (unbind) bound SO_2 to then be able to measure the total amount of SO_2 as is done for FSO2.

The AO method requires some special labware and apparatus as well as laboratory skills; samples have to be heated for measuring TSO2. You may be able to find easy-to-use AO SO_2 test kits (Figure 8.7) on the market.

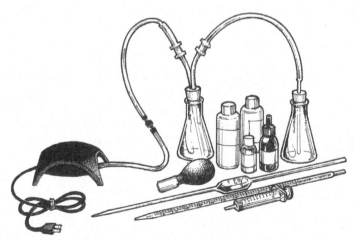

Figure 8.7: AO SO_2 test kit for measuring FSO2 — this specific kit does not measure TSO2

8

In the Ripper method, an iodine titrant is added to a wine sample to react with SO_2. The sample is first treated with a dilute sulfuric acid solution to reduce oxidation of polyphenols by iodine. The sample is then titrated to an endpoint, detected using a starch indicator or an oxidation–reduction potential (ORP) electrode and meter. FSO2 is then calculated from the amount of iodine titrant used. This method is simpler to implement as there is no aspiration or heating involved but is less accurate because, unlike the AO method, polyphenols, ascorbic acid, sugars and other so-called "reductones" are also oxidized by iodine during the analytical procedure; however, the error can be assumed to be small for all practical purposes in a home winemaking context. If you want to obtain a more accurate measurement, first determine FSO2 in a wine sample, then treat a second sample with 2–3 mL of 40% glyoxal to oxidize reductones, re-measure FSO2, and subtract that value from the first FSO2 value.

There are various Ripper-method products and equipment for measuring FSO2 (Figure 8.8).

The Vinmetrica test unit measures both FSO2 and TSO2. It requires a significant up-front investment but is well worth it if you expect to measure these parameters often.

CHEMetrics Titrets measure FSO2 in whites with relatively good accuracy, if there are negligible polyphenols and no ascorbic acid, but cannot be used in reds because of interfering substances, primarily polyphenols.

Accuvin Quick Tests strips measure FSO2, but these rely on color changes that need to be matched against a supplied color chart to determine FSO2, and therefore these tend to be less accurate.

Always measure SO_2 levels *after* processing wine, i.e., if the wine needs racking, first rack, then take a sample and measure SO_2 as the racking will cause a small drop in FSO2 due to dissipation.

 Do not dump or flush spent reagents and other chemicals down the sink or toilet. Always dispose in an environmentally responsible way according to your local laws. Your municipality may have a program for collecting hazardous waste.

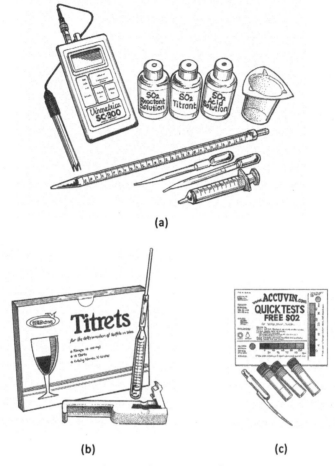

8

Figure 8.8: Products and equipment for measuring FSO2 and, with some, also TSO2: a) Vinmetrica SC-300; b) CHE-Metrics Titrets; c) Accuvin Free SO2 Quick Tests

8.4 ADJUSTING SO$_2$ LEVELS

Now that you know how to measure SO$_2$ levels and how to add KMS for desired FSO2 and MSO2 levels, here you will learn how and when to make SO$_2$ adjustments based on analytical data.

Winemakers have different approaches to managing FSO2 and SO$_2$ additions. One approach is to make smaller but more frequent adjustments to compensate for SO_2 binding and maintain the required FSO2 level. Another approach is to make larger but less frequent adjustments. These larger adjustments upfront will actually, albeit counterintuitively, result in lower TSO2 when time comes to bottle [1]. With experience in managing your wines and with a critical evaluation of your test data, you will come to adopt and adapt the method that best suits you. Another approach is to add a specific amount of FSO2 without considering MSO2 or pH, but I do not recommend this method as it always adds too little or too much SO_2, never the "right" amount, which is risky at elevated pH.

Following are some guidelines to help you implement a solid SO_2-adjustment protocol in your winemaking.

1. Always calculate the required FSO2 based on pH using a MSO2 level for the style of wine as per Table 8.1. If you are using an on-line calculator (e.g., SO2 CALCULATOR downloadable at ModernHomeWinemaking.com) that allows entering temperature and ethanol concentration, enter the *cellar* temperature — not the temperature of the sample during lab analysis — and the actual or estimated % ABV (i.e., PA). Large temperature swings can have a significant impact on the amount of FSO2 needed.

Table 8.1: Recommended MSO2 levels for various styles of wines

Style of wine	MSO2 (mg/L)
Fruity, light white or rosé	0.8
Fuller-bodied (e.g., oak aged) white	0.5
Light- or medium-bodied red	0.5
Full-bodied red	0.2

2. As acetaldehyde is at its highest concentration at the end of AF and takes about three (3) days to metabolize, make the *first* KMS addition as follows:

 • For white wines, add KMS three (3) days after completion of the AF *and* MLF, if any;

 • For rosé wines, add KMS seven (7) days after completion of the AF *and* MLF, if any; and

- For red wines, add KMS ten (10) days to 2 weeks or more after completion of the AF *and* MLF, if any.

The objective here is to reduce the amount of KMS to add on the first addition and, for rosés and reds, to allow acetaldehyde to bridge anthocyanins and tannins during polymerization in stabilizing color (see Section 9.1).

In all cases, in one alternative approach, measure FSO2 three (3) days later after the KMS addition, and re-adjust FSO2 as needed to compensate for SO_2 binding and to ensure the wine has sufficient protection until the next checkpoint, as per the frequency established below.

3. As another alternative approach for red wines, for those intended to be aged a minimum of 18 months, on the very *first* KMS addition after completion of AF and MLF, add 100% more (i.e., double) KMS in full-bodied reds and 30–50% more in medium-bodied reds to allow for binding. Adjust a further 50% in full-bodied reds on the second KMS addition. Measure TSO2 to monitor the efficacy of your SO_2 additions.

   For reds to be bottled within 12 months and consumed shortly thereafter, add the required amounts of KMS *without* any further adjustments for binding; the higher amount of SO_2 may become detectable by smell if you bottle early.

   For full-bodied, barrel-fermented whites add 10% more KMS on the very *first* KMS addition after completion of AF and MLF to account for binding. No adjustments are necessary on subsequent additions.

4. Measure and adjust FSO2 every three (3) months for wine aging in glass carboys and stainless steel tanks. Increase the frequency to once a month for wine aging in barrels and "breathable" HDPE tanks given the greater consumption of FSO2 due to oxygen ingress into these types of containers. In all cases, measure TSO2 every three (3) months to get an understanding of the extent of binding. Adapt these frequencies according to your cellar's temperature and humidity as well as historical FSO2 trend data.

8

When topping up vessels after taking samples, spray the surface of the wine with a light mist of 1% sulfite–citric solution (see Section 4.5.1) for extra protection against oxygen and microorganisms in the headspace.

Change the sulfite solution in airlocks at each 3-month interval when you measure and adjust FSO2. If you use vodka, it's still good — no need to change.

5. When transferring wine into *new* barrels, add 50% more KMS than the calculated amount needed to account for the extra oxygen transferred from the new wood into the wine. New wood can contain as much as 60–70% of air by volume, which represents about 13–15% of oxygen [2].

6. Never let FSO2 fall below 10 mg/L; it could otherwise compromise microbial protection.

Figure 8.9: DO meter

If you have the ability to measure dissolved oxygen (DO) with a DO meter (Figure 8.9) or Vinmetrica unit and DO probe, measure DO in wine every time you measure FSO2 (and pH), and increase your FSO2 addition by an amount of 2.5–4 mg/L for each mg DO/L to compensate SO_2 consumption by oxygen radicals. The theoretical amount of FSO2 consumed by 1 mg DO/L is 4 mg/L, but it may be closer to 2.5 mg/L according to some experimental data as some oxygen oxidizes other wine compounds [3,4]. For example, if you measured 1.0 mg DO/L, increase the calculated FSO2 by 2.5–4.0 mg/L (the SO2 CALCULATOR uses 2.5 mg/L). This may not seem much when DO is below 1 mg/L, but it can be 3 mg/L or 4 mg/L after a racking or filtration run (see Table 8.2), possibly considerably more if executed carelessly and the wine picks up excessive amounts of oxygen. In a low-pH wine where much less FSO2 is needed, excessive DO can quickly consume whatever little FSO2 there is and bring it below the critical 10 mg/L level. You will better manage your wine and FSO2 adjustments if you make measuring DO a routine part of your winemaking; measure DO *before and immediately after*

Table 8.2: Empirical data of typical average oxygen uptake during various operations at 20 °C (60 °F). Data adapted from references [5] and [6].

Operation	Oxygen uptake (mg/L)
Racking	
with aeration	3–8
without aeration	0.2–2
Pumping	
light	1–2
heavy	2–6
Barrel aging (per year)	
new barrel	20–28
used barrel[1]	10
Barrel topping	0.3
Filtration (plate)	4
Bottling	3

[1]Barrel (225 L) used for 5 wines over 5 seasons

8

any processing, for example, racking or filtering, to understand how much oxygen the wine has absorbed.

KMS can be added in powder form, Campden tablets, effervescent self-dissolving granules (e.g., Efferbaktol (Martin Vialatte), Effergran (Esseco)), or most conveniently using a 5%, 10% or 20% KMS solution (the percentage doesn't matter).

The powder form works well when you only have one or two batches to adjust. It is not as practical if you have to treat, for example, 10 or 20 batches as you would need to weigh the required amount for each batch, dissolve the powder in water, and then add each sulfite solution to its corresponding batch. You would also need a very good lab balance with an accuracy of 0.1 g (100 mg) or better to weigh small amounts of powder if you work with small volumes. Buy only as much KMS powder as you expect to use in 6 months, and store in a dry, cool place. Toss in a couple of silica desiccant packs in the opened bag or container to help absorb moisture and protect the powder.

Campden tablets are available, for example, in 0.44-g tablets, and therefore no weighing is required but they have be crushed to a powder using a mortar and pestle before dissolving in water. Their advantage is in recipes with standard wine volumes; it gets trickier when only a portion of a tablet is required, making measurements very imprecise. Just be sure to use the potassium form of Campden tablets as some may be produced from sodium metabisulfite, which is not recommended as an additive. And follow the same storage recommendations as powder.

Follow product instructions for effervescent self-dissolving granules; they will indicate how much SO_2 a certain weight of granules adds per volume of wine.

A dilute KMS solution, for example, 10%, is most practical as you quickly calculate FSO2 needs and the corresponding amounts of solution to add for each batch and then use an accurate pipette to transfer the calculated amount into each batch.

To prepare a 10% KMS solution, dissolve 10 g of KMS powder in approximately 75 mL of cool (never hot), distilled or fresh water in a 150-mL beaker. Stir well until completely dissolved. Transfer the solution to a 100-mL volumetric flask, rinse the beaker with water using a squeeze-type wash bottle, transfer that too to the volumetric flask, add water to the 100-mL mark, cap the flask and invert several times to mix thoroughly. Label the flask as "10% KMS SOLUTION" along with the date. You can also use a good-quality graduated cylinder in lieu of the flask; then transfer the solution to a small 100-mL bottle. You can keep this solution for one month if stored in a cool, dry place.

 A 10% SO_2 solution is not the same as a 10% KMS solution. Make sure you understand the difference when using calculators or doing manual calculations using a 10% SO_2 solution.

Table 8.3: SO_2 additions using a 10% KMS solution

Incremental FSO2 amount (mg/L)	Volume of 10% KMS solution to be added to each **liter** of wine (mL)	Volume of 10% KMS solution to be added to each **gallon** of wine (mL)
1	0.02	0.07
5	0.09	0.33
10	0.17	0.66

Use Table 8.3 to determine how many mL of 10% KMS solution is needed per liter or gallon of wine to increase FSO2 by a desired amount.

EXAMPLE 8.6

Determining how much 10% KMS solution to add

You would like to add 56 mg/L FSO2 to a 23-L (6-gal) batch.

From Table 8.3, an increase of 56 mg/L is achieved as (5×**10** + 1×**5** + 1×**1**), and therefore, calculate the required amount of 10% KMS solution as follows:

$$Amount\ of\ 10\%\ solution\ (mL)$$
$$= (5 \times 0.17 + 1 \times 0.09 + 1 \times 0.02) \times 23\ L$$
$$= 22\ mL$$

8

EXAMPLE 8.7

First KMS addition after fermentation

Your medium-bodied Cabernet Sauvignon just completed both AF and MLF. And it's time to stabilize the wine with SO_2. You transferred the wine to a single 23-L (6-gal) carboy for aging in your cellar at a temperature of 13 °C (55 °F). You don't know the actual % ABV but you had measured a PA of 14.5% and fermented the wine completely dry. Wine pH is 3.55 and you assume that, since you don't measure SO_2 levels, both FSO2 and TSO2 are 0 mg/L for all practical purposes.

Summary of wine parameters and measurements

Time (months)	Batch size	% ABV	pH	Temp.	Measured FSO2 (mg/L)	Measured TSO2 (mg/L)
0	23 L 6 gal	14.5	3.55	13 °C 55 °F	0	0

Since this is a medium-bodied red, you decide to use 0.5 mg/L MSO2. Using the equation in Section 8.2, calculate the required FSO2 as follows:

$$FSO2\ (mg/L) = 0.5 \times \left[1 + 10^{(3.55-1.81)}\right]$$
$$= 28\ mg/L$$

Since this is the first KMS addition to a medium-bodied red, adjust FSO2 by 100% from 28 mg/L to 56 mg/L.

Now calculate the amount of KMS powder to add to the 23-L (6-gal) carboy:

$$KMS\ (mg) = \frac{56\ mg/L}{0.57} \times 23\ L$$

$$= 2260\ mg\ (2.3\ g)$$

If you are using a 10% KMS solution, you would add 22 mL based on the calculations in Example 8.6.

EXAMPLE 8.8

SO_2 control at 3-month intervals

You are now at the *first 3-month mark* and you are ready to do a control of SO_2 levels in your 23-L (6-gal) batch of medium-bodied Cabernet Sauvignon with the same parameters as in Example 8.7, but here you measure 40 mg/L FSO2 and 50 mg/L TSO2.

Summary of wine parameters and measurements

Time (months)	Batch size	% ABV	pH	Temp.	Measured FSO2 (mg/L)	Measured TSO2 (mg/L)
3	23 L 6 gal	14.5	3.55	13 °C 55 °F	40	50

You had added 56 mg/L FSO2 three months ago and it is now at 40 mg/L, which means that there was a drop of 16 mg/L with 10 mg/L becoming bound and 6 mg/L consumed or lost by dissipation since TSO2 is 50 mg/L. We see that there was some binding, and you expect little binding from here on, but you still do a 1/3 (33%) adjustment anyways.

Since none of the wine parameters have changed and still using 0.5 mg/L MSO2, the wine requires the same 28 mg/L FSO2 plus about 9 mg/L (the 33% for binding) for a total of 37 mg/L. Since the wine already contains 40 mg/L, no adjustment is required.

At the 6-month mark, you measure 30 mg/L FSO2 and 55 mg/L TSO2, which means that there was a FSO2 drop of 10 mg/L with 5 mg/L becoming bound and 5 mg/L consumed or lost since TSO2 is 55 mg/L. There was much less binding between the third and sixth months, therefore, we can assume that there will be very little binding from here on.

Summary of wine parameters and measurements

Time (months)	Batch size	% ABV	pH	Temp.	Measured FSO2 (mg/L)	Measured TSO2 (mg/L)
6	23 L 6 gal	14.5	3.55	13 °C 55 °F	30	55

Assuming the same wine parameters and a MSO2 of 0.5 mg/L, the wine requires the same 28 mg/L FSO2, but it contains 30 mg/L, therefore, again, no adjustment is necessary.

At the 9-month mark, you measure 25 mg/L FSO2 and 55 mg/L TSO2, which means that there was an FSO2 drop of 5 mg/L, all of it consumed or lost since TSO2 is 55 mg/L — there was no additional binding.

Summary of wine parameters and measurements

Time (months)	Batch size	% ABV	pH	Temp.	Measured FSO2 (mg/L)	Measured TSO2 (mg/L)
9	23 L 6 gal	14.5	3.55	13 °C 55 °F	25	55

Assuming the same wine parameters and a MSO2 of 0.5 mg/L, the wine requires the same 28 mg/L FSO2, but it contains 25 mg/L, therefore you need to add 3 mg/L with no adjustment for binding.

Calculate the amount of KMS powder or 10% KMS solution (using Table 8.3) to add to the 23-L (6-gal) carboy:

$$KMS \ (mg) = \frac{3 \ mg/L}{0.57} \times 23 \ L$$

$$= 121 \ mg \ (0.12 \ g)$$

Amount of 10% solution (mL)

$$= (3 \times 0.02) \times 23 \ L$$

$$= 1.4 \ mL$$

This example illustrates why adding KMS in small amounts can be difficult without a good lab balance; it is best to add as a 10% KMS solution. The SO2 CALCULATOR greatly simplifies all these calculations.

Here is an important observation with respect to binding adjustments in relation to the total amount of KMS added.

In Example 8.8, no KMS addition was necessary until the ninth month, and only a minor adjustment was required. After the FSO2 adjustment at the 9-month point, FSO2 and TSO2 would be around 28 mg/L and 58 mg/L, respectively.

Had you not made any adjustments to account for binding, there would have been more binding — quite counterintuitively but that is how binding chemistry works — with FSO2 falling below the 28-mg/L level that was required for this wine, and which would have required KMS additions at each 3-month interval and in greater amounts that would have resulted in a higher TSO2. It is also likely at the 3 and 6-month control points that FSO2 would have dropped below the critical 10-mg/L threshold.

EXAMPLE 8.9

Adjusting FSO2 to account for dissolved oxygen (DO)

You completed filtering your medium-bodied red wine; you did a coarse filtration and a medium filtration (see Chapter 17) in preparation for bottling. You take a sample to the lab and measure the following parameters:

Summary of wine parameters and measurements

Batch size	% ABV	pH	Temp.	Measured FSO2 (mg/L)	Measured TSO2 (mg/L)	DO (mg/L)
23 L 6 gal	14.5	3.55	13 °C 55 °F	25	55	2.3

You go with the assumption that 1 mg/L DO consumes 2.5 mg/L FSO2. The recommended FSO2 without accounting for DO is still 28 mg/L, as calculated in previous examples. To that amount, add 2.5 × 2.3 mg/L or 5.8 mg/L for a new recommended FSO2 level of about 34 mg/L to account for DO.

Calculate using Table 8.3 the volume of 10% KMS solution to add to increase FSO2 by 9 mg/L in your 23-L (6-gal) batch:

$$Amount\ of\ 10\%\ solution\ (mL)$$
$$= (9 \times 0.02) \times 23\ L$$
$$= 4.1\ mL$$

I ADDED TOO MUCH SULFITE. WHAT DO I DO?

You took the time to perform all your calculations diligently but then you realize you added 100 mg/L FSO2 instead of 25 mg/L, you're ready to bottle, but you can't — you can smell the sulfite in the wine.

8

If so equipped, first measure FSO2 to confirm the extent of the problem as FSO2 may have already dropped due to binding.

You then have several options, in decreasing order of preference based on possible adverse impacts on wine quality: blending, waiting, sparging with inert gas, aerating by splash-racking, or treating with hydrogen peroxide.

Blending the over-sulfited wine with (ideally) the same wine is the ideal solution as it does not impact wine quality. The same wine and the required volume may not always be readily available, and therefore, this solution is not always practical. If you have a low-sulfite wine available for blending, you can run bench trials until you get to a blend in which you can no longer smell sulfite. Alternatively, if you are able to measure FSO2, then you can determine the amount of the low-sulfite wine needed to bring FSO2 of the problem wine down to a desired target using the Pearson Square (see Section 16.5).

Waiting for FSO2 to drop, via consumption, binding and dissipation, does not adversely impact wine quality, however, assuming a reasonable loss of 5 mg/L per month at cool cellar conditions, you would have to wait 15 months for FSO2 to drop by 75 mg/L! Assuming a loss of 10 mg/L per month at warmer storage conditions, you would still have to wait 7–8 months. These long wait periods may not be practical.

Sparging with inert gas, such as nitrogen, is an effective way of "blowing" FSO2 and has no adverse effects on wine quality. It does however require the use of a gas tank and inert gas along with a sintered stone. The sintered stone can be placed at the bottom of a tank through, for example, a Tri-Clover port, if so equipped, or drawn down from the top using a stainless steel tube or rigid hose. The idea is to inject inert gas and let it displace gaseous SO_2 throughout the wine volume until you can no longer smell the SO_2 or FSO2 has dropped to a desired level. The sparging time depends on the amount of FSO2 to "blow off" and wine volume: As a guideline, sparge for 10–15 minutes for 100 L (25 gal) of wine, then measure FSO2 and repeat as required.

The idea in aerating wine vigorously via splash-racking is to saturate it with oxygen (O_2) by racking into an open vessel, such as a pail or VCT, and letting the wine splash to the bottom by placing the racking hose high at the top of the vessel, then letting the oxygen consume FSO2 over the next few days, re-measuring FSO2, and repeating the procedure until FSO2 drops to the desired level or until you can longer pick up the sulfite smell. There are two drawbacks to this technique. First, the FSO2–O_2 reaction can take 5–7 days, and based on the amount of oxygen needed to react with FSO2, you would need to perform the procedure at least four times, which will take a total of perhaps a month. Second, any oxygen that does not react with and consumes FSO2 will oxidize other wine substances, as per the reactions we have seen in Section 8.1.

 From our SO_2 chemistry lesson, you'll recall that there is a greater proportion of molecular SO_2 (the form you can smell) at lower pH compared to bisulfite ions, which you cannot smell. This means that the lower the pH, the more likely you are to smell excessive sulfite additions.

The most effective method, albeit the most risky if not executed perfectly, to quickly reduce FSO2 is to treat the wine with a solution of pharmacy-grade hydrogen peroxide (H_2O_2). According to our chemistry lesson in Section 8.1, H_2O_2 reacts with bisulfite ions to drop FSO2, and produces sulfate (aqueous sulfuric acid) — the same oxidation reaction that occurs during the normal evolution of wine.

 You should only use the hydrogen peroxide method to reduce FSO2 if you can accurately measure FSO2 levels and that you are absolutely comfortable and able to measure small amounts of H_2O_2. First confirm the concentration of your pharmacy-

grade (H_2O_2) solution — 3% w/w or w/v are the most common, but you'll also find 0.3% w/w. The amount of H_2O_2 in 3% wt/wt versus 3% wt/vol is just about the same; you can use either.

Using a 3% w/v H_2O_2 solution, you will need 0.18 mL of solution for every 10 mg FSO2. For example, if you need to drop FSO2 by 75 mg/L in a 100-L (25-gal) batch, you will need 75 × 0.18 × 100 ÷ 10 or 135 mL of solution. You can make use of the downloadable worksheet at Modern-HomeWinemaking.com to help you with these calculations.

Before treating the entire batch, it is highly recommended to run bench trials with a 100-mL sample and measuring and confirming the drop in FSO2. In our example, you would need 0.14 mL of solution — use a good 1-mL syringe.

When you come to treat the entire batch, add the H_2O_2 solution very slowly while stirring gently. Measure FSO2 when you have added half the calculated amount of solution to confirm the drop is as expected, then complete the addition.

Now let's go back to sulfuric acid (H_2SO_4) as a by-product and understand the impact to acidity (TA). For every 10 mg/L FSO2 reacted with H_2O_2, 15 mg/L H_2SO_4 is produced, which represents a TA increase of approximately 23 mg/L expressed as tartaric acid equivalents. In our example, the 75 mg/L FSO2 drop translates into a TA increase of 172 mg/L, or 0.17 g/L (0.017%), and therefore still only a very small increase considering the large drop in FSO2.

8.5 MAKING BLIND SULFITE ADDITIONS

If you are not inclined or equipped to measure SO_2 or weigh KMS powder, you can make blind sulfite additions at regular intervals, for example, every 3 months in inert vessels and once a month in barrels as many home winemakers do to keep it simple.

You can add about ¼ teaspoon of KMS into a 23-L (5- or 6-gal) carboy or ¾ teaspoon KMS per 54-L (14-gal) demijohn at the end of fermentation and every 3 months thereafter, a method often recommended by those who do blind additions. Each ¼ teaspoon (roughly 1.5 g) of KMS added to a carboy adds about 40 mg/L FSO2. This method is okay for wines to be bottled within a year as the total amount of sulfite added would still be within the accepted maximum. But if you will be aging the wine for an extended period of time, reduce the additions to ⅛ teaspoon at each 3-month interval.

But beware! Teaspoons are not very accurate, and trying to measure ¼ teaspoon and especially ⅛ teaspoon makes it all that much more inaccurate. It is easy to add too little or too much. 50 mg/L FSO2 might be very low for a high-pH wine, making the wine vulnerable to microbial spoilage. And excessive sulfite can mute precious aromas, reduce color in reds, and can potentially be smelled easily by some tasters.

To make great wines, flawlessly and consistently, invest in knowledge and equipment to measure SO_2 levels.

8.6 ADDING SULFITE TO GRAPES OR FRESH JUICE

When working with grapes or fresh juice for which no SO_2 was added, you need to add KMS at crush or when you receive juice regardless of pH or desired MSO2 to inhibit indigenous yeast, spoilage microorganisms and oxidative enzymes (PPOs) to allow for a trouble-fee fermentation.

For sound grapes and juice, add 50 mg/L KMS, which gives approximately 30 mg/L free SO_2. For damaged fruit or juice pressed from moldy grapes, add up to 100 mg/L depending on the state of the fruit or juice. Table 8.4 provides the amount of KMS to add to sound grapes and juice to achieve 30 mg/L FSO2. You can sprinkle the KMS powder over the crushed grapes or juice and then stir thoroughly. Under normal fermentation conditions and using cultured (not indigenous) yeast, 30 mg/L FSO2 at this stage will leave the wine with very little FSO2, for example, in the order of 10 mg/L, and perhaps around 25 mg/L TSO2 at the end of fermentation. Be aware that yeast produces some SO_2 during fermentation; the amounts vary by strain.

Table 8.4: Amount of KMS to add to sound grapes and juice to achieve approximately 30 mg/L free SO_2

JUICE		GRAPES	
mg KMS per liter	mg KMS per gallon	mg KMS per kg	mg KMS per lb
50	200[1]	35	15[1]

[1]Numbers have been rounded to simplify calculations to determine KMS additions.

EXAMPLE 8.10

Adding KMS at crush

You just received ten (10) 36-lb cases of Merlot for a total of 360 lbs or 164 kg, and the grapes look good with no signs of spoilage. Calculate the amount of KMS to add at crush to achieve 30 mg/L FSO2 as follows:

$$KMS\,(mg) = 35\ ^{mg}/_{kg} \times 164\,kg$$
$$= 5740\,mg\,(5.7\,g)$$

$$KMS\,(mg) = 15\ ^{mg}/_{lb} \times 360\,lbs$$
$$= 5400\,mg\,(5.4\,g)$$

8.7 ALTERNATIVE STRATEGIES FOR REDUCING SULFUR DIOXIDE USAGE

As a first strategy in reducing SO_2 use, or at least making SO_2 additions more efficient, delay the *first* KMS addition, as outlined in Section 8.4, to allow acetaldehyde produced by yeast metabolism during the AF to be metabolized and to become bound. Hasty KMS additions would result in high SO_2 binding and having to replenish with more KMS.

Then, ascorbic acid, glutathione, specific inactivated yeast, enological tannins or yeast lees can be used as complementary antioxidant strategies for reducing the use of sulfite. Although these substances may have higher antioxidant power than SO_2 — and significantly higher in the case of glutathione and enological tannins — none can entirely replace sulfite as a broad-spectrum preservative.

Ascorbic acid, which is better known as vitamin C, is an additive used to protect transient oxidant effects when bottling whites, but is not recommended for red wines as the acid degradation product can interact with tannins and anthocyanins to cause bleaching (color loss) and premature oxidation of other wine compounds. There are small amounts naturally occurring in grapes but ascorbic acid does not survive long after crushing due to exposure to air.

The issue with ascorbic acid is that it plays a dual role — switching from acting as an antioxidant to a pro-oxidant, in what is referred to as a "crossover effect." If used without sulfite or if free SO_2 quickly becomes bound soon after the addition of the acid, ascorbic acid can actually cause oxidation. And therefore, the primary use of ascorbic acid is to scavenge oxygen in white or rosé wine at bottling or in other operations where the wine will be subjected to temporary aeration, such as at rackings or filtration; but it should always be used in conjunction with sulfite, always. For reducing sulfite, simply go with a lower molecular SO_2 in the recommended range for a desired style of wine (see Table 8.1).

To calculate the amount of ascorbic acid to add, simply multiply the FSO2 level by 4.4, making sure not to exceed 250 mg/L.

EXAMPLE 8.11

Adding ascorbic acid

You are about to bottle a 23-L (6-gal) carboy of Sauvignon Blanc; pH is 3.40. You have added sulfite to achieve about 25 mg/L FSO2 with 0.5 mg/L MSO2, and you want to complement this with ascorbic acid. (The wine would need about 35 mg/L FSO2 at 0.8 mg/L MSO2.) Calculate the amount of ascorbic acid to add as follows:

$$\textit{Amount of ascorbic acid to add (g)}$$

$$= 4.4 \times 25 \, ^{mg}/_L \times 23 \, L$$

$$= 2530 \, mg \, (2.5 \, g)$$

2530 mg of ascorbic acid in a 23-L (6-gal) batch represents 110 mg/L, well below the 250 mg/L recommended maximum.

We had briefly mentioned glutathione (GSH) in Section 1.1. GSH is a naturally occurring tripeptide in grapes and a powerful antioxidant. There are commercial glutathione preparations, such as OptiMUM White or Glutastar (Lallemand) and FreshArom (Laffort), which you can add at crush or pressing in white or rosé winemaking and forego or reduce the use of SO_2. Some of these products have the ability to preserve free SO_2, and therefore less SO_2 is needed, and which can also be used to protect wine during storage and aging.

Specific inactivated yeasts (SIY), such as Noblesse and Pure-Lees Longevity (Lallemand), and FreshArom and PowerLees Rouge (Laffort), are other excellent alternatives for scavenging oxygen, therefore reducing the use of SO_2, and for preserving aroma freshness. They can be used at any stage of winemaking but recommended at the must (juice) stage in oxidation-prone varieties or processes, especially where aroma preservation is the primary objective.

Enological tannins have high antioxidant power but they may not be suitable for certain styles of wine as these may impart undesirable astringency and bitterness. Ellagitannins and gallotannins are preferred over grape tannin mixtures as these have much less impact on astringency and bitterness; however, gallotannins are more reactive to oxygen than odoriferous compounds, which need oxygen to express their full aromatic potential, and are therefore not recommended for varieties such as Gewürztraminer and those in the Muscat family. Gallotannins (gallic tannins) are particularly effective as must additives to inhibit PPOs. Products that contain gallotannins and which have proven very effective include Scott'Tan FT Blanc Soft (Scott Laboratories), and Galalcool SP and Suprarom (Laffort); the latter is a formulation of gallotannins, ascorbic acid and KMS.

Wines aged on yeast lees are known to have greater aging potential as they are better protected against oxidative damage. Yeast lees possess strong reducing properties owing to the ability of nonviable yeast cells to consume considerable amounts of dissolved oxygen. We'll discuss yeast lees and aging on the lees in more details in Section 15.5.

If you are dealing with high pH wines, you can reduce the large amounts of SO_2 needed for microbiological control using fungi-derived chitosan (see Section 13.4.3.1), which can lower populations of various spoilage yeasts and bacteria, depending on the formulation of commercial products. Examples of chitosan-based products for microbial control include: Bactiless (Lallemand), which works against acetic acid and lactic acid bacteria populations, and BactiControl and MicroControl (Laffort) and EnartisStab Micro (Enartis/Esseco), which also work against spoilage yeast populations.

REFERENCES

1. Blouin, J. 2014. *Le SO₂ en œnologie*. Dunod, Paris.

2. Renouf, V., Y. Qiu, H. Klebanowski, A. Monteau and M. Mirabel. 2016. *L'apport d'oxygène durant l'élevage en fûts: L'importance du phénomène de désorption de l'oxygène contenu dans le bois*. Revue des œnologues et des techniques vitivinicoles et œnologiques. 43(161):52-54.

3. Pascal, C., J. Diéval and S. Vidal. 2019. *Prédiction de l'évolution de la concentration de sulfites post-embouteillage et durée de vie du vin*. Revue des œnologues et des techniques vitivinicoles et œnologiques. 46(173 Spécial):55-57.

4. Schneider, V. 2008. *Önologische Aspekte fruchtiger Weine: Die Rolle von Oxidation und Reduktion*. Österreichischer Agrarverlag (Av Buch), Sturzgasse (Austria).

5. Taillandier, P. and J. Bonnet. 2005. *Le vin: Composition et transformations chimiques*. Éditions Tec & Doc (Lavoisier), Paris.

6. Vivas, N. 1999. *Les oxydations et les réductions dans les moûts et les vins*. Éditions Féret, Bordeaux.

9 Understanding Tannins

....

The topic of tannins is fundamental in understanding red wine structure and body, and managing the red winemaking process. Tannin chemistry is an advanced topic; however, you will often come across the different types of tannins occurring in wine or which are added during winemaking, and you will need to understand how these work — at a functional level — so that you can make informed decisions on if, when and how to use tannins to, for example, stabilize color, or how to correct for deficiencies in structure and body. As you browse through a vendor's product catalog to choose an appropriate tannin product, you will often see tannins split into three categories: fermentation, aging and finishing tannins.

In this chapter, you will learn what tannins do, the different kinds of tannins, where they come from, and how tannin products are used in winemaking. There is a lot of terminology — some of it can be very confusing — so we'll clear it all up.

9.1 TANNINS: WHAT ARE THEY, WHAT DO THEY DO, WHERE DO THEY COME FROM?

....

Tannins are a broad class of heterogeneous compounds, known as polymerized flavonoid phenols or simply polyphenols, found in grape skins, seeds and stems, certain types of woods and nuts, plants, green tea and dark chocolate, and which are mainly known for their bitter taste and astringency. Astringency is a tactile sensation of dryness and roughness on the palate, or what is often described as a "puckery mouthfeel," and is due to tannins binding with saliva proteins when we taste and drink red wine. High acidity will reinforce bitterness and astringency of tannins, hence why tannic reds typically have lower acid levels.

Tannins provide structure or body to wine. When a red wine is said to be "full-bodied," it means that it not only contains a relatively high amount of ethanol but also great amounts of tannins and is typically richly colored. That is to say that a high-ethanol wine with little tannins is not considered full-bodied.

Tannins are extracted from grape skins and seeds during maceration and fermentation and from wood during barrel aging, or added by the winemaker in specific applications. Punchdowns favor more gentle extraction of tannins, whereas pumpovers with the aggressive use of pumps tend to extract more tannins.

Tannins tend to polymerize, that is, form long tannin chains, in part with the aid of oxygen from processing and aging. As tannin polymers grow, they become less bitter and less astringent making the wine taste "softer," "silkier." But tannins also polymerize with anthocyanins (then called polymeric pigments) to stabilize color; this polymerization is often mediated by acetaldehyde, which acts as a bridge, and which is produced by yeast during alcoholic fermentation (AF).

Anthocyanins are the color pigment molecules that give red wines their color; they too belong to the class of polyphenols. These are extracted from grape skins during maceration and fermentation and transferred into the juice, and generally, the hotter the fermentation, the greater the color extraction. As with tannins, pumpovers using pumps can extract more anthocyanins from grape skins. In teinturiers, such as Alicante Bouschet, Chambourcin and Marquette, the pulp too is colored with great amounts of anthocyanins.

 Pumpovers are generally not recommended in home winemaking as amateurs are not equipped with the larger kinds of pumps and hoses needed to move the dense and "slushy" mass of grape solids from the bottom of a vessel to the top.

Anthocyanins on their own are highly reactive and very unstable and tend to precipitate or stick to the side of vessels, and therefore, winemakers must make every effort possible to achieve an optimal balance between tannins and anthocyanins to ensure a stable color throughout the life of the wine.

Tannin–anthocyanin and tannin–acetaldehyde–anthocyanin complexes are much more stable than anthocyanins on their own. A deeply colored, anthocyanin-rich wine with very little tannin content will quickly lose its color as there aren't sufficient tannins to stabilize all those anthocyanins. On the other hand, a poorly colored wine with high amounts of tannins will have a more stable color, sure, but will taste overly bitter and may require years of aging to mellow out. Winemakers work arduously to achieve that perfect balance, often having to call upon the use of enological products to address any shortcomings.

Given tannins' affinity for proteins, tannins can be used for fining for proteins in making white wines stable against the ill-effects of protein instabilities, which become exacerbated with increasing temperatures (see Section 14.3), and vice versa, that is, proteins can be used to fine for harsh tannins in reds and barrel-aged whites.

9

Because of these tannin–anthocyanin and tannin–protein interactions, red Native American and hybrid grape varieties (see Section 2.2.2) require special processing consideration as they tend to produce wines with lower tannin concentrations than *V. vinifera* varieties, likely due to significantly stronger binding by flesh cell wall proteins. Red Native American varieties and hybrids may need to be treated with proteases — enzymes that break down proteins (see Section 10.1.4) — to reduce protein binding and increase tannin levels in wine, or alternatively tannins can be subsequently added, to stabilize color.

As we have seen in Section 8.1, tannins are also efficient antioxidants, having a great ability to consume oxygen, and enhance aging potential. Tannins provide further protection against oxidation and browning effects at the juice stage by inhibiting polyphenol oxidases (PPOs), naturally occurring oxidative enzymes, as well as, and, particularly laccases, highly damaging oxidative enzymes found in moldy fruit affected by *Botrytis cinerea,* the so-called "noble rot." And tannins provide some protection against microorganisms too, hence why reds generally require less molecular sulfur dioxide (SO_2) than whites.

You will often hear tannins being referred to as "condensed" or "hydrolyzable."

Condensed tannins, which are more commonly referred to as proanthocyanins because they release anthocyanins in an acidic medium when heated, are those tannins found in grape skins, seeds and stems. Grape skin tannins are most desirable as these are riper and therefore the least bitter and least astringent. Grape skin tannins are what winemakers try and extract as much as possible in making full-bodied reds. Seed tannins are more bitter and more astringent and are only extracted so much during fermentation. Stem tannins are the harshest, and particularly so in green stems (as opposed to brown stems), and tend to contain greater amounts of potassium (K^+), which affects color, pH, and tartrate stability, and therefore winemakers generally avoid stems altogether by destemming grape bunches at the crusher.

Hydrolyzable tannins are so-called because they release (hydrolyze into) ellagic or gallic acid in an acidic medium, and refer to tannins found in oak and chestnut wood and gallnuts, respectively. Oak and chestnut tannins are known as ellagitannins (or ellagic tannins) while those from gallnuts are known as gallotannins (or gallic tannins). Ellagitannins and gallotannins are highly desirable as they have greater antioxidant power than proanthocyanins, and therefore, you will often find ellagitannins and gallotannins in commercial enological preparations and specifically recommended in whites and rosés to boost protection against oxidation.

What happens during maceration and fermentation in red winemaking is that, as grape skin tannins are extracted and transferred into the juice and wine, naturally occurring proteins bind and precipitate these tannins. But these are the "good" tannins that winemakers want to preserve to give wine its structure, and therefore, they add what are called "sacrificial tannins" in winemaking-speak. Then proteins bind with and precipitate sacrificial tannins, and whatever grape skin tannins are extracted during maceration and fermentation go towards building structure. To reduce the use of sacrificial tannins, proteases can optionally be used at crush to break down proteins.

9.2 FERMENTATION, CELLARING AND FINISHING TANNINS

Winemakers often have to make use of tannin products, for example, to address a deficiency, for specific processing, such as dealing with proteins, or to adjust mouthfeel and body. These products are classified as: fermentation, cellaring or aging, and finishing tannins. These are commercial liquid or powdered preparations of different types of tannins designed for specific applications.

Fermentation tannins include sacrificial grape or wood tannins for use in reds for dealing with proteins and to stabilize color and enhance structure, and ellagitannins or gallotannins for added protection against oxidation in reds but particularly more so in whites and rosés. As the name implies, these tannins are added at the maceration or fermentation stage.

Cellaring or aging tannins include a vast variety of tannins, including those from exotic wood, which are added post fermentation to accomplish several objectives: to further stabilize color and build mid-palate structure in reds; to increase aroma complexity and mask any potential herbaceous character due to green pyrazine compounds found in Cabernet-related grape varieties (see Sections 2.1.2 and 22.9); and to further increase anti-oxidant potential. To avoid adding too much tannins and having to deal with an overly bitter or astringent wine, add the lowest recommended dosage, give the wine and tannins a couple weeks to integrate, then reassess before making any further adjustments.

Finishing tannins include many different types of tannins to fine-tune mouthfeel and body, to increase organoleptic complexities by adding, for example, hints of coconut and vanillin from toasted oak wood, or by increasing the perception of sweetness without the sweetness, what is better described as *sucrosité* in French. These tannins are typically added shortly before bottling. Here too, to avoid adding too much tannins, conduct bench trials to determine the dosage that best suits your palate, give the wine and tannins a couple weeks to integrate, reassess before making any further adjustments, then bottle.

Table 9.1 summarizes the different kinds of tannins along with some product examples that we will use in the winemaking protocols presented in later chapters as well as to address specific needs.

Table 9.1: Summary of the different kinds of tannins and commercial products used in winemaking. Consult product specifications and instructions regarding proper applications and dosages.

Type of tannins	Timing	Purpose	Examples of Products
Fermentation	Maceration/ Fermentation	• Remove proteins	• Granular oak • Tanin VR Supra (Laffort)
		• Stabilize color • Enhance structure	• Tanin VR Color (Laffort) • Tan'Cor Grand Cru (Laffort) • Scott'Tan FT Rouge (Scott Laboratories) • Vinitannin Multi-Extra (2B FermControl)
		• Protect against oxidation (whites and rosés)	• Suprarom (Laffort) • Tanin Galalcool SP (Laffort) • Scott'Tan FT Blanc Soft (Scott Laboratories)
Cellaring	Aging/ Cellaring	• Stabilize color	• Tan'Cor Grand Cru (Laffort) • Scott'Tan Tannin Complex (Scott Laboratories)
		• Build mid-palate structure • Increase aroma complexity • Increase antioxidant potential	• Scott'Tan Tannin Riche (Scott Laboratories) • ViniTannin SR (2B FermControl) • Tanin VR Grape, Tanin VR Supra and Quertanin (Laffort)
		• Mask herbaceous character	• Untoasted oak
Finishing	Pre-bottling	• Fine-tune mouthfeel and body • Increase organoleptic complexities	• Scott'Tan Tannin Riche (Scott Laboratories) • Tanin VR Grape, Tanin VR Supra and Quertanin (Laffort)
		• Protect against oxidation (whites and rosés)	• Tanin Galalcool SP (Laffort)

10 Understanding Enzymes

....

Enzymes are proteins that enable or catalyze specific reactions without themselves undergoing any change. These reactions could otherwise not happen or could take much longer to occur. You may already be familiar with, for example, sucrase, the enzyme that hydrolyzes sucrose into glucose and fructose.

Microbiological processes in juice and wine are all enabled by a plethora of enzymes, from the transformation of sugars into alcohol by yeast during fermentation, to the conversion of malic acid into lactic acid by lactic acid bacteria during malolactic fermentation (MLF), and to microbial spoilage reactions, such as the oxidation of ethanol into acetic acid by acetic acid bacteria. All these enzyme-enabled reactions are said to be of microbiological nature as they involve microorganisms.

Many other enzymatic reactions in juice and wine are of a chemical nature, that is, they do not involve microorganisms. We have already encountered many such reactions, such as phenolic browning caused by naturally occurring polyphenol oxidases (PPOs) in grapes that cause juice to oxidize and turn brown if not protected from oxygen, and pectin breakdown by naturally occurring pectinases in grapes.

Winemakers add specific enological enzymes to enable or hasten reactions that act on specific substrates, such as breaking down grape cell walls and proteins, and releasing aromas from their non-volatile part (see Section 1.1).

Enzymes are easily identifiable by their prefix, usually the name of the substance they act on or how they perform that action, plus the suffix –ases; for example, pectinases break down pectin, and glycosidases cleave a specific bond that releases a sugar molecule from an aroma molecule.

This chapter provides an overview of the wide variety of enzymes winemakers use in such as applications as enhancing aroma complexity to improving clarification and filterability, and which will help you understand manufacturers' product descriptions and choose suitable products for your applications.

10.1 DIFFERENT ENZYMES FOR DIFFERENT APPLICATIONS

Enological enzymes may contain one or more specific enzymes described in this section to accomplish several winemaking objectives at once. Some products are suitable for white and rosé winemaking or reds only, or all types of musts and wines. The timing of enzyme addition is important too; some are added at crush, some before or after pressing, others during fermentation, and some strictly in wine, and therefore, be sure to read and follow product instructions.

Enzymes are available in liquid or dry, powder form, and are usually added as a 10% solution using cool water. Some dry enzymes require to be rehydrated for several hours.

Specific products are used in the white, rosé and red winemaking protocols presented in Chapters 19, 20 and 21, respectively.

10.1.1 PECTINASES

Pectolytic enzymes, or pectinases, break down pectin to hasten color and tannin extraction in red winemaking, and, more generally, to improve flocculation, sedimentation, clarification, and filterability of wines.

Pectin is a viscous, structural polysaccharide found in the cell walls of all plant tissues; it acts as the "cement" between cellulose fibers. Pectin in grapes is found predominantly in the skins and therefore it is present in much higher levels in red must owing to greater extraction into juice during maceration. It can become a source of clarification and filtration problems; for example, excessive residual pectin can cause filter media to clog (see Section 14.2).

Pectin is usually not an issue in wines made from viniferas as it is almost completely broken up during fermentation by naturally occurring pectinases as well as any pectinases added by the winemaker. But non-vinifera varieties, particularly *V. labrusca* and notably Concord, can have very high levels which, if not treated sufficiently, can result in residual pectin that will become insoluble in ethanol as juice is fermented and give rise to colloidal instabilities that can cause clarification and filtration problems. If you have made wine from Concord grapes or fruit wine from, for example, peaches or apricots, you know firsthand about pectin problems.

Pectinases also ease pressing, improve juice and wine flow through the grape solids in the press, and increase press yield.

Pectinase products may also contain hemicellulases, cellulases, glycosidases and proteases, and are often described in manufacturers' literature as having such "side activities," for example, "glycosidase side activities." We explore these enzymes below.

10.1.2 HEMICELLULASES, CELLULASES AND BETA-GLUCANASES

Hemicellulases and cellulases break down large polysaccharides — hemicellulose and cellulose strands — found in grape cell walls and membranes, and improve pressing, anthocyanin and tannin extraction for greater color stability and mouthfeel, wine structure, and clarification and filterability. These enzymes are essential in red winemaking for maximizing color extraction, particularly with low-anthocyanin varieties.

In conjunction with pectinases, hemicellulases and cellulases also ease pressing, improve juice and wine flow through the grape solids in the press, and increase press yield. These are often packaged with pectinases into products referred to as macerating enzymes.

Beta-glucanases, or β-glucanases, are cellulase-type enzymes specifically used for releasing mannoproteins during yeast autolysis as wine is aging on the lees (see Section 15.5). Mannoproteins increase mouthfeel and improves wine structure.

M O D E R N   H O M E   W I N E M A K I N G

10.1.3 GLYCOSIDASES

Glycosidasic enzymes, or glycosidases, break specific bonds in compounds, for example, to free aroma molecules from their binders and enhance aroma complexity and varietal expression.

We saw in Section 1.1 how some aromas are non-volatile and therefore not perceptible until these are cleaved and freed from their non-volatile parts (mainly sugars) to become volatile. For example, many aromatic varieties contain terpenes, but which only express their aromas once cleaved from their binding sugar molecules. It's more complex with thiols, but glycosidases are responsible for breaking up specific bonds and releasing thiolic aromas in such grape varieties as Sauvignon Blanc in white winemaking and Grenache in rosé winemaking. Thiols impart aromas of grapefruit, passion fruit and box tree.

Grapes contain naturally occurring glycosidases that could cleave those bonds and release aromas during fermentation, but these enzymes have poor stability at the low pH found in wine and are also inhibited by ethanol. The bonds may eventually break by acid hydrolysis as wine ages, but winemakers add enological glycosidases to accelerate aroma release.

Some glycosidases may be inhibited by the presence of high amounts of sugars, and therefore, these should only be used in wine post fermentation when sugars have been consumed.

10.1.4 PROTEASES

Proteases (also known as peptidases) break down naturally occurring proteins in grapes that could otherwise cause protein instability and the wine to become cloudy.

Proteins are very large, naturally occurring molecules formed by amino acids. Due to their large size, proteins can form colloids in wine and become a source of haze.

Proteins are generally not an issue in reds because they bind to and precipitate with tannins; proteases can be added as a preventative measure in varieties that have high protein but low tannin levels. But in whites, and particularly in fruity, early-drinking styles of wines where there are negligible amounts of tannins, proteins must be removed using a suitable fining agent.

Here too when proteases are packaged with pectinases, products are referred to as macerating enzymes.

10.1.5 LYSOZYME

Lysozyme (also known as muramidase) is a glycosidase-type proteinaceous enzyme isolated from egg white, and is used to suppress specifically lactic acid bacteria to prevent a renewed MLF and ensure microbial stability in cases where malic acid was not completely converted to lactic acid. Lysozyme has no effect on acetic acid bacteria.

Lysozyme activity is most effective in white wines and is more active at higher pH; in reds, the increasing concentration of tannins during maceration and alcoholic fermentation reduce lysozyme activity as tannins interact with proteins, as we have seen in Section 9.1.

The use of lysozyme is discussed further in Section 14.1.2.

10.2 FACTORS AFFECTING ENZYME PERFORMANCE

Certain wine compounds, additives and environmental conditions can inactivate enzymes or reduce their performance. These include: the presence of fining agents, high amounts of sugars, polysaccharides and tannins, ethanol concentration, sulfur dioxide (SO_2) levels, temperature, dosage rate, and contact time.

Because of their proteinaceous nature and their typical positive charge in a wine medium, enzymes have an affinity for binding with negatively charged compounds, including fining agents, such as bentonite, polysaccharides and tannins, and can therefore become inhibited. Bentonite is well known to interfere with enzyme performance, even at low dosage, e.g., below 0.1 g/L, and therefore, enzymes should be used prior to any bentonite treatment (see Section 13.4.1.1). Otherwise, if bentonite was already added, the wine must be racked off the bentonite before adding enzymes. Usually it is best to add enzymes, let them perform their action, and then treat with bentonite where required.

We have already seen how high amounts of sugars can inhibit glycosidases, and therefore, these must be added at the wine stage. Tannins too can inhibit certain enzymes, and therefore where a tannin addition is needed, it should be done 6–8 hours following the enzyme addition or as per product instructions.

Post-fermentation enzymes, i.e., those added to wine, may require higher doses to be effective as high amounts of alcohol can inhibit their performance. As ethanol also decreases the solubility of enzymes, first dissolve enzymes in water, or as per instructions, then add to wine and stir thoroughly.

SO_2 is seldom an issue as enzymes have good tolerance, some capable of performing well with up to 200–300 mg/L of free SO_2, some up to 500 mg/L, and therefore, normal dosages should not be a problem. A potential problem may occur when potassium metabisulfite (KMS) and enzymes are added simultaneously and without adequately dispersing the first substance added. You can add the enzymes and KMS in whichever order, but thoroughly stir the juice, must or wine to completely disperse the first addition of enzymes or KMS before the next addition. The safest approach is to allow at least two hours when adding enzymes before adding KMS.

Under normal winemaking conditions, temperature should not be an issue, but at high temperatures, above 60 °C (140 °F), proteinaceous enzymes can break down and completely lose their potential for any activity. And at low temperatures, below 5 °C (40 °F), activity may slow down considerably so as to become ineffective.

Dosage rate and contact time influence reaction rate and, ultimately, the time to completion of the intended process. Reactions occur at different rates depending on the enzymes, wine matrix and environmental conditions, and so, enzymes must be given the opportunity to fully react. Manufacturers' literature recommends the optimum conditions and dosage rate on product packaging.

11 Alcoholic Fermentation

....

Alcoholic fermentation (AF) is the transformation of fermentable sugars — glucose and fructose — by yeast into ethanol and vast amounts of carbon dioxide (CO_2) gas as the main products, plus a plethora of by-products that give wine a multitude of aromas and flavors. These by-products include aroma-carrying esters and terpenes, glycerol, acids and higher alcohols. Yeast will benefit from a good supply of nutrients in the form of nitrogen, minerals and vitamins to carry out the AF successfully and avoid sensory deviations.

11

The common practice is to add commercially produced cultured yeast in dry or liquid format. Cultured dry yeast comes in 5-g packets for home winemaking use or in larger sizes, for example, 500-g and 1-kg "bricks" for bigger operations; cultured liquid is available, for example, in 35 mL and 125 mL formats to make a standard, carboy-sized batch of wine. Cultured yeast comprises strains from the *Saccharomyces cerevisiae* (abbreviated to *S. cerevisiae*) species as they are best suited for making wine. *S. cerevisiae* yeast can withstand the harsh conditions of increasing alcohol and ferment to 16% ABV with some strains capable of reaching 18% ABV.

Many winemakers, especially those that espouse natural winemaking, rely on indigenous yeast that comprise *S. cerevisiae* as well as non-*S. cerevisiae* strains, the latter being much weaker and usually cannot complete fermentation on its own, but which can add aroma and flavor complexities. Most non-*S. cerevisiae* yeast can initiate fermentation but then die off at around 3–5% ABV at which point *S. cerevisiae* yeast takes over and completes fermentation.

Unless you manage your own backyard vineyard and are familiar with its microflora and the kinds of wines it can produce, relying on opportunistic indigenous yeast can cause off-aromas and flavors or possibly a stuck fermentation — a condition when yeast is no longer able to metabolize sugars or other essential nutrients and cannot complete fermentation without intervention. Having grapes shipped across the country or from one hemisphere to another and wanting to rely on indigenous yeast is highly risky. Indigenous yeast is generally not well adapted for making wine, and particularly less so now due to climate change, which creates more difficult conditions, such as high sugar levels or high pH, and therefore more difficult fermentations.

If you are intent on using indigenous yeast, you can let it initiate fermentation and when SG has dropped by 10–15 points (about 3 Brix), inoculate with a strong culture of *S. cerevisiae* yeast to ensure complete fermentation to dryness.

Alternatively, you can use a commercial non-*S. cerevisiae* yeast, for example, from *Torulaspora delbrueckii* species, which can be used in what is known as sequential yeast inoculation to initiate fermentation and, after a certain amount of sugar consumption (SG/Brix drop), cultured *S. cerevisiae* yeast is added to complete the fermentation.

Choosing a suitable wine yeast for the variety and winemaking conditions at hand is one of the most important decisions, and as critically important as managing nutrients in ensuring a successful fermentation.

This chapter first provides a review of the yeast growth cycle during fermentation to help us understand nutritional requirements, followed by an overview of yeast nutrients and their role in yeast fermentation, considerations on choosing a suitable yeast, how to conduct fermentation successfully, how to restart a sluggish or stuck fermentation, and how to stop an active fermentation when wanting to preserve some natural residual sugars.

11.1 YEAST GROWTH PHASES AND FERMENTATION

What is called "fermentation" can be divided into two general phases (Figure 11.1): respiration, which, as the name implies, yeast needs a good supply of oxygen; and fermentation, which by definition, occurs in the absence of oxygen.

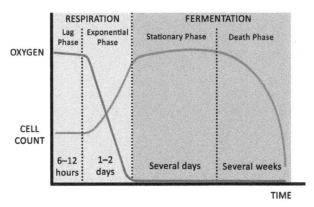

Figure 11.1: Yeast cell growth phases

Respiration comprises a lag phase and an exponential phase.

The lag phase refers to the first 6–12 hours when yeast acclimatizes to the must environment (temperature, sugar, etc.) and readies to build up its biomass for the next phase. A minimum yeast cell population is required along with sufficient essential nutrients needed for yeast growth and metabolic activities in carrying out fermentation.

In the exponential phase, which lasts 1–2 days depending on the temperature of the must, yeast grows and reproduces as it consumes sugars, oxygen and nutrients to build up sufficient biomass. By the end of the exponential phase, as much as about one-third of fermentable sugars have been converted, and most of the nutrients essential for yeast metabolism are depleted, including sterols that yeast is no longer able to synthesize as there is no more oxygen available. It is at about when one-third of fermentable sugars have been converted that the fermenting juice needs to be replenished with more complex yeast nutrients to compensate for depletion of important fermentation factors.

The fermentation phase comprises a stationary phase and a death phase.

The stationary phase is the active, vigorous part of the fermentation process as we know it, where we see a lot of foaming, and lasts just a few days in most fermentations but which can be made to last weeks in some types of fermentations, such as cool-fermented whites where winemakers try to express a more fruity character.

The death phase occurs at the tail end of fermentation when there is very little sugar left to convert, but which yeast struggles to complete conversion; it can last several weeks.

11.2 YEAST NUTRITION

Yeast needs plenty of essential micronutrients — nitrogen, minerals (trace elements), vitamins and sterols — for its growth and to support metabolic activities in carrying out fermentation in what is a relatively hostile environment of high sugar followed by increasing alcohol. And the greater the sugar concentration (SG/Brix) of the must, the greater the nutritional needs. Different strains also have different nutritional needs with some having a greater appetite than others. You will find this bit of information on any yeast strain chart; it will say something like: Low, Medium or Normal, and High.

Nitrogen is the most important of nutrients and is found in must in inorganic and organic forms as ammonium and amino acids, respectively. The amount of nitrogen available to yeast and which it can assimilate is referred to as yeast assimmilable nitrogen, or YAN. Inorganic nitrogen is less beneficial and is consumed much faster than organic nitrogen, which is assimilated and metabolized more efficiently.

Nutrient deficiencies can cause fermentation problems and the production of undesirable mercaptans, particularly sulfides, such as hydrogen sulfide (H_2S), which impart very unappealing smells of rotten eggs, sewage, cooked cabbage, struck flint or burnt rubber. As grapes are often deficient in nutrients, usually a consequence of less-than-ideal climatic conditions in a growing season or because of poor vineyard soil conditions, the must may need to be supplemented with more nutrients. Moldy grapes also reduce the availability of nitrogen that can cause a sluggish fermentation.

Excessive nutrients too can cause problems, not only with H_2S-related off-odors, but yeast may not necessarily consume all the nutrients, and particularly if added after the exponential phase, which could result in leftover nutrients in the wine. Leftover nutrients can be used by residual yeast and cause a renewed fermentation after adding sugar to sweeten wine (see

Section 16.1), or possibly by spoilage microorganisms that can cause flaws or faults.

There are many commercial preparations for adding nutrients: rehydration nutrients, yeast nutrients, and diammonium phosphate (DAP).

Rehydration nutrients, such as Go-Ferm (Lallemand) and Superstart (Laffort), are essentially inactivated yeast containing inorganic and organic nitrogen, minerals, vitamins, sterols and yeast autolysates (i.e., intracellular material). These nutrients are specifically used to rehydrate active dry yeast (ADY), or cultured yeast, in non-chlorinated, non-distilled water. Water is a much less stressful environment than must where there is also no interference from other substances such as acids, polyphenols, polysaccharides and sulfur compounds. Rehydration nutrients "condition" and help protect yeast so that it adapts more readily with less risk of problems once introduced into must. DAP is lethal to yeast at this stage and therefore should never be used for rehydrating ADY. Section 11.4 gives specific instructions on using rehydration nutrients when preparing yeast.

11

Yeast nutrients (also referred to as complex nutrients and fermentation nutrients) are added to must at two critical points to replenish depleted nutrients. Fermaid K and Fermaid O (Lallemand), Nutristart (Laffort), and Superfood (BSG) are examples of yeast nutrient products.

The first addition is done shortly after yeast inoculation, towards the end of the lag phase or after SG has dropped by 10–15 points (2–3 Brix), as some yeast and nutrients manufacturers suggest, to make sure yeast has sufficient nutrients (YAN) for the critical exponential phase.

Nutrients may be completely depleted by the end of the exponential phase and it is recommended to supplement for the stationary phase. This second addition is done when about one-third of sugars — the equivalent to a SG drop of about 30–35 points (7–8 Brix) in most cases — has been metabolized.

 Rehydration nutrient and yeast nutrient additions are completely separate and should not be interchanged; you have to add both — one does not replace the other.

Diammonium phosphate (DAP) is a source of inorganic nitrogen and, given its higher nitrogen content compared to amino acids, is most useful when large nitrogen additions are needed, for example, in severely YAN-deficient must, and should only be used in combination with complex nutrients. If you are not able to measure YAN to confirm the extent of deficiency, it's best not to use straight DAP as excessive DAP in must can be lethal to yeast.

DAP is often used as a yeast energizer in conjunction with yeast hulls for reviving a sluggish or stuck fermentation. Yeast hulls are purified yeast cell walls and are rich in sterols and fatty acids, which can help with a stuck fermentation, especially where there is an oxygen deficiency. Yeast hulls also help absorb toxic substances that may inhibit yeast cell functions and help restart a stuck fermentation.

Commercial nutrient preparations for organic winemaking will contain organic nitrogen, i.e., no inorganic nitrogen (DAP), with no additions of vitamins and minerals, where small amounts are naturally found in inactivated yeast.

HOW MUCH NUTRIENTS TO ADD?

As a home winemaker you are likely not equipped nor inclined to measure YAN; and therefore it's really guesswork trying to determine the nutritional status of the must and how much nutrients to add. If you want to up your game and make consistently greater wines, make YAN measurements part of your winemaking. You can either send samples to a lab or use a kit, such as Vinmetrica's YAN Test Kit. The drawback going the lab route is the turnaround time for results as you typically need to adjust YAN in must within 24 hours of crush or receiving must. A sample can be sent a few days before harvest if you grow and process your own grapes.

 YAN testing involves handling and disposing formaldehyde (37% aqueous solution) — a hazardous substance considered a possible carcinogen. Use a fume hood or work in a well-vented area when handling formaldehyde, making sure to wear protective clothing and googles.

If you are not measuring YAN, consider using the minimum recommended nutrient dosage in product instructions to ensure the yeast has access to key vitamins, minerals and nitrogen. An ounce of prevention can avoid a lot of headaches later in the fermentation. Split the calculated amount in half between the first and second additions.

Here's a simple way to determine a rate of addition based on SG/Brix of your must and the yeast strain you intend to use for fermentation.

- If the SG is in the range 1.090–1.100 (22–24 Brix) and you'll be fermenting using a yeast strain with medium nutritional needs, choose a dosage midway in the range.

- If the SG is less than 1.090 (<22 Brix) or you'll be fermenting using a yeast strain with low nutritional needs, choose a lower or the lowest dosage in the range.

- If the SG is more than 1.100 (>24 Brix) or you'll be fermenting using a yeast strain with high nutritional needs, choose a higher or the highest dosage in the range.

If you are working with Native American varieties or hybrids, which tend to be low in YAN, here too choose a higher or the highest dosage in the range.

If you buy nutrients in large packs, or if you consult a manufacturer's specification sheet, you will find the dosage expressed in g/hL — that's grams per hectoliter (hL), which is 100 liters or about 25 gallons — so you'll have to do some careful calculations. You can also simply multiply the g/hL number by 10 to get the equivalent in mg/L (ppm); for example, 5 g/hL = 50 mg/L.

If working with straight juice, for example, when making white wine, use the *exact volume of juice* in your calculations. If working with must, for example, when making red wine, use the *total volume of juice and grape solids* in your calculations.

Let's look at an example.

EXAMPLE 11.1

Determining the amount of complex nutrients to add if you are NOT measuring YAN

You just crushed and destemmed a batch of Sangiovese grapes and the total must volume is 100 L (25 gal). You measured SG 1.110 (26.0 Brix). You want to supplement nutrients with Fermaid K and ferment using Lalvin BM4X4 yeast — a strain known to have high nutritional needs.

Summary of wine parameters and measurements

Batch size	SG	Brix	PA
100 L (25 gal)	1.110	26.0	14.9

The dosage for Fermaid K is 25–50 g/hL; that's equivalent to 250–500 mg/L.

Given the relatively high SG/Brix and high-nutritional needs of BM4X4 yeast, add Fermaid K at the full rate of 500 mg/L. Calculate the total amount of Fermaid K needed, as follows:

$$Total\ amount\ of\ Fermaid\ K\ needed\ (g) = 500\ ^{mg}/_L \times 100\ L$$
$$= 50{,}000\ mg\ (50\ g)$$

Add this amount as follows:

• Add 25 g some 6–12 hours after inoculation

• Add 25 g when SG drops to around 1.075, or Brix drops to around 18.5.

Follow the manufacturer's instructions on preparing the slurry; you typically will have to dissolve the nutrients in about 10 times the weight in water, or 250 mL in each of the 25-g additions above.

If you are able to or can have a lab measure YAN, things get a bit more complicated, but you will better manage your nutrients additions and fermentations.

Use Table 11.1 to determine the target YAN based on your measured SG or Brix and your yeast's nutritional needs. Note that YAN is expressed in mg of nitrogen per L, or mg N/L; it is also simply expressed as mg/L or ppm when the context is known to be YAN.

Now convert the incremental YAN needed into the amount of nutrients (the actual product you are using) to add. This is where it gets tricky: read the product's instructions to find out how much nitrogen the product delivers; for example, it might say that 10 g/hL (100 mg/L) of product adds the equivalent of 10 mg N/L, and therefore, if you need to add 75 mg N/L, you have to add 750 mg/L of the product.

Table 11.1: Recommended YAN levels at various sugar levels and yeast nutritional needs (adapted from reference [1])

SG[1]	Brix[1]	YAN (mg N/L)		
		Low	Med	High
1.080	20	150	180	250
1.085	21	160	190	260
1.090	22	165	200	275
1.095	23	175	210	290
1.100	24	180	220	300
1.105	25	190	230	315
1.110	26	195	240	325
1.115	27	200	250	350

[1]For the purpose of this table, SG and Brix are rounded to the nearest 0.005 and 1 Brix, respectively.

11

Then follow your product instructions on adding the nutrients as manufacturers will instruct adding the required amount of nutrients just once at one-third sugar drop if the incremental YAN is only 50 mg N/L, or if greater, to split the additions between the lag phase and one-third sugar drop.

And if you need to add large amounts of YAN, the manufacturer may recommend using complementary products, for example, Fermaid K and Fermaid O (Lallemand), or Nutristart and Thiazote (Laffort). Fermaid O is an organic product and is very efficient as it delivers 4–6 times the measurable YAN, or "equivalent" YAN, as, for example, Fermaid K. Table 11.2 lists these and other common products and the amount of measurable and equivalent YAN they deliver.

You can make use of the downloadable worksheet at ModernHomeWinemaking.com to help you with the above calculations.

Table 11.2: Measurable and equivalent YAN for various yeast nutrient products

Product	Measurable YAN at 100 mg/L dose (mg N/L)	Equivalent YAN at 100 mg/L dose (mg N/L)
Fermaid K	10	10
Fermaid O	4	16–24
Nutristart	15	15
Nutristart Org	10	10
Thiazote	21	21
Superfood	10	10
Mauriferm Gold	10	10

11.3 CHOOSING A SUITABLE WINE YEAST

One of the most important decisions you will routinely make as a wine-maker is choosing the "right" yeast for making your wine.

Yeast does not simply convert sugars into alcohol; it metabolizes and transforms many other substrates, such as aroma compounds, amino acids, proteins and acids, into a plethora of substances which, when the process is well controlled, will add organoleptic complexity to create a great wine.

There is a vast selection of *S. cerevisiae* strains, many of which have been isolated from specific winemaking regions of the world and then produced commercially, each having specific fermenting properties that are intended to replicate the wines of those regions when matched to the same grape variety. For example, Lalvin BM4X4 is a strain isolated from Montalcino in Tuscany, a winemaking region famous for its Brunellos, and which is specifically intended for Sangiovese grapes. And therefore, specific strains can bring out favorable qualities in specific grape varieties. Where one strain may work well with one variety, it may not add anything to another variety.

And as tempting as it might be, do *not* use two different yeast strains for fermenting the same batch in the hope of benefiting from the positive characteristics of each strain — the two strains may produce aromas or flavors or both that are not necessarily compatible. Both strains will perform suboptimally as they will compete for sugar, nutrients and other substrates, and likely not produce the desired results. A better strategy is to split the batch into two and ferment each with the desired strain, then see how each turns out and blend the wines as desired.

As you ponder the decision of which yeast, consider the grape variety at hand, the condition of the grapes, your desired style of wine, and your processing objectives, techniques and environment, and choose a yeast strain that best meets your criteria without jeopardizing fermentation.

First and foremost, make sure that you are fermenting within the strain's alcohol tolerance and temperature range, or pick a strain that best meets your fermenting conditions, and be sure to account for the strain's nutritional needs. This means that if you have a high-SG/Brix must that you want to ferment to 15% ABV or more, then you'll have to choose a strain that can ferment to at least 16% and that you supply lots of nutrients. Temperature too is important; if it is too low or too high, it can lead to flaws such as H_2S or other off-aromas or flavors, or possibly result in a stuck fermentation. And if you are dealing with poor fruit condition, choose a fast-fermenting yeast strain so that it will out-compete microbial spoilers and won't contribute to VA [2].

If you intend to process your wine for malolactic fermentation (MLF), choose a strain that is more compatible with lactic acid bacteria performing the MLF, especially if you intend to do a concurrent MLF with your AF. We will discuss MLF in details in Chapter 12.

If you are working with high-malic acid grapes or must and you need to lower acidity ahead of, for example, putting the wine through MLF, choose a strain known to degrade large amounts of malic acid (into ethanol, or water and CO_2, depending on fermentation conditions — not into lactic acid). S. cerevisiae yeast strains degrade malic acid, some in more significant amounts. Examples of such strains and the amount of malic acid they can metabolize in brackets, according to manufacturers, include: Lalvin 71B-1112 (20–40%), Actiflore BO213 (40–80%), Renaissance Andante (30%), and Maurivin B (up to 56%).

And look for any potential red flags as some strains produce, for example, high levels of undesirable H_2S. Red Star's Premier Classique (formerly Montrachet) strain is known to produce lots of H_2S. If you have had H_2S

problems in the past, other than looking at where in your process you're causing H_2S production, try any of the so-called "no-H_2S" or "H_2S-preventing" yeast strains, such as those from Renaissance or those identified as being developed by QTL (Quantitative Trait Loci) Process. Use a no-H_2S strain if you had to add high amounts of SO_2 to deal with poor grape conditions at crush.

Section 11.7 lists by manufacturer some of the most common yeast strains — dry and liquid formats — available in small packets for fermenting standard carboy batches as well as larger formats, along with suggested varieties and important fermentation parameters. There are many, many other strains in larger formats for bigger batches. You can consult your favorite winemaking supply shop or each manufacturer's website for information on other products or for more information on those strains listed here.

Dry yeast packets can be stored in a dry, cool area unopened for 12–18 months or for up to 6 months in a refrigerator once opened. Liquid cultures should be stored in a refrigerator and used within 6 months.

11.4 CONDUCTING THE AF

Conducting the AF to ensure it completes successfully to dryness involves preparing cultured yeast (if not relying on indigenous yeast), inoculating the must with cultured yeast or waiting for indigenous yeast to kick in, supplementing the must with nutrients, managing fermentation temperature, and monitoring fermentation progress.

ADJUSTING TEMPERATURE

Before you inoculate the must or are ready to let indigenous yeast start fermentation, make sure that the must is just below the desired fermentation temperature for the style of wine you want to create. As fermentation takes off, there will be an increase in temperature, possibly a sharp and significant increase depending on your choice of yeast and must chemistry, perhaps necessitating that you lower the temperature. You will need to be ready and able to swiftly adjust temperature to within the desired range. We will look at specific temperature recommendations when we look at the various styles of wines in Chapters 19, 20 and 21.

To raise temperature, it may simply be a matter of raising the room temperature and then dialing it back once fermentation becomes vigorous, or if you are working with a carboy, pail or similarly small vessels, you can wrap a heating belt around the vessel. For larger vessels, you can link multiple heating belts.

Lowering temperature may be trickier depending on how much you need to reduce it. You can try lowering the room temperature, moving the vessel to a cooler area if possible, perhaps placing the vessel in a cool- or cold-water bath, or making use of your glycol chiller.

 Only use PET carboys or plastic fermentors if you need to transfer a batch into a cool- or cold-water bath. Placing a glass carboy in a water bath can be very difficult and slippery to handle.

11

PREPARING THE YEAST CULTURE AND INOCULATING THE MUST

Inoculation refers to the action of adding yeast to must to start fermentation.

If using liquid yeast, follow the manufacturer's instructions for inoculating the must.

If using dry cultured yeast, although some winemakers simply sprinkle it on the surface of the must, it is always best to first rehydrate the yeast in conjunction with rehydration nutrients to help the yeast build up critical biomass. You will need approximately 0.25 g of yeast per liter of juice or must, or 1 g per gallon; a 5-g packet is therefore sufficient for a standard 23-L (6-gal) batch. Increase that rate to 0.35 g/L (1½ 5-g packets, but 2 packets is fine) if you are working with high SG/Brix must, i.e., over 1.110 (26 Brix). If you are fermenting straight juice, i.e., with no grape solids, as in white and rosé winemaking, simply use the volume of juice to calculate the amount of yeast needed. In red winemaking, where you will be adding yeast to the whole volume, juice and grape solids, use the whole volume in your yeast calculations; estimate that volume based on the capacity of your fermenting vat.

To rehydrate and prepare dry cultured yeast (Figure 11.2), add rehydration nutrients as per manufacturer's instructions to fresh, clean, chlorine-free water at around 43 °C (110 °F) in a suitably sized, sanitized beaker. As an example, if using Go-Ferm as rehydration nutrients, add 0.3 g/L or 0.4 g/L to must with SG below or over 1.110 (26 Brix), respectively. The amount of water needed is typically about 20 times the weight of rehydration nutrients to be added; for example, if instructed to add 0.3 g/L for a 23-L (6-gal) batch, you will need to add about 7 g to 140 mL of water — let's say 150 mL; it's an easier number to work with beakers or flasks. Stir well while adding the nutrients and continue stirring until completely dissolved; there should be no clumps.

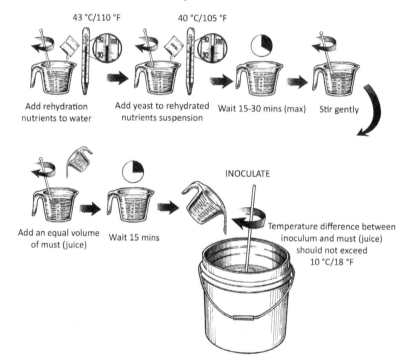

Figure 11.2: Rehydrating yeast

Although rehydration nutrients contain plenty of minerals to provide yeast with a balanced environment, as a precaution, do *not* use distilled water as it may inhibit or kill yeast if there is a mineral deficiency.

Let the suspension drop to around 40 °C (105 °F), then add the yeast while *very gently* stirring with a sanitized spoon for no more than a minute.

Let hydrate for approximately 20 minutes or as per the yeast manufacturer's instructions without ever exceeding 30 minutes. Use a stopwatch with an alarm as it is easy to get distracted and lose track of time. At this point the yeast–nutrient suspension, now called inoculum, should be foaming, more or less depending on strain. Stir thoroughly but gently — there should be no clumps.

Now add an equal volume of must to the inoculum, stir thoroughly and wait for about 15 minutes to let the yeast acclimatize; for example, if you prepared 150 mL of suspension, add about 150 mL of must. After the wait time, pour the inoculum (often referred to as yeast starter at this point) over the entire surface of the must and stir thoroughly to disperse completely throughout the whole volume of must. Stir vigorously to introduce oxygen to help yeast in building biomass and growing in the respiration phase. Place an airlock and stopper if fermenting in a carboy or cover the open-top vessel with a tarp or blanket to protect the must from the elements, dust and flies.

 The difference in temperature between the must and inoculum should not exceed 10 °C (18 °F); otherwise, add an equal volume of must to the inoculum, let acclimatize 15–20 minutes until there is a sign of activity, and repeat as required until the temperature difference is less than 10 °C (18 °F).

6–12 hours after inoculation, do your first yeast nutrients addition, if needed, as outlined in Section 11.2.

Within 24–36 hours of yeast inoculation, you should see signs of yeast launching into the exponential phase; there should be bubbles forming at the edge and at the surface of the must. Gently stir the must during that period to provide oxygen but also to avoid ambient aerobic bacteria and other microorganisms from taking hold on the surface.

MANAGING THE FERMENTATION

During fermentation, once a day, retrieve a sample and measure and record SG/Brix/PA and temperature in your log book to monitor progress. Use your favorite spreadsheet app, for example, Microsoft Excel, to plot these numbers on a graph. The graph should show a steady decline in sugar and relatively stable temperature during the stationary phase of fermentation;

the graph will help you identify if you have a sluggish fermentation. Figure 11.3 shows a typical (actual) graph mapping Brix and temperature over the fermentation period.

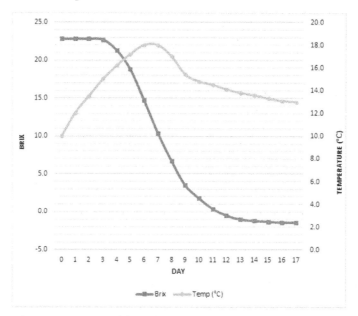

Figure 11.3: A typical (actual) graph of a white wine mapping Brix and temperature over the fermentation period. The juice was cold settled and then warmed up in preparation for fermentation, albeit a cooler kind. The juice was inoculated on day 1 at 22.8 Brix (SG 1.095) and 12.0 °C (53.6 °F). On day 3, fermentation started as temperature climbed to 15.0 °C (59.0 °F). As fermentation picked up and became vigorous, temperature spiked to 18.0 °C (64.4 °F) by day 6. There was a steady consumption of sugars between days 3 and 13. Fermentation was complete by day 16 with 2 days of steady readings at −1.4 Brix (0.995).

 Be sure to use a sanitized wine thief, cylinder and hydrometer to measure SG/Brix in samples. This is particularly important if you are working with small batches and you want to return samples back to carboys.

This next step is critical.

As the now-fermenting wine approaches the end of the exponential phase when approximately one-third of sugars have been converted, yeast will have consumed most of the available nutrients, and you therefore need to replenish the wine with the second addition of complex nutrients you had calculated to ensure that fermentation proceeds optimally. Follow instructions on yeast nutrient calculations and additions outlined in Section 11.2.

To determine the one-third sugar depletion point, take the decimal part (called points) of the starting SG, and divide by 3. For example, if your starting SG was 1.100, a one-third drop on the 100 points (the 100 part of 1.100) is about 33 points (let's call it 35 points to keep this simple); and therefore, when SG has reached around 1.065 (i.e., 1.100 − 0.035), do the second nutrients addition. If you're working with Brix, subtract one-third the original Brix or simply multiply the original Brix by 2/3; for example, if the starting Brix was 26, do the second addition at around 17 Brix.

 When doing the second nutrients addition, or when adding anything to fermenting wine, stir ever so gently making sure that you have plenty of headspace as there can be considerable foaming. Stirring vigorously will cause excessive foaming and possibly wine gushing out of your fermentor.

If the starting SG was high, for example, above 1.110 (26 Brix), thoroughly stir the wine when fermentation has reached the last third of sugar depletion, i.e., when the SG reaches about 1.030 (close to 8 Brix), to inject some oxygen to give yeast their last breath and complete conversion of the remaining sugar.

Usually, you will ferment wine to complete dryness in your pail, vat or carboy, i.e., when SG < 0.995 (Brix < −1.5), before transferring to another vessel (what is commonly called a racking from the primary to secondary fermentor by home winemakers). However, depending on the style of wine you are making, for example, if you want to limit polyphenol extraction when making red wine, or if you want to press earlier with Native American varieties or hybrids to limit extraction of less desirable flavors, or if you are following instructions provided in a kit or by your juice or grapes supplier, you can rack to another vessel before dryness, for example when SG has reached 1.010–1.020 (2.5–5 Brix).

As you get close to the end of the AF, a thick layer of dense, creamy sludge will have formed at the bottom of the vessel. This sludge is referred to as gross lees and contains primarily dead yeast cells, grape particulates, tartrate crystals, polysaccharides and, in red wines, seeds and protein–tannin complexes.

Rack the wine off the gross lees promptly as soon as the AF is complete, at the latest, or as instructed; otherwise, the strong reductive conditions, i.e., lack of oxygen, at the bottom of the vessel will cause sulfur-containing substances to turn into mercaptans, i.e., H_2S and other sulfides, as dead yeast cells break down in what is known as yeast autolysis. H_2S causes a very unappealing rotten-egg smell — it is an obvious marker for wine left too long on the gross lees. Gross lees can also impart a vegetal character.

Reds will receive one such racking when drawing the free-run wine and transferring the pomace to the press to extract press-run wine. As the press-run wine will still contain gross lees, a second racking is performed 24–36 hours later to a maximum 3 of days. Whatever precipitates from there on are fine lees, which still contain some small amounts of dead yeast cells but with little risk of causing reductive aromas. The fine lees also contain nitrogen-rich micronutrients that lactic acid bacteria can utilize for the MLF.

To add complexity, enhance mouthfeel and increase aging potential, it is possible to age wine on the lees, a topic discussed in Section 15.5.

If you detect any traces of H_2S in your wine, first try aerating the wine by doing a gentle racking. If that does not eliminate the odor completely, try treating the wine with copper sulfate ($CuSO_4$) as described in Section 22.4.

FIRST SULFITE (KMS) ADDITION

As described in Section 8.1, yeast produces small amounts of acetaldehyde as part of its metabolism during AF. Acetaldehyde is at its highest at the end of AF and takes about three (3) days to metabolize, and therefore, delay your first KMS addition according to the guidelines set out in Section 8.4. The objective here is to reduce the amount of KMS to add on the first addition.

Waiting those extra days before the first KMS addition also gives greater assurance that any residual sugars still remaining when the SG reads just about 0.995 (Brix reads around −1.5), but which you cannot (are not able to) measure, is completely metabolized.

11.5 DEALING WITH A STUCK AF

When yeast prematurely and unexpectedly stops converting sugars into alcohol and the SG/Brix does not change for more than 24 hours, the condition is termed a stuck fermentation.

During what should be an active fermentation, if sugar is *above* SG 1.005 (1.0 Brix) and you measure a drop of less than 5 SG points (1 Brix), or if approaching dryness and sugar is *below* SG 1.005 (1.0 Brix) and you measure a drop of less than 2 SG point (0.5 Brix), then you likely have what is called a sluggish fermentation and that a stuck fermentation is imminent, assuming temperature and all other fermentation parameters are favorable. This is where the fermentation progress graph — e.g., Figure 11.3 — comes in handy.

Here we will treat both conditions as a stuck fermentation for the purpose of implementing a restart protocol. A stuck fermentation can open the door to undesirable microorganisms that can cause undesirable organoleptic deviations or outright spoilage if fermentation is not restarted swiftly.

There can be several reasons, usually very difficult to pinpoint, for a stuck fermentation, and your ability to relaunch the fermentation depends on wine chemistry and conditions. The closer you are to dryness, the more difficult it will be to restart fermentation. You may be unable to restart fermentation when, for example, the SG is 1.000 (0 Brix), and if you decide to bottle it as such without proper stabilization (see Section 14.1.1), you may soon find out that yeast can kick in again under seemingly harsh conditions and finish fermenting whatever residual sugar there is, even under high alcohol and nominal SO_2.

The first step in trying to restart a stuck fermentation is to consult your winemaking records to make sure you have followed the protocol to the letter, and then to identify the most likely cause and take swift remedial action. First ensure that:

- Your starting SG was less than 1.110 (26 Brix) and that you had chosen a suitable yeast strain that could ferment to dryness within its alcohol tolerance;

- You had properly rehydrated the recommended amount of (dry) yeast with rehydration nutrients, or used the right amount of liquid yeast culture;

- You had supplied a good amount of oxygen at inoculation;

- You had supplied sufficient complex yeast nutrients after inoculation;

- You are fermenting within the yeast's temperature range and not fermenting whites or rosés excessively cold or reds excessively hot, as outlined in Chapters 19, 20 and 21;

- You had added complex yeast nutrients at one-third sugar drop, usually after a SG drop of 30 points (7–8 Brix drop); and

- You had not added excessive amounts of sulfite at crush or in preparing the must. Recheck your calculation.

If a stuck fermentation occurs early on or during the stationary phase, you likely did not observe one of the above instructions.

If you have followed the protocol to the letter, first try increasing the temperature, stir the wine, and look for signs of renewed activity within 24 hours. If fermentation does not restart within 24 hours, the wine likely has a significant concentration of fermentation inhibitors and toxic substances (e.g., fatty acids); you need to implement a restart protocol. The priority is to restart fermentation as quickly as possible to reduce the possibility of spoilage microorganisms taking hold, and to ensure that once restarted, it will go to completion. This may involve foregoing the use of your initial choice of yeast and going with a much stronger strain, such as Lalvin K1V-1116 or Uvaferm 43 RESTART (Lallemand), or Premier Cuvée (Red Star), specifically known for restarting stuck fermentations; consult the yeast charts in Section 11.7.

RESTART PROTOCOL

The protocol to restart a stuck fermentation involves treating the problem wine with yeast hulls, e.g., Oenocell (Laffort), preparing the booster yeast, which will be added to a small volume of wine (what is called a *pied-de-cuve*), and then adding the pied-de-cuve to the whole batch of wine. Be sure to use fresh yeast hulls as they contain fats that oxidize when exposed excessively to air and may develop an unappealing rancid taste.

Step 1: If treating wine in a carboy or tank without grape solids, first *carefully* rack the wine off its lees and into another vessel while avoiding oxygen pick-up to the extent possible, and immediately add 10–20 mg/L free SO_2 (FSO2). Make sure wine temperature is in the range 20–25 °C (68–77 °F).

Add 0.1–0.25 g/L of yeast hulls, or as per your product's instructions, while stirring thoroughly but gently, again, to minimize oxygen uptake.

Stir every 12 hours until Step 4.

11

Step 2: Take 10% of the wine volume, for example, about 2 L (½ gal) if dealing with a 23-L (6-gal) batch, and transfer to a suitably sized container. This is for preparing the pied-de-cuve.

Add and dissolve enough table sugar to raise the SG to around 1.020 (5 Brix) if it is below that. You need about 25 g/L of sugar to raise SG by 10 points (2.5 Brix).

Add complex nutrients, such as Fermaid K or O (Lallemand), as per product instructions at the recommended rate. Keep wine at 20–25 °C (68–77 °F).

Step 3: In a separate container sufficiently large to hold more than the amount of wine drawn in Step 2 (you need to account for foaming), add the required amount of rehydration nutrients to fresh, clean (non-distilled) water, as per instructions in Section 11.4 on *PREPARING THE YEAST CULTURE AND INOCULATING THE MUST*, for example, 0.30 g/L in 20 times its weight of water.

Rehydrate 0.30 g/L of your yeast strain of choice in the suspension as per the yeast rehydration instructions in Section 11.4.

Add about 10% of wine from the volume drawn in Step 2; for example, if you are making a 23-L (6-gal) batch and had drawn out 2 L (½ gal), then transfer about 0.2 L (200 mL) into the yeast–nutrient suspension. This is now the pied-de-cuve — it should start fermenting fairly quickly. Let cool and maintain at 20–25 °C (68–77 °F), and stir occasionally *until the SG drops to 1.000 (0 Brix)*.

Once the pied-de-cuve SG has dropped to 1.000 (0 Brix), double the volume by adding another 10% of wine from the volume drawn in Step 2. Maintain temperature at 20–25 °C (68–77 °F) and stir occasionally. If fermentation becomes vigorous, proceed to Step 4, otherwise, double the volume again.

Step 4: Once the pied-de-cuve is fermenting vigorously, add to the batch of wine and stir thoroughly, add more complex nutrients at a rate midway in the recommended range for your product, and stir again thoroughly. Place an airlock on the carboy or tank. The entire batch of wine should restart fermenting and proceed to completion, i.e., SG below 0.995 (–1.5 Brix).

11.6 STOPPING AN ACTIVE FERMENTATION

There may be times when you will want to stop an active fermentation at some desired low SG above 1.000 (Brix above 0.0) to keep some of the natural sugars when making an off-dry or sweeter-style of wine as an alternative to sweetening (see Section 16.1).

 As we have seen in Section 6.5, estimating the amount of sugar in wine at low SG/Brix is very complicated, but you can use the tables in Appendix B to establish a rough target SG/Brix at which to stop fermentation. This should get you close enough to your desired level of sweetness. You can fine-tune, if you need more sweetness, as per instructions in Section 16.1.

Stopping an active fermentation involves racking the wine, then shocking yeast with refrigeration followed by an aggressive sulfite addition. The instructions below are suited for standard carboy batches that you can fit in your refrigerator.

Keep in mind that you will have to start halting fermentation at a slightly higher SG/Brix than your desired target since fermentation will not stop immediately. For example, if you want to stop fermentation at a SG of about 1.002 (0.5 Brix), you need to initiate the halting procedure just above that, maybe at around 1.004 (1.0 Brix), perhaps higher, depending on the SG/Brix at which you start halting fermentation and how efficiently you are able to halt it. The higher the SG/Brix, the more active the fermentation and the greater the population of yeast cells; this is to say that it will be more difficult to stop fermentation at SG 1.010 (2.5 Brix) than at 1.004 (1.0 Brix).

First rack the wine if you are able to do it quickly to remove yeast lees and give you a better chance at inhibiting fermentation faster. Then immediately refrigerate at the coldest temperature possible in your refrigerator without freezing, or use your glycol chiller. The colder the temperature, the faster you will be able to inhibit fermentation. After 24 hours, add 180 mg/L KMS, or about 4 g for a 23-L (6-gal) carboy, to give you about 100 mg/L FSO2. Don't worry about the high KMS dose; you won't need to add anymore until FSO2 falls below the recommended level based on pH as outlined in Section 8.4.

11

The wine will start clearing very quickly during refrigeration. After several days, take the wine out of the refrigerator and carefully rack into another carboy, then coarse filter, for example, at 10 microns (see Section 17.4). Do a second pass with a medium filter at, for example, 5 microns. If you can measure FSO2 (and pH), determine if more KMS is needed and make the necessary adjustments. Also measure the SG/Brix to see how close you are to the desired final SG/Brix.

Now add potassium sorbate at the maximum rate of 200 mg/L, or 4.6 g to a 23-L (6-gal) batch. See Section 14.1.1 for more information on the use of potassium sorbate. Store and age the wine in your usual winemaking area. There should be no risk of a renewed fermentation if you implemented the procedure correctly, but keep a close eye on the wine as a precaution, being sure to maintain an adequate FSO2 level until bottling.

 Potassium sorbate cannot be used to stop an active fermentation; it only inhibits a renewed fermentation after the wine has been properly stabilized.

As an alternative to stopping an active fermentation or sweetening, you can try *Torulaspora delbrueckii* yeast, for example, BioDiva (Lallemand), or Zymaflore Alpha (Laffort), which ferment to a maximum of 10% ABV and preserve some of the natural sugars.

11.7 YEAST CHARTS BY MANUFACTURER

This section provides a chart by manufacturer of the most popular wine-making yeast strains along with key fermentation data including: temperature range, alcohol tolerance, nutrient needs, if they can be used to restart a stuck fermentation, if they can be used to degrade malic acid relatively significantly, as well as types of wines and recommended grape varieties for each strain with red varieties identified in bold. Varieties are abbreviated as listed in Section *GRAPE VARIETY ABBREVIATIONS* below. Recommended varieties are based from a mix of manufacturer or vendor literature, and from input from amateur and commercial winemakers as well as from personal experience. Those identified as "Rosé" can be any red variety that can produce rosé wine (see Sections 2.1.2 and 2.2.2).

Cultured dry yeast available in 5-g packets and cultured liquid yeast available, for example, in 35 mL and 125 mL formats, to make a standard, carboy-sized batch of wine are identified in bold.

Additional information and specifications, such as extent of SO_2, H_2S and VA production, MLF compatibility and rate of fermentation, can be obtained from reference [3], and from manufacturers' or vendors' references as follows: Lallemand [2,4], Laffort [5,6], Enartis (Esseco) [7], Red Star (Fermentis) [8], White Labs [9], Wyeast [10], Renaissance [11], and AB Biotek [12]. Some of the information and specifications listed in charts were obtained from personal communication with manufacturers.

You can make use of the downloadable worksheet at ModernHome-Winemaking.com to help you select a yeast strain for your desired grape variety and yeast manufacturer, and to determine the quantity needed for your volume of must or juice.

 The data presented in the following charts are believed to be correct and up to date at the time of publication. Data may change without prior notice due to, but not limited to, changes in manufacturer's specifications.

GRAPE VARIETY ABBREVIATIONS

WHITE VINIFERAS

AL = Albariño
AU = Auxerrois
CB = Chenin Blanc
CH = Chardonnay
GW = Gewürztraminer
MU = Muscat
PG = Pinot Gris
RI = Riesling
SB = Sauvignon Blanc
VI = Viognier

RED VINIFERAS

AB = Alicante Bouschet
AG = Aglianico
BB = Barbera
CF = Cabernet Franc
CM = Carménère
CS = Cabernet Sauvignon
GR = Grenache
GY = Gamay
MA = Malbec
ME = Merlot
MV = Mourvèdre
NB = Nebbiolo
PN = Pinot Noir
PS = Petite Sirah
PT = Pinotage
PV = Petit Verdot
SG = Sangiovese
SY = Syrah
TN = Touriga Nacional
TP = Tempranillo
ZF = Zinfandel

WHITE NON-VINIFERAS

CW = Cayuga White
LC = La Crescent
NI = Niagara
SN = Scuppernong
SV = Seyval Blanc
TR = Traminette
VB = Vidal Blanc

RED NON-VINIFERAS

BN = Baco Noir
CN = Chambourcin
CO = Concord
CT = Catawba
FR = Frontenac
LM = Léon Millot
MF = Maréchal Foch
MQ = Marquette
NR = Noiret
NT = Norton
SC = St. Croix

11

11.7.1 LALLEMAND

Yeast[1]	Temp. range (°C)	Temp. range (°F)	Alcohol tolerance	Nutrient needs	Restart stuck ferm.[2]	Malic degradation	White	Rosé	Red	Recommended varieties[3,4]
71B-1122	15–29	59–84	14%	Low		★	★	★	★	AL, AU, **BN, CN, CO, GY,** LC, **GY,** LM, MF, MQ, NI, NR, NT, PG, RI, **FR, GR, SC,** SV, VB, Rosé
Alchemy I	13–16	55–61	15.5%	Med			★			CH, CB, LC, PG, RI, SB, SV, TR, VB
BDX	18–30	64–86	16%	Med					★	**CF, CM, CS, ME, PV, SY, TN,** VB
BM45	18–28	64–82	15%	High					★	CH, **CN, CS, GR, MF, SG,** ZF
BM4X4	18–28	64–82	16%	High					★	AG, CH, **CN, CW, CS, FR, GR, MQ, PS, PT, SG,** ZF
BRG	18–31	64–88	15%	High			★		★	CH, **GY, PN**
BRL97	16–29	61–84	16%	Med					★	**BB, MA, ME, MF, NB, NR, NT, PN, PV,** ZF
CLOS	14–90	57–90	17%	Med					★	AB, AG, BB, **CN, GR, MA, MQ, NR, NT, PS, PV, SC, SY, TN, TP,** ZF
Cross Evolution	14–20	57–68	15%	Low			★	★		AL, CH, GW, MU, VI, Rosé
CSM	15–32	59–90	14%	Med					★	CF, **CM, CN, CS, FR, ME, MQ, PV, SC**
CY3079	15–25	59–77	15%	High			★			CB, CH, PG
DV10	10–35	50–95	17%	Low	★		★	★		AL, CH, GW, PG, Rosé
EC-1118	10–30	50–86	18%	Low	★		★	★		All varieties
ICV-D21	16–30	61–86	16%	Med					★	CH, **CS, ME, SY, TN,** ZF
ICV-D254	12–28	54–82	16%	Med					★	CH, VI, CF, **CN, CS, MA, MQ, NT, PV, SG, SY, TN,** ZF
ICV-D47	15–28	59–82	15%	Low			★	★		CH, VI, Rosé
ICV-D80	15–28	59–82	16%	High					★	AB, AG, **CM, CN, CS, ME, PS, PT, SY, TN,** ZF
ICV-GRE	15–28	59–82	15%	Med		★		★	★	CB, RI, VI, **CF, CS, GR, ME, SY, TN,** Rosé
K1V-1116	10–35	50–95	18%	Med	★		★	★	★	CB, **CW,** VB, Rosé
Lalvin C	15–30	59–86	16%	Low	★		★	★	★	**LC, FR, NT, SN,** Rosé
QA23	15–32	59–90	16%	Low			★			AL, CB, CH, CW, GW, LC, MU, PG, RI, SB, SV, TR, VB, VI
R2	10–30	50–86	16%	High			★	★		AL, CB, GW, LC, MU, PG, RI, SB, TR, VB, VI
RC 212	15–30	59–86	16%	Med					★	**BN, CN, CS, FR, GR, GY, MF, MQ, PN**
RP15	20–30	68–86	17%	Med					★	**CF, CS, FR, GR, LM, MA, ME, MF, MQ, NT, PS, PV, SY, TN, TP,** ZF
SVG	16–28	61–82	15%	Med			★	★		LC, PG, RI, SB, SV, VI, Rosé
SYRAH	15–32	59–90	16%	Med	★				★	AB, AG, **ME, MV, PS, PV, SY, TN**
Uvaferm 43 RESTART	13–35	55–95	17%	Low			★	★		All varieties
VIN 13	12–16	54–61	17%	Low			★	★		AL, CH, CB, LC, MU, SB, SN, TR, VI, Rosé

[1] Yeast identified in **bold** are available in 5-g packet for fermenting standard carboy-sized batches.
[2] Can be used for all varieties.
[3] "Rosé" means any variety that can be used for making a rosé wine.
[4] Red varieties are identified in bold.

11.7.2 LAFFORT

Yeast[1]	Temp. range (°C)	Temp. range (°F)	Alcohol tolerance	Nutrient needs	Restart stuck ferm.[2]	Malic degradation	White	Rosé	Red	Recommended varieties[3,4]
ZYMAFLORE										
F15	20-32	68-90	16%	Med		★			★	AB, AG, BN, CF, CM, CN, CO, CS, CT, FR, GY, LM, ME, MF, MQ, NR, NT, PN, PS, PT, SC, TN, ZF
F83	20-30	68-86	16.5%	Med					★	BB, CM, CN, GR, ME, MV, SG, SY, TN
FX10	20-35	68-95	16%	Low					★	AG, CM, CS, MA, ME, PS, PT, PV, TN
RB2	20-32	68-90	15%	Low		★			★	BN, GY, ME, MF, MQ, NT, PN
RX60	20-30	68-86	16.5%	High					★	CN, GR, MQ, NB, PT, SY, TN, TP
CX9	14-22	57-72	16%	Low			★			AU, CH
DELTA	14-22	57-72	14.5%	High			★	★		AL, CB, CW, GW, LC, NI, PG, RI, SB, SN, SV, TR, VB, VI, Rosé
VL1	16-20	61-68	14.5%	High			★			AL, AU, CB, CH, GW, LC, MU, RI, SB, TR, VB
VL2	14-20	57-68	15.5%	Med			★			CH, CW, SV, VB, VI
VL3	15-21	59-70	14.5%	High			★			CB, GW, RI, SB
X5	13-20	55-68	16%	High			★	★		RI, SB, Rosé
X16	12-18	54-64	16.5%	Med		★		★		AL, AU, CB, CH, Rosé
ACTIFLORE										
BO213	10-32	50-90	>18%	Low	★	★	★			All varieties
ROSÉ	13-18	55-64	15%	Med				★		Rosé

[1] Yeast identified in **bold** are available in 5-g packet for fermenting standard carboy-sized batches.
[2] Can be used for all varieties.
[3] "Rosé" means any variety that can be used for making a rosé wine.
[4] Red varieties are identified in bold.

11

11.7.3 ENARTIS (ENARTISFERM BY ESSECO)

Yeast[1]	Temp. range (°C)	Temp. range (°F)	Alcohol tolerance	Nutrient needs	Restart stuck ferm.[2]	Malic degradation	White	Rosé	Red	Recommended varieties[3,4]
Aroma White	14–24	57–75	15%	Med/High			★	★		CB, CW, GW, PG, RI, SB, TR, VI, Rosé
D20	18–38	64–100	17%	Med					★	CF, CS, GR, ME, PS, PV, SG, SY, ZF
ES123	15–25	59–77	14%	High			★	★		CH, MU, RI, Rosé
ES181	10–20	50–68	16.5%	Low			★			AU, CB, CW, GW, RI, SB, VI
ES401	15–30	59–86	15%	Med/High		★		★	★	CT, FR, NT, Rosé
ES454	18–28	64–82	16%	Med					★	AG, BB, CS, MA, ME, MV, NB, PN, SC, SY, ZF
ES488	15–28	59–82	16%	High		★			★	BN, CF, CM, CS, FR, GR, LM, ME, MF, MQ, NT, PN, SC
EZ Ferm 44	15–30	59–86	17.5%	Low	★		★	★	★	All varieties
MB15	18–30	64–86	16%	Low/Med			★		★	BB, GR, NB, PN, PT, SG, ZF
Q Citrus	10–20	50–68	15%	Med			★			AL, CB, CW, GW, LC, MU, PG, RI, SB, TR, VB, VI
Q5	15–30	59–86	16%	Med					★	BB, BN, CN, GY, LM, MF, MQ, MV, NR, PS, PT, TN, TP, SY
Q7	20–32	68–90	16.5%	Med					★	PT, SY, ZF
Q9	15–20	59–68	14%	Med/High			★	★		AL, CB, CH, GW, LC, MU, NI, PG, RI, SB, SV, TR, VB, VI, Rosé
Red Fruit	14–32	57–89	15.5%	High				★	★	AB, CO, GY, LM, NR, Rosé
Top Essence	15–25	59–77	15%	Med				★		SN, SV, Rosé
Vintage Red	15–32	59–89	16%	Med					★	BN, CF, CM, CS, ME, MF, MQ, MV, NB, NT, PV, SG, SY, TN, TP, ZF
Vintage White	14–24	57–75	15.5%	Med/High			★			AU, CB, CH, SV, VB
VQ Assmanshausen	20–30	68–86	15%	Med					★	BB, GW, NB, PN, RI, SG, SY, TR, ZF
VQ10	10–25	50–77	17%	Low			★			AU, CH, GW, PG, RI, SB, TR, VB
VQ51	20–30	68–86	16%	Med					★	BB, CF, CM, CN, CS, GR, GY, MA, ME, MV, NB, PV, SG, SY, ZF
WS	16–30	60–86	18%	Low	★		★		★	PN, ZF, Rosé

[1] Yeast identified in **bold** are available in 5-g packet for fermenting standard carboy-sized batches.

[2] Can be used for all varieties.

[3] "Rosé" means any variety that can be used for making a rosé wine.

[4] Red varieties are identified in bold.

11.7.4 RED STAR (FERMENTIS BY LESAFFRE)

Yeast[1]	Temp. range (°C)	Temp. range (°F)	Alcohol tolerance	Nutrient needs	Restart stuck ferm.[2]	Malic degradation	White	Rosé	Red	Recommended varieties[3,4]
Premier Rouge (Pasteur Red)	18–30	64–86	15%	High					★	**AG, BN, CF, CM, CN, CS, FR, GR, GY, LM, ME, MF, MV, NR, PN, PS, PT, PV, SC, SG, SY, TN, ZF**
Premier Classique (Montrachet)	14–30	57–86	15%	Low			★	★	★	CH, **CF, CS**, Rosé
Côte des Blancs	14–30	57–86	14%	High		★	★	★		AL, AU, CB, CH, GW, LC, MU, NI, RI, SB, SV, TR, VB, Rosé
Premier Blanc (Pasteur Champagne)	10–30	50–86	18%	Very Low	★	★	★	★	★	AL, AU, CB, CH, **CF, CS**, LC, MU, SN, VI, Rosé
Premier Cuvée	10–30	50–86	16%	Very Low	★		★	★	★	BN, CH, **CS**, CW, **FR, LM, MF, MQ, NR, NT, SC, SV, TR, VB**, Rosé

[1]Yeast identified in **bold** are available in 5-g packet for fermenting standard carboy-sized batches.
[2]Can be used for all varieties.
[3]"Rosé" means any variety that can be used for making a rosé wine.
[4]Red varieties are identified in bold.

11

11.7.5 WHITE LABS

Yeast[1]	Temp. range (°C)	Temp. range (°F)	Alcohol tolerance	Nutrient needs	Restart stuck ferm.[2]	Malic degradation	Types of wines White	Rosé	Red	Recommended varieties[3,4]
California Pinot Noir (WLP707)	16–32	60–90	>15%	Med			★		★	CH, **CS**, **GY**, **PN**
Champagne (WLP715)	21–24	70–75	>15%	Med			★			AU, LC, VB, VI
Avize (WLP718)	16–32	60–90	15%	Med			★			CH
Sweet Wine (WLP720)	21–24	70–75	15%	Med			★	★		GW, MU, NI, RI, SN, Rosé
Steinberg-Geisenheim (WLP727)	10–32	50–90	15%	Med			★	★		GW, RI, Rosé
Chardonnay (WLP730)	10–32	50–90	15%	Med			★	★		AL, AU, CH, Rosé
French White (WLP735)	16–32	60–90	>15%	Med			★			CB, CW, SV, VI
Merlot Red (WLP740)	16–32	60–90	>15%	High			★	★	★	**AG**, **BN**, CH, **CM**, **CN**, **CT**, **ME**, **PN**, **PS**, **PT**, **PV**, **SB**, **SC**, **SY**, **TN**
Assmanshausen (WLP749)	10–32	50–90	>15%	Med			★	★	★	**PN**, RI, **ZF**, Rosé
French Red (WLP750)	16–32	60–90	>15%	Med			★	★	★	**AG**, **CF**, **CM**, **CS**, **FR**, **LM**, **MA**, **ME**, **MF**, **MQ**, **MV**, **NR**, **NT**, **PS**, **PT**, **PV**, **SB**, **SC**, **TP**
Cabernet Red (WLP760)	16–32	60–90	>15%	Med			★		★	**BB**, **CF**, CH, **CM**, **CS**, **FR**, **GR**, **LM**, **MF**, **MQ**, **MV**, **NB**, **NR**, **NT**, **PV**, **SG**, **TP**, **ZF**
Suremain Burgundy (WLP770)	16–32	60–90	>15%	High			★		★	**BN**, CH, **CO**, **CT**, **GY**, **PN**, SB, Rosé

[1]Yeast identified in **bold** are available in 5-g packet for fermenting standard carboy-sized batches.
[2]Can be used for all varieties.
[3]"Rosé" means any variety that can be used for making a rosé wine.
[4]Red varieties are identified in bold.

11.7.6 WYEAST

Yeast[1]	Temp. range (°C)	Temp. range (°F)	Alcohol tolerance	Nutrient needs	Restart stuck ferm.[2]	Malic degradation	White	Rosé	Red	Recommended varieties[3,4]
Dry White/Sparkling (4021)	13–24	55–75	17%	Med			★			AU, CH, **CF**, CW, GW, LC, MU, PG, **PT**, SB, SV, TR
Red (4028)	13–32	55–90	14%	Med			★		★	AG, AL, **BB**, CB, **CF**, CH, CM, **CO**, **CS**, **CT**, **FR**, **GR**, **GY**, **LM**, **MA**, **ME**, **MQ**, **MV**, **NR**, **PN**, **PS**, **PV**, SB, **SC**, **SG**, SN, SV, **SY**, **TN**, TP, **ZF**, VI
Fruity White (4242)	13–24	55–75	12%	Med			★	★		CB, CH, CW, GW, **GY**, LC, MU, NI, PG, TR, Rosé
Italian Red (4244)	13–24	55–75	14%	Med					★	**BB**, **MA**, **NB**, **PV**, **SG**, TP
Summation Red (4267)	13–32	55–90	14%	Med			★		★	AG, **BB**, **BN**, **CF**, **CM**, **CO**, **CS**, **FR**, **LM**, **MA**, **ME**, **MQ**, **MV**, **NR**, **PS**, **PV**, SB, **SC**, **SG**, **SY**, TP, VI
Dry/Fortified (4767)	16–32	60–90	14%	Med			★		★	**ME**, **MV**, **SG**, **TN**, TP, **ZF**
Sweet White (4783)	13–24	55–75	14%	Med			★			AL, AU, GW, RI, SN, SV, TR, VB
Bold Red/High Alcohol (4946)	16–29	60–85	18%	Med	★				★	AG, **BN**, **CN**, **CS**, **FR**, **LM**, **MF**, **MQ**, **PN**, **PS**, **PT**, **SY**, **TN**, **ZF**

Types of wines: White, Rosé, Red

[1] Yeast identified in **bold** are available in 5-g packet for fermenting standard carboy-sized batches.
[2] Can be used for all varieties.
[3] "Rosé" means any variety that can be used for making a rosé wine.
[4] Red varieties are identified in bold.

11

11.7.7 RENAISSANCE

Yeast[1]	Temp. range (°C)	Temp. range (°F)	Alcohol tolerance	Nutrient needs	Restart stuck ferm.[2]	Malic degradation	Types of wines			Recommended varieties[3,4]
							White	Rosé	Red	
Allegro	15–28	59–82	16%	Med		★	★			AL, CB, CH, CW, NI, PG, SN, SV, VI
Andante	18–35	64–95	17%	Med		★			★	BN, CM, CO, CS, CT, FR, LM, MF, MQ, NB, NT, SG, SY, ZF
Bella	14–30	57–86	17%	High			★			AU, CH, CT, GW, LM, MU, RI, VB
Bravo	16–30	61–86	17%	Med					★	AG, BB, CF, CM, CN, CS, MA, ME, MF, MV, NB, PS, PV, SC, SY
Brio	17–28	63–82	16%	Med				★		CM, GR, GY, NR, PN, PV, SY, Rosé
Maestoso	18–25	64–77	16%	High					★	AB, AG, BN, LM, ME, MF, MV, PS, PT, TN, TP
TR-313	14–25	57–77	16%	Med			★			CB, GW, LC, RI, SB, TR
Vivace	14–28	57–82	16%	High			★			CH, PG, RI, SB

[1]Yeast identified in **bold** are available in 5-g packet for fermenting standard carboy-sized batches.
[2]Can be used for all varieties.
[3]"Rosé" means any variety that can be used for making a rosé wine.
[4]Red varieties are identified in bold.

11.7.8 AB BIOTEK

Yeast[1]	Temp. range (°C)	Temp. range (°F)	Alcohol tolerance	Nutrient needs	Restart stuck ferm.[2]	Malic degradation	Types of wines			Recommended varieties[3,4]
							White	Rosé	Red	
Maurivin B	20–30	68–86	15%	Low		★			★	**BN, CO, CS, FR, GR, GY, LM, MF, MQ, NT, PN, PT, SY, ZF**

[1]Yeast identified in **bold** are available in 5-g packet for fermenting standard carboy-sized batches.

[2]Can be used for all varieties.

[3]"Rosé" means any variety that can be used for making a rosé wine.

[4]Red varieties are identified in bold.

11

REFERENCES

1. Scott Laboratories. *Fermentation Management: A Focus on Nutrition.* https://scottlab.com/content/files/Documents/FermentationManagementNutrition.pdf. Last accessed March 18, 2021.

2. Scott Labs Canada. 2020. *2020 Winemaking Handbook.* Scott Laboratories Ltd. Niagara-on-the-Lake, ON.

3. Pambianchi, D. 2008. *Techniques in Home Winemaking: A Practical Guide to Making Château-Style Wines.* Newly-Revised and Expanded. Véhicule Press, Montréal (Québec).

4. Lallemand website. https://lallemandwine.com/.

5. Laffort. 2020. *Catalog 2020/21.* Laffort. Bordeaux, France.

6. Laffort website. https://laffort.com/.

7. Enartis website. https://www.enartis.com/.

8. Fermentis (Lesaffre) team. Email correspondence with Hugo Picard. January 11, 2021.

9. White Labs website. https://www.whitelabs.com/.

10. Wyeast website. http://wyeastlab.com/.

11. Renaissance website. https://www.renaissanceyeast.com/.

12. AB Biotek website. https://www.abbiotek.com/.

12 Malolactic Fermentation

Most red wines and only a handful of whites go through what many call a "second" and even "secondary" fermentation where lactic acid bacteria (LAB) convert naturally occurring, sharper-tasting malic acid (think green apples) into the softer, weaker lactic acid (think dairy products) and reduce overall acidity (and increase pH) in what is known as malolactic fermentation, or MLF. The sight of tiny, slow-rising carbon dioxide (CO_2) bubbles post alcoholic fermentation (AF) is usually a telltale sign of an active MLF. And just as with indigenous yeast, some winemakers familiar with the microflora in their vineyards and wineries may rely on indigenous LAB, but it's otherwise very risky as there are many more rogue bacteria that can outcompete "good LAB" and produce off-aromas and flavors, biogenic amines, and possibly outright spoilage. Biogenic amines are contaminant substances, some of which have physiological effects, such as headaches, and include histamine, putrescine and cadaverine. Modern winemakers appreciate the predictability and reliability of commercial cultured LAB, which are screened to remove the enzymes responsible for biogenic amine production.

 If you make wine from kits, you can skip this chapter. Juice and concentrate in kits have been prepared to produce balanced wines. Putting such wines through MLF can compromise quality and yield unexpected results that can be very different than the style the kit vendor intended.

MLF produces many by-products that contribute positive aromas and flavors. Diacetyl — the same substance that's added to your popcorn at the movies — is produced by some LAB strains used in MLF and is partially responsible for the buttery aroma in, for example, barrel-aged and barrel-fermented Chardonnays.

MLF and complete malic conversion are almost always desired in reds to add aroma and flavor complexity but also as a way to reduce high acidity, i.e., total acidity (TA). It also improves microbial stability as malic acid is no longer available to rogue malic-craving bacteria as an energy source. The style of white wine, and the strain of bacteria being used for the LAB addition will impact the decision when to start the MLF. A light, fruity white wine will benefit from an earlier LAB addition to avoid the development of more dominant aromas which will develop more in a post-AF LAB addition.

Where only a partial MLF is desired, wines have to be actively stabilized against renewed MLF in bottles using sulfur dioxide (SO_2) and lysozyme (see Section 14.1.2), or chitosan (see Section 13.4.3.1) or, alternatively, if possible, sterile filtration (see Section 17.3).

Wines acidified with citric acid should not be subjected to MLF as many LAB convert the acid into acetic acid (vinegar) and a commensurate increase in volatile acidity (VA) and copious amounts of diacetyl.

This chapter describes timing of inoculation for MLF, nutrition for LAB, how to choose a LAB culture for a desired style of wine, how to conduct the MLF, how to monitor MLF progression and test for completion, and how to deal with a stuck MLF.

12.1 TIMING OF INOCULATION: CONCURRENT VERSUS SEQUENTIAL MLF

The very first decision you will be making when wanting to conduct a MLF is the timing of LAB inoculation and MLF — a topic of much discussion. There are processing considerations, including when to add nutrients in ensuring that the MLF goes to completion, and the desired diacetyl character.

Some winemakers believe that LAB can better complete the MLF in a much shorter timeframe when inoculated at the start of the AF, or shortly thereafter, or later in the AF in a co-inoculation scenario. This allows the LAB to adapt to the wine environment and increasing alcohol, to complete the MLF more quickly and the wine to be stabilized sooner, decreasing the need to keep the wine warm while waiting for the MLF to start in a sequential MLF. Although LAB are active and healthy during the AF, the LAB population does not really start to grow until the yeast is tailing off and dying, which means that the MLF will always take longer to complete than the AF. A concurrent AF and MLF can also be used to minimize diacetyl production. The risk with co-inoculation is in the case of the AF unexpectedly becoming stuck; the restart protocol may jeopardize the active MLF.

There are those who believe that sequential inoculation is best, i.e., waiting for the AF to complete before inoculating for the MLF and eliminating competition for nutrients between yeast and bacteria. A sequential AF and MLF can also be used to maximize diacetyl production, when desired. The risk with a sequential MLF is that it extends the duration the wine is not protected with SO_2, especially if the MLF takes much longer than expected to complete, all the while maintaining the wine at warmer temperatures.

Experiment with the different MLF inoculation methods and see what works best for you, making sure to use nutrients as outlined in Section 12.2. If you are starting with a high-SG/Brix must, consider starting the MLF as soon as possible, concurrently with the AF, to minimize the risk of a stuck MLF due to high alcohol inhibiting LAB. Beware though! If you use processed juice or must in which processors have added SO_2 and you intend to carry out a concurrent AF and MLF, be sure to measure total SO_2 to ensure that it is not beyond the LAB's specifications. If it is, you may have to delay the MLF until after the AF when there will be less free SO_2, and likely lower total SO_2.

12.2 BACTERIAL NUTRITION

LAB need essential micronutrients — even more so than yeast — for their growth and to support metabolic activities in carrying out MLF in what could be a relatively hostile environment depending on wine chemistry and timing of MLF. LAB nutrients are different from yeast nutrients, and are therefore not interchangeable.

Just like yeast, there are rehydration nutrients for LAB too, and MLF nutrients.

Rehydration nutrients, such as Acti-ML (Lallemand), which contains inactivated yeast and cellulose, are used when rehydrating freeze-dried culture to give LAB a greater chance of carrying out the MLF to completion. According to product literature, cellulose is used in Acti-ML to "increase the surface area and keep bacteria in better suspension for optimizing activity." Rehydration nutrients are particularly recommended when conducting the MLF concurrently with the AF to help LAB be more robust through the AF.

MLF nutrients, such as Opti'Malo Plus (Lallemand), are complex nutrients that, in addition to inactivated yeast and cellulose, contain organic nitrogen, cell wall polysaccharides, vitamins and essential minerals. MLF nutrients are always recommended in both co-inoculation and sequential MLF scenarios.

In a co-inoculation scenario, LAB are present from the (almost) start and can therefore access some of the nutrients available in the must early on, and therefore MLF nutrients should only be added at the tail end of the AF so that the yeast does not use up the nutrients before the LAB can get to them.

Nutrients are also used in wine, for example, when the MLF is initiated after completion of the AF, if the wine has been racked clean of its lees. Nutrients are not necessarily needed if there are lees present, as lees contain abundant amounts of nutrients that LAB can use. But nutrients are always recommended when the MLF will be performed under difficult conditions related to alcohol level, pH, malic acid level, SO_2 presence, and temperature, and the presence of inhibitors, such as polyphenols in reds.

 Rehydration nutrients and MLF nutrients are quite different and should not be interchanged.

 For adding MLF nutrients, follow your product's instructions on dosage and proper use; some nutrients may need to be added a day or two before initiating MLF.

12.3 CHOOSING A SUITABLE LAB CULTURE

The most common LAB strains used for MLF are from the species *Oenococcus oeni* (*O. oeni*). There are also new strains of *Lactobacillus plantarum* bacteria that have shown greater malolactic activity, resulting in faster conversion of malic acid and shorter MLF, although the bacteria may have stricter operating tolerances than *O. oeni* LAB or can only be used in co-inoculation scenarios. Here, the focus will be on *O. oeni* LAB.

Compared to yeast, LAB are much more fastidious and have stricter tolerances, which you can find in LAB specification sheets. Different strains have different tolerances, but in general, *O. oeni* LAB prefer an alcohol level (% ABV) below 15%, a pH over 3.1 or 3.2, a maximum *total* SO_2 level around 40–50 mg/L, and temperature in the range 18–22 °C (64–72 °F). You'll need to be particularly mindful of choosing an appropriate LAB culture for MLF in high-acid wines with very low pH (less than 3.0).

Being anaerobic microorganisms, LAB are not only sensitive to oxygen and become inhibited, but under oxidative conditions and particularly at high pH (>3.5) and low SO_2, LAB can metabolize tartaric acid into objectionable levels of lactic, acetic and succinic acids, but higher pH, which can make wine limp and flat and turn the wine cloudy in what is called *tourne* [1,2]; this is one of the reasons why MLF should be completely protected from oxygen.

If any of the above parameters are out of the specification range or the wine has excessive amounts of dissolved oxygen, you can expect a difficult MLF that can take several weeks or months to complete, or perhaps become stuck. This exposes the wine to microbial risks as there is very little or no SO_2. Therefore you have to be extra vigilant and maintain very strict sanitary conditions when conducting the MLF, especially with high-pH wines, as LAB thrive at higher pH, like most microorganisms and particularly spoilage ones.

Note that LAB are sensitive to bound SO_2 (see Section 8.2), not just free SO_2, which means you need to respect the LAB strain's specifications on *total* SO_2. This should not be an issue under normal winemaking conditions as any SO_2 added at crush or produced by yeast during the AF has been consumed or dissipated and only a small amount has become bound. Total SO_2 will generally be under 25 mg/L and therefore not an issue.

12

The other important consideration is how much butter — diacetyl — you want in your wine. Copious amounts of diacetyl may be fine in an oak-style Chardonnay, but likely not in a bold Cab or refined Pinot Noir. There are LAB strains and winemaking techniques that limit diacetyl production and its buttery aromas and flavors; we'll explore those techniques in Section 12.4.

The only issue with LAB culture, particularly freeze-dried formats, for home or small-scale winemakers is that the smallest format available can inoculate large volumes of wine; for example, a 2.5-g packet is good for 250 L (65 gal) of wine. These packets can be expensive, so plan carefully, splitting a packet across different wines. A 2.5-g packet is good for about 10 standard 23-L (6-gal) carboys and preferably added at the same time, or with a very short delay, to all carboys. If inoculating all at once, suspend the contents of the 2.5-g packet in non-chlorinated, non-distilled water, stir gently, and then pipette the required amount of suspension into each carboy.

Alternatively, you can use a liquid format culture, such as those from White Labs and Wyeast, which are better suited for smaller volumes.

Section 12.7 lists by manufacturer some of the most common LAB cultures — dry and liquid formats along with important MLF parameters. There are many other cultures from other manufacturers. You can consult your favorite winemaking supply shop or each manufacturer's website for information on other products or for more information on those cultures listed here.

Be sure to follow product instructions as some cultures can be added directly to the juice or wine while others may need to be first rehydrated in water and perhaps with some rehydration nutrients. Visit manufacturers' websites for additional information.

 Freeze-dried culture packets can be stored generally for up to 18 months in the fridge at 4 °C (40 °F) or up to 36 months in the freezer at −18 °C (0 °F) in their original sealed packaging. The entire packet should be used as quickly as possible once opened. Liquid cultures should be stored in the fridge and used within 6 months. Always follow the manufacturer's instructions for your specific product.

12.4 CONDUCTING THE MLF

There are several important processing considerations for ensuring a successful MLF and the extent of diacetyl production.

MALIC ACID LEVEL

High malic acid levels are converted into high levels of lactic acid. Above a certain threshold (typically around 3 g/L) and specific to each bacterium strain, these lactic acid levels can inhibit LAB. If you suspect high malic levels in your grapes, must or wine, for example, when making wine from Native American varieties or hybrids or from viniferas from a very poor vintage, it is recommended to metabolize some malic acid using a malic-degrading yeast for the AF. This will reduce the amount of lactic acid produced during the MLF.

ADJUSTING TEMPERATURE

Before you inoculate, first make sure that the must or wine temperature is within your LAB's operating range, typically in the range 18–22 °C (64–72 °F), taking into account temperature increases during the AF if doing a concurrent MLF. Refer to Section 11.4 on tips for adjusting temperature.

INOCULATING THE MUST OR WINE

Before initiating the MLF, run a paper chromatography test, described below in Section 12.5, to establish a baseline view of the acid situation in the must or wine — it's basically to see how much malic acid there is. This will give you something to compare when you run your final chromatography test at the end of the MLF. It's good practice, and it's fun to visualize the progress of your MLF.

If you are adding MLF nutrients, follow the manufacturer's instructions as some may need to be added a day or two in advance of LAB inoculation. This may also depend on whether you intend to use the lees as nutrients.

12

For direct-inoculation culture, follow the manufacturer's instructions; the culture is usually just added to the must or wine with a good stir.

If your culture requires rehydration, add rehydration nutrients as per manufacturer's instructions to fresh, clean, chlorine-free tap water at the recommended temperature in a suitably sized, sanitized beaker. For example, if using Acti-ML, add at a rate of 200 mg/L by first dissolving the powder in 10 times its weight of water at 25 °C (77 °F) — that's 4.6 g of Acti-ML for a 23-L (6-gal) batch to be dissolved in about 50 mL of water. Add the required amount of LAB, wait approximately 15 minutes, then add the suspension to the must or wine while stirring very gently. If using a freeze-dried packet with a listed dosage of 2.5 g per 250 L (that's 0.01 g/L), you need 0.2–0.3 g for the 23-L (6-gal) batch. If you don't have a gram scale, just scoop with a spatula what would be about one-tenth of the contents of the packet. When adding such small amounts, a little more bacteria is fine; it may allow the MLF to start faster. Put the airlock and stopper back on the carboy or vessel if the MLF is done in a closed container.

MANAGING THE MLF

During the MLF, you can stir the wine *very gently* — to avoid oxygen pickup — once or twice a week just to get the lees and bacterial cells back into suspension to favor a smooth and faster MLF. Be sure to maintain temperature within the LAB's specifications.

MLF activity can be a bit difficult to detect as it produces tiny CO_2 bubbles, far and few in between. Therefore be careful as lack of detection of bubbles does not necessarily signify lack of activity. Point a flashlight at an angle towards the top of the carboy neck and look for slowly rising bubbles. Run a paper chromatography test, described below in Section 12.5, or an enzymatic test, every week or at least every two weeks to monitor progress. Do not rely strictly on bubbles; these can be misleading. Progress and completion can only be monitored with paper chromatography or enzymatic testing.

When the MLF is complete and according to the schedule set out in Section 8.4, either add SO_2 according to pH to ensure microbial stability, without racking if you intend to age the wine further on the lees, or first rack then add SO_2.

If you had opted for a partial MLF, add SO_2 according to pH and lysozyme at a dosage based on bench trials and as per instructions outlined in Section 14.1.2, or add a commercial formulation of chitosan (see Section 13.4.3.1). If you wish not to add lysozyme or chitosan, your only other option is sterile filtration (see Section 17.3).

And if you intend to sweeten (see Section 16.1) to make an off-dry or sweeter style of wine, do not add sorbate if the wine has undergone MLF, as lactic acid bacteria will metabolize sorbate and produce a very off-putting geranium-like smell (see Sections 14.1.1 and 22.10).

MANAGING DIACETYL PRODUCTION

This section has been adapted from reference [3].

To *maximize* diacetyl production:

1. Use a LAB strain known for high diacetyl production (refer to the bacterium charts in Section 12.7).

2. Wait for the AF to complete, rack the wine off the gross lees and wait several days to further allow yeast cells to die, and then inoculate for a sequential MLF. The presence of yeast lees during MLF would otherwise metabolize diacetyl.

3. While managing inherent risks, because of the lack of protection from SO_2, lower the temperature within the LAB's range to extend the duration of MLF. Note that lower pH too favors higher diacetyl production.

4. Stir the wine twice or more per week, a touch vigorously to inject some oxygen and favor diacetyl production.

5. Diacetyl level is highest right when all malic acid has been converted. At the point of full malic conversion, as determined by paper chromatography (see Section 12.5), rack the wine and add SO_2 according to pH — this would be your first post-AF, post-MLF addition.

To *minimize* diacetyl production:

1. Choose a neutral LAB strain with low diacetyl production (refer to the bacterium charts in Section 12.7).

2. Conduct concurrent AF and MLF to allow yeast and bacteria to metabolize any diacetyl being produced.

3. Favor a speedier and shorter MLF by increasing temperature within the LAB's range. Note that higher pH favors lower diacetyl production.

4. If MLF does not complete before the end of AF and you need to rack and continue MLF separately, do not stir the wine during MLF so as to maintain a reductive environment and not favor diacetyl production.

5. When malic acid has been completely converted, as determined by paper chromatography (see Section 12.5), wait 10–14 days to allow yeast and bacteria to further metabolize diacetyl, rack the wine, then add SO_2 according to pH — this would be your first post-AF, post-MLF addition. If aging on the fine lees, racking can be delayed until the first opportune moment, for example, following fining.

12.5 TESTING FOR MLF COMPLETION

Wines that have been subjected to MLF have to be tested for the complete disappearance of malic acid. Any residual malic acid will make the wine unstable, meaning that a spontaneous MLF can restart unexpectedly at a later time, for example, in the bottle and spoil the wine.

MLF is generally considered completed when there is 100 mg/L or less of residual malic acid. Commercial labs may have a stricter threshold of 30 mg/L.

Paper chromatography is the most common method used to test for MLF. There are more advanced enzymatic methods, such as Vinmetrica's SC-50 MLF Analyzer Kit and Accuvin Quick Tests Malic Acid, which can be used to test for MLF and quantify malic acid.

In paper chromatography, a special sheet of paper is "spotted" with samples of each wine to be tested, then the bottom edge of the paper is immersed in a solvent. As the solvent is absorbed and travels up the paper, the different acids in the samples travel up, stopping at different levels depending on the chemical nature of each acid. Each acid creates a spot on the paper, and the position of each spot is used to identify each acid. MLF is said to be complete when the malic acid spot disappears completely; a lactic acid spot appears at the top, but we'll come back to this as there is a nuance to clarify.

Following are detailed instructions on how to run a paper chromatography test.

 Paper chromatography makes use of a strong and irritating solvent that requires extra handling care and should only be used in a well-ventilated area.

To run the test, you need the following material, apparatus and chemicals, which you can purchase as a kit (Figure 12.1) from your winemaking supplier of choice:

12

- Whatman #1 chromatography paper approximately, 184 mm × 230 mm (7¼ in × 9 in)

- 4-L (1-gal) wide-opening jar with a tight-closing lid

- Disposable capillary tubes

- Chromatography solvent (a solution of n-butanol, formic acid and bromocresol-green indicator) — color of solvent is a bright orange

- 3.0 g/L (0.3%) tartaric acid reference solution

- 3.0 g/L (0.3%) malic acid reference solution

- 3.0 g/L (0.3%) lactic acid reference solution

And you will also need a small sample — a few mL — of each wine to be tested.

First wash your hands thoroughly as you don't want to transfer any dirt or substances while handling Whatman paper.

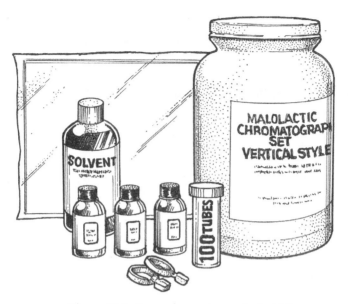

Figure 12.1: Paper chromatography test kit

Using a *lead pencil* (not a pen as ink will run when absorbed by the solvent), draw a horizontal line on the long side of a sheet of a Whatman #1 paper about 2.5 cm (1 in) from the bottom edge, as shown in Figure 12.2. On the line just drawn, put an X for each acid reference and wine sample to be tested, spacing these out 2.5 cm (1 in) with the first and last spot at least 2.5 cm (1 in) away from each edge. As you become more experienced running this test, you will be able to leave out the acid references and also pack in more samples somewhat tighter than 2.5 cm (1 in). Label each acid reference (e.g., T for tartaric, M for malic and L for lactic) and wine sample below each X with your pencil. Also jot down the date of the test in the bottom corner of the paper as you will likely be looking at the result later on during your winemaking.

Place the Whatman paper flat on a table and slide a pencil under the paper so that it is parallel to the drawn line, the idea being that the edge of the paper is slightly elevated off the table. You will be "spotting," i.e., placing tiny drops of acid or wine, on the X marks and you don't want the liquid on the underside touching the table.

Start with the tartaric reference. Draw a small sample using a capillary tube; hold a finger on the top opening to prevent the sample from running

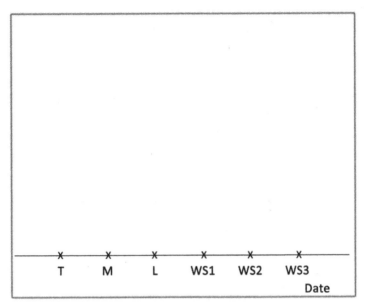

Figure 12.2: Spotting a Whatman #1 paper with acid standards and wine samples (WS) for running a paper chromatography test

12

out. Use a Kimwipe to wipe off any excess drop. Spot the matching X mark with one drop being careful not to let the paper absorb too much liquid. Release your finger from the top and accurately spot the X mark with 3 more drops. You want the spot nice and tight and not use too much of the sample; otherwise, the spots on the paper will become large and will make the analysis of results more difficult. Using a different capillary tube, repeat for each acid reference and wine sample making sure to apply the same exact number of spots — a total of 4 here.

When done spotting all acid reference solutions and wine samples, let the spots dry for a few minutes; use a hair dryer to speed up the drying.

Curl the paper into a perfect cylindrical shape along the short axis of the paper, making sure that there is no overlap — this is important — and staple the sides of the paper at the top, middle and bottom.

Pour approximately 100 mL of chromatography solvent in the jar and insert the curled paper into the solvent (Figure 12.3). The line drawn on the chromatography paper should be just above the solvent level. Close the jar tightly with a lid, making sure that the curled paper remains perfectly standing vertically. Let stand for 3–4 hours or until the solvent has reached the top of the paper. As the solvent travels up the paper, it will "drag" each acid up and separate the acid components out of the wine samples.

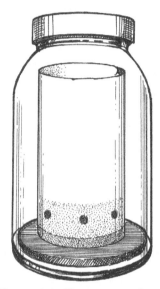

Figure 12.3: Chromatography test

When the solvent has reached the top of the paper, remove the paper from the jar and, using plastic clips, hang to dry in a warm, well-ventilated area or over a source of gentle heat to volatilize the solvent and to allow spots to form.

Return the leftover solvent to its container and thoroughly rinse the jar with plenty of water and let dry.

 The solvent can be reused but will need to be replaced after 6 months, perhaps up to a year. If the spots don't develop clearly, if there is excessive streaking of spots, or if the paper remains yellowish and does not develop to a bluish color, you need to replace the solvent.

At this point, there is nothing really visible on the paper; it will look orange. Drying will take several hours, therefore plan on leaving the paper hanging overnight.

As the paper dries, it will turn a blue–green color with yellowish spots corresponding to each acid. When dry, remove the staples and uncurl the paper — it is now called a chromatogram. Figure 12.4 shows an example of an actual (digitally-enhanced) chromatogram illustrating separation of acids.

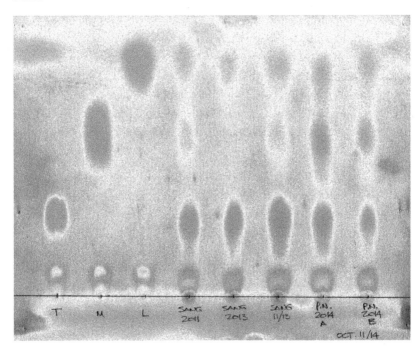

Figure 12.4: Example of a chromatogram showing separation of acids. MLF is in progress in wine samples SANG 2011, SANG 11/13, P.N. 2014A and P.N. 2014B, with the SANG (Sangiovese) much further ahead than the P.N. (Pinot Noir) samples. The absence of a malic spot for the SANG 2013 sample indicates that this batch has completed MLF.

Using the yellow spots formed by each of the reference acids, you can now see the component acids for each wine sample. Since all (grape) wines have tartaric acid, there will be a tartaric acid spot in each sample at the same height as the tartaric reference spot. For each sample, moving up the paper from its tartaric acid spot, look for the presence of a malic acid spot. If there is no visible sign of a yellow spot, it means that the MLF has completed and converted all malic acid into lactic acid for that sample, and therefore, if you move up the paper for that sample, there should be a bright yellow spot at the same level as the lactic acid reference spot. The malic spot has to have *completely* disappeared to give you some confidence that the amount of residual malic acid is less than the critical threshold of 100 mg/L. Depending on your spotting techniques, you may or may not see a spot at as much as 500 mg/L of residual malic acid.

If you have trouble deciphering the presence (or absence) of spots, try holding the chromatogram up against a strong light source. Here's another helpful technique to better detect the presence of malic acid in seemingly invisible spots. Scan the chromatogram at full color and upload to your PC. Using your favorite photo-editing software, decrease hue (towards green) and increase saturation (towards red) to create a visible contrast among spots. If there is residual malic acid, you will now see a faint orange spot.

If MLF is complete, you can proceed with microbial stabilization and add SO_2. It is however recommended to let the wine stand for another week or two to ensure that any residual malic acid that is not visible on the test is allowed to complete conversion. If there is even a slight hint of a yellow (or orange) spot, then MLF is not complete and you should allow for more time; there will still be a lactic spot towards the top of the paper.

If the MLF is stuck and you do not intend to take action to complete it, you will need to stabilize the wine against a renewed MLF using sulfite and lysozyme, or chitosan (see Section 14.1.2).

A word of caution.

If you see yellow spots at the malic acid position and a lactic acid spot at the top, it does not necessarily mean that the MLF has begun. Yeast produces another acid, succinic acid, during the AF and which appears in approximately the same positon as lactic acid on the chromatogram — it is very difficult to separate out and distinguish the two acids. If you see tiny bubbles rising up the side of the carboy, it is a sign that MLF has *likely* begun. And this is the value of doing a test before initiating MLF — to have a baseline for comparison.

12.6 DEALING WITH A STUCK MLF

When LAB prematurely and unexpectedly stop converting malic acid into lactic acid where there is no sign of activity or progress judging from chromatography analysis, the condition is termed a stuck MLF. If LAB are still working but the MLF is taking an unusual amount of time, more than a couple of months, the condition is termed a sluggish MLF. Here we will treat both conditions as a stuck MLF for the purpose of implementing a restart protocol.

A stuck MLF that takes several months to complete can open the door to spoilage microorganisms that can cause undesirable organoleptic deviations or outright spoilage as the wine is not yet protected with SO_2.

The most common causes of a stuck MLF are usually related to environmental and wine chemistry conditions outside the specifications of the LAB, for example, the temperature might be too cold, pH is too low, ethanol level is very high, there is too much SO_2, or from a lack of nutrients.

It can be very difficult to relaunch a stuck MLF depending on the cause and the amount of malic acid available. You have to try and complete the MLF, or else, you will have to stabilize the wine with SO_2 and lysozyme (see Section 14.1.2) or chitosan (see Section 13.4.3.1) to avoid a renewed MLF in bottles.

Unless pH has dropped below the LAB's critical level during MLF, wine pH is seldom the problem, unless combined with an addition of SO_2. And if you had started with a high-SG/Brix must, it was recommended to initiate the MLF as early as possible to avoid the LAB having to work in a high-alcohol environment. Trying to relaunch an MLF in a high-alcohol wine — greater than 16% ABV — may be a futile exercise.

Measure total SO_2, if so equipped, to make sure that it is not beyond the LAB's specification. This would only happen if you added excessive amounts of potassium metabisulfite (KMS) prior to the MLF or if the yeast strain used for the AF has produced large amounts of SO_2. Adding KMS post AF, but pre MLF, is a common mistake with beginners. Removing SO_2 is not simple, and if this is the problem, your best bet is to stabilize the wine with lysozyme or chitosan.

12

If all looks good, try increasing the temperature towards the upper range of the LAB's specification, and if that does not work, you will need to implement a restart protocol.

RESTART PROTOCOL

The protocol to restart a stuck MLF involves treating the problem wine with yeast hulls (purified yeast cell walls), e.g., Oenocell (Laffort), adding an MLF activator (nutrients), and re-inoculating the batch of wine with a stronger LAB strain.

Step 1: Make sure the wine is at 18–22 °C (64–72 °F). Add 0.1–0.25 g/L of yeast hulls, or as per your product's instructions, while stirring thoroughly but gently, again, to minimize oxygen uptake. Stir thoroughly every 6–12 hours for 48 hours, and then *carefully* rack the wine off its lees and into another vessel while minimizing oxygen pick-up to the extent possible.

Step 2: Dissolve your choice of MLF activator, such as ML Red Boost (Lallemand) or MaloBoost (Laffort), in a small volume of water or wine, for example, 50 mL for a 23-L (6-gal) batch, then add to the batch of wine and stir thoroughly but gently to avoid oxygen pickup. Keep the wine at 18–22 °C (64–72 °F). Wait 24 hours before proceeding to Step 3.

Step 3: Choose a strong LAB strain specifically known to be good at restarting a stuck MLF, such as Lalvin MBR VP41 (Lallemand), Lactoenos B16 Standard (Laffort), Er1A & Ey2d Blend (Wyeast) or Viniflora CH35 (Chr. Hansen), and prepare or add directly to the wine, as per product instructions, at *double the normal rate* for the product used. Stir thoroughly but gently. Keep the wine at 18–22 °C (64–72 °F) until MLF completes. Monitor progress using paper chromatography, and sulfite immediately when malic acid has been completely converted.

12.7 LACTIC ACID BACTERIUM CHARTS BY MANUFACTURER

This section provides a chart by manufacturer of the most popular wine-making lactic acid bacterium strains along with key fermentation data including: temperature range, alcohol tolerance, nutrient needs, minimum pH, maximum total SO_2, diacetyl production, if they can be used to restart a stuck MLF, and types of wines each can be used in.

Some freeze-dried LAB cultures can be added directly to must or wine or first rehydrated; liquid LAB cultures can be added directly to must or wine. Always follow manufacturer's instructions.

Additional information and specifications can be obtained from manufacturers' or vendors' references as follows: Lallemand [4,5], Laffort [6,7], White Labs [8], Wyeast [9], and Chr. Hansen [10]. Some of the information and specifications listed in charts were obtained from personal communication with manufacturers.

The data presented in the following charts are believed to be correct and up to date at the time of publication. Data may change without prior notice due to, but not limited to, changes in manufacturer's specifications.

12

12.7.1 LALLEMAND

Bacteria[1]	Format	Addition method	Temp. range (°C)	Temp. range (°F)	Alcohol tolerance	Nutrient needs	Minimum pH	Maximum Total SO$_2$ (mg/L)	Diacetyl production	Restart stuck MLF	Types of wines		
											White	Rosé	Red
Enoferm Beta	Freeze-dried	Direct[2]	14–27	57–81	15%	High	3.2	60	Seq.: High Co-inoc: Low		★	★	★
Lalvin MBR 31	Freeze-dried	Direct[2]	13–28	55–82	14%	Med	3.1	45	High		★	★	★
Lalvin MBR VP41	Freeze-dried	Direct[2]	16–28	61–82	16%	Low	3.1	60	Low	★	★	★	★
PN4	Freeze-dried	Direct[2]	16–28	61–82	16%	Med	3.1	60	High				★
ML Prime	Freeze-dried	Direct[2]	20–26	68–79	10%	Very Low	3.4	50	Very Low		★		★

[1] All strains are from the species Oenococcus oeni, except ML Prime, which is from Lactobacillus plantarum.

[2] Direct inoculation possible with or without rehydration.

12.7.2 LAFFORT

Bacteria[1]	Format	Addition method	Temp. range (°C)	Temp. range (°F)	Alcohol tolerance	Nutrient needs	Minimum pH	Maximum Total SO$_2$ (mg/L)	Diacetyl production	Restart stuck MLF	Types of wines		
											White	Rosé	Red
Lactoenos B16 Standard	Freeze-dried	Rehydrate in must/wine	16–25	61–77	16%	Low	2.9	60	Low	★	★	★	★
Lactoenos B7 Direct	Freeze-dried	Direct[1]	16–25	61–77	16%	Low	3.2	60	Low	★	★	★	★

[1] Direct inoculation possible with or without rehydration.

12.7.3 WHITE LABS

Bacteria	Format	Addition method	Temp. range (°C)	Temp. range (°F)	Alcohol tolerance	Nutrient needs	Minimum pH	Maximum Total SO$_2$ (mg/L)	Diacetyl production	Restart stuck MLF	Types of wines		
											White	Rosé	Red
WLP675	Liquid	Direct	13–24	55–75	15%	Low	White: 3.1 Red: 3.3	40	Low		★	★	★

12.7.4 WYEAST

Bacteria	Format	Addition method	Temp. range (°C)	Temp. range (°F)	Alcohol tolerance	Nutrient needs	Minimum pH	Maximum Total SO$_2$ (mg/L)	Diacetyl production	Restart stuck MLF	Types of wines		
											White	Rosé	Red
Er1A (4114)	Liquid	Direct	21–32	70–90	>12%	N/R[1]	3.4[2]	50	no data				★
Ey2d (4221)	Liquid	Direct	13–24	55–75	>12%	N/R[1]	3.4[2]	50	no data		★	★	
Er1A & Ey2d Blend (4007)	Liquid	Direct	13–32	55–90	>12%	N/R[1]	3.4[2]	50	no data	★	★	★	★

[1]None required.
[2]Time to complete MLF is less than 1 month at pH>3.4 at 18°C (64°F).
At pH<3.3, time to complete MLF for Er1A, Ey2d and Blend are 1-2 months, 2-3 months, and 1-3 months, respectively.

12

12.7.5 CHR. HANSEN

Bacteria[1]	Format	Addition method	Temp. range (°C)	Temp. range (°F)	Alcohol tolerance	Nutrient needs	Minimum pH	Maximum Total SO₂ (mg/L)	Diacetyl production	Restart stuck MLF	Types of wines White	Rosé	Red
Viniflora CH16	Freeze-dried	Direct[1]	17–25	63–77	16	Low	3.4	40	Med				★
Viniflora CH35	Freeze-dried	Direct[1]	15–25	59–77	14	Low	3.1	45	High	★	★	★	★
Viniflora Oenos	Freeze-dried	Direct[1]	17–25	63–77	14	Low	3.2	40	Med		★	★	★

[1]Direct inoculation possible with or without rehydration.

REFERENCES

1. Jackson, R.S. 2008. *Wine Science: Principles and Applications.* Third Edition. Academic Press, Burlington (MA).

2. Taillandier, P. and J. Bonnet. 2005. *Le vin: Composition et transformations chimiques.* Éditions Tec & Doc (Lavoisier), Paris, France.

3. Scott Laboratories. *Managing Diacetyl Production.* https://scottlab.com/manage-diacetyl.

4. Scott Labs Canada. 2020. *2020 Winemaking Handbook.* Scott Laboratories Ltd. Niagara-on-the-Lake, ON.

5. Lallemand website. https://lallemandwine.com/.

6. Laffort. 2020. *Catalog 2020/21.* Laffort. Bordeaux, France.

7. Laffort website. https://laffort.com/.

8. White Labs website. https://www.whitelabs.com/.

9. Wyeast website. http://wyeastlab.com/.

10. Chr. Hansen website. https://www.chr-hansen.com/.

12

13 Clarifying and Fining for Taste and Visual Appeal

....

The terms "clarification" and "fining" are used interchangeably although they have different meanings to experienced winemakers.

Clarification is the process of treating or processing must or wine for the purpose of achieving clarity, or limpidity in winemaking-speak. It is achieved by natural sedimentation by gravity, by the use of processing aids (referred to as fining agents in this context) to aid in flocculation, by filtration, or a combination of these. Sedimentation and the use of fining agents cause a more or less voluminous mass of sediment to form at the bottom of vessels. The liquid portion is separated from the sediment and transferred to another vessel by what is referred to as racking.

Fining is the process of treating the must or wine with fining agents for the purpose of achieving clarity, modifying or correcting color, mouthfeel, flavors and aromas, removing unwanted compounds, and stabilizing against potential instabilities. You will also often hear the terms counterfining or two-stage fining; these refer to the practice of adding a second fining agent or other processing aid to either improve the efficacy of the first fining agent or, for example, to help it sediment. If you have made wine from kits, you will be very familiar with the duo-pack of kieselsol and chitosan at the clarification stage where chitosan is used to counterfine kieselsol — we'll learn why and how.

This chapter discusses how to carry out clarification and fining operations, and given their controversy, it also address their impacts on color, mouthfeel, aromas and flavors. Filtration is discussed separately in Chapter 17.

13

13.1 JUICE (COLD) SETTLING

In white and rosé winemaking or where these is no maceration of grape solids with juice *during* fermentation, colloidal matter, such as proteins and pectin, and other large, heavy particulates can interfere with yeast and possibly negatively affect fermentation. By removing unwanted colloidal matter and particulates, fermentation will proceed more smoothly and give rise to a "cleaner" aroma profile with higher levels of esters — those compounds responsible for the wonderful fruity aromas. This is accomplished by allowing freshly pressed white or rosé juice to settle at cold temperatures prior to fermentation — this is known as juice settling or cold settling. The juice is then racked to separate the liquid from the sediment, and the liquid (now called must) is fermented.

To cold settle a carboy-sized batch of white or rosé juice, transfer the carboy to a refrigerator set at the coldest temperature as close to 0 °C (32 °F) as possible, or use your glycol chiller, and let settle 24–36 hours to allow colloidal matter and particulates to sediment; this cold temperature also prevents fermentation from starting spontaneously. For large batches that cannot be transferred into refrigeration, add dry ice at a rate of 2 g per kg of grapes (1 g per 1 lb) and replenish as needed, likely every 4–6 hours.

As we will see in Chapters 19 and 20, whites and rosés have to be first treated for pectin before cold settling.

At the end of the settling period, take the carboy out and place in a warmer area, or turn off your glycol chiller and let the juice warm up, then carefully rack or use a pump with a pre-filter strainer to transfer the juice to another carboy or vessel to separate the juice from the heavy sediment. Racking is best performed at a warmer temperature to minimize oxygen pickup — gases are more soluble at colder temperatures.

 Use PET carboys for cold settling to avoid glass breakage and possibly injuries. If you use glass carboys, handle gently as glass can crack and break at cold temperatures.

13.2 RACKING

Racking, the process of separating juice or wine from its sediment while transferring from one vessel to another, is done at various intervals, the frequency being at the discretion of the winemaker, to obtain a progressively clearer wine. Racking can be done by gravity or more efficiently using a positive-pressure or vacuum pump (Figure 13.1).

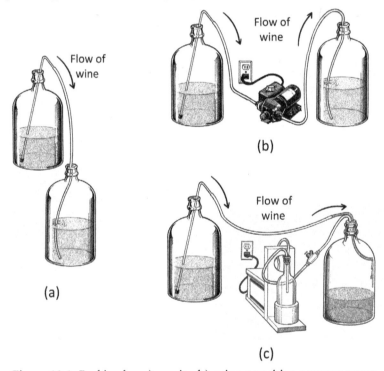

13

Figure 13.1: Racking by: a) gravity, b) using a positive-pressure pump, or c) using the All In One Wine Pump

Exercise care during racking operations so as not to disturb the sediment back into suspension, which can then cause fining or filtration problems. Make sure to use the anti-dreg tip on the racking cane and to keep it above the sediment. To minimize disturbing the sediment, you can hold the racking cane and anti-dreg tip just below the surface of the wine and let the racking cane slide down gently during racking until you reach the sediment; then slant the vessel to rack the last bit of wine. Again, be careful not to pick up sediment.

Racking by gravity or using a positive-pressure pump will expose juice or wine to air and may cause some oxygen pickup. This is generally not a concern if the racking is performed gently and correctly without turbulence, i.e., without vigorous or aggressive aeration. Alternatively, you can blanket the receiving carboy or vessel with inert gas (argon or nitrogen, carbon dioxide too is fine) prior to racking. Racking using a vacuum pump better protects juice or wine in the receiving vessel as it is transferred under vacuum.

Expect foaming in the receiving vessel due to residual carbon dioxide (CO_2) gas in the wine when racking, particularly on the first racking after the alcoholic fermentation (AF) and especially if using an electric pump. Therefore rack slowly and let the CO_2 settle in the receiving vessel before topping up. The extent of foaming decreases at each racking as wine releases CO_2 during aging and other processing, for example, when stirring in additives.

Following a racking operation, you will be faced with a carboy or vessel with some headspace due to wine loss, and therefore you will need to top those up to protect the wine from oxygen and spoilage microorganisms. Use the same or similar wine from the current or a past vintage for topping; otherwise, you can use a similar commercial wine. Alternatively, remove the air and create a vacuum using, for example, the Headspace Eliminator (Figure 13.2), or use a device, such as Better Top Ups (Figure 13.2), to displace wine and reduce headspace.

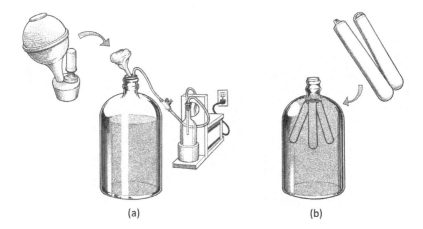

(a)   (b)

Figure 13.2: a) Headspace Eliminator; b) Better Top Ups

If you are using a PET carboy and it is just short of a full top-up, simply squeeze the body of the carboy to cause the wine level to reach up into the neck and quickly snap a PET carboy closure into place. The closure forms a perfect seal and keeps the wine from falling back down.

RACKING WHITE AND ROSÉ WINES

In white and rosé winemaking, you will want to keep the number of rackings to a minimum to protect wine from oxygen as much as possible.

Following is a typical racking schedule in making white and rosé wines:

- First racking: done immediately following the completion of the AF to separate the wine from the gross lees and likely tartrates.

- Second racking: done following clarification and stabilization.

- Third racking: done prior to bottling or, optionally, prior to filtration if there are any concerns of agitating sediments back into suspension.

A racking is performed on pressed, cold-settled juice, though this racking is not counted, to avoid confusion when referring to a "first racking," as it only applies when pressing grapes; there is no such racking when working with juice, either fresh or reconstituted from concentrate.

13

This racking schedule and number of rackings will also depend on your processing, for example, if you are using fining agents or just natural clarification, and the style of wine you are making, for example, if the wine is to be aged in oak barrels.

RACKING RED WINE

In red winemaking, rackings are often done with some aeration or splashing — in what is known a splash-racking — to introduce some oxygen into the wine, but never excessively, to favor polymerization of tannins to give them a smoother sensation on the palate. The racking schedule for reds can vary significantly depending on processing techniques and desired style of wine. There can be many variations, and with experience, you will come to develop your own that best suits your winemaking.

Following is a typical racking schedule for barrel-aged red wine from grapes with no fining and to be bottled in 12–18 months.

- First racking: done 1–3 (max) days after pressing to separate wine from the gross lees. This is typically the wine that goes into barrels for oak aging and MLF, if sequential, or microbial stabilization if MLF was done concurrently with AF.

- Second racking (optional): done 3–6 months after the first racking to start natural clarification.

- Third racking (optional): done up to 6 months after the second racking as part of natural clarification.

  If aging for longer periods, there may be optionally more rackings, for example, every 6 months. After the second racking, you will likely come to see that there is little sedimentation in 3 months, and therefore, you'll likely want to rack every 6 months, if not longer.

- Fourth racking: done in preparation for bottling with optionally a prior coarse filtration, depending on the clarity of the wine achieved with prior rackings.

 The second and third rackings are a personal choice and are optional, particularly if you are not doing any fining; you can otherwise rack only when ready to bottle.

13.3 DEGASSING

Wine is saturated with CO_2 following AF, especially whites and rosés. When making wine from grapes, fresh juice or frozen must, CO_2 naturally dissipates to an imperceptible level in all types of wines — reds, whites, and rosés — by bottling time. Processing and aging are usually sufficient to rid of CO_2 — at least using the proposed protocols described in this book.

When making wine from a kit and bottling as per instructions, or if you want to bottle wine soon after fermentation and the required clarification and stabilization, say within 6 months or just several weeks, then you have to degas the wine.

If you will be clarifying using a fining agent, be sure to degas *before* you add in the fining agent — the wine will not clarify if there is excessive CO_2 still. This is an all-too-common cause of fining problems in "rushed" wines.

Degassing is accomplished by mechanical means (Figure 13.3), either by agitation or using a vacuum pump. You can use the handle of a long-handled spoon and lots of elbow grease, or better yet, a lees stirrer mounted on an electric drill, or a vacuum pump or compressor with one of several attachments or devices available on the market, such as the Headspace Eliminator (it's also a degassing device) and Gas Getter (Figure 13.3).

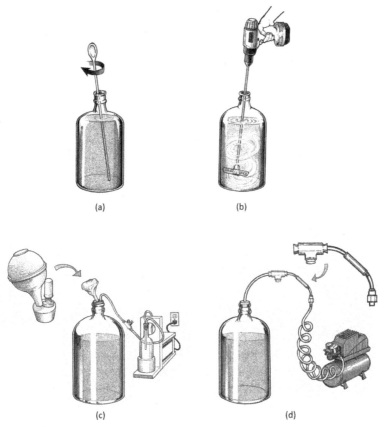

(a)   (b)

(c)   (d)

Figure 13.3: Degassing with a) handle of a long spoon, b) a lees stirrer, c) a Headspace Eliminator, and d) Gas Getter

First transfer the wine to a larger vessel as there can be a lot of foaming. You can degas immediately or transfer the vessel to a warmer area and wait

24 hours; the warmer temperature helps release CO_2 gas faster and reduces oxygen uptake.

Since wine is saturated with CO_2, there is no real concern of wine absorbing oxygen when degassing by agitation — that is, when using a long-handled spoon or a lees stirrer — provided that you stop when the wine is sufficiently degassed. It should take 5–10 minutes to degas a standard carboy when done properly. There should be no more foaming. Taste the wine as you degas and stop when you no longer detect CO_2 (no prickly sensation) on the palate. If you continue degassing by agitation past this point, then yes, you will start introducing oxygen into the wine, which can start oxidative reactions depending on availability of sulfur dioxide (SO_2).

Kit instructions have you degas *before* you add any KMS so as to preserve the total desired amount of SO_2 to be added and not lose any during degassing. Alternatively, if you are able to measure and adjust free SO_2, add the required amount of KMS based on pH (see Section 8.4), degas, then re-measure and re-adjust free SO_2 once degassing is completed.

13.4 FINING

Colloidal matter and particulates that affect the limpidity of wine and which cannot or do not always precipitate naturally can be made to flocculate and sediment with the aid of a fining agent.

Although fining is usually associated with clarifying wine, fining is also used for removing undesirable substances that may have adverse effects on color, mouthfeel, aromas and flavors, and fermentation. Products and techniques to address specific cases not discussed here are presented in other sections: yeast hulls for removing toxic fermentation substances (see Section 11.2), mannoproteins for increasing body and reducing astringency (see Sections 15.5 and 16.2), copper sulfate for dealing with hydrogen sulfide problems (see Section 22.4), and inactivated dry yeast for dealing with methoxypyrazines (see Section 22.9).

Fining agents have specific modes of action, such as binding to colloidal matter by electrical attraction, bond formation, or absorption/adsorption. And therefore, you need to assess the nature of the colloids or substances to be treated to choose a suitable fining agent and which will not otherwise adversely affect the quality of the wine. Those that work by electrical attraction carry a charge that acts upon an oppositely charged substance; for example, haze-causing proteins have a positive charge in wine and can be removed using bentonite, which carries a negative charge.

 Always store additives and processing aids in well-sealed containers and stored away in a cool, dry place. Many of these are hygroscopic and can absorb odors.

As with any other additives and processing aids, *always* perform comprehensive bench trials with fining agents before treating an entire batch as results can vary greatly depending on the kinds of colloids, their concentrations, pH and acidity, temperature, and the presence and concentration of protective colloids. Bench trials are particularly important in assessing organoleptic impacts as some fining agents can adsorb and strip aromas and flavors. Excessive use of a fining agent can also cause a charge reversal and result in clarification problems or other instabilities, or have a detrimental impact on organoleptic qualities. Chapter 5 describes how to conduct bench trials.

Dosage quantities listed under each fining agent can be used for generic products; otherwise, follow the instructions of the product you are using.

Fining agents may also have specific rehydration and addition procedures. Some need to be rehydrated into an aqueous suspension *before* being added to wine for their fining action to work properly while some need to be boiled, or boiled and cooled, before use. Add the suspension to must or wine very slowly while gently stirring continuously to keep the fining agent in suspension to maximize available surface area for binding. And whenever possible, cool the must or wine down to, for example, around 13 °C (55 °F), and maintain at the cooler temperature during the fining operation to speed up flocculation and sedimentation.

And remember! Be sure that the wine to be treated is sufficiently degassed.

Let's look at some of the most common fining agents used by home winemakers. We'll sort them by type, e.g., mineral, proteinaceous, etc., describe their applications, and discuss pros and cons of each agent. Table 13.1 at the end of this chapter summarizes fining agents discussed in the following sections.

13.4.1 MINERAL AGENTS

Mineral fining agents are natural or prepared inorganic substances and include clays and sands; the most widely used are bentonite and silicon dioxide.

13.4.1.1 BENTONITE

Primary application: Clarification of whites and rosés; removal of proteins in whites and rosés

Dosage: 0.25–1.0 g/L

Bentonite is a heavy, soft clay with an extraordinary ability to swell in water as well as juice or wine. It is one of the most common fining agents used for both clarification and treating proteins in whites and rosés. It is less popular in red winemaking as it strips color.

Sodium bentonite is the most common form of bentonite because it has greater binding capacity but creates more sediment than calcium bentonite.

As bentonite swells up during rehydration, layers within the clay structure become negatively charged and then attract and flocculate positively charged proteins that can otherwise cause a perfectly clear wine to go cloudy, especially if subjected to warmer temperatures (see Section 14.3). This mode of action is also the reason why bentonite is not recommended in reds — anthocyanins are positively charged at wine pH, which would cause color stripping.

Bentonite can also adsorb polyphenol oxidases (PPOs), the enzymes responsible for oxidation in juice, hence one of the reasons it is often added at cold settling. But bentonite can also deactivate enological enzymes, therefore it should not be used concurrently, for example, with pectinases or lysozyme — a minimum wait time is usually recommended in the enzymes' product specifications.

Given the potentially high metal content in bentonite, its use may increase metal content and alkalinity in juice and wine, and therefore potentially impact tartrate stability, which, in practical terms means, always fine with bentonite *before* cold stabilization (see Section 14.4).

Within the recommended dosage range, there should be no aroma or flavor stripping although research and anecdotal evidence are very contradictory. Avoid exceeding the 1-g/L maximum if possible. Musts and wines from high-protein grape varieties, such as Gewürztraminer and Sauvignon Blanc as well as some hybrids and Native American varieties, may require the full dosage. Bench trials are particularly essential here as bentonite properties can vary greatly depending on the source.

In must, you can sprinkle the bentonite clay on the surface and stir it in quickly before it sinks to the bottom, or, preferably, you can swell it in water a day ahead.

To swell bentonite, add the required amount in 10 times its weight of hot, soft (low mineral content) water in a suitable container that can be closed tightly with a lid — you will be doing a lot of shaking. For example, if you need 10 g of bentonite, rehydrate the clay in about 100 mL of hot water. Hard water can negatively affect the clay's binding efficiency. Slowly add the clay to the water while stirring to make sure it swells up properly and that it does not form clumps. Over the next 12–24 hours, shake the container as vigorously and as often as you can. You should end up with a very homogenous bentonite suspension with absolutely no clumps. If working with large volumes of bentonite solution, you can use a lees stirrer mounted on a cordless drill.

When properly rehydrated, slowly introduce the bentonite suspension into the juice or wine while gently stirring, and continue stirring until thoroughly dispersed. Bentonite is optionally added to juice, that is, before the AF, to start shedding proteins earlier and to ferment a cleaner must for better fermentation kinetics; it also reduces foaming during AF.

When fining wine with bentonite, rack in two (2) weeks or when completely clear. If you will be chilling wine for tartrate stabilization (see Section 14.4), you can rack just once after the stabilization treatment — this helps compact the bentonite lees.

13

Sodium bentonite's vast swelling power is also its biggest disadvantage; it settles into voluminous lees that can result in significant wine volume losses, in the order of 5–10%, following racking. Some bentonite manufac- turers now recommend rehydrating the clay directly into wine as an alter- native; this reduces the volume of lees but at the expense of flocculation capacity. Bentonite lees can also be compacted by counterfining with kie- selsol or gelatin (see below). Alternatively, you can use calcium bentonite, such as Albumex (Keller), or calcium–sodium bentonite, such as Canaton (Keller).

13.4.1.2 SILICON DIOXIDE

Primary application: Clarification of whites, rosés and reds; removal of proteins and tannins in whites and rosés

Dosage: 0.25–0.50 mL/L (1–2 mL/gal) as a 30% suspension

Silicon dioxide, or silica, is simply sand and therefore abundantly available. It is manufactured into silica gel or colloidal silica, usually a 30% aqueous silica suspension, or what is most commonly known as kieselsol in wine- making.

Silica particles acquire a negative charge and very efficiently attract and flocculate positively charged colloids, including proteins. Its fining efficacy can be further increased by counterfining with gelatin, isinglass or chitosan — these are described further below. As you notice, counterfining involves using a second fining agent with an opposite charge to help flocculate and sediment the first fining agent and the particulates attached to it.

Silica gel results in more compact lees and therefore less volume loss, faster precipitation, better clarity, and less stripping of wine character. It can also be used with proteinaceous agents to reduce phenolics as it can precipitate protein–tannin complexes, and therefore, it can be used for clarifying reds, whites and rosés or for addressing tannin issues in whites and rosés.

Add the kieselsol suspension directly into the wine while stirring gently but continuously, followed by a counterfining treatment after 24 hours.

13.4.2 PROTEINACEOUS FINING AGENTS

Proteinaceous substances have an affinity for tannins and are therefore very effective in fining red wines. Conversely, tannins are effective in fining proteins to prevent protein instabilities (see Section 14.3). The efficacy is reduced in the presence of protective colloids, such as polysaccharides.

Proteinaceous fining agents includes casein, egg white, gelatin, isinglass, and others from non-animal sources.

13.4.2.1 CASEIN

Primary application: Removing bitter tannins and reducing browning in whites and rosés

Dosage: 0.50–1.0 g/L as a caseinate suspension

Casein is a type of protein found in milk. In winemaking, it is added as a powdered sodium or potassium salt as it readily dissolves in water. Powdered caseinate is highly effective for improving color in white wines affected by oxidation.

13

Casein becomes positively charged and attracts and flocculates negatively charged colloids. It acts and precipitates very quickly because it has very low solubility in wine medium (due to pH). For this reason, it must be mixed thoroughly when added to wine. Another advantage is that it is only minimally affected by protective colloids.

Casein is primarily recommended for reducing bitter tannins in over-oaked or overly tannic white wines, and for reducing browning resulting from oxidation of polyphenols.

Casein has several drawbacks. It strips aromas and color when used excessively. It requires a counterfining with bentonite to avoid clogging filter pads when wine is to be filtered. And it may not be suitable if you have a gluten intolerance.

Add powdered potassium caseinate within the recommended rate based on bench trials. Dissolve the powder in 10 times its weight of cold water and let the powder swell for several hours. Then add to the wine very slowly while stirring continuously making sure that all the suspension is stirred in completely and uniformly. Allow to settle for a few days to a week, then rack, counterfine with bentonite, and rack once again.

If dealing with a browning problem due to oxidation, treat with PVPP (see Section 13.4.4) instead of bentonite. There are products, such as Poly-lact (Laffort), which combine casein and PVPP specifically for treating browning problems.

13.4.2.2 EGG WHITE

Primary application: Taming aggressive tannins in barrel-aged reds

Dosage: 2–3 fresh egg whites per 100 L; 3–8 fresh egg whites per standard 225-L (59-gal) barrel

Fining with egg white (albumen) is a traditional and still popular method for softening aggressive tannins in red wines.

The fining action is provided by albumin proteins that take on a positive charge and which therefore have great affinity for tannins. This is the same interaction that precipitates proteins during fermentation in red winemaking as we had seen in Section 9.1. Egg white is ideal for fining highly tannic red wines or reds undergoing barrel aging, and with minimal impact on color, but it tends to be too aggressive for young or low-tannin wines as it can negatively affect mouthfeel.

Separate the eggs — being sure to discard the yolks — into a small stainless steel bowl. Dissolve a pinch of salt in 250 mL of water in a small beaker or glass. Salt is needed to increase the solubility of albumin, which has low solubility in wine; it would otherwise not fine effectively. Gently stir the saline solution into the egg whites being careful not to froth the preparation. Then *very slowly* introduce the saline egg-white solution in the wine directly into the barrel while stirring continuously. It is absolutely important to add the solution as slowly as possible and with continuous stirring to maximize fining efficacy. As you add the solution you will see protein–tannin clumps forming very rapidly, confirming the efficacy of egg white. Rack the wine in 1–2 weeks.

Instead of using eggs, you can use pure, refrigerated egg whites — the type sold in small cartons in your grocer's dairy section. Enological liquid or powdered albumen preparations are also available. Generally, 3 mL of liquid albumen and 4–5 g of albumen powder are equivalent to one fresh egg white.

13.4.2.3 GELATIN

Primary application: Taming aggressive tannins in whites, rosés and reds

Dosage: 0.01–0.05 g/L

Gelatin is a collagenic protein derived from animal tissues and bones. It carries a positive charge making it ideal for fining negatively charged substances, particularly for counterfining bentonite to compact loose lees and for fining aggressive tannins in reds. Gelatin fining is also often used with kieselsol to preserve polyphenols and improve antioxidant activity in reds. In whites and rosés, gelatin requires the addition of an equivalent weight of grape tannins to ensure fining efficacy, or a counterfining with kieselsol to avoid over-fining and possibly making wine unstable with respect to heat-labile proteins.

13

As gelatin includes a great diversity of products with varying levels of effectiveness due to their method of manufacture and what is called Bloom units, follow product instructions on preparing and adding gelatin to wine. The Bloom number, which you will find on product labels, simply describes a gelatin's gelling ability, and the stiffer the gelatin, the higher the Bloom number. Most enological gelatin preparations are in the range 80–150; choose one in the range 90–100, and only use unflavored gelatin specifically designed for winemaking. And be careful as there is a risk of overfining and stripping flavors if not used properly.

First soak the gelatin powder in warm water not exceeding 50 °C (122 °F) — higher temperatures may denature the proteins and render them ineffective. Some gelatin manufacturers may recommend soaking the gelatin in cold water and then heating it to parboil. Add the still-warm gelatin solution to a small volume of wine — about twice the amount of water used — then add to the rest of the wine and stir thoroughly. Let settle for 1–2 weeks and then rack.

13.4.2.4 ISINGLASS

Primary application: Clarifying whites and rosés

Dosage: 0.01–0.03 g/L

Isinglass is a protein that consists mainly of collagen fibers and which is prepared from the swim bladders of cichlids (tropical spiny-finned freshwater fishes) though traditionally from sturgeons. It is an excellent fining agent because of its high molecular weight and is only minimally affected by protective colloids. It is positively charged and therefore ideal for fining negatively charged colloids. It is most effective in clarifying white and rosé wines, particularly oak-aged whites, where it enhances aromas without affecting tannins. It strips color to a lesser extent than other proteinaceous fining agents such as gelatin or casein.

Isinglass performs best at cool cellar temperature, around 13 °C (55 °F); it can hydrolyze and lose its effectiveness at warmer temperatures. Completely dissolve isinglass powder in *cool* water and allow to swell for the recommended amount of time making sure to follow manufacturer's instructions on rehydration and addition protocols. Slowly introduce the solution into wine while stirring continuously. Let settle and rack in 1–2 weeks or when the wine is completely clear.

Isinglass can throw a fluffier deposit that tends to cling to carboy glass or tank walls making racking a little cumbersome. Either gently stir the wine close to the perimeter of the vessel to dislodge particles, let sediment, then rack, or counterfine with bentonite to alleviate this problem and to avoid clogging filter pads when wine is to be filtered.

13.4.2.5 PROTEINS FROM NON-ANIMAL SOURCES

There are now many other proteinaceous fining agents of plant origins, such as peas, corn, lentil flour and potatoes, and of yeast origins, some of which have become common for use in winemaking by those looking for non-animal alternatives. Since these are relatively new, you may only find them in packages for treating large volumes of wine.

Potato proteins are particularly efficient in removing oxidized and oxidizable compounds in white wines, and in fining high-turbidity reds and reducing astringent tannins, making these proteins a suitable replacement to gelatin.

Yeast protein extracts, which comprise various proteins of differing molecular weights, have also been shown to be efficient in fining both red and white wines.

13.4.3 POLYSACCHARIDES

Polysaccharides are very long polymers of carbohydrates. Certain polysaccharides have specific fining action.

This section describes chitosan, alginates, and gum arabic. Mannoproteins, polysaccharides derived from the cell walls of dead yeast cells, are not considered fining agents but they are used for taming bitter and astringent tannins in reds and barrel-aged whites. Mannoproteins are discussed in Sections 15.5 and 16.2.

13.4.3.1 CHITOSAN

Primary application: Clarifying whites; reducing Brett character

Dosage: Varies by product

Chitosan is a polysaccharide derived from chitin, a major structural component of the exoskeleton of crustaceans and insects as well as in the cell walls of yeasts and filamentous fungi, such as *Aspergillus niger*. If seafood allergies are a concern, look for chitosan derived from *A. niger* fungi; it also contains less proteins, which minimizes possible protein instabilities unless counterfined with a suitable agent, such as silica gel (kieselsol).

At wine pH, chitosan is positively charged and is very effective in treating negatively charged colloids, particularly when first counterfined with silica gel. Fining is complete in just a couple of days. You will often find kieselsol and chitosan packaged together, as in DualFine (Fermfast) and Super-Kleer

K.C. (Liquor Quik) though the chitosan is derived from shellfish. As there are different chitin/chitosan formulations and procedures, use as per manufacturer's directions.

Fungi-derived chitosan can also be used to treat wines tainted with *Brettanomyces*, a dreaded rogue yeast that can impart an unappealing barnyard smell or other off-aromas (see Section 22.12). Chitosan can also be used as a preventative against *Brettanomyces* and other spoilage yeasts as well as spoilage bacteria, including acetic acid and lactic acid bacteria (see Section 14.1.2).

13.4.3.2 ALGINATES

Primary application: Clarifying whites and reds with pH<3.5

Dosage: 0.04–0.08 g/L

Alginates are high molecular weight polysaccharides obtained from alginic acid salts, and which make for effective fining but only in wines with a pH below 3.5. Alginic acid ions are positively charged at wine pH and can electrostatically bind and precipitate negatively charged particles in wine without stripping color, aromas or flavors.

Lees are fairly compact though voluminous that can result in appreciable wine loss; the compactness does however ease the racking operation and increase filter throughput. Flocculation is fairly quick at low pH but precipitation is relatively slow compared to other fining agents. You can accelerate precipitation by counterfining with a suitable fining agent chosen based on the type of wine to be treated. Alginates can also be used to remove haze left by other fining agents and to help compact lees when processing with other fining agents known to produce less compact lees.

Sparkolloid is one such common alginate-based fining agent that, for improved fining efficacy, also includes diatomaceous earth and silicon dioxide.

Older alginate formulations required that the powder be added to boiling water and stirred continuously for up to 20 minutes, and then added to the wine to be treated. There are now new alginate formulations which can be dissolved in cold water.

13.4.3.3 GUM ARABIC

Primary application: Preventing glass staining in early bottled or heavily pigmented reds

Dosage: 0.15–0.6 g/L or 1–2 mL/L (4–8 mL/gal) as a 15–30% solution

Gum arabic (or Arabic gum, acacia gum) is not a fining agent per se, but rather, a protective colloid with fining-like properties and many uses in winemaking (see Section 14.4.2). It can be used in small doses in unfiltered or very lightly filtered *young* reds meant for early consumption to prevent coloring matter from depositing on glass and staining bottles. It is not recommended for wines destined for aging as those much desirable polyphenol chemical reactions are inhibited (see Section 9.1); the wine can then take on a milky appearance that can affect its normal clarity [1].

First dissolve gum arabic powder in water at the desired rate, and perform bench trials to establish a desired dosage. Commercial preparations are readily available as 15–30% solutions; some common ones include Liqui-Gum (25%, Keller), Stabivin (30%, Laffort), Arabinol (20–30%, AEB) and Maxigum (>20%, Enartis/Esseco).

Only add gum arabic to clear, ready-to-bottle wine as it can otherwise foul filter media. Do not treat wine with any other agents following addition of gum arabic.

13.4.4 SYNTHETIC POLYMERS: PVPP

Primary application: Taming bitter tannins; preventing or dealing with browning problems; avoid pinking in whites

Dosage: 0.25–0.50 g/L or as per product instructions

PVPP, short for polyvinylpolypyrrolidone, is a high molecular weight synthetic polymer with great affinity for polyphenols. It is used to tame excessive bitterness in red wines due to, for example, over-extraction of tannins or extensive barrel aging (see Section 16.3), and eliminate oxidized and oxidizable polyphenols responsible for browning and for trapping

13

aromas in whites and rosés. It is often used with a proteinaceous fining agent, separately or within a commercial product, as a preventative against oxidation in musts.

PVPP is also useful for avoiding pinking in whites caused by oxidation of colorless tannins, which then discolor the wine and also affect its flavor and freshness. Both Sauvignon Blanc and Viognier are white varieties at high risk of pinking in a warm, dry vintage, when the skins have much higher levels of phenolics. When this is a concern, separate the pressings, then add PVPP to the free- and press-run fractions before fermentation.

Dissolve PVPP in 10 times its weight in water while stirring vigorously, then let the suspension swell for at least one hour before adding to wine. Always perform bench trials to determine the optimal rate of addition as PVPP can strip aromas, flavors and especially color, and also affect mouthfeel if used excessively.

Settling occurs quickly, as fast as 1–2 hours depending on the type of PVPP used, though usually within several days. Rack the wine immediately after settling followed by a coarse filtration.

A PVPP–bentonite co-fining can be very successful in clarifying white wine, especially if slightly or overly tannic. First, slowly add PVPP and stir thoroughly but gently, then follow with a bentonite treatment. PVPP interacts with tannins to form PVPP–tannin complexes, which then bind to bentonite and precipitate. Rack as soon as the wine is completely clear.

13.4.5 POLYPHENOLS: TANNINS

Primary application: Removing proteins

Dosage: 0.05–0.10 g/L

Tannins are usually associated with red wine structure; they affect bitterness and astringency, and color stability. But tannins can also be used as a fining agent in white wine for removing proteins or as counterfining agent to complement the action of other fining agents. Tannins acquire a negative charge and act on positively charged protein molecules.

Commercial tannin preparations can be sourced and produced from various trees and shrubs but predominantly from grape seeds for condensed tannins as well as skins, and oak wood, chestnuts or gallnuts for hydrolyzable tannins, or as any combination of these. Chapter 9 discusses the different kinds of tannins in further details.

As with all fining agents, always follow your product's instructions for the dosage and mode of addition, but in general, you can add tannins up to 0.05 g/L in whites and up to 0.10 g/L when fining high-protein wines with gelatin or when needing to increase mouthfeel.

Dissolve tannin powder in a small volume of wine, preferably warmer than cellar temperature, and add the suspension to the batch. If counter-fining, allow 3–5 days before adding the second fining agent.

13.4.6 CARBONS: ACTIVATED CARBON

Primary application: Correcting browning due to oxidation; addressing color problems in whites; and removing thiol off-odors

Dosage: 0.10–0.50 g/L

Activated carbon (charcoal) is used to treat juice or wine affected by different types of faults, such as correcting phenolic browning, removing unwanted, unsightly color in white wines, and reducing thiol off-odors, particularly where a copper sulfate ($CuSO_4$) treatment is not desired for fixing hydrogen sulfide (H_2S) and thiol problems (see Section 22.4). There are specific charcoal products for decolorizing as well as for "de-odorizing" to treat off-aromas and flavors.

Activated carbon is produced from carbon-containing material, like wood, that is heated at high temperatures to create charcoal, and which is then "activated" by treating it with (typically) oxygen or certain acids and bases. Its mode of action is adsorption; it traps molecules along the pores of its very large surface area.

It is usually considered a last resort to salvage affected wine as carbon is non-selective and can therefore remove other desirable aromas and flavors or strip color excessively. It also tends to be a messy and tedious process requiring careful fining and filtration to remove all traces of carbon.

The dosage depends on the size of granules as finer powders have a larger surface area with which to adsorb molecules, and therefore, the finer the powder, the lower the required dosage. Bench trials are absolutely essential with activated carbon.

REFERENCE

1. Ribéreau-Gayon, P., Y. Glories, A. Maujean and D. Dubourdieu. 2012. *Traité d'œnologie, Tome 2 - Chimie du vin. Stabilisation et traitements*. 6e édition. Dunod, Paris.

SUMMARY CHART OF FINING AGENTS

Table 13.1: Fining agents

Fining Agent (charge, if any)	Application	Recommended Dosage	Comments
Bentonite (−)	• Clarifying of whites and rosés • Removing of proteins in whites and rosés	0.25–1.0 g/L	• Creates heavy, voluminous lees; counterfine with kieselsol or gelatin • Strips color in reds
Silicon dioxide (−)	• Clarifying of whites, rosés and reds • Removal of proteins and tannins in whites and rosés	0.25–0.50 mL/L (1–2 mL/gal) as a 30% suspension	• Very efficient, compact lees • Counterfine with gelatin, isinglass or chitosan
Casein (+)	• Reducing bitter tannins in over-oaked or overly tannic white wines • Reducing browning due to oxidation of polyphenols	0.50–1.0 g/L as a caseinate suspension	• Can strip aromas and color • Requires a counterfining with bentonite or PVPP depending on application
Egg white (+)	• Taming aggressive tannins in barrel-aged reds	2–3 fresh egg whites per 100 L (25 gal) 3–8 fresh egg whites per standard 225-L (59-gal) barrel	• Too aggressive for young or low-tannin wines
Gelatin (+)	• Taming aggressive tannins in whites, rosés and reds • Counterfining bentonite to compact lees	0.01–0.05 g/L	• May strip flavors if not used properly
Isinglass (+)	• Clarifying whites and rosés	0.01–0.03 g/L	• Use at cool cellar temperature • Throws fluffier deposit; counterfine with bentonite
Chitosan (+)	• Clarifying whites • Reducing Brett character	Varies by product	• Allergy risk with products derived from shellfish

(continued)

13

SUMMARY CHART OF FINING AGENTS

Table 13.1, *continued*

Fining Agent (charge, if any)	Application	Recommended Dosage	Comments
Alginates (+)	• Clarifying whites and reds with pH<3.5	0.04–0.08 g/L	• Does not strip color, aromas or flavors • Compact but voluminous lees • Slow precipitation; best to counterfine
Gum arabic	• Preventing glass staining in early bottled or heavily pigmented reds	0.15–0.6 g/L or 1–2 mL/L (4–8 mL/gal) as a 15–30% solution	• Only add to clear, ready-to-bottle wine
PVPP	• Taming bitter tannins • Preventing or dealing with browning problems • Avoid pinking in whites	0.25–0.50 g/L or as per product instructions	• Can strip aromas, flavors and color if used excessively
Tannins (−)	• Removing proteins	0.05–0.10 g/L	• Dissolve in a small amount of wine
Activated carbon	• Correcting browning due to oxidation • Addressing color problems in whites • Removing thiol off-odors	0.10–0.50 g/L	• Non-selective; aggressive treatment • Can easily strip aromas, flavors and color • Very messy to handle • Requires careful fining and filtration

14 Mitigating Microbial, Chemical and Physical Instabilities

Once wine has completed fermentation, both alcoholic and malolactic, the latter if performed, it must remain stable throughout its sojourn in carboys, tanks and barrels, and in bottles; that is, it should not undergo any unwanted or unexpected changes, and certainly not spoilage. Sulfur dioxide (SO_2) is added as an antimicrobial and antioxidant agent, as described in Chapter 8. But it does not end there. What about residual sugar that could trigger a renewed alcoholic fermentation? Or proteins in whites that can cause a perfectly clear wine to go cloudy? Or tartrates that can form in bottles?

As a winemaker you have to anticipate any such potential instabilities and proactively implement proper stabilization protocols to avoid problems.

This chapter describes four of the most important topics in wine stabilization — microbial, pectin, protein and tartrate. It describes how to predict or test for instabilities, and how to stabilize wine.

14

 Blending two or more stable wines does not guarantee that the final blend will be stable; the blended wine must be tested and treated, if necessary, for stability.

14.1 MICROBIAL STABILITY

There exists a very varied and broad population of microorganisms — yeasts and bacteria — in juice and wine. These can become active and start effecting spoilage under favorable environmental conditions if they can find something to feed on. Many microorganisms can feed on minuscule amounts of sugar, even under fairly hostile conditions, for example, of high alcohol or in the absence of oxygen. Lactic acid bacteria have a preference for malic acid; acetic acid bacteria prefer ethanol but need oxygen to start their spoilage effect. Most spoilage microorganisms can be inhibited with SO_2, perhaps in conjunction with other inhibitors, or be removed to an acceptably low level by sterile filtration.

But as home winemakers, we are not equipped to perform microbiological analysis of wine, and therefore we should assume that microorganisms are always present, which they are, and that they will strike at a most opportune time if there is sufficient food. We are primarily concerned with residual fermentable sugars above 2 g/L (0.2%) and residual malic acid above 100 mg/L (0.01%) in wines that have undergone malolactic fermentation (MLF). Many microorganisms, such as acetic acid bacteria and surface yeasts, such *Candida mycoderma* (see Section 22.3), which thrive and cause spoilage in the presence of oxygen, and therefore, you have to minimize exposure to air. And remember — microorganisms flourish at higher pH, therefore you will need to always factor in pH in your SO_2 adjustments.

14.1.1 MICROBIAL STABILIZATION AGAINST RESIDUAL FERMENTABLE SUGARS

 Residual sugar (RS) amounts are expressed in g/L here. Simply divide that by 10 to convert to a percent figure; for example, 2.0 g/L is equivalent to 0.2%.

 Please review the sidebar on WHAT DOES RESIDUAL SUGAR REALLY MEAN? in Section 6.5 before tackling this section. What's important to remember here is that RS is a good approximation of the amount of residual fermentable sugars, albeit probably a tad higher. For simplicity of it all, we will just assume that the amount of residual fermentable sugars is the measured amount of residual sugar (RS) — reducing sugars, really — using one of the methods or kits described in Section 6.5.

If wine contains sufficient residual fermentable sugars, it can restart fermenting, and it if happens in bottles, corks can pop out or, in the worst case, bottles can explode. SG 0.995 (−1.5 Brix) is the generally accepted threshold when residual sugars (RS) cannot be measured analytically. Measuring RS (see Section 6.5) gives much greater confidence; here, we rely on RS too.

Many winemakers consider the residual fermentable sugar threshold to be 4 g/L, the level at which yeast can restart metabolizing sugars if the wine has not been adequately stabilized. But some yeasts can metabolize lower levels, down to 2 g/L, and therefore, for added confidence, it is best to assume a threshold of 2 g/L. Some enologists and commercial analytical services laboratories recommend no more than 1.0 g/L, but that's usually to mean glucose+fructose, which is always smaller then RS, and therefore, 2 g/L is a very safe threshold. What this all means is that any wine that contains more than 2 g/L of residual fermentable sugars must be treated either with SO_2 in conjunction with sorbate, or be sterile filtered.

If you cannot measure RS, err on the side of caution and add SO_2 and sorbate in wines that have *not undergone MLF*. For those that have undergone MLF, the only options are higher doses of SO_2 *without* sorbate and drink the wine young and fairly quickly before SO_2 levels drop below critical levels, or sterile filtration. If you add sorbate to a wine that has undergone MLF and lactic acid bacteria (LAB) have not been removed by sterile filtration (see Section 17.3), LAB will metabolize sorbate and produce a very off-putting geranium-like smell (see Section 22.10).

The amount of potassium metabisulfite (KMS) and free SO_2 (FSO2) to add should be a function of a wine's pH, as described in Section 8.4. Sorbate, which is sorbic acid, is added as potassium sorbate as it has much greater solubility than sorbic acid.

To stabilize wine with RS greater than 2 g/L, add potassium sorbate at a rate of 1.34 times the amount of sorbic acid needed based on ethanol level as per Table 14.1. For wines with pH greater than 3.5, use the next higher dosage as the amount of molecular sorbic acid (the active form) available drops from about 95% to 85% at pH 4.0. If sweetening wine with sugar, be sure to add the sorbate *before* adding sugar. Sorbate is not needed when using commercially produced wine conditioners as these already contain sorbate (see Section 16.1).

At the levels recommended in Table 14.1, sorbate does not impart any off-aromas or flavors. Such flaws result from the use of old, stale sorbate

Table 14.1: Amounts of sorbic acid to add based on % ABV; use the next higher dosage for wine with pH>3.5

% ABV	Sorbic acid (mg/L)
10	150
11	125
12	100
13	75
14	50

or in excessive amounts. Only buy sorbate on an as-need basis — toss out any sorbate that is older than 6 months.

Add potassium sorbate *before* cold stabilization making sure to dissolve the powder thoroughly in a little water and to *add the sorbate solution to wine very slowly while stirring continuously* to minimize the possibility of crystals forming and precipitating later on in bottles. Wait at least 2 weeks *before and after* sweetening, or before bottling to make sure there is no sedimentation; if there is, rack before sweetening or bottling. Do not rush the sorbate treatment, sweetening and bottling or you will likely find tiny white deposits forming.

Let's look at an example.

EXAMPLE 14.1

Adding sorbate

You have a 23-L (6-gal) batch of white wine with approximately 12% ABV and 3.65 pH and with perhaps just a touch of residual sugar. You are not equipped to measure RS but your final hydrometer reading was just under 1.000 (0 Brix); the wine does taste a touch sweet.

You now need to stabilize with KMS and potassium sorbate. This is the first KMS addition after fermentation (and after the first racking), and therefore, you assume that FSO2 is zero.

According to the SO2 CALCULATOR or using Figure 8.4 in Section 8.2, you need about 50–60 mg/L FSO2 using a molecular SO_2 of 0.8 mg/L for a white wine with 3.65 pH, as recommended in Table 8.1 in Section 8.4. That works out to around 2 g of KMS for the 23-L (6-gal) batch.

 You can download the SO2 CALCULATOR at ModernHome-Winemaking.com.

At 12% ABV, 100 mg/L of sorbic acid is recommended, but since pH is above 3.5, we will go with 125 mg/L. The amount of potassium sorbate to add to the entire batch then is calculated as follows:

$$Potassium\ sorbate\ to\ add\ (g) = 1.34 \times 125\ ^{mg}/_L \times 23\ L$$

$$= 3853\ mg\ (3.9\ g)$$

And what should you do if you suspect refermentation in bottles?

If you notice corks being pushed out of bottles, or if you see fine sediment with the wine remaining clear or going cloudy, or the wine tastes slightly fizzy, then you likely have refermentation, and you need to take immediate action before bottles potentially explode and create a big mess.

14

You have to uncork all bottles and re-process the wine. Pour all bottles back in a carboy, retrieve and degas a sample (see Section 6.3 for instructions on degassing samples), and measure the SG (Brix) with your hydrometer. Top up the carboy and place a stopper with an airlock, and let fermentation run its course if you had intended to make a dry wine. When you see no more activity in the airlock, take another sample, degas, and measure the SG (Brix). You can stabilize with SO_2 and re-bottle when SG is 0.995 or lower (–1.5 Brix or lower) or, if you can measure RS, when RS is less than 2 g/L. As a precaution, you can add sorbate with the SO_2 addition.

If you had intended an off-dry or sweeter style of wine, you can stop fermentation as per instructions in Section 11.6, and then stabilize the wine as described in this section.

14.1.2 MICROBIAL STABILIZATION AGAINST
RESIDUAL MALIC ACID

A wine that has undergone MLF having a residual malic acid level below 100 mg/L is considered to be stable against a renewed MLF; some wine-makers use 30 mg/L for added confidence, but since you cannot measure malic acid, if you run a paper chromatography test, as described in Section 12.5, and the malic spot has *completely disappeared*, you can assume that the wine has completed MLF. If there is the slightest hint of a malic spot and you cannot complete the MLF, you have to stabilize the wine against a renewed MLF using SO_2 and lysozyme, or fungi-derived chitosan (see Section 13.4.3.1). This is done independently of whether the wine has re-sidual sugar or not, though you are reminded *never* to add sorbate to a wine that has undergone MLF. Lysozyme and chitosan can also be used where MLF is not desired and needs to be inhibited as a precaution, such as in young, fruity white wines or if blending a wine that has undergone MLF with one that hasn't. Avoid possible stability problems by only using wine that has undergone MLF for topping barrels, for example.

Lysozyme acts on lactic acid bacteria (LAB) used for MLF as well as spoi-lage LAB that can produce a range of off-odors and flavors, but it has no effect on acetic acid bacteria or yeast.

Lysozyme must be used with SO_2 to be effective. The recommended dosage is 100–500 mg/L, or as per your product's instructions; use a low dosage in reds or if the amount of residual malic acid is small (faint malic spot from the paper chromatography test) or up to 500 mg/L in whites and if the amount of residual malic acid is more significant (brighter malic spot).

As lysozyme binds with tannins and other polyphenols, you can expect a slight decrease in mouthfeel and color in reds. Run bench trials (see Chapter 5) at various rates, for example, 100, 200 and 300 mg/L to assess impacts. Treat samples at the desired rate, let stand overnight, and assess mouthfeel and color the next morning.

When stabilizing white wine with lysozyme, you have to treat lysozyme proteins with a suitable fining agent, such as bentonite, to avoid protein instability (see Section 14.3).

To stabilize wine with residual malic acid and against a renewed MLF, first add KMS to the required FSO2 level. Rehydrate the required amount of lysozyme powder in 5 times its weight of *warm* water, stir gently for one minute, and allow to soak for at least 45 minutes. Stir periodically during the soaking period. Add the lysozyme suspension to the wine very slowly while stirring gently, and let the wine stand for a minimum of one week, preferably two, before racking or any further treatment.

EXAMPLE 14.2

Adding lysozyme

You have a 23-L (6-gal) batch of red wine with what you assess to be a small amount of residual malic acid. Now you want to add lysozyme to stabilize the wine against a renewed MLF. You already did your SO_2 addition and, based on your bench trials, you want to add 200 mg/L of lysozyme.

Calculate the amount of lysozyme needed as follows:

$$Lysozyme\ to\ add\ (g) = 200\ ^{mg}/_L \times 23\ L$$
$$= 4600\ mg\ (4.6\ g)$$

Rehydrate the lysozyme powder as per instructions in about 25 mL of warm water.

14

Fungi-derived chitosan, which, unlike lysozyme, not only acts on LAB — MLF and spoilage LAB — but also on acetic acid bacteria and spoilage yeasts, depending on the formulation of commercial products. Chitosan works by lowering the population of spoilage yeasts and bacteria, and therefore reduces the need for SO_2, making it an attractive alternative in high-pH wines. Bactiless (Lallemand), BactiControl (Laffort) and Enartis-Stab Micro (Enartis/Esseco) are examples of commercial chitosan-based products for microbial control.

14.2 PECTIN STABILITY

As discussed in Section 10.1.1, pectin is usually not an issue in wines made from viniferas, but non-vinifera varieties, particularly *V. labrusca* and notably Concord, can have very high levels, which can result in residual pectin that can cause clarification and filtration problems if not treated sufficiently. Pectin is more problematic in high-acid wines because pectin molecules become less stable with increasing acidity, causing them to break up into smaller compounds.

Residual pectin cannot be removed using fining agents or by filtration — it must first be broken down using pectinases. Pectinases are added to must at crush or at pressing (pre-ferment stage), or to wine to resolve a clarification or filtration problem. If clarification or filtration problems persist after fining, it is an indication that the wine may contain excessive pectin.

14.2.1 TESTING FOR PECTIN STABILITY

You can test very easily for the presence of pectin. Pour 25 mL of wine in a 100-mL graduated cylinder, add 50 mL of acidified alcohol, for example, 95% isopropanol with, optionally, 1% strong acid (e.g., HCl), cap the cylinder or use paraffin film, and shake thoroughly. If the wine sample remains clear, it is considered pectin stable; if a jelly-like solid forms, a pectinase treatment is required.

14.2.2 PECTIN STABILIZATION

If a pectin test was positive, treat the wine with pectinases. There are many enzyme products that contain pectinases for other applications, such as macerating reds. Just look for a straight pectinase product to deal with the pectin issue, and follow the product's instructions, paying particular attention to dosage for use in must versus wine. Typical dosage is 0.5 g/L in must; wine usually requires slightly larger doses. Dissolve the powder in *cold* water, never warm or hot as it could render the enzymes ineffective.

If you are to treat must or wine with bentonite for clarification or to deal with proteins (see Section 14.3), allow the pectinase treatment to complete until the must or wine is clear before treating with bentonite; bentonite will bind the pectinase and render it inactive.

14.3 PROTEIN STABILITY

Proteins occur naturally in juice and can still be present in significant amounts in wine. A wine may appear perfectly clear, but if unstable, proteins can break down *at normal cellaring temperatures* and cause a haze and possibly form white specks or sediment, and more so with increasing temperatures. Since temperature is the main factor in protein stability, it is also referred to as heat stability.

Proteins are generally not an issue in reds, at least not tannic reds, because they bind to and precipitate with tannins; proteases can be added as a preventative measure. But in whites, and particularly in fruity, early-drinking styles of wines where there are only tiny amounts of tannins, proteins have to be removed using a suitable fining agent.

14

14.3.1 TESTING FOR PROTEIN STABILITY

Protein stability is assessed using a heat stability test that involves subjecting wine samples to various temperatures for various durations and looking for signs of turbidity. A simplified protein (heat) stability test is possible too at home.

Pour into a heat-resistant glass about 50 mL of wine sample filtered at 0.45 micron using a syringe filter (Figure 14.1). Heat the wine sample for 2 hours at 80 °C (176 °F) in a small toaster oven, then take out the sample and let cool for 3 hours at 20 °C (68 °F). If the sample becomes cloudy, the wine is not protein-stable and must be treated with a suitable fining agent;

bentonite or silica–gel are best. To help you assess the cloudiness of samples, cut a small slit in a small cardboard box, place a light bulb in the box, turn off the lights in the room, and hold the sample near the slit.

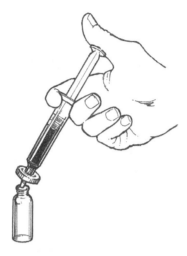

Figure 14.1: Filtering a wine sample with a syringe filter

Here we will use bentonite — the industry standard — to demonstrate how to perform protein stabilization.

14.3.2 PROTEIN STABILIZATION

You can reduce the amount of fining agent needed for protein stabilization in wine by treating must, i.e., before fermentation, to remove some of the proteins. This early treatment reduces proteins that would have to be treated later; however, it does not guarantee total removal as new proteins are produced by yeast during fermentation. You cannot achieve complete protein stability at the juice stage — you will need to test for stability in the wine and treat it accordingly. There is, however, less impact of a treatment at the juice stage to aroma and flavor compounds, many of which are not yet formed since there has been no fermentation yet.

You will need to perform bench trials to determine the minimum amount of fining agent needed to obtain a sample that remains clear after heating.

Here is a simplified way of performing bench trials with bentonite. If the procedure is beyond your abilities, you can simply go with the maximum recommended amount of bentonite, i.e., 1 g/L. Chapter 5 describes how to conduct bench trials, but bentonite bench trials are a little more involved as you have to visually assess the clarity of samples.

First prepare a 5%-bentonite slurry several hours in advance of the bench trials by slowly introducing 5 g of bentonite into 75 mL of hot water in a graduated bottle while stirring vigorously — there should be no clumps. When completely absorbed, add warm water to the 100-mL mark. Over the next couple of hours or so, shake the bottle vigorously as often as possible to allow the clay to absorb water and swell up and perform as it should.

In the next step, you will introduce varying amounts of bentonite to wine samples — *these must be filtered*. Filter about a bottle's worth, some 750 mL, using a vacuum filtering kit (Figure 14.2) and qualitative filter paper with a retention of around 5 μm (microns), such as Whatman #93 paper or equivalent.

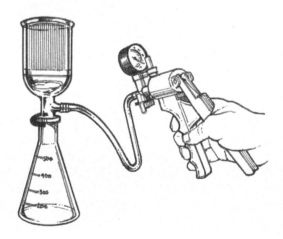

Figure 14.2: Vacuum filtering kit

Prepare six 100-mL *filtered* samples in graduated cylinders and label them 0, 0.10, 0.25, 0.50, 0.75 and 1.00, corresponding to the amount of bentonite to be added to each cylinder; the "0" sample is the control, i.e., no bentonite added.

Stir the bentonite slurry again just prior to use. Using a good 1-mL or 2-mL syringe or graduated pipette, accurately transfer the required amount of 5% bentonite slurry into each wine sample as per Table 14.2.

Table 14.2: Amounts of 5% bentonite slurry to add for targeted rates of addition

Target rate of addition (g/L)	Volume of 5% bentonite slurry to add (mL)
0.00	0
0.10	0.2
0.25	0.5
0.50	1.0
0.75	1.5
1.00	2.0

Seal the graduated cylinders or bottles with paraffin film or lid, shake each sample to mix the wine and bentonite thoroughly, and let stand for 24 hours.

After the 24-hour wait period, discard samples that show any sign of haze or cloudiness as those contain too little bentonite to remove proteins to an acceptable level.

Heat the remaining samples in a small toaster oven at 80 °C (176 °F) for 2–6 hours; the longer the heating, the greater the confidence in the results.

Take the samples out of the oven and let cool to room temperature. Examine each sample and assess turbidity, and pick the sample with the lowest rate of bentonite addition for which there is no haze. Then scale up the addition for the batch to treat based on the rate of bentonite addition just determined.

EXAMPLE 14.3

Adding bentonite

You have a 23-L (6-gal) batch of white wine to be tested and possibly treated for protein stability.

You run bench trials and the control sample and the one labeled 0.10 are hazy after the 24-hour period, and therefore, you know that the wine must be treated and at a rate greater than 0.10 g/L. You then heat the remaining samples and let cool.

Now the samples labeled 1.00 and 0.75 are perfectly clear but the ones labeled 0.25 and 0.50 show a slight haze. The required bentonite dosage then is 0.75 g/L.

Calculate the amount of bentonite needed to treat the batch, as follows:

$$Bentonite\ to\ add\ (g) = 0.75\ ^g/_L \times 23\ L$$

$$= 17.3\ g$$

14.4 TARTRATE STABILITY

As we have seen in Section 7.4.1, juice and wine contain tartaric acid and potassium that form potassium bitartrate (KHT), which can become a source of instability.

KHT can crystallize and precipitate as tartrate crystals (cream of tartar) as it becomes more insoluble as ethanol increases and temperature decreases. Although completely harmless, tartrates may cause some stern looks when serving white or rosé wine; it is tolerated much more in reds.

From wine chemistry and taste perspectives, there can be significant changes depending on the relative amounts of tartaric acid and potassium ions, storage temperature, and the presence of other inhibitory substances, such as polyphenols, proteins and polysaccharides, which can cause more or less tartrates to form, reduce total acidity (TA) and alter pH — the latter two can impact taste and microbial stability. And therefore wine must be properly stabilized against tartrates before bottling. There are two challenges for home winemakers: first, assessing with some level of confidence if a wine is stable, and second, how to stabilize.

To minimize the risk of tartrates forming in bottles, wines, and especially whites and rosés, are subjected to a cold-temperature treatment known as cold stabilization and often simply referred to as "cold crashing" in home winemaking. Protective colloids can also be used to inhibit the

14

formation of tartrates. Cold stabilization and the use of protective colloids are referred to as tartrate stabilization.

Reds are not usually treated specifically for tartrate stabilization as these are not chilled for drinking, although the technique is commonly used to lower acidity in high-TA wines.

14.4.1 TESTING FOR TARTRATE STABILITY

The fridge test is a test you can easily implement at home to predict tartrate stability.

Filter about 100 mL of wine down to 0.45 μm using a syringe filter (Figure 14.1) to minimize any potential protective effects of other colloids — this will improve the confidence of the test.

Pour the sample in a glass bottle, cap, place in the coldest spot in the refrigerator, and hold for 7–10 days. Typical fridge temperature is around 4 °C (40 °F), but the test is more effective and shorter if you can chill the sample to around 0 °C (32 °F) or even lower. Just keep in mind that whatever temperature you perform the test at, that's the temperature you have to chill your batch, and that means having sufficient space in the fridge for your batch or taking advantage of cold weather, or using a glycol chiller to cold stabilize.

At the end of the wait period, take the bottle out, flip it over and hold it up against a bright light to see if any tartrate crystals have formed.

If there are no crystals, the wine is *considered tartrate stable to the test temperature* (i.e., the temperature in your refrigerator) and requires no further processing against tartrates. Tartrate precipitation may still occur if the wine is stored at colder temperatures than the test temperature. What this means is that if you stabilized your wine in your fridge where the coldest temperature was only 6 °C (43 °F) and you give a bottle to a friend who puts it in his fridge at 4 °C (40 °F) and leaves it there for a week, he/she will likely find tartrates in your wine.

If crystals are visible (Figure 14.3), then the test is positive, i.e., the wine is not tartrate stable, and therefore it needs to be stabilized.

Figure 14.3: : Tartrates

There is a variant of the fridge test — called the freezer test — where a sample is held overnight at much lower temperature in a freezer and not have to wait for a week or more. Since cold stabilization is in practice usually carried out at cold temperatures, perhaps close to freezing but not freezer temperatures, you may get different results cold stabilizing than from the freezer test.

14.4.2 TARTRATE STABILIZATION

14

You can stabilize wine against tartrates by one of two methods: chilling or, if that is not an option, adding a protective colloid as an inhibitor. The mode of action of protective colloids is simply to interfere with KHT formation and crystallization. Protective colloids include: metatartaric acid, carboxymethyl cellulose, and potassium polyaspartate.

The choice of method depends on the wine to be treated, how quickly you want to bottle, and your ability to hold the wine at a steady cold temperature for up to two weeks, perhaps longer. Whatever your choice of method, tartrate stabilization should be the last step in the winemaking process, before filtering and bottling — you should not be using any additives or processing aids that can otherwise alter tartrate stability and require a second treatment; you can still add KMS.

And remember to stabilize a blended wine — that the blend components are tartrate-stable does not guarantee that the blend will be stable. For example, wine A can be stable if it has a low tartaric acid and high potassium while wine B can also be stable if it has a high tartaric acid level and low potassium, but the blended wine A+B would likely not be stable since it would have high tartaric acid and high potassium levels.

CHILLING

Cold stabilizing by chilling involves holding the wine at cold temperatures for a minimum amount of time to allow tartrates to form and precipitate. The colder the temperature — without freezing the wine — the shorter the cold stabilization time needed. Generally, the practice is to hold wine at a temperature around 0 °C (32 °F) or lower for 2–3 weeks — the extra time compared to the fridge test is to achieve greater confidence that the wine is stabilized, especially if your wine has not been filtered; this is because the wine may still have protective colloids that impede tartrate formation.

I strongly recommend not to rush this step and not to rush to bottle after cold stabilizing, and to wait another couple of weeks to a month, if possible. Tartrates can still form, albeit, ever so slowly, at warmer temperatures after cold stabilization.

As mentioned in Section 7.4.1, potassium bitartrate becomes more insoluble with increasing alcohol, which means that you cannot expect to cold stabilize juice (i.e., pre-fermentation) and hope for a stable wine — the wine will still likely be unstable post fermentation.

Either place the wine in a fridge at the coldest possible temperature or use your glycol chiller, or, if you live in a northern climate and your wine is ready to be stabilized during a cold stretch, you can place it outdoors — being careful that temperature does not drop below –5 °C (23 °F). Stabilizing in a fridge has the advantage of providing a steady temperature whereas outdoor temperatures can fluctuate greatly, especially at nighttime.

If done outdoors, keep in mind that wine starts freezing at around –5 °C (23 °F); sweeter wines freeze at lower temperatures still. If you can maintain the wine *steady* at –5 °C (23 °F), that would be most ideal as the wines can be stabilized within a week. But as temperatures will likely fluctuate above and below, the wine will only be stable to the highest temperature during the cold stabilization period. For example, if daytime and nighttime temperatures fluctuate between 5 °C (41 °F) and –5 °C (23 °F), respectively, you will have to assume that wine will only be stable to 5 °C (41 °F), in which case, you will need to allow for a longer stabilization period.

In all cases it is best to transfer the wine from glass to PET carboys to allow for possible expansion, particularly if the wine accidentally freezes, and to avoid glass breakage. To the extent possible, do not let the wine freeze and be sure to cover the carboys with a heavy tarp to protect the wine from the sun. You can also use a stainless steel tank making sure to leave a small headspace, flushed with inert gas, to allow for expansion.

 Never cold stabilize wine in oak barrels; tartrates will stick to the wood surface on the inside of the barrel and will form a barrier between wine and wood that will prevent future wines from acquiring all those wonderful oak substances. Tartrates on wood can prove to be a challenge to remove.

Once the wine has been cold stabilized by chilling, bring the wine back to your cellar area and allow tartrates to settle. It's possible depending on the type of vessel you are using that tartrates "stick" to the wall of the vessel. To dislodge the crystals, gently stir along the wall perimeter of the vessel with the handle of a long-handle spoon or lees stirrer, and wait for the crystals to precipitate. Rack the wine before your final filtration or bottling.

If you had done a bentonite treatment for protein stability and did not rack, be careful not to shake the carboy or vessel so as not to disturb the layer of sediment.

METATARTARIC ACID (MTA)

Metatartaric acid, or MTA, has long been used in winemaking to stabilize young, early-drinking wines because it was inexpensive and readily available but it has fallen out of favor to newer, more efficient protective colloids. It is very effective in whites, rosés and light reds, but its protection lasts less than 12 months when stored above 15 °C (59 °F) as the acid slowly hydrolyzes into tartaric acid, or up to 18 months when stored at 12–15 °C (54–59 °F) and approximately 2 years at 10–12 °C (50–54 °F).

First filter wine as desired, then add MTA at a rate of 0.05–0.10 g/L of wine. Measure the required amount carefully because metatartaric acid is strong and it is therefore easy to over-compensate. Dissolve the powder in 10 times its volume of *cold* water — this to avoid hydrolysis of the acid — and stir well.

 Only use freshly purchased MTA and from an unopened bag as MTA will solidify and lose efficiency as it picks up moisture.

You can also add gum arabic at a rate of 1 mL of 30% suspension per L of wine, or 4 mL per gallon, to enhance the action of MTA.

CARBOXYMETHYL CELLULOSE (CMC)

Carboxymethyl cellulose, or CMC, a cellulose gum polymer, has become an industry favorite for tartrate stabilization in whites, rosés and light reds as its action lasts much longer than that of metatartaric acid and at wider temperature ranges. CMC is a common food additive used as a thickener and to stabilize emulsions.

It does interact with anthocyanins and may therefore reduce color slightly in rosés and light reds; it is, however, not recommended in medium- and fuller-bodied reds. This interaction can be reduced by adding gum arabic.

CMC is available in powder form or as, for example, a 10% solution. Add CMC at a rate of 1 mL/L as a 10% solution. Wait 24–48 hours before filtering and bottling. Be sure that the wine is protein stable before treating with CMC.

POTASSIUM POLYASPARTATE (KPA)

Potassium polyaspartate, or KPA, is a relatively newcomer in tartrate stabilization quickly gaining popularity owing to its stabilization efficacy in not only whites and rosés but also in reds with minimal impact on color, if any. It is available in powder form or as an aqueous solution, such as Zenith Uno (Enartis/Esseco).

Follow your product's instructions for the recommended dosage being sure to perform bench trials before treating an entire batch.

The wine to be treated should be clear, stabilized against proteins, and not contain lysozyme. You can filter and bottle immediately after the KPA treatment.

14

15 Aging Wine for Greatness

···

Wine is a "living" beverage; it progresses and transforms during aging, or what is also referred to as maturation, what the French call *élevage*, akin to raising a kid. These transformations are the results of many seemingly surreptitious reactions occurring throughout the life of wine. For example, aroma compounds come slowly freed from their other binding components, as we had seen in Section 1.1. Once freed, those aroma compounds are volatile and can then be smelled. New esters are also created as alcohol and acids interact to give rise to other wonderful aromas. Oxygen also enters bottles, and once it becomes dissolved in wine, it enables other reactions, some good, some not so good. One of the favorable reactions involving oxygen we have seen in Section 9.1 is tannin polymerization; it's what causes tannins to soften.

Well-made wines produced from sound raw material and having good structure and balance will improve with "some" aging. They can improve over just a few months or over several years depending on many factors, such as wine pH, tannin content and cellaring conditions. Far too often wines are consumed before they have reached their peak, and that's okay for those who are partial to the fruitier aromas instead of the more complex, more subtle tertiary aromas that develop during aging.

In this chapter, we will first look at the phases of wine progression and aging potential to set the context, and then we will look at specific techniques for aging wine.

15

15.1 THE THREE PHASES OF WINE PROGRESSION

Wines progress through three phases of aging: improvement, plateau and decline.

In the improvement phase, transformations bring about positive changes to wine to increase overall quality. The rate of transformations depends on many factors, as we will see in Section 15.2. Wine then reaches a peak and plateaus out. It will maintain this plateau for months, years or decades, again, depending on the same factors. It reaches a point where quality starts to decline, where the wine will become "tired," taking on a deeper perhaps golden color in whites and an orange-to-brown color in reds as the wine becomes oxidized.

Let's consider three hypothetical wines — A, B, and C — of different qualities and compare what happens to quality as the wines evolve over time. The graph in Figure 15.1 maps out hypothetical progression curves for each.

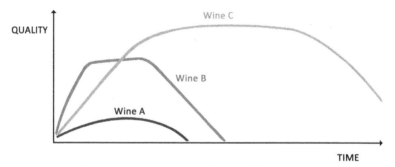

Figure 15.1: Evolution of three different wines

Wine A will only get so good, and in relatively short order, and also decline relatively quickly.

Wine B improves considerably and quite rapidly; it reaches its plateau in fairly short order. It remains at its plateau for a short time and then declines.

Wine C is aging more gracefully and more progressively over a longer period of time before it reaches its plateau. It remains there for a much longer period of time than wines A and B, and then declines at a slower rate.

How do you know when wines peak, how long they will stay at their plateaus, or how quickly they will decline? That comes with experience and knowing your wines. A simple solution: Make sufficient wine so that you can taste a bottle every so often to see how it is evolving. Be patient and let your wines age to understand how they are evolving and to discover their potential and your likings.

Table 15.1 gives general timelines for making and bulk-aging wine, i.e., from crush to bottle, and recommended additional bottle aging for different styles of wines. Some bulk aging is always recommended as wine ages more gracefully than in bottles owing to the smaller ratio of oxygen-containing headspace to wine volume. Note that recommended cellar and bottle-aging periods are best achieved at an ideal cellar temperature of 13 °C (55 °F); as temperature increases, a wine's aging potential decreases.

Table 15.1: Suggested aging durations at 13 °C (55 °F) for different styles of wines

Style of wine	Crush to bottle (months)	Recommended additional bottle aging (months)
Fruity, light whites and rosé	6–9	6–9
Full-bodied, oak-aged whites	12–18	12–18
Light-bodied reds	9–12	9–12
Medium-bodied reds	12–18	9–12
Full-bodied reds	18–24	12–18
Premium full-bodied reds	24–36+	18+

15

Let's look at factors that impact aging potential.

15.2 AGING POTENTIAL

The aging potential of a wine depends on the grape variety, quality of the vintage, viticultural practices, winemaking techniques and the style of wine, use of sulfite, wine chemistry, whether aging the wine in bulk, possibly on the lees in inert vessels or in barrels, or aging in bottles, and cellaring conditions.

Grapes contain a naturally occurring substance called glutathione (see Section 1.1), or GSH, which has very high antioxidant power, greater than sulfur dioxide (SO_2) and tannins, yet winemakers seldom talk about glutathione. The amounts of GSH found in grapes vary by grape variety, viticultural practices, soil and climate, and therefore they will vary from one vintage to another. Some GSH is also produced by yeast during alcoholic fermentation (AF). GSH protects wine until it is exhausted during oxidation reactions. There are commercial preparations, such as OptiMum White and Glutastar (Lallemand), which contain GSH and which can be added to white and rosé must or wine for extra protection, or FreshArom (Laffort), which allows yeast to assimilate substances to manufacture GSH. Unfortunately, we home winemakers cannot measure the amount of GSH in must, and therefore we cannot assess the antioxidant power of must and wine. But the use of these products will prove beneficial.

Tannins too have high antioxidant power, and any winemaking technique that extracts tannins to create a fuller-bodied style of wine will boost aging potential. That's why an oak-aged Chardonnay or rich Cabernet Sauvignon have greater aging potential. But as we have seen in Section 8.1, SO_2 is essential in prolonging aging. SO_2 is involved in the regeneration of tannins and other polyphenols and protects against oxidation reactions, including oxidation of aromas. When SO_2 is exhausted, the wine's antioxidant power becomes compromised and spoilage reactions will begin in earnest.

Ethanol, acids and pH too are important wine chemistry factors warding off spoilage microorganisms. Low-pH (high-acid) wines are better protected against microorganisms than high-pH (low-acid) wines as microorganisms thrive at higher pH. Similarly, higher alcohol levels afford greater protection against microorganisms.

Wines age slower and better in bulk and in larger vessels because there is a much smaller ratio of headspace to wine volume and because oxygen enters well-sealed vessels at a much slower rate through and around closures in bottled wine. As oxygen enters bottles, it dissolves in wine, and that starts oxidation of the many oxidizable substances. Poor-quality closures increase the rate of oxygen ingress and dramatically shorten wine's aging potential.

The rate of reactions are generally faster as temperature increases, and in wine, increasing temperature speeds up that early improvement phase of the aging curve and compresses the plateau. Wine ages most gracefully at cellar temperature of around 13 °C (55 °F); any colder and the wine will develop too slowly. And there will be greater loss of fruity aromas and greater intensity of aged character in white, rosé and lighter, fruity red wines stored above 20 °C (68 °F).

Wine in barrels will also evaporate at a faster rate in a dry cellar, therefore increasing the rate of headspace created and the amount of oxygen exposing the wine to oxidative and microbial spoilages. The recommended relative humidity is 55–75%.

15.3 AGING WINE IN GLASS AND STAINLESS STEEL VESSELS

Aging wine in inert glass or stainless steel vessels is straightforward and requires very little intervention other than periodic control and adjustments of free SO_2 (FSO2) levels. HDPE plastic is inert too but we'll discuss HDPE vessels and their use in wine aging in Section 15.4.

During aging, taste wine on a regular basis — every month for whites and light reds, and every 3 months or at every racking for fuller-bodied reds — to assess evolution, and measure and adjust FSO2 every 3 months. Make sure you keep vessels fully topped up. If there is any headspace, you can flush air out with inert gas, such as argon or nitrogen, or even carbon dioxide (CO_2), or by creating a vacuum, making sure to repeat at least once a month as there is a slow loss of gas or vacuum. The best strategy is to always have vessels completely topped up. And CO_2 does not become dissolved in wine, at least not easily, as many fear after finally having rid of the gas by degassing. CO_2 becoming dissolved in wine is only a concern if it is applied under pressure or while processing wine (turbulence increases the rate of gas solubilization).

Taste wine and measure and adjust FSO2 more frequently when using stainless steel variable-capacity tanks (VCTs), maybe at least once a month, as VCTs tend to let air in from around the bladder. Inflate the bladder well

15

past the red line to ensure a tight seal, and check the bladder pressure regularly and inflate some more if required.

When the wine is to your liking, you can bottle it and perhaps allow it to age some more in bottles; enjoy a bottle once in a while to see how it is evolving. Give reds a chance to evolve and open up and for tannins to soften — reds need time, particularly full-bodied styles. It is quite possible that you may need to "tweak" some wines during aging, just before bottling, to adjust mouthfeel, or tame some still harsh tannins. In Chapter 16, we'll look at techniques and products used for fine-tuning wine.

You can also use pieces of oak wood, referred to as oak adjuncts or oak alternatives, to impart oak aromas and flavors while aging wine in inert vessels. Don't use oak chips for aging as the large surface area of exposed grain results in very quick transfer of oak compounds — they are not meant for aging. You can however use oak chips, as well as oak extract, for fine-tuning.

Oak adjuncts are available in different shapes, sizes, American or French oak, and toast levels for any desired oak profile, smokiness and perceived sweetness. Shapes include chips, cubes, balls (spheres), whole or notched segments, staves, spirals and infusion sleeves. Toast levels include light (LT), medium (MT), medium-plus (MT+) and heavy toast (HT) — the higher the toast level, the greater the smoky, spicy aromas and flavors. Follow instructions for your product as different adjuncts transfer extractable compounds at different rates and therefore require different durations of exposure to wine, and which also depends on your desired style. Use an infusion tube (Figure 15.2) with cubes to allow easy retrieval when the desired oak level is reached. And there is no need to rinse or sanitize oak adjuncts when taken out from sealed or properly re-sealed packages. The sanitizing will simply leach out and reduce those much desirable oak compounds.

Figure 15.2: Infusion tube for oak cubes

Always store oak products in well-sealed bags as they can absorb odors.

Note that the use of oak adjuncts in inert vessels is *not* the same as aging wine in barrels as there is no oxygen entering vessels and therefore no oxygen-mediated polyphenol polymerization, except for HDPE tanks specifically designed for this purpose.

15.4 AGING WINE IN OAK BARRELS, AND HDPE TANKS WITH OAK ADJUNCTS

Aging wine in toasted-oak barrels adds another dimension to a wine's aroma and flavor profiles. Although other types of woods such as redwood and chestnut may be used, white oak species from among those in the *Quercus* genus are most common in winemaking. And as a trend that is becoming more popular, consider aging wine in used whiskey barrels. Depending on the level of charring and age of the barrel, and how recently whiskey has been pulled out, you may be getting a dramatically different wine than what went in; be sure to taste often to avoid overdoing it, especially if you have never tried whiskey barrels before.

Toasted oak adds a multitude of smoky, spicy aromas and flavors, and tertiary aromas of almonds, caramel, coconut and sweet vanilla. It also enhances body, structure and mouthfeel, stabilizes color in reds, helps with clarification, and improves aging potential. There are two key elements at play here: oxygen entering barrels and oak wood tannins.

Barrels are said to "breathe," a phenomenon referred to as micro-oxidation, owing to the infinitesimally small and gradual amounts of atmospheric oxygen in through wood, via stave and head segment joints (Figure 15.3), and around the bunghole. Wood is a porous material, and therefore it acts as an exchange system between the cellar atmosphere and the wine. Oxygen becomes dissolved in wine where it enables polymerization of tannins and anthocyanins (see Section 9.1), which causes a "softening" of tannins for a smoother mouthfeel, and also stabilizes color. You'll recall that anthocyanins are not very stable on their own; they become

15

much more stable once bound to tannins. And here, there are not only condensed, grape-derived tannins but also oak wood tannins, i.e., ellagitannins.

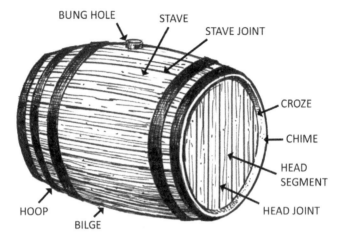

Figure 15.3: Oak barrel anatomy

The terms micro-oxidation and micro-oxygenation are often used interchangeably in barrel aging discussions. Here, micro-oxidation is used to refer to the passive transfer of oxygen through a material and into wine; micro-oxygenation refers to the deliberate, active injection of oxygen into wine using specialized equipment in conjunction with oak adjuncts.

Ellagitannins share a lot of the same tactile sensations and chemistry as condensed tannins (proanthocyanins), but they have greater antioxidant power that confers greater aging potential.

In addition to ellagitannins, toasted oak wood contains many other extractable compounds, such as furfurals, phenolic aldehydes, volatile phenols and lactones, which are transferred into the wine and which impart favorable organoleptic properties and which react with other wine compounds to form tertiary aromas and flavors. These, as well as color, become more concentrated as alcohol and water evaporate through the wood and joints — a phenomenon observed mainly in standard 225-L (59-gal) barrels or bigger as a controlled study using 55-L (14-gal) barrels found no difference [1]. There is also dissipation of CO_2 in similar fashion.

This evaporation and that wood absorbs wine cause a headspace to form above the wine and a commensurate loss of wine. The rate of evaporation is a function of environmental factors, namely, cellar humidity, temperature and ventilation, as well as barrel size and age. The drier and warmer the cellar, and the newer or smaller the barrel, the greater the rate of evaporation. The headspace is mostly vacuum, but because of oxygen ingress, there is still sufficient oxygen in the headspace to cause wine to oxidize, acetic acid bacteria to produce acetic acid, and surface yeast to form surface film. Therefore you have to be vigilant and top up barrels and adjust FSO2 on a regular basis.

At a minimum, top up with the same or similar wine and measure and adjust FSO2 once a month, more often in a drier cellar. As a guideline, I work with 55-L (14-gal) barrels kept at 13 °C (55 °F) and 55–75% relative humidity, and I top up every 2 weeks, requiring about 125 mL, and adjust FSO2 once a month. FSO2 does drop considerably from being consumed by oxygen and polyphenols, from binding with polyphenols and other binders, such as aldehydic compounds from toasted oak, and a tiny amount from dissipation of molecular SO_2. And you'll want to be extra vigilant the first couple of months when introducing wine into a *new* barrel. New wood can contain 60–70% air, of which 21% is oxygen, and therefore you need to do more frequent FSO2 checks and adjustments.

The barrel aging duration depends on size and age (new versus old oak), the type of oak and how it was seasoned and manufactured into barrels, and the desired style of wine. A small-volume barrel will impart oak substances at a faster rate than a larger barrel owing to the higher surface-to-volume ratio in a smaller barrel. Different grape varieties also have different barrel maturation requirements as some may have more of an affinity for oak than other varieties; for example, high-tannin varietals require less barrel aging. Therefore, monitor and taste regularly wines undergoing barrel maturation to avoid imparting too much oak.

As a general guideline for your first batch of red wine into a new barrel, figure one week of aging per gallon; for example, for a 55-L (14-gal) barrel, that would be about 14 weeks, or 3–4 months. Then, double the aging period on each subsequent use of the same barrel. Taste the wine at least once a month to assess evolution, and adapt the duration accordingly. Barrels made from kiln-dried wood impart oak substances at a much faster

15

rate. Those manufactured from premium two, or better yet, 3-year air-dried French (*Quercus robur*) and American (*Quercus alba*) oak impart more subtle oak aromas and flavors and softer tannins at a much slower rate for a longer aging cycle. Kiln-drying is a quicker and cheaper production process than air-drying. Consult reference [2] for more information on oak types and barrel-production methods.

Be extra careful with high-acid wines. If you extract too much tannins, these will taste very bitter and the acidity will seem that much sharper (see Section 1.2). Look at reducing acidity if you intend to barrel-age high-acid wines.

Aging on the lees in barrels, which we discuss next in Section 15.5, can greatly increase organoleptic complexity, body and structure, and aging potential. Where oak influence in whites is desired but *without* lees inter-actions, transfer wine to barrels after the AF and MLF although the wine will likely lose some of its fruit character and develop oxidative odors in the absence of lees. It is best not to oak delicately aromatic or fruit-forward wines to avoid losing freshness or the oak masking the fruit.

To the extent possible, try and time the transfer of wine into a barrel when the barrel-aged one is ready to be transferred out. Simply rinse the barrel with fresh, clean water after transferring the wine out, let the water drip out, and then introduce the new wine. This saves on having to store empty barrels, which require burning discs or pieces of sulfur (Figure 15.4) or filling the barrel with a sulfite–citric solution. Consult reference [2] for more information on storing empty barrels, how to care and maintain barrels, and how to deal with barrel problems.

Barrels are a significant investment with a limited lifespan and require care and maintenance. In general, barrels can be reused three, perhaps four times, then they become "*neutral*," i.e., they have no more extractable compounds to offer although they still allow oxygen in for micro-oxidation, albeit at a much slower rate, and therefore, you can use oak adjuncts in neutral barrels to achieve similar results as aging in newer barrels.

If you want to replicate the benefits of micro-oxidation in barrels, use neutral barrels or "breathable" HDPE tanks, and *always* in conjunction with oak adjuncts.

Figure 15.4: Burning sulfur in a barrel

Breathable HDPE tanks, such as Flextanks (see Figure 3.7 in Section 3.2), are specifically designed for wine aging by allowing in minuscule amounts of air (oxygen). These are manufactured from resin into extremely durable, food-safe polyethylene that can last many years, significantly longer than the useful life of an oak barrel, and are designed with specific oxygen transfer rates (OTR) to emulate micro-oxidation in barrels.

Another advantage of HDPE tanks is that there is no evaporation, and therefore no wine loss or need for topping. Tanks may need an initial topping as the HDPE material "stretches" a wee bit when wine is first introduced into tanks. But since these tanks allow oxygen to interact with wine, taste the wine and monitor and adjust FSO2 on a regular basis as with barrels. Follow the same instructions and guidelines described above on the use of oak adjuncts.

15.5 AGING WINE ON THE LEES

White wines that have been cold settled, produced in a full-bodied style and fermented with no sulfide problems, can benefit greatly from extended aging on the lees *without racking* post AF.

If you detected hydrogen sulfide (H₂S) or any other sulfide-related off-odors at any point, it is best not to age on the lees to avoid the risk of sulfides resurfacing.

During aging and lees contact, or what is known as *sur-lie aging* (from the French to mean aging on the lees), dead yeast cells undergo autolysis and release mannoproteins from their cell walls. Mannoproteins are polysaccharides that add body, increase mouthfeel and reduce astringency. Mannoproteins also have high antioxidant power owing to their high reductive power and their ability to consume dissolved oxygen. They also improve protein and tartrate stability therefore reducing the need for bentonite and cold stabilization, respectively. What's not to like about mannoproteins? Mannoproteins can also be supplemented with a commercial preparation, such as Mannofeel (Laffort), and UltiMA Fresh or Soft (Institut Œnologique de Champagne).

Yeast autolysis also releases many other compounds from within cells that impart yeasty or nutty aromas and flavors, including peptides that can increase sweetness. And therefore, wines aged on the lees are richer, creamier and fuller, and have greater organoleptic complexity. This richness, creaminess, and intensity of aromas and flavors are a function of contact time between lees and wine. The use of β-glucanases, for example, Extralyse (Laffort), can enhance the effects of yeast autolysis (see Section 10.1.2).

And wines aging in oak barrels benefit further from sur-lie aging as mannoproteins bind to ellagitannins and other tannins for a softer mouthfeel.

The lees need to be stirred back into suspension to not only release all those wonderful substances from dead yeast cells but also to avoid those same reductive conditions that may produce stinky sulfides. This technique is called lees stirring, or what is called *bâtonnage* in French, and is widely used in crafting creamy, buttery, full-bodied whites, Chardonnay being the most popular. It is less popular in reds, certainly big reds given their robust flavors and greater organoleptic complexity, but it can be beneficial in turning that medium-bodied wine into a fuller-bodied style.

You can age on the lees for as long as needed to achieve a desired style; it can be weeks, months, or several months up to a year as the enzymes responsible for yeast autolysis can remain active for many months.

The frequency of stirring depends on the type of vessel the wine is aging in, the surface area of wine exposed to air when the vessel is opened for stirring, and cellar temperature. But stir every other day for the first couple of weeks and relatively vigorously to provide sufficient oxygen to the lees to avoid reductive conditions if you have voluminous lees.

Then stir the lees once a week if aging in inert vessels, and at every topping, for example, every 2 weeks or once a month if in barrels. Reduce the frequency if your cellar temperature is warmer than 13 °C (55 °F). Stir *gently* to minimize oxygen pickup, particularly if a large surface area of wine is exposed to air — the exposed area in a carboy is much smaller than in a barrel that has developed a headspace because of wine loss into the wood and evaporation out of the barrel.

Taste the wine on a regular basis to make sure it is progressing according to your taste and that no sulfides are forming, then rack the wine when you have reached your desired style.

Even though mannoproteins in the lees have antioxidant power, keep in mind that this provides protection against chemical oxidation, not microbial protection, and therefore, be sure to maintain proper FSO2 levels based on pH during the aging period. This means that you can go with a lower molecular SO_2 (MSO2); for example, if you typically use 0.8 mg/L for your fruity whites, you can go down to 0.5 mg/L MSO2.

You can augment the benefits of aging on the lees via complementary use of inactivated dry yeast products, such as Oenolees (formerly Biolees) (Laffort) (see Section 16.2). Inactivated dry yeast enhances mouthfeel and mid-palate structure, reduces polyphenols that are responsible for bitterness and astringency, increases aromatic intensity and freshness, improves color stability in reds, inhibits premature oxidation and phenolic browning, and reduces production of undesirable volatile sulfur compounds (VSCs) such as hydrogen sulfide (H_2S).

15

REFERENCES

1. Pambianchi, D. 2021. *A Comparative Study on the Evolution of Wine Aged for 12 Months in a Flextank vs. a Two-Year-Old Oak Barrel.* https://techniquesinhomewinemaking.com/attachments/File/Report%20on%20a%20Comparative%20Study%20on%20the%20Evolution%20of%20Wine%20Aged%20in%20a%20Flextank%20vs%20Oak%20Barrel.pdf.

2. Pambianchi, D. 2008. *Techniques in Home Winemaking: A Practical Guide to Making Château-Style Wines.* Newly-Revised and Expanded. Véhicule Press, Montréal (Québec).

16 Fine-Tuning and Blending Wine

You're at the maturation/aging or pre-bottling stage and your great wine is missing a little something — it's just not quite perfect. Perhaps it's a dry white wine with just a tad too much acidity in spite of your best efforts to deacidify down to the "right" level. Maybe it's a full-bodied red that needs a little more bite, or, on the flip side, that needs to be tuned to reduce some slight bitterness or astringency, or you just didn't get enough oak from your barrel aging.

Almost invariably when making wine from grapes or frozen must you will need to make minor tweaks to satisfy your palate. This is not about fixing flaws or faults — those are discussed in Chapter 22.

This chapter will help you fine-tune your wine post fermentation or pre bottling to improve balance between acidity and sweetness, to improve body and structure or increase mouthfeel, to tame tannins to reduce bitterness and astringency, to increase oak aromas and flavors, and to create a greater wine by blending two or more wines.

16.1 SWEETENING: BALANCING ACIDITY AND SWEETNESS

You did a judicious pre-ferment deacidification of your juice or must and you cold stabilized the wine specifically to reduce the high acidity further in wanting to make a dry white wine, but acidity (i.e., TA) is still just a tad high, or perhaps you want to create more of an off- or medium-dry style and make the fruit aromas and flavors stand out a smidgen more. This is easily accomplished by sweetening, or what is commonly referred to as "backsweetening" in home winemaking, that is, by adding sugar in the form of sucrose, glucose or fructose. Since you already cold stabilized the wine, a deacidification with a carbonate salt is not recommended, particularly not just before bottling, as the wine would require another tartrate stabilization treatment.

You could alternatively use a wine conditioner specifically designed for sweetening finished wine, or maybe try using reserved press-run grape juice or grape-juice concentrate in cans or from a kit to also add different aromas and flavors.

Keep in mind that adding sugar, reserved juice or concentrate adds *fermentable* sugars, and therefore you need to treat the wine with sorbate (see Section 14.1.1) and sulfur dioxide (SO_2) *before* sweetening to prevent a renewed fermentation in bottles. Wine conditioners already contain sorbate but may not contain some sulfite, and perhaps glycerin for extra mouthfeel, therefore be sure to read and follow your product's instructions and conduct bench trials.

 Never use sorbate in wine that has undergone malolactic fermentation (MLF); lactic acid bacteria can metabolize sorbic acid and cause a series of reactions resulting in an off-putting geranium odor.

ADDING SUGAR

You can add sugar as sucrose, glucose or fructose. Sucrose, a disaccharide of glucose and fructose, is extracted and refined into table sugar from either sugar cane or sugar beet. Glucose (dextrose) and fructose are derived from sucrose; glucose can also be produced from starch isolated from, for example, corn or potatoes.

Other sources of sugars, such as honey, brown or caramelized sugar, and artificial sweeteners (e.g., stevia, sucralose, xylitol) may not necessarily complement grape wines, but you can certainly experiment with those if wanting to create a different style — be sure to conduct bench trials first to avoid disappointments. And if using honey, brown or caramelized sugar, or any other kind of fermentable sugar, you will need to stabilize the wine with sorbate, here too, but only if it did not go through MLF.

With sucrose, you have to prepare a sugar solution, referred to as liquid-invert sugar, which you heat to break down (invert) the disaccharide into glucose and fructose. This adds water to wine, and therefore there will be some dilution, more or less, depending on the extent of sweetening. It is not recommended to add sugar directly to wine as a lot of stirring would be required and which could cause excessive oxygen uptake and oxidation reactions. It would also require time until the sucrose is hydrolyzed by the wine's acids to taste the same sweetness as in your bench trials.

The advantage of glucose and fructose is that these sugars readily dissolve in wine and no hydrolysis is required, and therefore, the effect on taste is immediate. As for sweetness, using sucrose as reference, glucose is 0.75 as sweet while fructose is 1.75 times as sweet [1,2]. That means you will need more glucose or less fructose to achieve the same perception of sweetness as sucrose. Use fructose if you want the greatest sweetness impact, for example, when making a sweeter style of wine. Run bench trials using a 10% solution of your sugar of choice to determine how much sugar to add to achieve your desired style and taste.

If using glucose or fructose, prepare 100 mL of 10% solution in a 100-mL graduated cylinder by first dissolving *exactly* 10 g of sugar in about 75 mL of good, fresh tap water in a beaker, and transfer to the graduated cylinder. Rinse the beaker with a little tap water and transfer to the cylinder, and add water as needed to bring the volume to exactly 100 mL.

If using sucrose, first heat about 75 mL of water in a small beaker sufficiently hot to dissolve *exactly* 10 g of sugar, then add a pinch of acid, either tartaric acid or citric acid, or potassium bitartrate (cream of tartar), to hydrolyze the sucrose. Stir well until all is perfectly dissolved. Let cool down to room temperature, then transfer the syrupy solution to a 100-mL graduated cylinder. Rinse the beaker with a little tap water and transfer to the cylinder, and add water as needed to bring the volume to exactly 100 mL.

16

Each mL of 10% solution in 100 mL of wine sample adds *approximately* 1 g/L of sugar.

If you are not sure of your desired sweetness, pick a fairly large range of sugar additions to run your trials; for example, conduct bench trials by adding 10 g/L, 20 g/L and 30 g/L of sugar, and if you find that 20 g/L is not enough but that 30 g/L is too sweet, then you can perform a second round of trials by adding, for example, 22 g/L, 25 g/L and 27 g/L.

See Example 5.1 in Section 5.3 for specific instructions on how to conduct bench trials to determine the amount of sugar to add to sweeten a batch of wine to taste.

Once you have determined the right dosage for your taste and desired style, simply scale up the dosage to your batch, and add the sugar to the wine. Remember that, if using sucrose, you need to dissolve the sugar in heated water with a little acid, letting that cool down before adding to wine.

 Home winemakers often work with target SG numbers and use some conversion factor or table to determine the amount of sugar to add to hit that SG. This doesn't work given the complexity of wine and estimating sugars at low SG, as we have seen in Section 6.5. Adding the "right" amount of sugar to a desired sweetness can only be performed by conducting tasting bench trials as described above.

16.2 IMPROVING BODY AND STRUCTURE: ADDING TANNINS AND POLYSACCHARIDES

If your wine has good overall balance but which you feel lacks mouthfeel or body, perhaps tasting just a tad thin, or maybe just missing that extra bite, tannins, mannoproteins, gum arabic or glycerin are very effective additives to increase mouthfeel, the perception of more body, and overall structure.

There is now a wide range of specialized finishing tannins derived from grape skins or oak wood to fine-tune mouthfeel and body and develop mid-palate structure in reds. Some recommended products include: Scott'Tan Tannin Riche (Scott Laboratories), ViniTannin SR (2B Ferm-Control), and Tanin VR Grape, Tanin VR Supra and Quertanin (Laffort). These products contribute many other positive attributes, such as increased organoleptic complexities, longer aging potential, and perhaps increased perception of sweetness. The recommended dosage is typically a fairly large range, therefore be sure to run bench trials at different rates. Follow product instructions as some may require the wine to be filtered before the addition. Taste and mouthfeel impacts are almost immediate, but they need a minimum bulk-aging contact time, usually 1–3 weeks, then the wine is racked and bottled.

We had already learned in Section 15.5 how mannoproteins from autolysis of dead yeast cells during aging on the lees can add body, increase mouthfeel and fullness, and reduce astringency in reds as well as in full-bodied, barrel-fermented or barrel-aged whites. Here too there are specialized products for adding *S. cerevisiae* yeast cell mannoproteins, such as Mannofeel (Laffort), or UltiMA Fresh or Soft (Institut Œnologique de Champagne); both UltiMA products comprise gum arabic too.

Other products, such as Oenolees (formerly Biolees) (Laffort), incorporate not only yeast cell wall mannoproteins but also other inactivated yeast substances, such as peptides, which increase mid-palate sensations or sweetness. A peptide, and more specifically a yeast protein called HSP12 (look for this protein in product literature, though it may be referred to as "specific peptide fraction" only), is known to increase the perception of sweetness [3].

Gum arabic, which we had described as a protective colloid in Section 13.4.3.3, can be used on its own to add body and increase mouthfeel in whites and young reds. These usually come in 15–30% solutions, therefore it's very important here to run bench trials to determine the "right" dosage. Common gum arabic products include Liqui-Gum (25%, Keller), Stabivin (30%, Laffort), Arabinol (20–30%, AEB) and Maxigum (>20%, Enartis/ Esseco).

Glycerol is one of the major metabolites of yeast fermentation. It is a colorless, odorless, sweet tasting, viscous liquid with a sweetness of about half that of sucrose, and therefore, less than glucose. It is also known as glycerin or its commercial name, glycerine. Its use as an additive is typically not allowed in commercial wines but it is very popular with many home winemakers as it not only improves mouthfeel but also adds sweetness without the worries of refermentation — glycerin cannot be metabolized by yeast. Bench trials are absolutely necessary here, particularly if you have never used glycerin, as results can be mixed.

When we'll look at a typical red winemaking protocol in Chapter 21, we'll see how to use inactivated yeast derivative products to impact body, mouthfeel and structure right from the get-go at the fermentation stage.

16

16.3 TAMING TANNINS: REDUCING BITTERNESS OR ASTRINGENCY

If your wine has slightly bitter or astringent tannins because of over-extraction of, for example, seed tannins or oak tannins during barrel aging, and you are wanting to bottle the wine, a fining treatment can be used to tame the tannins. The choice of a fining agent will depend on restrictions you may have self-imposed on the kinds of additives you use and how soon you expect to bottle. You'll just need to be a little patient and perhaps delay bottling for a couple of weeks or so.

RED WINES

There are many options for dealing efficaciously with bitter and astringent tannins in reds; these include PVPP, egg white, particularly for barrel-aged reds, gelatin and mannoproteins. Refer to Section 13.4 on the specific use and dosage of fining agents.

PVPP can be used preventatively or as a cure for removing astringency or browning — it is the most effective fining agent to remove both monomeric and polymerized flavonoid phenols, i.e., small, bitter phenols and larger, less bitter polyphenols. PVPP has the advantage that its impact can be assessed immediately in bench trials and that the treated wine can be racked the same day although it is recommended to wait several days in case of slower precipitation (see Section 13.4.4).

Mannoproteins are most interesting in that they have many other benefits as we have seen in Section 15.5. There is a vast choice of products that contain mannoproteins and specifically designed for taming tannins.

WHITE AND ROSÉ WINES

For treating bitter and astringent tannins in whites and rosés, options include casein, gelatin in conjunction with silica although not as effective in low-phenol wines, mannoproteins, and PVPP. Casein is very effective but will need a further treatment with bentonite to hasten flocculation. Proteinaceous fining agents from plant origins can be used in lieu of other fining agents derived from animal sources. Refer to Section 13.4 on the specific use and dosage of fining agents.

16.4 INCREASING OAK AROMA AND FLAVOR COMPLEXITY

If you want to add oak aromas and flavors quickly to wine, use a high-impact oak adjunct, such as oak chips or oak extract (see Section 15.3).

Use oak chips at a rate of 1–2 g/L in whites or 2–4 g/L in reds. Experiment with both toasted and untoasted oak and consider blending. Use an oak cube infusion tube (Figure 15.2 in Section 15.3) to allow easy retrieval when the desired oak level is reached. Start tasting the first week to assess aromas and flavors, and taste regularly at least once a week until you hit your desired level of oak. Follow instructions on the product package as different oak products transfer extractable compounds at very different rates; every wine gives different results even with the same kind of chips.

Oak extract, produced by macerating oak chips in ethanol, is an inexpensive alternative to impart oak aromas and flavors to wine. There are new liquid-extract formulations comprising ellagitannins and gallotannins for near-instant integration into wine. The dosage depends on the specific product and concentration of oak aromas and flavors. Follow your product's instructions.

Oak can also be used to mask undesirable methoxypyrazines, or vegetative aromas, in red wines made from underripe fruit with Cabernet-related varieties — Cabernet Franc, Cabernet Sauvignon, Merlot and Carménère (see Section 22.9).

16

16.5 BLENDING WINES

Blending is the practice of mixing two or more different wines primarily for creating a desired style, such as a traditional Bordeaux, Super Tuscan or GSM (Grenache, Syrah, and Mourvèdre) blend, but which is also used for correcting deficiencies, such as low acidity, high pH, high alcohol, or poor aromatics.

The blending components may be different varietals, from different vintages, vineyards or grape-growing areas, or wines from the same varietal but which may have been processed differently, for example, free- and press-run wines. But you should never blend a faulty wine with a perfectly good wine; the results are seldom satisfactory, particularly when it comes to masking oxidation problems.

 Blending two or more stable wines does not guarantee that the final blend will be stable; the blended wine must be tested and treated, if necessary, for stability, i.e., for tartrates as well as for proteins in whites and rosés.

To blend wines, first determine your objectives, that is, are you wanting to adjust, for example, % ABV, TA, pH or Brix, or are you looking to create a specific style or blend of wine — and then run bench trials before blending batches.

To blend wines for the purpose of achieving a desired % ABV, TA or Brix using two component wines of known % ABV, TA and Brix values, respectively, the proportion of component wines is easily determined using the Pearson Square.

The Pearson square (Figure 16.1) is a simple tool to calculate the *number of parts* of wine of a given concentration required to bring the concentration of another wine to a desired level. It can be used for any linear relationship, such as % ABV, TA, Brix and free SO_2 — it cannot be used for pH or SG.

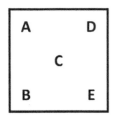

Figure 16.1:
Pearson square

In Figure 16.1, A, B, C, D and E are defined as follows:
A = the concentration of the wine to be used
B = the concentration of the wine to be "corrected"
C = the desired concentration
D = the number of parts of wine to be used and is equal to C−B
E = the number of parts of wine to be "corrected" and is equal to A−C
If D or E results in a negative value, enter the absolute (positive) value.

Let's look at an example.

EXAMPLE 16.1

Pearson Square; blending two wines to increase TA

You have a 23-L (6-gal) batch of low-acid Chambourcin wine with a TA of 5.2 g/L (this is the B value) that you would like to increase to 6.0 g/L (this is the C value) using Frontenac wine with a TA of 10.0 g/L (this is the A value). Determine as follows how much Frontenac you need to add to the Chambourcin to achieve the desired TA:

$$
\begin{array}{|ccc|}
\hline
\textbf{10.0} & & \textbf{0.8} \\
& \textbf{6.0} & \\
\textbf{5.2} & & \textbf{4.0} \\
\hline
\end{array}
$$

The Pearson Square says that you need 0.8 parts of Frontenac wine for 4.0 parts of Chambourcin wine, or:

$$Volume\ of\ Frontenac\ needed\ (L) = 23\ L \times \frac{0.8}{4.0}$$

$$= 4.6\ L$$

This example illustrates that, even for what may seem like a small adjustment in TA from 5.2 to 6.0 g/L, blending to make such corrections may require not insignificant amounts of the second wine (20% here), which could substantially alter the character of the original wine.

EXAMPLE 16.2

Pearson Square; adding concentrate to must to increase SG/Brix/PA

In Example 6.4 in Section 6.4.1, we looked at chaptalizing must by adding concentrate from a kit. Specifically, we needed to determine the amount of concentrate having a SG of 1.155 (35 Brix) to add to 26 L (7 gal) of must to increase SG from 1.091 to 1.102, or Brix from 22.0 to 24.5, to achieve a desired PA of 14.0% ABV.

16

In the Pearson Square, we can use Brix or PA, but not SG; we will use
Brix along with Metric volumes.

35.0	2.5
24.5	
22.0	10.5

The Pearson Square says that you need 2.5 parts of 35.0 Brix concentrate
for 10.5 parts of must at 22.0 to raise Brix to 24.5, or:

$$Volume \ of \ concentrate \ needed \ (L) = 26 \ L \times \frac{2.5}{10.5}$$

$$= 6.2 \ L$$

To blend for a desired style or to address poor aromatics, perform bench
trials by trying various combinations of the component wines and in different proportions, being sure to taste and evaluate wines at the serving
temperature — that means chilling samples if blending whites and rosés.
Have ready one 750-mL bottle for each component wine. You may need
more depending on the number of wines you are trialing, the number of
combinations, and of course, the number of friends — "wine expert"
friends — who will be helping you out tasting the trial blends.

You will find many blending suggestions for grape varieties described
in Chapter 2, including blending vinifera with non-vinifera wines, or perhaps blending one or more wines but from different barrels, choosing the
best barrels for your top blend. There can be significant variations of the
same wine from different barrels. You can also experiment blending wines
of the same varietal but produced from grapes sourced from geographically
different growing regions. And don't limit yourself to blending wines from
the same vintage; sometimes adding a small portion of a more recent vintage to an older wine can add freshness and restore some of the fruity character.

This is where you need experience in assessing the various blends during the trial — it's not always easy or straightforward. You are looking for the "right" blend that brings together each of the component wine's organoleptic characteristics, i.e., aromas, flavors and mouthfeel, into a superior wine. Enlist an experienced eno-friend who can guide you through the process if you're just starting out. You may also have one or two other friends to give you honest feedback.

Once you have determined the blending components and proportions, blend your batches accordingly in a single vessel, such as a variable-capacity tank (VCT), to ensure a homogeneous blend. If for logistical reasons you need to blend entire batches of the component wines, you can do that too. Either way, you'll want to know the resulting % ABV and TA of the final blend; for pH, you will have to measure, though you should confirm TA too by titration. There are online calculators to help you with these calculations, or download the worksheet at ModernHomeWinemaking.com, or if you are mathematically inclined, you can use the following equation where V_1 and ABV_1 are the volume and % ABV of wine component #1, respectively, V_2 and ABV_2 are the volume and % ABV of wine component #2, etc. (you can use it for TA too, but not pH):

$$Final\ \%\ ABV = \frac{V_1 \times ABV_1 + V_2 \times ABV_2 + V_3 \times ABV_3 + \cdots}{V_1 + V_2 + V_3 + \cdots}$$

Let's look at an example.

EXAMPLE 16.3

16

Calculating % ABV of a blended wine

You have created a Bordeaux-style blend with the following component wines:

Wine component	Volume (L)	% ABV
Cabernet Sauvignon	50	14.2
Merlot	25	13.5
Petit Verdot	10	14.5

Calculate the final % ABV as follows:

$$Final\ \%\ ABV = \frac{50\ L \times 14.2\% + 25\ L \times 13.5\% + 10\ L \times 14.5\%}{50\ L + 25\ L + 10\ L}$$

$$= 14.0\%$$

REFERENCES

1. Belitz, H.D., W. Grosch and P. Schieberle. 2004. *Food Chemistry*. 3rd. Springer-Verlag Berlin, Heidelberg, Berlin.

2. Carr, C.J., F.F. Beck and J.C. Krantz Jr. 1936. *Sugar Alcohols. V. Chemical Constitution and Sweet Taste*. J. Am. Chem. Soc. 58:1394-1395.

3. Marchal, A., P. Marullo, V. Moine and D. Dubourdieu. 2011. *Influence of yeast macromolecules on sweetness in dry wines: role of the Saccharomyces cerevisiae protein Hsp12*. J. Agric. Food Chem. 59:2004-2010.

17 Filtering Like the Pros

Filtration is the mechanical process of removing particulates and colloids, including yeast and bacterial cells, using a filter medium for the purpose of achieving greater clarity or removing unwanted yeast and bacteria left over from alcoholic and malolactic fermentations. Filtration intended for clarifying wine is referred to as clarifying filtration and that for removing yeast and bacterial cells to achieve microbial stability is referred to as sterile filtration.

This chapter describes the equipment necessary for clarifying and sterile filtrations, and how to filter efficiently. But first, let's understand the need for filtering.

17.1 WHY FILTER?

Filtration is a very controversial topic because, interventionism notwithstanding, many believe that it strips wine of aromas, flavors and color, or that it causes excessive oxygen uptake.

Aroma and flavor molecules are so much smaller than the porosity of filter media used in winemaking that filtration cannot strip aromas and flavors. Yes, the filter medium can affect aromas and flavors, particularly pads, *if not properly prepared*. If you filter wine though pads without adequately rinsing with plenty of water, the wine can indeed pick up a cardboard smell and taste. Some winemakers will also point out that wine tastes different after filtration, once bottled. This is not a filtration problem but, rather, a condition where the wine is temporarily "knocked out" from processing, a condition known as "bottle sickness," often referred to as "bottle shock" although the two have slightly different meanings in winespeak.

Bottle sickness refers to a wine with muted aromas and flavors, seemingly devoid of prior fruity aromas, believed to be the result of rapid oxidation during the bottling process that causes a small amount of acetaldehyde to form. Once the bottle is corked, the condition slowly disappears over the course of the next few days, weeks, or even months, as acetaldehyde reacts with sulfur dioxide (SO_2) and polyphenols and the fruity aromas shine through again. Bottle shock is about wine stress that results from excessive handling or vibrations from, for example, a long journey in a car.

As for filtration stripping color, it is simply removing what will eventually drop out and sediment, and, as is often witnessed in reds processed too quickly, what will stain bottles.

If executed attentively with a suitable filtration system, oxygen uptake can be limited to 1–2 mg/L, which can be easily mitigated by adjusting free SO_2 (FSO2) by 5 mg/L before or after filtration.

Sure, you can certainly make great wine, very clear wine, without ever filtering. And you may never need to filter if you bottle and drink wine quickly. But if you offer a bottle of 12-month-old unfiltered Petite Sirah to a friend who may store it away for months, your friend may well discover sediment or wonder at the deeply stained bottle. And if you enter wines into competitions, judges always look for perfectly clear, brilliant wines, always.

17.2 CLARIFYING FILTRATION

Clarifying filtration is concerned with removing suspended particulates and colloids that affect the clarity of wine, and involves passing wine, either by gravity or using a pump, through a filter medium. Clarifying filtration generally involves successively performing a coarse filtration, followed by a polishing filtration, and a fine filtration. But depending on the colloidal state of the wine, i.e., the amount of particulates in suspension, a clear white wine, for example, can go straight to a fine filtration.

There are different types of filter media for processing small and large batches. Disposable, single-use media include cartridges made of polypropylene spun microfibers in various sizes, for example, 2, 5 and 10 inches, the latter being the most common in home winemaking, and depth filter pads manufactured from layers of cellulose fibers in sizes ranging from 10 cm × 10 cm or 20 cm × 20 cm for small operations, or as 22-cm discs. Reusable media include cartridges made of a variety of materials, such as polyester microfiber, polypropylene or glass. Consult your filter housing vendor to choose a suitable reusable cartridge as these are available in many kinds of end cap and O-ring configurations.

The porosity or retention rating of filter media is expressed in microns as either nominal or absolute. A micron is a micrometer (μm), or 1×10^{-6} meter, which, to give you an idea of size, is 10–100 times smaller than the diameter of human hair.

Nominal means that the filter medium will filter, more or less, at the specified micron rating, but that larger particles may be allowed through or smaller particles may be blocked. There can be a fairly large variance between the rating and actual retention. For example, if a filter cartridge is rated for "2 microns nominal," it might let through somewhat larger particles than 2 microns and likewise block smaller particles.

Absolute rating is much more precise and with much smaller variance; it means that more than 99%, often more than 99.99%, of particles greater in size than the stated micron rating will be filtered out. These differences are due to manufacturing processes and materials, physicochemical properties of the filter medium, filtering pressure and wine chemistry.

Filter media in the 5–10 microns range are used for coarse filtering, 2–5 microns for polishing filtering, and 0.5–1 micron for fine filtering. These are all nominal ratings.

17

We will discuss sterile filtration in Section 17.3 below, but to put things into perspective, sterile filtration requires filtering wine at, most commonly, 0.45 micron absolute-rated filter media to provide a high level of confidence of microbial stability (see Section 14.1) by removing at least 99.9% of spoilage yeast and bacteria; this cannot be accomplished with 0.45 micron nominal-rated filter media.

Figure 17.1 illustrates the many types of filtration systems for home winemaking applications, both small and large.

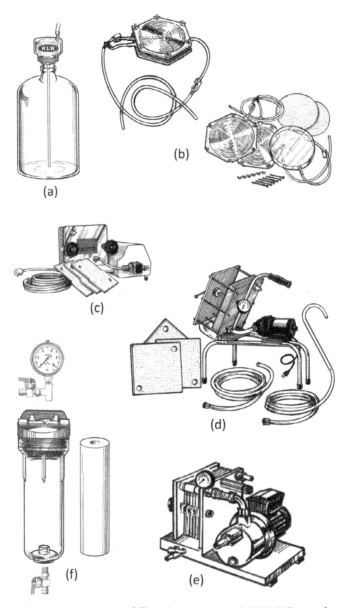

Figure 17.1: Types of filtration systems: a) KLR Wine and Beer Filter; b) round plate-and-frame filter and pads; c) Buon Vino Mini Jet and filter pads; d) Buon Vino Super Jet and filter pads; e) Pillan F6 plate-and-frame filter; f) 10-inch filter housing and cartridge with optional gauge and purge and drain valves, such as a Sioux Chief ¼" PDQ × ⅛" MIP.

A gravity-type filter, such as the KLR Wine and Beer Filter (Figure 17.1a), which uses cartridges rated 1 and 5 microns nominal, will serve you well if you filter infrequently and only small batches from a gallon (4 L) to a standard 23-L (6-gal) carboy.

A round plate-and-frame filter and pads (Figure 17.1b) coupled to a small pump or an integrated filter system such as the Buon Vino Mini Jet (Figure 17.1c) will also work well for standard carboy batches. Round filter pads are identified as AF1, AF2, AF3, AF4 and AF5 corresponding to 8, 4.5, 2.5, 0.8 and 0.5 micron nominal, respectively, while Buon Vino filter pads are identified as No. 1, No. 2 and No. 3 corresponding to 5, 1.8 and 0.5 micron nominal.

Table 17.1 summarizes the various types of nominal-rated filter media available for filtering small batches. These media are designed to filter up to a standard carboy of wine.

Table 17.1: Summary of nominal rated filter media available for filtering small batches

Type of filtration	Approximate microns range	KLR Cartridges	Round pads	Buon Vino pads
Coarse	5–10	5 microns	AF1, AF2	No. 1
Polishing	2–5		AF3	No. 2
Fine	0.5–1	1 micron	AF4, AF5	No. 3

For larger batches, upgrade to, for example, an integrated system like the Buon Vino Super Jet (Figure 17.1d) or Pillan F6 filtration system (Figure 17.1e), which both use 20 cm × 20 cm (7⅞ in × 7⅞ in) pads, or a 10-inch cartridge setup that uses disposable or reusable cartridges (Figure 17.1f) in any nominal rating and which requires a positive-pressure or vacuum pump. Buon Vino Super Jet filter pads are bigger than the Mini Jet's but are similarly rated.

17

Positive-pressure-type filtration systems filter by moving wine from a vessel, through the pump and filter media, and into a receiving vessel. Vacuum-type filtration systems filter by "pulling" wine from a vessel, then through the filter medium, and into the receiving vessel — the wine never flows through the pump. The advantage of a vacuum-type system is that the wine is protected from air in the receiving vessel. You can accomplish this with a positive-pressure-type system too: simply flush the air out of the receiving vessel with inert gas and install a one-way vent valve on the stopper to let gas out as the vessel fills up with wine.

You can also set up two filter housings in series and equipped with cartridges of different ratings when you want to step-filter, that is, filter through two successive grades, for example, through a 5-micron cartridge followed by a 2-micron cartridge. Use cartridges with closely matched ratings; do not use, for example, a 10-micron cartridge with a 1-micron cartridge — the latter will clog very quickly. Step-filtering with serial media requires a good pump that can generate sufficient pressure to move wine efficiently through both filter cartridges. Section 17.4.2 outlines additional instructions for step-filtering with two filter housings in series.

Some systems come pre-equipped with a pressure gauge to monitor filtering efficiency. When pressure reaches the manufacturer-specified threshold, the filter medium is clogged and is no longer filtering efficiently and is causing excessive strain on the pump and the entire line. You can easily install a pressure gauge on a cartridge filter housing. If you choose the right filter medium rating, there should be no clogging under normal operating conditions. Of course, a filter medium will start clogging at some point if you are trying to filter much larger volumes than the medium was designed for. The volume that each type of medium can filter depends on the clarity of the wine. You can easily filter 100, 200 or more liters (25, 50 gal or more) with 10-inch cartridges. The Buon Vino pads in a Super Jet can easily filter a standard 54-L (14-gal) demijohn.

Most often you will filter wine into another vessel, but there will be instances where you will want to filter right into bottles, i.e., filter to the bottler to fill bottles, for example, if doing only a coarse filtration of a red wine. This is possible and most efficient with a vacuum-type filter system as it provides flow-control of wine through the filter system and into bottles, whereas a filtration system using a positive-pressure pump does not allow such control.

Consult reference [1] for additional information on clarifying filtration.

17.3 STERILE FILTRATION

Sterile filtration at bottling is concerned with removing unwanted yeast and bacteria through a filter medium down to a level that these microorganisms pose no further risks of spoilage for all practical purposes. Given that yeast cells are 1–2 microns and most lactic acid and spoilage bacterium cells are 0.5–0.8 micron, sterile filtration with a filter medium rated a minimum of 0.5 micron *absolute* is required; the standard is 0.45 micron *absolute*.

 The term "sterile filtration" is commonly used when discussing this type of filtration in winemaking, however, it is a misnomer as true sterile filtration is only possible with specialized equipment that removes 99.9999% of microorganisms but which is really not required for processing wine. But it is understood that sterile filtration in winemaking involves treating the filter line with steam and using absolute-rated filter media. In a home winemaking setting where the use of steam is not feasible, or at least not easily accessible, properly sanitizing the filter system and using absolute-rated filter media can achieve acceptable results. Since the term is in common use, we will refer to "sterile filtration" here too.

If any of the following criteria apply to your wine, then it needs to be sterile filtered *at bottling*:

- The wine has more than 2 g/L (0.2%) of residual sugar and you cannot use sorbate because it has gone through malolactic fermentation (MLF).

- The wine has more than 100 mg/L of residual malic acid (a spot is still visible from the chromatography test) due to an incomplete MLF.

- The wine was affected by spoilage yeast, including surface yeast and *Brettanomyces*, or spoilage bacteria, including acetic acid bacteria and lactic acid bacteria.

17

Sterile filtration is not required in wines that have not been subjected to MLF and which are protected with sufficient SO_2. Keep in mind, however, that if a wine is protected with only a small amount of SO_2 and it is to be aged in bottles, it is at risk of microbial activity as the SO_2 level becomes critically low as some free SO_2 is consumed over time.

There are no specific filtration systems per se for sterile filtration for home winemaking — it is simply a matter of using, for example, a cartridge rated for 0.45 micron *absolute*, and protecting wine from air and the elements when filtering into another vessel or into bottles.

But beware!

Unless you can bottle under "sterile" conditions, your wine will still be at risk of microbial activity as microorganisms are always present in your winemaking area, on your equipment, and in your wine. Bottling under sterile conditions implies filtering wine in-line through a sterile filter medium and into nitrogen-sparged bottles using a vacuum-type bottling system. There is otherwise a risk as ambient microorganisms can be present in bottles waiting to be filled or in filled bottles moved from the filler to the corker. And therefore, sterile filtration and sterile bottling are very difficult to implement in home winemaking. You can still sterile filter using sanitary conditions to minimize risks.

Consult reference [1] for additional information on sterile filtration.

17.4 FILTERING WINE

Filtering wine involves preparing the equipment, sanitizing the filtration line and equipment, filtering the wine, and cleaning up. The cleanup time and effort varies on whether you are using disposable or reusable media.

17.4.1 FILTERING WITH DEPTH FILTER PADS

Figure 17.2 illustrates two typical filtration setups using depth filter pads: a) round plate-and-frame filter, and b) Buon Vino Super Jet.

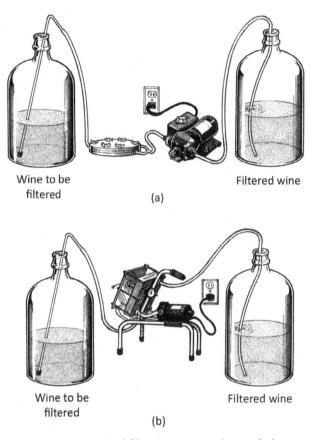

Wine to be filtered

Filtered wine

(a)

Wine to be filtered

Filtered wine

(b)

Figure 17.2: Typical filtration setups: a) round plate-and-frame filter, and b) Buon Vino Super Jet

There are three very important points to remember when setting up a filtration system using disposable depth filter pads:

1. Filter pads have a smooth side and a rough side and must be positioned correctly between filtration plates as per the system's instructions so that wine flows in from the rough side and out the smooth side. Because of how filtration plates and systems are designed, pads may need to be inserted in alternating fashion. Be sure you understand the configuration and setup of your system.

   In the Buon Vino Mini Jet, pads are inserted between plates with the rough side of all pads pointing away from the back plate, and

17

in the Buon Vino Super Jet, all pads are inserted between plates with the rough side pointing towards the pump. Be sure that the holes in pads all line up with the holes in plates. Each of these set-ups uses three filter pads.

2. If you intend to step-filter, you will need to do successive filter runs; do *not* use a mix of pads with different ratings.

 Plate-and-filter systems making use of, for example, 3, 10 or 20 depth filter pads, are designed to distribute wine by a manifold so a portion of the wine goes through each single pad; the wine does not flow through the set of pads successively. This is the reason why pads cannot be mixed in these systems.

3. Rinse the pads to avoid imparting a cardboard taste to wine. The procedure is described below.

Prepare approximately 10 L (2½ gal) of 1% sulfite–citric solution. See Section 4.5.1 for instructions on preparing a sulfite–citric solution.

 Never use alkaline (caustic) products or products containing detergents or foaming agents for cleaning or sanitizing depth filter pads. Such products can leave residues that can negatively affect the taste or appearance of wine.

Dip the pads in clean, fresh water and allow them to become completely saturated with water, until there is no more bubbling. Insert pads one at a time in the frame as per your system's instructions, and tighten all bolts as hard as you can by hand. If you prefer to insert the pads dry, only loosely tighten all bolts, run water through the filter system and allow the pads to swell up completely (this will cause leakage), and only then completely tighten all bolts until leakage stops.

Install the racking hose and cane and outlet hose. Insert both the racking cane and outlet hose in the container with the sulfite–citric solution, turn on the pump, and let the solution recirculate for approximately 10 minutes to sanitize the whole system — pump, filter plates, filter pads and hoses.

To complete this step, slightly raise the racking cane just above the level of the sulfite–citric solution and let run for just a few seconds to empty the filter system of any leftover solution.

Transfer the racking cane to a pail filled with about 20 L (5 gal) of clean, fresh water, and place the out tube into another pail or carboy. Start the pump and allow water to rinse and flush the entire system. Collect the out water for possible reuse. While flushing, taste the water regularly; you can stop the rinsing when the water has no cardboard taste.

To complete this step, slightly raise the racking cane just above the water level and let run for just a few seconds to empty the filter system of any leftover water.

You are now ready to filter wine.

 At this point, the filter pads still contain some water, and therefore, when you start the filtration run, you will first get some water; you will need to decide when water becomes wine and start collecting wine in the receiving vessel.

Insert the racking cane in the vessel with previously racked wine to be filtered. Hold the out hose over a small container. Start the pump and watch for the water at the out hose. As soon as the water turns to wine, judging from the color, place the out hose into the receiving vessel and let filtration run its course.

If your system is equipped with a pressure gauge, monitor the pressure to make sure it is well within the maximum as specified by the manufacturer; if not, just make sure that wine flows consistently at a good rate. If pads clog up, you may not be able to complete this filtration run, in which case you will need to start over with a coarser grade of pads.

 Plate-and-frame filter systems will leak — just a little — during filtration; this is normal. If there is excessive leakage, try tightening the plates; if it persists, you are likely trying to filter with pads of too low a rating or the wine is not filter-ready.

17

 Once the pump is working and wine is being filtered, do not turn the pump off/on as it can decrease filter efficiency and clarity of the wine.

Once complete, take a wine sample to the lab and measure pH, FSO2 and DO (dissolved oxygen), if so equipped, and adjust FSO2 as needed. Place a stopper and airlock on your vessel.

Dispose of the pads — they can be composted — and flush the pump and hoses with clean water or the water you had saved from the sanitizing step. Clean the pump by running and recirculating a mild solution of carbonate or percarbonate cleaner, such as PBW. Immerse in a similar solution all hoses and parts that have come into contact with wine. Rinse the pump, hoses, and parts with fresh, clean water, let dry and store away.

17.4.2 FILTERING WITH CARTRIDGES

You can use disposable or reusable cartridges right out of the *unopened* package without sanitizing if they had been stored properly; however, it is always recommended to clean and sanitize cartridges to reduce spoilage risks in the event they contain contaminants left over from manufacturing.

Cartridges filter incoming wine from the outside towards the inside, channeling wine up or down the housing, depending on the filtration system configuration, and to the out hose.

To filter efficiently, wine must be filtered across the whole length of a cartridge, and this means that *the filter housing should always be full during filtration*. All too often those inexperienced with cartridge filtration will have wine only partially fill the housing and leave a good portion of the cartridge not filtering. This happens when the filter housing is above the wine (to be filtered) level or has not been properly primed. Some filter housings, such as Tenco's Tandem used with the Enolmatic bottler, are equipped with a bypass/purge valve to purge air out of the housing and equilibrate pressure.

When you purchase a filter housing, choose a model with a bypass/purge valve; otherwise, you can easily install one (see Figure 17.1f), and while you're at it, install a drain valve too to empty the housing at the end of sanitizing and rinsing cycles or filtration. Sioux Chief ¼" PDQ × ⅛" MIP valves work great for this purpose. Note that, any wine left in and drained from the housing has *not* been filtered, and therefore, you should not bottle it — simply save it to enjoy with dinner. A variable-speed positive-displacement diaphragm pump with a bypass valve on the housing will greatly simplify filling and emptying the housing. You can also install a pressure gauge on the housing (see Figure 17.1f) to monitor operating pressure and filtering efficiency; you will need a tee (plastic fitting) to connect the purge valve and gauge onto the filter housing.

In the following procedure, you can use a filtration configuration with one or two filter housings and media using a positive-pressure pump or a vacuum pump (Figure 17.3). If using two housings, make sure that wine to be filtered first flows through the higher-micron cartridge.

 Make sure that the vessel of wine to be filtered is ABOVE the filter housing so that the filter housing fills up completely and filtering uses the entire length of the cartridge. This means having the bottom of the vessel always above the highest point of the housing, as shown in Figure 17.3 where two housings are used in series.

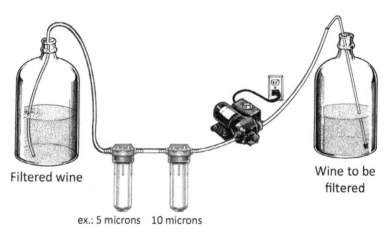

Filtered wine   Wine to be filtered

ex.: 5 microns   10 microns

Figure 17.3: Filtering using a positive-displacement diaphragm pump with two cartridges (e.g., 10 and 5 microns in series); note that the wine level is above the housings

 If you are re-using a reusable-type cartridge that has been stored in a 70%-ethanol solution (see Section 17.4.3 below), you can skip the next step as sanitizing is not required.

Secure all hose connections extra tight with proper clamps, keeping in mind that wine is less dense than water, and therefore, you might still get a leak once you start filtering wine even though there was no leak during sanitizing and rinsing.

To sanitize a new (disposable or reusable) cartridge, first prepare approximately 10 L (2½ gal) of 1% sulfite–citric solution. Note that since you have to sanitize the filter housing, you will be sanitizing the cartridge too even if it is not required. With the pail of solution sitting higher than the filter housing, insert both the racking cane and out hose in the container with the sulfite–citric solution, turn on the pump, and allow the housing to fill up completely, then let the solution recirculate for approximately 5 minutes.

To complete this step, slightly raise the racking cane just above the level of the sulfite–citric solution and let run for just a few seconds to empty the filter system of any leftover solution.

Transfer the racking cane to a pail filled with about 20 L (5 gal) of clean, fresh water, and the out tube into another pail or carboy. Start the pump and allow the housing to fill up completely, then allow all the water to rinse the entire system. Collect the out water for possible reuse.

To complete this step, slightly raise the racking cane just above the water level and let run for just a few seconds to empty the filter system of any leftover water. If there is any water left in the housing, unscrew the housing, drain and replace, or simply drain via the drain valve if you had installed one.

You are now ready to filter wine.

 At this point, the cartridge may still contain a significant amount of water, and therefore, when you start the filtration run, you will first get some water; you will need to decide when water becomes wine and start collecting wine in the receiving vessel.

Insert the racking cane in the vessel with previously racked wine to be filtered. Hold the out hose over a small container. Start the pump and allow the housing to fill up completely, and watch for the water at the out hose. As soon as the water turns to wine, judging from the color, place the out hose into the receiving vessel and let filtration run its course.

If your system is equipped with a pressure gauge, monitor the pressure to make sure it is well within the maximum as specified by the manufacturer; if not, make sure that wine flows constantly at a good rate and that the *housing remains full to the top until the end of the run*. If the cartridge clogs up, you may not be able to complete this filtration run, in which case you will need to start over with a coarser grade cartridge.

Once complete, take a wine sample to the lab and measure pH, FSO2 and DO, if so equipped, and adjust FSO2 as needed. Place a stopper and airlock on your carboy.

If you used a disposable cartridge, dispose of it and flush the pump, hose and housing with clean water or the water you had saved from the sanitizing step. Clean the hose and housing by running and recirculating a mild solution of carbonate or percarbonate cleaner, such as PBW. Rinse the hose and housing with fresh, clean water, let dry and store away.

 If you used a reusable cartridge, follow the instructions in Section 17.4.3 on cleaning and storing the cartridge.

17.4.3 CLEANING AND STORING REUSABLE FILTER CARTRIDGES

At the end of the filtration run, the *reusable* filter cartridge will still contain wine as well as filtered organic residues that need to be broken down and removed before the cartridge can be stored away for the next use. The most effective way to deal with organic residues as well as removing color from processing red wine is to treat with a 3% NaOH (sodium hydroxide) solution.

Prepare a 3% NaOH solution by dissolving about 120 g (about 8 tbsp) of NaOH pellets in 4 L (1 gal) of water — always add the pellets to the water, *not the other way around* — in a suitable chemical-resistant plastic (not glass) container.

 A 3% NaOH solution is very caustic and can burn eyes and skin. The solution will also become quite hot while pellets dissolve. Wear protective face shield, clothing and gloves.

First flush the entire line and filter housing (with cartridge) of wine, then rinse completely and abundantly with about 20 L (5 gal) of fresh, clean water from a pail using your filter pump. When done, stop the pump and drain or empty the housing and entire line.

Run and recirculate the 3% NaOH solution for just a few minutes through the entire line and filter medium and housing making sure that the entire housing fills up. If you have previously filtered red wine, the NaOH solution will take on a greenish-gray color, pretty much like when you titrate for total acidity (TA). Turn the pump off and leave the whole setup to soak overnight if you filtered white or rosé wine or up to 24 hours if you filtered red wine. The idea is to let the cartridge soak in the NaOH solution to break down organic matter and to restore the color of the cartridge to an almost-perfect white; it will also remove any red color that had stained equipment.

The next day, turn on the pump and recirculate the NaOH solution once again through the entire line for a few minutes. When done, collect the NaOH solution in its container, drain or empty the housing and entire line of the NaOH solution, and rinse the entire line with about 20 L (5 gal) of fresh, clean water.

At this point the entire system is clean and free of NaOH, but run and recirculate a 1% sulfite–citric solution to neutralize any residual NaOH, and complete with one final water rinse. You can save this water from the final rinse for other use to minimize waste.

Drain or empty the housing and entire line, remove the cartridge, and transfer to a suitable tall, cylinder jar and completely fill with a 70% ethanol solution, and seal the jar. You can prepare a 70% ethanol solution by appropriately diluting 90–95% ethanol, such as grain alcohol (the label might say "180 proof"; just divide that by two to get the percent ethanol) available from your local liquor store. Do *not* use denatured ethanol as it contains methanol and other hazardous substances.

REFERENCE

1. Pambianchi, D. 2008. *Techniques in Home Winemaking: A Practical Guide to Making Château-Style Wines*. Newly-Revised and Expanded. Véhicule Press, Montréal (Québec).

18 Packaging and Bottling

·····

"'Winemaking' continues after bottling." [1]

You have invested considerable money in sourcing the best fruit or must from one of the finest grape-growing regions of the world, and many months, if not years, in crafting a superlative wine. You are now ready to bottle and start enjoying the wine or, perhaps, cellar it for a few more months or years to give it additional time to evolve into an even greater wine. It's time now to choose a type of bottle, closure and capsule, design and print labels, and plan your bottling.

Bottling involves washing and sanitizing bottles, if these had been previously used, filling bottles, corking, and dressing bottles with capsules and labels.

This chapter looks at packaging choices and considerations, the necessary equipment for washing and sanitizing bottles, and bottling small or large batches, then outlines the bottling process.

18.1 PACKAGING

You will be making many, many decisions related to packaging: types of bottles, closures, capsules and labels. There's a lot of advance planning to do here.

18.1.1 BOTTLES

Glass bottles with a "cork finish" remain by far the predominant type of packaging in home winemaking — and the focus of this section — as they are easily sourced and recycled, and can be resealed with a new closure. Screw cap-type bottles too can be recycled but there is no affordable equipment for amateurs to reseal bottles with new screw caps; used screw caps do not provide for a perfect seal and will compromise the wine's aging potential.

Glass bottles come in various shapes (Figure 18.1), sizes, thicknesses and colors.

(a)   (b)   (c)

Figure 18.1: Most common wine bottle shapes: a) Bordeaux, b) Burgundy, and c) Alsace or Hoch

Bottle shape is purely for form and does not impact wine quality or aging potential. But many winemakers still follow tradition and only use high-shouldered Bordeaux bottles for varietals such as Cabernet Sauvignon, Merlot and Sauvignon Blanc, sloping-shouldered Burgundy bottles for Pinot Noir and Chardonnay, and tall sloping-shouldered Alsace or Hoch-style bottles for Riesling and Gewürztraminer. The decision on a type of bottle may come down to how you intend to store bottles for aging: individually in a wine rack, stacked in a wooden case or crate, or perhaps just left in their cardboard boxes. Bordeaux-type bottles stack the best; Burgundy ones less so; and Hoch bottles make stacking a risky proposition.

Size does matter here; wine ages more gracefully and longer in bigger bottles as the ratio of headspace — and therefore the amount of air — to total wine volume is smaller than in smaller bottles. 750 mL is the standard size; 375 mL and 1.5 L are also common. The indentation at the bottom of some bottles, or what is called a "punt" (or push-up, and identified as

P/U on cardboard cases), has no function other than to make bottles look bigger.

But of bottle characteristics, thickness and color are most important as these can impact the evolution of the wine, namely, color, aromas and flavors, and aging potential, particularly under adverse conditions, such as exposure to sunlight or strong light, or high temperatures during storage.

Standard bottle colors and common industry names include: green (Antique Green, Champagne Green, Dead Leaf Green), amber/brown, blue (Royal, Arctic, Aquamarine), clear with a light shade of green (Half Green, Georgia Green), and clear (Flint).

Each color has some filtering power against the damaging effects of exposure to light, especially fluorescent lighting and UV rays from sunlight: the lower the filtering power, the lower the protection. The photo-oxidation reaction, known as light-strike reaction, which can occur in as little as several hours, imparts unpleasant corn chip or asparagus off-odors, what the French call *goût de lumière*, literally "taste of light."

Green and amber or brown-colored glass offer the greatest filtering power and, therefore, provide the best protection; these are the best choice for aging wine. Blue and Half Green/Georgia Green glass offer much less filtering power, and Flint glass provides practically no protection.

As for sourcing bottles, your best bet is to buy new, cased bottles if you are just getting started in making wine at home; you can then re-use those for future batches. You can simply rinse new bottles with fresh, clean water or do the whole wash–sanitize–rinse process, though not necessary, and then fill bottles. And of course you can use recycled bottles although you must wash, sanitize and rinse. If sourcing used bottles of commercial wine, you have the extra and time-consuming step of removing labels — that can be a pain.

18

One easy way to remove labels is to fill bottles with hot water and soak for an hour or so in hot water in a laundry sink. Labels will either come off on their own, more or less depending on the kind of adhesive, or they can be scraped off with a paring knife. Wineries use permanent adhesives on their white-wine bottles to avoid labels coming off when wine is chilled in an ice bucket — those can be a chore to remove. If you really insist on saving those bottles, try adding some percarbonate (see Section 4.4.1) to the hot-water soak. After scraping labels off, using a soft-bristle brush or steel wool to remove any remaining stubborn adhesive, then rinse bottles thoroughly with a sulfite–citric solution and water. The use of solvents is not recommended as these tend to leave a smell and also affect the integrity of the glass.

18.1.2 CLOSURES

Beyond providing a proper seal, bottle closures should not adversely affect the quality or the evolution of the wine. That means that closures should allow for a slow transfer of atmospheric oxygen, which helps wine age gracefully, and that the material is relatively inert such that it does not adversely react with wine and does not impart any off-aromas or flavors.

Natural-cork stoppers have been the traditional choice of closure for wine bottles. But the high occurrence of spoiled wine and increasing frustration with TCA-contaminated corks due to cork taint (see Section 22.11), premature oxidation, bottle variation due to the natural variability of cork, and leakage, have spawned alternative closures as well as new cork processes to guarantee the quality and performance of cork closures.

Home winemakers now have access to a greater choice of closures, and each available with different oxygen transfer rates (OTR) — an ever-increasingly important cork manufacturing criterion — to better match styles of wines and desired aging.

Here we look at stoppers produced from natural cork or cork fragments, and from synthetic materials. Screw caps are not recommended and therefore not described here as *used* screw caps do not provide for a perfect seal and can compromise the wine's aging potential. New screw caps must be applied with a screw capping machine, something still out of reach for home winemakers.

 Never reuse stoppers — of any kind — as they will not seal properly.

CORK STOPPERS

There are three general types of cork stoppers (Figure 18.2): natural cork, agglomerated and technical.

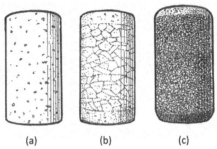

(a)   (b)   (c)

Figure 18.2: Cork stoppers: a) natural,
b) agglomerated, and c) technical

Natural-cork stoppers are manufactured and punched out as single pieces entirely from cork material extracted from the outermost layer of the bark of Cork Oak (*Quercus suber*). But quality varies greatly, and therefore, prices too range widely. The best stoppers have no holes or cracks bigger or larger than some specifications, for example, no holes larger than 2 mm ($^5/_{64}$ in), and few lenticels — the small imperfections or crevices in cork.

Colmated corks are natural-cork stoppers manufactured from lower-quality parts of the cork bark and which have had cork dust applied with an adhesive to fix defects and imperfections for improved performance and greater visual appeal.

Cork suppliers and vendors use different quality grading systems; for example, 1–10 or A–C, with 1 and A being the highest and most expensive, and which are rated for up to 20 years of aging, or perhaps something more cryptic, such as, in decreasing quality, USS, US+, US, UFS, UF, UFB, UFB1, UFBB and UFB4.

Extruded agglomerated stoppers are manufactured using coarsely ground granules derived from rejected cork or from manufacturing left-overs or other cork by-products, i.e., the material came from a source with a higher rate of defects. The granules are glued together with a binding agent, such as food-grade polyurethane or a plant-based compound, and then hot-press molded into their cylindrical shape. These are relatively

18

brittle and are rated for less than 2 years. They tend to break down when pulled from a bottle if allowed to age too long.

Molded agglomerated stoppers, also known as micro-agglomerate technical stoppers, are of much higher quality than their extruded counterpart as they are manufactured from very finely ground, TCA-free granules that provide a more uniform structure with a much denser and stronger body, and a more reliable and consistent seal for a longer rating, some up to 20 years. And they are cheaper compared to high-quality, natural-cork stoppers.

Technical stoppers are composites manufactured with an agglomerated body and then finished with a natural disc at each end. These are also known as twin-disc and 1+1 technical stoppers. The idea is that the end with a natural disc is the only material in contact with wine during bottle storage. Given their extruded agglomerated body, they are rated for up to two years only. But they are relatively cheap and ideal for early-drinking wine.

The standard stopper diameter for 750-mL bottles is 24 mm ($^{15}/_{16}$ inch) — these are known as a #9 corks in home winemaking and come in standard lengths of 38 mm (1½ in) and 44 mm (1¾ in); some may have chamfered rims at the top and bottom to ease insertion into bottles. Use a good floor corker (see Section 18.4) for driving #9 corks into bottles; if using a double-lever corker, use #8 stoppers — they have a slightly smaller diameter.

Use cork stoppers within 6 months of receiving. If stored longer in a previously opened package, stoppers will become dry and hard to insert, and may not provide a good seal. There is no need to soak, boil or sanitize stoppers if fresh out of an unopened bag. Soaking or boiling in water are in fact not recommended as it compromises the integrity of stoppers and removes the silicone coating that manufacturers apply to ease stopper insertion into bottles. If you need to sanitize stoppers, for whatever reason, refer to the procedure outlined in Section 18.5.

SYNTHETIC STOPPERS

Synthetic stoppers got a bad rap when first introduced in the 1980s and 90s as an alternative to natural-cork closures prone to TCA taint, as they had their own problems, including: difficulty in pulling out of bottles, aroma and flavor scalping, and high OTRs. But they have come a very long way. There has been significant progress in synthetic materials and production technologies, and manufacturers now provide a range of synthetic corks that alleviate problems of the past.

Modern high-performance synthetic stoppers are manufactured entirely from polymers, such as low-density polyethylene (LDPE), styrene-butadiene-styrene (SBS) and ethylvinyl alcohol (EVA), or from plant-based biopolymers such as sugar cane.

The material is injected into a cork-shaped mold or is continuously extruded through a cylindrical die to form the core of the stopper and then cut to desired length. Some stoppers have a foam core and a thermoplastic elastomer sleeve forming the outer skin. The sleeve too is manufactured by extrusion and applied over the foam core immediately following extrusion of the core, and then thermally bonded to the core. Co-extruded stoppers are manufactured with a wide range of OTRs to meet closure needs of the various styles of wines.

Beware, however, as not all synthetic stoppers work well with manual corkers. Some stoppers are very hard to compress and others seem to pick up grooves from the jaws of corkers. Seek advice from stopper manufacturers or your supplier when evaluating the purchase of new stoppers that you have never used previously.

Here too you should not have to sanitize stoppers if fresh out of an unopened bag. If you need to sanitize stoppers, place the stoppers in a pail and lightly spray with a sulfite–citric solution.

18

18.1.3 CAPSULES

Capsules are part of the finishing touch in packaging; they have a purely aesthetic function.

PVC heat-shrink capsules (Figure 18.3) are by far the most common type used in home winemaking due to their low cost and ease of application. They can be applied on standard 375, 750 and 1500-mL bottles and shrunk using heat, such as water vapor from boiling water, from a heat gun (Figure 18.4), either the kind for stripping furniture or the type specifically designed for winemaking, or a heat tunnel (Figure 18.4). It is best not to dip bottles in water to shrink capsules as excessive moisture can get trapped over the cork and possibly form mold. Look for capsules with a tear-off tab; these are easier to tear off and get to the cork without looking clumsy trying to cut off the capsule with a corkscrew. Just be careful not to apply excessive heat as it can compromise the function of the tear-off tab.

Figure 18.3: Capsules

You can also dress bottles with wax, but be sure to use a soft wax that can be easily removed; hard wax can be very difficult and messy to remove. You will need a device, such as a deep fryer, to melt chunks of wax. You can either dip a bottle upside down into the wax to get a capsule-like look, or you can apply a small amount to the closure area with a spatula or knife to give bottles a classier, more refined look.

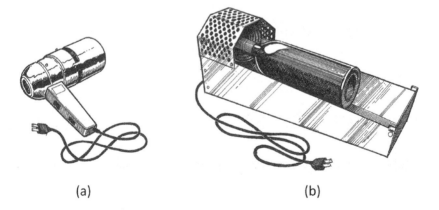

(a)   (b)

Figure 18.4: a) Heat gun and b) tunnel for shrinking PVC capsules

18.1.4 LABELS

Wine labels are a lot fun as they convey your artistic side and, most important, your pride of what's in the bottle and the effort you put into it. The whole labeling process, from designing to printing and applying labels, can be as simple as 1-2-3 using off-the-shelf solutions or it could become a laborious project if you create your own artwork and cut labels into fancy shapes. And there are many solutions in between to fit any budget, skills, and time you invest.

There are many online one-stop shops that have predesigned, preprinted labels, some removable and reusable, or which you can download and print. Some will have standard templates where you simply add your specific wine information. And others will accept your artwork and create and print custom labels for you. You can also design and create your very own using your favorite art or photo-editing software, or simply use the Label feature in MS Word (under the MAILINGS tab) to print on standard Avery labels of your choice.

Applying labels can be tedious if done freehand, assuming that you are not inclined to invest in an expensive labeling machine since you are a home winemaker and not labeling thousands of bottles at a time. But even if you make, for example, the US legal limit of 200 gal (758 L) per year for a household with at least two adults, that's still over 1,000 labels to stick on bottles. Getting them consistently lined up at the right level, if that matters, can be a daunting task. You can build or buy a simple jig (Figure 18.5) to help you align and apply labels (more) consistently.

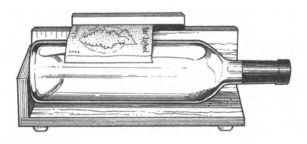

Figure 18.5: Label Wizard jig for applying labels

18

Here are some key points to keep in mind in designing, printing and applying labels.

Always design your label to fit the size and shape of the bottle, and this is particularly important if you use recycled bottles of different sizes and shapes; trying to apply a label on a curved surface will usually result in wrinkles. For best results, apply labels to clean, oil-free, room-temperature bottles. Cold surfaces or condensation on a cold container will prevent labels from adhering properly.

And keep printing in mind when designing labels, making sure fonts are big enough (computer screens are big, labels are small) and there is enough contrast to read them.

You will be reusing bottles for your next batches, and that means removing labels, and therefore, you'll want labels that can be easily peeled off or removed. There are self-adhesive, removable labels, e.g., Avery, or labels made from plain paper that you apply with a water-soluble glue or paste and which you can easily remove by running hot water over the label or by soaking bottles in a hot-water bath.

Print waterproof labels — that means, either print using a laser printer, or apply a spray varnish if printing using an inkjet printer. You don't want ink starting to run off labels in a humid cellar, and certainly not with gifted bottles.

Provide as much useful data as possible on labels as well as something interesting or important about you or the wine or both. Communicate the passion that made you make the wine (the label is the first interaction people have with the wine, it makes the first impression). Consider adding a back label to keep the front label visually appealing and easy to read. There are no restrictions or requirements as a home winemaker. But make your labels informative, particularly as you'll be gifting bottles. Include the following information:

- The varietal or, if a blend, the varieties or use a descriptor that is understood to represent a specific style, for example, Meritage or Bordeaux Red for Cabernet-based blends;

- Your name or your home winery's name or logo;

- Vintage, if it is a vintage wine, and which corresponds to the season in which the grapes were grown;

- % ABV, which can simply be an estimate based of your initial Potential Alcohol (PA) measurement or a calculation for a blend; and

- Residual sugar (RS), if known. Wine consumers (your friends) are becoming more aware of the amount of sugar in wines, either to understand their carb intake or the style of wine they're drinking.

18.2 BOTTLE WASHING AND SANITIZING EQUIPMENT

You will be washing and sanitizing countless bottles in your winemaking, particularly if you reuse bottles. If reusing bottles, simply wash and rinse them thoroughly with water when you have finished consuming the wine, let drip dry, and store away for your next bottling. If you want to skip this tedious part of the process, buy cased bottles that are ready to receive wine, otherwise, roll up your sleeves and get ready for some painstaking work.

As with any winemaking equipment, the key to avoiding spoilage in bottled wine is to thoroughly wash and sanitize bottles. You can simply rinse clean, previously used bottles with hot water, then treat with a sanitizing solution, and, if you have fresh, clean water, rinse one last time. Let bottles drip dry before filling.

For washing and sanitizing bottles, you need a bottle washer/rinser, a bottle rack or tree for letting bottles drip dry, and some device for sanitizing bottles.

BOTTLE WASHER/RINSER

For small productions, a single-bottle washer/rinser (Figure 18.6) works very well. It goes mounted directly on a faucet and uses tap-water pressure to wash and rinse. It has a built-in valve actuated by pressing a bottle against it to start and stop the flow of water. For higher throughput, use a 2-in-1 Bottle Washer or FastWasher (Figure 18.6) that can wash or rinse 12 bottles at a time.

18

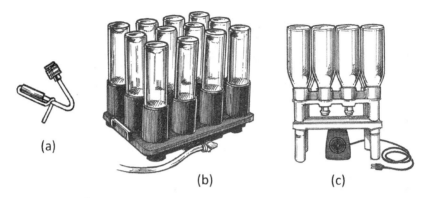

Figure 18.6: a) Single-bottle washer/rinser; b) 2-in-1 Bottle Washer; c) Fast-Washer

The 2-in-1 Bottle Washer sits in a deep sink, and connects to a faucet and delivers a strong jet of water to bottles held in a tray. Wash or rinse water drains out. A second tray comes in handy to load another case of bottles while the previous case is being washed or rinsed. You could also rig the 2-in-1 Bottle Washer with a pump to deliver a sanitizing solution.

The FastWasher sits in a deep sink with sufficient clean water to fully cover the submersible pump plugged into a GFCI outlet adapter for protection against electrocution. The submersible pump delivers a strong jet of water or sanitizing solution. With this washer, wash and rinse water is reused; it is not drained. You should however change the water for every rinse cycle to avoid re-contaminating bottles.

BOTTLE TREE

A bottle tree (Figure 18.7) is used to hold bottles upside down to drip dry when rinsing and sanitizing. It consists of several levels of bottle racks or modules that can be configured for any number of bottles; however, most vendors sell trees to hold, for example, 45 or 90 bottles. Although you can grow the tree by adding more racks, 90 is really the practical limit; more than this and the tree becomes very heavy when fully loaded. You might find it more efficient to have a second tree if you are cleaning, sanitizing and rinsing; you will be moving a lot of bottles between each operation.

A bottle sanitizer can be fitted at the top of the bottle tree. Some models also have a separate rotating base that makes easier access to bottles during the bottle cleaning and sanitizing process.

Figure 18.7: Bottle tree with bottle sanitizer

BOTTLE SANITIZER

The bottle sanitizer (Figure 18.7), or sanitizer injector, is used to squirt a sanitizing solution into a bottle — only one at a time. It consists of a bowl to hold the solution and a spring-loaded injector. A bottle is placed on the injector and pushed down to squirt a strong jet of sanitizing solution. It can be repeated several times as desired, then the bottle is transferred to a bottle tree to drip.

18

18.3 BOTTLE FILLERS

There are many types of bottle fillers to suit any budget and production volume. These operate either by gravity, or using a positive-pressure or vacuum pump.

BOTTLING WAND

The bottling wand (Figure 18.8) is the most basic of gravity-fed bottle fillers and works well for small batches. The filler has a springless or spring-activated "foot valve" to control the flow of wine into a bottle and goes connected to a hose and racking cane. One small awkward challenge with this filler is priming, i.e., getting the flow of wine going. You could suck on the bottom of the wand, pushing the valve open, to start the flow of wine. Then you insert the wand in the bottle and push the valve open against the bottom to start the flow, which can be a bit tricky with some models when

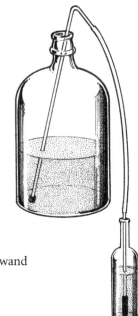

Figure 18.8: Bottling wand

filling punted bottles. Use a hand-pump type siphon starter or auto-siphon to start the flow while holding the valve open against the bottom of the bottle. As the bottle fills, pull the wand out when the wine reaches the top of the bottle. The wine drops back down to the proper fill level to allow insertion of a standard 38 or 44-mm (1½ or 1¾-in) closure.

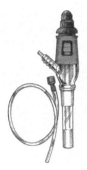

FERRARI AUTOMATIC BOTTLE FILLER

The Ferrari Automatic Bottle Filler (Figure 18.9) is a gravity-fed filler also ideal for small batches. Once primed by suction, the filler is inserted in the top of the bottle and the flow of wine is started at the push of a button. The flow stops automatically at a (adjustable) preset level. When a bottle is filled, the filler is moved to the next bottle.

Figure 18.9: Ferrari Automatic Bottle Filler

BUON VINO SUPER AUTOMATIC GRAVITY BOTTLE FILLER

The Buon Vino Super Automatic Bottle Filler (Figure 18.10) is a gravity-fed filler, very similar in operation to the Ferrari Automatic Bottle Filler, and comes with a racking tube and tip. The filler head mechanism includes a flow regulator, filler nozzle and overflow tube. The flow of wine is started by suction using the overflow tube. The nozzle has a diverter that pours wine down the glass of the bottle to minimize agitation. The flow stops automatically at a (adjustable) preset level and excess wine goes into an overflow bottle. When a bottle is filled, the filler is moved to the next bottle and flow is restarted by pushing down on the flow regulator.

BUON VINO ELECTRIC FILL JETS

The Buon Vino Tabletop and Floor Model Electric Fill Jets (Figure 18.11) use a similar filler-head mechanism as the gravity-fed Super Automatic Bottle Filler but are powered by a self-priming, positive-pressure pump for faster bottling. These are stationary fillers in that, when a bottle is filled, it is removed and an empty bottle is placed on the spring platform and under the filler nozzle. The operation is otherwise identical. Their advantage is that the carboy or other vessel can be at the same level as the filler.

18

Figure 18.10: Buon Vino Super Automatic Bottle Filler

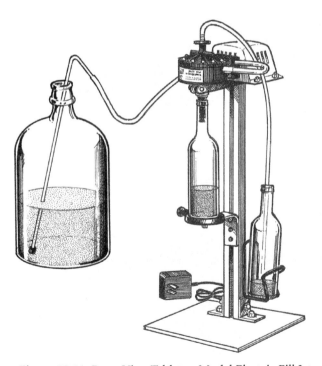

Figure 18.11: Buon Vino Tabletop Model Electric Fill Jet

ALL-IN-ONE WINE PUMP AND VACUUM BOTTLE FILLER

The All-in-One Wine Pump bottle filler (Figure 18.12) uses an electric vacuum pump to displace wine and fill bottles, one at a time, to a (adjustable) preset fill level using a stopper attachment that includes an adjustable vacuum valve to control the flow of wine and down the side of the glass to minimize foaming. Overflow wine is sucked back to the carboy or vessel, and so, it must sit below the level of bottles during the filling operation.

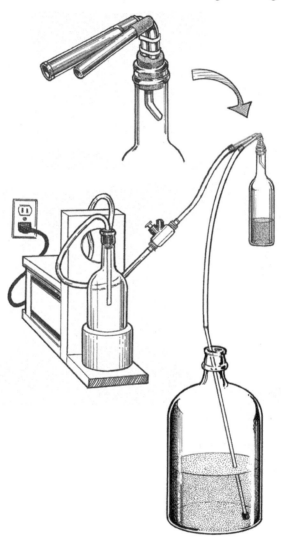

Figure 18.12: All-in-One Wine Pump bottler filler; note that the carboy is below the level of bottles

18

TENCO ENOLMATIC BOTTLE FILLER

The Tenco Enolmatic Bottler Filler (Figure 18.13) is a tabletop filler that uses an electric vacuum pump to displace wine and fill bottles, one at a time, to a (adjustable) preset fill level. This is a stationary model in that bottles are positioned under and moved out of the filler. It also includes an adjustable vacuum valve to control the flow of wine down the side of the glass to minimize foaming. Overflow wine is sucked into an integrated bowl, the same bowl used to create the vacuum and so, the carboy or vessel can be set at the same level as bottles during the filling operation.

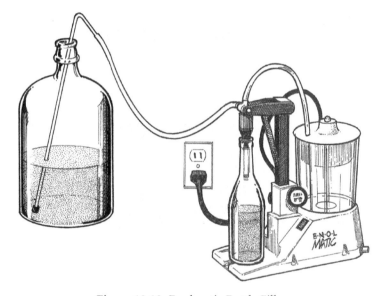

Figure 18.13: Enolmatic Bottle Filler

MULTI-SPOUT BOTTLE FILLERS

As you scale up your production to hundreds of liters or gallons of wine, you will want to speed up your bottling operation using a multi-spout filler (Figure 18.14), for example, a 3 or 5-spout filler.

Wine is moved by gravity into a large holding reservoir during the filling operation. The reservoir is equipped with a float ball to adjust and maintain the fill height and to control the flow of wine. Some models have clasps

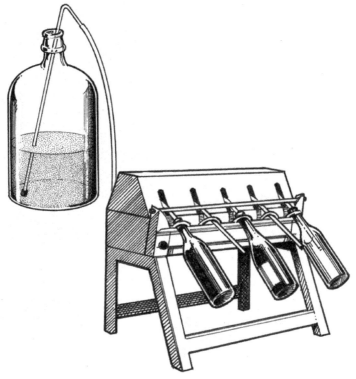

Figure 18.14: Multi-spout Filler

to hold bottles once inserted over the spouts during the filling operation while other models have a bottle tray that makes it more convenient to insert and retrieve bottles than clips. Filler heads are primed using a handheld siphon starter.

18.4 CORKERS

There are two general kinds of corkers for inserting closures into standard 750-mL bottles as well as demis (375 mL) and magnums (1.5 L): double-lever corker and tabletop or floor corkers (Figure 18.15).

The double-lever corker works well for small batches and with #8 stoppers. You'll need a lot of muscle power with #9 stoppers; these can be very hard to drive in all the while keeping the bottle steady and pushing

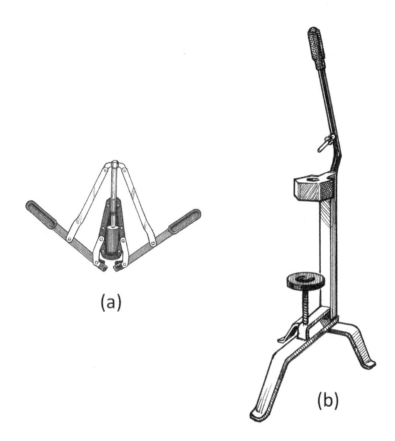

Figure 18.15: a) Manual corker; b) Floor corker

down on the corker. Micro-agglomerates are much too hard for this type of corker, and synthetic stoppers can get damaged during insertion and compromise the closure. You'll soon want to upgrade to a tabletop or floor corker for anything more than a standard 23-L (6-gal) batch.

Tabletop or floor corkers are very efficient. The corker head has a set of crimping jaws that squeeze the closure, which is inserted into a bottle when the lever is pulled down. The bottle stand locks into position during corking to ensure a flawless insertion. The most popular models are the tabletop model with plastic jaws, and the more robust Italian (Ferrari in blue, others red) and Portuguese (smaller, red) corkers, which have brass or stainless steel jaws.

18.5 THE BOTTLING PROCESS

Bottling requires some careful planning; most important, is the wine ready for bottling? Do not be tempted to bottle wine immediately after you performed significant processing, such as fining or even tweaking mouthfeel with tannins. It often leads to disappointment — sediment appears in bottles just days after bottling, mouthfeel just isn't right, or tartrates are still forming.

Try and complete all processing as far in advance of bottling as possible to ensure the wine is stable and bottle-ready, and that you are absolutely confident it will not undergo any changes in bottles beyond normal evolution. If possible, transfer all batches into a single tank or vessel to ensure a homogeneous product. And if blending different varietals, only blend component wines that have undergone the same exact treatments, as blending stable but different component wines does not guarantee a stable blend.

Depending on the volume of wine you intend to bottle and if you will apply capsules and labels that same day, get some extra pairs of hands for the various tasks. You will need one person filling bottles, one person corking, one applying capsules, and one person applying labels and placing bottles in cases, this all after you have washed and sanitized bottles. The most critical aspects from a wine quality perspective are to minimize the amount of time from filling to corking bottles, and protecting the wine from excessive exposure to air.

Get all your bottles ready making sure you have calculated the right amount; get some extra ones in case your volume calculations are not exact. If you are using natural-cork closures, buy a fresh bag. You can use natural-cork closures right out of the bag — there is no need to soak or sanitize corks. If the bag had been previously opened and you need to sanitize the corks, you can build a simple "sulfite humidor." You need to do this several days in advance of bottling.

Pour a small amount of 1% sulfite–citric solution (see Section 4.5.1) in a 23-L (6-gal) pail. Place the required number of corks in a sanitized light-weight bowl, seat it on the surface of the solution, and close the pail tight

18

with its lid. Let stand for several days in an area at room temperature to allow humidity in the pail to rise and to allow sulfur dioxide (SO_2) gas to sanitize the corks without soaking.

On the day of bottling, wash, sanitize and, optionally, rinse all bottles, and let drip dry.

A typical wash–sanitize–rinse process would consist of washing bottles with a good cleaning agent (see Section 4.4), immediately sanitizing with a 1% sulfite–citric solution or other sanitizing agent (see Section 4.5), placing bottles on a bottle tree to let the sanitizing solution do its work for a few minutes, and then doing one final water rinse and letting bottles drip dry on the bottle tree. If you have good, clean municipal water, the last water rinse is strongly recommended; its removes any trace of substances that, although not harmful, are not really compatible with wine — the sulfite–citric solution is perfectly compatible. A water rinse is also recommended because it minimizes the possibility of bottle variation due to slightly different amounts of sulfite–citric in bottles.

Next, wash and sanitize your bottling equipment using a similar wash–sanitize–rinse process. Scrupulously sanitize anything — hoses, racking cane, bottle filler, and filter system if you are filtering in-line with your bottling — and everything that will come into contact with wine. The procedure for sanitizing a filter system is described in Section 17.4.

As you sanitize equipment, use this opportunity to test your bottling procedure and equipment with the water and sanitizing solution to get a hang of the process — you should do it no matter how many times you have bottled before. Check fill levels and the flow rate of liquid into bottles. You will want to avoid turbulence to minimize oxygen uptake during bottle-filling; this is not an issue with vacuum-type fillers.

 As there is always some small amount of residual carbon dioxide (CO_2) in wine, expect some foaming. This should not be a problem and the foaming should quickly subside as bottles fill up — you can immediately insert the closure. But if your wine still has a tad too much CO_2, you can expect significant foaming and which may impact the filling process. Bottles may foam so much that you won't be able to fill them to the desired level; you will have to wait for the foaming to subside, then fill the bottles

again. This can be frustrating and make you waste precious time, and expose the wine to the elements. Therefore be sure to bottle only properly degassed wine. Refer to Section 13.3 for instructions on degassing wine.

And don't forget to also sanitize the corker jaws. Simply spray a 70% ethanol solution (*not denatured ethanol*), work the lever up and down a few times to let the ethanol cover as much of the jaw mechanism as possible, then wipe the ethanol with a clean paper towel. Repeat this procedure a couple of times.

Fill bottles to allow between ¼ inch and ½ inch of headspace, i.e., the space between the wine and the bottom of the cork in the bottle (Figure 18.16). This small headspace, or ullage, is to allow for wine expansion and contraction when temperature fluctuates. A headspace much greater than ½ inch in a standard 750-mL bottle will store a bit too much oxygen that can impact microbial protection or wine evolution.

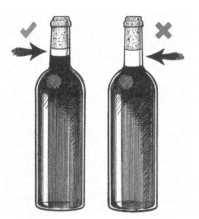

Figure 18.16: Correct and incorrect headspace

18

Once done, if using natural-cork closures, store bottles upright for a few days to allow the cork material to re-expand completely to its original shape and provide a good seal.

Should you store bottles horizontally (or upside down) to keep corks moist, as per conventional wisdom, to minimize wine loss and prevent corks from drying out?

Recent studies have shown that storing bottles *upright* has advantages [2]. Corks were shown to still absorb wine from the saturated headspace, and therefore do not dry out. There was also much less wine loss, and wine was "cleaner," tasting more pure.

Bottles with agglomerate-type and synthetic closures need not be stored horizontally either, but do allow about 30 minutes for closures to properly set up against the bore of the bottles if you still intend horizontal storage.

And here's a heads-up as you uncork a bottle of that great wine you just bottled only days or maybe a couple of weeks ago.

The wine may not smell or taste what it was the day you bottled it — at least not as you remember it. The wine suddenly has muted flavors and seemingly devoid of fruity aromas. This temporary condition is known as "bottle sickness" and is believed to be the result of rapid oxidation during the bottling process, which causes a small amount of acetaldehyde to form. Once the bottle is corked, the condition slowly disappears over the course of the next month or so as acetaldehyde reacts with SO_2 (another reason why the use of SO_2 is a good thing) and phenols, and the fruity aromas come out again.

REFERENCES

1. Capone, D., M. Sefton, I. Pretorius and P. Høj. 2004. *Flavor 'scalping' by wine bottle closures — 'Winemaking' continues after bottling.* Practical Winery & Vineyard Journal, July/August 2004. 262:44-55.

2. Hülsemann, C. *Counselor: … from Geisenheim.* http://www.griff korken.com/deutsch/products_services/ratgeber/geisenheim/ ratgeber_aus_geisenheim.html. Last accessed March 21, 2021.

19 Making Fruity and Full-Bodied White Wines

This chapter describes the protocols for making two styles of white wines from grapes — purchased or from your backyard vineyard — or from fresh, unprocessed juice.

You may want to first refresh your memory on the white winemaking process; refer back to the process flowchart presented in Figure 1.2 in Section 1.3.2.

The general process for making white wine involves crushing and pressing grapes, cold settling the juice, carrying out alcoholic fermentation (AF), clarifying and stabilizing the wine followed by a short aging period, then filtering and bottling. There is usually no maceration, or perhaps just a very short maceration, of grape skins in juice.

There is, however, orange wine, which is made by macerating and fermenting on the skins, much like is done in red winemaking. Orange wine is a deep, orange-hued, bold, somewhat sour and tannic style of white wine with intense aromas of honey, bruised apples and nuts, all resulting from limited oxidation.

As there are many different variations of making white wine, some involving fermenting or aging in oak barrels, two of the more common protocols are presented here — one for making a dry, light, fruity style and one for making a dry, full-bodied, oaked style. As you gain experience with varieties you work with and depending on your preferred style, you will come to develop your own variations.

Review and understand the protocols *before you start* making wine to be sure you are equipped and prepared to execute all the necessary steps. And, although not essential, if you are able to implement techniques and use equipment that minimize wine exposure to air during processing,

19

particularly during racking operations, you will make even greater wine. For ideas on techniques and equipment, consult the protocol for making rosé wine in Chapter 20 — oxygen exclusion is more critical in rosé winemaking.

And a reminder to keep a meticulous log of all processing activities, additives and processing aids used, measurements taken, as well as progress tasting notes (see Section 1.4). You can use the log sheet in Appendix C, which can be downloaded at ModernHomeWinemaking.com.

19.1 MAKING A DRY, LIGHT, FRUITY-STYLE WHITE WINE

Light, fruity whites are fermented relatively cool and slow to preserve delicate fruity esters while light whites meant to feature more of the varietal characteristics are fermented warmer and faster. Both styles of wines are seldom put through malolactic fermentation (MLF) so as to preserve the fruity character as well as freshness from their higher acidity that characterizes these styles. These wines are bottled within 6–9 months and are meant to be consumed relatively quickly, within another 6–9 months.

Figure 19.1 illustrates a typical timeline for making a dry, fruity-style white wine from grapes, with no MLF, and bottled 6–9 months from the start of the process.

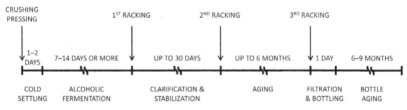

Figure 19.1: Typical timeline for making a dry, fruity-style white wine from grapes, with no MLF, and bottled in 6–9 months

Generally, you will want a wine with 11–12.5% ABV, which means you need a starting SG in the range 1.080–1.090 (19–22 Brix), and TA in the range 5–8 g/L for a dry style with residual sugar (RS) less than 5 g/L.

"Dry style" does not equate to microbially stable. Only dry wines with less than 2 g/L RS are considered microbially stable; those with 2–5 g/L RS (or more) would still require to be properly stabilized, as outlined in Section 14.1.1.

Almost all white grape varieties can be used to make fruity-style wines. Chenin Blanc, Gewürztraminer, Muscat varieties, Riesling, and of course, Sauvignon Blanc, are all excellent choices where thiol expression is desired. As thiols are very sensitive to oxygen, every precaution should be taken to avoid excessive exposure to air during processing to prevent varietal character loss. Consult Chapter 2 for other processing considerations and tips for your variety.

The log chart in the CONTROL CHECKPOINTS section at the end of this chapter provides a view of which measurements you should be taking at the various steps in the protocol described below. In my own winemaking, I measure dissolved oxygen (DO) at every checkpoint when adjusting free SO$_2$ (FSO2); it also flags any potential oxygen ingress issues.

19.1.1 CRUSHING AND PRESSING

If you are making wine from fresh juice that has not been cold settled, proceed to Section 19.1.2. If you are making wine from fresh juice that has already been cold settled and is ready to be fermented, proceed to Section 19.1.3.

Clean, sanitize and thoroughly rinse all equipment, tools and fermentors.

Ideally work with cold grapes, or set up in an area where you can drop the temperature to as cold as possible or, alternatively, use your glycol chiller or place carboys and small vessels in a refrigerator. Work as fast as possible to get press-run juice into vessels and protected from air.

Once you have harvested or received your grapes, first remove any MOG (material other than grapes) and meticulously remove any and all moldy grapes or raisined berries that may otherwise reduce the availability of nitrogen and cause a sluggish fermentation or premature oxidation. There is no need to wash grapes; it is actually not recommended as leftover water will dilute the juice.

19

In the next step, we will assume that the entire mass of grape solids can be loaded into your press. You may need to do multiple press runs if you cannot load all the mass into the press at once.

Crush–destem grapes into a vat, or into pails and then transfer to a vat if your crusher–destemmer is equipped with a chute.

Add gallotannins to avoid uncontrolled skin extraction and juice oxidation using one of the many commercial preparations. Suprarom (Laffort) is a preparation of gallotannins, ascorbic acid and potassium metabisulfite (KMS); add at a rate of 10–25 g per 100 L (25 gal) of *volume of crushed grapes*. Scott'Tan FT Blanc Soft (Scott Laboratories) contains gallotannins; add at a rate of 5–15 g per 100 L (25 gal) of *volume of crushed grapes*. I suggest using the lowest dosage if the harvest is healthy, and then doing another complementary addition after pressing.

Add 35 mg of potassium metabisulfite (KMS) per kg (15 mg per lb) of crushed grapes. You can determine the approximate weight from your harvest data or from the number of 18-lb (8.2 kg) lugs or 36-lb (16.3 kg) cases you crushed. Alternatively, you can add 50 mg/L KMS (which gives approximately 30 mg/L FSO2) if you can estimate the total crush volume. Mix thoroughly with your punchdown tool.

Immediately transfer to the press, press and collect the juice in a pail and transfer to a vessel as quickly as possible to minimize exposure to the elements. If possible, use a single vessel, such as a variable-capacity tank (VCT); this will greatly facilitate managing additions of processing aids and additives. Otherwise, transfer to as many carboys, demijohns or other suitable vessels that you need. Fill vessels as much as possible to minimize headspace.

You may find that certain grape varieties, particularly slipskin varieties, such as Niagara and Muscat, don't drain their juice well out of the press. To improve internal drainage during pressing, add some stems back to the crushed grapes as you load the press or, better yet, to eliminate the possibility of extracting harsh stem tannins, add rice hulls at a rate of 1:100, i.e., 1 kg per 100 kg or 1 lb per 100 lbs of crushed grapes. Sprinkle rice hulls over the crushed grapes during the transfer to the press. Alternatively, open the press after the first pressing cycle, break up and stir the pomace, then start another press cycle.

To get "cleaner" juice or to minimize juice exposure to air when working with more delicate varieties, you can press whole clusters if you have a good press, that is, without crushing or destemming grapes, although this tends to reduce juice yield. But stems do facilitate pressing as they act as a pressing aid, which allows for better juice flow through the grape mass and out of the press. Just be careful not to over-press as you can start extracting harsh stem tannins.

As you load the press, add pressing enzymes, specifically pectinases, at the rate recommended for your product to break down grape-skin pectin to increase pressing efficiency and improve juice yield. Specially formulated pectinases with glycosidasic side activities, such as Lafazym Press (Laffort), can also help extract more aroma precursors.

Press the pomace and transfer juice into the VCT or vessels as quickly as possible and with as little agitation as possible. Press as much as you want to within the maximum pressure your press can handle or until there is no more juice flowing, keeping in mind that the more pressure you exert to extract more juice, the more tannins you will extract.

Add pectinases, such as Lafazym CL (Laffort), to hasten juice settling and clarification. Add up to the maximum dosage in the recommended range based on the lowest temperature you expect to settle the juice in the next step; enzyme activity slows down considerably below 10 °C (50 °F).

For extra protection against oxidation, optionally add gallotannins, such as Tanin Galalcool SP (Laffort), and/or glutathione, such as OptiMUM White or Glutastar (Lallemand), or specific inactivated yeast, such as Pure-Lees Longevity (Lallemand).

Purge any headspace with inert gas, if possible, in all vessels and seal with solid stoppers.

Unload the press and discard the pomace to the compost.

19

WILL YOU BE MACERATING?

There is typically no maceration of crushed grape solids and juice in white winemaking, but you can macerate for a short duration at *cold temperature* (8 °C/46 °F or lower) and with macerating enzymes with glycosidase side activity, such as Lallzyme Cuvée Blanc (Lallemand), *before* pressing to extract more aromas and flavors from skins. Macerate an hour to several hours depending on grape variety, desired level of extraction and the style of wine, and your ability to keep the must cold to avoid a spontaneous fermentation.

A longer maceration in the order of days, weeks or even months, is possible for making orange wine with certain grape varieties (see Sections 2.1.1 and 2.2.1) that are less prone to oxidation.

When you have completed crushing, add macerating enzymes and mix thoroughly with a punchdown tool. Place a heavy tarp or lid on your vat or fermentor to protect the must from the elements and to keep fruit flies out. Now wait 2–4 hours before adding KMS in the next step.

After the wait period, add 35 mg of KMS per kg (15 mg per lb) of crushed grapes and mix thoroughly with a punchdown tool.

For extra protection against oxidation, optionally add gallotannins, glutathione or ascorbic acid at this stage, as opposed to after pressing.

For dropping temperature, use your glycol chiller, refrigerate the must if working with small volumes, or use plastic jugs of frozen water or dry ice at a rate of 2 g per kg of grapes (1 g per 1 lb). If using frozen jugs, have more jugs in the freezer ready to go as you will need to rotate jugs in and out of the juice every 6–12 hours. And be sure to sanitize the jugs before every use and rotation. If using dry ice, replenish as needed to maintain cold temperature, likely every 4–6 hours.

 Wear proper safety gear when handling dry ice. At −78 °C (−108 °F), dry ice is cold to the touch and can cause severe freeze burns if it comes in contact with skin.

Place a heavy tarp or lid on your vat or fermentor to protect the must from the elements and to keep fruit flies out. As there is no active fermentation generating carbon dioxide (CO_2), the surface of the must is not well protected against the elements, fruit flies and spoilage microorganisms. If possible, and especially if you intend to macerate for more than 6 hours, protect the must with inert gas, preferably CO_2 since it is heavier than air. If your fermentor has a lid or if you can tie down a tarp with rubber straps on your vat, try injecting CO_2 gas from a cylinder to displace air out and to form a protective layer over the surface of the must. Make sure to keep doing punchdowns during the cold-soak period and to flush out air again with CO_2.

After the desired maceration period, proceed with pressing.

19.1.2 COLD SETTLING

 If you are making wine from fresh juice that has already been cold settled and is ready to be fermented, proceed to Section 19.1.3.

Use your glycol chiller, or transfer vessels to a fridge, if possible, or to the coldest area, ideally below 8 °C (46 °F), and hold cold for 24–48 hours to allow the juice to settle. If you cannot maintain a cold temperature, let settle for no more than 24 hours, or you'll risk a spontaneous fermentation.

After the cold settling period, transfer all vessels to a warmer area or warm up all vessels according to the kind of fermentation you are planning, i.e., cold versus warm.

19.1.3 MUST ANALYSIS AND ADJUSTMENTS

While you wait for the juice to warm up, take a sample to the lab for analysis. If you have all the juice in a single vessel, take a 250-mL sample. If you have multiple vessels, take proportional amounts from each to get a homogeneous sample, assuming that the wine will eventually all be blended. If you intend to return samples to their vessels, which is never recommended but frugal winemakers still do, be doubly sure to sanitize all equipment that will come into contact with the juice — you don't want to pick up any spoilage microorganisms lurking in your hydrometer cylinder and infect batches.

Record the volume of juice in each batch, if in separate vessels. Measure and record temperature, SG/Brix, TA and pH of the sample, and determine

19

the PA, and making sure to make any adjustments to compensate for the measured temperature if different from the hydrometer's calibration temperature. Measure yeast assimmilable nitrogen (YAN), if so equipped.

Determine your target SG/Brix, TA, pH and YAN, and if you need to adjust any of these parameters, plan the adjustments so that you will be ready to implement them the next day after the cold settling period.

Once the settling period completed, carefully rack the juice off the sediment into your vessels of choice making sure to minimize oxygen uptake by placing the racking hose at the bottom of the receiving vessel. If you need to make adjustments, it's best to rack all the juice into a single vessel to have it all homogenous and make single adjustments. Then make the adjustments. We're not quite ready to make YAN adjustments just yet.

The juice is referred to as must from here on; it's what gets fermented.

If working with a thiolic grape variety and you want to get more of the thiol aromas, add specific pectinases with glycosidase activities, such as Lafazym Thiols[+] (Laffort), designed to bring out grapefruit, passion fruit and box tree aromas. Be sure to choose a complementary yeast known to enhance thiol-type varietal aromas, such as Alchemy I (Lallemand), Zymaflore VL3 (Laffort) or EnartisFerm Q9 (Esseco).

If you cannot ferment in a single vessel, like a VCT, where you need headspace, transfer to as many vessels as you need, but *only fill to 75% capacity*, maybe a little more if fermenting cool, to allow for foaming during fermentation. CO_2 produced during fermentation will displace any air in the headspace out of vessels.

Place the floating lid several inches above the must in the VCT to allow for foaming and insert a stopper with airlock, or similarly if using different vessels.

19.1.4 ALCOHOLIC FERMENTATION

 Conduct the AF in an area with good ventilation when fermenting large volumes as there will be considerable amounts of CO_2 gas produced that can pose an asphyxiation hazard.

By now, you know what style of white wine you want to create and you had chosen an appropriate yeast that best matches your variety and fermentation conditions.

Set the temperature of your fermentation area or glycol chiller to match the desired style, making sure it is within the temperature range of your yeast of choice. For a fruitier style, such as a fruit-forward Sauvignon Blanc or Vidal Blanc, ferment cool, around 13 °C (55 °F), to increase ester production. For a style that exhibits more varietal character, such as a New Zealand-style Sauvignon Blanc that expresses box tree and passion fruit aromas, ferment warmer, around 20 °C (68 °F) to increase thiol production.

You are now all set to prepare the yeast inoculum and to inoculate batches.

Prepare the inoculum using the required amount of yeast and add to a suspension of rehydration nutrients, as per instructions in Section 11.4.

Add the inoculum to the vessel or proportionally to however many vessels you have. Stir the must well. Seal all vessels with stoppers and airlocks.

Based on your target YAN, calculate the total amount of complex nutrients needed, as per Section 11.2, and 6–12 hours *after* yeast inoculation, add *half the calculated total amount* of complex nutrients. Stir well and reseal all vessels.

Within 24–36 hours of inoculation, you should see signs of fermentation with bubbles rising towards the surface of the must. From here on until the end of AF, monitor fermentation progress by measuring, recording and charting temperature and temperature-adjusted SG/Brix, once a day and at the same time every day, to make sure all is proceeding according to plan. Smell and taste the wine to make sure there are no off-aromas or flavors.

A simple way to monitor fermentation temperature is to insert a floating thermometer into the must — just leave it in for the duration of fermentation — or use a handheld thermometer equipped with a long probe. Be sure to sanitize any tool or device going into the wine and to minimize air exposure.

19

In about 24 hours, you will be adding bentonite to get a jump-start on protein stabilization, and therefore, you need to rehydrate the bentonite clay now to give it time to swell up. Rehydrate 0.5 g/L of bentonite in ten times its weight of *hot* water, as per instructions outlined in Section 13.4.1.1.

24 hours after the start of fermentation, add the *previously rehydrated* bentonite suspension, and stir gently but thoroughly.

This next step is very important.

When SG (Brix) has dropped by one-third — that's usually 30–35 SG points (7–8 Brix) — add the second half of complex nutrients you had calculated above. Stir well to also introduce some oxygen to help the ferment move along. You do not need to otherwise stir during an active fermentation, i.e., during the stationary phase.

As fermentation nears SG 1.010 (2.5 Brix), give the wine a good stir to get the lees back into suspension and to help yeast carry fermentation to dryness.

Ferment to complete dryness, that is, when SG is below 0.995 (Brix is below −1.5) with a steady reading for at least two consecutive days. This can take a week if fermenting at warmer temperatures, or several weeks at cooler temperatures. Make sure to fully degas samples when measuring the final SG/Brix; use a precision, low-range hydrometer for more accurate results.

By the end of fermentation, there will be a fairly thick layer of lees at the bottom of vessels. You're ready for your first post-AF racking.

19.1.5 FIRST (POST-AF) RACKING

Rack the wine off the sediment in all vessels; this is your first post-AF racking.

Minimize the amount of lees you pick up during racking, which will otherwise offset your efforts in clarifying the wine. Lees also contain still-viable yeast cells that may kick back into action if your wine has sufficient residual sugar, if you have not fermented dry, or after you sweeten.

You will likely lose an appreciable amount of wine with the lees from this first racking. If you want to salvage some of the wine, transfer the sludge into the smallest glass vessel possible, purge the headspace with inert gas, if possible, and transfer to a refrigerator. Hold 24–48 hours and then carefully rack (it's easier with a small pump) the wine layer to another vessel leaving the sediment behind. Let the wine warm up to cellar temperature, smell and taste, and if there are no flaws, such as hydrogen sulfide (H_2S), add this wine to the rest of the batch. If the wine has any detectable flaws, discard it.

Take a sample, and measure and record temperature (of the wine, not the sample), TA and pH. TA helps you understand how acidity has changed during fermentation while pH will indicate microbial stability of the wine and how much SO_2 you need to add in the next step.

And definitely smell and taste the wine to see how you like it and to make sure it has not developed any undesirable smells or flavors.

At this stage, you should not be making (or have to make) significant acidity changes. If the wine is not quite to your liking, perhaps it lacks a bit of acidity, you can make a small addition not exceeding 0.5 g/L using tartaric acid or malic acid. Always conduct bench trials before treating an entire batch.

If acidity is too high, it is best not to deacidify at this stage as it can be very difficult to achieve the desired results. You may have more success dropping TA through chilling. You can always balance acidity with a little sugar when making a fruity style of wine, or if you prefer an off-dry or slightly sweet wine, you can sweeten by adding table sugar or wine conditioner, but don't add anything just yet, not until you have stabilized the wine.

19.1.6 DEGASSING

Wine will contain a lot of CO_2 left over from fermentation. Normal wine processing will naturally dissipate CO_2 to an imperceptible level by the time you come to bottle. But if you need to accelerate the process and you need to degas, follow the instructions outlined in Section 13.3. Be sure to degas *before* adding any fining agent for clarification, or the wine will not clear properly.

19.1.7 MICROBIAL STABILIZATION

Three (3) days after completion of the AF, you are ready to stabilize with SO_2.

Re-measure temperature and pH, and using a molecular SO_2 (MSO2) of 0.8 mg/L, as recommended for a fruity-style wine, determine the required free SO_2 (FSO2) level using the SO2 CALCULATOR or Figure 8.4 in Section 8.2, add the required amount of KMS, stir thoroughly, and place the stoppers and airlocks on again.

If you cannot measure pH, simply add ¼ teaspoon (about 1.5 g) KMS per 23-L (6-gal) carboy or ¾ teaspoon (about 4 g) KMS per 54-L (14-gal) demijohn.

At this point, it is also a good idea to measure % ABV and residual sugar (RS), if so equipped.

19.1.8 CLARIFICATION AND STABILIZATION

At this point, the wine needs to be clarified to a crystal-clear appearance, and stabilized against proteins and tartrates.

You can clarify either naturally by sedimentation or using fining agents, although natural clarification will take longer and may not yield a perfectly crystal-clear wine; you still have the option of filtering before bottling.

You can also forego stabilization if you expect to bottle the wine soon and consume it relatively quickly, and you don't want to be concerned with protein and tartrate stability. But here we are obsessed with only making consistently great wine — remember? You have to eliminate any and all risks of potential problems during aging, whether in bulk or in bottles.

You also have the option of aging wine before and/or after clarification and stabilization. Here, for our fruity style of wine, we will perform clarification and stabilization, then age the wine in bulk before bottling.

You can also combine clarification and stabilization steps and rack once at the completion of both; however, you must respect two important rules: 1) always cold stabilize during or after protein stabilization, *never before*, and 2) never make changes to wine chemistry after cold or tartrate stabilization, such as adding tartaric acid or deacidifying with a potassium salt, which would otherwise require that you tartrate stabilize again.

For clarification and protein stabilization, you can use a combination of kieselsol and gelatin or chitosan, or just bentonite. If you are able to perform a protein stability test and bentonite bench trials (see Section 14.3), determine the extent of protein instability and how much bentonite you need. With most vinifera varieties, you should not need more than — and you should not exceed — a total of 1 g/L of bentonite, and since you had already added 0.5 g/L during fermentation, you should not need more than another 0.5 g/L. Protein-rich Native American and hybrid varieties may require more than 1 g/L. Allow 2–3 weeks for the wine to clarify.

You can concurrently chill the wine for tartrate stabilization to hasten clarification; in this manner, you will only need to rack once, when both protein and tartrate stabilization have completed. Alternatively, instead of chilling the wine for tartrate stabilization, you can use a protective colloid (see Section 14.4).

At the end of stabilization, your wine will be stable against proteins and tartrates, and against any renewed AF if it was fermented completely dry; there was no MLF, and therefore, there are no concerns with residual malic acid here.

Rack the wine from its lees, and re-measure temperature, TA and pH, then measure FSO2, TSO2 and DO, and adjust FSO2 based on pH, MSO2 and DO.

TA and pH help you understand how acidity and microbial stability have changed during cold stabilization.

If your fermentation did not run completely dry to SG below 0.995 (Brix below −1.5) and you measure (or suspect) more than 2 g/L RS either using

19

an RS kit or your hydrometer, or if you have any concerns about possible refermentation due to residual sugar, play it safe and add sorbate (see Section 14.1.1) or sterile filter (see Section 17.3).

You can also fine-tune your wine here to balance acidity by adding sugar or a wine conditioner, or you can do it later after bulk aging.

If you want to sweeten by adding sugar, run bench trials to determine the amount of sugar to add to please your palate, then add sorbate. If you use a wine conditioner, it (should) already contains sorbate. Refer to Section 16.1 on sweetening to balance acidity and sweetness.

19.1.9 AGING

You can bulk age the wine some more or you can proceed to filtering and bottling. Fruity wines meant to be drunk young will still benefit from a short aging. Guidelines and techniques for aging wine are described in Chapter 15.

If aging for long periods of time, be sure to measure temperature, pH, FSO2 and DO, and adjust FSO2, as required, every 3 months.

Taste and assess the wine periodically to ensure that it is still to your liking, especially the balance between dryness/sweetness and acidity.

19.1.10 FILTERING

At this point, your wine should be very clear, but likely not quite crystal clear. If you want to filter the wine to give it that extra sparkle, first rack all similar batches ideally into a single holding tank or vessel for homogeneity, then filter. If you try and filter without racking, you can accidentally suck sediment and cause premature clogging of the filter medium. Similarly, never try to filter a cloudy wine.

If the wine is very clear, you can proceed directly to a polishing filtration using a 1-micron or 2-micron cartridge or polishing-grade pads, for example, Buon Vino No. 2 pads, followed by a fine filtration using a 0.45-micron (nominal) cartridge or equivalent, for example, Buon Vino No. 3 pads.

It's wise to again measure temperature, pH, FSO2 and DO, and adjust FSO2, as required, to make sure everything is in order and especially if you don't intend to bottle immediately after filtering.

19.1.11 BOTTLING

As a pre-bottling precaution, it's a good idea to re-measure RS to confirm your measurement taken at the end of fermentation, just to make sure that the wine is microbially stable and a sorbate treatment is not required. RS should not have changed, unless you added sugar for an off-dry or sweeter style of wine.

When ready to bottle, you know the drill — measure temperature, pH, FSO2, TSO2 and DO one last time, and adjust FSO2 based on pH, desired MSO2 and DO. You may want to bump up the FSO2 addition by 5–10 mg/L to account for oxygen uptake during bottling and bottle aging.

If you are set up to sterile filter and deliver wine directly into bottles under vacuum, filter with a 0.45-micron (*absolute*) cartridge and bottle immediately.

You can start drinking the wine now but it will benefit from a short aging between 6–9 months.

LOG CHART — CONTROL CHECKPOINTS: FRUITY WHITE WINE

19

Highlighted boxes represent those measurements you should be making and recording at the various checkpoints as described in the protocol outlined in Section 19.1.

Create a *separate log sheet for each batch* if the wine spans more than one vessel.

LOG CHART — CONTROL CHECKPOINTS: FRUITY WHITE WINE

Date	CHECKPOINT	Volume (L or gal)	Temp. (°C/°F)	SG / BRIX	Temp-adjusted SG / BRIX	PA or Actual % ABV	TA (g/L)	pH	FSO2 (mg/L)	TSO2 (mg/L)	DO (mg/L)	YAN (mg N/L)	RS (g/L)
	MUST ANALYSIS												
	ALCOHOLIC FERMENTATION												
	FIRST (POST-AF) RACKING												
	MICROBIAL STABILIZATION												
	CLARIFICATION AND STABILIZATION												
	AGING												
	FILTERING												
	BOTTLING												

19.2 MAKING A DRY, FULL-BODIED, OAKED WHITE WINE

Full-bodied whites, particularly those barrel-fermented or barrel-aged, will have greater complexity defined by more subtle aromas and flavors of toasted oak, and lighter acidity as they are usually put through MLF. Their exposure to oak gives them more of a bite due to tannins, and longer aging potential. These wines are bottled within 12–18 months and can be drunk young but are best appreciated after 12–18 months more bottle aging.

Figure 19.2 illustrates a typical timeline for making a dry, full-bodied, oaked white wine from grapes, with sequential MLF, no sweetening, and bottled 12–18 months from the start of the process.

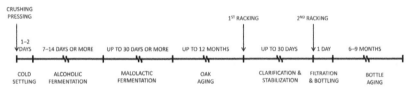

Figure 19.2: Typical timeline for making a dry, full-bodied, oaked white wine from grapes, with sequential MLF, and bottled in 12–18 months

Generally, you will want a wine with 12.5–13.5% ABV, which means you need a starting SG in the range 1.090–1.100 (22–24 Brix), and TA around 5.0 g/L for a dry style with residual sugar (RS) less than 2 g/L.

 "Dry style" does not equate to microbially stable. Only dry wines with RS less than 2 g/L are considered microbially stable; those with 2–5 g/L RS (or more) would still require to be properly stabilized, as outlined in Section 14.1.1.

Chardonnay, Seyval Blanc, Vidal Blanc and Viognier are all excellent choices for this style of wine. Consult Chapter 2 for processing considerations and tips for your variety.

The log chart in the CONTROL CHECKPOINTS section at the end of this chapter provides a view of which measurements you should be taking

19

at the various steps in the process described below. Here too I measure dissolved oxygen (DO), which gives interesting, if not enlightening, information when aging on the lees and seeing how it impacts DO and FSO2.

BARREL-FERMENT OR BARREL-AGE? BARRELS OR OAK ALTERNATIVES?

If you invested in oak barrels and want to use those to create a full-bodied, oaked style, first decide whether you want: a) to ferment in barrels and then age the wine in inert vessels or perhaps some more in barrels, or b) vice versa, to ferment in inert vessels and then age in barrels.

Because of how yeast interacts with oak compounds, barrel fermentation results in less wood, less almond and toasted aromas, and is deemed better integrated than the same wine barreled after fermentation. If you decide to age in barrels after AF and MLF, make sure to keep the lees to introduce into barrels; these are essential for aging whites in barrels (see Sections 15.4 and 15.5).

Alternatively if you're on a budget, instead of barrels, you can use oak alternatives, and again, either during fermentation or aging.

The protocol presented here is for both fermenting and aging in barrels and using oak alternatives.

19.2.1 CRUSHING AND PRESSING

 If you are making wine from fresh juice that has not been cold settled, proceed to Section 19.2.2. If you are making wine from fresh juice that has already been cold settled and is ready to be fermented, proceed to Section 19.2.3.

Follow the same instructions — without maceration — as set out in Section 19.1.1.

19.2.2 COLD SETTLING

 If you are making wine from fresh juice that has already been cold settled and is ready to be fermented, proceed to Section 19.2.3.

Follow the same instructions as set out in Section 19.1.2.

 We'll be using the gross lees after fermentation for aging the wine on the lees. If you detect any reductive smells, i.e., sulfides, after cold settling or after fermentation, do not use the gross lees, or you will risk having a sulfide problem.

19.2.3 MUST ANALYSIS AND ADJUSTMENTS

Follow the same instructions as set out in Section 19.1.3: record the volume of juice in each batch, if in separate vessels, and measure and record temperature, SG/Brix, TA and pH of the sample, and determine the PA, and making sure to make any adjustments to compensate for the measured temperature if different from the hydrometer's calibration temperature. Measure yeast assimmilable nitrogen (YAN), if so equipped.

Determine your target SG/Brix, TA, pH and YAN, and if you need to adjust any of these parameters, plan the adjustments so that you will be ready to implement those the next day after the cold settling period.

 If you are making wine from fresh juice, the juice vendor likely added KMS. As a precaution, you should also measure total SO2 (TSO2), if so equipped, to make sure that TSO2 does not exceed the maximum TSO2 for the lactic acid bacteria culture you will be using for the MLF. If TSO2 is too high, it can inhibit the MLF.

19

Following the settling period, carefully rack the juice off the sediment into barrels, if barrel fermenting, or inert vessels of choice if using oak alternatives, making sure to minimize oxygen uptake in the process by placing the racking hose at the bottom of the receiving vessel.

If you need to make adjustments, it's best to first rack all the juice into a single vessel to have it all homogenous and make single adjustments. Then make the adjustments. We're not quite ready to make YAN adjustments just yet.

The juice is referred to as must from here on; it's what gets fermented.

When working with barrels, there is a bit of planning you need to do as you cannot fill barrels completely; you have to leave some headspace for fermentation and foaming. That means that you will have to ferment a small amount of wine separately, in inert vessels, which you will use to top up barrels when fermentation is nearing completion or has completed.

Place a stopper with airlock on each vessel to protect the juice.

19.2.4 ALCOHOLIC FERMENTATION

Follow the same instructions as set out in Section 19.1.4, but ferment at around 18 °C (64 °F).

If you are using oak alternatives, add 1–2 g/L of oak chips of your choice. Place the chips in a sanitized mesh bags with a drawstring or in an infusion tube for easy retrieval later on. Use the mesh bag if making wine in a vessel with a large opening, such as an open-top tank like a VCT, and the infusion tube if making wine in carboys or similar vessels with a small opening. You can use staves or spirals if you prefer a "softer" impact of oak and tannins. Staves and spirals do not need a bag as they can be removed easily after racking out the wine. We'll use staves later on for aging.

Monitor fermentation progress by measuring, recording and charting temperature and temperature-adjusted SG/Brix, once a day and at the same time every day, to make sure all is proceeding according to plan. Smell and taste the wine to make sure there are no off-aromas or flavors.

Remember to add the second half of complex nutrients when SG (Brix) has dropped by one-third, and to give the wine a good stir as fermentation nears SG 1.010 (2.5 Brix) to get the lees back into suspension and to help yeast carry fermentation to dryness.

Ferment to complete dryness, that is, when SG is below 0.995 (Brix is below −1.5) with a steady reading for at least two consecutive days.

By the end of fermentation, there will be a fairly thick layer of lees at the bottom of vessels. Unlike making a fruity-style wine, we'll make use of these lees here for sur-lie aging and not rack the wine, but, again, only if you had cold settled the juice and had not detected any reductive smells during winemaking.

The first post-AF racking will be done after the aging period. But take this opportunity to taste the wine for oak and tannins to make sure you're not overdoing it. If you are using oak chips, you will likely have considerable oak influence and tannins; if so, and also to avoid the risk of adding too much oak and tannins, take out the mesh bag or infusion tube and replace with staves or spirals if you will be aging the wine on the lees.

Take a sample, and measure and record temperature, TA, pH, FSO2 and TSO2. TA helps you understand how acidity has changed during fermentation while pH will indicate microbial stability of the wine and how much SO_2 you need to add in the next step. The TSO2 measurement is to make sure it is well within specifications of the lactic acid bacterium you will be using for the MLF.

19.2.5 MALOLACTIC FERMENTATION

Fuller-bodied styles of whites can greatly benefit from an MLF; it adds aromas and flavors that bode well with the variety and style, and also decreases acidity (TA) to better complement oak tannins.

As discussed in Section 12.1, there are pros and cons for carrying out the MLF either concurrently with the AF or sequentially at the end of the AF. Here, we will perform a sequential MLF.

First run a paper chromatography test to get a baseline view of the malic acid content in the wine to help you monitor malic conversion.

You typically don't need to add malolactic nutrients as there should be sufficient nutrients in the lees. But if you have very little lees, which can

19

happen if you are making wine from processed juice, add malolactic nutrients at least 24 hours before lactic acid bacteria (LAB) inoculation.

Inoculate the wine with a suitable commercial LAB culture of *O. oeni* (see Section 12.7) that meets all the wine chemistry criteria making sure to follow the product instructions on any rehydration protocol — some LAB may require to be rehydrated with nutrients.

Maintain temperature in the range 18–22 °C (64–72 °F) for the duration of the MLF.

MLF should start within a couple of days; you should see tiny CO_2 bubbles rising ever so slowly — you may need a flashlight to see this, or stick your ear close to the bunghole of a barrel and listen for a faint popping sound. Be sure to maintain absolutely sanitary conditions throughout the MLF period as the wine has no SO_2 and therefore no protection against spoilage microorganisms.

Once a week, gently stir the lees into suspension to favor a healthy MLF. Be sure to stir *very gently* to avoid oxygen uptake and affecting oxygen-sensitive LAB.

Run a paper chromatography test every week or at least every two weeks to monitor MLF progress. Do not rely strictly on bubbles; these can be misleading. Progress and completion can only be monitored with paper chromatography. MLF can take several weeks, perhaps months, to complete depending on wine chemistry and temperature. Be sure to run a test for each batch if the wine is in several vessels. Wines in different vessels may complete at different times, and therefore, you need to monitor MLF progress separately in each. This means that wines may move to the microbial stabilization step at different times.

When the test confirms complete conversion of malic acid, measure and record temperature, TA and pH, taste the wine for oak and tannins, aromas, flavors and overall quality, and proceed with microbial stabilization. Repeat for all vessels.

TA helps you understand how acidity has changed during MLF while, here too, pH indicates microbial stability and how much SO_2 you need to add in the next step.

19.2.6 MICROBIAL STABILIZATION

If you had carried out the MLF in another, warmer area, transfer all vessels *for which wines have completed MLF* to your cellar or cooler area. From here on, maintain wine at cellar temperature, ideally around 13 °C (55 °F).

Three (3) days after completion of the AF and MLF, you are ready to stabilize with SO_2. If you want to minimize diacetyl and any buttery character, you can extend this to 10–14 days to allow yeast and bacteria to further metabolize diacetyl. As wines in different vessels may complete at different times, you will need to continue monitoring MLF progress until completion, then stabilize each after the wait period.

Re-measure temperature and pH, and using a molecular SO_2 (MSO2) of 0.5 mg/L, as recommended for a full-bodied style, determine the required free SO_2 (FSO2) level using the SO2 CALCULATOR or Figure 8.4 in Section 8.2, making sure to increase the SO_2 addition by about 10% to account for binding, add the required amount of KMS, stir thoroughly, and place the stoppers and airlocks on again.

If you cannot measure pH, simply add ¼ teaspoon (about 1.5 g) KMS per 23-L (6-gal) carboy or ¾ teaspoon (about 4 g) KMS per 54-L (14-gal) demijohn.

At this point, it is also a good idea to measure % ABV and residual sugar (RS), if so equipped.

Now we will age the wine, possibly on the lees if it was not racked, *then* perform clarification and stabilization using the same procedure as for the fruity style, and again perhaps age some more in bulk before bottling.

19.2.7 AGING

19

At this point, you either have wine sitting on the lees in inert vessels with staves, or whichever other oak alternative you had picked, or in oak barrels. Now we'll be aging the wine sur-lie with *bâtonnage* (stirring the lees) for up to 12 months. You can add β-glucanases, for example, Extralyse (Laffort), if you wish to enhance the effects of yeast autolysis.

There are different stirring regimens for short or long periods depending on how much oak and lees influence you want. Refer to Sections 15.4 and 15.5 for techniques and guidance for aging in barrels and on the lees, and a reminder of what β-glucanases do.

If aging in inert vessels, every 3 months and for *all vessels*, taste the wines, measure temperature, pH, FSO2 and DO, and adjust FSO2, as required.

If aging in barrels, every month and for *all barrels*, taste the wines, measure temperature, pH, FSO2 and DO, and adjust FSO2, as required, and be sure to top up barrels.

These short check intervals will help you identify early on any potential problems and take preventive and corrective action if required.

By the end of the aging period, there will be a fairly thick layer of lees at the bottom of vessels. You're ready for your first post-AF racking.

19.2.8 FIRST (POST-AF) RACKING

Follow the same instructions as set out in Section 19.1.5 to rack the wine.

Take a sample, and measure and record temperature (of the wine, not the sample), TA and pH. TA helps you understand how acidity may have changed during aging while pH will indicate microbial stability of the wine and how much SO_2 you need to add in the next step.

And definitely smell and taste the wine to see how you like it and to make sure it has not developed any undesirable smells or flavors.

19.2.9 CLARIFICATION AND STABILIZATION

Follow the same instructions as set out in Section 19.1.8 to clarify and stabilize the wine against proteins and tartrates.

Rack the wine from its lees, and re-measure temperature and pH, then measure FSO2, TSO2 and DO, and adjust FSO2 based on pH, MSO2 and DO.

If the wine has residual malic acid in excess of 100 mg/L, as evidenced by a visible spot from a chromatography test, you will need to add KMS and lysozyme (see Section 14.1.2) or sterile filter (see Section 17.3).

You can also fine-tune your wine here to, for example, tame aggressive tannins, or, on the flip side, to add more tannins. If you need to add more tannins, add oak-type finishing tannins, i.e., ellagitannins, to maintain compatibility. Sections 16.2 and 16.3 describe techniques to address tannins.

19.2.10 FILTERING

Follow the same instructions as set out in Section 19.1.10.

It's wise to again measure temperature, pH, FSO2 and DO, and adjust FSO2, as required, to make sure everything is in order and especially if you don't intend to bottle immediately after filtering.

19.2.11 BOTTLING

As a pre-bottling precaution, it's a good idea to re-measure RS to confirm your measurement taken at the end of fermentation, just to make sure that the wine is microbially stable and a sorbate treatment is not required. RS should not have changed.

When ready to bottle, measure temperature, pH, FSO2, TSO2 and DO one last time, and adjust FSO2 based on pH, desired MSO2 and DO. You may want to bump up the FSO2 addition by 5–10 mg/L to account for oxygen uptake during bottling and bottle aging, although this is optional given that the wine has high antioxidant power owing to aging on the lees.

19

If you are set up to sterile filter and deliver wine directly into bottles under vacuum, filter with a 0.45-micron (*absolute*) cartridge and bottle immediately.

You can certainly start drinking the wine now but it will greatly improve in the bottle between 6–9 months, perhaps even longer.

LOG CHART — CONTROL CHECKPOINTS:
FULL-BODIED WHITE WINE

Highlighted boxes represent those measurements you should be making and reducing at the various checkpoints as described in the protocol outlined in Section 19.2.

Create a *separate log sheet for each batch* if the wine spans more than one vessel.

LOG CHART — CONTROL CHECKPOINTS: FULL-BODIED WHITE WINE

Date	CHECKPOINT	Volume (L or gal)	Temp. (°C/°F)	SG / BRIX	Temp-adjusted SG / BRIX	PA or Actual % ABV	TA (g/L)	pH	FSO2 (mg/L)	TSO2 (mg/L)	DO (mg/L)	YAN (mg N/L)	RS (g/L)	MLF Check
	MUST ANALYSIS													
	ALCOHOLIC FERMENTATION													
	POST AF/PRE MLF													
	MALOLACTIC FERMENTATION													
	MICROBIAL STABILIZATION													
	AGING													
	FIRST (POST-AF) RACKING													
	CLARIFICATION AND STABILIZATION													
	FILTERING													
	BOTTLING													

19

20 Making Attractive Rosé Wine

This chapter describes the protocol for making rosé wine from grapes — purchased or from your backyard vineyard.

You may want to first refresh your memory on the rosé winemaking process; refer back to the flowchart presented in Figure 1.3 in Section 1.3.3.

The general process for making rosé wine is very similar to making white wine except that there is a short maceration phase following crushing to extract the desired amount of color. Highly pigmented varieties might go straight to the press as whole bunches or perhaps destemmed because they would otherwise liberate too much color with even the shortest of maceration if first crushed.

As there are many different variations of making rosé wine and particularly with achieving a desired color profile, a common protocol for making a light, fruity-style rosé is presented here. The *saignée* method, a French term that translates to "bleeding," is a variation involving running off some juice from crushed red grapes to make a rosé wine though the primary objective is usually to concentrate flavors and color in the rest of the juice in making the red wine. As you gain experience with the varieties you work with and depending on your preferred style and color, you will come to develop your own variations.

There are two challenges in making rosé wine, great rosé, that is: limiting oxygen exposure and minimizing tannin extraction.

One of the appeals of rosé wine is color. Red dominates, or it should, but orange hues may make the wine appear more orange than red — the result of phenolic browning due to polyphenol oxidation. In rosé winemaking, you should make every effort possible to limit oxygen exposure and "rough" processing to minimize oxidation of juice and wine. This will be particularly important when working with thiolic varieties to prevent

20

varietal character loss as thiols are very sensitive to oxygen. There are specific complementary treatments, for example, adding gallotannins or glutathione, to further protect juice and wine from oxidation and let the red color shine.

Maceration inevitably causes some tannin extraction. The amount of tannins depends on grape variety, extent of maceration, the amount of pressure exerted at pressing, and processing temperature. It's easy to over-extract tannins, especially with tannic varieties like Mourvèdre, and that would not bode well with the style of wine. You will need to manage this extraction and likely have to fine-tune tannins during aging or before bottling.

The following section describes a method for making rosé wine from grapes in a dry style that can be sweetened to taste. The protocol implements techniques and uses equipment that minimize wine exposure to air during processing and is adapted from *Rosé from Saignée Protocol by Laffort* [1]. I experimented extensively with this protocol and I was able to achieve greater red color and significantly less orange hues; the extra effort required to implement some of the procedures is well worth it.

Review and understand the protocol *before you start* making wine to be sure you are equipped and prepared to execute all the necessary steps.

And a reminder to keep a meticulous log of all processing activities, additives and processing aids used, measurements taken, as well as progress tasting notes (see Section 1.4). You can use the log sheet in Appendix C, which can be downloaded at ModernHomeWinemaking.com.

20.1 MAKING A FRUITY-STYLE ROSÉ WINE

As in making fruity-style whites, rosés too are fermented relatively cool and slow to retain delicate fruity esters. Malolactic fermentation (MLF) is generally not desirable so as to let all the fruity aromas shine unimpeded and preserve the higher acidity desired in this style of wine. In cases of very high acidity, MLF may be required to partially convert malic acid if the varietal is compatible with MLF. Rosés are bottled within 6–9 months and are meant to be consumed relatively quickly, within another 6–9 months.

Figure 20.1 illustrates a typical timeline for making a dry, fruity-style rosé wine from grapes, with no MLF, sweetened if desired, and bottled 6–9 months from the start of the process.

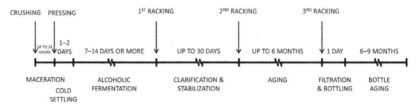

Figure 20.1: Typical timeline for making a dry, fruity-style rosé wine from grapes, with no MLF, and bottled in 6–9 months

Generally, you will want a wine with 11–12.5% ABV, which means you need a starting SG in the range 1.080–1.090 (19–22 Brix), and TA in the range 5–8 g/L for a dry style with residual sugar (RS) less than 5 g/L. Be careful with high-sugar varieties as you may end up with a rosé charged with 13% ABV or more, which may require you to ameliorate if you are wanting a lighter style.

 "Dry style" does not equate to microbially stable. Only dry wines with less than 2 g/L RS are considered microbially stable; those with 2–5 g/L RS (or more) would still require to be properly stabilized, as outlined in Section 14.1.1.

Grenache is one of the most popular varieties for making rosé wine, but there is no shortage of options for producing outstanding rosés using the protocol outlined in this section. Recommended varieties include: Aglianico, Barbera, Catawba, Léon Millot, Merlot, Mourvèdre, Pinot Noir, Pinotage, Sangiovese, Tempranillo and Zinfandel. Marquette (a teinturier), Petite Sirah and Syrah are excellent choices too though they would go straight to the press without any crushing and maceration. Consult Chapter 2 for other processing considerations and tips for your variety.

The log chart in the CONTROL CHECKPOINTS section at the end of this chapter provides a view of which measurements you should be taking at the various steps in the protocol described below. In my own winemaking, I measure dissolved oxygen (DO) at every checkpoint when adjusting the free SO_2 (FSO2); it also flags any potential oxygen ingress issues.

20

20.1.1 CRUSHING AND DESTEMMING

This protocol makes use of Lafazym Press (Laffort) pectinases that must be prepared and chilled up to 6 hours before adding to crushed grapes in the press. Use 2 g per 100 kg (220 lbs) of crushed grapes for thin-skinned varieties and up to 5 g per 100 kg (220 lbs) for thick-skinned varieties. Prepare a suspension as per product instructions.

Install a 1-inch bottom valve in your vat to easily run off and transfer juice to fermentation vessels at the end of maceration when you are ready to press the grape solids. Position the vat sufficiently high to be able to place a pail under the valve to collect juice. Alternatively, you can transfer juice and grape solids to the press using a plastic scoop, pan or similar device and collect all the juice at once.

Clean, sanitize and thoroughly rinse all equipment, tools and fermentors.

Ideally work with cool grapes at a maximum temperature of 14 °C (57 °F) to slow down uncontrolled enzymatic reactions. If your grapes are warmer, you can cool the grapes once crushed in the next step during maceration.

Once you have harvested or received your grapes, first remove any MOG (material other than grapes) and meticulously remove any and all moldy grapes or raisined berries that may otherwise reduce the availability of nitrogen and cause a sluggish fermentation or premature oxidation. There is no need to wash grapes; it is actually not recommended as leftover water will dilute the juice.

Crush–destem grapes into a vat, or into pails and then transfer to a vat if your crusher–destemmer is mounted on a chute.

Add gallotannins to avoid uncontrolled skin extraction and juice oxidation using one of the many commercial preparations. Suprarom (Laffort) is a preparation of gallotannins, ascorbic acid and potassium metabisulfite (KMS); add at a rate of 10–25 g per 100 L (25 gal) of *volume of crushed grapes*. Scott'Tan FT Blanc Soft (Scott Laboratories) contains gallotannins; add at a rate of 5–15 g per 100 L (25 gal) of *volume of crushed grapes*. I suggest using the lowest dosage if the harvest is healthy, and then doing another complementary addition after pressing. Mix thoroughly with your punchdown tool.

Add the *previously prepared* Lafazym Press suspension and mix thoroughly with your punchdown tool. These pectinases increase pressing efficiency and improve juice yield, and also help extract aroma precursors.

Add 35 mg of potassium metabisulfite (KMS) per kg (15 mg per lb) of crushed grapes. You can determine the approximate weight from your harvest data or from the number of 18-lb (8.2 kg) lugs or 36-lb (16.3 kg) cases you crushed. Alternatively, you can add 50 mg/L KMS (which gives approximately 30 mg/L FSO2) if you can estimate the total crush volume. Mix thoroughly with your punchdown tool.

Place a heavy tarp or lid on your vat to protect the must from the elements and to keep fruit flies out.

20.1.2 MACERATION

 If working with a highly pigmented grape variety where no maceration is required, proceed to Section 20.1.3.

In this step, you need to hold the must at 14 °C (57 °F) or lower for a couple of hours, perhaps several, or maybe even a day, until you obtain your desired color extraction.

If you need to drop the temperature of the must, use plastic jugs of frozen water or dry ice. If using frozen jugs, have more jugs in the freezer ready to go as you will need to rotate jugs in and out of the must as frequently as necessary to maintain the desired temperature. Be sure to sanitize the jugs before every use and rotation. If using dry ice, add at a rate of 700 g per 100 L (25 gal) of volume of crushed grapes for every 1 °C (2 °F) drop in temperature, mix thoroughly to homogenize, and replenish as needed to maintain the desired temperature.

20

Wear proper safety gear when handling dry ice. At −78 °C (−108 °F), dry ice is cold to the touch and can cause severe freeze burns if it comes in contact with skin.

Place a heavy tarp or lid on your vat to protect the must from the elements and to keep fruit flies out. As there is no active fermentation generating carbon dioxide (CO_2), the surface of the must is not well protected against the elements, fruit flies and spoilage microorganisms. If possible, and especially if you intend to macerate for more than just several hours, protect the must with inert gas, preferably CO_2 since it is heavier than air, if not already using dry ice. If your vat has a lid or if you can tie down a tarp with rubber straps on your vat, try injecting CO_2 gas from a cylinder to displace air out and to form a protective layer over the surface of the must. Make sure to keep doing punchdowns during the cold-soak period and to flush out air again with CO_2.

Monitor the color hourly to gauge extraction keeping in mind that there will be some significant color loss, in the order of 30–40%, from fermentation and processing, therefore, extract more color.

Once you have obtained your (overcompensated) desired color, you are ready to press grape solids and transfer juice to vessels for cold settling.

20.1.3 PRESSING

To the extent possible, drop the temperature of your winemaking area as much as possible, or use your glycol chiller, as you will need to store the juice at low temperature for cold settling following pressing.

Clean, sanitize and thoroughly rinse all equipment, tools and fermentors.

Here, we will assume that you have one single holding tank, such as a stainless steel variable-capacity tank (VCT), or vessel to accommodate the entire juice volume to keep it all homogeneous and not have to split across multiple vessels.

Throughout the following procedure, protect the juice from oxidation to the extent possible while you transfer juice into the holding tank or other vessel. The easiest way to protect juice is to add dry ice pellets into the holding tank or vessel at a rate of about 1 g/L (4 g/gal) based on your estimated volume of juice. Alternatively, if so equipped and inclined, you can flush air out of the tank with CO_2 and transfer juice into the tank via the bottom valve using a pump and under cover of CO_2.

Rack free-run juice from the vat from the bottom valve into a pail using a coarse, plastic or stainless steel strainer, and transfer into the holding tank. If your vat is not equipped with a bottom valve, use a plastic scoop or stainless steel pan to scoop must into the pail, still using a strainer. You can use a pump for the transfer of juice from pail into the holding tank.

When done transferring free-run juice, cover the holding tank or vessel with loose fabric or a loosely fitted lid to protect the juice from the elements, dust and fruit flies until you are ready for the pressing operation next.

Set up the press close to the vat as you will be scooping up and transferring grape solids to the press — it can get messy.

In the next step, we will assume that the entire mass of grape solids can be loaded into your press. You may need to do multiple press runs if you cannot load all the mass into the press at once.

Using a plastic scoop or stainless steel pan, scoop up grape solids and transfer to the press. Still using a strainer to keep grape fragments out of the juice, press into a pail as quickly as possible to minimize juice exposure to the elements while transferring press-run juice to the holding tank.

You may find that certain grape varieties, particularly slipskin varieties, such as Catawba, don't drain their juice well out of the press. To facilitate internal drainage during pressing, add rice hulls at a rate of 1:100, i.e., 1 kg per 100 kg or 1 lb per 100 lbs of crushed grapes. Sprinkle rice hulls over the crushed grapes during the transfer to the press. Alternatively, open the press after the first pressing cycle, break up and stir the pomace, then start another press cycle.

20

Press the pomace and transfer press-run juice into the holding tank or vessel as quickly as possible and with as little agitation as possible. Press as much as you want to within the maximum pressure your press can handle or until there is no more juice flowing, keeping in mind that the more pressure you exert to extract more juice, the more tannins you will extract too.

Add pectinases, such as Lafazym CL (Laffort), to hasten juice settling and clarification. Add up to the maximum dosage in the recommended range based on the lowest temperature you expect to settle the juice in the next step; enzyme activity slows down considerably below 10 °C (50 °F).

For extra protection against oxidation, optionally add gallotannins, such as Tanin Galalcool SP (Laffort), and/or glutathione, such as OptiMUM White or Glutastar (Lallemand), or specific inactivated yeast, such as Pure-Lees Longevity (Lallemand).

Place the floating lid on the juice in the VCT and seal with a solid stopper. If using other types of vessels, purge any headspace with inert gas, if possible, and seal with a solid stopper.

Unload the press and discard the pomace to the compost.

20.1.4 COLD SETTLING

Hold the VCT cold or transfer vessels to a fridge, if possible, or to the coldest area, ideally below 8 °C (46 °F), and hold cold for 24–48 hours to allow the juice to settle. If you cannot maintain a cold temperature, let settle for no more than 24 hours, or you'll risk a spontaneous fermentation.

After the cold settling period, transfer the VCT or vessel to a warmer area or raise the temperature to the planned fermentation temperature.

20.1.5 MUST ANALYSIS AND ADJUSTMENTS

While you wait for the juice to warm up, take a 250-mL sample to the lab for analysis. If you intend to return the sample to the VCT or vessel, which is never recommended but frugal winemakers still do, be doubly sure to sanitize all equipment that will come into contact with the juice — you don't want to pick up any spoilage microorganisms lurking in your hydrometer cylinder and infect your batch.

Record the volume of juice in each batch, if in separate vessels. Measure and record temperature, SG/Brix, TA and pH of the sample, and determine the PA, and making sure to make any adjustments to compensate for the measured temperature if different from the hydrometer's calibration temperature. Measure yeast assimmilable nitrogen (YAN), if so equipped.

Determine your target SG/Brix, TA, pH and YAN, and if you need to adjust any of these parameters, plan the adjustments so that you will be ready to implement those the next day after the cold settling period.

Once the settling period completed, carefully rack the juice off the sediment into another VCT or intermediate transfer vessel making sure to minimize oxygen uptake by placing the racking hose at the bottom of the receiving vessel. Use the same inerting techniques described above in Section 20.1.3 to reduce the effects of juice oxidation. Then make the adjustments. We're not quite ready to make YAN adjustments just yet.

The juice is referred to as must from here on; it's what gets fermented.

If working with a thiol-rich grape variety, such as Grenache, Cabernet, Merlot or Mourvèdre, and you want to get more thiol aromas, add specific pectinases with glycosidase activities, such as Lafazym Thiols[+] (Laffort), specifically designed to bring out grapefruit, passion fruit and box tree aromas. Be sure to choose a complementary yeast known to enhance thiol-type varietal aromas, such as Alchemy I (Lallemand), Zymaflore VL3 (Laffort) or EnartisFerm Q9 (Esseco).

If you cannot ferment in a single vessel, like a VCT, where you need headspace, transfer to as many vessels as you need, but *only fill to 75% capacity*, maybe a little more if fermenting a bit cooler, to allow for foaming during fermentation. CO_2 produced during fermentation will displace any air in the headspace out of vessels.

Place the floating lid several inches above the juice in the VCT to allow for foaming and insert a stopper with airlock, or similarly if using different vessels.

20

20.1.6 ALCOHOLIC FERMENTATION

 Conduct the AF in an area with good ventilation when ferment-ing large volumes as there will be considerable amounts of CO_2 gas produced that can pose an asphyxiation hazard.

Set the temperature of your fermentation area or glycol chiller to match the desired style, making sure it is within the temperature range of your yeast of choice. For a fruitier style, ferment cool, around 13 °C (55 °F), to increase ester production. For a style that exhibits more varietal character that expresses box tree and passion fruit aromas, as in this protocol, fer-ment warmer, around 20 °C (68 °F) to increase thiol production.

You are now all set to prepare the yeast inoculum and to inoculate your batch.

Prepare the inoculum using the required amount of yeast and add to a suspension of rehydration nutrients, as per instructions in Section 11.4.

Add the inoculum to the VCT or vessel, or proportionally to however many vessels you have. Stir the must thoroughly. Seal all vessels with stoppers and airlocks.

Based on your target YAN, calculate the total amount of complex nu-trients needed, as per Section 11.2, and 6–12 hours *after* yeast inoculation, add *half the calculated total amount* of complex nutrients. Stir well and re-seal all vessels.

Within 24–36 hours of inoculation, you should see signs of fermenta-tion with bubbles rising towards the surface of the must.

Now add a commercial preparation of proteins and PVPP, such as Poly-must Rosé (Laffort), at the recommended dosage to control oxidation and stabilize color — this is key — and stir thoroughly but gently, and reseal all vessels.

From here on until the end of AF, monitor fermentation progress by measuring, recording and charting temperature and temperature-adjusted SG/Brix, once a day and at the same time every day, to make sure all is pro-ceeding according to plan. Smell and taste the wine to make sure there are no off-aromas or flavors.

A simple way to monitor fermentation temperature is to insert a floating thermometer into the must — just leave it in for the duration of fermentation — or use a handheld thermometer equipped with a long probe. Be sure to sanitize any tool or device going into the wine and to minimize air exposure.

In about 24 hours, you will be adding bentonite to get a jump-start on protein stabilization, and therefore, you need to rehydrate the bentonite clay now to give it time to swell up. Rehydrate 0.5 g/L of bentonite in ten times its weight of *hot* water, as per instructions outlined in Section 13.4.1.1.

24 hours after the start of fermentation and addition of proteins and PVPP, add the *previously rehydrated* bentonite suspension, and stir gently but thoroughly.

This next step is very important.

When SG (Brix) has dropped by one-third — that's usually 30–35 SG points or 7–8 Brix — add the second half of complex nutrients you had calculated above. And to further protect the wine from oxidation effects and to preserve aromas, add a glutathione-rich inactivated yeast preparation, such as Fresharom (Laffort), and stir gently but thoroughly. You do not need to stir during an active fermentation, i.e., during the stationary phase.

As fermentation nears SG 1.010 (2.5 Brix), give the wine a good stir to get the lees back into suspension and to help yeast carry fermentation to dryness.

Ferment to complete dryness, that is, when SG is below 0.995 (Brix is below −1.5) with a steady reading for at least two consecutive days. This can take a week if fermenting at warmer temperatures, as in our thiol-style protocol, or several weeks at cooler temperatures. Make sure to fully degas samples when measuring the final SG/Brix; use a precision, low-range hydrometer for more accurate results.

By the end of fermentation, there will be a fairly thick layer of lees at the bottom of vessels. You're ready for your first post-AF racking.

20

20.1.7 FIRST (POST-AF) RACKING AND
MICROBIAL STABILIZATION

Rack the wine off the sediment into another VCT or vessel *and one (1) week after the end of the AF*, add 50 mg/L FSO2 (that's 87 mg/L KMS) during racking. The wait period before adding SO_2 is to allow for sufficient acetaldehyde bridging with tannins and anthocyanins, resulting in less astringency and greater color stability. SO_2 would otherwise bind to acetaldehyde and interfere with that process.

Minimize the amount of lees you pick up during racking, which will otherwise offset your efforts in clarifying the wine. Lees also contain still-viable yeast cells that may kick back into action if your wine has sufficient residual sugar, if you have not fermented dry, or after you sweeten. Protect the wine in the receiving VCT or vessel using dry ice pellets or CO_2 gas.

You will likely lose an appreciable amount of wine with the lees from this first racking. If you want to salvage some of the wine, transfer the sludge into the smallest glass vessel possible, purge the headspace with inert gas, if possible, and transfer to a refrigerator. Hold 24–48 hours and then carefully rack (it's easier with a small pump) the wine layer to another vessel leaving the sediment behind. Let the wine warm up to cellar temperature, smell and taste, and if there are no flaws, such as hydrogen sulfide (H_2S), add this wine to the rest of the batch. If the wine has any detectable flaws, discard it.

Take a sample, and measure and record temperature (of the wine, not the sample), TA and pH. TA helps you understand how acidity has changed during fermentation while pH indicates microbial stability of the wine. At this point, it is also a good idea to measure % ABV and residual sugar (RS), if so equipped.

And definitely smell and taste the wine to see how you like it and to make sure it has not developed any undesirable smells or flavors.

At this stage, you should not be making (or have to make) significant acidity changes. If the wine is not quite to your liking, perhaps it lacks a bit of acidity, you can make a small addition not exceeding 0.5 g/L using tartaric acid or malic acid. Always conduct bench trials before treating an entire batch.

If acidity is too high, it is best not to deacidify at this stage as it can be very difficult to achieve the desired results. You may have more success dropping the TA through chilling. You can always balance acidity with a little sugar when making a fruity style of wine, or if you prefer an off-dry or slightly sweet wine, you can sweeten by adding table sugar or wine conditioner, but don't add anything just yet, not until you have stabilized the wine.

Degassing is not recommended here as we are trying to eliminate all oxygen ingress, however small it might be. Be patient. Give the wine time to degas naturally during clarification and stabilization, processing and aging.

20.1.8 CLARIFICATION AND STABILIZATION

At this point, the wine needs to be clarified to a crystal-clear appearance, and stabilized against proteins and tartrates.

You can clarify either naturally by sedimentation or using fining agents, although natural clarification will take longer and may not yield a perfectly crystal-clear wine; you still have the option of filtering before bottling.

You can also forego stabilization if you expect to bottle the wine soon and consume it relatively quickly, and you don't want to be concerned with protein and tartrate stability. But here we are obsessed with only making consistently great wine — remember? You have to eliminate any and all risks of potential problems during aging, whether in bulk or in bottles.

You also have the option of aging wine before and/or after clarification and stabilization. Here, we will perform clarification and stabilization, then age the wine in bulk before bottling.

You can also combine clarification and stabilization steps and rack once at the completion of both; however, you must respect the same two important rules as in making white wine: 1) always cold stabilize during or after protein stabilization, *never before*, and 2) never make changes to wine chemistry after cold or tartrate stabilization, such as adding tartaric acid

20

or deacidifying with a potassium salt, which would otherwise require that you tartrate stabilize again.

For clarification and protein stabilization, you can use a combination of kieselsol and gelatin or chitosan, or just bentonite. If you are able to perform a heat stability test and bentonite bench trials (see Section 14.3), determine the extent of protein instability and how much bentonite you need. With most vinifera varieties, you should not need more than — and you should not exceed — a total of 1 g/L of bentonite, and since you had already added 0.5 g/L during fermentation, you should not need more than another 0.5 g/L. Protein-rich Native American and hybrid varieties may require more than 1 g/L. Allow 2–3 weeks for the wine to clarify.

You can concurrently chill the wine for tartrate stabilization to hasten clarification; in this manner, you will only need to rack once, when both protein and tartrate stabilization have completed. Alternatively, instead of chilling the wine for tartrate stabilization, you can use a protective colloid (see Section 14.4).

At the end of stabilization, your wine will be stable against proteins and tartrates, and against any renewed AF if it was fermented completely dry; there was no MLF, and therefore, there are no concerns with residual malic acid here.

Rack the wine from its lees, and re-measure temperature, TA and pH, then measure FSO2, TSO2 and DO, and adjust FSO2, if required, based on pH, MSO2 and DO.

TA and pH help you understand how acidity and microbial stability have changed during cold stabilization.

If your fermentation did not run completely dry to SG below 0.995 (Brix below –1.5) and you measure (or suspect) more than 2 g/L of residual sugar (RS) either using an RS kit or your hydrometer, or if you have any concerns about possible refermentation due to residual sugar, play it safe and add sorbate (see Section 14.1.1) or sterile filter (see Section 17.3).

You can also fine-tune your wine here to balance acidity by adding sugar or a wine conditioner, or you can do it later after bulk aging.

If you want to sweeten by adding sugar, run bench trials to determine the amount of sugar to add to please your palate, then add sorbate. If you use a wine conditioner, it (should) already contains sorbate. Refer to Section 16.1 on sweetening to balance acidity and sweetness.

20.1.9 AGING

You can bulk age the wine some more or you can proceed to filtering and bottling. Fruity wines meant to be drunk young will still benefit from a short aging. Guidelines and techniques for aging wine are described in Chapter 15.

If aging for long periods of time, be sure to measure temperature, pH, FSO2 and DO, and adjust FSO2, as required, every 3 months.

Taste and assess the wine periodically to ensure that it is still to your liking, especially the balance between dryness/sweetness and acidity. Pay particular attention to tannins here. There should not be any taste or sensation of bitter or astringent tannins. Refer to Section 16.3 on instructions for taming tannins.

20.1.10 FILTERING

At this point, your wine should be very clear, but likely not quite crystal clear. If you want to filter the wine to give it that extra sparkle, first rack all similar batches ideally into a single holding tank or vessel for homogeneity, then filter. If you try and filter without racking, you can accidentally suck sediment and cause premature clogging of the filter medium. Similarly, never try to filter a cloudy wine.

If the wine is very clear, you can proceed directly to a polishing filtration using a 1-micron or 2-micron cartridge or polishing-grade pads, for example, Buon Vino No. 2 pads, followed by a fine filtration using 0.45-micron (nominal) cartridge or equivalent, for example, Buon Vino No. 3 pads.

20

It's wise to again measure temperature, pH, FSO2 and DO, and adjust FSO2, as required, to make sure everything is in order and especially if you don't intend to bottle immediately after filtering.

20.1.11 BOTTLING

As a pre-bottling precaution, it's a good idea to re-measure RS to confirm your measurement taken at the end of fermentation, just to make sure that the wine is microbially stable and a sorbate treatment is not required. RS should not have changed, unless you added sugar for an off-dry or sweeter style of wine.

When ready to bottle, you know the drill — measure temperature, pH, FSO2, TSO2 and DO one last time, and adjust FSO2 based on pH, desired MSO2 and DO. You may want to bump up the FSO2 addition by 5–10 mg/L to account for oxygen uptake during bottling and bottle aging.

If you are set up to sterile filter and deliver wine directly into bottles under vacuum, filter with a 0.45-micron (*absolute*) cartridge and bottle immediately.

You can start drinking the wine now but it will benefit from a short aging between 6–9 months.

LOG CHART — CONTROL CHECKPOINTS: ROSÉ WINE

Highlighted boxes represent those measurements you should be making and recording at the various checkpoints as described in the protocol outlined in Section 20.1.

Create a *separate log sheet for each batch* if the wine spans more than one vessel.

LOG CHART — CONTROL CHECKPOINTS: ROSÉ WINE

Date	CHECKPOINT	Volume (L or gal)	Temp. (°C/°F)	SG / BRIX	Temp-adjusted SG / BRIX	PA or Actual % ABV	TA (g/L)	pH	FSO2 (mg/L)	TSO2 (mg/L)	DO (mg/L)	YAN (mg N/L)	RS (g/L)
	MUST ANALYSIS												
	ALCOHOLIC FERMENTATION												
	FIRST (POST-AF) RACKING & MICROBIAL STABILIZATION												
	CLARIFICATION AND STABILIZATION												
	AGING												
	FILTERING												
	BOTTLING												

20

REFERENCE

1. Laffort. *Rosé from Saignée Protocol by Laffort.* https://laffort.com/
   wp-content/uploads/Protocols/ITI_EN_Rose_Saign%C3%A9e-1.
   pdf. Last accessed March 24, 2021.

21 Making Blockbuster Red Wine

This chapter describes the protocol for making red wine from grapes — purchased or from your backyard vineyard — or frozen must.

You may want to first refresh your memory on the red winemaking process; refer back to the flowchart presented in Figure 1.4 in Section 1.3.4.

The general process for making red wine involves crushing grapes with an optional cold soak to start extracting color from skins, macerating grape solids and juice while carrying out alcoholic fermentation (AF) with frequent punchdowns or pumpovers to hasten color and tannin extraction, pressing grapes, carrying out malolactic fermentation (MLF), clarifying and stabilizing the wine whilst aging in barrels or inert vessels with oak alternatives, optionally filtering, and bottling.

Although the common practice is to crush and ferment each grape variety into a varietal and then possibly blending different varietals during aging or at bottling, it is also possible to crush and coferment different varieties, possibly viniferas with non-viniferas, as a single wine in what is known as "field blending" or cofermentation. Field blending can simply be used for practical reasons where you have only one wine to manage, or to address a deficiency, for example, to add tannins or improve color, to balance sugar by blending high and low-sugar grapes, or to extract complementary aromas and flavors.

Cofermentation is also used in a very interesting application where a small amount of white variety grapes, up to 5%, for example, are added to a batch of red variety grapes, for example, Viognier added to Syrah, right at crush to increase red color intensity and stability via a phenomenon known as copigmentation whereby anthocyanins link in a stacking fashion to only other anthocyanins, but also colorless compounds. These colorless compounds include naturally occurring polyphenols called flavonols, and which are found abundantly in Viognier; quercetin is a familiar example of a common flavonol found in grapes.

As for pre-fermentation cold soak, there are mixed reviews and much contradictory information on the benefits, or any benefits, for that matter. The theory is that, since anthocyanins are more soluble in juice (an aqueous solution) than in wine (an alcoholic solution), grape solids can be macerated cold in the juice for a longer maceration period to favor anthocyanin extraction while inhibiting the start of AF. Some home winemakers consider the additional risk of spontaneous fermentation or growth of spoilage organisms to outweigh any theoretical improvement in anthocyanin extraction and therefore avoid cold soaking altogether.

Maceration and AF can be carried out in inert vessels, such as large plastic vats or in open-top barrels. MLF can be carried out concurrently with the AF or sequentially post pressing; there are pros and cons in either approach (see Section 12.1).

When working with *V. labrusca* varieties, you may need to shorten the maceration and fermentation duration to help reduce the foxy character, which can be a challenge in extracting sufficient color with light-colored varieties such as Catawba. Alternatively to "mask" the foxy character, as discussed in Section 2.2.2, you can add untoasted oak at a rate of 1–4 g/L at crush or during fermentation to intensify the fruity expression and bring forward "ripe" fruit notes without the aromas of toasted oak.

Similarly for methoxypyrazine-prone varieties from a weak vintage or if you have underripe fruit, you may need to go with a shorter maceration and also add untoasted oak at crush or during fermentation to mask the vegetal, bell pepper aromas (see Section 2.1.2).

Free-run and press-run fractions can be processed separately or combined if their chemistry and organoleptic profiles are similar.

Free-run wines will typically taste less harsh, have more intense and more stable color, lower pH due to less potassium extracted, be richer in glutathione (GSH), a natural antioxidant, and have less soluble solids. Lower pH translates into greater tartrate stability, greater protection against microbial spoilage, and reduced need for sulfur dioxide (SO_2) for protection.

Press-run wines tend to taste harsher, have higher pH, and less color or lower color intensity than their free-run counterparts. The higher pH not only destabilizes color, it also increases both tartrate and microbial instabilities.

Clarification is usually allowed to occur naturally when wine is aged for an extended period of time, say, more than 12 months. Aging can be as short as just a few months and done in inert vessels with or without oak alternatives, or up to 18 months or more in barrels for premium full-bodied reds. Wines racked periodically over long aging periods and which are deemed completely stable from a microbial perspective can be bottled without filtering. Early-drinking reds bottled within a few months are filtered to prevent color pigments from staining bottles.

Whereas the focus is on creating and preserving delicate aromas and flavors in white and rosé winemaking, red winemaking is largely focused on extracting color and tannins based on the desired style of wine while also extracting flavors from the skins and juice. Each variety and vintage poses extraction challenges. The skins of some varieties, such as Pinot Noir, may have much less color and tannins to offer, while many hybrids have much greater amounts of proteins, all of which necessitate special consideration during maceration and fermentation. As an added challenge, reds tend to shed some of their color during winemaking and aging, necessitating special treatments to stabilize color and maximize retention.

Reds can be made into a variety of styles, from light and fruity to a medium-bodied style with more tannins and to a full-bodied style with relatively high alcohol and tannins that can give wine long aging potential. And of course the ability to make a certain style of red depends on the variety and the quality of the vintage; you cannot expect to make a full-bodied red from poorly colored grapes in a poor, cold and rainy vintage.

Given the great diversity of styles and the many different variations of making red wine, this chapter describes one common protocol for making a full-bodied style. Keep in mind that there are many different techniques and products — not to mention opinions — in any step of the process. With experience, you will come to develop your own techniques — and opinions — and adapt the process accordingly. You can make different varietals and styles separately, and then blend later.

21

Review and understand the protocol *before you start* making wine to be sure you are equipped and prepared to execute all the necessary steps. Roll up your sleeves and get ready to get dirty — red winemaking, and particularly from grapes, is a lot of work, messy work, but oh the rewards.

And the usual reminder to keep a meticulous log of all processing activities, additives and processing aids used, measurements taken, as well as progress tasting notes (see Section 1.4). You can use the log sheet in Appendix C, which can be downloaded at ModernHomeWinemaking.com.

21.1 MAKING A PREMIUM FULL-BODIED RED WINE

Full-bodied reds are fermented relatively warm, if not hot, to extract as much color as possible — this results in much quicker fermentations compared to white and rosé winemaking. Reds are almost invariably put through MLF primarily to reduce acidity to better balance high tannins. These wines are bottled within 18–24 months, perhaps more, with additional bottling aging. Patience is a virtue in making red wine, but, again, you will be richly rewarded.

Figure 21.1 illustrates a typical timeline for making a premium, full-bodied dry red wine with sequential (post-pressing) MLF, and bottled 18–24 months from the start of the process.

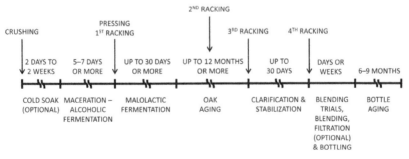

Figure 21.1: Typical timeline for making a premium, full-bodied dry red wine with sequential MLF, and bottled 18–24 months from the start of the process

Generally, you will want a wine with 13.5–14.5% ABV, which means you need a starting SG in the range 1.100–1.107 (24–25.5 Brix), and TA in the range 4–6 g/L for a dry style with residual sugar (RS) less than 2 g/L.

"Dry style" does not equate to microbially stable. Only dry wines with less than 2 g/L RS are considered microbially stable; those with 2–5 g/L RS (or more) would still require to be properly stabilized, as outlined in Section 14.1.1.

There is a vast choice of grape varieties — vinifera, Native American varieties and hybrids — for making full-bodied reds, with endless blending possibilities. Consult Chapter 2 for processing considerations and tips for your variety, and for blending ideas.

The log chart in the CONTROL CHECKPOINTS section at the end of this chapter provides a view of which measurements you should be taking at the various steps in the process described below. In my own winemaking, I measure dissolved oxygen (DO) at every checkpoint when adjusting free SO_2 (FSO2); it also flags any potential oxygen ingress issues.

21.1 CRUSHING AND DESTEMMING

If you are making wine from frozen must with skins, proceed to Section 21.1.2.

Install a 1-inch bottom valve in your vat to easily draw and transfer free-run wine to other vessels at the end of fermentation or when you are ready to press the grape solids. Position the vat sufficiently high to be able to place a pail under the valve to collect free-run wine. Alternatively, you can transfer wine with grape solids to the press using a plastic scoop, pan or similar device and collect all the wine at once.

Clean, sanitize and thoroughly rinse all equipment, tools and fermentors.

21

In this first step, ideally work with cold grapes, use your glycol chiller, or set up in an area where you can drop the temperature to as cold as possible, perhaps making use of dry ice. You also need to decide if you will want to do a pre-fermentation cold soak of the crushed and destemmed grapes to hasten and prolong color extraction, as described in Section 21.1.3.

Once you have harvested or received your grapes, first remove any MOG (material other than grapes) and meticulously remove any and all moldy grapes, or raisined or damaged berries that may otherwise reduce the availability of nitrogen and cause a sluggish fermentation or premature oxidation.

Sort berries and only keep those that you deem of utmost quality and which will produce only the greatest wine. This is particularly important with Native American varieties and hybrids as they tend to be less forgiving of compromised fruit. You can still make a "second" wine with rejected — though not moldy or raisined — berries. There is no need to wash grapes; it is actually not recommended as leftover water will dilute the juice.

Crush–destem grapes into a vat or into pails and then a vat if your crusher–destemmer is mounted on a chute. If you are not equipped to destem, remove as many stems as possible by hand, especially green stems. Green stems contain harsh tannins and "green" substances that can make wine unappealing; they can also reduce color owing to their higher pH due to higher potassium levels. Brown stems are better as they have much less impact on tannins and can help with wine drainage in the press.

The purpose of crushing is not to mash grapes, but rather, to gently split berries to allow yeast to interact with the juice, and release wine during fermentation.

If you want to concentrate color, tannins, aromas and flavors, particularly if you are working with a light-colored variety, run off a small amount of juice, say 10–15% or more, and process that juice as white or *saignée* rosé depending on how much color has already been extracted.

Add pectinases, such as Lafase HE Grand Cru (Laffort) or Lallzyme EX (Lallemand), to break down grape skin pectin, according to instructions for your product. Mix thoroughly with your punchdown tool. Place a heavy tarp or lid on your vat or fermentor to protect the must from the elements and to keep fruit flies out. Wait 6–8 hours to allow the pectinases to do their work before proceeding with the next step of adding tannins.

After the pectinase wait period, add "sacrificial tannins" (see Chapter 9) to bind and precipitate naturally occurring proteins using any fermentation tannin product recommended for this purpose, such as Tanin VR Supra (Laffort) or granular oak, which contains strong protein-binding ellagitannins. Follow the rate of addition for your product making sure to use the *total must volume* — not the expected juice or wine yield — for your calculations. For granular oak, add at a rate of 1–2 g/L based on the *total must volume*. You can add sacrificial tannins in conjunction with untoasted oak chips or powder where you need to reduce the vegetal or foxy character of the variety.

Alternatively to using sacrificial tannins and pectinases, you can use macerating enzymes, such as Scottzyme Color Pro (Scott Laboratories), which include pectinases and proteases into a single product. Be sure to allow at least two hours when adding macerating enzymes before adding potassium metabisulfite (KMS) in the step below.

If you will be doing a cold soak, add the above enzymes at up to the maximum dosage in the recommended range based on the lowest temperature you expect to achieve; enzyme activity slows down considerably below 10 °C (50 °F).

Add 35 mg of KMS per kg (15 mg per lb) of crushed grapes and mix thoroughly with your punchdown tool. You can determine the approximate weight from your harvest data or from the number of 18-lb (8.2 kg) lugs or 36-lb (16.3 kg) cases you crushed. Alternatively, you can add 50 mg/L KMS (which gives approximately 30 mg/L FSO2) if you can estimate the total crush volume.

I recommend punchdowns over pumpovers here for the simple reason that home winemakers are not equipped with the kinds of pumps and hoses to be able to do pumpovers efficiently. You can install a strainer inside a plastic fermentor vat or tub (see Figure 3.8 in Section 3.2) and use a good enological impeller-type pump with minimum 2-inch hoses.

21

If working with varieties known to lack body or impart harsh tannins, you can also start impacting mouthfeel and tannin structure right from crush and during fermentation using specific inactivated yeast products, such as Opti-Red, Noblesse and REDStyle (Lallemand) and PowerLees Rouge (Laffort). These products add polysaccharides and peptides that contribute body, enhance mouthfeel, enhance perception of sweetness, smoothen tannins, and further stabilize color.

Place a heavy tarp or lid on your vat or fermentor to protect the must from the elements and to keep fruit flies out.

Until you are ready to inoculate and start fermentation, punch down and stir the must at least twice daily to favor phenolic extraction, homogenize temperature, and keep aerobic surface microorganisms in check.

21.1.2 MUST ANALYSIS AND ADJUSTMENTS

If you have all the must in a single vat, take a 250-mL sample for analysis by, for example, dipping a cone-shaped stainless steel strainer into the grape mass and using a wine thief or baster. If you have multiple vessels, take proportional amounts from each to get a homogeneous sample, assuming that the wine will eventually all be blended. If you intend to return samples to their vessels, which is never recommended but frugal winemakers still do, be doubly sure to sanitize all equipment that will come into contact with the juice — you don't want to pick up any spoilage microorganisms lurking in your hydrometer cylinder and infect batches.

Record the estimated volume of juice in each batch. Measure and record temperature, SG/Brix, TA and pH of the sample, and determine the PA making sure to make any adjustments to compensate for the measured temperature if different from the hydrometer's calibration temperature. Measure yeast assimmilable nitrogen (YAN), if so equipped; you can delay this measurement until the end of cold soak if you choose to go that route.

Determine your target SG/Brix, TA and pH, and make any desired adjustments. Determine your target YAN but do not make any adjustments just yet.

21.1.3 COLD SOAK

 If you are making wine from frozen must with skins, proceed to Section 21.1.4.

Pre-fermentation cold soaking does require a bit of work depending on how you intend to lower and maintain temperature to a cold level.

Bring the temperature of your must down to as close as possible to around 5 °C (40 °F) using your glycol chiller, plastic jugs of frozen water or dry ice, and hold for anywhere between a couple of days to a week. If using frozen jugs, have more jugs in the freezer ready to go as you will need to rotate jugs in and out of the must as frequently as necessary to maintain the desired temperature. Be sure to sanitize the jugs before every use and rotation. If using dry ice, add at a rate of 700 g per 100 L (25 gal) of volume of crushed grapes for every 1 °C (2 °F) drop in temperature, mix thoroughly to homogenize, and replenish as needed to maintain the desired temperature.

 Wear proper safety gear when handling dry ice. At −78 °C (−108 °F), dry ice is cold to the touch and can cause severe freeze burns if it comes in contact with skin.

Place a heavy tarp or lid on your vat to protect the must from the elements and to keep fruit flies out. As there is no active fermentation generating carbon dioxide (CO_2), the surface of the must is not protected against the elements, fruit flies and spoilage microorganisms. If your vat has a lid or if you can tie down a tarp with rubber straps on your vat, try injecting CO_2 gas from a cylinder to displace air out and to form a protective layer over the surface of the must. Make sure to keep doing punchdowns during the cold soaking and to flush out air again with CO_2.

Remove the frozen jugs, if any, when ready to proceed with fermentation.

It's a good idea at this point to take another set of measurements to see if there have been any changes in SG/Brix, TA, pH and YAN.

21

21.1.4 MACERATION AND ALCOHOLIC FERMENTATION

 Conduct the AF in an area with good ventilation when ferment-ing large volumes as there will be considerable amounts of CO_2 gas produced that can pose an asphyxiation hazard.

 In this protocol, the MLF is conducted sequentially immediately after pressing; this can be right after completion of the AF or when pressing before having reached dryness.

Set the temperature of your fermentation area to be warm — but not hot — and allow the must to warm up. The idea is to have the must warm up fairly quickly to the 18–20 °C (65–68 °F) range to be able to inoculate swiftly without wild yeast jump-starting a spontaneous fermentation while you wait. Keep in mind that you want a relatively "hot" fermentation but that temperature will increase significantly as yeast gets to work, therefore don't overheat your area. You will need higher temperatures when using smaller fermentors as smaller vessels retain less heat during fermentation. You'll want fermentation to be in the range 25–30 °C (77–86 °F) to favor color extraction, but never allow it to exceed 32 °C (90 °F) as it can inhibit yeast and cause a stuck fermentation or possibly produce some stinky sulfides and other off-odors.

You are now all set to prepare the yeast inoculum and to inoculate your batch.

Prepare the inoculum using the required amount of yeast and add to a suspension of rehydration nutrients as per instructions in Section 11.4.

Add the inoculum to the vat or proportionally to however many fermentors you have. Stir the must thoroughly with your punchdown tool.

Based on your target YAN, calculate the total amount of complex nutrients needed, as per Section 11.2, and 6–12 hours *after* yeast inoculation, add *half the calculated total amount* of complex nutrients. Stir the must with your punchdown tool. Cover the vat and all fermentors with a heavy tarp or lid.

Within 24–36 hours of inoculation, you should see signs of fermentation with bubbles rising towards the surface of the must.

From here on until the end of AF, monitor fermentation progress by measuring, recording and charting temperature using, for example, a handheld thermometer equipped with a long probe, and temperature-adjusted SG/Brix, once a day and at the same time every day, to make sure all is proceeding according to plan. Smell and taste the wine to make sure there are no off-aromas or flavors.

As fermentation becomes more vigorous, CO_2 gas will push grape solids up to the surface and form a cap, and seeds are released from berries and slowly fall to the bottom.

At least twice daily, break and punch down the cap (Figure 21.2), and mix thoroughly. *Never let the cap go dry*. The idea is to re-submerge the solids into the fermenting wine to favor color, tannin and flavor extraction, to homogenize temperature, to keep aerobic surface microorganisms in check, and — very important — to avoid the production of stinky sulfides at the bottom of the vat. Reach close to the bottom of the vat or fermentors with your punchdown tool to ensure a good and thorough mixing of the must and to get the lees into suspension. And remember to sanitize the punchdown tool before each use and rinse after use.

Figure 21.2: Punching down the cap

21

Alternatively, if you are equipped with a good pump and you had fitted your vat with a bottom valve, drain free-run wine into a pail or other smaller recipient and let it splash vigorously to introduce oxygen to hasten anthocyanin–tannin polymerization. You'll recall from Section 9.1 that this is key to stabilizing color and softening tannins.

Throughout fermentation, smell the wine to make sure there are no off-aromas. Be particularly careful of any hydrogen sulfide (H_2S) smell.

Now we're going to start stabilizing color.

When SG (Brix) has dropped by about 25–30 SG points (5–7 Brix), add grape tannins, such as Tanin VR Color (Laffort), and mix in thoroughly using your punchdown tool.

This next step is very important.

When SG (Brix) has dropped by one-third — that's usually 30–35 SG points (7–8 Brix) and which will happen almost immediately after the color-stabilization tannin addition — add the second half of complex nutrients you had calculated above.

Closely monitor color to gauge extraction progress. You will need to make a call as to when you have reached maximum color and there is no more color being extracted. Remember: By stabilizing color here, wine will retain more of its color during aging.

Once color is at maximum, add anthocyanin-binding fermentation tannins, for example, Tan'Cor Grand Cru (Laffort) or Vinitannin Multi-Extra (2B FermControl), to "lock in" and stabilize color.

When making full-bodied red wine from viniferas, and particularly when wine is to go into barrels and where you want to reduce the risk of microbial problems arising from residual sugar, you will typically want to ferment to complete dryness, i.e., when SG is below 0.995 (Brix below −1.5) before pressing; this can take 5–7 days, more at cooler temperatures. Fermentation is complete when you get a steady hydrometer reading for at least two consecutive days. Degas wine samples when measuring the final SG/Brix to confirm end of fermentation, and, ideally, use a high-precision hydrometer.

If you prefer a more fruit-forward style and the wine will not go into barrels, you can press earlier, for example, at SG 1.010 (around 2–3 Brix) or higher and then complete fermentation in glass vessels or stainless steel tanks.

With Native American varieties and hybrids, long macerations may cause wine to pick up odd aromas and flavors and lose its fruity character. Closely monitor aromas and flavors during fermentation to make sure there are no flaws developing and perhaps move to pressing earlier, say, at around SG 1.020–1.030 (5–7 Brix) provided you extracted sufficient color.

Some winemakers prefer to press well before the wine has reached dryness, regardless of variety, because, aside from keeping more of its fruity character, it's a lot easier to separate the floating cap from the wine and to transfer the solids to the press. There is much less CO_2 gas at dryness, and therefore, there is no more cap and the grape solids fall back into the wine, complicating the separation process.

At this point, some winemakers perform what is called an "extended maceration," much like a pre-ferment cold soak, which involves soaking the grape solids in the wine for days or weeks at cold temperatures for the purpose of softening tannins, making the wine more approachable in its youth. This technique carries risks and requires work and know-how to implement. It is only recommended for advanced winemakers. For more information on doing an extended maceration, please consult reference [1].

21.1.5 PRESSING

Clean, sanitize and thoroughly rinse your press, all equipment, tools and vessels — anything that will come into contact with wine. Have ready vessels of different sizes so that you end up with all vessels fully topped up at the end of pressing.

When fermentation is complete or when you are ready to press, rack the free-run wine from the vat and into a pail using a plastic or stainless steel colander or strainer to keep grape solids out of the wine, and transfer into vessels using a large funnel (Figure 21.3). Don't fill the vessels just yet as you will have more free-run wine as you load the press in the next step. It's

21

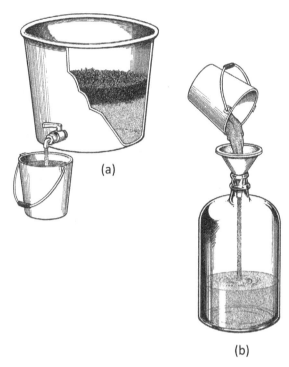

Figure 21.3: a) Racking free-run wine from a vat and
b) transferring to a glass carboy

always best to transfer all free-run wine into a single holding tank or vessel, such as a variable-capacity tank (VCT). This will make the whole volume of free-run wine homogeneous and will greatly facilitate racking into smaller vessels, including barrels, in the next step.

Smell and taste the wine to make sure all is progressing well and that it has not developed any flaws.

Place some loose fabric or loosely-fitted lids on all vessels to protect wine from fruit flies and dust until you have completed this next step — pressing.

Set up the press close to the vat as you will be scooping up grape solids and transferring them to the press — it will get messy.

You may want to keep press- and free-run wines separate until you run some analytical and taste tests to assess differences. If the wines are similar, you can blend at this stage. Keep in mind that if you segregate the wines, you will need to measure, log and adjust all parameters, i.e., TA, pH, FSO2, etc., separately.

In the next step, we will assume that the entire mass of grape solids — the pomace — can be loaded into your press. You may need to do multiple press runs if you cannot load all the pomace at once.

Place a pail and a plastic or stainless steel colander or strainer at the bottom of the press to collect free-run wine released from pressure on the grape solids as you load the press.

Using a plastic scoop or stainless steel pan, scoop up some pomace and transfer to the press. If you are using a bladder press, refer to Section 3.1 for instructions on properly loading the press. Do *not* transfer seeds to the press.

To facilitate internal drainage, add rice hulls at a rate of 1:100, i.e., 1 kg per 100 kg or 1 lb per 100 lbs of crushed grapes. Sprinkle rice hulls over the crushed grapes during the transfer to the press. Alternatively, open the press after the first pressing cycle, break up and stir the pomace, then start another press cycle.

Continue loading the press, collecting free-run wine and transferring it to the holding tank or vessels.

Once the press is fully loaded and there is no more flow of free-run wine, you are now ready to collect press-run wine.

Start pressing into pails and transfer the press-run wine into a separate holding tank or vessels from the free-run wine. Press as much as you want to within the maximum pressure your press can handle or until there is no more press-run wine flowing.

Unload the press and discard the pomace to the compost or make "piquette" (see below). Repeat this cycle if you have more grape solids to press.

Ideally all vessels should be fully topped up at this point. Alternatively, use inert gas to displace air out from partially filled vessels. If neither is possible, you will be racking the wine in 24–36 hours; it's not ideal but the wine will be exposed to a little air for only a short period.

Place a stopper and airlock on all vessels.

21

Do an inventory of volume in each vessel — keeping free- and press-run wines separate for now — to determine your *actual* yield. Update your records accordingly. Going forward, all your calculations for additives and processing aids will be based on this volume.

MAKING PIQUETTE

Piquette, also known as second-run wine, is a light-bodied, low-alcohol wine in the 5–10% ABV range made by adding water to pressed grape pomace to leach out alcohol, color, tannins and flavors still trapped in the skins, and fermenting on the skins or re-pressing the pomace and then fermenting. It's meant to be an easy-drinking wine for consumption soon after it has fermented and been stabilized.

To make piquette, add about half the volume of wine in water to the pomace in a large vat; for example, if you got a yield of 50 L (13 gal) of free- and press-run wine, add 25 L (6 gal) of water. Add sufficient sugar to the pomace or pressed wine to bring SG (Brix) to a PA in the 5–10% range. Measure TA and pH, and make any adjustments you want.

Wait 24 hours. Fermentation will likely take off on its own; if not, inoculate with a strong fermenting yeast, for example, Lalvin EC-1118 (Lallemand).

Ferment to dryness, press if fermented on the skins, then follow the process for rosé winemaking for clarifying, stabilizing, filtering and bottling.

21.1.6 FIRST RACKING

Free-run wine and especially press-run wine in holding tanks or vessels will have a heavy layer of sediment, or gross lees, which contains dead yeast cells, grape fragments and other substances that, if not removed, can cause flaws, H_2S being the most common.

Gross lees sediment within 24–36 hours; those that sediment after that are referred to as fine lees, and can be beneficial and not cause any H_2S problem. You can extend this to a *maximum of three days* to get the gross lees to form a more compact layer of sediment for easier and cleaner racking.

After the settling period, rack each tank or vessel into other tanks, vessels, or barrels if you intend to carry out the MLF in barrels, to separate wine from the gross lees. Keep free- and press-run wines separate. Oxygen pick-up during this racking is not an issue at this point; a splash-racking is actually favorable as it begins the process of polymerizing tannins and further stabilizing color. But do make sure that all vessels (including barrels) are completely topped up when done; you will likely need to use a few smaller vessels. Place a stopper and airlock on all vessels.

 You will likely lose an appreciable amount of wine with the gross lees from this first racking. If you want to salvage some of the wine, transfer the sludge into the smallest glass vessel possible, purge the headspace with inert gas, if possible, and transfer to a refrigerator. Hold 24–48 hours and then carefully rack (it's easier with a small pump) the wine layer to another vessel leaving the sediment behind. Let the wine warm up to cellar temperature, smell and taste, and if there are no flaws, no H_2S, add this wine to the rest of the batch. If the wine has any detectable flaws, discard it.

Measure temperature, TA, pH, FSO2 and TSO2 in representative samples of free- and press-run wines. TA helps you understand how acidity has changed during fermentation while pH indicates microbial stability. The TSO2 measurement is to make sure it is well within specification of the lactic acid bacterium you will be using for the MLF.

Also smell and taste each wine and assess color to make sure they have not developed any undesirable smells or flavors, and to decide if you want to keep free- and press-run wines separate or blend them. If the wines taste and look different or there is a significant gap in pH values, then keep the wines separate.

21.1.7 MALOLACTIC FERMENTATION

Most reds and certainly tannin-rich, fuller-bodied styles will greatly benefit from an MLF because of the added aromas and flavors that bode well with the variety and style, but also because the decrease in acidity will better

21

balance tannins. Keep in mind that you'll want lower acidity as the wine acquires more tannins during barrel aging.

You have several options in terms of barrel interactions. The preferred method if you want more exposure to oak is to perform MLF in barrels, and specifically new barrels where you will obtain better integration of oak. Alternatively, perform MLF in inert vessels for the rest of the process or maybe re-introduce the wine into barrels for further aging after MLF. Be sure to keep vessels completely full during MLF as lactic acid bacteria (LAB) are sensitive to oxygen and as other undesirable microorganisms can set in and effect spoilage.

First run a paper chromatography test for both free-run and press-run wines (preferably all batches) to get a baseline view of the malic acid content to help you monitor malic conversion.

At least 24 hours before inoculation, add malolactic nutrients to all batches (see Section 12.2). During the wait period, run a paper chromatography test.

Inoculate all batches with a suitable commercial diacetyl-neutral LAB culture of *O. oeni* that meets all the wine chemistry criteria, making sure to follow the product's instructions on any rehydration protocol. Some LAB require to be rehydrated with nutrients, such as Acti-ML (Lallemand), specifically designed for rehydrating freeze-dried LAB.

Maintain temperature in the range 18–22 °C (64–72 °F) for the duration of the MLF.

MLF should start within a couple of days; you should see tiny CO_2 bubbles rising ever so slowly — you may need a flashlight to see this. Be sure to maintain absolutely sanitary conditions throughout the MLF period as the wine has no SO_2 and therefore no protection against spoilage microorganisms.

Once a week, gently stir the lees into suspension to favor a healthy MLF. Be sure to stir *very gently* to avoid oxygen uptake and affecting oxygen-sensitive LAB.

Run a paper chromatography test every week or at least every two weeks to monitor MLF progression. Do not rely strictly on bubbles; these can be misleading. Progress and completion can only be monitored with paper chromatography. MLF can take several weeks, perhaps months, to complete depending on wine chemistry and temperature. Be sure to run a test for each batch if the wine is in several vessels. Wines in different vessels may complete at different times, and therefore, you need to monitor MLF progress separately in each. This means that wines may move to the microbial stabilization step at different times.

When the test confirms complete conversion of malic acid, measure and record temperature, TA and pH, taste the wine for oak and tannins, aromas and flavors, and overall quality, and proceed with microbial stabilization. Repeat for all vessels.

TA helps you understand how acidity has changed during MLF while, here too, pH indicates microbial stability and how much SO_2 you need to add in the next step.

At this stage, you should not be making (or have to make) significant acidity changes. If the wine is not quite to your liking, perhaps it lacks a bit of acidity, you can make a small addition not exceeding 0.5 g/L using tartaric acid — do *not* use malic acid as that would likely trigger another MLF. Always conduct bench trials before treating an entire batch.

If acidity is too high, it is best not to deacidify at this stage as it can be very difficult to achieve the desired results. You may have more success dropping TA through cold stabilization. If you do make any acidity adjustments, re-measure TA to confirm your adjustment, but, more important, re-measure your pH as this may have changed. We will not consider adding sugar here as we are going for a totally dry style.

21.1.8 MICROBIAL STABILIZATION

If you had carried out the MLF in another warmer area, transfer all vessels *for which wines have completed MLF* to your cellar or cooler area. From here on, maintain wine at cellar temperature, ideally around 13 °C (55 °F).

Wait 10 days to 2 weeks after the end of the MLF before stabilizing with SO_2. This wait period is to allow for sufficient acetaldehyde bridging with tannins and anthocyanins, resulting in less astringency and more color stability. SO_2 would otherwise bind to acetaldehyde and interfere with that process, and require more KMS to be added.

21

As wines in different vessels may complete at different times, you will need to continue monitoring MLF progress until completion, then stabilize each after the wait period.

Re-measure temperature and pH, and using a molecular SO_2 (MSO2) of 0.2–0.5 mg/L (the fuller bodied the wine, the lower the MSO2 you can use), determine the required free SO_2 (FSO2) level using the SO2 CALCU-LATOR or Figure 8.4 in Section 8.2, and increase that amount by 50% if making a medium-bodied style or 100% if making a full-bodied style to account for binding, add the required amount of KMS, stir thoroughly, and place the stoppers and airlocks on again.

If you cannot measure pH, simply add ¼ teaspoon (about 1.5 g) KMS per 23-L (6-gal) carboy or ¾ teaspoon (about 4 g) KMS per 54-L (14-gal) demijohn.

At this point, it is also a good idea to measure % ABV and residual sugar (RS), if so equipped.

21.1.9 AGING

At this point, you have wine in inert vessels or, possibly, in barrels, and which you intend to age.

Medium- and full-bodied reds will greatly benefit from 12–18 months of aging, perhaps more, in oak barrels or in "breathable" HDPE tanks in conjunction with oak segments and at cool cellar temperature, ideally at around 13 °C (55 °F) and a relative humidity in the range 55–75% if in barrels. The long sojourn will provide for natural clarification and the cooler temperatures will allow for a very slow and graceful maturation as well as further tartrate stabilization.

First add cellaring/aging tannins comprising both grape tannins and el-lagitannins, such as Tan'Cor Grand Cru (Laffort) or Scott'TanTannin Complex (Scott Laboratories), at the recommended dosage rate for the product you are using to further stabilize color for the long aging period.

If aging in inert vessels, every 3 months and for *all vessels*, taste the wines, measure temperature, pH, FSO2 and DO, and adjust FSO2, as required.

Since there is no oxygen ingress in inert vessels as there is in barrels and therefore no acetaldehyde is being produced, you can optionally rack the wine every month to aerate it to hasten tannin–anthocyanin bridging by acetaldehyde to help stabilize color.

If aging in barrels or breathable HDPE tanks, every month and for *all barrels and HDPE tanks*, taste the wines, measure temperature, pH, FSO2 and DO, and adjust FSO2, as required, and top up barrels.

You should also measure TSO2 every 3 months in all vessels and barrels to understand binding in your wine. You will likely notice different binding patterns between barrels and HDPE tanks (equipped with oak segments) depending on the difference of oak extraction and oxygen consumption in each.

These short check intervals will help you identify early on any potential problems and to take preventive and corrective action if required.

Rack all vessels, barrels and tanks every 6–12 months, making sure to *rack each wine back into its barrel* to preserve the individuality of each barrel. You may get more or less sediment depending on your varietal and your winemaking process, and therefore, adjust your racking schedule accordingly also taking into account the expected aging period. Rack less frequently the longer you intend to age the wine. Racking every 3 months is not necessary and might in fact be excessive as great amounts of oxygen are absorbed, which, in turn, will require more frequent KMS replenishment to make up for consumed FSO2.

21.1.10 CLARIFICATION AND STABILIZATION

Depending on the extent of aging, varietal, wine chemistry and cellar temperature, your wine may be so clear that it might not necessarily need any fining or filtering; a simple final racking before bottling may be all that is needed.

If you want to further clarify your wine, you can fine with kieselsol and chitosan, or gelatin. If the wine is aging in barrels and you wish to "round out" tannins, you can fine with egg whites right in the barrels or,

21

alternatively, first rack to an inert vessel, then fine with your choice of fining agent.

When the wines taste to your liking with the right level of oak extraction, you can pull the oak segments out of inert vessels and rack wine out of barrels and into inert vessels.

At this point the wine is tartrate stable down to the lowest temperature at which you held the wine. If you were only able to hold the wine down to, for example, 15 °C (60 °F), and the wine has high acidity, consider a cold stabilization treatment, if possible, to reduce acidity and reduce the risk of tartrates forming later on.

If the wine has residual malic acid in excess of 100 mg/L, as evidenced by a visible spot from a chromatography test, you will need to add KMS and lysozyme (see Section 14.1.2) or sterile filter (see Section 17.3).

And there should be no issues with pectin or proteins, and therefore, no further processing is required.

If you intend to age the wine some more, be sure to take periodic measurements and adjust FSO2 as needed.

21.1.11 PREPARATION FOR BOTTLING AND BLENDING

In preparation for bottling, if your wine spans many inert vessels, first transfer all batches to a single holding tank or vessel to ensure homogeneity.

If your wine spans many oak barrels, you can expect variances among barrels. Taste each barrel, one by one, and assess quality based on aromas, flavors, mouthfeel, color and overall impressions. Rate each barrel according to quality to decide if you want to create different quality-based blends. For example, you can create one blend with wines from the highest-rated barrels and a second blend with wines from the second highest-rated barrels. Set aside any barrels that do not meet the highest standards; you can bottle those batches on their own or blend with similarly lower-quality batches for quick consumption. Then transfer batches into holding tanks or vessels according to your rating.

If you are considering blending other component wines, run bench trials to determine the proportions of each, then blend all wines into a single holding tank.

Taste and evaluate the final wine, what will be bottled, and make any final adjustments you wish. It's a good idea to measure key parameters of the blended wine at this point and make FSO2 adjustments, if needed. If you do blend, it is a good idea to re-measure % ABV and residual sugar (RS), if so equipped. Measuring RS of the varietal or blended wine is a precaution to ensure that the wine to be bottled is microbially stable and that a sorbate treatment is not required.

If you have blended batches, and particularly if you made tannin adjustments, wait at least two weeks to allow the component wines to integrate, then re-assess aromas, flavors, mouthfeel, color, and overall impressions again to make sure the wine to be bottled tastes as expected. You may need to rack it again if you added tannins.

21.1.12 FILTERING

At this point, your wine should be very clear and may not need filtering. If however you aged for a very short period and did not allow for anthocyanin–tannin complexes to precipitate and be racked off, the wine will be acceptably clear, but you can expect those complexes to stain bottles. It will make bottle cleaning quite the chore for reuse.

If you simply want to "clean up" the wine so that it does not drop sediment or stain glass, coarse filter using a 5-micron (nominal) cartridge or pads, for example, Buon Vino No. 1 pads. If you have to sterile filter for microbial stability, either because of residual sugar or malic acid, first filter again using a 2-micron (nominal) cartridge or pads, for example, Buon Vino No. 2 pads, with another pass recommended using a 1-micron (nominal) cartridge or pads, for example, Buon Vino No. 3 pads, then a final filter using a 0.45-micron (absolute) cartridge, ideally right into bottles.

It's wise to again measure temperature, pH, FSO2 and DO, and adjust FSO2, as required, to make sure everything is in order and especially if you don't intend to bottle immediately after filtering.

21

21.1.13 BOTTLING

When ready to bottle, measure pH, FSO2, TSO2 and DO one last time if there was any delay since preparative work or filtering, and adjust FSO2 based on pH, desired MSO2 and DO. You may want to bump up the FSO2 addition by 5–10 mg/L to account for oxygen uptake during bottling and bottle aging.

If you are set up and wanting to sterile filter and deliver wine directly into bottles, successively filter as described above in Section 21.1.12, with the final filtration at 0.45 micron (*absolute*) right into bottles.

You can start drinking the wine now but it will benefit from another 6–9 months or more of aging in bottles. Open and taste a bottle every so often, say every 3 to 6 months, to assess evolution, making sure to save sufficient bottles to gauge evolution over long periods of time — it's the best way to learn and to be able to feed those learnings back into your winemaking.

LOG CHART — CONTROL CHECKPOINTS: RED WINE

Highlighted boxes represent those measurements you should be making and recording at the various checkpoints as described in the protocol outlined in Section 21.1.

Create a *separate log sheet for each batch*, and definitely separate sheets for free- and press-run wines, if the wine spans more than one vessel.

LOG CHART — CONTROL CHECKPOINTS: RED WINE

Date	CHECKPOINT	Volume (L or gal)	Temp. (°C/°F)	SG / BRIX	Temp-adjusted SG / BRIX	PA or Actual % ABV	TA (g/L)	pH	FSO2 (mg/L)	TSO2 (mg/L)	DO (mg/L)	YAN (mg N/L)	RS (g/L)	MLF Check
	MUST ANALYSIS													
	COLD SOAK													
	ALCOHOLIC FERMENTATION													
	FIRST RACKING													
	MALOLACTIC FERMENTATION													
	MICROBIAL STABILIZATION													
	AGING													
	CLARIFICATION AND STABILIZATION													
	PREPARATION FOR BOTTLING													
	BLENDING													
	FILTERING													
	BOTTLING													

21

REFERENCE

1. Pambianchi, D. 2008. *Techniques in Home Winemaking: A Practical Guide to Making Château-Style Wines.* Newly-Revised and Expanded. Véhicule Press, Montréal (Québec).

22 Troubleshooting and Fixing Common Faults and Flaws

Making wine is relatively easy but making *great* wine is a perpetual challenge because the raw material is often not balanced and winemakers must therefore make important decisions on how best to make adjustments and ensure success.

In spite of all the care and caution, things can — and will — go wrong, even for the most seasoned winemaker. Experience is key here, but a winemaker is only as good as his/her ability to resolve a problem. Faults and flaws happen, and you must be able to identify them, assess them, and take corrective actions. This entails first carrying out a root-case analysis to evaluate possible causes; never jump to unfounded conclusions. The challenge is in recognizing faults and flaws, and this depends on your experience and detection threshold. We all have different thresholds on detecting, for example, volatile acidity (VA), and therefore, training will be important as well as asking other winemakers or wine enthusiasts for their opinions. And always look beyond what you see when trying to identify root causes — leaky corks may not necessarily point to a cork problem, but perhaps to a bottle refermentation issue.

Jamie Goode, in *Flawless: Understanding Faults in Wine*, uses two terms to describe defects: faults and taints [1]. Faults refer to defects resulting from the fermentation process, though this should be understood to mean the winemaking process. Oxidation, volatile acidity (VA) and *Brettanomyces* are examples of faults. Taints refer to defects resulting from an extraneous flavor chemical or some external factor, such as cork taint. Here we make no distinction, as Goode goes on to discuss faults and taints as one, as both are defects. However, a flaw is considered less serious than a fault, and may become a fault if left uncontrolled and cause a wine to be rejected. For example, tartrates are considered a flaw as they do not adversely affect the taste of wine, whereas VA was said to be fault because it would cause the wine to be rejected outright.

22

This chapter describes twelve of the most common defects, and how to resolve them confidently and expertly, where possible, towards salvaging a problem batch of wine.

For dealing with a stuck or sluggish alcoholic fermentation (AF), or stuck or sluggish malolactic fermentation (MLF), refer to Sections 11.5 and 12.6, respectively.

22.1 PREMATURE OXIDATION

DESCRIPTION

Oxidation occurs in every wine, ever so slowly during the winemaking process and aging, including bottle aging, but it should not occur prematurely or unexpectedly in young wines, either in bulk or bottled.

Premature oxidation is a condition of uncharacteristic early browning of wine and smell of acetaldehyde (bruised apple) and nutty aromas and flavors, which mute other desirable aromas.

CAUSES

Reference Sections: 8.1–8.4

Premature oxidation is the result of chemical oxidation of polyphenols and ethanol due to prolonged exposure to oxygen with very low or no sulfur dioxide (SO_2) protection. This is usually a result of poor oxygen and SO_2 management, most often due to leaving too much headspace in carboys or other vessels, or excessive processing in the absence of SO_2 protection. In bottled wine, it can also result from the use of poor closures with high oxygen transfer rates (OTR).

Aging and storage temperatures are also important factors as warmer temperatures accelerate oxidation reactions.

This fault is often accompanied by volatile acidity (VA), described below in Section 22.2, and possibly by a whitish surface film, described in Section 22.3.

ASSESSMENT

A wine affected by premature oxidation will have a very distinctive smell of bruised apple from acetaldehyde, a sure sign that free SO_2 (FSO2) has been depleted. If you are able to measure FSO2, confirm to what extent free SO_2 has been used up — in all likelihood, it is below the critical 10 mg/L threshold, or possibly completely depleted.

Acetaldehyde is easily detected given its very low detection threshold, in the 500 µg/L (that's parts per billion, or ppb) range. Once detectable, wine quality is seriously compromised and remedial actions can make the wine drinkable, maybe, or it may have to be discarded depending on the severity. Unfortunately, there is no simple analytical tool for home wine-makers to monitor acetaldehyde concentration; you will need to rely on your nose.

Whites affected by premature oxidation will exhibit a dark or brownish color.

In reds, you will need to assess the wine in a glass; tilt the glass and look for an orange, brownish hue at the rim. It can be very difficult, if not impossible, to fix an oxidation problem in a red wine; it is best left alone.

If a whitish film has formed on the surface of the wine, you have advanced oxidation and a surface yeast problem; refer to Section 22.3.

REMEDIAL ACTIONS

If you detect acetaldehyde, add potassium metabisulfite (KMS) immediately to bind the acetaldehyde to make it non-volatile. Add KMS to the recommended FSO2 level based on pH. Then taste the wine again, and if you still smell the acetaldehyde, try adding 50% of the amount of FSO2 just added, then repeat another time if the smell persists. For example, if you first added 50 mg/L FSO2, try adding another 25 mg/L and another 25 mg/L. At this point, you would have added twice the recommended FSO2 level; if you can still smell the acetaldehyde, your wine is likely beyond fixing and is best discarded.

For whites affected by limited oxidation and showing a darkish yellow color with light-brown hues, first treat with casein at a rate based on bench

22

trials, then treat with bentonite to assist in settling the casein. If your bench trials conclude that casein strips out too much aromas, try using PVPP instead. You can also try specially formulated casein–bentonite preparations, such as Bentolact S (IOC – Institut Œnologique de Champagne). Refer to Section 13.4 for fining agent dosages.

Following a successful treatment to an acceptable color without excessive loss of aromas and flavors, add specific inactivated yeast with high antioxidant properties containing polysaccharides and/or glutathione (GSH), such as OptiMUM White or Glutastar (Lallemand), to protect against further oxidation.

If a white wine is affected by advanced oxidation and has a dark-brown color, it is likely not salvageable. As an absolute last resort only and when other treatments have not been effective, you can try removing some of the brown color using activated carbon. Perform bench trials first to make sure the treatment produces acceptable results. Add the activated carbon powder directly to the wine and stir thoroughly; never add more than the maximum because it will strip color excessively and leave an off carbon-like flavor. Add bentonite at the maximum rate of 1 g/L immediately after the activated carbon treatment, rack after a few days, and filter the wine before bottling.

If you have managed to cure the wine, be sure to top up whichever carboy or vessel it was in.

PREVENTIVE ACTIONS

To prevent premature oxidation, avoid prolonged oxygen exposure during processing and particularly during storage and aging. Top up carboys and barrels with the same or similar wine making sure to top up barrels regularly — at least once a month — due to evaporative losses. Although you can use inert gas or create a vacuum to protect wine in partial carboys or tanks — but not in barrels — this is only a short-term strategy; it's always best to top up.

Maintain adequate FSO2 levels based on pH and molecular SO_2 (MSO2) for the type of wine. *Never* allow FSO2 to fall below 10 mg/L.

For whites and rosés, minimize the amount of phenols extracted during processing and perform a preventive addition of PVPP when fining, and store at cool temperature, ideally around 13 °C (55 °F).

Invest in a dissolved oxygen (DO) meter and make DO monitoring a regular task of your quality control protocol. By monitoring DO (at the same time as pH and FSO2), you will be able to detect a potential problem before acetaldehyde develops to detection threshold levels. You may have a defective bung on a carboy but you may never know that without knowledge of both FSO2 and DO measurements.

For wines that may be more fragile and prone to oxidation, or if you want to reduce the use of sulfite, consider other antioxidants and techniques, such as the use of tannins, glutathione, specific inactivated yeast (SIY), mannoproteins or aging on the lees. There is a vast selection of products specifically designed as preventive against oxidation in white and rosé wines.

22.2 VOLATILE ACIDITY (VA)

DESCRIPTION

Volatile acidity (VA) in wine is due primarily to one acid, acetic acid, which imparts a distinctive vinegar-like smell. It is most often accompanied by another volatile substance, ethyl acetate, which confers a smell of nail polish remover and imparts a particularly hot sensation on the tongue.

All wines have a little VA; it adds organoleptic complexity. Wines produced from late-harvest or botrytized grapes will have higher levels as shriveled or (good) moldy grapes will produce VA within affected berries on the vines.

VA magnifies the taste of fixed acids and tannins but, itself, is masked by high levels of sugar and alcohol.

Acetic acid detection threshold is around 600–700 mg/L, depending on the type of wine and a taster's sensitivity, and becomes defective as it approaches 1200 mg/L; wine is considered spoiled at 2000 mg/L. Ethyl acetate detection threshold is in the 150–200 mg/L range. The significance of these

22

detection thresholds is that they are fairly high, meaning once detected, wine contains large amounts of acetic acid and ethyl acetate, and is perhaps beyond repair. Unfortunately, here too there are no simple analytical tools for home winemakers to monitor VA and ethyl acetate.

Reference Section: 7.2

Acetic acid and VA are the result of ethanol oxidation by acetic acid bacteria, which thrive in the present of oxygen (air), hence why this fault is common in wines in poorly topped up carboys, tanks, and particularly barrels. Acetaldehyde is an intermediate of ethanol oxidation, and therefore, if you detect acetaldehyde, you likely have an imminent VA problem. Ethyl acetate is due to esterification of acetic acid. Esterification is a chemical reaction between alcohol and an acid — ethanol and acetic acid here — to form an ester, a volatile substance.

VA is a common problem in poorly managed wines aging in barrels. Due to evaporative losses in barrels, a headspace is created above the wine volume. Although the headspace is a vacuum, it is not a perfect vacuum and still has some oxygen, making it a good breeding ground for acetic acid bacteria. VA in barreled wines will creep up a little, this is normal, but it should never be excessive or detectable by smell — never.

VA is also a small by-product of AF, and therefore, expect VA to increase a little from juice to wine, but again, it should not be detectable by smell; if it does, then the wine was affected by acetic acid bacteria during AF. Yeast produces more VA during a stressful AF, for example, when the AF is conducted at very low or excessively high temperatures, or when nutrients have been depleted.

VA can also result from the degradation of citric acid by lactic acid bacteria during MLF, or from a spoilage reaction involving indigenous lactic acid bacteria. Small inconsequential amounts of citric acid occur naturally in grape juice, but because of the spoilage risks, never add citric acid to acidify wines that will go through MLF. If citric acid is metabolized into acetic acid, it will also produce excessive amounts of diacetyl, a substance that imparts a buttery aroma.

And if you manage your own vineyard, beware of fruit flies; they can cause a disease known as sour rot, which shrivels grape berries causing whole bunches to turn brown and ooze with a distinct vinegar smell due to acetic acid being formed.

ASSESSMENT

Home winemakers are not equipped to measure VA or ethyl acetate, and therefore, you need to rely on your ability to smell and detect these. If you do detect VA or ethyl acetate, you may want to send a sample to a certified lab for evaluation to give you a sense of how big a problem you have.

REMEDIAL ACTIONS

VA is impossible to remove except by reverse osmosis — it involves equipment outside the domain (and budget) of home winemaking.

If the wine is objectionable, discard it — there is no sense in keeping VA-affected wine in your winemaking area as it is a source of further contamination. And it is never a good idea to blend a faulty wine with a perfectly good wine.

If you detect acetaldehyde, it is a sign of imminent VA spoilage; sulfite immediately to bind the acetaldehyde, as per instructions in Section 22.1.

If high levels of VA are detected in a barrel, discard the barrel too. Yes, it hurts, but it is very difficult to eradicate acetic acid bacteria from a barrel, and you will simply be infecting any wine you transfer into that barrel. If VA is only slightly detectable, there is hope in salvaging the barrel. Fill the barrel with a 300 mg/L SO_2 (about 500 mg/L KMS) solution and let soak for two days to extract VA out of the wood. Empty the barrel out and rinse abundantly with water, then smell the barrel. If there is any hint of VA, it is best to discard the barrel.

PREVENTIVE ACTIONS

To avoid VA infections and spoilage:

1. Reject damaged or rot-affected fruit.

22

2. Use a low-VA producing yeast; consult the yeast manufacturer's specifications — they will usually include a qualitative descriptor of how much VA (e.g., low, medium, high) a yeast produces.

3. Avoid prolonged oxygen exposure, top up carboys, tanks and barrels.

4. Maintain adequate FSO2 levels based on pH, MSO2 and DO.

5. Do not store wine above 15 °C (60 °F), at least not for extended aging.

Fungi-derived chitosan is another option to prevent VA problems, particularly when working with high-pH wines. Chitosan works by reducing the population of acetic acid bacteria, which therefore also reduces the need for SO_2. Bactiless (Lallemand), BactiControl (Laffort) and Enartis-Stab Micro (Enartis/Esseco) are examples of commercial chitosan products used for preventive microbial control.

22.3 WHITE SURFACE FILM

DESCRIPTION

A whitish film on the surface of wine is the result of surface spoilage yeast that thrive because of the presence of oxygen. The condition is often referred to as mycoderma, named after the most common of these aerobic surface yeasts, *Candida mycoderma*. It is most commonly seen in seemingly forgotten wines aging in poorly topped up barrels.

This condition always results in some oxidation and increase in VA although there may not be any perceptible organoleptic flaws if caught early.

CAUSES

Reference Sections: *14.1 and 15.4*

Surface spoilage yeast needs oxygen to grow and develop. It starts off by forming a small islet that grows and is able to do so even in the presence of SO_2, and therefore, this clearly points to an oxygen ingress problem, typically because of poor topping in barrels or a defective bung or airlock in barrels or carboys.

ASSESSMENT

Any surface film points to the presence of excessive oxygen and surface spoilage yeast activity. The cause is readily obvious in barreled wines that have not been topped up properly or stored above 15 °C (60 °F). Remember that a barrel acts an oxygen-transfer system and, although the headspace is largely a vacuum, there is sufficient oxygen for aerobic spoilage yeasts (and bacteria) to start their destructive effects.

As you assess the problem, do *not* disturb the film; the film will otherwise break up and disperse on the entire surface and possibly drop into the wine.

Perform a visual examination of both the bung or seal and airlock to see if there are any obvious defects that would allow air to enter into the vessel.

Certain kinds of bungs tend to lose their form or elasticity and not form a proper seal when seated in a carboy.

S-style airlocks too can be a source of air infiltration. These airlocks have a seam that can split open ever so slightly, invisible to the eye, and let air in from below the liquid level in the airlock. It happens. You can test the integrity of the (empty) airlock by blowing into one end and blocking the other with a finger. If you are able to keep blowing or if you feel some air through the seam, then you have a defective airlock. Another problem is the extra plastic material protruding from the seam, which, when inserted into a bung, creates a small air gap into the carboy (see Section 3.3).

If you are using dry airlocks, verify that they work properly. If you blow from the bottom end of a dry airlock, it should vent properly at the other end, but once you blow from the other end at the top, the airlock should provide an absolutely tight seal. Marble-type airlocks on variable-capacity tanks (VCTs) are notorious for letting air in; it is best to change those with better airlocks.

22

Also assess for potential oxidation and VA problems as described in Sections 22.1 and 22.2, respectively.

REMEDIAL ACTIONS

As a short-term solution, if the surface film is high in the neck of a full carboy, which definitely points to a defective bung or airlock, try and remove the film by gently inserting a paper towel and giving it a gentle twist to scoop up as much film as possible. Be gentle as it is very easy to break up the film and cause it to spread further into the wine. You can also try sucking the film up with a kitchen baster although this may prove more difficult.

The best technique though is the "overflow" or "flooding" method. If you are able to insert a small tube into the wine without disturbing the film too much, add wine via the tube into the carboy until the film overflows and floats out. Wrap the top of the carboy with paper towels to avoid making a mess.

Use the same overflow technique for film in barrels as you will not be able to scoop it out given the large surface area and headspace. With a baster or wine thief, remove wine to bring it down to a level where you can properly insert a bung. If still using an airlock, make sure that it is not defective and sand off the excess plastic material on the seam to a smooth finish to avoid creating that air gap into vessels.

Since this technique never completely removes all the surface film, no matter how careful you are, the recommended longer-term solution is to gently insert a racking cane to just above the sediment, if any, and transfer the wine to another vessel being careful not to transfer film particles as the surface of the wine approaches the bottom. As it has surface tension characteristics, most film will cling to the wall of the vessel as the wine surface drops. Stop the transfer when you see film particles approaching the racking tube inlet; discard the leftover wine.

A coarse filtration in conjunction with the above techniques helps separate excess film if you were not able to remove it effectively and particularly if some dropped back into the wine. Remove as much film as possible to avoid carrying it through.

Measure FSO2 to see if there was any significant depletion, and make any necessary adjustments according to pH and perhaps an additional 10–15 mg/L to deal with DO.

If you detect oxidation or VA problems, refer to Section 22.1 or 22.2, respectively, for further remedial actions.

PREVENTIVE ACTIONS

Always keep vessels, and especially barrels, ideally at around 13 °C (55 °F), never exceeding 20 °C (68 °F), completely full and topped up, and wines at the proper FSO2 level according to pH. Make sure bungs are inserted as tight as possible. Aerobic spoilage yeast cannot thrive in the absence of oxygen.

Sand off to a smooth finish the extra plastic material at the seam on new airlocks. Visually inspect bungs, seals and airlocks before use.

22.4 HYDROGEN SULFIDE (H_2S)

DESCRIPTION

Hydrogen sulfide (H_2S) is the most common of a very broad class of volatile sulfur compounds, or VSCs, or mercaptans. It is the reduced form of sulfur — "reduced" means the opposite of oxidized — hence why it is said to impart a reductive character in certain cases where it might be expected, for example, in wine bottled under screw cap, which allows H_2S to manifest itself due to the low-oxygen environment.

H_2S imparts a familiar smell of rotten eggs, perhaps even sewage, cooked cabbage, struck flint or rubber. It can be detected at levels as low as 1 μg/L (ppb).

CAUSES

Reference Sections: 11.2–11.4

There can be various causes for H_2S in wine. It can be due to low nitrogen supply during the AF, wine aging on the gross lees for too long, or from

22

metabolism of such substances as sulfur-containing amino acids, inorganic sulfur, SO_2 and sulfate.

Yeast cells can become overly stressed and produce excessive amounts of H_2S if the amount of nitrogen found in nutrients needed for a healthy fermentation is too low or also too high, or if fermentation temperature is too low or too high. It can occur if juice is highly turbid (see Section 22.6) with a large amount of soluble solids, and therefore, as red winemaking involves maceration of wine with grape solids, H_2S is a much more common occurrence in red wines.

But the most common cause of H_2S in home winemaking is the degradation of sulfur-containing compounds from autolysis when wine is left too long on the gross lees.

The presence and concentration of naturally occurring or yeast-derived sulfur-containing amino acids in the juice is another significant source of H_2S. During yeast fermentation, yeast cells generate sulfur to synthesize sulfur-containing amino acids as part of their sulfur metabolism; however, if these amino acids cannot be synthesized, sulfur can turn into sulfides.

Other causes include: the degradation by yeast of inorganic sulfate from elemental sulfur from the overuse of sulfur-based vineyard sprays to control mildew; a harvest that was too close to spraying; and from spent wicks accidentally dropped at the bottom of barrels during sulfuring [2].

H_2S can also result from the excessive use of SO_2 and sulfate from exogenous additions of KMS and copper sulfate ($CuSO_4$), respectively.

During AF, yeast produces small amounts of H_2S (as well as SO_2), but because of its volatility, much of that H_2S produced early in winemaking is lost through entrainment in carbon dioxide (CO_2). And different yeast strains produce different amounts of H_2S and SO_2, the latter becoming a substrate for H_2S production.

And in a lesser-known cause, H_2S and other sulfides that had become bound — and therefore non-volatile — can become released during aging. This factor can be particularly problematic as it may resurface well after an initial problem with H_2S had been resolved.

If there is excessive H_2S or if left untreated, H_2S can react with ethanol to form ethanethiol, another VSC and which imparts a smell of raw onions, rubber or natural gas, or a skunk smell. Ethanethiol can then become esterified to the sulfurous-smelling ethyl thioacetate or oxidized into diethyl disulfide, two compounds that impart unpleasant odors of onions. These compounds are easier to smell and detect but can be almost impossible to remove.

ASSESSMENT

There are no tools to quantify H_2S in home winemaking, and therefore, you must rely on your sense of smell. H_2S smells of rotten eggs or burnt rubber; it should never be detectable in sound wine.

REMEDIAL ACTIONS

Very mild cases of H_2S can be treated through volatilization by sparging the wine with inert gas, e.g., nitrogen, or, for *red wine only*, by aerating via, for example, a vigorous racking. Affected white and rosé wines should not be aerated, or you'll risk oxidizing the wines.

For more serious cases, treat with a 1% $CuSO_4$ solution. Run bench trials *first* to determine how much $CuSO_4$ is needed to treat the entire batch. High doses of residual copper can become a source of oxidation problems and, more important, pose a health hazard. Treated wine will form a copper sulfide (CuS) precipitate; rack and filter in one week.

Some amateurs resort to the use of copper piping for treating H_2S because of its simplicity. This practice is *not recommended* — it is in fact very dangerous as the amount of copper transferred into the wine cannot be controlled and easily becomes excessive and toxic. For reference, legal limits in commercial wines are typically in the 0.2–1 mg/L range, 1.0 mg/L in the United States.

As copper can possibly react with other VSCs, the copper sulfate treatment should be weighed against the likelihood of reducing desirable volatile thiol aromas in, for example, Sauvignon Blanc and Chenin Blanc. Copper is non-selective on thiols — in addition to reacting with other volatile thiols, it can react with non-VSCs, such as the naturally occurring antioxidant glutathione (GSH), and the wine could become more prone to spoilage.

22

For bench trials and to treat the affected batch, use a commercially available 1% $CuSO_4$ solution, such as Sulfidex (Vintner), or make one by dissolving precisely one gram of cupric sulfate pentahydrate ($CuSO_4 \cdot 5H_2O$) crystals in approximately 75 mL of distilled water in a 100-mL volumetric flask or good 100-mL graduated cylinder, then bring to volume with more distilled water.

There are excellent alternative commercial products for treating H_2S. Reduless (Lallemand) comprises inactivated yeast with "biologically bound copper" and some bentonite [3], and Kupzit (Erbslöh), a relatively new product that uses copper citrate to remove H_2S; it too contains bentonite.

Following are instructions on how to run proper bench trials and to treat a batch using a 1% $CuSO_4$ solution.

1. Label two wine glasses, one as *control* and one as *copper*. Pour 50 mL of the affected wine into each glass. With a 1-mL pipette or syringe, transfer one drop of 1% $CuSO_4$ solution into the *copper* glass. Swirl each glass, let them stand for about five minutes, then smell each, but do not taste. If the *copper* glass still has the stinky smell, no safe amounts of $CuSO_4$ can eliminate the H_2S smell. The single drop represents roughly 1 mg/L of copper, and therefore just at the acceptable limit used in many winemaking regions of the world.

   If the single drop does neutralize the smell, continue the trial to determine how much $CuSO_4$ you need to treat your entire batch. Here, 1 L (¼ gal) of wine in a 1000-mL graduated cylinder works best.

2. Transfer a single drop of $CuSO_4$ solution into the wine in the 1000-mL graduated cylinder. Each drop in 1000 mL of wine is now about 0.05 mg/L of copper. Stir the wine to thoroughly dissolve the $CuSO_4$. Pour some wine into the *copper* glass (not in the *control* glass), swirl both the *control* and *copper* glasses, let stand for about five minutes, then smell each.

   If the smell of H_2S persists, return the sample from the *copper* glass back to the graduated cylinder (you don't want to change your 1000-mL reference volume), add another drop of $CuSO_4$ solution, and repeat the process until the H_2S smell disappears, *without exceeding 20 drops* to stay within the safe maximum of 1 mg/L.

3. Once the smell is neutralized, scale up the volume used in the 1-mL pipette or syringe for the entire batch. For example, if you used 0.1 mL to rid of the H_2S smell in the 1000-mL sample and you need to treat a 23-L (6-gal) batch, then you need to add 0.1 × 23 or 2.3 mL of 1% $CuSO_4$ solution.

4. Once the batch is treated, let settle for one week, then rack and coarse filter to remove the black powder-like copper sulfide precipitate. Complete removal of copper sulfide by racking or filtration may not always be possible.

PREVENTIVE ACTIONS

There are many preventive actions to mitigate the possibility of H_2S forming in wine:

1. Don't harvest too close to vineyard spraying.

2. Add complex nitrogen-containing nutrients to must prior to inoculating for AF and add more complex nutrients when SG/Brix has dropped by one-third.

3. Avoid yeast strains (e.g., Red Star Premier Classique, formerly Montrachet) known to produce large amounts of H_2S, or consider using a so-called "H2S-preventing" yeast (e.g., Renaissance).

4. Avoid stressing yeast by, for example, ameliorating high-SG/Brix juice, and fermenting at recommended temperatures.

5. Go easy with KMS prior to or during AF.

6. Aerate reds during AF; rack wine off the gross lees within 2 days or 3 maximum of completion of AF.

7. Be careful not to spill burning sulfur wicks in barrels during sulfuring.

22

22.5 TARTRATES

DESCRIPTION

Tartrates are potassium bitartrate crystals (also known as cream of tartar), the result of tartaric acid and potassium interacting in wine and precipitating when subjected to cold temperatures. Often referred to as wine diamonds, tartrates are considered by some wine connoisseurs as a sign of good winemaking — it is not!

The crystals look like little tiny shards of broken glass and which precipitate to the bottom of the bottle — some might stick to the side of carboys and tanks — or stick to the exposed surface of the cork in bottles stored horizontally. A small amount is usually acceptable in reds, but an unsightly distraction in whites and rosés, particularly if poured into the glass during service. The problem is only visual with the odor and flavor of the wine unaffected. If you discover tartrate crystals in a long-cellared bottle of red wine, you can decant it through a small stainless steel strainer to avoid unsightly crystals in the wine you pour for guests.

CAUSES

Reference Sections: *7.4.1 and 14.4*

Tartrates are due to no or incomplete cold stabilization. The extent of crystal formation depends primarily on the cold stabilization temperature, and tartaric acid and potassium concentrations, and to a smaller extent on the amounts of ethanol, polyphenols, proteins and polysaccharides.

ASSESSMENT

Making a definitive assessment on tartrate stability is tricky, and definitely not an exact science. And the only practical method for home winemakers is a fridge test, as outlined in Section 14.4.1.

If a fridge test is positive, you will need to cold stabilize the batch or add a protective colloid.

If crystals formed in the bottle, you will need to treat the wine to stabilize against tartrates.

REMEDIAL ACTIONS

If the fridge test is positive, cold stabilize the batch or add a protective colloid, either metatartaric acid, carboxymethyl cellulose in conjunction with some gum arabic, or polyaspartate.

If crystals formed in the bottle, pour all bottles back into a carboy or suitable vessel, then cold stabilize the batch or add a protective colloid, and re-bottle the wine.

PREVENTIVE ACTIONS

To prevent tartrates in bottles, perform a fridge test and cold stabilize if positive, or add a protective colloid. This stabilization procedure should be performed after any fining procedure to ensure that the addition of a fining agent after cold stabilization does not alter that stability.

Cold stabilize at the coldest temperature possible within the recommended range.

There are three important points worth repeating here to minimize the risk of tartrates forming in bottles:

1. The warmer the cold stabilization temperature, the longer you have to allow for tartrates to form and precipitate.

2. Wine is only tartrate stable to the coldest temperature at which it was stabilized.

3. Do *not* add anything (e.g., bentonite) or perform adjustments (e.g., acidification with tartaric acid) *after* cold stabilization.

22.6 WINE NOT CLEARING OR HAS BECOME CLOUDY

DESCRIPTION

It is not an uncommon occurrence that a previously crystal-clear wine unexpectedly becomes cloudy, or that, in spite of clarification treatments, a wine remains cloudy or causes filtration problems.

22

CAUSES

Reference Sections: 14.2 and 14.3

There are two main sources of persistent cloudiness or clarification problems in wines: pectin and proteins.

Residual post-fermentation pectin can cause poor sedimentation or clarification problems in wines made from high-pectin grape varieties, usually Native American varieties and hybrids, which have not been sufficiently treated with pectinases. These varieties are also more prone to pectin-related problems given their typically higher acidity, which causes pectin to become less stable and to break up into smaller compounds. Pectin is not an issue in viniferas as it is completely broken down during fermentation.

Proteins can cause white or rosé wine to remain cloudy in spite of attempts at clarifying, or cause a previously crystal-clear wine to unexpectedly become cloudy even at room temperature, but more so at warmer temperatures. It occurs in wines which were insufficiently treated; Sauvignon Blanc and Gewürztraminer are examples of wines which are typically high in proteins and therefore at greater risk of protein instability. Proteins are not an issue in reds because they bind to and precipitate with tannins. But in whites and rosés where there are hardly any tannins, proteins must be removed using a suitable fining agent.

ASSESSMENT

First determine if it is a pectin or protein instability by performing a pectin or protein test on samples.

Test for pectin (see Section 14.2.1): if pectin becomes hydrolyzed and the wine sample remains clear, it is then considered pectin stable; if pectin flocculates, a pectinase treatment is required.

Test for proteins (see Section 14.3.1): if the sample becomes cloudy, the wine is not protein-stable and must be treated. Perform bench trials to determine the minimum amount of fining agent needed to obtain a sample that remains clear after heating.

REMEDIAL ACTIONS

To treat sedimentation or clarification problems due to pectin, add pectinase to the problem wine, let settle, then rack and filter. Be sure to use an appropriate product that is effective in wine, not just juice, and follow the product instructions as doses may need to be increased in wine compared to those in juice (see Section 10.1.1).

To remedy a cloudy condition due to proteins, treat with bentonite or silica–gel (e.g., kieselsol/gelatin), let settle, then rack and filter.

PREVENTIVE ACTIONS

To prevent pectin problems, treat the must with pectinases, using higher doses for known high-pectin varieties.

To prevent a protein haze, perform a heat stability test on wine and treat with bentonite or silica–gel as needed.

22.7 REFERMENTATION IN BOTTLES

DESCRIPTION

A previously still wine — that is, wine that had no perceptible fizz on the palate — now tastes slightly fizzy or even carbonated, and there may be visible sediment. In the worst case, corks can pop or bottles explode due to pressure build-up. The powdery sediment is often mistaken for tartrates by those not familiar with tartrates — the latter are crystals, not powder-like.

CAUSES

Reference Sections: *6.5, 11.4 and 14.1.1*

This problem is due to refermentation in bottles; this happens when the wine has not fermented to complete dryness, i.e., there is an appreciable amount of residual fermentable sugars, and which has not been properly stabilized. This is a common occurrence in sweetened wines, or with novice winemakers rushing to bottle wine but not understanding the implications

22

of residual sugar and incomplete or improper stabilization. Unless wine is sterile filtered at 0.45 micron (absolute) to remove yeast and bacteria that may cause refermentation or other unwanted reactions, these microorganisms are always present — or should be assumed to be always present — and waiting for an opportune moment to strike if conditions are good, for example, if there is residual sugar.

ASSESSMENT

Do a visual inspection followed by a taste test.

If you suspect that wine has started refermenting in bottles, look for any visible *fine* sediment — these are the fine lees that form during AF — making sure not to confuse these with tartrates, which are bigger and more shiny having a crystal-like appearance. Hold the bottle by the neck and turn it upside down; if the lees make the wine cloudy, it is a sure sign of refermentation. Open the bottle and taste the wine; if it tastes fizzy, then it is definitely a refermentation problem.

REMEDIAL ACTIONS

To avoid corks popping out or bottles exploding, uncork all bottles and pour the wine back into a carboy or appropriate holding vessel, let the wine complete AF to dryness, i.e., SG below 0.995 (Brix below −1.5), fine with a fining agent, stabilize with KMS, optionally filter, and re-bottle.

If you have no means of measuring the amount of residual sugar (RS), add sulfite *and* sorbate before re-bottling. If you can measure RS, add sulfite *and* sorbate if RS is greater than 2 g/L; if RS is less than 2 g/L, you only need to add KMS but sorbate is recommended as a safeguard.

Sorbate cannot be used to stop an active AF; you must stop AF or let it complete before adding sorbate.

Never use sorbate in wine that has undergone MLF; lactic acid bacteria can metabolize sorbic acid and cause a series of reactions resulting in an off-putting geranium odor.

PREVENTIVE ACTIONS

To avoid refermentation problems, always ferment to dryness to a SG below 0.995 (Brix below −1.5). At SG 0.995 (−1.5 Brix), wine can still have up to 7–8 g/L or more of residual sugar, sufficient for yeast to happily restart fermentation when conditions improve, primarily when FSO2 decreases, especially if temperature increases.

If you can measure RS and it is greater than 2 g/L or if SG is 0.995 or greater (Brix greater than −1.5), add KMS *and* sorbate; if RS is less than 2 g/L, only KMS is needed but sorbate is recommended as a safeguard. In all cases, sterile filter the wine down to 0.45 micron (absolute), if so equipped, to reduce yeast and bacterium populations to insignificant levels.

22.8 POOR OR LIGHT COLOR IN REDS

DESCRIPTION

Red wine, even previously deeply colored, exhibits a very light color and subdued intensity.

CAUSES

Reference Section: 9.1

If the (red) wine was already light-colored since the completion of fermentation, then there was insufficient extraction of anthocyanins during maceration and fermentation, or there was an anthocyanin deficiency due to a poor vintage, e.g., a rainy growing season.

If there was good color extraction but the wine is unexpectedly shedding color, then color was not adequately stabilized during maceration and fermentation.

Red wines also normally shed color during aging, but much more so if there is an anthocyanin–tannin imbalance. Anthocyanins are very unstable molecules and need to polymerize with tannins to become stable and exhibit their red color. If there is a large amount of anthocyanins, i.e., the

22

wine has a deep-red color, but very little tannins, anthocyanins precipitate and wine loses some color.

Anthocyanins are also sensitive to pH; they exhibit a redder color at low pH and lose their red color as pH increases towards and beyond 4.0 — anthocyanins start becoming almost colorless. The difference in color due to pH is often very visible between free- and press-run fractions; the latter often has a higher pH due to a higher potassium content.

Blind, excessive sulfite additions too will bleach anthocyanins due to the high binding attraction between anthocyanins and SO_2.

ASSESSMENT

Color is assessed by visual inspection, naturally, but you can also taste the wine to assess its tannin profile. If the wine is richly colored but tastes unusually light and seems to lack body (due to low tannins), then the wine has an anthocyanin–tannin imbalance and is at risk of shedding some of its color during aging.

REMEDIAL ACTIONS

A simple way to restore the red color is to increase acidity, for example, by adding tartaric acid, if the wine's acidity profile and tartrate stability status allow it; you do not want to create a taste imbalance or stability problem just to fix color. By acidifying, you are in effect lowering pH, and that causes anthocyanins to change from their more colorless form to their redder form.

Another simple way is to add cellaring tannins, particularly when there is a deficiency. Tannins stabilize color by polymerizing with anthocyanins.

If you are dealing with a variety or a poor harvest that have yielded poor color in spite of all extraction efforts, you can add exogenous anthocyanins, ideally to the must but it can also be added to wine. Commercial exogenous anthocyanins are natural dye obtained from skin extraction of red grape berries, but such products may prove to be very difficult to find.

PREVENTIVE ACTIONS

Richly colored red varietals that have had limited tannin extraction or hybrids with high protein content (which will precipitate larger amounts of essential tannins) will need an extra dose of tannins at crush and during fermentation to balance anthocyanins and stabilize color.

Before bottling, you can also add gum arabic — a protective colloid — to prevent flocculation of anthocyanins and anthocyanin complexes in *young* red wines meant for early consumption. It is not recommended for wines destined for aging as desirable polyphenol reactions would be inhibited; the wine can then take on a milky appearance that can affect its normal clarity [4].

Following are techniques to increase color extraction and improve color stability:

1. Destem grapes at crush; potassium-rich stems increase pH.

2. Run off approximately 10% of juice at crush to increase the skin-to-juice ratio to improve color in low-anthocyanin varieties, such as Pinot Noir and St. Croix.

3. Use macerating enzymes at crush.

4. Add sacrificial grape or oak tannins at crush, and do a second tannin addition to lock in color when it has peaked.

5. Consider doing a pre-ferment cold soak to get an extended maceration to extract more color.

6. Ferment at warmer temperatures in the range 25–30 °C (77–86 °F).

7. Increase frequency of punchdowns or consider doing pumpovers if you have a good pump; these improve polyphenol extraction and polymerization.

8. Supplement with inactivated yeast derivative nutrients to augment tannin-complexing polysaccharides.

9. Inoculate with an appropriate yeast strain suitable for the variety and desired wine style.

22

10. Watch out for large acidity drops, for example, in high-malic wines during MLF, which can cause pH spikes.

11. Coferment with a teinturier, such as Alicante Bouschet or Marquette.

12. Coferment complementary white and red varieties, for example, Viognier with Syrah, to increase color intensity and stability, and for copigmentation to shift color towards purple.

13. Consider adding pasteurized, crushed and destemmed grapes, such as Allgrape Pack, when making small volumes from lightly colored juice.

14. Process free- and press-run fractions separately; blend only if similar.

15. Consider freezing must (or buying frozen must); the freezing process ruptures grape skin cell walls and releases more anthocyanins.

16. Use SO_2 judiciously as it can bleach anthocyanins.

22.9 VEGETAL CHARACTER IN CABERNET VARIETIES

DESCRIPTION

Red cabernet-related varieties — Cabernet Franc, Cabernet Sauvignon, Merlot and Carménère — as well as Malbec, have naturally occurring compounds known as methoxypyrazines, or simply pyrazines, which impart vegetative aromas of green peppers, freshly cut grass and asparagus, and are considered a flaw, particularly when excessive. Pyrazines can mask fruity aromas and become objectionable and can be very difficult to treat where they can linger for a very long time. They are easily detected given their extremely low detection thresholds in the 1–2 ng/L range, some in the pg/L range — that's parts per trillion (ppt) and parts per quadrillion (ppq), respectively!

CAUSES

Reference Section: 2.1.2

Pyrazines still present in grapes are due to underripe fruit from a wet or cold vintage or precocious harvest, or possibly from poor canopy management. The canopy of a grapevine refers to the parts of the vine visible above ground — the trunk, cordon, stems, leaves, flowers and fruit. A canopy with excessive leaves may cause too much shade therefore delay the ripening process and cause high levels of pyrazines. Pyrazines also increase if vines are allowed to carry more fruit than they can properly mature; dropping fruit just before harvest (after veraison) may be too late.

Pyrazines are found predominantly in skins, and therefore, this flaw is found mainly in red Cabernet varieties due to the maceration process.

ASSESSMENT

This flaw is easily detected by smell and assessed qualitatively; wine has an unmistakable smell of green peppers and freshly cut grass.

REMEDIAL ACTIONS

Pyrazines are very difficult to treat and their offending odors cannot always be attenuated or removed. There are, however, two solutions worth trying: treating with inactivated dry yeast or adding oak chips, or both.

Inactivated dry yeast products, such as Noblesse (Lallemand), have been shown, as well as in my own personal experience in dealing with an overly "green" Carménère, to be able to adsorb and reduce the offending substances [5].

Add Noblesse at a rate of 0.2–0.3 g/L while stirring the wine. Noblesse must be dissolved in 10 times its weight of water. Rack the wine in 3–4 days, then add more Noblesse at a rate of 0.1 g/L while stirring the wine. Once a week for the next month, stir the wine gently but thoroughly to get the sediment back into suspension to allow the inactivated dry yeast to continue its adsorbing action. After this first month, taste, smell and assess

22

the wine. If the pyrazine odors are still present, repeat the treatment with more Noblesse at a rate of 0.05–0.1 g/L, but now, stirring the wine every second week for one month. At the end of the treatment, either after the first or second month, rack the wine and continue aging as per your program, or filter if close to bottling.

Alternatively, or if the above treatment was not sufficient, you can add oak chips to try and mask pyrazine-related odors. Here you have to use untoasted or lightly toasted oak, or a blend, and at a rate of 2–4 g/L. Taste, smell and assess the wine once a week, and remove the chips (if held in a nylon mesh bag) or rack the wine when the odors are sufficiently masked. Complete the treatment by adding finishing tannins (see Section 9.2) to increase organoleptic complexities, being sure to conduct bench trials first.

If you grow your own grapes in your backyard vineyard, manage the canopy to maximize grape bunch exposure to sunlight and heat, avoiding any fruit shading, and drop fruit to balance each vine shortly after veraison. Dropping fruit is hard for home winemakers to do, leaving grapes on the ground, but it can really improve quality and uniformity at harvest.

PREVENTIVE ACTIONS

If you manage your own home vineyard, open the canopy to let the sun shine onto grape bunches to promote ripening and reduce pyrazines, particularly in a difficult vintage or in cool-climate growing areas. And don't harvest too early, making sure to have good balance among sugar (SG/Brix), acidity, pH and phenolic ripeness.

Mitigate methoxypyrazines and their vegetal aromas by adding untoasted oak right at crush or during fermentation if you are working with a poor harvest or a variety known to have high methoxypyrazines. Untoasted oak masks the vegetal character in wines by intensifying the fruity expression and bringing forward "ripe" fruit notes without the aromas of toasted oak. And opt for a short maceration and quick fermentation to minimize extraction of methoxypyrazines.

22.10 UNPLEASANT SMELL OF GERANIUMS

DESCRIPTION

Geraniums are great flowering plants, much appreciated for their wonderful scents. But alas, a detectable geranium-like smell in wine is considered a serious fault.

CAUSES

Reference Sections: 12.4 and 14.1.1

The smell of geraniums is caused by the addition of sorbate (sorbic acid), used to prevent a renewed fermentation in wines with residual sugars, in wines which have a high population of lactic acid bacteria (LAB), either indigenous or due to a malolactic fermentation (MLF).

LAB metabolize sorbate into a compound known as hexadienol that then goes on to react with ethanol to form the culprit compound, 2-ethoxyhexa-3,5-diene, which imparts a strong, disagreeable (in wine) and irreversible odor of geraniums, detectable at 0.1 μg/L (ppb).

ASSESSMENT

This fault is easily detected from the strong, unpleasant smell of geraniums that masks other aromas.

REMEDIAL ACTIONS

This fault cannot be reversed or cured, and the wine is best discarded. Do not be tempted to blend it with another wine – you may be propagating the problem.

PREVENTIVE ACTIONS

Do not use potassium sorbate in any wine that has undergone MLF.

22

For wine that will be put through MLF, ferment to total dryness – no sorbate will be required as there will be no residual fermentable sugars and the wine will be microbially stable.

For those that have undergone MLF and which have residual fermentable sugars, the only options are higher doses of SO_2 *without* sorbate and to drink the wine young and fairly quickly before SO_2 levels drop below critical levels, or sterile filtration.

22.11 CORK TAINT

DESCRIPTION

Cork taint is a condition where wine has a moldy, musty smell, often described as a damp basement or wet newspaper smell, and which has become devoid of its anterior aromas and flavors. This fault almost always, but not exclusively, occurs in bottled wine under natural-cork closures.

CAUSES

Reference Sections: 4.3, 4.5.2, and 18.1.2

Cork taint is the result of microbial contamination of cork material; it causes a chemical reaction between phenols from lignin degradation (of cork material) and chlorine in the environment or which was used in bleaching natural corks in the manufacturing process. It is often referred to as TCA, short for its molecular name, 2,4,6-trichloroanisole, a powerfully odorant molecule with a detection threshold in the 1–4 ng/L (ppt) range, but which poses no health concerns. It can, however, easily contaminate your winemaking area as wood barrels and pallets and cardboard boxes can harbor these contaminants, which can then infect wine.

ASSESSMENT

This fault can be assessed qualitatively by smell. It is easily detected by wine drinkers who are familiar with the smell of TCA although detection can vary by individual; many only detect TCA at 10 ng/L or more.

REMEDIAL ACTIONS

There is no remedy for a TCA-infected wine; it is best discarded. There is anecdotal evidence that some have had some success in at least reducing the musty smell by pouring wine over plastic wrap made from PVC (poly-vinyl chloride) — not LDPE (low-density polyethylene) plastic — although this is believed to scalp other aromas and flavors.

PREVENTIVE ACTIONS

Given that this fault occurs almost exclusively in wines bottled with natural corks, use a TCA-free alternative closure, such as micro-agglomerates or synthetic closures, if you intend to age wine for years. Or you can use bottles with a crown-cap finish if you can source these; you will need a crown-capper to crimp caps on bottles.

Alternatively, consider kegging wine. Wine is protected and "pushed" by inert gas, such as nitrogen or argon; you simply pour as much wine as desired into a carafe for your dinner needs.

And avoid any and all chlorine-based cleaning or sanitizing products in your winemaking area; these are common and high-risk sources of TCA infections. In cellar construction or maintenance, avoid using pressure-treated lumber as these products too are a source of similar contaminants.

22.12 BRETTANOMYCES

DESCRIPTION

Brettanomyces, or "Brett," as it is affectionately referred to, is a condition where wine (almost exclusively red wine) has an unappealing barnyard smell or medicinal, sweaty, "Band-Aid" and rancid aromas. Affected wine can also have some secondary symptoms including biofilm formation, cloudiness, color loss and volatile acidity (VA).

Winemakers partial to the barnyard smell may find that a little Brett adds complexity and may argue that it is part of their terroir, but others consider any amount of Brett an outright fault.

22

This fault is due to indigenous *Brettanomyces* yeast that metabolizes naturally occurring phenolic acids into volatile ethyl phenols, the compounds responsible for the offending odors and which have a detection threshold of about 600 µg/L (ppb).

Brettanomyces yeast can be very difficult to inhibit, even preventatively, in that it only needs very low levels of sugar, less than 275 mg/L (0.0275%), and very little nutrients to jump into action. Acetic acid is a by-product of Brett metabolism, and therefore, although VA seldom becomes detectable, there is an increase.

ASSESSMENT

This fault can be assessed qualitatively by smell; however, it can be very difficult to detect as the metabolic conversion by *Brettanomyces* yeast is very, very slow. The range of smells can vary greatly depending on strains and can be categorized more generally as animal, savory, woody, putrid, chemical/solvent, veggie, fruit, floral spice, fermentation, dairy and earthy. Detection of specific smells depends on the relative concentrations of *Brettanomyces* compounds in the wine matrix, not just their absolute detection thresholds.

Brettanomyces yeast has strong physiological resistance and can persist in the winemaking area and particularly in the barrel cellar for very long periods of time during which it can easily contaminate equipment and wine. Although some incorrectly equate this fault to poor hygiene in the cellar, it can aggravate the infection.

Brettanomyces can persist long periods of time in bottled wine too, having very good tolerance to typical wine alcohol levels and being only moderately sensitive to SO_2.

REMEDIAL ACTIONS

Brettanomyces is very difficult to eradicate and can easily propagate to the entire winemaking area.

Chitosan has been shown to have some efficacy in treating infected wines (see Section 13.4.3.1). No Brett Inside (Lallemand) is a chitosan product specifically formulated to treat Brett infections.

PREVENTIVE ACTIONS

Assume that *Brettanomyces* yeasts are always present, therefore be extra vigilant and practice good cellar hygiene. If you have had Brett infections in the past, consider using chitosan after completion of the MLF as a preventive measure. And don't accept any wine (e.g., to supplement your production) from other producers known to have had *Brettanomyces* in their wines. Some wineries have strict rules of not accepting wine — any wine — from outside the estate for fear of contaminating their cellar.

Reds are at higher risk because of their greater phenolic content, higher pH, and that the wines are produced by macerating skins in juice. Ferment to complete dryness, i.e., SG below 0.995 (below −1.5 Brix).

Barrels pose a greater risk because they can harbor the yeast and because of their cellobiose content. Cellobiose is a sweet disaccharide produced from cellulose hydrolysis during manufacture of oak barrels. If you have access to an ozone generator and are knowledgeable in its use, an ozone treatment can reduce *Brettanomyces* yeast populations in barrels.

Choose a so-called "cinnamic esterase-negative" *O. oeni* lactic acid bacterial strain for barrel-aged or barrel-fermented red wines for conducting the MLF; do *not* rely on indigenous lactic acid bacteria. And minimize the time to complete the MLF and sulfite aggressively using a 100% FSO2 adjustment on the first KMS addition upon completion of the MLF, as prescribed in Section 8.4. A minimum MSO2 of 0.5 mg/L is recommended for reds where *Brettanomyces* is a potential problem or as preventive.

Store and age wine at cool temperature, ideally at 13 °C (55 °F).

And sterile filter at 0.45 micron (absolute) directly into bottles, if possible.

22

REFERENCES

1. Goode, J. 2018. Flawless: *Understanding Faults in Wine*. University of California Press, Oakland, CA.

2. Pambianchi, D. 2008. *Techniques in Home Winemaking: A Practical Guide to Making Château-Style Wines*. Newly-Revised and Expanded. Véhicule Press, Montréal (Québec).

3. Lallemand. *Reduless Technical Datasheet*. https://catalogapp.lallemandwine.com/uploads/siy/docs/c83c53ae9f87e4bd7cbc7638321e7f0f1507d772.pdf. Last accessed March 25, 2021.

4. Ribéreau-Gayon, P., Y. Glories, A. Maujean and D. Dubourdieu. 2012. *Traité d'œnologie, Tome 2 - Chimie du vin. Stabilisation et traitements*. 6e édition. Dunod, Paris.

5. Delteil, D. 2010. *Noblesse's adsorptive sponge effect: Practical guideline for Virginia Varieties*. http://www.delteil-consultant.com/pdf/RD/ENG_Noblesse_guidelines.pdf. Dominique Delteil Consultant, Lallemand. Last accessed March 25, 2021.

23 Entering Wines into Competitions

Entering wines into competitions is an excellent way to get feedback from respected judges. Sure, medals can be rewarding, but without feedback, you won't know why your wines did not score higher; you will have no idea of what the judges didn't like or if they identified flaws or faults. There are many local, state or provincial, national and international competitions run by reputable organizations. Choose those that will provide feedback, not just medals. Remember! You want to elevate your hobby to making *great* wines.

And if going after medals, be sure you understand how these are awarded. Some competitions will award medals based on total score for each wine, for example, 12–14 (out of 20) points is awarded bronze, 15–17 points is awarded silver, and 18–20 points is awarded gold. All wines scoring in medal range are awarded medals. Other competitions award bronze, silver and gold medals only to the highest-scoring wine, that is, only three wines will be awarded first, second and third place. As there are several judges tasting and scoring each wine, the final score may be an average of all the judges' scores, or in some cases, to remove biases or scoring abnormalities, the highest and lowest scores are removed and an average is calculated from the remaining scores.

23.1 WHAT JUDGES LOOK FOR IN WINE

Different competitions have different scoring systems. The most common ones (Figure 23.1) score wines on a 0-to-20 scale awarding, for example, 0–3 points for appearance, 0–6 points for aroma and bouquet, 0–6 points for taste, 0–3 points for aftertaste or finish, and 0–2 points for overall impressions.

23

Wine Assessment Scoresheet	Awarded Points
Appearance (maximum 3 points) ❏ Excellent – Brilliant with outstanding characteristic color (3 points) ❏ Good – Clear with characteristic color (2 points) ❏ Needs Improvement – Slight haze and/or slight off color (1 point) ❏ Objectionable – Cloudy and/or off color (0 points) Comments	———
Aroma and Bouquet (maximum 6 points) ❏ Exceptional – Wonderful characteristic aroma of grape variety or wine type. Outstanding and complex bouquet. Exceptional balance of aroma and bouquet. (6 points) ❏ Excellent – Strong characteristic aroma of grape variety or wine type. Complex bouquet. Good balance of aroma and bouquet. (5 points) ❏ Good – Good characteristic aroma of grape variety or wine type. Admirable bouquet. (4 points) ❏ Pleasant – Good characteristic aroma of grape variety or wine type. Pleasant bouquet. (3 points) ❏ Acceptable – No perceptible or bouquet or with slight off odors. (2 points) ❏ Needs Improvement – Off odors very detectable (1 point) ❏ Objectionable – Offensive odors (0 points) Comments	———
Taste (maximum 6 points) ❏ Exceptional – Wonderful characteristic flavor of grape variety or wine type. Outstanding balance. Smooth, full-bodied and outstanding. (6 points) ❏ Excellent – Strong characteristic flavor of grape variety or wine type. Excellent balance and body, but not quite outstanding. (5 points) ❏ Good – Good characteristic flavor of grape variety or wine type. Good balance. May have some minor imperfections. (4 points) ❏ Pleasant – Pleasant flavor of grape variety or wine type. May be slightly out of balance and/or have minor off flavors. (3 points) ❏ Acceptable – A hint of flavor of grape variety or wine type. Detectable out of balance flavors with more pronounced faults than above. (2 points) ❏ Needs Improvement – Disagreeable off flavors and a poor balance (1 point) ❏ Objectionable – Offensive flavors (0 points) Comments	———
Aftertaste (maximum 3 points) ❏ Excellent – Lingering outstanding aftertaste (3 points) ❏ Good – Pleasant aftertaste (2 points) ❏ Needs Improvement – Little or no distinguishable aftertaste (1 point) ❏ Objectionable – Unpleasant aftertaste (0 points) Comments	———
Overall Impression (maximum 2 points) ❏ Excellent (2 points) ❏ Good (1 point) ❏ Objectionable (0 points) Comments	———
Total Scores: 18–20 Extraordinary 9–11 Pleasant 15–17 Excellent 6–8 Acceptable 12–14 Good 0–5 Needs Improvement	——— Total Points Awarded

Figure 23.1: A typical wine competition scoring sheet

The visual aspect of the wine creates a first impression and provides clues — good or bad — as to what to expect from the wine, therefore appearance is very important. Judges look for a brilliant wine free of any particulates, sediment, including tartrates, carbon dioxide (CO_2) gas, and certainly free of any haze or cloudiness. This is particularly important with white wines, which are expected to be brilliant and where flaws are much more obvious. Therefore if your wine has suffered from heat or extreme cold exposure during shipping, your perfectly, crystal-clear wine may develop a haze or tartrates by the time it reaches the competition site. And whites will definitely score better if filtered. But then the question is: Do you make wines to enter competitions or to enjoy them in the style and manner you created them?

Color too is important. Color should not show any signs of fatigue or oxidation, and should be characteristic of the style of wine submitted. If you are submitting a lightly colored Cabernet Sauvignon, you may lose a couple of points right there as this varietal is expected to be deeply colored. Similarly, if your Seyval Blanc is a golden color, it likely suffered from oxidation, in which case you will also lose points in the other categories.

Although aroma and bouquet are most often combined to mean all the aromas detected in wine, some may use the term "aroma" to refer to those aromas arising from naturally occurring aroma compounds in grapes, and from yeast or bacterial metabolism during alcoholic or malolactic fermentation, while the term "bouquet" is used to refer to tertiary aromas that develop over the course of aging in inert vessels or wood barrels. Here you have to give careful consideration to the wines you wish to enter. A very young wine bottled soon after the alcoholic fermentation, without any aging, may not show much aromas. And older wines may have complex bouquets but without much of the fruity aromas found in younger wines. Therefore, if you submit an aged Cabernet Sauvignon, keep in mind that it will be evaluated in its category against fruit-bomb Cabs.

Judges assess if the wine aromas are characteristic of the grape varieties, the intensity of aromas, bouquet complexity, and if there are any off-odors. The more aromas (primary, secondary and tertiary) and complexity, the higher the wine will score. But no one aroma should be so dominant that it mutes other aromas, as with overly oaked wines or an excessive barnyard character in reds.

Varietal expression is important. If a Muscat Blanc à Petits Grains (Moscato Bianco) wine has none of the characteristic floral, grapey aromas, it will not score well as judges expect varietals to exhibit specific aromas. But if a Riesling does not show any petrol aroma, that's ok, as that aroma tends to develop with aging and may not necessarily be present in a younger Riesling.

23

The wine should have absolutely no off-odors, such as the smell of vinegar (acetic acid) due to volatile acidity (VA) from, for example, a poorly barrel-aged wine, or Sherry-like odors due to oxidation, or bad smells from poorly cleaned or sanitized equipment. VA and oxidation are the most common faults in wines at competitions. And if you use sulfite as a preservative, it should never be detectable; this should never be a problem if molecular SO_2 is below 0.8 mg/L and free SO_2 adjusted according to pH.

For taste, here too judges look how expressive a wine is, and the more flavors and complexity, the higher the score. The wine should exhibit characteristic flavors of the varietal or blend. Balance is very important in taste. All components — alcohol, acidity, sweetness and tannins — should all be in harmonious balance; no one component should dominate for the style of wine in a specific category. Reds are judged very critically here for body, structure and mouthfeel. Uncharacteristically light-bodied reds from rich varieties or overly tannic wines from excessive extraction of harsh tannins will be considered poorly balanced and will score low. And there should be no off-flavors that would be considered a flaw or a fault.

If you submit an off-dry wine into a dry-wine category, you will lose points. Here you have to be careful and anticipate how wines may be tasted. Not all competitions have the luxury of keeping whites and rosés chilled until pouring and tasting time. Perceived acidity will be lower in a warmer wine, and therefore, a dry wine can quite possibly taste off-dry when tasted at a warmer temperature.

For aftertaste, judges look for persistence and intensity of flavors and a smooth finish, i.e., no bitter aftertaste.

For overall impression, judges consider all the elements, if they exist in harmony, and how well the wine was made. Judges often ask themselves if they would buy the wine to rate their impression.

23.2 DOS AND DON'TS OF SUBMITTING WINES

Here is a list of dos and don'ts that will help you improve your chances of your wines scoring well in competitions.

- Do not rush to complete a wine simply to be able to submit it into a competition. The wine will neither be as good as you had planned nor will it show well. Ensure that the wine has been adequately clarified and stabilized.

- Realize that not all judges, especially at smaller competitions, are familiar with obscure varietals, and that, therefore, your wines may not be judged entirely objectively.

- Only submit wine that had been previously bottled and given a chance to rest. Wine may suffer bottle sickness and not show well if bottled just a couple of days before being shipped. And don't submit wines that are cloudy or have any kind of sediment, even reds — they will be turbid (cloudy) once poured.

- Submit wines for which you have already received honest feedback from trusted friends and family. Don't simply rely on your own assessment — it is biased. You need objective feedback from different tasters. Don't submit wines with flaws or faults unless you are looking for specific feedback on those, though the use of a professional lab would be money better spent.

- Only submit wine that reflects the expected style of the varietal or blend. Submitting a lightly colored Cab will not score well.

- Do not ship wine during a heat wave or a cold snap. And always use the fastest shipping method possible, and avoid shipping late in the week. Your precious wines may be sitting in transit in some warehouse or, worse, in a truck, over the weekend. Pack bottles ideally in Styrofoam packs specifically designed for shipping wine bottles; they provide some protection against temperature spikes.

- For blends, identify all the blending components and their percentages.

- Enter wines into their appropriate categories, including if they were made from kits or grapes if the competition distinguishes those wines. This may not always be clear, especially for blends, depending on how many categories there are and how they have been defined. Some competitions may not allow, for example, a wine to have a hybrid component in a vinifera blend, or may allow

23

a small percentage, perhaps up to 15%. There may also be categories based on the perceived or actual amount of residual sugar (RS), e.g., dry (0–1% RS), semi-dry (1–2% RS), etc. Read the competition rules very carefully.

- When you do receive scores and feedback, accept it all with a view of improving your winemaking, however disappointing the results may be. And if you don't receive any medals, that's ok. Just be sure to understand how medals are awarded.

Good luck!

Appendixes

A-C

Appendix A: Conversion Factors Between Metric, U.S. and Imperial Systems

Table A-1: List of abbreviations for systems and units of measure used in this book.

Unit of measure	Abbreviation	Unit of measure	Abbreviation
atmosphere	atm	micrometer	micron *or* mm
bar	bar	milligram	mg
Baumé	B° *or* Bé°	milligram per liter	mg/L
degrees Brix (Brix)	°B *or* °Bx	milliliter	cc *or* mL
centimeter	cm	millimeter	mm
cup	cup	millimeter of mercury	mmHg
degrees Celsius	°C		
degrees Fahrenheit	°F	Oechsle	°Oe
fluid ounce	fl oz	ounce	oz
foot (feet)	ft	parts per billion	ppb
gallon	gal	parts per million	ppm
gram	g	parts per quadrillion	ppq
gallon per liter	gal/L	parts per trillion	ppt
gram per liter	g/L	Pascal	Pa
hectoliter	hL	percent alcohol by volume	% ABV *or* % alc/vol
hectoPascal	hPa		
inch	in	pound(s)	lb(s)
inch of mercury	inHg	pound per square inch	psi
International System of Units	SI		
		Specific Gravity	sp gr or SG
kilogram	kg	tablespoon	tbsp
kilogram per square centimeter	kg/cm^2	teaspoon	tsp
		temperature	T
kiloPascal	kPa	ton	T
liter	L	United States	U.S.
meter	m	volume	vol *or* v
metric ton (tonne)	MT	weight	wt *or* w

LENGTH						
Metric/SI				U.S.		
m	cm	mm		ft	in	
	1	10	=		0.39	
	2.54	25.4	=		1	
1	100		=	3.28	39.37	
0.3			=	1		

MASS AND WEIGHT						
Metric/SI				U.S.		
MT	kg	g	mg	U.S. T	lb	oz
	1	1000		=	2.2	
		1	1000	=		0.035
		454		=	1	16
		28.35		=		1
1	1000			=	2200	
	910			=	1	2000

TEMPERATURE	
°C to °F	°F to °C
°F = 9/5 × (°C) + 32	°C = 5/9 × (°F) − 32

Example

10.0 °C converts to 9/5 × 10.0 + 32 = 50.0 °F

 Shaded boxes represent the base number used for deriving con-verted numbers. Converted numbers are approximate due to rounding.

VOLUME									
Metric/SI			U.S.					Imperial	
hL	L	mL	gal	fl oz	cup	tbsp	tsp	gal	fl oz
1	100		= 26.4					= 22.0	
	3.79		= 1	128				= 0.83	
	4.55		= 1.2	154				= 1	160
		1	= 0.034					=	0.035
		29.6	=	1				=	1.04
		28.4	=	0.96				=	1
		237	=	8	1			=	
		14.8	=			1	3	=	
		4.9	=				1	=	
	11.4		= 3						
	19.0		= 5	Standard					
	22.7		= 6	Carboy					
	24.6		= 6.5	Sizes					

PRESSURE									
Metric/SI						U.S.		Other	
kPa	hPa	Pa	kg/cm²	bar	mmHg	psi	inHg	atm	
1	10	1000	0.01	0.01	7.5 =	0.15	0.30 =	0.01	
100	1000	100,000	1.0	1	750 =	14.5	29.5 =	1	
6.9	69	6895	0.07	0.07	51.7 =	1	2.0 =	0.07	

 Shaded boxes represent the base number used for deriving converted numbers. Converted numbers are approximate due to rounding.

A-C

Appendix B: Sugar Concentrations, Potential Alcohol, and Conversions

Use Table B.1 to convert between °Brix, Specific Gravity (SG), sugar concentrations expressed in Metric and U.S. units, and Potential Alcohol (PA) expressed in % alc/vol (% ABV), for measurements at 20 °C (68 °F).

°Brix and SG data in Table B.1 is partly derived and adapted from data from Table II – Evaluation of sugar by refractometry of Method OIV-MA-AS2-02 in the OIV Compendium of International Methods of Analysis of Wines and Musts [1]. Sugar concentrations in g/L are approximated to 10 times the °Brix value, and a factor of 17.5 is used to derive PA. For further information, please refer to Section 6.2.

Use Table B.2 to correct readings to compensate for temperature differences when taking hydrometer readings at temperatures other than 20 °C (68 °F).

Use Table B.3 to estimate the amount of residual sugars in wine based on initial SG and total acidity (TA) in g/L, as per the method outlined in Section 6.5 [2].

Use Table B.4 to estimate the amount of residual sugars in white and rosé wines at a given final SG (Brix) and % ABV in the range 10.0–12.5, and Table B.5 in red wines at a given final SG (Brix) and % ABV in the range 12.5–15.0.

Table B.1: Conversions between °Brix, SG, sugar concentrations and PA (adapted from [1])

°Brix	SG	Approx. sugars (g/L)	Approx. sugars (g/gal)	PA
-2.3	0.991			
-2.2	0.992			
-2.1	0.992			
-2.0	0.993			
-1.9	0.993			
-1.8	0.993			
-1.7	0.994			
-1.6	0.994			
-1.5	0.994			
-1.4	0.995			
-1.3	0.995			
-1.2	0.995			
-1.1	0.996			
-1.0	0.996			
-0.9	0.997			
-0.8	0.997			
-0.7	0.997			
-0.6	0.998			
-0.5	0.998			
-0.4	0.998			
-0.3	0.999			
-0.2	0.999			
-0.1	1.000			
0.0	1.000	0	0	0.0
0.1	1.000	1	4	0.1
0.2	1.001	2	8	0.1
0.3	1.001	3	11	0.2
0.4	1.002	4	15	0.2
0.5	1.002	5	19	0.3
0.6	1.002	6	23	0.3
0.7	1.003	7	27	0.4
0.8	1.003	8	30	0.5
0.9	1.003	9	34	0.5
1.0	1.004	10	38	0.6
1.1	1.004	11	42	0.6
1.2	1.005	12	45	0.7
1.3	1.005	13	49	0.7
1.4	1.005	14	53	0.8
1.5	1.006	15	57	0.9
1.6	1.006	16	61	0.9
1.7	1.006	17	64	1.0
1.8	1.007	18	68	1.0
1.9	1.007	19	72	1.1
2.0	1.008	20	76	1.1
2.1	1.008	21	80	1.2
2.2	1.008	22	83	1.3
2.3	1.009	23	87	1.3
2.4	1.009	24	91	1.4
2.5	1.010	25	95	1.4
2.6	1.010	26	99	1.5
2.7	1.010	27	102	1.5
2.8	1.011	28	106	1.6
2.9	1.011	29	110	1.6
3.0	1.011	30	114	1.7
3.1	1.012	31	117	1.7
3.2	1.012	32	121	1.8
3.3	1.013	33	125	1.8
3.4	1.013	34	129	1.9
3.5	1.013	35	133	1.9
3.6	1.014	36	136	2.0
3.7	1.014	37	140	2.1
3.8	1.015	38	144	2.1
3.9	1.015	39	148	2.2
4.0	1.015	40	152	2.2
4.1	1.016	41	155	2.3
4.2	1.016	42	159	2.3
4.3	1.016	43	163	2.4
4.4	1.017	44	167	2.5
4.5	1.017	45	171	2.6

(continued)

Table B.1, *continued*

°Brix	SG	Approx. sugars (g/L)	Approx. sugars (g/gal)	PA	°Brix	SG	Approx. sugars (g/L)	Approx. sugars (g/gal)	PA	°Brix	SG	Approx. sugars (g/L)	Approx. sugars (g/gal)	PA
4.6	1.018	46	174	2.6	6.9	1.027	69	262	3.9	9.2	1.036	92	349	5.3
4.7	1.018	47	178	2.7	7.0	1.027	70	265	4.0	9.3	1.036	93	352	5.3
4.8	1.018	48	182	2.7	7.1	1.028	71	269	4.1	9.4	1.037	94	356	5.4
4.9	1.019	49	186	2.8	7.2	1.028	72	273	4.1	9.5	1.037	95	360	5.4
5.0	1.019	50	190	2.9	7.3	1.028	73	277	4.2	9.6	1.038	96	364	5.5
5.1	1.019	51	193	2.9	7.4	1.029	74	280	4.2	9.7	1.038	97	368	5.5
5.2	1.020	52	197	2.9	7.5	1.029	75	284	4.3	9.8	1.038	98	371	5.6
5.3	1.020	53	201	3.0	7.6	1.030	76	288	4.3	9.9	1.039	99	375	5.7
5.4	1.021	54	205	3.1	7.7	1.030	77	292	4.4	10.0	1.039	100	379	5.7
5.5	1.021	55	208	3.1	7.8	1.030	78	296	4.5	10.1	1.040	101	383	5.8
5.6	1.022	56	212	3.2	7.9	1.031	79	299	4.5	10.2	1.040	102	387	5.8
5.7	1.022	57	216	3.3	8.0	1.031	80	303	4.6	10.3	1.040	103	390	5.9
5.8	1.022	58	220	3.3	8.1	1.032	81	307	4.6	10.4	1.041	104	394	5.9
5.9	1.023	59	224	3.4	8.2	1.032	82	311	4.7	10.5	1.041	105	398	6.0
6.0	1.023	60	227	3.4	8.3	1.032	83	315	4.7	10.6	1.042	106	402	6.1
6.1	1.024	61	231	3.5	8.4	1.033	84	318	4.8	10.7	1.042	107	406	6.1
6.2	1.024	62	235	3.5	8.5	1.033	85	322	4.9	10.8	1.042	108	409	6.2
6.3	1.024	63	239	3.6	8.6	1.034	86	326	4.9	10.9	1.043	109	413	6.2
6.4	1.025	64	243	3.7	8.7	1.034	87	330	5.0	11.0	1.043	110	417	6.3
6.5	1.025	65	246	3.7	8.8	1.034	88	334	5.0	11.1	1.044	111	421	6.3
6.6	1.026	66	250	3.8	8.9	1.035	89	337	5.1	11.2	1.044	112	424	6.4
6.7	1.026	67	254	3.8	9.0	1.035	90	341	5.1	11.3	1.044	113	428	6.5
6.8	1.026	68	258	3.9	9.1	1.036	91	345	5.2	11.4	1.045	114	432	6.5

(continued)

A–C

Table B.1, *continued*

°Brix	SG	Approx. sugars (g/L)	Approx. sugars (g/gal)	PA
11.5	1.045	115	436	6.6
11.6	1.046	116	440	6.6
11.7	1.046	117	443	6.7
11.8	1.046	118	447	6.7
11.9	1.047	119	451	6.8
12.0	1.047	120	455	6.9
12.1	1.048	121	459	6.9
12.2	1.048	122	462	7.0
12.3	1.049	123	466	7.0
12.4	1.049	124	470	7.1
12.5	1.049	125	474	7.1
12.6	1.050	126	478	7.2
12.7	1.050	127	481	7.3
12.8	1.051	128	485	7.3
12.9	1.051	129	489	7.4
13.0	1.051	130	493	7.4
13.1	1.052	131	496	7.5
13.2	1.052	132	500	7.5
13.3	1.053	133	504	7.6
13.4	1.053	134	508	7.7
13.5	1.054	135	512	7.7
13.6	1.054	136	515	7.8
13.7	1.054	137	519	7.8
13.8	1.055	138	523	7.9
13.9	1.055	139	527	7.9
14.0	1.056	140	531	8.0
14.1	1.056	141	534	8.1
14.2	1.056	142	538	8.1
14.3	1.057	143	542	8.2
14.4	1.057	144	546	8.2
14.5	1.058	145	550	8.3
14.6	1.058	146	553	8.3
14.7	1.059	147	557	8.4
14.8	1.059	148	561	8.5
14.9	1.059	149	565	8.5
15.0	1.060	150	569	8.6
15.1	1.060	151	572	8.6
15.2	1.061	152	576	8.7
15.3	1.061	153	580	8.7
15.4	1.062	154	584	8.8
15.5	1.062	155	587	8.9
15.6	1.062	156	591	8.9
15.7	1.063	157	595	9.0
15.8	1.063	158	599	9.0
15.9	1.064	159	603	9.1
16.0	1.064	160	606	9.1
16.1	1.065	161	610	9.2
16.2	1.065	162	614	9.3
16.3	1.065	163	618	9.3
16.4	1.066	164	622	9.4
16.5	1.066	165	625	9.4
16.6	1.067	166	629	9.5
16.7	1.067	167	633	9.5
16.8	1.068	168	637	9.6
16.9	1.068	169	641	9.7
17.0	1.069	170	644	9.7
17.1	1.069	171	648	9.8
17.2	1.069	172	652	9.8
17.3	1.070	173	656	9.9
17.4	1.070	174	659	9.9
17.5	1.071	175	663	10.0
17.6	1.071	176	667	10.1
17.7	1.072	177	671	10.1
17.8	1.072	178	675	10.2
17.9	1.072	179	678	10.2
18.0	1.073	180	682	10.3
18.1	1.073	181	686	10.3
18.2	1.074	182	690	10.4
18.3	1.074	183	694	10.5

(continued)

Table B.1, *continued*

°Brix	SG	Approx. sugars (g/L)	Approx. sugars (g/gal)	PA
18.4	1.075	184	697	10.5
18.5	1.075	185	701	10.6
18.6	1.076	186	705	10.6
18.7	1.076	187	709	10.7
18.8	1.076	188	713	10.7
18.9	1.077	189	716	10.8
19.0	1.077	190	720	10.9
19.1	1.078	191	724	10.9
19.2	1.078	192	728	11.0
19.3	1.079	193	731	11.0
19.4	1.079	194	735	11.1
19.5	1.080	195	739	11.1
19.6	1.080	196	743	11.2
19.7	1.080	197	747	11.3
19.8	1.081	198	750	11.3
19.9	1.081	199	754	11.4
20.0	1.082	200	758	11.4
20.1	1.082	201	762	11.5
20.2	1.083	202	766	11.5
20.3	1.083	203	769	11.6
20.4	1.084	204	773	11.7
20.5	1.084	205	777	11.7
20.6	1.085	206	781	11.8
20.7	1.085	207	785	11.8
20.8	1.085	208	788	11.9
20.9	1.086	209	792	11.9
21.0	1.086	210	796	12.0
21.1	1.087	211	800	12.1
21.2	1.087	212	803	12.1
21.3	1.088	213	807	12.2
21.4	1.088	214	811	12.2
21.5	1.089	215	815	12.3
21.6	1.089	216	819	12.3
21.7	1.090	217	822	12.4
21.8	1.090	218	826	12.5
21.9	1.090	219	830	12.5
22.0	1.091	220	834	12.6
22.1	1.091	221	838	12.6
22.2	1.092	222	841	12.7
22.3	1.092	223	845	12.7
22.4	1.093	224	849	12.8
22.5	1.093	225	853	12.9
22.6	1.094	226	857	12.9
22.7	1.094	227	860	13.0
22.8	1.095	228	864	13.0
22.9	1.095	229	868	13.1
23.0	1.095	230	872	13.1
23.1	1.096	231	875	13.2
23.2	1.096	232	879	13.3
23.3	1.097	233	883	13.3
23.4	1.097	234	887	13.4
23.5	1.098	235	891	13.4
23.6	1.098	236	894	13.5
23.7	1.099	237	898	13.5
23.8	1.099	238	902	13.6
23.9	1.100	239	906	13.7
24.0	1.100	240	910	13.7
24.1	1.101	241	913	13.8
24.2	1.101	242	917	13.8
24.3	1.102	243	921	13.9
24.4	1.102	244	925	13.9
24.5	1.102	245	929	14.0
24.6	1.103	246	932	14.1
24.7	1.103	247	936	14.1
24.8	1.104	248	940	14.2
24.9	1.104	249	944	14.2
25.0	1.105	250	948	14.3
25.1	1.105	251	951	14.3
25.2	1.106	252	955	14.4

(continued)

A-C

Table B.1, *continued*

°Brix	SG	Approx. sugars (g/L)	Approx. sugars (g/gal)	PA
25.3	1.106	253	959	14.5
25.4	1.107	254	963	14.5
25.5	1.107	255	966	14.6
25.6	1.108	256	970	14.6
25.7	1.108	257	974	14.7
25.8	1.109	258	978	14.7
25.9	1.109	259	982	14.8
26.0	1.110	260	985	14.9
26.1	1.110	261	989	14.9
26.2	1.110	262	993	15.0
26.3	1.111	263	997	15.0
26.4	1.111	264	1001	15.1
26.5	1.112	265	1004	15.1
26.6	1.112	266	1008	15.2
26.7	1.113	267	1012	15.3
26.8	1.113	268	1016	15.3
26.9	1.114	269	1020	15.4
27.0	1.114	270	1023	15.4
27.1	1.115	271	1027	15.5
27.2	1.115	272	1031	15.5
27.3	1.116	273	1035	15.6
27.4	1.116	274	1038	15.7
27.5	1.117	275	1042	15.7
27.6	1.117	276	1046	15.8
27.7	1.118	277	1050	15.8
27.8	1.118	278	1054	15.9
27.9	1.119	279	1057	15.9
28.0	1.119	280	1061	16.0
28.1	1.120	281	1065	16.1
28.2	1.120	282	1069	16.1
28.3	1.121	283	1073	16.2
28.4	1.121	284	1076	16.2
28.5	1.121	285	1080	16.3
28.6	1.122	286	1084	16.3
28.7	1.122	287	1088	16.4
28.8	1.123	288	1092	16.5
28.9	1.123	289	1095	16.5
29.0	1.124	290	1099	16.6
29.1	1.124	291	1103	16.6
29.2	1.125	292	1107	16.7
29.3	1.125	293	1110	16.7
29.4	1.126	294	1114	16.8
29.5	1.126	295	1118	16.9
29.6	1.127	296	1122	16.9
29.7	1.127	297	1126	17.0
29.8	1.128	298	1129	17.0
29.9	1.128	299	1133	17.1
30.0	1.129	300	1137	17.1
30.1	1.129	301	1141	17.2
30.2	1.130	302	1145	17.3
30.3	1.130	303	1148	17.3
30.4	1.131	304	1152	17.4
30.5	1.131	305	1156	17.4
30.6	1.132	306	1160	17.5
30.7	1.132	307	1164	17.5
30.8	1.133	308	1167	17.6
30.9	1.133	309	1171	17.7
31.0	1.134	310	1175	17.7
31.1	1.134	311	1179	17.8
31.2	1.135	312	1182	17.8
31.3	1.135	313	1186	17.9
31.4	1.136	314	1190	17.9
31.5	1.136	315	1194	18.0
31.6	1.137	316	1198	18.1
31.7	1.137	317	1201	18.1
31.8	1.138	318	1205	18.2
31.9	1.138	319	1209	18.2
32.0	1.139	320	1213	18.3
32.1	1.139	321	1217	18.3

Table B.2: Approximate SG/Brix corrections for hydrometer readings taken at temperatures other than 20 °C (68 °F)

Temperature		SG	°Brix	Temperature		SG	°Brix
(°C)	(°F)			(°C)	(°F)		
10.0	50.0	− 0.003	− 0.6	20.0	68.0	0.000	0.0
10.5	50.9	− 0.003	− 0.5	20.5	68.9	0.000	0.0
11.0	51.8	− 0.003	− 0.5	21.0	69.8	0.000	+ 0.1
11.5	52.7	− 0.003	− 0.5	21.5	70.7	0.000	+ 0.1
12.0	53.6	− 0.003	− 0.5	22.0	71.6	0.000	+ 0.1
12.5	54.5	− 0.002	− 0.4	22.5	72.5	+ 0.001	+ 0.2
13.0	55.4	− 0.002	− 0.4	23.0	73.4	+ 0.001	+ 0.2
13.5	56.3	− 0.002	− 0.4	23.5	74.3	+ 0.001	+ 0.2
14.0	57.2	− 0.001	− 0.3	24.0	75.2	+ 0.001	+ 0.3
14.5	58.1	− 0.001	− 0.3	24.5	76.1	+ 0.001	+ 0.3
15.0	59.0	− 0.001	− 0.3	25.0	77.0	+ 0.001	+ 0.3
15.5	59.9	− 0.001	− 0.3	25.5	77.9	+ 0.002	+ 0.4
16.0	60.8	− 0.001	− 0.2	26.0	78.8	+ 0.002	+ 0.4
16.5	61.7	− 0.001	− 0.2	26.5	79.7	+ 0.003	+ 0.5
17.0	62.6	− 0.001	− 0.2	27.0	80.6	+ 0.003	+ 0.5
17.5	63.5	− 0.001	− 0.2	27.5	81.5	+ 0.003	+ 0.5
18.0	64.4	0.000	− 0.1	28.0	82.4	+ 0.003	+ 0.6
18.5	65.3	0.000	− 0.1	28.5	83.3	+ 0.003	+ 0.6
19.0	66.2	0.000	− 0.1	29.0	84.2	+ 0.003	+ 0.6
19.5	67.1	0.000	0.0	29.5	85.1	+ 0.003	+ 0.7
20.0	68.0	0.000	0.0	30.0	86.0	+ 0.003	+ 0.7

Example

A reading of SG 1.100 (24.0 Brix) at 15.0 °C (59 °F) should be corrected to 1.100 − 0.001, or SG 1.099 (23.7 Brix).

A-C

Table B.3: Correction factors for estimating the amount of residual sugars based on initial SG and total acidity (TA) (adapted from [2])

TA (g/L)	Specific Gravity (SG)												
	1.075	1.076	1.077	1.078	1.079	1.080	1.081	1.082	1.083	1.084	1.085	1.086	1.087
4.5	4.6	4.8	5.0	5.2	5.4	5.6	5.8	6.0	6.2	6.4	6.6	6.8	7.0
5.0	4.4	4.6	4.8	5.0	5.2	5.4	5.6	5.8	6.0	6.2	6.4	6.6	6.8
5.5	4.2	4.4	4.6	4.8	5.0	5.2	5.4	5.6	5.8	6.0	6.2	6.4	6.6
6.0	4.0	4.2	4.4	4.6	4.8	5.0	5.2	5.4	5.6	5.8	6.0	6.2	6.4
6.5	3.8	4.0	4.2	4.4	4.6	4.8	5.0	5.2	5.4	5.6	5.8	6.0	6.2
7.0	3.6	3.8	4.0	4.2	4.4	4.6	4.8	5.0	5.2	5.4	5.6	5.8	6.0
7.5	3.4	3.6	3.8	4.0	4.2	4.4	4.6	4.8	5.0	5.2	5.4	5.6	5.8
8.0	3.2	3.4	3.6	3.8	4.0	4.2	4.4	4.6	4.8	5.0	5.2	5.4	5.6
8.5	3.0	3.2	3.4	3.6	3.8	4.0	4.2	4.4	4.6	4.8	5.0	5.2	5.4
9.0	2.8	3.0	3.2	3.4	3.6	3.8	4.0	4.2	4.4	4.6	4.8	5.0	5.2
9.5	2.6	2.8	3.0	3.2	3.4	3.6	3.8	4.0	4.2	4.4	4.6	4.8	5.0
10.0	2.4	2.6	2.8	3.0	3.2	3.4	3.6	3.8	4.0	4.2	4.4	4.6	4.8
10.5	2.2	2.4	2.6	2.8	3.0	3.2	3.4	3.6	3.8	4.0	4.2	4.4	4.6
11.0	2.0	2.2	2.4	2.6	2.8	3.0	3.2	3.4	3.6	3.8	4.0	4.2	4.4
11.5	1.8	2.0	2.2	2.4	2.6	2.8	3.0	3.2	3.4	3.6	3.8	4.0	4.2
12.0	1.6	1.8	2.0	2.2	2.4	2.6	2.8	3.0	3.2	3.4	3.6	3.8	4.0
12.5	1.4	1.6	1.8	2.0	2.2	2.4	2.6	2.8	3.0	3.2	3.4	3.6	3.8
13.0	1.2	1.4	1.6	1.8	2.0	2.2	2.4	2.6	2.8	3.0	3.2	3.4	3.6
13.5	1.0	1.2	1.4	1.6	1.8	2.0	2.2	2.4	2.6	2.8	3.0	3.2	3.4
14.0	0.8	1.0	1.2	1.4	1.6	1.8	2.0	2.2	2.4	2.6	2.8	3.0	3.2
14.5	0.6	0.8	1.0	1.2	1.4	1.6	1.8	2.0	2.2	2.4	2.6	2.8	3.0

(continued)

Table B.3, *continued*

TA (g/L)						Specific Gravity (SG)							
	1.088	1.089	1.090	1.091	1.092	1.093	1.094	1.095	1.096	1.097	1.098	1.099	1.100
4.5	7.2	7.4	7.6	7.8	8.0	8.2	8.4	8.6	8.8	9.0	9.2	9.4	9.6
5.0	7.0	7.2	7.4	7.6	7.8	8.0	8.2	8.4	8.6	8.8	9.0	9.2	9.4
5.5	6.8	7.0	7.2	7.4	7.6	7.8	8.0	8.2	8.4	8.6	8.8	9.0	9.2
6.0	6.6	6.8	7.0	7.2	7.4	7.6	7.8	8.0	8.2	8.4	8.6	8.8	9.0
6.5	6.4	6.6	6.8	7.0	7.2	7.4	7.6	7.8	8.0	8.2	8.4	8.6	8.8
7.0	6.2	6.4	6.6	6.8	7.0	7.2	7.4	7.6	7.8	8.0	8.2	8.4	8.6
7.5	6.0	6.2	6.4	6.6	6.8	7.0	7.2	7.4	7.6	7.8	8.0	8.2	8.4
8.0	5.8	6.0	6.2	6.4	6.6	6.8	7.0	7.2	7.4	7.6	7.8	8.0	8.2
8.5	5.6	5.8	6.0	6.2	6.4	6.6	6.8	7.0	7.2	7.4	7.6	7.8	8.0
9.0	5.4	5.6	5.8	6.0	6.2	6.4	6.6	6.8	7.0	7.2	7.4	7.6	7.8
9.5	5.2	5.4	5.6	5.8	6.0	6.2	6.4	6.6	6.8	7.0	7.2	7.4	7.6
10.0	5.0	5.2	5.4	5.6	5.8	6.0	6.2	6.4	6.6	6.8	7.0	7.2	7.4
10.5	4.8	5.0	5.2	5.4	5.6	5.8	6.0	6.2	6.4	6.6	6.8	7.0	7.2
11.0	4.6	4.8	5.0	5.2	5.4	5.6	5.8	6.0	6.2	6.4	6.6	6.8	7.0
11.5	4.4	4.6	4.8	5.0	5.2	5.4	5.6	5.8	6.0	6.2	6.4	6.6	6.8
12.0	4.2	4.4	4.6	4.8	5.0	5.2	5.4	5.6	5.8	6.0	6.2	6.4	6.6
12.5	4.0	4.2	4.4	4.6	4.8	5.0	5.2	5.4	5.6	5.8	6.0	6.2	6.4
13.0	3.8	4.0	4.2	4.4	4.6	4.8	5.0	5.2	5.4	5.6	5.8	6.0	6.2
13.5	3.6	3.8	4.0	4.2	4.4	4.6	4.8	5.0	5.2	5.4	5.6	5.8	6.0
14.0	3.4	3.6	3.8	4.0	4.2	4.4	4.6	4.8	5.0	5.2	5.4	5.6	5.8
14.5	3.2	3.4	3.6	3.8	4.0	4.2	4.4	4.6	4.8	5.0	5.2	5.4	5.6

(continued)

A-C

Table B.3, *continued*

TA (g/L)	Specific Gravity (SG)												
	1.101	1.102	1.103	1.104	1.105	1.106	1.107	1.108	1.109	1.110	1.111	1.112	1.113
4.5	9.8	10.0	10.2	10.4	10.6	10.8	11.0	11.2	11.4	11.6	11.8	12.0	12.2
5.0	9.6	9.8	10.0	10.2	10.4	10.6	10.8	11.0	11.2	11.4	11.6	11.8	12.0
5.5	9.4	9.6	9.8	10.0	10.2	10.4	10.6	10.8	11.0	11.2	11.4	11.6	11.8
6.0	9.2	9.4	9.6	9.8	10.0	10.2	10.4	10.6	10.8	11.0	11.2	11.4	11.6
6.5	9.0	9.2	9.4	9.6	9.8	10.0	10.2	10.4	10.6	10.8	11.0	11.2	11.4
7.0	8.8	9.0	9.2	9.4	9.6	9.8	10.0	10.2	10.4	10.6	10.8	11.0	11.2
7.5	8.6	8.8	9.0	9.2	9.4	9.6	9.8	10.0	10.2	10.4	10.6	10.8	11.0
8.0	8.4	8.6	8.8	9.0	9.2	9.4	9.6	9.8	10.0	10.2	10.4	10.6	10.8
8.5	8.2	8.4	8.6	8.8	9.0	9.2	9.4	9.6	9.8	10.0	10.2	10.4	10.6
9.0	8.0	8.2	8.4	8.6	8.8	9.0	9.2	9.4	9.6	9.8	10.0	10.2	10.4
9.5	7.8	8.0	8.2	8.4	8.6	8.8	9.0	9.2	9.4	9.6	9.8	10.0	10.2
10.0	7.6	7.8	8.0	8.2	8.4	8.6	8.8	9.0	9.2	9.4	9.6	9.8	10.0
10.5	7.4	7.6	7.8	8.0	8.2	8.4	8.6	8.8	9.0	9.2	9.4	9.6	9.8
11.0	7.2	7.4	7.6	7.8	8.0	8.2	8.4	8.6	8.8	9.0	9.2	9.4	9.6
11.5	7.0	7.2	7.4	7.6	7.8	8.0	8.2	8.4	8.6	8.8	9.0	9.2	9.4
12.0	6.8	7.0	7.2	7.4	7.6	7.8	8.0	8.2	8.4	8.6	8.8	9.0	9.2
12.5	6.6	6.8	7.0	7.2	7.4	7.6	7.8	8.0	8.2	8.4	8.6	8.8	9.0
13.0	6.4	6.6	6.8	7.0	7.2	7.4	7.6	7.8	8.0	8.2	8.4	8.6	8.8
13.5	6.2	6.4	6.6	6.8	7.0	7.2	7.4	7.6	7.8	8.0	8.2	8.4	8.6
14.0	6.0	6.2	6.4	6.6	6.8	7.0	7.2	7.4	7.6	7.8	8.0	8.2	8.4
14.5	5.8	6.0	6.2	6.4	6.6	6.8	7.0	7.2	7.4	7.6	7.8	8.0	8.2

(continued)

Table B.3, *continued*

TA (g/L)	Specific Gravity (SG)												
	1.114	1.115	1.116	1.117	1.118	1.119	1.120	1.121	1.122	1.123	1.124	1.125	1.126
4.5	12.4	12.6	12.8	13.0	13.2	13.4	13.6	13.8	14.0	14.2	14.4	14.6	14.8
5.0	12.2	12.4	12.6	12.8	13.0	13.2	13.4	13.6	13.8	14.0	14.2	14.4	14.6
5.5	12.0	12.2	12.4	12.6	12.8	13.0	13.2	13.4	13.6	13.8	14.0	14.2	14.4
6.0	11.8	12.0	12.2	12.4	12.6	12.8	13.0	13.2	13.4	13.6	13.8	14.0	14.2
6.5	11.6	11.8	12.0	12.2	12.4	12.6	12.8	13.0	13.2	13.4	13.6	13.8	14.0
7.0	11.4	11.6	11.8	12.0	12.2	12.4	12.6	12.8	13.0	13.2	13.4	13.6	13.8
7.5	11.2	11.4	11.6	11.8	12.0	12.2	12.4	12.6	12.8	13.0	13.2	13.4	13.6
8.0	11.0	11.2	11.4	11.6	11.8	12.0	12.2	12.4	12.6	12.8	13.0	13.2	13.4
8.5	10.8	11.0	11.2	11.4	11.6	11.8	12.0	12.2	12.4	12.6	12.8	13.0	13.2
9.0	10.6	10.8	11.0	11.2	11.4	11.6	11.8	12.0	12.2	12.4	12.6	12.8	13.0
9.5	10.4	10.6	10.8	11.0	11.2	11.4	11.6	11.8	12.0	12.2	12.4	12.6	12.8
10.0	10.2	10.4	10.6	10.8	11.0	11.2	11.4	11.6	11.8	12.0	12.2	12.4	12.6
10.5	10.0	10.2	10.4	10.6	10.8	11.0	11.2	11.4	11.6	11.8	12.0	12.2	12.4
11.0	9.8	10.0	10.2	10.4	10.6	10.8	11.0	11.2	11.4	11.6	11.8	12.0	12.2
11.5	9.6	9.8	10.0	10.2	10.4	10.6	10.8	11.0	11.2	11.4	11.6	11.8	12.0
12.0	9.4	9.6	9.8	10.0	10.2	10.4	10.6	10.8	11.0	11.2	11.4	11.6	11.8
12.5	9.2	9.4	9.6	9.8	10.0	10.2	10.4	10.6	10.8	11.0	11.2	11.4	11.6
13.0	9.0	9.2	9.4	9.6	9.8	10.0	10.2	10.4	10.6	10.8	11.0	11.2	11.4
13.5	8.8	9.0	9.2	9.4	9.6	9.8	10.0	10.2	10.4	10.6	10.8	11.0	11.2
14.0	8.6	8.8	9.0	9.2	9.4	9.6	9.8	10.0	10.2	10.4	10.6	10.8	11.0
14.5	8.4	8.6	8.8	9.0	9.2	9.4	9.6	9.8	10.0	10.2	10.4	10.6	10.8

A-C

Table B.4: Estimated amount of residual sugars in white and rosé wines in the range 10.0–12.5% ABV (adapted from [3], [4])

SG	Brix	% ABV (WHITE/ROSÉ WINE)					
		10.0	10.5	11.0	11.5	12.0	12.5
0.990	−2.6	0.0	0.0	0.0	0.0	0.0	0.0
0.991	−2.4	0.0	0.0	0.0	0.0	0.0	0.0
0.992	−2.2	0.0	0.0	0.0	0.0	0.0	1.0
0.993	−1.9	0.0	0.0	0.0	0.8	2.2	3.6
0.994	−1.6	0.0	0.6	2.0	3.4	4.8	6.2
0.995	−1.3	1.8	3.2	4.6	6.0	7.4	8.7
0.996	−1.0	4.3	5.7	7.1	8.5	9.9	11.3
0.997	−0.8	6.9	8.3	9.7	11.1	12.5	13.9
0.998	−0.5	9.5	10.9	12.3	13.7	15.1	16.4
0.999	−0.3	12.1	13.4	14.8	16.2	17.6	19.0
1.000	0.0	14.6	16.0	17.4	18.8	20.2	21.5
1.001	0.1	17.2	18.6	19.9	21.3	22.7	24.1
1.002	0.4	19.7	21.1	22.5	23.9	25.3	26.6
1.003	0.8	22.3	23.7	25.0	26.4	27.8	29.2
1.004	1.0	24.8	26.2	27.6	28.9	30.3	31.7
1.005	1.3	27.4	28.7	30.1	31.5	32.9	34.2
1.006	1.6	29.9	31.3	32.6	34.0	35.4	36.7
1.007	1.8	32.4	33.8	35.2	36.5	37.9	39.3
1.008	2.1	34.9	36.3	37.7	39.0	40.4	41.8
1.009	2.3	37.5	38.8	40.2	41.5	42.9	44.3
1.010	2.6	40.0	41.3	42.7	44.1	45.4	46.8
1.011	2.9	42.5	43.8	45.2	46.6	47.9	49.3
1.012	3.1	45.0	46.3	47.7	49.0	50.4	51.8
1.013	3.4	47.5	48.8	50.2	51.5	52.9	54.2
1.014	3.6	50.0	51.3	52.7	54.0	55.4	56.7
1.015	3.9	52.4	53.8	55.1	56.5	57.8	59.2

Table B.5: Estimated amount of residual sugars in red wines in the range 12.5–15.0% ABV (adapted from [3], [4])

SG	Brix	% ABV (RED WINE)					
		12.5	13.0	13.5	14.0	14.5	15.0
0.990	−2.6	0.0	0.0	0.0	0.0	0.0	0.0
0.991	−2.4	0.0	0.0	0.0	0.0	0.0	0.0
0.992	−2.2	0.0	0.0	0.0	0.0	0.0	0.0
0.993	−1.9	0.0	0.0	0.0	0.0	1.2	2.6
0.994	−1.6	0.0	0.0	1.0	2.4	3.8	5.1
0.995	−1.3	0.7	2.1	3.5	4.9	6.3	7.7
0.996	−1.0	3.3	4.7	6.1	7.5	8.9	10.3
0.997	−0.8	5.9	7.3	8.7	10.1	11.4	12.8
0.998	−0.5	8.4	9.8	11.2	12.6	14.0	15.4
0.999	−0.3	11.0	12.4	13.8	15.2	16.5	17.9
1.000	0.0	13.5	14.9	16.3	17.7	19.1	20.4
1.001	0.1	16.1	17.5	18.9	20.2	21.6	23.0
1.002	0.4	18.6	20.0	21.4	22.8	24.1	25.5
1.003	0.8	21.2	22.5	23.9	25.3	26.7	28.0
1.004	1.0	23.7	25.1	26.4	27.8	29.2	30.5
1.005	1.3	26.2	27.6	29.0	30.3	31.7	33.1
1.006	1.6	28.7	30.1	31.5	32.8	34.2	35.6
1.007	1.8	31.3	32.6	34.0	35.3	36.7	38.1
1.008	2.1	33.8	35.1	36.5	37.9	39.2	40.6
1.009	2.3	36.3	37.6	39.0	40.3	41.7	43.1
1.010	2.6	38.8	40.1	41.5	42.8	44.2	45.5
1.011	2.9	41.3	42.6	44.0	45.3	46.7	48.0
1.012	3.1	43.8	45.1	46.5	47.8	49.2	50.5
1.013	3.4	46.2	47.6	48.9	50.3	51.6	53.0
1.014	3.6	48.7	50.1	51.4	52.8	54.1	55.4
1.015	3.9	51.2	52.5	53.9	55.2	56.6	57.9

A-C

REFERENCES

1. OIV. 2019. *Compendium of International Methods of Wine and Must Analysis: Volume 1.* Organisation Internationale de la Vigne et du Vin (OIV), Paris, France.

2. Dienstleistungzentrum Ländlicher Raum Mosel. 2020. *Praxisleitfaden Oenologie 2020.* Rheinland Pfalz. https://www.dlr-mosel.rlp.de/Internet/global/themen.nsf/Web_DLR_Mosel_Aktuell_All_XP/6F65 3FCBE0D5CD93C125830B00361153/$FILE/2020-08-13%20Praxis leitfaden%20Oenologie%202020%20DLR.pdf, pp. 87 –88.

3. Ims, D. *Extract, Residual Sugar & ABV: Developing a simple way to estimate Residual Sugar and Alcohol in finished wine.* http://www.rochesterwinemakers.org/winemaking-information/winemaking-articles-by-members/determining-abv-and-residual-sugar/.

4. Ims, D. *Quick Reference Guide: Estimating a Wine's ABV and Residual Sugar in 3 Easy Steps.* http://www.rochesterwinemakers.org/wine making-information/winemaking-articles-by-members/guide-est-abv-and-res-sugar/.

Appendix C: Winemaking Log Chart

Use the following example *Winemaking Log Chart* to track all your wine-making activities and lab measurements. You can download a printable version of the chart from ModernHomeWinemaking.com. You can also download a version, created in Microsoft Excel, which makes use of drop-down lists to enter data, such as grape variety and type of operation, and which has a DASHBOARD that populates summary fields at the top of the chart as you enter data to provide a single, simple view of the status of your batch.

As each batch of the same wine can potentially be different, create a separate log chart for each batch. Then, for example, if you blend batches, create a new log chart for the now-blended wine.

Maintain meticulous records of all activities, making sure to enter the date and, where needed, the time of day where you might be performing several activities in a few hours or day. This level of tracking and commitment to maintaining accurate and complete records will allow you to perform a root-cause analysis if a problem occurs; it will be guesswork trying to figure out what went wrong without that data.

Under "Operation or Checkpoint," enter the specific activity, such as crushing/destemming, must analysis, pressing, alcoholic fermentation, free SO_2 adjustment, etc., and record any pertinent analytical data. Use the suggested control checkpoints in the log charts presented in the respective winemaking sections in Chapters 19, 20 and 21.

A-C

Variety: _____
Source: _____
Vintage: _____
Style: _____
Quantity: _____
Price: _____
Batch ID: _____

DASHBOARD:

Date	Operation or Checkpoint	Additive or Processing aid	Quantity added	Volume (L or gal)	Temp. (°C/°F)	SG / BRIX	Temp-adjusted SG / BRIX	PA or Actual % ABV	TA (g/L)	pH	FSO2 (mg/L)	TSO2 (mg/L)	DO (mg/L)	YAN (mg N/L)	RS (g/L)	MLF Check	Comments

Index

....

Page numbers in **bold** type indicate important and most relevant references, particularly where there are multiple page entries.

"*See*" refers to another, more appropriate index entry; "*See also*" refers to another index entry for additional, related information.

A semi-colon separates references to key index entries; for example, "astringency" and "balance" are two key index entries in "bitterness, 35, ... , **406**. *See also* astringency; balance."

A comma separates a key index entry and a sub-entry; for example, "bound SO_2. *See* sulfur dioxide, bound" refers to the key entry "sulfur dioxide" and sub-entry "bound."

Notes